The Windows NT Windows 2000 Answer Book

A Complete Resource from the Desktop to the Enterprise

John Savill

Addison-Wesley
An imprint of Addison Wesley Longman, Inc.

Reading, Massachusetts • Harlow, England • Menlo Park, California
Berkeley, California • Don Mills, Ontario • Sydney
Bonn • Amsterdam • Tokyo • Mexico City

The publisher offers discounts on this book when ordered in quantity for special sales. For more information, please contact

AWL Direct Sales
Addison Wesley Longman, Inc.
One Jacob Way
Reading, Massachusetts 01867
(781) 944-3700

Visit AW on the Web: www.awl.com/cseng/

Library of Congress Cataloging-in-Publication Data

Savill, John, 1975—
    The Windows NT and Windows 2000 answer book : a complete resource
from the desktop to the enterprise / John Savill.
        p.   cm.
    ISBN 0-201-60636-4
        1. Microsoft Windows NT.   2. Operating systems (Computers)
    I. Title.
    QA76.76.063S3567   1999
    005.4'4769—dc21   99.25868
                                                              CIP

Acquisitions Editor: Gary Clarke
Editorial Assistant: Rebecca Bence
Production Manager: John Fuller
Cover Designer: Jennifer Collins

Text printed on recycled and acid-free paper.
ISBN 0201606364

2 3 4 5 6 7   MA   02 01 00 99

2nd Printing September 1999

For Emmaline,
without whose support and understanding
this book would not have been possible

Brief Contents

Contents

Chapter 27   Batch Files   561

Foreword

Spending more than twenty years in the computer industry, I've seen various operating systems, products, languages, and fads come and go. It is certainly a pleasure to see some durability in something as fundamental as an operating system like Microsoft's premier operating system—Windows NT or the soon to be released Windows 2000.

The combination of research, knowledge, and sheer development power that created Windows NT has created an operating system that is robust, powerful, and widespread. The only downside to this beauty is that Windows NT can be daunting to configure and administer. Once configured, though, Windows NT runs like a well-tuned sports car, but if it is configured incorrectly, then, well, like any poorly tuned car, it can have problems. When you want to tune a car you go to the owner's manual. It would be nice to see such a manual for Windows NT also.

Well, John Savill's *The Windows NT and Windows 2000 Answer Book* is just such a book. Although I have worked with and programmed for Windows NT right from its inception in version 3.1, there were always questions in my mind, like "How can I configure NT to run better?" or "What switch was it that I need to set to change that setting?" After reviewing John's work I realized very quickly that this was it—this was the book that I had been waiting for. Not only did John's work answer all of my outstanding questions, but also I found answers to questions I didn't think I had. I discovered that there are many more ways to configure Windows NT, not only to run more smoothly, but also to run faster than I thought possible.

If you use, work with, or administer Windows NT, then I would highly recommend that you read this book from cover to cover. Yes, there may be topics
that may not directly concern you, but as you will probably find when you read
the book, there are probably more topics that do concern you than not.
This one book is like having your own personal technical support team waiting
for you. Whatever your question or difficulty with Windows NT, you can be
assured that *The Windows NT and Windows 2000 Answer Book* will most likely
contain an answer or solution.

—Robert Coleridge
Software Design Engineer
A large software company
in the Pacific Northwest

Introduction

Windows NT was first inaugurated in 1993. Four versions later (3.1, 3.5, 3.51, 4.0), we are now waiting for Windows 2000. Many sites, however, are just now upgrading to NT 4.0 and many expect to continue to use NT 4.0 for several years, making a comprehensive resource on NT 4.0 a vital and necessary item for the NT 4.0 user or system administrator. As Windows NT has stabilized and developed over time, it has become known for certain strengths—easy-to-use GUI, excellent security, and a very rich feature set—in spite of its comparatively weak reliability and hardware support, which is improving with Windows 2000.

Particularly as a result of NT's ease of use and large feature set (and not forgetting the Microsoft name), Windows NT is rapidly becoming the server operating system of choice and—in the corporate market—the desktop system of choice. In the future, all Microsoft operating systems will be NT based with the introduction of Windows 2000. With advanced technologies such as built-in application repair and full plug-and-play support, the use of NT will not be restricted to the workplace and the home office but will be made easily accessible to general users as well. With NT here to stay, learning how to get the most out of it is critical. In the corporate setting in particular, Windows NT system administrators must deal with many common challenges and tasks, but until now, there has been no one resource that addresses all of these common tasks and challenges. The goal of this book is to provide Windows NT users and system administrators with valuable know-how for handling these day-to-day tasks and proven solutions to the many common challenges. Just as the administrator is task-driven, so too is this book task-focused. How do I terminate a trust relationship? How do share and file system permissions interact? Over 800 such frequently asked questions (FAQs) and their answers are provided in this book!

The tasks and challenges addressed as questions cover all facets of Windows NT, from the simple to the complex, and should appeal to both experienced and inexperienced administrators and users. When first using NT, everyone has the same challenges (or issues, to use Microsoft-speak), such as

- How do I install NT on a machine with Windows 98 installed?
- How do I convert a FAT partition to NTFS?
- How can I change the My Computer icon?

Every answer is structured in a step-by-step format, with examples and an explanation of exactly what is being carried out.

If answers to some questions are well known to you, you can skip over these sections. This book is designed to appeal to readers with different levels of experience with NT. My hope is that, with over 800 questions, all readers will find something helpful and informative.

How It Began

I've been using Windows NT since its first version, 3.1; however, my first use was accidental. I only noticed I was using NT when the machine hung—I pressed Ctrl+Alt+Del and, instead of rebooting, a strange dialog appeared. From that point forward I was hooked and have been ever since, learning all I can about the Windows NT operating system (OS) and even participating on the Windows 2000 beta team.

In developing my understanding of Windows NT, I've always been very active in the Windows newsgroups. About three years ago I started to notice that the same questions were being asked by both system administrators and average users within these different newsgroups. Because I often knew the answers to these questions, I put together a short list of Frequently Asked Questions (FAQs) and posted this list on my Logica Web page (where I worked at the time). I quickly began to get requests and suggestions from many other NT users, and over the past two years I've expanded the FAQs and added details about various back-office components, such as Internet Information Server, Proxy Server, and Exchange Server—all topics covered in this book. The Web version of the FAQ (http://www.ntfaq.com) now gets thousands of hits a month and is used by many large companies as a vital technical resource, including U.S.

government agencies and many large computer and financial institutions. It is due in part to the creation and up-to-date maintenance of this Web-based FAQ that I was awarded the Microsoft Most Valuable Professional Award (MVP) in 1997 and 1998.

Turning the Web-based FAQ into a book seemed to be a natural and worthwhile progression. I didn't want this to be just a print version of the online FAQ, however, so I've expanded the text to be more comprehensive, provided many additional explanatory examples, and added as much information on Windows 2000 as is practical at this time. This book has over 800 answers to common NT questions asked by real people attempting to solve real problems, and I hope it will prove invaluable for users and system administrators alike.

Who Should Read This Book?

Anybody who has an interest in learning more about Windows NT will benefit from reading this book. Indeed, I've written the book to be usable by both NT novices and experienced NT administrators.

I, of course, hope everyone will read the whole of this book from start to finish. More likely, you will want to pick out those chapters of the book that will help you in your daily NT tasks. I also encourage you to read chapters that cover aspects of Windows NT that lie outside of your daily tasks. You will be surprised at the power of NT and will doubtless find new ways of accomplishing your day-to-day tasks. My hope is that this book can serve as the one Windows NT reference guide that will help you be successful as a user and system administrator.

Book Organization

So you can get to solutions quickly, I've structured the book so each entry is self-contained and does not require you to read previous entries. The book starts off covering the basic installation and NT fundamentals and then goes into more specific tasks, such as configuring the Active Directory or setting up a remote access service (RAS).

Sections generally start with what the chapter is about, how the item is installed and configured (where appropriate), and further customizations and common actions.

What Version of Windows NT Is Covered in This Book?

Both Windows NT 4.0 and Windows 2000 are covered in this book. Although the operating system has been modified substantially from NT 4.0 to Windows

2000, much of the user interface and other elements remain basically the same. This means some FAQs apply to both NT 4.0 and Windows 2000, but some only to NT 4.0 or only to Windows 2000. To help you navigate the book, we have used icons to indicate what version is covered by each FAQ. If no icon is present, the FAQ applies to both NT 4.0 and Windows 2000. If the FAQ applies to only NT 4.0 or Windows 2000, you'll see the following icons:

2000 ONLY   4.0 ONLY

A Big Thanks to . . .

There are many people I would like to thank. First, I'd like to thank Stuart Chapman and Andy Rose from Logica. They gave me my first big break by hiring me at Logica and allowed me to learn and experiment with all things digital. Without their help, I doubt I'd be where I am today.

I would also like to thank the technical reviewers of this book: Jeff Dunkelberger, Erik Olson, Paul Nelis, Michael Chacon, Robert Coleridge, Dharma Shukla, and Krishnan Menon. A big thanks to Rebecca Bence for organizing the technical reviews and to Gary Clarke of Addison Wesley for keeping the whole thing together. Their patience and professionalism helped transform my rough draft manuscript into this coherent, perfect work of art.

Many people have helped and encouraged me through life. I would especially like to thank my fiancée, Emmaline (we are to be married August 14, 1999), for putting up with my "always being on that computer" and for her love and support.

Also a big thanks to my parents, who first introduced me to the computer bug with a ZX Spectrum, who always encouraged me to try everything, and who taught me that anything is possible.

Let us begin…

John Savill
London, England
February 1999

1 CORE CONCEPTS

This book is split into a large number of sections, each dealing with an aspect of the Windows NT operating system. This chapter starts with some pieces of information I consider "core"—among the first and most important questions users want answered.

Although many "users" of this book are looking for solutions to a particular problem, I recommend reading through this brief chapter to lay a foundation for future learning and understanding. A basic appreciation of an operating system and its goals is vital to competently utilizing its capabilities.

I use the term Windows NT here, but Windows 2000 is NT at heart and the information applies equally to Windows 2000.

Here's a point I would like to make clear. Throughout the book, whenever I describe methods that involve editing the Registry, I have put REGEDIT.EXE or REGEDT32.EXE in brackets. If I say REGEDT32.EXE, you **have** to use REGEDT32.EXE because you are manipulating a data type or performing a function not supported by REGEDIT.EXE. If I say REGEDIT.EXE, you can use REGEDT32.EXE if you wish.

 ## What is Windows NT?

Both the Workstation and Server Windows NT products are 32-bit operating systems. Windows NT Server and Windows NT Workstation actually share much of the same code, and it is only Registry settings and performance optimizations that separate them.

Windows NT is a preemptive, multitasking operating system, which means that the operating system controls allocation of CPU time, not the applications running on it. This prevents one application from using as much CPU time as it feels necessary and thus hanging the OS.

Windows NT supports multiple CPUs, giving true multitasking. It also uses symmetrical multiprocessing, meaning the processors share all tasks, as opposed to asymmetrical multiprocessing in which the OS uses one CPU and the applications another.

NT is also a fault-tolerant operating system, with each 32-bit application operating in its own protected virtual memory address space (4GB) so one application cannot interfere with another's memory space. Among other features, Windows NT has built-in software RAID (mirroring and disk striping with parity), file system journaling, and the capability to boot into a "last known good" configuration in the event of a system start failure.

Unlike earlier versions of Windows (such as Windows for Workgroups and Windows 95), NT is a complete 32-bit operating system and not an addition to DOS. Although NT has a command window (CMD.EXE), this is not a normal DOS window and offers enhancements over standard DOS boxes, which are explored in Chapter 26, Command Prompt Configuration. Windows NT does support some 16-bit calls through a process called "thunking"; however, it is thanks to its shedding of basic 16-bit support that NT was able to gain significant performance advantages over Windows 9x.

NT supports several processor architectures: Intel x86, IBM PowerPC (not to be supported for Windows 2000), and DEC Alpha.

NT's other main plus is security. NT includes a special NT file system (NTFS) that allows permissions to be set on a file and directory basis extending to nearly all objects in the operating system.

Windows 2000 introduces version 5.0 of NTFS with yet more security and performance gains, including its built-in encrypted file system (EFS).

 ## What is the history of NT?

In the late 1980s, the Windows environment was created to run on the Microsoft DOS operating system. Microsoft and IBM joined forces to create a

DOS replacement that would run on the Intel platform. That effort led to the creation of OS/2, and at the same time Microsoft was working on a more powerful operating system that would run on other processor platforms. The idea was that the new OS would be written in a high-level language (such as C) so it would be more portable.

Microsoft hired Dave Cutler (who also designed Digital's VAX / VMS) to head the team for the New Technology operating system (NT). Originally, the new OS was to be called OS/2 NT.

In the early 1990s, Microsoft released version 3.0 of its Windows OS, which gained a large user base. It was at this point that Microsoft and IBM's split started, as the two companies disagreed on the future of their OSs. IBM viewed Windows as a stepping stone to the superior OS/2, whereas Microsoft wanted to expand Windows to compete with OS/2, so they split. IBM kept OS/2 and Microsoft changed OS/2 NT to Windows NT.

The first version of Windows NT (3.1) was released in 1993 and had the same graphical user interface (GUI) as the normal Windows operating system. It was a pure 32-bit OS, but also provided the capability to run older DOS and Windows applications as well as character mode OS/2 1.3 programs.

For a detailed history, consider buying a book called *Show Stopper* by G. Pascal Zachary. In it, the author has interviewed a large number of Microsoft employees and charted the entire development cycle brilliantly.

 ## What does NT stand for?

NT, as a trademark, actually stands for Northern Telecom, but Microsoft licensed it, and in the Windows sense, it stands for New Technology.

It's also interesting to note its heritage:

RSX -> VMS -> ELN -> NT (all major designs of David Cutler)

Also VMS +1 letter = WNT (Windows NT), just as HAL + 1 = IBM in 2001.

Windows 2000 as a name has hit a problem encountered by NT—a Web information site already owns the name Windows 2000 and the www.windows2000.com Web address.

What are the differences between NT Workstation and NT Server?

As has been mentioned, Windows NT Server and Windows NT Workstation share a common code base, with Windows NT Server shipping with extra modules (such as DNS, WINS). In fact, many of the advanced features of NT Server—such as disk mirroring—would be available in NT Workstation but for a single Registry entry that is checked when Disk Administrator is started.

Table 1-1 shows the major changes between the two versions of the OS.

Table 1-1. Comparison of Windows NT Server and Windows NT Workstation

	Workstation	Server
Connection to other clients	10	Unlimited
Connection to other networks	Unlimited	Unlimited
Multiprocessing	2 CPUs	4 CPUs*
RAS	1 connection	255 connections
Directory replication	Import	Import and export
Macintosh services	No	Yes
Logon validation	No	Yes
Disk fault tolerance	No	Yes
Network	Peer-to-peer	Server

* Special versions of NT Server can support up to 32 CPUs.

 ## What is the NT boot process?

Table 1-2 lists the files that are used in the initial phase of the boot process.

Table 1-2. Initial Phase Boot Files

NTLDR	A hidden, read-only system file that loads the operating system.
BOOT.INI	A read-only, hidden system file, used to build the boot loader operating system Selection menu on Intel x86-based computers.
BOOTSECT.DOS	A hidden file loaded by NTLDR if another operating system is selected. It basically contains the data the boot sector for the disk would contain for the OS.
NTDETECT.COM	A hidden, read-only system file used to examine the available hardware and to build a hardware list.
NTBOOTDD.SYS	A file used only by systems that boot from a SCSI disk when SCSI BIOS is enabled.

The common boot sequence (second phase) files are listed in Table 1-3.

Table 1-3. Second Phase Boot Files

NTOSKRNL.EXE	The Windows NT kernel.
SYSTEM	This file is a collection of system configuration settings.
Device drivers	Files that support various device drivers.
HAL.DLL	Hardware abstraction layer software.

The boot sequence is as follows:

1. Power-on self-test (POST) routines are run.
2. The BIOS reads the first physical sector on the disk, called the master boot sector, and loads an image of it into memory. The BIOS then transfers execution of the master boot sector to that image.
3. The master boot record is loaded into memory, which contains the partition table and a small amount of executable code. The master boot record then finds the active partition's starting location.
4. The boot sector from the active partition is loaded into memory and executed.
5. NTLDR is loaded and initialized from the boot sector.
6. Processor changes from real mode to 32-bit flat memory mode.
7. NTLDR starts the appropriate minifile system drivers. Minifile system drivers are built into NTLDR and can read FAT or NTFS.

8. NTLDR reads the BOOT.INI file.

9. NTLDR loads the selected operating system and one of two things happens:

   - If Windows NT is selected, NTLDR runs NTDETECT.COM.
   - For other operating systems, NTLDR loads and runs BOOTSECT.DOS and passes control to it. The Windows NT process ends here.

10. NTDETECT.COM scans the computer hardware and sends the list to NTLDR for inclusion in HKEY_LOCAL_MACHINE\HARDWARE.

11. NTLDR then loads NTOSKRNL.EXE, HAL.DLL, and the system hive.

12. NTLDR scans the system hive and loads the device drivers configured to start at boot time.

13. NTLDR passes control to NTOSKRNL.EXE, at which point the boot process ends and the load phases begin.

 ## What is virtual memory?

Virtual memory makes up for the lack of physical RAM in computers by using space on the hard disk as memory—virtual memory.

When physical memory starts to run low, the virtual memory manager chooses sections of memory that have not been recently used and are of low priority and writes them to the swap file on disk. This process is hidden from applications, and applications view both virtual and physical memory as the same.

The swap file is created at installation time and can be modified by using the System Control Panel applet (this is covered later in the book).

Each application that runs under Windows NT is given its own virtual address space of 4GB (2GB for the application, 2GB for the operating system). You should note that this 2/2 memory split can be modified in recent versions of NT 4.0 (Service Pack 3 and above) to use 3GB for applications, 1GB for the operating system. You do this by adding /3GB to your BOOT.INI file. All versions of Windows 2000 support this.

The problem with virtual memory is that it writes and reads to the hard disk and therefore is much slower than actual RAM. This is why if an NT system does not have enough memory, it runs very slowly.

 ## Is NT year 2000 compliant?

Yes, as long as the system has Service Pack 3 with the Year 2000 hotfixes applied or has Service Pack 4. For more information, see the Microsoft Year 2000 Information Center at http://www.microsoft.com/y2k or http://www.microsoft.com/ithome/topics/year2k/default.htm.

As you would expect, Windows 2000 will be fully Y2K compliant when released.

2 WINDOWS 2000 (A.K.A. WINDOWS NT 5.0)

Windows 2000 is the next generation of Microsoft's golden operating system. To mark its functional metamorphosis from Windows 9x, Microsoft decided to name it Windows 2000. Another reason for the new naming scheme is that Windows 98 is the last release of the Windows 9x software, and all future releases will be NT based.

The information in this section is about what is new in Windows 2000 and what is needed. There are other items relating to Windows 2000 functionality elsewhere in the FAQ.

This chapter also analyzes and explains the new Windows 2000 directory service, the Active Directory.

What is Windows 2000?

Microsoft has renamed NT 5.0 to Windows 2000 in an attempt to simplify their product lines. Four products make up the new Windows 2000 product line, all "built on NT technology."

Microsoft has expanded the Windows server line to allow greater flexibility in its products. This also helped them meet customer demands for solutions that are more powerful than Windows NT Server Enterprise Edition and for lower cost-clustering alternatives for branch-office servers.

The Windows 2000 line, which Microsoft will begin to roll out in 1999, will include four products. Windows 2000 Professional is a desktop operating system aimed at businesses of all sizes. Microsoft designed Windows 2000 Professional as the easiest Windows yet, with high-level security and significant enhancements for mobile users. The operating system is also designed to provide industrial-strength reliability and help companies lower their total cost of ownership with improved manageability.

Microsoft offers the Windows 2000 Server as the ideal solution for small- to medium-size workplace application deployments, Web servers, workgroups, and branch offices. Windows 2000 Server will support new systems with up to two-way symmetric multiprocessing (SMP); existing Windows NT Server 4.0 systems with up to four-way SMP can be upgraded to this product.

Windows 2000 Advanced Server is a more powerful departmental and application server that provides network operating system and Internet services. Supporting new systems with up to four-way SMP and large physical memories, this product is ideal for database-intensive work. In addition, Windows 2000 Server integrates clustering and load-balancing support to provide excellent system and application availability. Organizations with existing Windows NT 4.0 Enterprise Edition servers with up to eight-way SMP can install this product.

The Windows 2000 line will also include the new Windows 2000 Datacenter Server, which is the most powerful server operating system ever offered by Microsoft. Windows 2000 Datacenter Server supports up to 16-way SMP and up to 64GB of physical memory, depending on system architecture. Like Windows 2000 Advanced Server, it provides both clustering and load-balancing services as standard features. Microsoft designed this product especially for large data warehouses, econometric analysis, large-scale simulations in science and engineering, online transaction processing, and server-consolidation projects.

Microsoft believes its new Windows 2000 name will help both its partners and its customers.

In addition, Windows 98 marks the end of that product line and all future OS releases will be NT based.

The company believes that the Windows 2000 name and NT tagline will help people identify which operating system will work best in their environment.

What is new in Windows 2000?

Windows 2000 is the next major release of NT. It is expected to include the following new features:

- A new X.500-style directory service called Active Directory. In the Active Directory, Domain Controllers store the entire directory database for their domain. This directory information can be structured to create a hierarchical directory system.
- Active Directory uses DNS as a locator service and supports lightweight directory access protocol (LDAP) queries.
- A distributed file system (DFS), an add-on for NT4, enables multiple volumes on different machines (even if not Windows NT) to appear as a single logical volume.
- Support for more than one monitor, using new application program interface (API) commands (note that not all video cards are supported).
- Kerberos security, an MIT-developed security protocol. It is used for distributed security within a domain tree and is based on passwords and private-key encryption.
- 64-bit memory support on alpha processors (more than 4 gigs of memory supported, 32 gigs on 64-bit processors).
- Support for plug-and-play based on advanced configuration and power interface (ACPI).
- A common device driver model, so new drivers can work on both Windows NT and Windows 98.
- Built-in disk quota software; per user/per volume only.
- Encrypting file system; file encryption on a per file or per folder basis (like compression at present).

For more information on what's new, see http://www.microsoft.com/NTServer/Basics/Future/WindowsNT5/Features.asp.

Where can I get more information on Windows 2000?

Many computer-related publications are now including large amounts of information on Windows 2000 (I seem to be writing at least one a month). Among the best are *Windows NT Magazine* and *NT Explorer*.

Microsoft also has some information at its Web site, with the best found at

Windows NT Server 5.0 main page
http://www.microsoft.com/ntserver/windowsnt5/default.asp
Windows NT Beta page
http://ntbeta.microsoft.com/

How do I get the Microsoft Windows NT 5.0 beta?

Windows NT 5.0 is currently in beta test (the beta is still known as NT 5.0 and not Windows 2000). The technical beta program is closed and is not accepting additional requests at this time. The Windows NT 5.0 beta is not generally available at present for free. If you want this beta, you could consider one of these three approaches:

Send e-mail to betareq@microsoft.com. The technical beta is closed, and e-mail to this account is unlikely to get you onto the beta. If you do send e-mail, remember you need to justify why MS should send you the beta. Given that the technical beta is closed, this approach is unlikely to get you a beta copy.

Take out a subscription to Microsoft Developers Network (MSDN) Professional or Universal level. MSDN subscriptions offer comprehensive, timely, and convenient access to Microsoft Visual Tools, essential technical programming information, Microsoft operating systems, software development kits (SDKs), device driver kits (DDKs), Microsoft Office, BackOffice Test Platform, and more. See http://www.microsoft.com/msdn/join/subscriptions.htm for more details, including pricing.

Take the one-day course called Windows 2000 First Look (MS course # 1100, 1264, 1265, 1266, or 1267).

What hardware is needed to run Windows 2000?

Below is a list of the minimum hardware needed to install Windows 2000.

- 32-bit, Intel-based microprocessor computer (such as Pentium-compatible 166 MHz or higher) for both Windows NT Workstation and Windows NT Server.
- VGA or higher-resolution monitor.
- A keyboard.
- 32MB of RAM minimum (64MB of RAM for Windows NT Server).
- For Windows NT Workstation, a minimum of 300MB of free hard disk space. For Server, a minimum of 400MB of free disk space on the partition that will contain the Windows NT system files. Several factors affect free disk space required by Windows 2000 setup, including disk cluster size, amount of RAM in the system, the file system used (for example, NTFS uses a smaller disk cluster size than FAT file systems), and network compared to local installations (because local requires less free space). Setup determines if you have sufficient disk space to successfully complete the installation with the optional components you select.
- For CD-only installation, a bootable CD-ROM drive (so you can start setup without using a floppy disk drive).
- For floppy disk and CD installation, a high-density 3.5-inch disk drive as drive A and a CD-ROM drive.
- For network installation, one or more network adapters installed on your computer and access to the network share containing the setup files.
- A mouse or other pointing device.

The minimum memory **is** the minimum memory. The setup program performs a test to verify that you have that amount or the installation will not proceed (very annoying when I tried to install server on my portable, which—then—had only 32MB of RAM). You can hack the installation file to install either Server or Workstation on systems with less memory (this is covered in Question 3-44 in Chapter 3, Installation). You can also add memory to the server, install Windows 2000, and then take it out again (there is no boot-time check for memory and no check on CPU type).

This information is also in the file SETUP.TXT on the Windows 2000 (NT 5.0 beta) CD-ROM and is subject to change.

What is the Active Directory?

The Active Directory is Microsoft's implementation of a Directory Service, which basically stores data in an organized format and has the mechanisms needed to publish and access the data.

Active Directory is not a Microsoft innovation but rather an implementation of an existing model (X.500), an existing communication mechanism (LDAP), and an existing location technology (DNS). Each of these is covered in the FAQs.

Before considering the details of Active Directory, you need an overview of what it is trying to achieve. A directory in its most basic sense is just a container for other information. A telephone directory, for example, has various entries, and each entry has values. Name, address, and telephone number are the values that make up a single entry in a telephone directory, as shown here:

Name: John Savill
Address: 2 SavillTech Way, London
Tel: 353 3523
E-mail: john@serverfaq.com

In a large directory, entries may be grouped by location or by type—say, lawyers, pest control, or both—leading to a hierarchy of each type of person in each location. The actual telephone directory is a directory service, because it contains not only the data but also a means to access and use the data. The telephone operator is also a directory service, which has access to the data and presents it to you when you request it.

Active Directory is a type of directory service, holding information about all resources on the network. Clients can query the Active Directory for information about any aspect of the network. Active Directory has a number of powerful features:

- Information is stored in a secure form. Each object in the Active Directory has an Access Control List (ACL)—a list of resources that may access the object and to what degree.

- The flexible mechanism for queries is based on a global catalog generated by the Active Directory. Any client that supports Active Directory can query the catalog.
- Replication of the directory to all Domain Controllers in the domain means easier accessibility, higher availability, and greater fault tolerance.
- Extensible design means new object types can be added to the directory or existing objects can be expanded. For example, a salary attribute could be added to the user object.
- Because of the Active Directory's X.500 foundation, communication can be carried out over a number of protocols. These include LDAP version 2 and 3 and the HTTP.
- A domain name server (DNS), rather than NetBIOS names, is used for the naming and location of Domain Controllers.
- Information is partitioned in the directory by domain to avoid replicating excessive amounts of information.

Even though the information in the Active Directory is partitioned into different stores, the Directory can be queried for information from other domains. Each domain maintains a list of other domains, the location of the global catalog for each of these domains, and the schema of the domain.

2000 ONLY

What is X.500 and LDAP?

X.500 is the most common protocol used for directory management. There are currently two main standards—the 1988 and 1993 standards—with the 1993 standard providing a number of advances over the older one. The Windows NT 5.0 implementation of its directory services is derived from the 1993 X.500 standard as described here.

The X.500 model uses a hierarchical approach to objects in the namespace, with a root at the top of the namespace and children coming off of it (see Figure 2-1). Domains in Windows 2000 are DNS names. For example, SAVILLTECH.COM is a domain name and LEGAL.SAVILLTECH.COM is a child domain of SAVILLTECH.COM. Child domains are covered in Chapter 14, Domains.

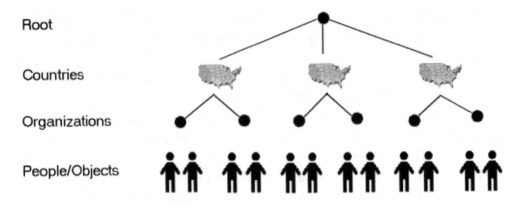

Figure 2-1. Example of X.500 hierarchy.

The example shows a root of the directory service and then a number of children. In this case, the first layer of children represents countries; however, there are no rules and you may break these down any way you want. Imagine each country as a child domain of the root (for example, USA.ROOT.COM and ENGLAND.ROOT.COM).

Each child domain can be broken into a number of organizations. These organizations can be broken down further into organizational units, with various privileges and policies applied to each organizational unit. Each organizational unit contains a number of objects, such as users, computers, or groups.

Although the directory service is based on X.500, the access mechanism actually uses lightweight directory access protocol (LDAP), which solves a number of problems with X.500.

X.500 is part of the Open Systems Interconnection (OSI) model. This does not translate well into a TCP/IP protocol environment, however, so LDAP uses TCP/IP for its communication medium. LDAP cuts down on the functions available with a full X.500 implementation, making a leaner, faster directory service but keeping the overall structure of X.500.

LDAP is actually the mechanism used to communicate with the Active Directory, and it performs basic read, write, and modify operations.

2000 ONLY

2.8 What is the global catalog?

The global catalog contains an entry for every object in the enterprise forest (the term "forest" is explained later) but contains only a few properties of each object. Searches in the whole enterprise forest can be done only on the properties in the catalog, whereas searches in the user's own domain tree can be for any property. Only directory services (or Domain Controllers) can be configured to hold a copy of the global catalog.

Don't configure too many global catalogs in each domain, because you will waste network bandwidth with the replication. One global catalog server per domain in each physical location is sufficient. NT sets servers as global catalogs as it deems necessary, so you should have no need to modify this unless you notice slow query response times.

Because full searches involve querying the whole domain tree rather than the global catalog, grouping the enterprise into a single tree will improve your searches. Grouping enables you to query on items not in the global catalog, thus providing more extensive search criteria.

2000 ONLY

2.9 How do I configure a server as a global catalog?

To configure a Windows 2000 Domain Controller as a global catalog server, perform the following:

1. Start the Active Directory Sites and Services Manager by choosing Start > Programs > Administrative Tools > Active Directory Sites and Services Manager (see Figure 2-2).
2. Select the sites branch.
3. Select the site that owns the server, and then expand the servers branch and the server in question.
4. Right-click on NTDS Settings and choose Properties.
5. Check or uncheck the Global Catalog box. Click Apply and then OK.

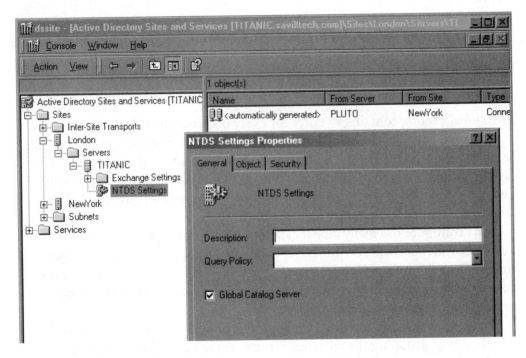

Figure 2-2. Configuring a Domain Controller as a global catalog server.

What is the schema?

The schema is a blueprint of all objects in the domain. When a domain is first created, a default schema exists that contains definitions for users, computers, domains, and so on. Because you cannot have multiple definitions of the same object, you can only have one schema per domain.

The default schema definition is defined in the SCHEMA.INI file, which also contains the initial structure for the NTDS.DIT (storage for the Directory data). This file is located in the %systemroot%\ntds directory. The SCHEMA.INI file is a plain ASCII format file and can be typed out. You will also notice a file NTDS.DIT, which is the storage location for the Active Directory.

What is a domain tree?

In Windows 2000, one domain can be a child of another domain. In other words, CHILD.DOMAIN.COM is a child of DOMAIN.COM (a child domain always has the complete domain name of the parent in it), and a child domain and its parent share a two-way transitive trust.

When you have a domain as a child of another, you have formed a domain tree. A domain tree has to have a contiguous namespace (see Figure 2-3).

The name of the tree is the root domain name, so the tree in the example would be referred to as ROOT.COM. Because the domains have DNS names and inherit the parent part of the name, renaming a part of the tree automatically renames all of its children. For example, if parent NTFAQ.COM of SALES.NTFAQ.COM were renamed BACKOFFICE.COM, the child would be renamed SALES.BACKOFFICE.COM. (Actually, this is not currently possible. Domain trees can currently be created only during the server-to-Domain Controller promotion process with DCPROMO.EXE, but this might change in the future.)

There are a number of advantages to placing domains in a tree. The first and most useful is that all members of a tree have Kerberos transitive trusts with its parent and all of its children. These transitive trusts mean that any user or group

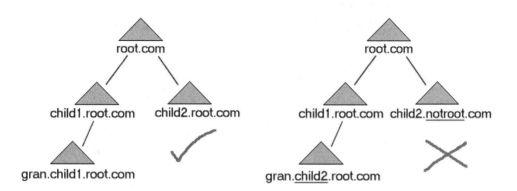

Figure 2-3. Notice in the second diagram that the lack of contiguous names means the domains are not part of the tree.

in a domain tree can be granted access to any object in the entire tree. They also mean that a single network logon can be used at any workstation in the domain tree.

2000 ONLY
FAQ 2.12   What is a domain forest?

You might want a number of separate domain trees in your organization to share resources. This can be accomplished by joining trees to form a forest.

A domain forest is a collection of trees that do not have to form a contiguous namespace (however, the trees themselves have to be contiguous). This might be useful if your company has multiple root DNS addresses.

As can be seen from the example in Figure 2-4, the two root domains are joined via a transitive, two-way Kerberos trust, as in the trust created between a child and its parent. Forests always contain the entire domain tree of each domain, and it is not possible to create a forest containing only parts of a domain tree.

Forests are created during the server-to-Domain Controller promotion process with DCPROMO and can currently not be created at any other time. (This will change in the next version.)

You are not limited to only two domain trees in a forest. You can add as many trees as you want and all domains within the forest will be able to grant access to objects for any user within the forest. Again, this cuts back on having to manu-

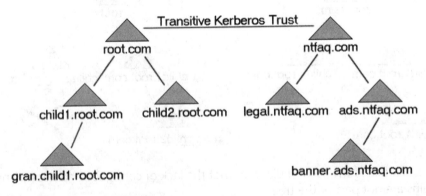

Figure 2-4. An example forest, consisting of the ROOT.COM and NTFAQ.COM domain trees.

ally manage the trust relationships. Creating a forest produces the following effects:

- All trees have a common Global Catalog, containing specific information about every object in the forest.
- The trees all contain a common schema. Microsoft has not yet confirmed what will happen if two trees have difference schemas before they are joined. I assume the changes will be merged.
- Searches in a forest perform a deep search of the entire tree of the domain from which the request is initiated. The search uses the Global Catalog entries for the rest of the forest.

You might, of course, choose not to join trees into a forest and might instead create normal trusts between individual elements of the trees.

What is a Kerberos trust?

Windows NT 4.0 trust relationships are not transitive. If domain2 trusts domain1, and domain3 trusts domain2, this does not mean domain3 trusts domain1.

This is not the case with the trust relationships used to connect members of a tree or forest in Windows 2000. Trust relationships used in a tree are two-way, transitive Kerberos trusts, which means any domain in a tree implicitly trusts every other domain in the tree or forest. This removes the need for time-consuming administration of the trusts, which are created automatically when a domain joins a tree.

Kerberos is the primary security protocol for Windows NT. Kerberos verifies both the identity of the user and the integrity of the session data. The Kerberos services are installed on each Domain Controller, and a Kerberos client is installed on each Windows NT workstation and server. A user's initial Kerberos authentication provides the user a single logon to enterprise resources. Kerberos is not a Microsoft protocol and is based on version 5.0 of Kerberos. For more information, see the Internet Engineering Task Force Requests for Comments (RFCs) 1510 and 1964, available on the Web from http://www.rfc-editor.org/.

3 INSTALLATION

The basic installation of Windows NT, both Workstation and Server, is fairly intuitive. A walkthrough of each is included in this chapter; however, many other advanced installation options are available. You also need to give careful consideration to the coexistence of two or more operating systems on the same computer.

Windows 2000's installation method is basically unchanged except that in Windows 2000 Server (the name for Windows NT 5.0), the role of the machine, whether Domain Controller or member server, is no longer defined at installation.

This chapter takes a detailed look at the various installation methods, including network and unattended installations. The problems of cloning installations are also discussed.

The first question about SMARTDRV is important. If you are performing unattended installations with WINNT.EXE, it could cut down your installation time by several magnitudes.

 ## How do I use SmartDrv?

Why am I talking about the MS-DOS SmartDrv utility? Well, if you use the WINNT.EXE installation method for NT and do not use SMARTDRV, the installation takes longer than if you do use it.

At the most basic level you can create a DOS bootable disk (format a: /s from DOS) that just maps to a network drive and starts the installation. To take advantage of SMARTDRV, copy these files onto the disk:

SMARTDRV.EXE
HIMEM.SYS

Then edit (or create) the file AUTOEXEC.BAT and add <path>smartdrv.exe /q, as in

```
a:smartdrv.exe /q
```

Now edit (or again create) the file CONFIG.SYS and add the line

```
device=himem.sys
```

HIMEM.SYS is needed by SMARTDRV and allows access to higher areas of memory. This applies equally to locally installed copies of DOS, although SMARTDRV.EXE is automatically installed. You can make sure you are using it by looking at AUTOEXEC.BAT.

How do I install NT Workstation 4.0?

Every installation of NT is different, depending on the optional subsystems added and options chosen. However, here is an example of an installation of a Workstation using TCP/IP and NetBEUI protocols connected to an NT Domain.

There are several methods of starting the installation. You can use the installation disk supplied with Windows NT, run WINNT32.EXE from the i386 installation folder (if you're using Windows NT), or run WINNT.EXE (if you're using an older 16-bit client). For this example, you use the boot disks.

1. Insert the first NT installation disk and boot the computer. The installation commences.
2. When prompted, put in the second installation disk and press Enter.

3. You are given a choice of options. Press Enter to choose Setup Windows NT (the default).

4. After you press Enter to Detect Hardware, insert disk 3. This disk contains the drivers for hardware and the basic keyboard, SCSI, file system, and other drivers.

5. When the detection is finished, if you have extra drivers to install, insert the OEM disk and press S to specify additional devices.

6. After you have installed all drivers, read the license agreement. Scroll down by using the Page Down key and press F8 at the end to agree.

7. A list appears of all hard disks and partitions. You can create partitions from here. Select the partition you want to install on and press Enter.

8. You are asked which file system to use. You can format FAT or NTFS. If you choose NTFS, it formats as FAT and schedules a conversion later in the installation process. Because of this initial FAT format, the largest partition you can create during the installation process is 4GB.

9. Select the directory name (you can accept the default of winnt) and press Enter.

10. Allow the setup program to check the hard disks for errors. Then press Enter.

11. After a number of core files are copied to the disk, you have to reboot the machine.

12. After the machine has rebooted, you are in the graphical portion of the installation procedure. (Note: If you selected to install on NTFS, the conversion would have occurred before this GUI phase of installation and an extra reboot would have occurred.)

13. Click Next for the installation procedure to check the computer and continue the installation.

14. Choose the type of installation. In this case, choose Custom to allow greater control over the subsystems installed.

15. Enter your name and organization (you can change this later by editing the values RegisteredOrganization and RegisterOwner from the HKEY_LOCAL_MACHINE\SOFTWARE\Microsoft\Windows NT\CurrentVersion key). Click Next.

16. Enter the CD Key, which is on the yellow sticker on the back of the NT installation CD-ROM case.

17. Enter a Computer Name and click Next.

18. Enter an Administrator password and click Next. This is the local machine's Administrator password and not that of the domain you will be joining.

19. Choose if you want an Emergency Repair Disk (ERD) and click Next. The Emergency Repair Disk is used in the event of a system corruption or problem. (For information about creating an ERD, see Question 11-1 in Chapter 11, Recovery.)

20. Select the components you wish to install (such as Messaging) and click Next.

21. Click the Next button to start the Networking set-up.

22. Select the connection type (in this case, Wired to the Network) and click Next. The other option is Remote Connection, such as over a modem.

23. If you choose Wired to the Network, the next request is for the adapter type. You can click Detect. If the program fails to find the device, click Select From List and pick the appropriate one. Then click Next.

24. Select the protocols you wish to install (in this case, TCP/IP and NetBEUI) and click Next.

25. When you are shown the Network services, again click Next.

26. If you installed TCP/IP, you are now asked if you want to use DHCP. For this example, say No. (DHCP is a process in which TCP/IP addresses are given out as needed, which can help with administration of the network. For more information about DHCP, see Chapter 18, Dynamic Host Configuration Protocol.)

27. Enter the IP address, subnet mask, and gateway, if applicable. Also, clicking on the DNS tab enables you to specify any DNS servers and enter your domain (for example, savilltech.com). Then click OK.

28. Click Next for services and then click Next to start the Network.

29. After the Network has been started, you are asked if you are to operate in a domain or a workgroup. Click the Domain check box and enter the domain name. If the domain administrator has already added your computer name to the domain (by using Server Manager), just click Next. If the name has not been added, click Create Account in Domain. Then you need to enter a Domain Administrator name and password.

30. Click Finish, select your time zone, and then click Close.

31. The last stage detects your graphics card. If it's correct, click OK. If it misdetects, just click Cancel to leave the standard VGA driver.

32. Finally, click Restart Computer.

You now have NT Workstation installed on the computer.

How do I install NT Server?

The installation of NT Server is the same as NT Workstation with a few exceptions. This is because NT Server is basically the same as Workstation with extra components and a number of different Registry-tuning parameters. You'll find these differences in the installation:

- You will need to choose the role of the NT Server, Server, PDC, or BDC. After you set this, it cannot be changed. For more information on these options, see Chapter 14, Domains.
- You can choose to install Internet Information Server.
- You need to choose a license mode: per server or per seat. This is covered more in Chapter 4, Licensing.

I want to install DOS and Windows NT. How should I do this, and how should I partition the hard disk?

A DOS installation was once useful for the configuration of some hardware that could be configured only from DOS. This is no longer such an issue, because most hardware has both NT drivers and NT configuration software.

Having DOS installed on an NT Server can pose a security risk, allowing easy access to data if physical access to the machine is possible.

If you still want to have DOS installed, the best method is to create at least two partitions. Make the first partition around 200MB and format it to FAT (DOS only works on FAT and must reside on the active partition, usually C:). You will install DOS on this partition.

I suggest 200MB because this is enough space to later install Windows 9x if needed. After you install DOS, install NT on the second partition (formatted to FAT or NTFS). After the installation, you will have a choice of booting into DOS or NT.

The advantage of having NT installed on a FAT partition is being able to boot up in DOS mode if there is a problem, so you can access the NT partition. You can possibly restore files this way, although the core NT startup files are located on the C: partition anyway (BOOT.INI, NTDETECT.COM, and NTLDR). The obvious disadvantage is you have none of the security advantages of NTFS on the C: partition.

Installation hangs when detecting the hardware. What should I do?

The program that detects hardware is NTDETECT.COM. The best course of action is to use the DEBUG version of NTDETECT.COM. A debug version of a program is one that gives extra diagnostic information.

In the support folder of the NT installation CD (CD-Rom:\support), you'll find a file NTDETECT.CHK. Follow these instructions to use it:

1. Using the diskcopy command, create a copy of the first installation disk:

```
diskcopy a: a: /v
```

This creates a copy of the first installation disk

2. Copy NTDETECT.COM from the support CD to the installation disk:

```
copy d:\support\ntdetect.chk a:ntdetect.com
```

3. Then reboot the machine with the new version of the installation disk. Each item is shown as it is detected.

This should give you an idea of the hardware at fault, and you can take further action based on the specific problem.

Is it possible to install NT without using boot disks or temp files?

On many new versions of BIOS, you can specify an IDE CD-ROM as a boot device, and the latest versions of the NT installation media have the files you need to boot directly from the CD-ROM. If your BIOS does support the CD-ROM as a boot device, just insert the CD and boot the computer.

If you have a SCSI CD-ROM drive, you can boot from the CD if the SCSI BIOS (such as from Adaptec) supports it.

If you cannot boot from the CD-ROM, you can either have it not using disks (winnt(32) /b) or not using temp files, but not both.

On the Alpha platform, it is possible to boot from the retail or MSDN CD of NT 4.0 and install so no boot disks or temp files are used.

Does NT have to be installed on the C drive?

No, you can install NT on any drive; however, it does place a few files on the active partition in order for NT to boot. Also, limitations of the computer architecture mean that the core NT operating system files have to reside in the first 7.8GB of a disk. This is due to the BIOS int 13H interface used by NTLDR to bootstrap up to the point when it can drive the native HDD IDE or SCSI. Int 13H presents a 24-bit parameter for cylinder/head/sector for a drive. You can find more details on the Microsoft Web site at http://support.microsoft.com.

I have NT installed. How do I install DOS?

The main problem with installing DOS after NT is that DOS replaces the boot information of the disk with its own, removing NT's boot loader. Follow these steps to back up this boot record and then restore it after the DOS installation. This procedure only works if the C drive is FAT—DOS cannot read NTFS.

1. Make an Emergency Repair Disk (ERD) by choosing RDISK.EXE > Update Repair Info.
2. Be sure you have NT installation disks (you can make these by using the winnt32 /ox command).
3. Reboot the machine and boot from the MS-DOS disks.
4. Install DOS (same as doing a SYS a: c: from a DOS bootable disk). The machine reboots into DOS.

5. Reboot the machine by booting off of your NT installation disks.

6. After disk 2, various options are displayed. Press R for repair.

7. Deselect all options except Inspect Boot Sector and press Enter to continue.

8. Press Enter to detect hardware and insert disk 3.

9. When asked if you have an Emergency Repair Disk, say Yes and insert the ERD.

10. The machine then boots into NT again.

11. From NT, go to a DOS session and type

```
> attrib c:\boot.ini -r -s
```

12. Edit BOOT.INI and insert the following at the bottom:

```
c:\=MS-DOS
```

13. Type > **attrib c:\boot.ini +r +s**.

14. Reboot the machine

You now have MS-DOS and NT options.

How do I convert NT Workstation to NT Server?

There are various discussions about the changing of two Registry keys that turn a Workstation into a Server, which in turn change a number of other keys. This is against license agreements, however, and should not be attempted.

A Workstation can be upgraded to a Server, but it cannot become a PDC or a BDC. To do this, you need a fresh installation of NT Server. You cannot upgrade a Workstation to a Domain Controller because of SID issues and incompatibilities between the Registry settings.

To convert a Workstation to a member or standalone server, follow these steps:

1. Boot off of the NT Server installation disks, or create them with winnt(32)/ox.

2. Press Enter to set up NT.

3. Press Enter to detect hardware.

4. Press Enter to continue (or S if you have special drivers).

5. Accept the license (use the Page Down key to read and then exit with F8).

6. When NT install detects the existence of Workstation and asks if you want to upgrade, press Enter.

7. When asked if you want to upgrade from Workstation to Server, press Enter.

8. Continue as usual. All Workstation components (Network, Print) are converted to Server.

9. When finished, you have NT Server and it will have kept all programs and groups.

If you have your NT Workstation upgraded with Service Packs, you need to upgrade the Server with the same service pack Workstation was running. This is best performed by an unattended installation, as described in Question 3-19. If you do not match service packs, you might get a lot of unpredictable problems—which might be small or might be a "blue screen of death."

I have bought a new disk; how do I move NT to this new disk?

Various methods for moving NT are available. The method you use will be governed by the equipment you have to enable you to move information, such as a backup device. You will also be affected by the type of disk you are copying to—for example, IDE or SCSI—and if SCSI, if it's on a different SCSI controller than before.

All of these methods are based on moving the entire structure to another disk, with the same partition configuration, so the NT partition does not change its letter. NT's drive letter is hard-coded in the Registry, which means moving to another partition is very complex and involves manually editing the Registry and changing all occurrences of the old drive name.

Here is the best method for moving NT:

1. Back up your NT disk to a tape.

2. Create a new, up-to-date ERD (rdisk /s).

3. Shut down NT and insert the new hard disk.

4. Perform a basic installation of NT to a directory with a different name than your final NT installation directory.

5. When the installation is finished, restore your backup tape.

6. There are sometimes problems with Registry entries, so reboot and boot off of the NT installation disks.

7. After disk 2, choose Repair and then choose everything except Check System Files. You need to insert disk 3 and then the ERD.

8. When you reboot, NT should work as required.

If the tape drive is not an option and the partition is NTFS, you still have a number of options. For example, you can set up the new disk as a mirror of your existing disk. Then you need to break the mirror and remove the old disk, setting the new disk as the boot disk.

You can also use the SCOPY utility, which is supplied with the NT Resource Kit. To do this, install the new hard disk, create an NTFS partition on it, and then use the following command:

```
scopy <source drive>: <target drive>: /o /a /s
```

To use the SCOPY command, you must have Backup and Restore user rights. After the copy is complete, shut down NT, remove the old drive, and set the new drive to master (if IDE) or SCSI 0/6 (if SCSI). Then boot off of the NT installation disks and again repair everything except Check System Files. If you have time, it can be worth your while to create a temporary NT installation on the drive before performing the copy. Then boot off of this minimal installation and perform the SCOPY from there. With this method, no files are locked and you only need to repair the boot sector.

Other methods include Norton Ghost from http://www.ghostsoft.com and DriveCopy from http://www.powerquest.com. These copy an entire disk, which should eliminate the need for performing a repair. I have used the Norton Ghost utility, and it works well.

If you are moving NT to a different type of disk (that is, one that needs a different driver), make sure you install the new driver before you perform the copy. This means NT has the needed drivers when it boots off of the new disk.

Can I upgrade from Windows 95 to NT 4.0?

There is no direct upgrade path from Windows 95 to NT 4.0. The best option would be to have a dual-boot system if you have 150MB of uncompressed space available. Install NT 4.0 into a *different* directory (if you install NT 4.0 into the same directory as Windows 95, you'll corrupt the 95 Registry), and when booting the machine, you'll have a choice of NT 4.0 or Windows 95.

Windows NT 4.0 does support an upgrade from Windows for Workgroups, but I'm not sure why you would want to.

Windows 2000 provides an upgrade path from Windows 95 and Windows 98.

How do I remove NT from a FAT partition?

If you have NT installed on a FAT partition, you need to remove the NT operating system files and the NT boot loader. To remove the files and the boot loader, boot an MS-DOS disk with the DELTREE utility copied and perform the following:

1. The first step is to ensure C: is the current drive. Type

```
C:
```

2. The entire WINNT directory tree and its contents should be deleted. To do so, use

```
DELTREE WINNT
```

3. Next, the Windows branch of the Program Folders folder should be deleted, so move to that directory:

```
CD PROGRA~1
```

4. Delete the Windows~1 tree (use the short names):

```
DELTREE WINDOW~1
```

5. Move back to the base directory:

```
CD \
```

6. Delete the NT Loader component:

```
DEL NTLDR
```

7. Delete the Windows NT detection command file:

```
DEL NTDETECT.COM
```

8. Now you can remove the boot menu:

```
DEL BOOT.INI
```

9. The pagefile NT uses should now be deleted; however, be aware that it might not reside on the system partition if you moved it.

```
DEL PAGEFILE.SYS
```

10. Delete the DOS boot sector code:

```
DEL BOOTSECT.DOS
```

11. Boot up, using a Win95 or DOS startup disk, and type the following to replace the NT boot loader:

```
SYS a: c:
```

12. Reboot the machine.

On reboot, the NT boot loader will have been removed and DOS/Windows 9x will start automatically.

 ## How do I remove NT from an NTFS partition?

The best way is to delete the partition, because other operating systems will not be able to read the partition, anyway.

Start the computer from the NT installation disks. At the option to create or choose partitions, select the NTFS partition where NT is installed. Press D to delete the partition and then L to confirm.

If NT was not on the active partition, you need to replace the boot loader as defined in Question 3-12.

 ## What are symbol files, and do I need them?

Symbol files are created when images are compiled. They are used for debugging an image. Symbol files enable someone with the correct tools to view code as the software is running. You do not need symbol files unless you are a developer.

Symbol files enable the developer to see the call stack—the sequence in which the calls were made—until a particular point in the execution of a program.

 ## How do I install the symbol files?

You are most likely to encounter symbol files when you're downloading a service pack and find a symbol file version in the region of twice the size of the normal service pack file. A common question is, do you need them?

Symbol files are produced during the link stage of the image compilation when a program is built. They're used to resolve global variables and function names in an executable. They are used only for debugging a program, so unless you are a developer, you do not need symbol files.

If you do want symbol files, perform the following:

1. Create a directory on your machine called SYMBOLS:

```
mkdir %systemroot%\symbols
```

2. Copy over the symbols from the NT installation CD-ROM:

```
xcopy <CD-ROM>:\Support\Debug\i386 %systemroot%\symbols /s
```

If you have any service pack symbols, you should extract these to the same directory. For Service Pack 2, for example, use

```
SYM_400I -d %systemroot%\symbols
```

How do I install NT and Linux?

Linux has a boot manager called LILO (which is a separate utility) that boots Linux on its native EXT2 partition and any other DOS/WIN bootimages residing on a FAT16 partition. LILO doesn't really care whether a file is dos/win95/NT; it will boot it. As long as NT is installed on a FAT16 partition, there is no problem with LILO. The latest Linux kernel has FAT32 support, so that might be an option, as well. Actually, Linux supports FAT16 and can mount the FAT16 partition under its filesystem and have all the DOS/WIN files visible. An alternative to LILO is Grub, which you can download from http://www. uruk.org/~erich/grub/.

You could use a program called LOADLIN to install Linux as an MS-DOS subdirectory in a DOS/WIN system. This enables Linux to be run as an application after you start DOS, but it does not work with NT because Linux needs to run in supervisor mode and not user mode. NT will not yield at all on this. Windows 95 is the same, but you can set LOADLIN to run in DOS mode, where it just sees DOS 7 and works fine.

Linux and NT work even if Windows NT is on NTFS. When using the FDISK utility, you need to set the Linux drive to be flagged bootable, not NT. Then install LILO and select to boot the Linux partition and NT (which is called OS/2 in LILO). This way you can use both NT and Linux and still have an NTFS partition. LILO must reside on the Linux root sector and not the MBR.

Another method follows:

1. Install NT as usual.
2. Download the BootPart freeware utility from http://www.winimage.com/bootpart.htm.
3. Install Linux. Make sure LILO is not installed on MBR but on the boot sector of the Linux root partition.
5. Boot NT.
5. Start a command prompt (CMD.EXE).
6. Run BOOTPART.EXE and add the Linux boot sector into the NT-OS loader. (This also works when the NT boot partition is NTFS.)

You can learn more about Linux from the Linux documentation project and the FAQ inside, which is mirrored in a large number of locations. One of the mirrors resides at ftp://ftp.ox.ac.uk/pub/linux/LDP_WWW/linux.html.

 # How do I install NT over the network?

If you do not currently have any operating system installed on your machine, you need to create a bootable floppy disk that contains a driver for your network card and network protocol. Provided with NT is the Network Client Administrator, which automatically creates a bootable disk used to install Windows 95 or Network Client. You can also use this tool to create a disk that can be used to install NT with a bit of tweaking.

1. Use DOS to format a system floppy drive:

   ```
   format a: /s
   ```

2. Create a share on the NT box containing the entire i386 structure from the NT installation CD-ROM and give everyone Read access.
3. Log on as the Administrator (or a member of the Administrators group).
4. Start the Network Client Administrator (Start > Programs > Administrative Tools > Network Client Administrator).
5. Choose the Make Network Installation Startup Disk option and click Continue.
6. Select Share files and accept the default of <CD-ROM>\clients.
7. When you click the OK button, the program performs some background actions.
8. Next, select the floppy drive and click Network Client V3.0 as the client. Choose your network card from the drop-down list and click OK.
9. Enter the name by which the computer will be known. The username and domain are completed automatically, using the current user.
10. You now need to choose the protocol. For this example, choose TCP/IP and uncheck DHCP. Enter an IP address, subnet mask, and gateway.

11. Insert the disk created in step 1 and click OK.

12. Files are copied to the floppy disk. When all have been copied, exit Network Client Administrator.

13. The disk needs to be edited to stop the automatic installation of the Network Client. Start Explorer and open the A: drive. Right-click on AUTOEXEC.BAT and choose Edit.

14. Remove the last two lines of the file (echo running setup and setup).

15. You can also change the net use command to point to the share where the NT installation files are located.

16. Choose Save from the File menu and close Notepad.

17. Insert the disk into the machine where you want to install NT and power up.

18. After startup has completed, change the directory to Z: (or whatever your net use pointed to).

19. Start a floppyless install:

```
winnt /b
```

If you plan to produce a large number of install disks, you can configure the Network Client Administrator to also create Workstation and Server network installation disks. To do this, you need to have the client directory on a hard disk and create two subdirectories under it (\\server\client).

1. winnt\netsetup (hierarchy of \i386 from NT Workstation CD-ROM)
2. winnt.srv\netsetup (hierarchy of \i386 from NT Server CD-ROM)

When you're creating the network disk, you will now also have options for Windows NT Workstation and Windows NT Server (see Figure 3-1).

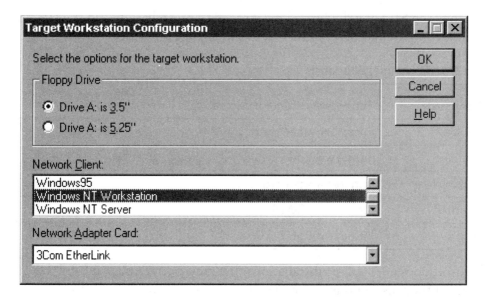

Figure 3-1. This version of Network Client Administrator has NT Workstation and NT Server options.

Is it possible to use disk duplication to distribute Windows NT?

It is okay to use disk duplication to install NT, but not a complete NT installation. To use disk duplication, follow these steps:

1. Use the winnt /b installation option on a machine.
2. Stop the setup at the second reboot, when it has finished the text portion of the installation and will be starting the GUI section.
3. Remove and duplicate the hard disk of the machine.
4. Install the duplicate hard drive in the new machine.
5. Start the new machine and the GUI sections will start.

The traditional problems with cloning were that the machine SID would be duplicated; however, several third-party products (see Table 3-1) now enable you to change the SID of a duplicated machine. After installation, add the machine as a new computer account on the PDC and change its name.

Table 3-1. Drive Image Products

NT Internals	http://www.sysinternals.com
ImageCast	http://www.netversant.com
DiskClone	http://www.qdeck.com
DriveCopy	http://www.powerquest.com
ImageBlast	http://www.keylabs.com
Ghost	http://www.ghostsoft.com

Microsoft does not support installations that have been duplicated and will stop support if they suspect duplication is the cause of the problem. Microsoft provides a tool, SYSPREP.EXE, that can be used to clone full NT Workstation installations.

How do I perform an unattended installation?

It is possible to specify a text file that can be passed to the Windows NT installation program containing answers to the questions asked by the installation procedure. This is useful for bulk installations.

This text file is usually called UNATTEND.TXT, and it's passed to the Windows NT installation program by using the /u:unattend.txt qualifier. The answer file has to adhere to a strict format, which can be very complex; however, the SETUPMGR.EXE utility on the NT Server CD (in the Support/Deptools/i386) lets you put the information into dialog boxes and then creates the file UNATTEND.TXT (or any other name) for you. Here is an example of how to use the SETUPMGR.EXE file:

1. Load the NT Server Installation CD-ROM.
2. Run <CD-ROM>:/Support/Deptools/i386/setupmgr.exe.
3. Click New and then OK in the advice dialog box.
4. Click the General Setup button.

5. Click the User Information tab and type your name (that is, John Savill, not your domain logon name), your company, a computer name, and the product ID (find it on the back of the NT installation CD).

6. Click the Computer Role tab. From the drop-down list, select the type (in this case, Workstation in Domain) and then type the Domain name.

7. Click Install Directory and choose the NT Install Directory.

8. Click the Time Zone tab and select your time zone from the drop-down list.

9. If you choose a PDC, you can click the License Mode tab and choose the licensing to be used.

10. Click OK.

11. Click the Networking Setup button.

12. Enter the information for adapters and protocols and then click OK.

13. If you want to use NTFS, click the Advanced button and click the File System tab. Then choose Convert to NTFS.

14. Click OK.

15. Click Save and enter a filename.

16. Click Exit.

Microsoft has a document on automated installations (Deployment Guide to Windows NT Setup) at http://www.microsoft.com/NTWorkstation.

 ## Is it possible to specify unique items during an unattended install?

The unattended installation file contains details for settings that apply to all machines; however, you might want some settings to be different from machine to machine, such as username, computer name, TCP/IP address. You can accomplish this by producing a text file in a certain format, with different sections for each computer. This Uniqueness Database File (UDF) is used by specifying the /UDF:ID[,<database filename>]. An example UDF file would be

```
[UniqueIds]
u1 = UserData,TCPIPParams
u2 = UserData,TCPIPParams
```

```
[u1:UserData]
FullName = John Savill
ComputerName = SavillComp
ProductID = xxx-xxxxxx
[u1:TCPIPParams]
IPAddress = 200.200.153.45
[u2:UserData]
FullName = Kevin Savill
ComputerName = KevinComp
ProductID = xxx-xxxxxx
[u2:TCPIPParams]
IPAddress = 200.200.153.46
```

The ID specified would be (in the case above) u1 or u2. If the example file were saved as UDF.TXT to perform an unattended installation for machine 1, you would use the following:

winnt /b /s:z: /u:unattend.txt /UDF:u1,udf.txt

This would set the installation as user John Savill, computer name SavillComp, and IP address 200.200.153.45. If a parameter is specified in both the unattended answer file and the UDF, the value in the UDF is used. (The /b means it's a floppyless installation, and the /s specifies the source for the installation files, UDF, and so on.) You would need to have already created the connection to z: (net use z: //savillcomp/dist).

The structure of the UDF uses a subset of the sections available in the unattended answer file.

How do I automatically install applications as part of the unattended installation?

The SYSDIFF.EXE utility supplied on the Windows NT Resource Kit is used to create a file containing files and Registry changes needed for an application or set of applications to be installed. To use SYSDIFF, copy it from the CD to your hard disk.

1. Insert the NT CD-ROM.
2. Move to the <CD-ROM>:\Support\Deptools\i386 directory.

3. Create a directory on your local hard disk (e.g. SYSDIFF).

4. Copy SYSDIFF.EXE and SYSDIFF.INF to the directory.

Alternatively, a newer version is available as a fix from ftp://ftp.microsoft.com/bussys/winnt/winnt-public/fixes/usa/NT40/utilities/Sysdiff-fix/. Download SYSDIFFA.EXE for Alpha or SYSDIFFI.EXE for Intel.

The basics behind SYSDIFF are that it creates a snapshot of the system before the application is installed. Then the application is installed and SYSDIFF is run again. It compares the current system to the snapshot, and any changes to the Registry and files are saved. Following is an example of how to perform this procedure:

1. Create an initial snapshot of the system by using SYSDIFF /snap <snapshot filename> (for example, snapfile, no extension).

2. Install the application to the machine (possibly Office 97).

3. Create a difference file based on the current system configuration and the snapshot file, using SYSDIFF /diff /c:<title> <snapshot file> <difference file>, such as <difffile, no extension>. For example, use

```
SYSDIFF /diff /c:officediff snap difffile
```

4. Have a look at the differences by using SYSDIFF /dump <difference file> <dump file>, as in

```
SYSDIFF /dump difffile dumpfile
```

5. Type out the dumpfile.

6. Edit your unattended installation file (UNATTEND.TXT) and change the [Unattended] section to include

```
OEMPreinstall = Yes
```

7. Copy SYSDIFF.EXE and SYSDIFF.INF to the OEM directory.

8. Copy DIFFFILE to the distribution directory.

9. If CMDLINES.TXT does not exist, create the file OEM\Cmdlines.txt and insert the following line, where /m makes the changes to the default user profile.

```
sysdiff /apply /m difffile
```

Note: When you use the /apply method, the %systemroot% has to be the same on all machines. In other words, if the difference file was created on a machine with a %systemroot% of d:\winnt\, all machines must be installed to d:\winnt\ ([Unattended] TargetPath).

If you are installing a large number of applications by using this method, the difference file might become too large. In this case, you can use an alternative method of creating an .INF file, using the SYSDIFF /INF switch. More information on the /inf switch can be found in the SYSDIFF Help file.

When I use an unattended installation, how do I avoid clicking "Yes" at the license agreement?

In the [unattended] section of your unattended answer file, insert the following line:

```
OemSkipEula = yes
```

How can I make domain users members of local Administrators groups during an unattended installation?

The easiest way to do this is to use the net localgroup command, but before you can use the command, you must be connected to the PDC and start the netlogon service. The following commands can be used in the unattended installation, using the CMDLINES.TXT file:

```
net use \\<machine name of the PDC> /user:<domain
name>\<username> <password>
net start netlogon
net localgroup Administrators <domain name>\<user> /add
```

I have problems running a program as part of the unattended installation. What should I do?

You can use the /e switch during the unattended installation to specify a program to run, like this:

```
winnt.exe /u:unattend.txt /s:w: /e:w:\servpack\update -u -z
```

The /e switch is used to install a service pack after the NT installation (-u for unattended, -z for no reboot); however, you might get the following error in SETUPLOG.TXT:

```
Warning:
Setup was unable to invoke external program
<drive>:\<directory>\<program> because of the following
error:
CreateProcess returned error 3.
```

This happens because network drives are no longer mapped after the installation and w: no longer exists. Any source files need to be locally stored to be run, and you need to use a local drive letter with the /e switch.

How do I delete the Recycle Bin as part of an unattended installation?

The Recycle Bin is just a Registry entry. If you delete the Registry entry, you will remove the recycle bin. To do so, create the following in a file REMRECYL.INF:

```
[Version]
Signature = $Windows NT$
Provider=%Provider%
[Strings]
Provider=SavillTech Ltd
[DefaultInstall]
```

```
AddReg = AddReg
DelReg = DelReg
UpdateInis = UpdateInis
[AddReg]
[DelReg]
HKEY_LOCAL_MACHINE\SOFTWARE\Microsoft\Windows\CurrentVersion\
Explorer\Desktop\NameSpace\{645FF040-5081-101B-9F08-
00AA002F954E}
[UpdateInis]
```

You should then create a OEM folder in your i386 installation directory and copy the file REMRECYL.REG into the directory.

If the file CMDLINES.TXT exists, edit it. If it doesn't exist, create it (in the OEM directory) and add the following:

```
[Commands]
rundll32 setupapi,InstallHinfSection DefaultInstall 128 .\
remreycl.inf
```

3.26 How do I disable the installation of Exchange during installation?

If you want to stop the installation of the Exchange client during installation of NT (or Windows Messaging, as it's now called), perform the following:

1. Copy the i386 directory from the Windows NT CD-ROM to a directory.
2. In the i386 folder expand the file SYSSETUP.IN_:

   expand Syssetup.in_ Syssetup.inf

3. Rename SYSSETUP.IN_ to SYSSETUP.OLD; otherwise, the installation uses the compressed version.
4. Edit the file SYSSETUP.INF and comment out the MSMAIL.INF entry in the [BaseWinOptionsInfs].
5. Save the file and install as usual.

Here is an example of the edited file:

```
[BaseWinOptionsInfs]
accessor.inf
communic.inf
games.inf
imagevue.inf
mmopt.inf
;msmail.inf
multimed.inf
optional.inf
pinball.inf
wordpad.inf
```

 3.27 ## During an unattended installation, I am prompted for an IP address if 0 is in the given address.

An error message appears if you have an unattended install file with information such as this:

```
[TCPIPParameters]
DHCP=NO
IPAddress=200.200.0.200
Subnet=255.255.0.0
```

This is the error message you'll receive during the installation:

"The IPAddress key has an invalid IP address. Please correct the problem after the property sheet is displayed."

If you click OK, the installation continues. The bug only applies if there is a 0 in the second or third octet—xxx.here.orhere.xxx.

Service Pack 2 or later corrected this problem, so you can avoid the message by replacing TCPCFG.DL_ on your distribution server (the i386 directory) with the TCPCFG.DLL from the latest service pack.

How do I map a network drive during an unattended installation?

This might be useful if you want to install software such as a service pack during installation.

Using the CMDLINES.TXT file, it is easy to map to a network share. CMDLINES.TXT must be stored in the OEM directory under your NT installation area (i386\OEM). A very basic CMDLINES.TXT would consist of

```
[Unattended]
OemPreinstall = yes
```

The map command should be under the [Commands] section of your unattended install file, like this:

```
[Commands]
.\net use <drive letter>: \\<server>\<share> /user:
<domain>\<user> [<password>] /persistent:no
```

It is important to add /user; otherwise the system attempts to use the system account. The system account does not have an actual user account, so the command fails. The /persistent:no is used because the connection should not be remapped at each logon.

One option would be to enable the Guest account and give it access to the share, which means you could connect at /user:<domain>\Guest. This allows a connection to be made to the share even if the Domain Controller cannot be contacted.

Install detects the wrong video card and locks the installation. What can I do?

When NT detects a video card, it insists that you click the Test button. If the NT installation procedure incorrectly detects the hardware (for example, the Number 9FX Reality card), it can cause the NT installation to hang until you press the Reset button. To solve this problem, just click the CANCEL button when the card is detected, and NT will leave the default VGA driver.

After the installation has finished, manually install the new driver supplied with the graphics card, or download the driver from the maker's Web site.

4.0 ONLY

How do I upgrade from NT 3.51 to NT 4.0?

The following scenario is for upgrading an NT Workstation 3.51 machine to an NT Workstation 4.0 machine. It is the same to upgrade an NT Server 3.51 to a NT Server 4.0, except that when you upgrade a server, you are also given the option to install Internet Information Server (IIS).

1. Although it is possible to upgrade by using the floppyless install, this example boots off of the three NT installation disks (which you can make by using winnt32 /ox). Insert the first NT installation disk and boot up the machine.
2. At the prompt, insert disk 2 and then press Enter.
3. You are given a choice of options. Choose Setup Windows NT by pressing Enter.
4. Press Enter to detect hardware. You now have to insert disk 3.
5. When the detection is finished, if you have extra drivers to install, insert the OEM disk and press S to specify additional devices.
6. After all drivers have been installed, read the license agreement. Scroll down by using the Page Down key and press F8 to agree at the end.
7. Install runs a check of the disks. When it detects your previous installation of NT, press Enter to upgrade this installation.
8. Press Enter to allow the program to perform a quick check of the disk.
9. The fonts on the system are upgraded and files copied over.
10. Remove any disks and press Enter to reboot.
11. When the system has rebooted, press Next to allow the Setup program to verify the computer information.
12. Enter the CD Key from the back of the NT installation CD-ROM case and click Next.
13. Select Yes if you want a repair disk and click Next.

14. Select components and click Next.
15. Click Next to upgrade Network Services.
16. Any nonstandard Network components are displayed and you are advised to remove them and add them after the installation.
17. Click Finish to copy the main files.
18. Click the Restart Computer button.

The only problem with the upgrade is it does not remove old applications that were part of 3.51, such as CARDFILE.EXE.

FAQ 3.31   I have Windows NT installed; how do I install Windows 98?

As with the installation of Windows 95, the system partition (the active partition, C:) must be FAT and not NTFS, because Windows 98 cannot read or write to an NTFS partition. Windows 98 places COMMAND.COM on the active partition (along with a blank AUTOEXEC.BAT).

If your system partition is not FAT, you should back up your data, reformat the partition as FAT, and restore the backup.

Windows 98 is NT-boot-menu friendly, which means it will not replace the boot loader code of the disk and instead automatically adds the following option to the boot menu (BOOT.INI) of the format:

```
C:\="Microsoft Windows 98"
```

This means either Windows 98 or NT can be chosen upon booting the machine.

Windows 98 cannot be installed from within Windows NT. If you have DOS also installed, boot from DOS (its boot menu item will be replaced with the Windows 98 name after the Windows 98 installation) and run SETUP.EXE on the Windows 98 installation disk.

If you do not have DOS installed, you should boot off of a DOS boot disk with a driver for your CD-ROM and again run SETUP.EXE.

After installation has started, you will be able to choose the installation drive and directory (only FAT partitions are allowed). If there are NTFS partitions on the system, a warning will be given that the contents will not be viewable under Windows 98.

When installation is complete, no user action is needed and you may boot off of either installation.

After you have completed the Windows 98 installation, be sure you do *not* upgrade the active partition to FAT32. Windows NT 4.0 cannot read FAT32, and converting the active partition to FAT32 renders the NT boot menu unusable and unbootable.

 ## I have Windows 95 and NT installed; how can I configure the applications to run on both?

Although it is possible to add the Windows 95 system directory to the NT path (which would mean you would find any DLLs or other files associated with applications), many applications write a large amount of information to the Registry that would be missing.

The best approach, and one I have tested, is to just install the application twice to the same directory—once when you are booted into NT and once when you are booted into 95. This has the effect of having only one set of EXEs, but duplicates both DLLs and Registry settings to both machines. Obviously, the applications cannot be on an NTFS or FAT32 partition.

 ## How do I remove Windows 95/DOS from my NT system?

The procedure below should be used on systems with either Windows 95 or DOS installed; however, be aware that it is sometimes a good idea to have a small DOS installation for use with such activities as hardware setup. Before you start this procedure, make sure you have an up-to-date ERD (use rdisk -s) and the three NT installation disks (use winnt32 /ox) in case you have a problem.

1. Modify the attributes on BOOT.INI to allow the file to be edited

```
attrib c:\boot.ini -r -s
```

2. Using Notepad (or another text editor), open c:\boot.ini and remove the lines for DOS or Windows 95 from the [operating systems] section. For example, the lines to remove might be

```
c:\=MS DOS 6.22
c:\bootsect.622=MS DOS 6.22
c:\=Windows 95
```

3. Lines to avoid removing are structured like this:

```
multi(0)disk(0)rdisk(0)partition(2)\WINNT=Windows NT
Workstation Version 4.00
```

4. Save the file, and put back the file attributes:

   attrib c:\boot.ini +r +s

5. If you are removing DOS, delete the DOS tree structure

   deltree c:\dos

6. If you are removing Windows 95, delete the Windows 95 tree structure, but make sure it is not the same directory where NT is installed (this is unlikely):

   deltree d:\window95

7. You also need to remove applications that were only installed for use with Windows 95 or DOS, such as programs under Program Files. Be careful, because NT also installs applications in this directory.

8. DOS and Windows 95 place a number of files on the boot partition that can be deleted, including
   - AUTOEXEC.BAT
   - CONFIG.SYS
   - IO.SYS
   - MSDOS.SYS
   - BOOTLOG.TXT
   - COMMAND.COM

It is probably safer to copy them somewhere before deleting them and just check that NT boots okay. You might need to set the files to be deletable by using

```
attrib <file> -r -h -s
```

9. You can usually delete all files at the base of the boot partition except these, which are needed for NT startup:
   - BOOT.INI
   - NTLDR
   - NTDETECT.COM
   - NTBOOTDD.SYS (FOR SCSI SYSTEMS)
10. When you reboot the machine, Windows 95 and DOS have been removed

4.0 ONLY
3.34 I can't create an NTFS partition over 4GB in size during installation. Why?

During the text-based portion of the NT installation, it is possible to create and format partitions. The maximum size for an NTFS partition is very large (16 exabytes); however, the maximum size for a FAT partition under NT is 4GB (2GB under DOS). If you format a partition as NTFS during NT installation, it is originally formatted as FAT and then converts in the final stages of the NT installation. Thus you are limited to a maximum partition size of 4GB during the NT installation.

To get around this problem, here are several possible solutions:

1. Before starting the installation, you can insert the disk into an existing NT installation and partition/format the disk by using Disk Administrator. Then insert the disk into the machine to be installed.
2. You can partition the disk into smaller partitions. For example, for a 5GB disk you can have a 1GB system partition and a 4GB boot partition. The system partition is where NT's core startup files are located (BOOT.INI, NTLDR, and NTDETECT.COM—or NTBOOTDD.SYS, if SCSI) and will normally be the active partition. The boot partition is the partition where NT stores the rest of its files (that is, the %systemroot% directory).

3. Finally, you can create a 4GB partition at installation time and then extend the NTFS partition after installation has completed, as follows:

   a. Start Disk Administrator (Start > Programs > Administrative Tools > Disk Administrator).

   b. Select the NTFS partition. Then, while holding down the Ctrl key, select the unpartitioned space of the rest of the disk.

   c. From the Partition menu, select Extend Volume Set.

Note: You cannot extend an NTFS partition if it is the boot or system partition (because the boot/system partition cannot be part of a volume set).

If you are performing an unattended installation, you can create a greater-than-4GB partition by using the ExtendOEMPartition flag in the unattended file. This key causes text-mode setup to extend the partition on which the temporary Windows NT sources are located into any available unpartitioned space that physically follows the partition on the disk. To perform this extension, include these lines under the [unattended] section:

```
FileSystem = convertNTFS
ExtendOemPartition = 1, NoWait
```

The NoWait is only available from Service Pack 1 and later.

Also, if you are installing from a distribution kit, you can copy the Service Pack 3 version of SETUPDD.SYS and replace the version in the i386 folder of the NT distribution set.

For more information, see these Knowledge Base articles:

- Q138364 at
  http://support.microsoft.com/support/kb/articles/q138/3/64.asp
- Q119497 at
  http://support.microsoft.com/support/kb/articles/q119/4/97.asp

I cannot upgrade my 4.0 NT installation with the NT 4.0 upgrade CD.

Microsoft has confirmed this to be a problem with the software, and they provide more information in Knowledge Base Article q154538 at http://support.microsoft.com/support/kb/articles/q154/5/38.asp.

A workaround is available. The setup procedure checks the Registry entry HKEY_LOCAL_MACHINE\SOFTWARE\Microsoft\Windows NT\ CurrentVersion\CurrentVersion for the version number, and only upgrades if the version is 3.1, 3.5, or 3.51. You can therefore edit this entry and change the current version number, as follows:

1. Start the Registry editor (REGEDIT.EXE).
2. Move to HKEY_LOCAL_MACHINE\SOFTWARE\Microsoft\ Windows NT\CurrentVersion.
3. Double-click on CurrentVersion in the right-hand pane.
4. Change 4.0 to 3.5 and click OK (see Figure 3-2).
5. Close the Registry editor.

You should now be able to upgrade.

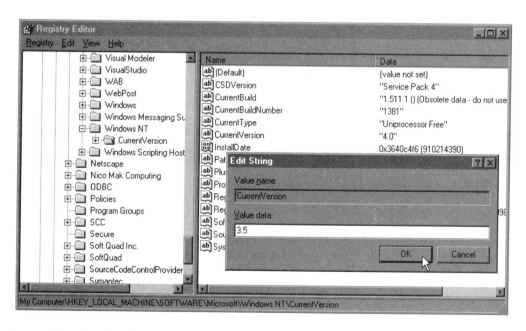

Figure 3-2. Modifying to 3.5 allows the upgrade version of NT to upgrade a 4.0 version of NT.

How do I create the NT installation disks?

Windows NT ships with three installation disks. If they get damaged or lost, perform the following to create a new set:

1. Insert your NT Workstation/Server CD.
2. From the Start Menu, select Run (or press Win key + R).
3. If you are not running NT on the machine from which you are making the disks, enter

   ```
   <CD-ROM drive>:\i386\winnt /ox
   ```

4. If you are running NT, enter

   ```
   <CD-ROM drive>:\i386\winnt32 /ox
   ```

5. You will have to put in three blank disks.

 ## How can I use a network card that is not one of those shown with Network Client Administrator?

The Network Client Administrator tool located in the Administrative Tools section is very useful for creating a bootable disk for installing an operating system over the network; however, it lacks the seemingly obvious function of Have Disk to use a NDIS 2.0 compatible driver supplied with the network card. You can get around this with a minimum of hassle, as follows:

1. Run Network Client Administrator as usual, selecting a network card similar to your card.
2. Locate the driver disk that was supplied with the network card.
3. On the disk, find the NDIS folder and DOS section.
4. Copy the .DOS file from this disk to the net subdirectory on the disk created by Network Client Administrator.

5. Also in the directory should be a sample PROTOCOL.INI file. Open this and look for the line with a driver with a $ on the end, for example, EL59X$, and write down that name:

```
DriverName = EL59X$
```

6. Insert the disk created by Network Client Administrator and move to the \net subdirectory.

7. Open the file SYSTEM.INI and edit the network drivers section. Change the netcard parameter to the name of the .DOS file you copied to the disk

```
[network drivers]
netcard=EL59X.dos
```

8. After saving SYSTEM.INI, open PROTOCOL.INI (in the same directory) and locate the DriverName parameter. Change to the name you found in the PROTOCOL.INI file supplied on the network card driver disk (the one you wrote down in step 5); for example,

```
[ms$elnk3]
DRIVERNAME=EL59X$
```

9. If the card is a PCI card, make sure the I/O, slot, and so on are commented out—or set these to the correct values—and save the file again.

The Network Client Administrator disk is now configured to use your network card. A known problem is with Irmatrac/Microdyne token ring adapters, which will not work unless the net subdirectory on the disk is renamed to dev.

This solution is fine for one-time disk creations; however, you might want to have the network card displayed as an option by the Network Card Administrator program. To do this, perform the following:

1. You have to have the client's directory shared on your hard disk, like this:

```
d:\clients
```

2. Copy the .DOS file from the network driver disk (Windows for Workgroups area) to <client share name>\msclient\netsetup directory.

3. Edit the file <client share name>\msclient\netsetup\wcnet.inf and enter the following details (this information will be on the Network card installation disk as an OEMSETUP.INF or similar file):

```
[netcard]
tcm$el59x=3Com Fast EtherLink/EtherLink III BusMaster
Adapter
(3C59x),0,ndis,ethernet,0x07,tcm$el59x,tcm$el59x_nif
```

4. Also in the OEMSETUP.INF will be two sections that correspond to the last two parameters (for example, tcm$el59x and tcm$el59x_inf). Append these to the end of WCNET.INF and save the file.

Network Client Administrator will now list the new card as a Network Card option.

I want to dial-boot Windows 98 and NT. What file system should I use?

Windows 98 supports two file systems, FAT and FAT32. Windows NT 4.0 supports two main file systems, FAT and NTFS. The only common file system is FAT, which means the active partition, C:, must be FAT and *not* FAT32.

If you then partition the hard disk into one partition for the active partition, one for 98 (D:), and one for NT (E:), you could have FAT32 on D: and NTFS on E:, but be aware that neither operating system will be able to see the partition of the other. If you ever want a partition that can be seen by both, you will need FAT.

Windows 2000 introduces support for FAT32, so in this case the active partition can be FAT32, and you need only one separate partition for NT if you want NTFS.

Tools are available that enable Windows 9x to read NTFS (such as NTFS-DOS from http://www.sysinternals.com), but these are mainly read-only and might lead to corruption if not used correctly. Also bear in mind that Windows NT 2000 introduces NTFS 5.0, which these utilities cannot read.

How can I stop the "Welcome to Windows NT" screen during setup?

Normally when a user logs on for the first time a welcoming splash screen is displayed. This can be disabled in a number of ways, one of which follows.

1. Copy the I386 directory structure from the Windows NT installation CD to a distribution server.
2. Create the UNATTEND.TXT file as normal.
3. In the I386 directory on the distribution server rename the file WELCOME.EX_ to WELCOME.BAK

   ```
   C:\> rename welcome.ex_ welcome.bak
   ```

4. Create a backup of the file TXTSETUP.SIF file (which is also in the I386 directory) to TXTSETUP.BAK.
5. Edit TXTSETUP.SIF and place a ; in front of the WELCOME.EXE line, so the line

   ```
   welcome.exe=1,,,,,,,1,0,0
   ```

   becomes

   ```
   ;welcome.exe=1,,,,,,,1,0,0
   ```

6. Save the modified file.
7. Create a backup of DOSNET.INF (again in the I386 directory) to DOSNET.BAK.
8. Edit DOSNET.INF and again place a ; in front of the WELCOME.EXE line, so the link

   ```
   d1,welcome.exe
   ```

   becomes

   ```
   ;d1,welcome.exe
   ```

9. Save the modified file.
10. Perform the unattended installation from the distribution share.

The above stops the installation of the WELCOME.EXE image and prevents it from executing. An alternative is to create a registry script that runs during installation that disables the Welcome dialog.

3.40 I have Windows 98 installed. How do I install NT?

The only requirement for installing Windows NT after Windows 98 is that the system partition (C:) is not FAT32. Windows NT cannot read FAT32 (at least until version 5.0 of NT, which has full FAT32 support).

If the active partition is FAT32, you need to convert it back to FAT16. A number of third-party applications can do this, such as Partition-It from QuarterDeck (http://www.symantec.com/corporate/quarterdeck/us_index.html). I have never used it, but other people have recommended it.

To begin the installation of NT, boot into Windows 98 and run WINNT32.EXE from the Windows NT installation. Then proceed as usual, but select Install, not Upgrade. The Windows NT installation procedure automatically detects the Windows 98 installation and adds it to the NT Boot menu.

Do **not** use the CONVERT.EXE command to upgrade the system partition to NTFS, because Windows 98 will no longer be able to boot.

 ## 3.41 I have Windows 2000 installed, but when I try to install Windows NT 4.0, the installation fails.

Windows 2000 changes the boot loader code, so if you try to install Windows NT 4.0 afterward, the Setup program might cause the machine to continuously restart each time the computer is started, without ever finishing.

Service Pack 4 provides an updated WINNT32.EXE that allows you to install Windows NT 4.0 after NT 5.0. You need to perform the following:

1. Copy the i386 directory structure from the Windows NT installation CD-ROM.
2. Rename WINNT32.EXE to WINNT32.OLD.
3. From the Service Pack 4 CD, copy WINNT32.EXE from the Support\Winnt32\i386 directory to your i386 directory structure.
4. Run WINNT32.EXE from your local stored copy.

How do I manually install SCSI drivers before the autodetect during installation?

Do this when you put the first boot disk in to install NT. There is a brief moment when, at the top of the screen in white lettering, it says Setup is inspecting your hardware. When you see that, press the F6 key. After the NT kernel is loaded, you are asked to select which drivers to install at the end of reading Disk 2 but before selecting the installation type.

2000 ONLY

During installation of Windows 2000 Server, the type of server cannot be set. Why?

Unlike in earlier versions of Windows NT, with Windows 2000 the role of a server can be changed at any time in its life—from a member server to a Domain Controller, and from a Domain Controller back to a member server. This means that *all* servers are initially installed as standalone member servers (even upgraded PDC/BDCs), which then have to be promoted to domain servers.

For information on promoting a server to a Domain Controller, see Question 14-12 in Chapter 14, Domains.

2000 ONLY

How can I install Windows 2000 on a machine with less than 64MB of memory?

By default, you need 64MB of memory installed on the machine to install Windows 2000 Server; however, you can avoid this limitation.

1. Copy the Windows 2000 i386 installation structure to a hard disk/network drive.
2. Edit the file TXTSETUP.SIF located in the root of the i386 structure.
3. Search for RequiredMemory.

4. Edit the line that allows you to change the amount of memory—but only change it if you know what you are doing. Here is an example:

```
RequiredMemory=66584576
```

5. Save the file.
6. Install as usual.

Be aware that this will not work with upgrades and installs using WINNT32.EXE, but only with WINNT.EXE.

An alternative approach is to temporarily add RAM to the machine during the installation and then remove it when the installation is complete.

My evaluation period has expired on my NT installation. Why?

Even if you don't use an evaluation CD but use setup disks created with an evaluation CD, the NT installation expires after 120 days.

You will get one hour's notice before you see a "blue screen of death" (BSOD) with the following message:

"END_OF_NT_EVALUATION_PERIOD (0x98)
Your NT System is an evaluation unit with an expiration date. The trial period is over. Information on the BSOD can be found in the recovery section."

To fix this, you need to upgrade your installation, using a full retail copy of NT. Don't use the upgrade version because it will not upgrade NT 4.0 to 4.0. Before you perform this upgrade, you must ensure that you have uninstalled Service Pack 2 or later. You might be wondering how you can uninstall anything if the machine has BSOD, but you can reboot and get another hour.

If Service Pack 3 was installed, make sure the following files are not replaced:

1. SAMSRV.DLL
2. SAMLIB.DLL
3. WINLOGON.ORG

To do this, copy your NT installation directory (i386) to the hard disk and expand the three files to the directory.

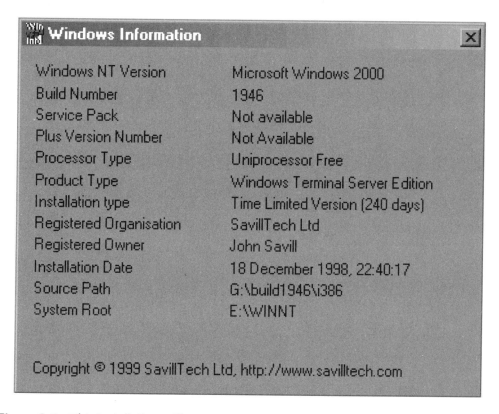

Figure 3-3. This installation will expire, as can be seen by the Time Limited Version (240 days) text. All beta versions of Windows 2000 expire in 240 days.

If you are not sure if your installation will expire, you can check it by downloading Win Info from http://www.savilltech.com/download/wininfo.zip (see Figure 3-3).

 ## There is a file ROLLBACK.EXE. What is it?

The ROLLBACK.EXE file is located on the NT installation CD in the Support folder. It is used by developers to remove post-installation Registry changes. It basically takes your installation back to the point when the GUI phase of installation was about to start.

4 LICENSING

As with any product, NT has a licensing scheme. However (rather against Microsoft tradition), it is an honor system with pieces of paper being purchased that are licenses. You just tell the software you have bought it, without having to provide any evidence (unless you get audited).

As you install other back-office products (Exchange, for example), they might add options to the NT license program; however, the licenses are all administered in the same manner.

 ## How is NT licensed?

The basic idea behind Windows NT licensing is that you purchase NT Server and licenses that allow you to have a number of connections to the server. A client license is just a piece of paper—no codes, no passwords—just a piece of paper saying you can use one more client. A client license costs around US$40. This means you have to buy the NT server software (around US$650) and then pay US$40 times the number of clients to the machine. In addition, you pay for the client software and licenses for any other software.

The two methods of licensing are *per seat* and *per server*. With per seat licensing, each network user has a license that allows the user to access any of the servers in the company. This is the most popular and cost-effective method if you have two or more NT servers.

With the second method, per server (also known as concurrent licensing) licenses are purchased and "installed" on the server. For example, if you purchase 50 client licenses and install them on the server, up to 50 connections are allowed at a time. If you then purchase another server, you will need to buy another 50 client licenses for connections to that server by the same 50 client machines.

From this explanation, you can see that if you have more than two NT servers, you will want per seat licensing. The exception would be a machine such as an Internet service server, which would have different people connecting to the site all the time. For that you would need x client licenses, where x is the maximum number of people you expect to connect at any one time. Current licensing does not require one license for each Internet connection.

It is possible to perform a once-only conversion of per server licenses to per seat licenses.

How can I view what licenses I have installed/used?

NT Server has a utility called License Manager that enables you to inspect the licenses and their use by doing the following:

1. Log on to the NT Server.
2. Start License Manager (Start > Programs > Administrative Tools > License Manager).
3. Click on the Products View tab to see a list of the licenses installed and used.

Windows 2000 has exactly the same interface and is currently not a Microsoft Management Console (MMC) snap-in. I'm not sure what the final product will do.

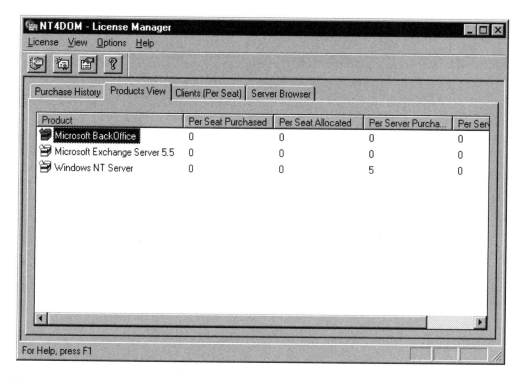

Figure 4-1. Viewing the licenses installed.

 # How do I install extra licenses?

This method is for per server licenses:

1. Log on to the NT Server.
2. Start License Manager (Start > Programs > Administrative Tools > License Manager).
3. Click on the Products View tab.
4. Click on Windows NT Server.
5. Either right-click on Windows NT Server and select Properties, or select Properties from the License menu.
6. Click the Server Browser tab, select the NT server, and click Edit.
7. Select Windows NT Server and click Edit.

8. Click Add Licenses and make sure the product selected is Windows NT Server. Then enter the number of licenses and click OK.

9. Click in the I Agree box and click OK.

10. Keep clicking OK until you are back to the main screen.

This method is for per seat licenses:

1. Start License Manager (Start > Programs > Administrative Tools > License Manager).

2. Select New License from the License menu.

3. Select Windows NT as the product.

4. Using the up and down arrows, increase the number of licenses.

5. If you wish, enter a comment.

6. Click OK.

7. Click in the I Agree box and click OK.

8. Keep clicking OK until you are back to the main screen.

 ## How do I convert from per server to per seat?

This is legally a one-way conversion process and can be carried out as follows:

1. Log on to the NT Server.

2. Start License Manager (Start > Programs > Administrative Tools > License Manager).

3. Click on the Products View tab.

4. Click on Windows NT Server.

5. Either right-click on Windows NT Server and select Properties, or select Properties from the License menu.

6. Click the Server Browser tab, select the NT server, and click Edit.

7. Select Windows NT Server and click Edit.

8. Click Per Seat and say Yes when asked if you're sure you wish to make this change.

9. Click in the I Agree box and click OK.

10. You are now using per seat licensing.

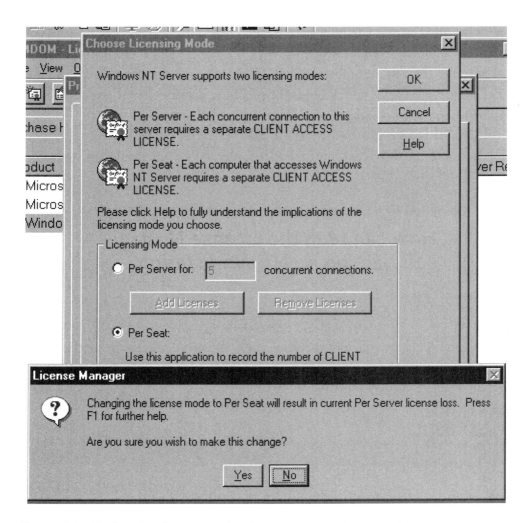

Figure 4-2. Performing the conversion from per server to per seat.

 # How can I reset the license information?

Here is the procedure (more information can be found in Knowledge Base article Q153140, which can be viewed from http://support.microsoft.com):

1. Start the Services Control Panel applet (Start > Settings > Control Panel > Services).

2. Select the License Logging Service and click Stop.
3. Start Explorer (Run > Explorer).
4. Move to the %systemroot%/system32 directory (d:\winnt\system32).
5. Delete CPL.CFG, which holds the purchase history.
6. Move to the Lls subdirectory of system32. Delete the files LLSUSER.LLS and LLSMAP.LLS if they exist.
7. Return to the Services Control Panel applet. Select License Logging Service and click Start.

 ## How can I run the License Manager software on an NT Workstation?

The NT Workstation server tools do not include this software. However, Server and Workstation share much of the same code; therefore, you can copy the following files from the %systemroot%/system32 directory on the server to the %systemroot%/system32 directory on the workstation:

LLSMGR.EXE
LLSMGR.HLP
LLSRPC.DLL
CCFAPI32.DLL

Then set up a shortcut to LLSMGR.EXE to complete the process.

5 SERVICE PACKS AND HOTFIXES

Although Microsoft provides very good quality code, there are always bugs in software. With increasing frequency, security hacks are found, to which Microsoft posts fixes.

A service pack contains images or other files that are required to fix the problems being addressed by its release. The files are compressed into a single executable, which self-extracts when executed.

Microsoft generally releases a service pack at least once a year. Instead of waiting until the next service pack to release fixes, small or "hot" fixes are made available on an as-needed basis and also included in the next full service pack release.

Service packs only provide the files that have changed and not the entire Windows NT build.

Service packs are cumulative, so you don't need to install Service Pack 1 before installing Service Pack 2, 3, and so on. This is why service packs get progressively bigger.

4.0 ONLY

FAQ 5.1 What service packs and fixes are available?

Table 5-1 lists the currently known service packs and hotfixes.

All directories are children of ftp.microsoft.com/bussys/winnt/winntpublic/fixes/usa/nt40. People in Europe might get faster access with ftp.sunet.se/pub3/vendor/microsoft/bussys/winnt/winnt-public/fixes.

Service packs can also be downloaded from certain Microsoft BBS numbers; however, the fixes tend to be a few days later than on the FTP site.

Resources such as TechNet—a monthly delivery of technical CDs to subscribers—provide the latest service packs. Also, they can usually be ordered on CD from Microsoft.

A complete, hyperlinked (clickable), and up-to-date version of Table 5-1 is available on the Web at http://www.ntfaq.com/ntfaq/servpack1.html. You might find them easier to use.

Table 5-1. Available Service Packs

Filename	Directory	Description (Microsoft Article No.)
Sp1_400i.exe	/ussp1/i386	Service Pack 1
Sp2_400i.exe	/ussp2/i386	Service Pack 2 (around 14MB)
Nt4sp3_i.exe	/ussp3/i386	Service Pack 3 (around 18MB)
NT4SP4I.EXE	http://support.microsoft.com/	Service Pack 4 (around 33MB)
SP5I386.EXE	http://support.microsoft.com/	Service Pack 5 (around 34.5MB)

The filenames in Table 5-2 are for the Intel platform (hence the ending I), but they might also be available for Alpha and PPC. For the I, substitute A (Alpha) or P (PPC).

Table 5-2. Service Pack 3 Hotfixes

Filename	Directory	Description (Microsoft Article No.)
2gcrashi.exe	/2gcrash	Q173277
aspfix.exe	/asp-fix	Q165335
ata-fixi.exe	/atapi-fix	Q183654
dnsfix_i.exe	/dns-fix	Q142047
eurofixi.exe	/euro-fix	Q182005
admnfixi.exe	/getadmin-fix	Q146965
idefix-i.exe	/ide-fix	Q153296

Table 5-2. Service Pack 3 Hotfixes *(continued)*

Filename	Directory	Description (Microsoft Article No.)
iis-fixi.exe	/iis-fix	Q143484
iis4fixi.exe	/iis4-fix	Q169274
joy-fixi.exe	/joystick-fix	Q177668
ndisfixi.exe	/ndis-fix	Q156655
nbtfix-i.exe	/netbt-fix	Q178205
pcmfix-i.exe	/pcm-fix	Q180532
pentfix.exe	/pent-fix	Q163852
pptpfixi.exe	/pptp2-fix	Q167040
pptpfixi.exe	/pptp3-fix	Q189595
privfixi.exe	/priv-fix	Q190288
prntfixi.exe	/Prnt-fix	Q181022
roll-upi.exe	/roll-up	Q147222
rrasfixi.exe	/rras20-fix	Q168469
rrasfixi.exe	/rras30-fix	Q189594
dcomfixi.exe	/SAG-fix	
scsifixi.exe	/scsi-fix	Q171295
sfm-fixi.exe	/sfm-fix	Q166571, Q170965, Q172511, Q177644, Q178364, Q180622, Q180716, Q180717, Q180718 & Q185722
chargeni.exe	/simptcp-fix	Q154460
snk-fixi.exe	/snk-fix	Q193233
srvfix-i.exe	/srv-fix	Q180963
ssl-fixi.exe	/ssl-fix	Q148427
tapi21fi.exe	/tapi21-fix	Q179187
tearfixi.exe	/teardrop2-fix	Q179129
wanfix-i.exe	/wan-fix	Q163251

Table 5-2. Service Pack 3 Hotfixes *(continued)*

Filename	Directory	Description (Microsoft Article No.)
winsfixi.exe	/winsupd-fix	Q155701
y2kfixi.exe	/y2k-fix	Q175093, Q180122, Q183123 & Q183125
zip-fixi.exe	/zip-fix	Q154094

Table 5-3. Service Pack 4 Hotfixes

Filename	Directory	Description (Microsoft Article No.)
DISCFIXI.EXE	/Disc-fix	Q221331
GINAFIXI.EXE	/Gina-fix	Q214802
MSMQFIXI.EXE	/MSMQ-fix	Q230050
MSV-FIXI.EXE	/Msv1-fix	Q214840
NPRPCFXI.EXE	/Nprpc-fix	Q195733
SP4HFIXI.EXE	/roll-up	Q195734
RNR-FIXI.EXE	/Rnr-fix	Q214864, Q216091, Q217001
SCRNSAVI.EXE	/Scrnsav-fix	Q221991
SMSFIXI.EXE	/Sms-fix	Q196270
SMSSFIXI.EXE	/Smss-fix	Q218473
TCPIPFXI.EXE	/Tcpip-fix	Q195725
Y2KUPD.EXE	/Y2KUPD	Q218877, Q221120

Table 5-4. Service Pack 5 Hotfixes

Filename	Directory	Description (Microsoft Article No.)
PWDFIXI.EXE	/RASPassword-fix	Q230681
RPWDFIXI.EXE	/RRASPassword-fix	Q233303
WINHLP-I.EXE	/Winhlp32-fix	NA

The following post–Service Pack 3 hotfixes have been replaced by newer fixes and are not listed above. They can be found at ftp://ftp.microsoft.com/bussys/winnt/winnt-public/fixes/usa/nt40/hotfixes-postSP3/archive.

- dbclclick-fix
- icmp-fix
- java-fix
- land-fix
- lsa-fix
- mdl-fix
- oob-fix
- pptp-fix

I should note a health warning: "If it ain't broke, don't fix it." I tend to agree with this, so unless you have a problem or require a new feature, think twice about installing a service pack. Also, if you are going to apply the service pack to a live system, try to test it first, because a service pack sometimes introduces new problems.

Microsoft publishes warnings about hotfixes, highlighting the fact that they have not been fully regression tested and should be applied only to systems experiencing the specific problem.

What are Q numbers and how do I look them up?

The Q numbers relate to Microsoft Knowledge Base articles and can be viewed at http://support.microsoft.com/support/ or TechNet. For example, Q214470 relates to moving locally cached profiles and can be viewed at http://support.microsoft.com/support/kb/articles/q214/4/70.asp.

How do I install a service pack?

If you receive the service pack by downloading from a Microsoft FTP site, copy the file to a temporary directory and then just enter the filename (for example, SP2_400I.EXE) to expand the file. Among the files created, find a file called UPDATE.EXE and run this file. If you find only .SYM files and no UPDATE.EXE, you have downloaded the symbols version used for debugging NT and need to download the standard version.

You can install Service Pack 3 and later ones by double-clicking on them. To just extract the files that make up a service pack without installing, enter this command:

```
<service pack name> /x
```

If you receive service packs via CD (for Service Pack 2 and later), insert the CD in the drive. The Internet Explorer window opens and you can click on Install for the service pack.

How do I install a hotfix?

Copy the file to a temporary directory and run the filename. A few files are created, including one called HOTFIX.EXE. Run HOTFIX/INSTALL to install the hotfix. Details about the hotfix are found in the created HOTFIX.INF file.

The newer hotfixes (Java fix for Service Pack 3 onward) will self-install if you just double-click on the downloaded file.

How do I remove a hotfix?

You need to expand the hotfix again by running the file (for example, JAVAFIXI.EXE). It will create HOTFIX.EXE and numerous other files, including HOTFIX.INF, which has the information needed to uninstall the hotfix. Use the following command to remove the hotfix:

```
Hotfix /remove
```

Remember: You **must** run hotfix /remove with the .INF file for the hotfix you want to remove. Otherwise, you will uninstall whatever hotfix was expanded last (the most recent HOTFIX.INF file).

Microsoft changed the method of removal and has used different switches on some recent fixes. If you're unsure, use **hotfix /?** to list the available options.

To force the removal by using the Registry editor (REGEDT32.EXE), go to HKEY_LOCAL_MACHINE\Software\Microsoft\Windows NT\ CurrentVersion\HOTFIX and delete the entry for the hotfix. Then use explorer to go to %SystemRoot%\HOTFIX\HF00?? and copy the backed-up files to their original location.

4.0 ONLY

FAQ 5.6 What are the Emergency Repair Disk issues after installation of Service Packs 3 and 4?

Because of changes in Service Packs 3 and 4, the Emergency Repair Disk (ERD) process has changed. The file SETUPDD.SYS that is on the second NT installation disk has been superseded by the one supplied with Service Pack 3. To extract the file from the Service Pack 3 executable, follow these instructions:

1. Copy NT4SP3_I.EXE to a temporary area.
2. Uncompress the service pack by typing

```
nt4sp3_i /x
```

3. Insert the second NT installation disk. (Do not use the originals; create a new set by using WINNT32 /OX.)
4. Set the file SETUPDD.SYS to write-enabled by typing

```
attrib -r a:\setupd.sys
```

5. Copy the new SETUPDD.SYS to the second installation disk by typing

```
copy setupdd.sys a:
```

This is discussed in the Service Pack 3 readme file and also in Knowledge Base article Q146887.

How do I install multiple hotfixes at the same time?

When you extract the files in a hotfix, you'll generally find the following:

HOTFIX.EXE
HOTFIX.INF
A number of executables/drivers/sys files etc. (usually one file)

The HOTFIX.EXE is the same executable for all hotfixes. The HOTFIX.INF is the same except for the files that are to be copied (for example, TCPIP.SYS) and a description of the hotfix. To install multiple hotfixes at the same time, you can decompress the hotfix files and update HOTFIX.INF with the information on which files to copy for each of the individual hotfixes. Here's what to do:

1. Create a directory called hotfix on a disk by typing

```
md hotfix
```

2. From the command line, decompress the hotfixes you wish to install. Note that each time you decompress a hotfix, a new HOTFIX.INF overwrites the existing one, so you might wish to back up the .INF files:

   a. Enter the hotfix name with /x (for example, **javafixi /x**).
   b. You are asked where to extract the hotfix files to. Enter the hotfix directory (for example, **d:\hotfix**) and click OK.
   c. Copy the HOTFIX.INF file to the name of the hotfix by using this command:

```
copy hotfix.inf javafix.inf
```

3. You now have a number of files in the hotfix directory: HOTFIX.EXE, HOTFIX.INF, and all the versions of the .INF files you copied. You need to merge the contents of the .INF files into one main HOTFIX.INF file. If the hotfix you extracted had file TCPIP.SYS (ignore the .DBG files), you need to update the HOTFIX.INF file to include the copying of this file. Because TCPIP.SYS lives in the system32/drivers directory, you add the line TCPIP.SYS to the [Drivers.files] section of the HOTFIX.INF file, like this:

```
[Drivers.files]
TCPIP.SYS
```

4. You also need to add TCPIP.SYS to the [SourceDisksFiles] section, like this:

```
[SourceDisksFiles]
TCPIP.SYS = 1
```

5. Finally, you need to add a comment at the end of the HOTFIX.INF file with a description of the hotfix in the [strings] section, the Q number, and a comment, like this:

```
[Strings]
..
HOTFIX_NUMBER="Q143478"
COMMENT="This fix corrects the port 139 OOB attack"
```

The reason for copying the .INF files is that you can copy and paste the hotfix-specific information to the common HOTFIX.INF. When you decompress a hotfix, you can see which files were created. You can then search the .INF file for the filename, which will be in two places: the directory in which it belongs and the [SourceDisksFiles] section. Now, from the bottom of the file, you can copy the hotfix number and comment and paste them to the end of HOTFIX.INF.

This is very hard to explain, and an example is probably the best way to demonstrate. Suppose you want to install these files:

The Java hotfix: JAVAFIXI.EXE
The OOB data hotfix: OOBFIX_I.EXE
The GetAdmin hotfix: ADMNFIXI.EXE

The procedure would be as follows:

1. Decompress the hotfixes to the hotfix directory. After each extraction, back up the HOTFIX.INF files in the order ADMNFIXI.EXE, JAVAFIXI.EXE, OOBFIX_I.EXE.

2. ADMNFIXI.EXE consists of NTKRNLMP.EXE and NTOSKRNL.EXE. Search ADMNFIXI.INF (the copy you made) for the files; they appear as follows:

   ```
   [Uniprocessor.Kernel.files]
   NTOSKRNL.EXE

   [Multiprocessor.Kernel.files]
   NTOSKRNL.EXE, NTKRNLMP.EXE

   [SourceDisksFiles]
   NTKRNLMP.EXE = 1
   NTOSKRNL.EXE = 1

   [Strings]
   HOTFIX_NUMBER="Q146965"
   COMMENT="This fix corrects GETADMIN problem"
   ```

3. JAVAFIXI.EXE consists of WIN32K.SYS, so search JAVAFIXI.INF for WIN32K.SYS:

   ```
   [MustReplace.System32.files]
   WIN32K.SYS

   [SourceDisksFiles]
   WIN32K.SYS = 1

   [Strings]
   HOTFIX_NUMBER="Q123456"
   COMMENT="This fix corrects the problem with True Color
   adapter cards and Java"
   ```

4. The current version of HOTFIX.INF already contains the information for the OOBFIX, because it was the last installed. The information for the other two must be added, resulting in these changes:

   ```
   [MustReplace.System32.files]
   WIN32K.SYS
   ```

```
[Drivers.files]
TCPIP.SYS

[Uniprocessor.Kernel.files]
NTOSKRNL.EXE

[Multiprocessor.Kernel.files]
NTOSKRNL.EXE, NTKRNLMP.EXE

[SourceDisksFiles]
NTKRNLMP.EXE = 1
NTOSKRNL.EXE = 1
TCPIP.SYS = 1
WIN32K.SYS = 1

[Strings]
;; this part needs modifying, only one HOTFIX_NUMBER can be
passed
;;so create your own internal reference,
;; e.g. Q99999 and also the comments need a unique number
at the end,
;;e.g. comment1, comment2, otherwise
;; only the first comment will be entered
HOTFIX_NUMBER="Q999999"
COMMENT1="This fix corrects the port 139 OOB attack"
COMMENT2="This fix corrects GETADMIN problem"
COMMENT3="This fix corrects the problem with True Color
adapter cards and Java"
```

To install, just type this from the directory you created (that is, hotfix):

`hotfix`

A dialog appears as the files are copied (the ones you specified in the HOTFIX.INF file), and then the system reboots. Here's how to see what hotfixes are installed:

1. Start the Registry editor (REGEDIT.EXE).
2. Look at the HKEY_LOCAL_MACHINE\SOFTWARE\Microsoft\ Windows NT\CurrentVersion\Hotfix values.

4.0 ONLY
5.8 How do I install hotfixes at the same time as I install Service Pack 3 onward?

UPDATE.EXE that ships with Service Pack 3 checks for the existence of a hot-fix subdirectory. If files HOTFIX.EXE and HOTFIX.INF are present, you are asked if you also want to install the hotfixes while you're running UPDATE.EXE.

1. Create a directory to hold the extracted service pack:

   md servpack

2. Extract the service pack:

   nt4sp3_i /x

3. You are asked for a directory. Enter the created directory and click OK. For example, type

   e:\servpack

4. Create a hotfix subdirectory:

   md hotfix

5. Extract the hotfixes to this directory by following the instructions in Question 5-7.
6. Run UPDATE.EXE in the servpack directory and click Yes when you're asked if you want to install hotfixes.

4.0 ONLY
5.9 I have installed Service Pack 3, but the Policy editor has not been updated. Why?

This is caused by a mistake in the Service Pack 3 UPDATE.INF file. The entry for POLEDIT.EXE (the executable for the Policy editor) is specified in the

[MustReplace.system32.files] section, but the file should actually be in the [SystemRoot.files].

To install the new Policy editor, perform the following:

1. Expand the service pack:

```
nt4sp3_i /x
```

2. You are asked for a directory. Enter a path and click OK. The service pack expands and an "Extraction complete" message is displayed.

3. Move to the directory where the service pack was extracted and copy the file POLEDIT.EXE to the %systemroot% directory:

```
copy poledit.exe %systemroot%
```

Alternatively, you can update the UPDATE.INF file and move the location of POLEDIT.EXE from [MustReplace.system32.files] to [SystemRoot.files].

How can I tell if I have the 128-bit version of Service Pack 3 installed?

The easiest way is to examine the secure channel dynamic link library (SCHANNEL.DLL):

1. Start Explorer (press Win key + E or choose Start > Programs > Windows NT Explorer).

2. Move to %systemRoot%/system32, where %systemRoot is the windows NT directory (for example, **d:\winnt**).

3. Right-click on SCHANNEL.DLL and select Properties.

4. Click the Version tab. You'll see one of the following:
   PCT / SSL Security Provider (United States and Canada for the 128-bit version.) *if you have the 128-bit version*

   or

   PCT / SSL Security Provider (Export Version) *if you have the non–128-bit version.*

5. Click OK when finished.

6. Close Explorer.

How do I install a service pack during an unattended installation?

There are various options; however, all of them require you to extract the service pack to a directory by using

```
NT4SP3_I /x
```

Then enter the directory to which you want the service pack to be extracted.

You could extract to a directory under the OEM installation directory, which would then be copied locally during the installation. You could add the following line to CMDLINES.TXT:

```
".\UPDATE.EXE -U -Z"
```

Because the contents have to be copied over the network, this increases the time of the text portion of the installation.

An alternative method is to install from a network drive, but it requires a bit more work:

1. Create a directory on a network server and copy the extracted service pack to this directory. Set up a share on this directory called SP.
2. Create a batch file in the OEM share of the installation area called SERVPACK.CMD. To do so, use

```
net use z:\\<server>\SP /persistent:no /user:<domain name>
\guest < password.txt
z:\update.exe -u -z
```

3. You need to create the PASSWORD.TXT file that contains the guest account password (usually blank). Therefore, perform the following:
   a. Type **copy con password.txt**.
   b. Press Enter once.
   c. Press Ctrl+Z to save the file.
   d. If the password is not blank, enter the password and then press Enter.
4. Copy the PASSWORD.TXT file to the OEM directory.
5. Edit CMDLINES.TXT and add **.\SERVPACK.CMD** to the end.

In what order should I apply the hotfixes for Service Pack 3?

The Service Pack 3 hotfixes are, for the most part, cumulative. This means that the latest binary also includes fixes previously made to the same binary.

For example, the 01/09/98 version of TCPIP.SYS (teardrop2-fix) also includes previous fixes to TCPIP.SYS (such as land-fix, icmp-fix, and oob-fix).

When you apply multiple fixes, install them in the following order to ensure that a newer fix is not replaced by an older one.

1. oob-fix
2. asp-fix
3. java-fix
4. dns-fix
5. iis-fix
6. lsa-fix
7. dblclick-fix
8. icmp-fix
9. zip-fix
10. roll-up (or roll-up/cluster)
11. mdl-fix
12. getadmin-fix
13. roll-up/cluster
14. winsupd-fix
15. ndis-fix
16. scsi-fix
17. 2gcrash
18. simptcp-fix
19. ide-fix
20. wan-fix
21. land-fix
22. pent-fix (x86 only)
23. joystick-fix (x86 only)
24. SAG-fix
25. iis4-fix
26. pptp-fix
27. teardrop2-fix
28. tapi21-fix
29. pcm-fix
30. srv-fix
31. y2k-fix
32. euro-fix
33. atapi-fix
34. netbt-fix
35. prnt-fix
36. sfm-fix
37. pptp2-fix
38. rras20-fix
39. lsa2-fix
40. ssl-fix
41. priv-fix
42. pptp3-fix
43. rras30-fix

For the Microsoft version of the list, see ftp://ftp.microsoft.com/bussys/winnt/ winnt-public/fixes/usa/nt40/hotfixes-postSP3/postsp3.txt.

4.0 ONLY

FAQ 5.13

I get an error message when I try to reapply a hotfix after installing a service pack. Why?

When you try to reapply a hotfix (after installing a service pack), you might get the following error:

> "Hotfix: The fix is already installed.
> Hotfix: Internal consistency error: Invalid Tree pointer = <garbage characters displayed>.
> You need to remove the hotfix before trying to reinstall."

To remove a hotfix, you would usually use **hotfix /r** or **hotfix -y**. (Which one you use depends on the version. Use **/?** on the hotfix to get the syntax.) However, in some situations, this method refuses to remove the hotfix and gives the following message:

> "Hotfix: Fix <name of hotfix> was not removed."

When you install a hotfix, all it actually does is check a Registry entry to see if the fix is already there. To get around this problem, you can go into the Registry and remove the hotfix's corresponding entry.

1. Start the Registry editor (REGEDIT.EXE).
2. Move to HKEY_LOCAL_MACHINE\SOFTWARE\Microsoft\ Windows NT\CurrentVersion\Hotfix.
3. Under this key you should see a number of subkeys. They are named according to the Knowledge Base article by which the hotfix is referenced (for example, Q123456 is the True Color Adapter fix).
4. To get more details about the hotfix, select the key (for example, Q123456) and look at the Fix Description value.
5. To remove NT's knowledge that the fix was installed, select the specific hotfix you want to remove (again, Q123456) and choose Delete from the Edit menu (see Figure 5-1). Click Yes to the confirmation message.
6. Close the Registry editor.

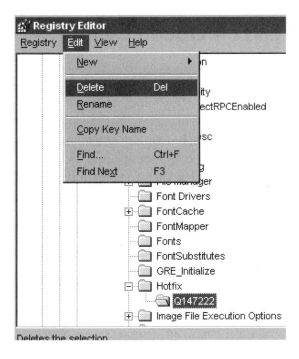

Figure 5-1. Manually removing NT's knowledge of a hotfix.

The fix is still installed on the system. All you have done is remove NT's knowledge of its installation so you can now reinstall the hotfix in the normal way.

 # When should I reapply a service pack?

You should reapply any service pack (and subsequent hotfixes) whenever you add any system utilities, services, hardware, or software. Here's a good guideline: when your computer says, "Changes have been made, you must shutdown and restart your computer," reapply your service pack before the reboot.

Be sure to uninstall the service pack before reinstalling, or you'll lose the ability to uninstall it.

What is NT 4 Option Pack?

Due to a lot of public pressure, Microsoft agreed they would no longer include any new functionality in service packs, but would instead produce separate add-ons that would update various option components. NT 4 Option Pack is the first of these (to keep in step with Service Pack 4). You can download NT 4 Option Pack (about 27MB) from http://www.microsoft.com/windows/downloads/contents/updates/nt40ptpk/default.asp. It is also supplied as part of MSDN.

If you download from the Web, you have to download a special program, DOWNLOAD.EXE, which downloads or installs the software.

The following are included in the NT 4 Option Pack:

- Internet Information Server 4.0 (which used the new Microsoft Management Console, standard in NT 5.0)
- Microsoft Transaction Server 2.0 (this is tied in with IIS)
- Microsoft Message Queue Server 1.0
- Internet Connection Services for Microsoft RAS
- Certificate Server
- Site Server Express
- SMTP Server
- NNTP Server (News Server)

You'll find more information at http://www.microsoft.com/NTServer/Basics/WhatNew.asp/.

1. To install the option pack, you must be running Service Pack 3 or later (I tested with Service Pack 4 and got a warning that it has not been tested on Service Pack 4, but it works fine) and you must have Internet Explorer 4.01 or later.

2. After you start the installation, you should click Next to go to the introduction screen, where you have two options:
   a. Upgrade Only
   b. Upgrade Plus

3. If you select Upgrade Only, only components existing on the system will be upgraded to the NT 4 Option Pack version. Clicking Upgrade Plus allows you to install extra software.

4. If you select Upgrade Plus, you can then choose which components to install. Some items have subcomponents you can choose to install. For example, IIS includes NNTP server (news).

5. Depending on the components you select, you are asked some minor questions and then the machine reboots.

4.0 ONLY

FAQ 5.16 How can I tell which version service pack I have installed?

The easiest way is to run WINVER.EXE, which tells you your current build and service pack version (see Figure 5-2).

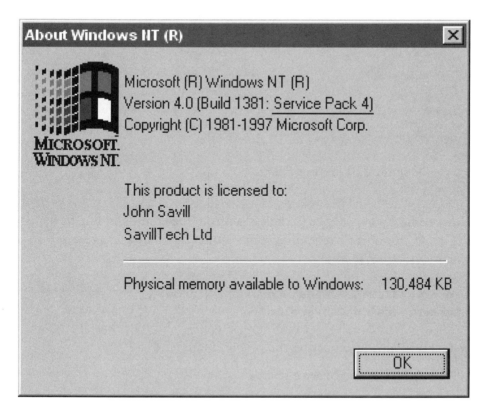

Figure 5-2. Viewing the NT service pack version by using WINVER.EXE.

Alternatively, when you install a service pack by using the normal method (not just copying the files to a build location), the service pack version is entered into the Registry value CSDVersion located under HKEY_LOCAL_MACHINE\SOFTWARE\Microsoft\Windows NT\CurrentVersion.

The value is in the form Service Pack n (for example, "Service Pack 4," as in Figure 5-3) but can have extra information if it is a beta or release candidate (for example, "Service Pack 4, RC 1.99").

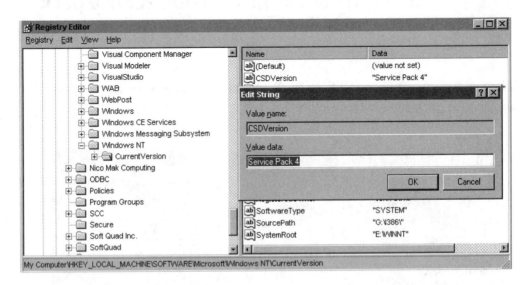

Figure 5-3. I'm up-to-date: Service Pack 4.

You can also check your service pack version from the command line by using the REG.EXE Resource Kit Supplement 2 utility, as follows (make sure you put the value in quotation marks):

```
reg query "HKLM\SOFTWARE\Microsoft\Windows
NT\CurrentVersion\CSDVersion"
```

The system responds by reporting the version number:

REG_SZ CSDVersion Service Pack 4

6 SYSTEM CONFIGURATION

Windows NT has become so complex and feature-rich, it can be configured in almost any way you could want. This chapter covers the most common system configurations and customizations.

It also looks at shortcuts, default settings for before a user logs in, and advanced new tools such as the Security Configuration Editor (SCE).

Chapter 7, User Configuration, and Chapter 8, Desktop Configuration, are also useful and relate to similar system configuration. Chapter 7 concentrates on settings relating to each user, and Chapter 8 relates to the look and feel of your desktop.

 ## How do I decrease the boot delay?

When Windows NT boots, the menu screen is displayed for 30 seconds by default and then the default choice chosen. This time can be modified.

Here are two ways of performing this change; the first method just automates the second method.

Method 1

1. Log on as Administrator.
2. Start the System Control Panel applet (Start > Settings > Control Panel > System).

3. Select the Startup/Shutdown tab.
4. In the Show List For box, set the number of seconds to the delay required (see Figure 6-1).

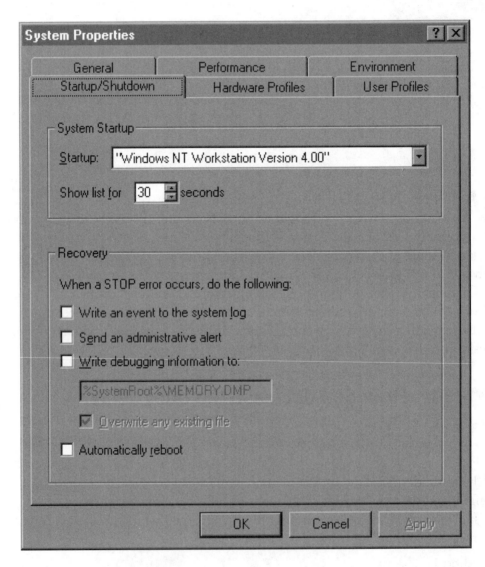

Figure 6-1. Modify the delay, using the Show List For box.

Method 2

Method 1 just updates the timeout value in the [boot loader] section of BOOT.INI; you can do this manually:

1. Set the file to non-system and non-read-only:

```
attrib c:\boot.ini -r -s
```

2. Edit the file and change the timeout value to whatever you want. For example, to make it wait for 5 seconds, change to

```
timeout= 5
```

3. Save your changes.
4. Set the file back to system and read-only:

```
attrib c:\boot.ini +r +s
```

 ## How do I configure the Boot menu to show forever?

You change the timeout by editing the BOOT.INI file (which is on the system partition) and changing the timeout parameter, like this:

1. Start a command session by choosing Start > Run > Command.
2. Set the attributes on c:\boot.ini to non-read and non-system:

```
attrib c:\boot.ini -r -s
```

3. Edit the file and change the timeout to -1:

```
[boot loader]
timeout = -1
```

4. Save your changes.
5. Set the file back to read-only and system using the following command:

```
attrib c:\boot.ini +r +s
```

Where do I load ANSI.SYS?

Some applications might still want ANSI.SYS; this can be loaded in NT.

There is a file in your system32 directory, CONFIG.NT, that tells NT how to run DOS 5 sessions. Add this to CONFIG.NT:

```
device=c:\winnt\system32\ansi.sys
```

or

```
device=%systemroot%\system32\ansi.sys
```

Now start a command line by using the COMMAND.COM that came with DOS 5.0 (dig out those old disks).

How do I schedule commands?

Windows NT has a built-in scheduler service that enables applications to be started at specified times. To schedule events, the Scheduler service must be started. Do the following:

1. Start the Services Control Panel applet (Start > Settings > Control Panel > Services).
2. Click Scheduler (or Task Scheduler on Workstation) and click Startup.
3. Select Automatic and click OK.
4. You can now reboot, or just click Start, which starts the Scheduler service.
5. Close the Services Control Panel applet.
6. The Scheduler service only needs to be started on the target machine, not the issuing machine. If the Scheduler service is not started on the target machine, the following error message is displayed:

   The service has not been started.

To schedule a command, you use the AT utility. AT is used with the following syntax:

AT [<computername>] <time> [/interactive] [/every:date/day..] [/next:date/day..] <command> (for example, AT \\savmain 22:00 /interactive /every:M,T,W,Th,F sol.exe)

This example would start the solitaire game on the SAVMAIN machine at 10 p.m. every weekday. The /interactive means the application can interact with the desktop—that is, the currently logged-on user. If /interactive is omitted and the application requires user interaction, it just starts and finishes instantly.

When a command is submitted, it is given an ID. To delete a scheduled command, use the following (*the /yes skips confirmation of the delete):*

AT [<computername>] <id> /delete /yes (for example, AT \\savmain 3 /delete /yes)

The above might seem like quite a lot to take in if all you want is a backup. (For an example of using AT with a backup, see Question 12-7, How do I schedule a backup? in Chapter 12, Backups.) A utility called WINAT (shipped with the NT Resource Kit) puts a graphical interface to the AT command that you might find easier, but the functionality is the same. The advantage is that WINAT automatically starts the Scheduler service on the target machine if it is not already running.

 ## How can I execute a batch file using WINAT with Administrator Permissions?

From the Services Control Panel applet (Start > Settings > Control Panel), double-click Scheduler. Change the account and password to that of a user in the administrative group. It might be wise to create a new account just for this use, which would require the following attributes:

Non-blank password
Non-expiring password
User rights: Log On As Service and Log On As Batch Job (select Advanced under the dialog to see them)

After changing the Scheduler information, you need to stop and start the service.

 ### 6.6 How do I change the Organization Name on NT?

Your company changed names again? By default, you enter your company name when you install NT, but it can be modified quite easily.

To change the company name in NT, do the following:

1. Start the Registry editor (REGEDIT.EXE).
2. Go to the HKEY_LOCAL_MACHINE\Software\Microsoft\ WindowsNT\CurrentVersion and select CurrentVersion.
3. On the right-hand side of the screen are a number of values.
4. Double-click on RegisteredOrganization and change the value data.
5. Click OK and exit the Registry editor.

 ### 6.7 How do I change the default location where NT expects to find NT software for installation (that is, CD)?

When you install new components to NT, you are asked for the i386 directory from which NT was installed, usually your CD-ROM drive (E:\i386).

To modify this location, perform the following:

1. Start the Registry editor (REGEDIT.EXE).
2. Move to HKEY_LOCAL_MACHINE\SOFTWARE\Microsoft\ Windows NT\CurrentVersion.
3. Double-click SourcePath and modify.
4. Click OK.
5. Close the Registry editor.

How can I remove the Shutdown button from the logon screen?

To remove the Shutdown button from the initial logon (thus forcing a user to log on before shutting down the server), perform the following:

1. Start the Registry editor (REGEDIT.EXE).
2. Move to HKEY_LOCAL_MACHINE\SOFTWARE\Microsoft\ Windows NT\CurrentVersion\Winlogon.
3. Double-click on ShutdownWithoutLogon and change the value from 1 to 0.
4. Close the Registry editor.

This can also be accomplished by using the Policy editor (POLEDIT.EXE). Expand the Windows NT System Logon tree and blank out Enable Shutdown From Authentication Dialog Box (see Figure 6-2).

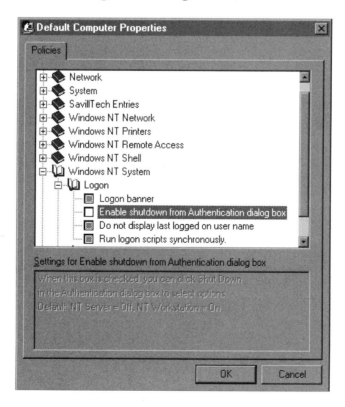

Figure 6-2. Disabling the Shutdown button by using the Policy editor.

6.9   How can I parse/not parse AUTOEXEC.BAT?

Command windows can be configured to use or not use the AUTOEXEC.BAT file. AUTOEXEC.BAT can be used by legacy applications, and items such as the path variable can be set.

The Registry value HKEY_CURRENT_USER\Software\Microsoft\ Windows NT\CurrentVersion\Winlogon\ParseAutoexec should be set to 1 for AUTOEXEC.BAT to be parsed or 0 for AUTOEXEC.BAT not to be parsed.

6.10   How do I add a path statement in NT?

To modify the Windows NT path—that is, the directories where NT will look for a program, dynamic link library (.DLL), and so on—perform the following:

1. Open the Control Panel (Start > Settings > Control Panel).
2. Double-click the System icon (or right-click on My Computer and select Properties).
3. Go to the Environment tab.
4. Choose whether to define a user or a system path. Click on the path variable and add the path statement to the end of the current string (including a ;).
5. Click Set and then click OK (see Figure 6-3).

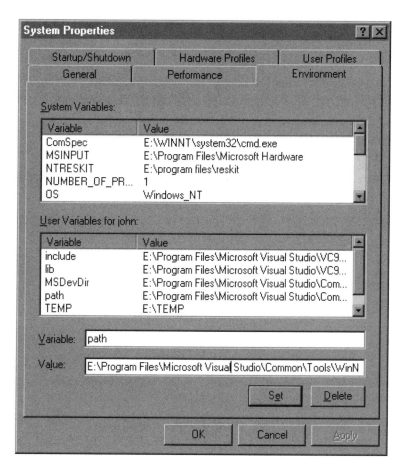

Figure 6-3. Modifying the path variable.

 # Can I change the default Windows background?

Before you log on, the background shows the WinNT logo and the green background; however, you can change this. Although some people recommend modifying the WINNT32.BMP picture, that is an ugly method, and the following method is much better.

1. Start the Registry editor (REGEDIT.EXE).
2. Move to HKEY_USERS\.DEFAULT\Control Panel\Desktop.

3. Double-click the Wallpaper Key and enter the pathname, including directory (for example, **c:\winnt\savlogo.bmp**).

4. You can also change the background color. To do so, type **HKEY_USERS\DEFAULT\Control Panel\Colors**. Then double-click Background and change the value (for example, 0 0 0 for black).

5. Close the Registry editor.

The default background and color that show before anyone logs on are now altered.

 ## How do I configure a default screen saver if no one logs on?

In the same way a different bitmap can be set before anyone logs on, a different screen saver can also be set. This is accomplished by using the Registry editor:

1. Start the Registry editor (REGEDIT.EXE).
2. Move to the HKEY_USERS\DEFAULT\Control Panel\Desktop.
3. Double-click ScreenSaveActive and set to 1.
4. Double-click SCRNSAVE.EXE and set to black16.scr.
5. Double-click ScreenSaveTimeOut and set to the number of seconds (for example, 600 for 10 minutes).
6. Close the Registry editor.

 ## How do I configure the default screen saver to be the OpenGL Text Screen Saver?

If you chose the OpenGL Text Screen Saver in Question 6-12, there are other settings you need to configure.

1. Start the Registry editor (REGEDIT.EXE).
2. Change the value HKEY_USERS\.DEFAULT\Control Panel\Desktop\SCRNSAVE.EXE to E:\WINNT\System32\sstext3d.scr.

3. Choose Edit > New > Key and create a key called HKEY_USERS\. DEFAULT\Control Panel\Screen Saver.3DText.

4. Under this new key, choose Edit > New > String Value and create two new values of string type, called Font and Text.

5. Set Font (double-click on it) to Arial.

6. Set Text to the string you want to be displayed (you are limited to 16 characters).

7. Close the Registry editor.

A word of caution: The OpenGL screen savers use a lot of system resources, so I would not advise you to use them; however, I was asked.

 How can I move shares and their contents from one machine to another?

Moving the actual files and directories is simple; however, share information is not contained in the directories in the Registry (under LanmanServer). Therefore, it's necessary to copy this Registry information from the machine currently containing the shares to the machine that will host the shares, as follows:

1. To copy the files, you need to use the SCOPY utility that is supplied with the resource kit to keep the current permission/audit settings.

```
SCOPY <current>:\<dir> <new>:\<dir> /o /a /s
```

2. On the machine that currently hosts the shares, start the Registry editor (REGEDT32.EXE, **not** REGEDIT.EXE).

3. Move to the key HKEY_LOCAL_MACHINE\SYSTEM\ CurrentControlSet\Services\LanmanServer\Shares.

4. Click on Shares and select Save Key from the Registry menu.

5. Enter the name of a file (for example, SHARES.REG) and click OK.

6. Copy this file to the target machine.

7. Again start the Registry editor (REGEDT32.EXE) and move to HKEY_LOCAL_MACHINE\SYSTEM\CurrentControlSet\Services\ LanmanServer\Shares and select Shares.

8. From the Registry menu, select Restore. Select the file you saved (it was SHARES.REG for this example) and click Open.

Warning: You will lose all currently configured shares on the machine.

9. When asked if you want to continue, click Yes.

10. Close the Registry editor.

Reboot the machine. When it starts again, you will see the new shares.

How can I restore the old Program Manager?

NT 4.0 by default uses the Explorer shell (EXPLORER.EXE). However, the old Program Manager (PROGMAN.EXE) is still delivered with NT 4.0 and can be configured to be the default shell by using the Registry.

1. Start the Registry editor (REGEDIT.EXE).
2. Go to the HKEY_LOCAL_MACHINE\SOFTWARE\Microsoft\ Windows NT\CurrentVersion\Winlogon.
3. Double-click on the value Shell.
4. Change from EXPLORER.EXE to PROGMAN.EXE (make sure you don't type *program.exe*—this will corrupt your machine, requiring a remote Registry edit to fix). Click OK.
5. Close the Registry editor.
6. Log off and then log on again.

Upon logon, the old Program Manager will start instead of Explorer.

Is there a way to start NT in DOS mode?

The command shell for NT is COMMAND.COM, and NT can be started in this mode with COMMAND.COM as the default shell. Just perform the steps in Question 6-15, but instead of changing the shell value to PROGMAN.EXE, change it to COMMAND.COM or CMD.EXE.

Be aware that this is not DOS but a command line version of NT, and DOS applications still will not run under this if they failed to run under NT.

How can I disable Lock Workstation when I press Ctrl+Alt+Del?

Service Pack 4 introduces a new Registry entry that will remove the Lock Workstation button from the Windows NT Security dialog.

You might not want users to be able to lock workstations, because this stops others from using them. You might prefer for them to fully log off instead. This might be especially useful in a school environment.

1. Start the Registry editor (REGEDIT.EXE).
2. Move to HKEY_CURRENT_USER\Software\Microsoft\Windows\CurrentVersion\Policies\System.
3. From the Edit menu, select New > DWORD Value.
4. Enter **DisableLockWorkstation** and press Enter.
5. Double-click on the new value and set to 1. Click OK.
6. Close the Registry editor.

Lock Workstation will now be grayed out.

This is also possible if you don't mind hacking one of the system .DLL files. The file in which the Ctrl+Alt+Del dialog is stored is msginA.DLL. Using any 32-bit resource editor (such as one with a Win32 C++ compiler, Visual C++, Borland C++), you can edit this .DLL and remove the Lock Workstation button. Below are instructions for performing this with Visual C++. If you're using a different resource editor, find dialog #1650 and edit the attributes of the Lock Workstation to Inactive or Invisible.

1. Rename %systemroot%\system32\msgina.dll to msgina_orig.dll (this is so you have a backup).
2. Copy the file back to be called msgina.dll, as follows:

```
copy d:\winnt\system32\msgina_orig.dll d:\winnt\system32\
msginA.dll
```

3. Start Visual C++ and select Open.

4. Change the type to Executable Files (.dll, .exe, .ocx).

5. Move to the %systemroot%\system32 directory, select msgina.dll, and click OK.

6. When it's open, click on the dialog tree and double-click 1650.

7. Double-click on the Lock Workstation button and deselect Visible.

8. Close the dialog box and choose Save from the File menu.

9. Exit Visual C++ and reboot the machine.

After the machine has booted up again, the Lock Workstation button will no longer be displayed.

How do I enable Ctrl+Esc to start Task Manager?

This was changed to Ctrl+Shift+Esc in release 4.0 of NT; however, you can restore it to Ctrl+Esc by editing the Registry:

1. Start the Registry editor (REGEDIT.EXE).

2. Go to the HKEY_LOCAL_MACHINE\Software\Microsoft\Windows NT\CurrentVersion\Winlogon.

3. Click Edit > New > String Value and enter the name **TaskMan**.

4. Double-click the entry, set the value to TASKMAN.EXE, and press Enter.

5. Close the Registry and reboot the machine.

How can I disable Alt+Tab?

Alt+Tab allows a user to "scroll" between currently running applications. This can be disabled via the Registry:

1. Start the Registry editor (REGEDIT.EXE).

2. Move to HKEY_CURRENT_USER\Control Panel\Desktop.

3. Double-click on Coolswitch.

4. Set to 0 and click OK.
5. Close the Registry editor.

You need to restart the computer for this to take effect.

How can I allow nonadministrators to issue AT commands?

By default, only Administrators can issue AT commands (which use the Scheduler service). AT commands are used to schedule commands to run at a certain time. You can do the following to allow Server Operators to also submit AT commands:

1. Start the Registry editor (REGEDIT.EXE).
2. Move to the HKEY_LOCAL_MACHINE\SYSTEM\ CurrentControlSet\Control\Lsa.
3. From the Edit menu, select New > DWORD Value.
4. Enter the name **Submit Control** and press Enter.
5. Double-click on the name and set the value to 1.
6. Exit the Registry editor and reboot the machine.

You should update your Emergency Repair Disk after making this change (see Chapter 11, Recovery, for information on RDISK.EXE).

4.0 ONLY

How do I control access to floppy drives and CD-ROM drives?

By default, Windows NT allows any program to access the floppy and CD-ROM drives. In a secure environment, you might want only the interactive user to be able to access the drives. This is accomplished by using the Registry:

1. Start the Registry editor (REGEDIT.EXE).
2. Move to the HKEY_LOCAL_MACHINE\SOFTWARE\Microsoft\ WindowsNT\CurrentVersion\Winlogon.
3. From the Edit menu, select New > Reg_SZ Type.

4. To allocate floppy drives, create a name AllocateFloppies; to allocate CD-ROM drives, create AllocateCDRoms.

5. Press Enter and then set the value to 1.

6. Log out and log in again.

The Windows NT Resource Kit also supplies a utility called FLOPLOCK.EXE, which runs as a service. When it is running, only members of the Administrators group can access the floppy drives.

 ## I have DOS, Windows 95, and NT installed, and I want them all to show on the Boot menu. How do I do it?

You need a handy utility called Bootpart (which you can get from http://www.ntfaq.com/ntfaq/download/bootpart.zip). Bootpart creates multiple operating .SYS files, enabling DOS and Windows 95 to be shown on the Boot menu:

1. The first thing to do is create an Emergency Repair Disk (RDISK /S).

2. Reboot the machine and boot into Windows 95.

3. When Starting Windows 95 is displayed, press F8.

4. Select option 8 to boot to previous version of DOS.

5. In DOS, go to where you unzipped BOOTPART.ZIP and type the following:

```
BOOTPART DOS622 c:\BOOTSECT.622 "MS-DOS 6.22"
BOOTPART WIN95 c:\BOOTSECT.W95 "Windows 95"
BOOTPART REWRITEROOT:C:
```

6. Edit the BOOT.INI file to remove the old MS-DOS/Windows95 option, as follows:

```
attrib c:\boot.ini -r -s
edit c:\boot.ini and remove c:\="MS-DOS"
attrib c:\boot.ini +r +s
```

7. Reboot the system.

Be aware that using Bootpart might cause problems if you select Previous Windows Version from Windows 95.

4.0 ONLY
6.23

How do I assign a drive letter to a removable drive?

It is not possible to assign a drive letter to a removable device by using Disk Administrator; however, you can assign drive letters to the other partitions and leave free the letter you want the removable drive to use. NT assigns drive letters to physical devices first (first partition), then to removable drives, and then to other partitions (secondary partitions). For example, if you had one hard disk with two partitions and a removable drive, the letter assignments would be

Physical drive, partition 1 = c:
Removable drive = d:
Physical drive, partition 2 = e:

To ensure that a removable drive receives a certain drive letter, follow the instructions below:

1. Shut down NT and disconnect the removable drive.
2. Start NT and assign drive letters to the partitions, leaving free the letter you want the removable drive to use.
3. Shut down NT, attach the removable drive, and start NT.

A fix is now available that allows you to actually set the letter for a removable drive. Find it at http://support.microsoft.com/support/kb/articles/q142/6/35.asp.

4.0 ONLY
6.24

How can I create a new hardware profile?

If you are about to change hardware, you might want to create a copy of your current hardware configuration before you start. This will enable you to revert to your old configuration:

1. Start the System Control Panel applet (Start > Settings > Control Panel) or right-click on My Computer and select Properties.

2. Click on the Hardware Profiles tab.
3. Select the current Hardware Profile Original Configuration (Current).
4. Click Copy and then type the new name in the dialog box that is shown.
5. Click OK and the Startup options will be set.

I have entries on the Remove software list that don't work. How can I remove them?

Each entry on the Remove list (reached by choosing Start > Settings > Control Panel > Add/Remove Programs) is an entry in the Registry under HKEY_LOCAL_MACHINE\SOFTWARE\Microsoft\Windows\CurrentVersion\Uninstall. In the Registry editor (REGEDIT.EXE), just remove the key for any entries you don't want by selecting the entry and clicking Del (see Figure 6-4).

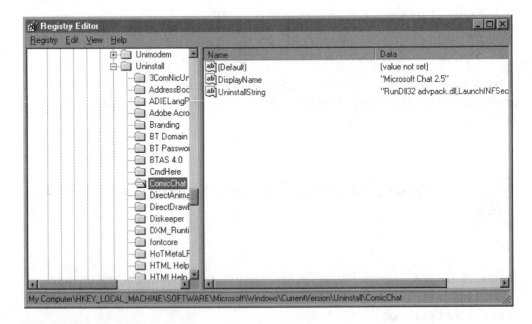

Figure 6-4. Press Del to remove the Comic Chat uninstall entry. This removes only the Remove entry, not the software.

How can I disable Dr. Watson?

Dr. Watson is displayed when a program crashes; however, it can be annoying, so you might want to disable it. You can disable Dr. Watson by using the Registry editor:

1. Start the Registry editor (REGEDIT.EXE).
2. Go to HKEY_LOCAL_MACHINE\SOFTWARE\Microsoft\ Windows NT\CurrentVersion\AeDebug.
3. Click on AeDebug and then click Del.

Alternatively, go to HKEY_LOCAL_MACHINE\SOFTWARE\Microsoft\ Windows NT\CurrentVersion\AeDebug\AUTO and set it to 0.

To reenable Dr. Watson, type **drwtsn32 -i**.

How can I configure the machine to reboot at a certain time?

A command line utility called SHUTDOWN.EXE is shipped with the Resource Kit. You can use this utility to reboot the local machine. Use the command

```
shutdown /l /r /y /c
```

where /l means to shut down the local machine, /r to reboot, /c to close all programs, and /y to avoid having to say yes to questions. You can then combine this command with the AT command to make the reboot happen at a certain time. (Don't forget you need to have the Schedule service running when you use the AT command; choose Start > Settings > Control Panel > Services.) The command is

```
AT <time> shutdown /l /r /y /c
```

(for example, AT 20:00 shutdown /l /r /y /c)

Additions to the AT command could be /every:M,T,W,Th,F so it happens every day:

```
AT 20:00 /every:M,T,W,Th,F shutdown /l /r /y /c
```

You will then be given 20 seconds before the machine is shut down. To abort the shutdown, type

```
shutdown /l /a /y
```

 ## How can I configure Explorer to start with a specific drive?

The procedure below is used to change the shortcut for Explorer in the Start menu. However, you could just as easily create a new shortcut on the desktop and then edit its properties and change the target.

1. Start Explorer (choose Start > Programs > Windows NT Explorer, or use Win key + E).
2. Move to %SystemRoot%/profiles/<your username>/Start Menu/Programs. For example, I would type the following:

```
d:/winnt/profiles/savillj/Start Menu/Programs
```

3. Right-click on Windows NT Explorer and select Properties, or select Properties from the File menu.
4. The target will be %SystemRoot%\explorer.exe. Change this to %SystemRoot%\explorer.exe /e, <drive letter>:\. For example, **%SystemRoot%\explorer.exe /e, e:** would make Explorer start at the E: drive (make sure you type the comma).
5. You can also use /root, which forces the right-hand pane to show only E:, as in **%SystemRoot%\explorer.exe /e, /root, e:**. Also note that instead of just a drive letter, you can specify a directory, as in **%SystemRoot%\explorer.exe /e, e:\winnt\system32**.
6. Click OK and exit Explorer.

How can I stop and start services from the command line?

To generate a list of the running services, enter this command:

```
net start
```

You can add > [filename] to the end to make the command output to a file, as in **net start > services.lst.** You can then try to shut down each service by entering the net stop command. To stop and start a service, use one of these:

```
net stop <service name>
net start <service name>
```

A full list of the exact services is found in the Registry (run REGEDIT.EXE) under the HKEY_LOCAL_MACHINE\SYSTEM\CurrentControlSet\ Services key.

Some services ask you to enter a y to confirm; for these, just add **/y** to the end.

You can also use the Resource Kit SC.EXE command to get a list of the services, as follows:

```
sc query
```

Then you can stop the service by using

```
sc stop <service name>
```

Alternatively, you can perform the stop and start, using the name shown in the Services control panel applet, by putting the name in quotes, like this:

```
net stop "<service>"
net start "<service>"
```

How do I delete a service?

To delete a service that has not been automatically removed by a software uninstall, you need to edit the Registry:

1. Start the Registry editor (REGEDIT.EXE).

2. Move to the HKEY_LOCAL_MACHINE\SYSTEM\
   CurrentControlSet\Services key.

3. Select the key of the service you want to delete.

4. From the Edit menu, choose Delete.

5. When you are prompted "Are you sure you want to delete this Key," click Yes.

6. Close the Registry editor.

There is also an INSTSRV.EXE utility supplied with the NT resource kit, which you can use to install and remove services, as follows:

```
instsrv <service name> remove
```

Alternatively, another Resource Kit utility, SRVINSTW.EXE, installs and removes services with a GUI Wizard format, allowing you to select the service either locally or remotely.

 ## How can I change the startup order of the services?

Each service belongs to a Service Group, and it is possible to modify the order in which the groups start:

1. Start the Registry editor (REGEDT32.EXE, **not** REGEDIT.EXE).

2. Move to HKEY_LOCAL_MACHINE\SYSTEM\CurrentControlSet\
   Control\ServiceGroupOrder.

3. Double-click on List in the right-hand pane.

4. You can now move the groups around in the list order.

5. Click OK and close the Registry editor.

For more information, see Knowledge Base Article Q102987 at http://support.microsoft.com/support/kb/articles/q102/9/87.asp.

What are the ErrorControl, Start, and Type values under the Services subkeys?

See the Tables 6-1 to 6-3 for a description of the main three values and their contents.

The values in Table 6-1 are used if the service fails to start up on boot.

Table 6-1. ErrorControl

Value	Meaning
0x00	If this driver can't be loaded or started, ignore the problem and display no error.
0x01	If the driver fails, produce a warning but let bootup continue.
0x02	Panic. If the current config is last known good, continue; if not, switch to last known good.
0x03	Record the current startup as a failure. If this is last known good, run diagnostic; if not, switch to last known good and reboot.

The values in Table 6-2 define when in the boot sequence the service should be started. You can also set these by using the Services control panel applet.

Table 6-2. Start

Value	Start Type	Meaning
0x00	Boot	The kernel loaded will load this driver first; it's needed to use the boot volume device.
0x01	System	This is loaded by the I/O subsystem.
0x02	Autoload	The service is always loaded and run.
0x03	Manual	This service does not start automatically and must be manually started by the user.
0x04	Disabled	The service is disabled and should not be started.

The values in Table 6-3 define the kind of service or driver. They are loaded in order, going down the list.

Table 6-3. Type

Value	Meaning
0x01	Kernel-mode device driver
0x02	Kernel-mode device driver that implements the file system
0x04	Information used by the Network Adapter
0x10	A Win32 service that should be run as a standalone process
0x20	A Win32 service that can share address space with other services of the same type

How can I decrease the time my machine takes to shut down or reboot?

Depending on what you have on your machine, it might take a long time to shut down because it has to shut all the services down.

It is possible to manually shut down most services and then shut down the machine. To identify which services are running, enter this command:

```
net start
```

You can add > [filename] to the end to make it output to a file, as in **net start > services.lst**. You can then try to shut down each service by entering the net stop command. For example, use

```
net stop "spooler"
```

Some services ask you to enter a "y" to confirm; for these, just add **/y** to the end. You will be able to build up a list of all the services that can be manually stopped, and you should put these in a .BAT file. Here's an example:

```
net stop "Computer Browser"
net stop "Messenger"
net stop "Workstation"
```

To the end of the file, add the following command to reboot the machine (leave off the /r to just shut down the machine):

```
shutdown /r /y /l /t:0
```

SHUTDOWN.EXE is part of the Windows NT Resource Kit. You might also want to add @echo off to the start of the file, and you could add a check to accept an input parameter to reboot or shut down. For example, save this file as SHUTFAST.BAT and call it by using

```
shutfast reboot, or shutfast shutdown
@echo off
net stop "Computer Browser"
net stop "Messenger"
net stop "Net Logon"
net stop "NT LM Security Support Provider"
net stop "Plug and Play"
net stop "Protected Storage"
net stop "Remote Access Autodial Manager"
net stop "Server"
net stop "Spooler"
net stop "TCP/IP NetBIOS Helper" /y
net stop "Workstation"

if %1==reboot goto reboot
shutdown /l /y /t:0
exit
:reboot
shutdown /l /y /r /t:0
exit
```

You could add a shortcut on the desktop for this batch file with the relevant parameters.

You can also do the following to decrease the time NT waits for a service to stop before terminating it:

1. Start the Registry editor (REGEDT32.EXE, **not** REGEDIT.EXE).
2. Move to HKEY_LOCAL_MACHINE\SYSTEM\CurrentControlSet\ Control.
3. Double-click on WaitToKillServiceTimeout (REG_DWORD) and change to the number of milliseconds to wait after the logoff/shutdown

before displaying the Wait, End Task and Close dialog box (for example, 10000 for 10 seconds; default is 20000).

4. Add HangAppTimeout (REG_DWORD) and change to the number of milliseconds to wait before displaying the Wait, End Task and Close dialog box after trying to close an application.

5. Add AutoEndTasks (REG_DWORD) and change to 1 to avoid the dialog asking to Wait, End Task and Close.

How can I configure the system so that certain commands run at boot time?

You can use a utility called AUTOEXNT.EXE, which you can download from http://www.ntfaq.com/ntfaq/download/autoexnt.zip. To use it, perform the following:

1. From the AUTOEXNT.ZIP file, extract the files AUTOEXNT.EXE, AUTOEXNT.BAT, and SERVMESS.DLL to %systemroot%/system32.

2. Also extract the file INSTSRV.EXE to any directory (a temp directory will do).

3. At the command prompt, enter the following to create a new service called AutoExNT:

```
instsrv install
```

4. Edit the file %systemroot%/system32/autoexnt.bat and put in any commands you want to be run when the machine boots (such as a CHKDSK).

When the system boots in future, the AutoExNT service will check for the existence of the file AUTOEXNT.BAT and execute any commands in it.

A version of this utility is also shipped with the Resource Kit; however, it is better to use the downloadable version. To install the Resource Kit version, type **instexnt install**.

What are the .CPL files in the system32 directory?

Each .CPL file represents one or more control panel applets (Start > Settings > Control Panel). Table 6-4 is a list of common .CPL files with the control panel applets they represent.

Table 6-4. Common .CPL Files

.CPL filename	control panel applet
ACCESS.CPL	Accessibility options
APPWIZ.CPL	Add/remove programs
CONSOLE.CPL	Console
DESK.CPL	Display
DEVAPPS.CPL	PCMCIA, SCSI adapters, and tape drives
INETCPL.CPL	Internet
INTL.CPL	Regional settings
JOY.CPL	Joystick
MAIN.CPL	Fonts, keyboard, mouse, and printers
MLCFG32.CPL	Mail
MMSYS.CPL	Sounds and multimedia
MODEM.CPL	Modems
NCPA.CPL	Network
NTGUARD.CPL	Dr Solomons
ODBCCP32.CPL	ODBC
PORTS.CPL	Ports
RASCPL.CPL	Dial-up monitor
SRVMGR.CPL	Server, services, and devices
SYSDM.CPL	System
TELEPHON.CPL	Telephony

Table 6-4. Common .CPL Files (continued)

TIMEDATE.CPL	Date/Time
TWEAKUI.CPL	TweakUI
UPS.CPL	UPS

If you rename any of these files, the items they represent in the Control Panel will not be shown. For example, the command **rename timedate.cpl timedate.non** would remove the Date/Time control panel applet.

Also, you can set HKEY_CURRENT_USER\Software\Microsoft\Windows\ CurrentVersion\Policies\Explorer\NoSetFolders (REG_DWORD) to 1 to hide the Control Panel, Printers, and My Computer in Explorer and the Start menu. You would need to create this value, because it does not exist by default.

How do I remove an application from the Control Panel?

Each item in the Control Panel corresponds to a .CPL file. When the Control Panel starts, it searches %systemroot%/system32 for all .CPL files. To remove an item from the Control Panel, rename the .CPL file (to .NOCPL, for example).

As an alternative, if you want to prevent only certain users from running a particular applet, you can have the boot partition on NTFS and remove the READ permission for these users or groups.

For more information on the .CPL files, have a look at Question 6-35.

How can I disable the Display Control Panel applet?

You can use Policies to disable the Display Control Panel applet. This can also be accomplished by using the Registry editor, as follows:

1. Start the Registry editor (REGEDIT.EXE).
2. Move to HKEY_CURRENT_USER\Software\Microsoft\Windows\ CurrentVersion\Policies\System.

3. From the Edit menu, select New > DWORD Value.
4. Enter **NoDispCPL** and press Enter.
5. Double-click the new value and set it to 1.
6. Close the Registry editor.

The change takes effect immediately. If you try to run the Display Control Panel applet now, either by right-clicking on the desktop and selecting Properties or by starting from the control panel applet, you will receive this message:

"Your system administrator disabled the Display control panel."

You could, of course, delete the DESK.CPL file; however, using the Registry editor is preferable because it allows greater control.

 ## How can I disable elements of the Display Control Panel applet?

Again, you can use Policies to disable elements of the Display Control Panel applet, but you can also do so by using the Registry editor.

1. Start the Registry editor (REGEDIT.EXE).
2. Move to HKEY_CURRENT_USER\Software\Microsoft\Windows\ CurrentVersion\Policies\System.
3. From the Edit menu, select New > DWORD Value.
4. Enter any of the options outlined in Table 6-5.
5. Double-click the new value and set it to 1.
6. Close the Registry editor.

Table 6-5. Disabling Elements of the Display Control Panel

NoDispAppearancePage	Removes the Appearance tab, which means users cannot change the colors or color scheme.
NoDispBackgroundPage	Removes the Background tab, which means no more Pamela Anderson background.
NoDispScrSavPage	Removes the Screen Save tab.
NoDispSettingsPage	Removes the Settings and the Plus tab.

These changes take immediate effect and any disabled tab is not displayed.

Of course, the user can go into the Registry and change these back, which is why it's better to implement these as policies (which is what I do).However, because they take immediate effect, nothing can stop someone from creating a reg script to run as part of the startup group that sets it to how they want to get around the policy. Of course, I would never condone this.

How can I run a control panel applet from the command line?

It is possible to run Control Panel applets from the command line by just typing

```
control <applet name>
```

In some instances the .CPL file represents more than one control panel applet. In that case, you need to pass a parameter of which applet to run, as in the following list:

SRVMGR.CPL: Services, Devices, or Server
MAIN.CPL: Fonts, Mouse, Printers, or Keyboard
MMSYS.CPL: Sounds or Multimedia

For example, **control main.cpl printers** will run the Printer Control Panel applet.

However, it is better to associate the .CPL extension with CONTROL.EXE, which means you only need to type the applet name. This is accomplished by using the assoc and ftype commands, as follows:

```
assoc .cpl=ControlFile
ftype ControlFile=control.exe %1 %*
```

You can now just enter the command and the applet will run (be sure to include the .CPL extension).

What Registry keys do the Control Panel applets update?

Table 6-6 shows the control panel applets and their corresponding Registry areas. Those not shown are stored in multiple areas.

Table 6-6. Control Panel Applet Registry Keys

Accessibility options	HKEY_CURRENT_USER\Control Panel\Accessibility
Date/time	HKEY_LOCAL_MACHINE\SYSTEM\CurrentControlSet\Control\TimeZoneInformation
Devices	HKEY_LOCAL_MACHINE\SYSTEM\CurrentControlSet\Services
Display	HKEY_CURRENT_USER\Control Panel\Desktop and HKEY_LOCAL_MACHINE\HARDWARE\RESOURCEMAP\VIDEO
Fonts	HKEY_LOCAL_MACHINE\SOFTWARE\Microsoft\Windows NT\CurrentVersion\Fonts
Internet	HKEY_LOCAL_MACHINE\SOFTWARE\Microsoft\Windows\CurrentVersion\Internet Settings
Keyboard	HKEY_CURRENT_USER\Control Panel\Desktop
Modems	HKEY_LOCAL_MACHINE\SOFTWARE\Microsoft\Windows\CurrentVersion\Unimodem
Mouse	HKEY_CURRENT_USER\Control Panel\Mouse
Multimedia	HKEY_LOCAL_MACHINE\SOFTWARE\Microsoft\Multimedia
Ports	HKEY_LOCAL_MACHINE\HARDWARE\RESOURCEMAP
Printers	HKEY_CURRENT_USER\Printers
Regional Settings	HKEY_CURRENT_USER\Control Panel\International
SCSI adapters	HKEY_LOCAL_MACHINE\HARDWARE\RESOURCEMAP\ScsiAdapter

Table 6-6. Control Panel Applet Registry Keys *(continued)*

Services	HKEY_LOCAL_MACHINE\SYSTEM\CurrentControlSet\ Services
Sounds	HKEY_CURRENT_USER\AppEvents\Schemes\Apps\.Default
Tape devices	HKEY_LOCAL_MACHINE\HARDWARE\ RESOURCEMAP\OtherDrivers\TapeDevices
Telephony	HKEY_LOCAL_MACHINE\SOFTWARE\Microsoft\ Windows\CurrentVersion\Telephony
UPS	HKEY_LOCAL_MACHINE\SYSTEM\CurrentControlSet\ Services\UPS

4.0 ONLY

6.41

How can I create a non-network hardware configuration?

You might have some machines that are not always connected to the network, and a solution is to create an alternative hardware profile that has all network devices and services disabled.

1. Open the control panel (Start > Settings > Control Panel).
2. Start the System Control Panel applet.
3. Select the Hardware Profiles tab.
4. Select the current configuration and click Copy.
5. In the To box, enter **No Network** and click OK.
6. From the Available Hardware Profiles box, select No Network and click Properties.
7. Click the Network tab. Check the Network Disabled Hardware Profiles box and click OK.
8. Make sure the Wait For time is set (for example, 30 seconds), and then click OK.
9. If you want, you can also change the name of Original Configuration to On Network by selecting it, clicking Rename, and typing the new name.

To actually use this configuration when you boot up the machine, you select the operating system to load as usual (for example, Windows NT Workstation 4.0).

Another menu displays, with your hardware profile choices. Select the required hardware and click Enter.

 4.0 ONLY

How can I remove the option "Press Spacebar for last known good config"?

The choice is hard-coded into NT and therefore cannot be removed; however, you can remove its functionality.

Several sets of configuration information are stored in NT: the current configuration and one or more sets of old configuration that are known to work. What NT does in the Registry is to point to the current configuration and also a link to one of the other sets. It is possible to change the link to the Last Known Good Config so that pressing the spacebar at bootup will have no effect.

1. Start the Registry editor (REGEDIT.EXE).
2. Move to HKEY_LOCAL_MACHINE\SYSTEM\Select (if you look at HKEY_LOCAL_MACHINE\SYSTEM, you can see the control sets).
3. Double-click on LastKnownGood and change its value to whatever Current's value is.
4. Click OK and close the Registry editor.

The Press Spacebar for Last Known Good Config option has caused lots of trouble because of its use with the Novell IntranetWare for Windows NT, which is unavailable after restoring the Last Known Good configuration. The same is true for any system-created hardware profile.

Here's an interesting solution for this and other related system crashes: save the whole registration key from the REGEDIT (interestingly, this method doesn't work with the more detailed REGEDT32) as a script file named—for example—SAVE.REG. If a system is then damaged, a simple double-click on this executable file regenerates the whole configuration without loss of information.

Moreover, you can zip this file—usually as large as 5MB—to a volume of nearly 500KB. With these tools in hand, it is possible to restore a crashed system from disk by using RDISK and afterward regenerate the system with the Registry file to the last known standard.

4.0 ONLY

6.43

How can I disable the OS/2 and POSIX subsystems?

Windows NT has built-in support for OS/2 and POSIX in the form of subsystems; however, it is possible to disable one or both of these.

1. Start the Registry editor (REGEDT32.EXE, **not** REGEDIT.EXE).
2. Move to HKEY_LOCAL_MACHINE\SYSTEM\CurrentControlSet\ Control\Session Manager\SubSystems.
3. Double-click on Optional (see Figure 6-5).
4. On each line is one subsystem; simply remove the one you wish to disable. If you want to disable both, set the value to Null.
5. Click OK.
6. Close the Registry editor and reboot.

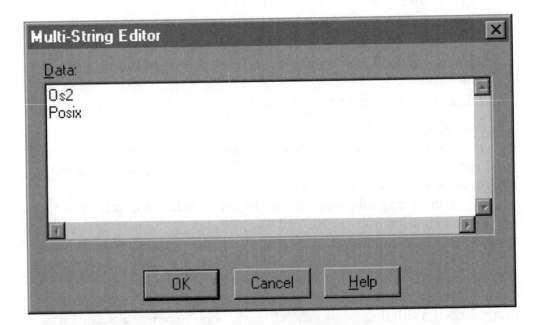

Figure 6-5. The Optional value. If it doesn't look like this, you are probably using REGEDIT.EXE instead of REGEDT32.EXE.

How can I configure a program/batch file to run every *x* minutes?

NT comes with a powerful built-in scheduling tool—the AT command—but it is not really suitable for running a command every 5 minutes. To do this, you would have to submit hundreds of AT jobs to run at certain times of the day. However, a number of helpful tools are supplied with the Windows NT Resource Kit.

The first is called SLEEP.EXE and is used to set a command file to wait for *n* seconds (like the timeout command). To use it, simply type (for example)

```
sleep 300
```

which would make the batch file pause for 5 minutes. If you want a command file or program to run every 5 minutes, you could write a batch file like the following (named RUN5.BAT):

```
<program name>
sleep 300
run5
```

This approach has a number of problems. For example, the command session has to stay open and the 5 minutes do not start until the program has closed. (You can solve this by running the program in a separate thread; put the word "start" in front of the program, as in **start <program>**).

Another program is SOON.EXE, which schedules a task to run in *n* seconds from now. To use SOON, the Scheduler service has to be running (Start > Settings > Control Panel > Services). Again, you could create a batch file for it:

```
(runsoon.cmd)
soon 300 runsoon.cmd
notepad.exe
```

Run the command file by using the AT command or SOON to get it started. For example, from the command line, type

```
soon 300 runsoon.cmd
```

If you want to stop the soon command after it is scheduled to run, you would first use the AT command to get a list of current scheduled jobs:

```
at
Status ID Day Time Command Line
_____
0 Today 9:04 AM runsoon.cmd
```

When you know the command's ID, you can stop it by using at [\\computer name] <ID> /delete. For example, type

```
at 0 /delete
```

How can I run a script at shutdown time?

There is no direct way to accomplish this; however, it is possible to write a script and then call the SHUTDOWN.EXE utility that is shipped with the NT Resource Kit:

```
shutdown /l /y
```

You could then add a shortcut to this script on the desktop. An alternative is to use a utility called ShutUp, which you can download from http://www.zdnet.com/pcmag/download/utils/shutup-A.htm/.

How can I make NT power down on shutdown?

Windows 98 users will be used to the powering down of the computer when they shut down the operating system. NT has a version of this:

1. Start the Registry editor (REGEDIT.EXE).
2. Go to the Key HKEY_LOCAL_MACHINE\Software\Microsoft\Windows NT\CurrentVersion\Winlogon.

3. If the value PowerdownAfterShutdown exists, change it to 1 and go to step 5.
4. If the value does not exist, add it as type REG_SZ and set it to 1.
5. Close the Registry editor.

You need an ATX power supply and an updated HAL.DLL from the computer manufacturer for this to work; otherwise, the machine just reboots.

Windows NT 4.0 Service Pack 4 ships with a HAL.DLL.SOFTEX file that works on many systems. This can be used in the event that an updated HAL.DLL is not available from the computer manufacturer. To install HAL.DLL.SOFTEX, perform the following:

```
cd %systemroot%\system32
WINNT\system32> rename hal.dll hal.old
WINNT\system32> copy g:\i386\hal.dll.softex hal.dll
```

Reboot, and your machine will now be able to power down on shutdown.

How can I create my own tips to be shown when NT starts?

The tips NT displays are stored in key HKEY_LOCAL_MACHINE\ SOFTWARE\Microsoft\Windows\CurrentVersion\Explorer\Tips and can easily be edited by using the Registry editor. You will notice that the names of the values are incremented by one, so to add a new tip, either edit an existing one or create a new value (of type string) and set its name to the next available number (see Figure 6-6).

The tips are displayed sequentially. The counter is stored in HKEY_ CURRENT_USER\Software\Microsoft\Windows\CurrentVersion\Explorer\ Tips\Next and can be changed, if you want. The values are stored in hexadecimal.

To control whether tips are shown, set the value HKEY_CURRENT_ USER\Software\Microsoft\Windows\CurrentVersion\Explorer\Tips\show to 01000000 to display and 00000000 to not display.

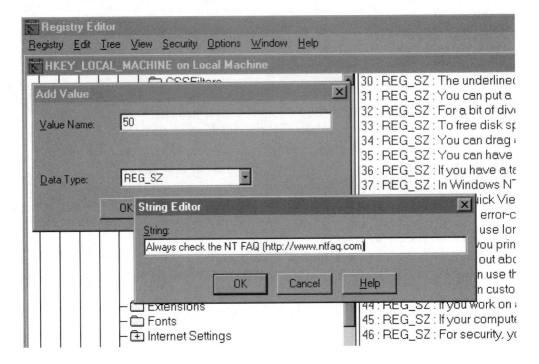

Figure 6-6. Essential!

How can I change the location of the event logs?

In Event Viewer, you will notice three different logs: Application, System, and Security. Each of these is mapped to an .EVT file in the %systemroot%/system32/config directory; however, for reasons of performance or disk space, you might wish to move them. You can do this by performing the following:

1. Start the Registry Editor (REGEDIT.EXE).
2. Move to the HKEY_LOCAL_MACHINE\SYSTEM\CurrentControlSet\Services\EventLog key. Under this key are three other subkeys: Application, Security, and System. Select one of them.
3. Under each of the subkeys is a value called File. Double-click this value.

4. Edit the value to the location you require and click OK.

5. Repeat for the other two log settings.

6. Close the Registry editor and reboot the machine for the change to take effect.

How can I configure the default Internet browser?

When you start an Internet browser, it usually performs a check to see if it is the default browser. However, you might have turned this check off and want to change the default browser. To do so, perform the following:

1. Start the Registry editor (REGEDIT.EXE).

2. Move to HKEY_CLASSES_ROOT\http.

3. Expand the tree and move to HKEY_CLASSES_ROOT\http\shell\ open\command. Double-click on Default and set the string to the command you wish to run for Internet addresses; for example, use this:

```
"E:\PROGRA~1\Plus!\MICROS~1\iexplore.exe" -nohome for
Internet Explorer
E:\Program Files\Netscape\Communicator\Program\
netscape.exe -h "%1" for Netscape
```

4. Click OK.

5. Move to HKEY_CLASSES_ROOT\http\shell\open\ddeexec\ Application. Again double-click Default and change to the browser: NSShell for Netscape or IExplore for Internet Explorer.

6. You might also want to change the associated icon. If so, move to HKEY_CLASSES_ROOT\http\DefaultIcon, double-click Default, and set to the icon, like this:

```
%SystemRoot%\system32\url.dll,0 Internet Explorer
E:\Program Files\Netscape\Communicator\Program\
netscape.exe,0 Netscape Navigator
```

You should repeat the above for https, as well: HKEY_CLASSES_ROOT\
https\shell\open\command, and so on.

How can I change the alert for low disk space on a partition?

By default, when a partition has less than 10% free disk space, an event ID 2013 is created with the following text:

"The disk is at or near capacity. You might need to delete some files."

To view these events, use Event Viewer; however, it is possible to change the percentage for which the alert is created.

1. Start the Registry editor (REGEDIT.EXE).
2. Move to HKEY_LOCAL_MACHINE\SYSTEM\ CurrentControlSet\Services\LanmanServer\Parameters.
3. If the value DiskSpaceThreshold exists, double-click on it and skip to step 5.
4. If the value does not exist, select New > DWORD Value from the Edit menu. Enter the name **DiskSpaceThreshold** and click OK.
5. Double-click on the new value, set the base to decimal, and enter a value from 0-99 for which you want the event to be generated.
6. Click OK and restart the machine.

How can I tell NT how much secondary cache (L2) is installed?

NT tries to detect how much L2 cache is installed at startup time; however, sometimes it cannot tell and uses a default of 256. If you have more, you can manually configure NT with your exact amount.

1. Start the Registry editor (REGEDIT.EXE).
2. Move to HKEY_LOCAL_MACHINE\SYSTEM\CurrentControlSet\ Control\Session Manager\Memory Management.

3. Double-click on SecondLevelDataCache.

4. Click the decimal base and then enter the amount. For example, enter **512** if you have 512K of cache.

5. Click OK, close the Registry editor, and reboot the machine.

 ## What are the long pathnames in the BOOT.INI file?

The pathnames in the BOOT.INI file are the ARC (Advanced RISC Computing) pathnames and they're used to locate the NT system partition. There are two main types of ARC names, depending on whether the disks are IDE or SCSI. For IDE, the pathnames follow this convention:

```
multi(x)disk(x)rdisk(x)partition(x)\%systemroot%
```

Both the multi and disk are not really used for IDE and should always be 0. The rdisk is the physical drive and will be 0 or 1 on the first IDE controller or 2 and 3 on the second IDE controller. Partition() is the partition number on the disk and starts from 1.

The scheme is slightly different for SCSI:

```
scsi(x)disk(x)rdisk(x)partition(x)\%systemroot%
```

Scsi() is the controller number of the SCSI identified in the NTBOOTDD. SYS. Disk() is the SCSI ID of the physical disk. Rdisk() is the SCSI logical unit number (LUN), which is nearly always 0. Partition is the same as with IDE and is the partition number starting with 1.

The multi() designation means that the drive can respond to INT 13 calls. Most SCSI drives can, so you might use multi() with a SCSI drive also.

In a pure IDE system, the multi() syntax will work for up to the four drives maximum on the primary and secondary channels of a dual-channel controller.

In a pure SCSI system, the multi() syntax will work for the first two drives on the first SCSI controller (that is, the controller whose BIOS loads first).

In a mixed SCSI and IDE system, the multi() syntax will work only for the IDE drives on the first controller.

4.0 ONLY
6.53

What switches can be used in BOOT.INI?

The BOOT.INI file has a number of lines. Some of these relate to the Windows NT operating system, such as

```
multi(0)disk(0)rdisk(0)partition(2)\WINNT="Windows NT
Workstation Version 4.00"
```

A number of switches can be appended to the Windows NT startup line to perform certain functions (the switches are shown in Table 6-7). To edit the file, perform the following:

1. Start a command session (CMD.EXE).
2. Modify the attributes on the file c:\boot.ini to make the file editable:

   attrib c:\boot.ini -r -s

3. Edit the file:

   edit c:\boot.ini

4. When you have edited the file, save it and reset the file's attributes:

   attrib c:\boot.ini +r +s

Table 6-7. Switches for the BOOT.INI Command

/3GB	New to Service Pack 3. This causes the split between user and system portions of the Windows NT map to become 3GB for user applications, 1GB for system. To take advantage of this, the system must be part of the NT Enterprise suite and the application must be flagged as a 3GB-aware application.
/BASEVIDEO	The computer starts up using the standard VGA video driver. Use this if you have installed a graphics driver that is not working.
/BAUDRATE	Specifies the baud rate to be used for debugging. If you do not set the baud rate, the default baud rate is 9600 if a modem is attached or 19200 for a null-modem cable.

Table 6-7. Switches for the BOOT.INI Command *(continued)*

/BURNMEMORY=	Makes NT forget about the given amount of memory in MB. For example, if /burnmemory=64 is given, 64MB of memory will be unavailable.
/CRASHDEBUG	The debugger is loaded when you start Windows NT but remains inactive unless a kernel error occurs. This mode is useful if you are experiencing random, unpredictable kernel errors.
/DEBUG	The debugger is loaded when you start Windows NT and can be activated at any time by a host debugger connected to the computer. This is the mode to use when you are debugging problems that are regularly reproducible.
/DEBUGPORT= comx	Specifies the COM port to use for debugging, where x is the communications port you want to use.
/HAL=<hal>	Allows you to override the HAL used; for example, using a checked version.
/KERNEL=<kernel>	Same as above but for the kernel.
/MAXMEM:n	Specifies the maximum amount of RAM Windows NT can use. This switch is useful if you suspect a memory chip is bad.
/NODEBUG	No debugging information is being used.
/NOSERIALMICE= [COMx | COMx,y,z...]	Disables serial mouse detection of the specified COM port(s). Use this switch if you have a component other than a mouse attached to a serial port during the startup sequence. If you use /NOSERIALMICE without specifying a COM port, serial mouse detection is disabled on all COM ports.
/NUMPROC=n	Only enables the first *n* processors on a multiple-processor system.
/ONECPU	Only uses the first CPU in a multiple-processor system.
/PCILOCK	Stops Windows NT from dynamically assigning IO/IRQ resources to PCI devices and leaves the devices configured by the BIOS.
/SOS	Displays the driver names while they are being loaded. Use this switch if Windows NT won't start up and you think a driver is missing. This option is configured by default on the [VGA] option on the Boot menu.

You can now edit the BOOT.INI file and either add Windows NT startup entries or modify existing entries; for example, you could add a debug entry in the file, as follows.

```
multi(0)disk(0)rdisk(0)partition(2)\WINNT="Windows NT
Workstation Version 4.00 [debug]" /debug /debugport=com2
```

I have duplicate entries on my Boot menu. What can I do?

This is easy to remedy and is usually caused by reinstalling Windows NT.

1. Start a command prompt (CMD.EXE).
2. Enter the following command:

   attrib c:\boot.ini -r -s

3. Now edit BOOT.INI:

   edit boot.ini

Under the [operating systems] section of the file, you will see lines such as these:

```
multi(0)disk(0)rdisk(0)partition(2)\WINNT="Windows NT
Workstation Version 4.00"
multi(0)disk(0)rdisk(0)partition(2)\WINNT="Windows NT
Workstation Version 4.00 [VGA mode]" /basevideo /sos
C:\ = "MS-DOS"
```

If you see any duplicates, delete them, making sure you delete the right ones. If they differ from the multi(0)disk(0)rdisk(0)partition(2) parts, it means you had NT installed on a different disk or partition before (or might still), so only delete the entries if you are sure that NT installation no longer exists.

How can I change the default editor used for editing batch files?

By default, if you right-click on a batch file and select Edit, the batch file will open in Notepad; however, the application used can be changed as follows:

1. Start the Registry editor (REGEDIT.EXE).
2. Move to HKEY_CLASSES_ROOT\batfile\shell\edit\command.
3. Double-click on Default.
4. Change the value to the editor you want to use. For example, for Word, change it to

```
D:\Program Files\Microsoft Office\Office\winword.exe %1
```

5. Click OK and close the Registry editor.

There is no need to reboot; the change takes effect immediately. To reset to Notepad, change the entry to:

```
%SystemRoot%\System32\NOTEPAD.EXE %1
```

4.0 ONLY

How can I add my own information to the General tab of the System Control Panel applet?

When you receive a PC from a manufacturer, you might see extra lines of description text and a company logo on the General tab of a System Control Panel applet. You can change this or add to it as follows:

1. Create a bitmap you want with dimensions 180 by 114.
2. Save the picture in the %systemroot%/system32 folder (for example, d:\winnt\system32) with the name OEMLOGO.BMP. If the picture is greater than this size, it will be clipped from the top left corner. If it is smaller, a black border will be added.

3. Create the file %systemroot%/system32/OEMINFO.INI (d:\winnt\ system32\oeminfo.ini) with the following format:

```
[general]
Manufacturer=SavillTech Ltd
Model=SuperDuper 1
[Support Information]
Line1=" "
Line2="For support…"
Line3=" "
```

You do not need to reboot the machine; the System Control Panel applet will pick up the files when it is started. The previous information would result in something that looks like Figure 6-7.

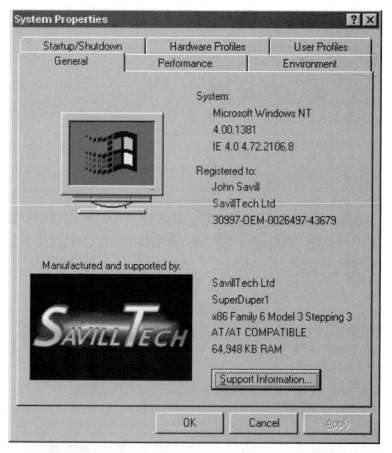

Figure 6-7. The SavillTech Computers logo now appears on the General tab.

6.57

How can I change the program associated with a file extension?

It is possible to associate a file extension with a default program or action. The easiest way to change this association is to perform the following:

1. Start Explorer (Run > Explorer).
2. Hold down the Shift key and right-click on a file with the extension you wish to change.
3. From the context menu displayed, select Open With.
4. Select an Application from the list (or click Other to find more) and check Always Use This Program to Open This Type of File.
5. Click OK.

An alternative method is to

1. Start Explorer (Run > Explorer).
2. Select Options (or Folder Options for IE 4.0 installations) from the View menu.
3. Click the File Types tab.
4. Select the File type and click Edit.
5. You can edit the Open and Print actions for the file type. For example, to change Open, select Open in the actions and click Edit. You can then change the command.
6. Click OK when finished.

 6.58

How can I open a file with an application other than the one with which it is associated?

Usually you can right-click on the file and select Open. Holding down Shift and right-clicking on the file gives you Open With.

4.0 ONLY
6.59 How do I set a process to use a certain processor?

This is called processor affinity. You set a process to use a specific processor on a multiprocessor system.

1. Start Task Manager (right-click on the taskbar and select Task Manager).
2. Click the Processes tab.
3. Right-click on the program and select Set Affinity.
4. You can check the processors on which you want the program to run (uncheck the ones you don't want it to use).

You cannot set affinity for a service or set affinity for a program that has not yet been started.

4.0 ONLY
6.60 How can I add the Printer panel to the Start menu?

To add a Printer panel to the Start menu, perform the following:

1. Create a new folder (right-click on the desktop and choose New > Folder). Name the folder

   ```
   Printers.{2227A280-3AEA-1069-A2DE-08002B30309D}
   ```

2. Right-click Start and choose Open.
3. Drag the new folder to the Start menu window.

The Printer panel will now be on the Start menu and will be cascading, meaning that all printers can be viewed as sub-items of the Printers menu item.

How can I hide the Administrative Tools on the Start menu?

There are several options open to you.

You can set the protections on the folder and its contents so only members of the Administrative group can read and execute it. This only works if the boot partition is NTFS.

1. Start Explorer (Run > Explorer).
2. Move to %systemroot%\Profiles\All Users\Start Menu\Programs.
3. Select Administrative Tools (Common) and select Properties from the File menu (or right-click the file and select Properties).
4. Click the Security tab.
5. Click the Permissions button.
6. Select Everyone and click Remove.
7. Click Add and select Domain Admins. Then click Add and select Access to Full Control.
8. Click OK to return to the Directory Permissions dialog box and click OK again.

Nonadministrative users will now see an empty Administrative Tools menu. You could select different users if you wish.

Alternatively, you could just move the Administrative Tools folder from the All Users section to a specific account area on the machine; however, there might be complications with roaming profiles and such.

The methods above just hide the items from the menu, but users can still run the applications from Run. This is not a problem, however, because the operating system prevents unauthorized users from altering the system by using these tools (you could set the protections on the executables as well if you don't want users to run them).

6.62 How do I change the Start menu items under the line?

Items above the line are part of the logged-in user's profile (winnt/profiles/ <user name>/Start Menu/Programs). Items under the line are part of the all-user group (winnt/profiles/All Users/Start Menu/Programs).

   To change the items under the line, choose Start > Settings > Taskbar & Start Menu > Start Menu > Advanced. Then move to the All Users directory and make changes. You can only set the All Users folder if you are logged on as a member with Administrative privileges.

6.63 How can I install a font from the command line or a batch file?

When you install a font, all you're doing is copying the .TTF file to the %systemroot%\fonts and adding an entry in HKEY_LOCAL_MACHINE\ SOFTWARE\Microsoft\Windows NT\CurrentVersion\Fonts. This can be automated with a batch file as follows:

```
Rem fontinst.bat
copy akbar.ttf %systemroot%\fonts
regedit /s font.reg
```

The FONT.REG would contain the following:

```
REGEDIT4
[HKEY_LOCAL_MACHINE\SOFTWARE\Microsoft\Windows
NT\CurrentVersion\Fonts]
"Akbar Plain (TrueType)"="akbar.ttf"
```

In this example, the batch file copies AKBAR.TTF, which is called Akbar Plain (TrueType)—yes, it's the Simpsons font. The reg script actually creates a value called Akbar Plain (TrueType) under HKEY_LOCAL_MACHINE\ SOFTWARE\Microsoft\Windows NT\CurrentVersion\Fonts with its contents AKBAR.TTF. The new font will be visible when the machine is rebooted.

If you have some older, 16-bit applications, you might want to add the font to WIN.INI, as well, in the [fonts] section. This can be accomplished by using an .INF file, like this:

```
[UpdateInis]
"E:\WINNT\WIN.INI","Fonts",,"Akbar Plain
(TrueType)=akbar.ttf"
```

4.0 ONLY

How do I restrict access to the floppy drive?

The NT Resource Kit and the Zero Administration Kit come with FlopLock service. To restrict access, perform the following:

1. First, install the FlopLock service:

   instsrv FloppyLocker c:\reskit\floplock.exe

2. Start the Service control panel applet (Start > Settings > Control Panel > Services).
3. Double-click on FloppyLocker and make sure the System Account is selected.
4. Set the startup to Automatic and click OK.
5. You can manually start the service to avoid the reboot by selecting FloppyLocker and clicking Start.

With the service started on Windows NT Workstation, only members of the Administrators and Power Users groups can access the floppy drives. With the service started on Windows NT Server, only members of the Administrators group can access the floppy drives.

To remove the service, perform the following:

1. Stop the FloppyLocker service (Start > Settings > Control Panel > Services > FloppyLocker > Stop).
2. Enter the following command:

   instsrv FloppyLocker remove

How do I enable AutoLogon?

The easiest way is to install TweakUI and go to the Network tab and just fill in the boxes. You can also enable AutoLogon manually through the Registry by following the instructions below:

1. Start the Registry editor (REGEDIT.EXE).
2. Open the HKEY_LOCAL_MACHINE\SOFTWARE\Microsoft\ Windows NT\Current Version\Winlogon.
3. Double-click the DefaultDomainName and fill in your domain name.
4. Double-click the DefaultUserName and fill in your login name.
5. From the Edit menu, select New > String Value and enter DefaultPassword as the name of the value.
6. Double-click DefaultPassword and enter the password.
7. From the Edit menu, select New > String Value and enter AutoAdminLogon as the name of the value.
8. Double-click the AutoAdminLogon and set the value to 1.
9. Close the Registry editor.
10. Log off and you will be automatically logged in again.

It is also possible to enable AutoLogon by using a program called AUTOLOG.EXE that comes with the Resource Kit. Just run the executable and you will be able to fill in the information.

To log on as a different user, you need to hold down the Shift key as you log off.

You will have to use REGEDT32.EXE to disable write permissions to HKEY_LOCAL_MACHINE\SOFTWARE\Microsoft\Windows NT\ Current Version\Winlogon if you want to be able to log off and log on as another user but still have the "original" user as the AutoLogon. Here's how:

1. Start the Registry editor (REGEDT32.EXE).
2. Move to HKEY_LOCAL_MACHINE\SOFTWARE\Microsoft\ Windows NT\Current Version\Winlogon.
3. Select Winlogon.
4. From the Security menu, select Permissions and adjust so write permission is removed for normal users.

How do I disable AutoLogon?

Again, use TweakUI. Or in the Registry editor, set AutoAdminLogon to 0 and clear the DefaultPassword.

How do I add a warning logon message?

You need to use the Registry editor.

1. Start the Registry editor (REGEDIT.EXE).
2. Move to HKEY_LOCAL_MACHINE/SOFTWARE/Microsoft/ Windows NT/CurrentVersion/Winlogon.
3. Double-click LegalNoticeCaption and enter the text you want to appear in the title bar. Then click OK.
4. Double-click LegalNoticeText and enter the warning text. Then click OK.
5. Close the Registry and log off. When you log on again, you will see the warning.

This can also be done via the Policy editor, as follows:

1. Start the Policy editor (POLEDIT.EXE).
2. Open the default Computer Policy.
3. Open the Windows NT system tree and then open Logon.
4. Put a tick in the Logon Banner check box and enter the caption and text.
5. Click OK and save the policy.

Alternatively, you can display a text message by creating the key LogonPrompt in HKEY_LOCAL_MACHINE/SOFTWARE/Microsoft/Windows NT/CurrentVersion/Winlogon.

How can I stop people from being authenticated by a server?

6.68

If you want to disable an NT server's capability to handle authentication, you can do so by stopping the Net Logon service:

1. Open the control panel (Start > Settings > Control Panel).
2. Double-click on Services.
3. Click Net Logon and then click Pause.
4. Close the control panel.

To disable all of NT's server services, click on Server and click Stop. This stops Net Logon, Computer Browser, and any other server services.

Users fail to log on at a server. Why?

6.69

By default, members of Domain Users will not be able to log on to a server (that is, a PDC or a BDC). If they try, they get the error message "The local policy of this system does not allow you to log on interactively." If you want users to be able to log on to a server (why, I don't know), follow this procedure:

1. Log on to the server as an Administrator.
2. Start User Manager for Domains (Start > Programs > Administrative Tools > User Manager for Domains).
3. Select User Rights from the Policies menu.
4. From the drop-down Rights list, select Log On Locally.
5. Click Add and select Domain Users. Click Add again and then click OK.
6. Close User Manager.
7. Log out and a user will now be able to log in.

6.70

How do I configure the default keyboard layout during logon?

You can change the keyboard layout by using the Keyboard control panel applet (Start > Settings > Control Panel > Keyboard > Input Locales); however, this does not affect the layout used during logon—which is by default English (United States). To change this layout, perform the following:

1. Start the Registry editor (REGEDIT.EXE).
2. Move to HKEY_USERS\.DEFAULT\Keyboard Layout\Preload.
3. Double-click on 1 and change the number to your local layout (you can get this by looking at HKEY_CURRENT_USER\Keyboard Layout\ Preload1). Click OK.
4. You might also change HKEY_USERS\.DEFAULT\Control Panel\ International\Locale to this value; however, doing so is not mandatory.
5. Close the Registry editor.
6. Log off and then on again.

Table 6-8 shows the codes to the countries.

Table 6-8. Keyboard Country Codes

00000402	Bulgarian
0000041a	Croatian
00000405	Czech
00000406	Danish
00000413	Dutch (Standard)
00000813	Dutch (Belgian)
00000409	English (United States)
00000809	English (United Kingdom)
00001009	English (Canadian)
00001409	English (New Zealand)
00000c09	English (Australian)

Table 6-8. Keyboard Country Codes (continued)

0000040b	Finnish
0000040c	French (Standard)
0000080c	French (Belgian)
0000100c	French (Swiss)
00000c0c	French (Canadian)
00000407	German (Standard)
00000807	German (Swiss)
00000c07	German (Austrian)
00000408	Greek
0000040e	Hungarian
0000040f	Icelandic
00001809	English (Irish)
00000410	Italian (Standard)
00000810	Italian (Swiss)
00000414	Norwegian (Bokmal)
00000814	Norwegian (Nynorsk)
00000415	Polish
00000816	Portuguese (Standard)
00000416	Portuguese (Brazilian)
00000418	Romanian
00000419	Russian
0000041b	Slovak
00000424	Slovenian
0000080a	Spanish (Mexican)
0000040a	Spanish (Traditional Sort)
00000c0a	Spanish (Modern Sort)
0000041d	Swedish
0000041f	Turkish

These can also be seen in the Registry at HKEY_LOCAL_MACHINE\ SYSTEM\CurrentControlSet\Control\Keyboard Layout\DosKeybCodes.

How do I enable NumLock automatically?

The Registry entry HKEY_CURRENT_USER\Control Panel\Keyboard\ InitialKeyboardIndicators can be used to set the initial state of the NumLock key. To change the state, perform the following to set it for the system before a user logs on:

1. Start the Registry editor (REGEDIT.EXE).
2. Move to HKEY_USERS\.DEFAULT\Control Panel\Keyboard.
3. Double-click on InitialKeyboardIndicators.
4. Set to 2 and click OK.
5. Close the Registry editor.

An easier way is to turn NumLock on and then log off by using Ctrl+Alt+Del logoff, which preserves the state of NumLock (Log Off from the Start menu does not do this).

4.0 ONLY

How do I limit the number of simultaneous logons?

You can limit the number of simultaneous connections by performing the following:

1. Start the Registry editor (REGEDIT.EXE).
2. Move to HKEY_LOCAL_MACHINE\SYSTEM\CurrentControlSet\ Services\LanmanServer\Parameters.
3. Double-click on the Users value in the right-hand pane. Set the type to Decimal and then enter the maximum number of simultaneous connections. This will be 10 on a workstation.
4. Click OK and close the Registry editor.

How can I configure the system to run a program at logon time?

The easiest way is to add the program to the Startup folder. You have two choices: to add the program to just your Startup menu (%systemroot%\Profiles\ <username>\Start Menu) or to add it to the all-users Start-up menu (%systemroot%\Profiles\All Users\Start Menu).

If you don't want to do it this way (which you don't if you don't want users to be able to remove it), there is a Registry key you can use to run programs.

1. Start the Registry editor (REGEDIT.EXE).
2. Move to HKEY_LOCAL_MACHINE\SOFTWARE\Microsoft\ Windows\CurrentVersion\Run.
3. From the Edit menu, select New > String Value.
4. Give it any name you want (for example, Notepad).
5. Double-click the new value and set it to the fully qualified pathname of the program (unless it is part of your system path, in which case you can just enter the executable's filename—for example, NOTEPAD.EXE). Click OK.
6. Close the Registry editor.
7. Log off and back on.

If you want a program to run only once and then never run again, perform the above but add the values under HKEY_LOCAL_MACHINE\SOFTWARE\ Microsoft\Windows\CurrentVersion\RunOnce. When the program has run once, it gets deleted from the RunOnce key.

You can also configure programs for only your account by adding values to HKEY_CURRENT_USER\SOFTWARE\Microsoft\Windows\ CurrentVersion\Run.

How can I stop the name of the last user to log on from being displayed?

When you log on, the name of the person who logged on before you is displayed. This might be considered a security risk.

There are two ways of remedying this. If you have the TweakUI utility installed, the easiest way is to perform the following:

1. Start the TweakUI control panel applet (Start > Settings > Control Panel > TweakUI).
2. Select the Paranoia tab.
3. Check the Clear Last User at logon box.
4. Click Apply and then OK.

If you don't have TweakUI or simply want to achieve the result through the Registry (maybe so you can set it from a logon script), perform the following:

1. Start the Registry editor.
2. Move to HKEY_LOCAL_MACHINE\SOFTWARE\Microsoft\ Windows NT\CurrentVersion\Winlogon.
3. If the value DontDisplayLastUserName does not exist, select New > String Value and enter the name **DontDisplayLastUserName**.
4. Double-click DontDisplayLastUserName and set it to 1.
5. Close the Registry editor.

%SystemRoot% is not expanded when I use it in a command. Why?

When you type SET or PATH at a command prompt, you might notice that the %SystemRoot% environment variable has not been expanded. This is a problem and needs to be corrected in the following manner:

1. Start the Registry Editor (REGEDT32.EXE).
2. Move to HKEY_LOCAL_MACHINE\SYSTEM\CurrentControlSet\ Control\Session Manager\Environment.
3. Look at the path in the right-hand pane and check the type of the Registry value (the second part). For example, the path might be

   Path: **REG_EXPAND_SZ:** %SystemRoot% [and so on]

4. If the type is **not** REG_EXPAND_SZ, perform the next steps. If it is, close the Registry editor.

5. Double-click on Path, select the contents, and press Ctrl+C to copy to the Clipboard.
6. While Path is still selected, select Delete from the Edit menu (or click the Del key). When prompted, confirm the deletion.
7. Make sure Environment is selected in the left-hand pane and select Add Value from the Edit menu.
8. Enter **Path** (note the capital P in path) and type **REG_EXPAND_SZ**. Then click OK.
9. Double-click Path and use Ctrl+V to copy back in the information you copied into the Clipboard.
10. Click OK and close the Registry editor.

You can also check HKEY_LOCAL_MACHINE\SOFTWARE\Microsoft\ Windows NT\CurrentVersion\SystemRoot and make sure that this REG_ SZ value contains the proper path (e:\winnt).

 ## How can I disable the Win key?

To disable both Windows keys (there is one on each side of the spacebar on newer Windows-enhanced keyboards), perform the following:

1. Start the Registry editor (REGEDT32.EXE).
2. Move to HKEY_LOCAL_MACHINE\SYSTEM\CurrentControlSet\ Control\Keyboard Layout.
3. From the Edit menu, select New > Binary Value.
4. Enter the name **Scancode Map** and press Enter.
5. Double-click on the new value and set to the following. Do not type the spaces—I included them only to help you view the data.

```
0000 0000 0000 0000 0300 0000 0000 5BE0 0000 5CE0 0000 0000
```

6. Click OK.
7. Close the Registry editor and reboot the machine.

When the machine restarts, the Win key will no longer work.

You can automate this by placing the command in a regini file. Create the file REMOVE_WIN.INI with the following contents:

```
\Registry\Machine\SYSTEM\CurrentControlSet\Control\Keyboard
Layout
Scancode Map = REG_BINARY 24 \
0x00000000 0x00000000 3 \
0xE05B0000 0xE05C0000 \
0x0
```

To run the script, enter this command:

regini remove_win.ini

REGINI.EXE is supplied with the Windows NT Resource Kit.

To reenable the Win key, delete the Scancode Map value you created.

What are the shortcuts available with the Win key?

The Win key was new to Windows 95 and NT 4.0. It enables quick access to some functions with a special key on enhanced keyboards (see Table 6-9).

Table 6-9. Win-key Shortcuts

WIN + R	Display the Run dialog
WIN + M	Minimize all windows
WIN + Shift + M	Undo minimize all windows
WIN + F1	Help
WIN + E	Explorer
WIN + F	Find files
Ctrl +WIN + F	Find computer
WIN + TAB	Cycle through minimized taskbar icons
WIN + BREAK	Systems properties

What keyboard shortcuts are available?

Table 6-10 shows some of the most popular keyboard shortcuts.

Table 6-10. Keyboard Shortcuts

F1	Help
F2	Rename
F3	Find
F4	Display combo box in Explorer
F5	Refresh
F6	Switch panes in Explorer
F10	Menu mode
ALT + ENTER	Properties
CTRL + Drag a file	Copy
CTRL + G	Goto
CTRL + Z	Undo
CTRL + A	Select all
CTRL + ESC	Start menu
CTRL + SHIFT + ESC	Task Manager

How do I set the number of cached logons a machine stores?

By default, an NT machine caches the last ten successful logons (since version 3.5—3.1 only stored the last one). However, you can change this to a value between 0 and 50.

1. Start the Registry editor (REGEDIT.EXE).
2. Move to HKEY_LOCAL_MACHINE\SOFTWARE\Microsoft\ Windows NT\CurrentVersion\Winlogon.
3. From the Edit menu, select New > String Value.
4. Enter the name **CachedLogonsCount** and press Enter.
5. Double-click on the new value and set it between 0 and 50. At 0, no logons will be cached; at 50, the last 50 will be cached.
6. Click OK, close the Registry editor, and reboot the machine.

When a user attempts to log on, if the domain controller is not available but the user's information is cached, the following message will be displayed but the logon will be successful:

"A domain controller for your domain could not be contacted. You have been logged on using cached account information. Changes to your profile since you last logged on may not be available."

If the user's information is not cached, this message will be displayed and the logon will not be successful:

"The system cannot log you on now because the domain <domain name> is not available."

4.0 ONLY

6.80 How do I disable the file delete confirmation?

If you use the Recycle Bin, you can disable the delete confirmation that appears when someone deletes a file.

1. Right-click on the Recycle Bin and Select properties.
2. Uncheck Display Delete Confirmation Dialog Box.
3. Click Apply and then OK.

How can I switch the time between 24-hour and 12-hour systems?

There are two ways to configure the time system. The first is using the Regional control panel applet, as follows:

1. Start the Regional control panel applet (Start > Settings > Control Panel > Regional Settings).
2. Select the Time tab.
3. HH in capitals means 24 hours; hh (lowercase) means 12 hours.
4. Click Apply and then OK.

The second method is to directly edit the Registry:

1. Start the Registry editor (REGEDIT.EXE).
2. Move to HKEY_CURRENT_USER\Control Panel\International.
3. From the Edit menu, select New > String.
4. Enter the name **iTime**.
5. Double-click and set to 0 for 12 hours or 1 for 24 hours.
6. Click OK and close the Registry editor.
7. Log off and then on again.

4.0 ONLY

How can I suppress boot error messages?

If you are performing development or know of a problem, you might decide you wish to suppress any of the error pop-ups that are usually displayed about a problem. An example would be a driver that can't be loaded or some other system component that is not acting correctly.

The pop-ups can be generated from either of the two main startup phases, and a separate Registry key needs to be set for each stage. Errors that are displayed as a result of the boot phase can be disabled as follows:

1. Start the Registry editor (REGEDIT.EXE).
2. Move to HKEY_LOCAL_MACHINE\SOFTWARE\Microsoft\Windows NT\CurrentVersion\Windows.

3. From the Edit menu, select New > DWORD Value. Enter the name **NoPopUpsOnBoot** and press Enter.

4. Double-click the new value and set it to 1 to suppress boot errors. Click OK.

5. Close the Registry editor and the change will take effect at the next reboot.

Error messages that are displayed as part of the post-boot startup phase include most device driver messages. To suppress such messages, perform the following:

1. Start the Registry editor (REGEDIT.EXE).

2. Move to HKEY_LOCAL_MACHINE\SOFTWARE\Microsoft\ Windows NT\CurrentVersion\Windows.

3. From the Edit menu, select New > DWORD Value. Enter the name **ErrorMode** and press Enter.

4. Double-click the new value and set it to 1 to display only application errors or 2 to suppress all error dialogs. Click OK.

5. Close the Registry editor and the change will take effect at the next reboot.

Instead of a blanket ban on all error messages, you might prefer to mark some services as "optional" instead of generating an error message if they don't start correctly. This can be accomplished by setting HKEY_LOCAL_ MACHINEM\SYSTEM\CurrentControlSet\Services\<service>\ErrorControl to 0. For more information about error messages, see Question 36-18 in Chapter 36, Hardware.

2000 ONLY

6.83 How can I enable or disable the Ctrl+Alt+Del to enter logon information?

In Windows 2000, you can do away with the necessity of pressing Ctrl+Alt+Del—called the Security Attention Sequence (SAS)—to log on. By default, this is no longer needed on a workstation. Although this is still necessary on a server, it can be reconfigured with a single Registry entry.

1. Start the Registry editor (REGEDIT.EXE).

2. Move to HKEY_LOCAL_MACHINE\SOFTWARE\Microsoft\ Windows NT\CurrentVersion\Winlogon.

3. Double-click on Disablecad.

4. Set it to 1 if you don't want to have to press Ctrl+Alt+Del, and set it to 0 if you do. Then click OK.

5. Close the Registry editor and reboot the machine.

Disabling this feature does not decrease the security of Windows NT. To gain access to the computer, users are required to log on to Windows NT with a valid username and password. The Windows NT logon process suspends all other user-mode processes for protection and is the only process that can create the access tokens used by the Windows NT security system.

The screen saver can only be configured to start up to 60 minutes after inactivity. Can this be changed?

This is a hard-coded restriction of Windows NT 4.0; however, Service Pack 4 increases this to 999 minutes.

I have lost the ADMIN$ share. Why?

Perhaps, by setting the relevant Registry entry AutoSharexxx, you have configured the system to not automatically create system shares at startup time. If so, this share will not be created, because that is what you are asking.

However, if you do not have this set and have just lost the ADMIN$ share that points to the %SytemRoot% folder (for example, d:\winnt), you can re-create it by entering the following command:

```
net share admin$
```

How can I configure Notepad to word-wrap?

By default, Notepad allows you to enter text and scroll right (not wrap) when the screen is full. This behavior can be altered.

Under the Edit menu of Notepad, you can check Word Wrap. However, you can also configure this in the Registry if you want to set Word Wrap as the default for policies, as part of a login script, or in an unattended installation.

1. Start the Registry editor (REGEDIT.EXE).
2. Move to HKEY_CURRENT_USER\Software\Microsoft\Notepad.
3. Double-click on Wrap.
4. Set to 1 and click OK.
5. Close the Registry editor.

4.0 ONLY

How do I modify the logon timer for profiles?

When you log on and, for instance, your local profile is newer than the one stored on the profile server, you have an option of which to use, with a timer of 30 seconds given to choose between them. This 30 seconds can be modified as follows:

1. Start the Registry editor (REGEDIT.EXE).
2. Move to HKEY_LOCAL_MACHINE\SOFTWARE\Microsoft\ Windows NT\CurrentVersion\Winlogon.
3. From the Edit menu, select New > DWORD Value. Enter the name **Show** and press Enter.
4. Double-click the new value and set to between 0 and 600. Make sure you set the Type to Decimal. Click OK.
5. Close the Registry editor and this will take effect at next logon.

How do I modify system variables?

As with user variables, system variables can be changed by using the System Control Panel applet, as follows:

1. Start the System Control Panel applet (Start > Settings > Control Panel > System).
2. Select the Environment tab.
3. Under System Variables, select a variable to see its value displayed. Modify it in the Value box and click Set.
4. After you have made all changes, click Apply and then OK.

Alternatively, you can directly edit the Registry to make these changes:

1. Start the Registry editor (REGEDIT.EXE).
2. Move to HKEY_LOCAL_MACHINE\SYSTEM\CurrentControlSet\ Control\Session Manager\Environment.
3. Double-click on the variable (for example, Path) and edit its value.
4. Click OK and close the Registry editor.

A final method is to use the SET command from the command line (but don't follow the example):

```
set OS=OS2
```

How do I disable the ability to change a password in the Security dialog?

Service Pack 4 introduces a new Registry entry:

1. Start the Registry editor (REGEDIT.EXE).
2. Move to HKEY_CURRENT_USER\Software\Microsoft\Windows\ CurrentVersion\Policies\System.

3. From the Edit menu, select New > DWORD Value.
4. Enter the name **DisableChangePassword** and press Enter.
5. Double-click on the new value and set it to 1.
6. Click OK and close the Registry editor.

When you press Ctrl+Alt+Del, Change Password will now be grayed out.

 ## How do I stop a process on a remote machine?

Say, for example, you are playing a multi-player game of Quake and are about to get killed for the sixth time. You can just stop the opponent's Quake process (always works for me). To stop a remote process, perform the following:

Note: The utilities discussed are part of the NT Resource Kit.

The target machine must have the RKILLSRV.EXE service running (either from the command line or installed as a service). To install RKILLSRV.EXE as a service, enter this command:

```
instsrv rkillsrv c:\ntreskit\RKILLSRV.EXE
```

This installs the executable as a service and sets its startup to automatic so it will restart at every bootup. After being installed, the service will not be started immediately. If it is to be used before a reboot, you should start it via the Services control panel applet or from the command line by using

```
net start rkillsrv
```

After the service has been configured and started on the remote machine, processes can be manipulated from client machines by users who have Administrative privileges. This is done via the command line with the RKILL.EXE and GUI WRKILL.EXE utilities.

To view the running processes with the command line tool, use rkill /view \\ <machine name>. For example, type

```
rkill /view \\nt4pdc
```

After you have identified the process, you can stop it with the rkill /
kill \\<machine name> <process id> command. For example, type

```
rkill /kill \\nt4pdc 84
```

With the GUI utility WRKILL.EXE, the process is simpler. To stop a process
by using this utility, perform the following:

1. Select the process and click Kill Selected Process (see Figure 6-8).
2. Click Yes to the confirmation message and then OK to the success dialog.

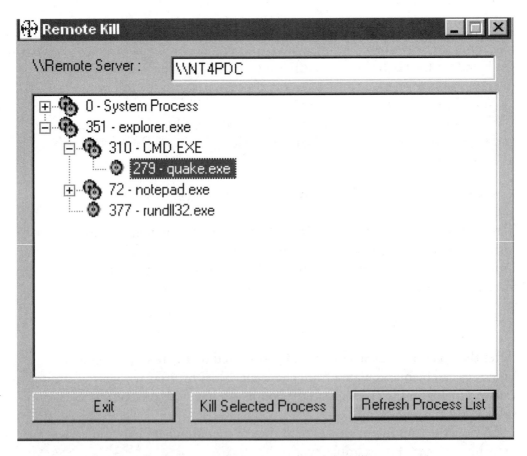

Figure 6-8. Using RKILLSRV.EXE to win a game of Quake.

4.0 ONLY

How do I install the Security Configuration Editor (SCE)?

The Security Configuration Editor, SECEDIT.EXE, is a new utility that forms part of Service Pack 4. However, due to Microsoft's pledge not to provide new functionality with service packs, the utility previously was only available on the Service Pack 4.0 CD. After public demand, a Web download version is available from ftp://ftp.microsoft.com/bussys/winnt/winnt-public/tools/SCM/SCESP4I.EXE.

After downloading, you should execute the file and select an extraction directory. When the extraction is complete, move to the extracted file directory and double-click on MSSCE.EXE to install. The installation installs two versions of SCE: a GUI version and a command line version. If you want to install only the command line tool, enter the following command. The /c means command line only, and the /s means silent install (no prompts).

```
mssce /c /s
```

The SCE is a Microsoft Management Console snap-in. To use it, you must follow these steps:

1. Start MMC (MMC.EXE).
2. From the Console menu, select Add/Remove Snap-in.
3. Click the Add button.
4. Select Security Configuration Manager and click OK.
5. Click OK to the main dialog.

You might want to save this configuration. To do so, perform these steps:

1. From the Console menu, select Save As.
2. Enter the name **secedit** and click Save.
3. The configuration icon has been added to the My Administrative Tools program folder.

To edit a configuration, expand the Configurations branch and the directory and select a configuration (see Figure 6-9).

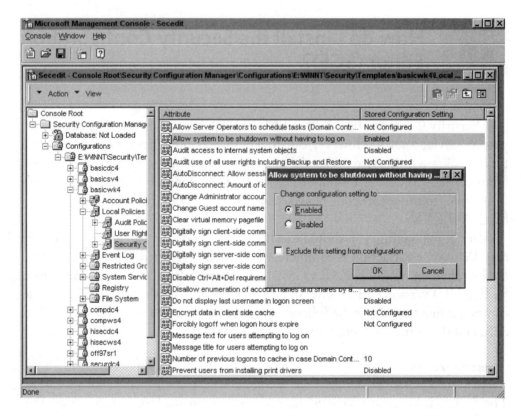

Figure 6-9. Setting the shutdown by using the Security Configuration Editor.

After you have modified a configuration and saved it, you need to activate it, as follows:

1. Right-click on Database and select Import Configuration.
2. Select a security configuration file (an .INF file) and click Open.
3. Right-click again and select Configure system now.
4. Select a log filename and location.
5. The policy will be applied to the system.

How can I get the cool UI effects to work on my P166 computer?

Windows 2000 comes with a number of nice user interface (UI) effects—gradient captions, menu fade-in, cursor shadow, and so on.

To see these, you must set your color depth to greater than 256 colors (use High Color or True Color). Also, the fade-in/out and shadow effects require Pentium Pro or better, or Alpha 21164 or better.

Most of the UI effects are controlled via a checkbox in the Display Properties applet. To find this, go to the Effects tab and choose Animate Windows > Menus and Lists. The cursor shadow effect can be turned on/off via the Mouse Properties applet (Pointers / Enable Pointer Shadow).

Sadly, there appears to be no Registry hack to circumvent minimum CPU requirements.

7 USER CONFIGURATION

This chapter deals with configuring your domains for managing the users rather than the basic look and feel of the user's desktop. Getting a basic Windows NT network running is fairly straightforward; however, enabling the more advanced features such as roaming profiles and quotas requires more thought.

Also covered are batch files and command line features to speed up and improve your administration of a domain or workgroup.

4.0 ONLY
FAQ 7.1 How do I add a user?

To add a new user to a domain, you need to log on to the server as an Administrator and run the User Manager for Domains utility. To add a user to a local workstation, you log on as an Administrator and run the normal User Manager utility.

Before adding a new user, however, you should consider the naming conventions that can be used. There are four main standards:

1. **Last name plus initial:** This is probably the most popular, and for John Savill would give SavillJ

2. **First name plus last name initial:** For example, JohnS. The problem is you will quickly run out and might need to use a middle initial as well.

3. **First name initial plus last name:** For example, JSavill

4. **First name plus number:** For example, John34. The problem with this is that it is not easy to recognize the person.

It is important to stick to a standard, and unless this is a new installation, there will already be a standard to follow at your company. To add a user, perform the following:

1. Start User Manager for Domains (Start > Programs > Administrative Tools > User Manager for Domains).

2. Select New User from the User menu to open the New User window shown in Figure 7-1.

3. In the Username field, enter the name the user will use to log on (for example, savillj). Case is not important, but it's good to stick to a common format. The username can be up to 20 characters in length, and you can use a combination of letters, numbers, and punctuation marks except for the following characters

   " [ ] ? / \ ; : | = ,

   You can use spaces in the username. This is not a good idea, however, because you then need to put the name in quotes whenever you enter a command relating to the account.

4. Although the Full Name field is not mandatory, filling it in with the person's real name is a good idea. Several NT utilities dump out the user information and display this name; with this in mind, you might like to put the person's last name first (Savill, John) for future readability.

5. The Description field is as the name implies—just a description of the person. This could be Sales Manager, for example, but you may put what you like for Description.

6. For new users, you need to enter a password, which they will use the first time they log on. You need to enter this twice, once in the Password field and again in the Confirm password field. The password is case sensitive, so make sure you enter the password in the correct

case both times and tell the user where you use capitals or lowercase.

7. You will see four check boxes:

   a. **User Must Change Password at Next Logon:** It is a good idea to select this so users need to change the password the first time they log on.

   b. **User Cannot Change Password:** Not a good idea; you would use this only for a shared account.

   c. **Password Never Expires:** Again not a good idea. Permanent passwords are frowned on because they are a security risk.

   d. **Account Disabled:** A means for suspending an account.

8. Click on the Groups button at the bottom of the dialog box. Select a group on the right side and click Add to make the new user a member of that group. Click OK when finished.

9. Click on the Profile button (this is only visible if you are adding the account to a domain rather than a local machine). In the Profiles, you can enter the path for the user's profile (for example, \\savpdc\ profiles).

10. In the Logon Script section, you can enter the name of a batch file to be run when the user logs on. You only need to enter the name of the batch file, and not the full UNC location, because the Server will assume the logon script is in the netlogon share.

11. You can also set up the user's home directory, which can be either a local area or—more commonly—a share on a network drive. Click OK when finished.

12. It is also possible to set logon hours for each user by clicking the Logon button.

13. By clicking the Logon To button, you can restrict the workstations to which the user can log on.

14. The Account button allows you to set up an account expiry time and an account type.

15. Finally, you can use the DialIn button to give accounts the ability to dial in and to choose whether to allow callback.

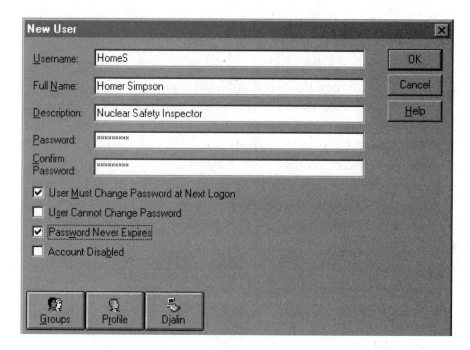

Figure 7-1. Homer Simpson, an essential employee of any company.

7.2 How can I add a user from the command line?

The simple answer is to use this:

```
net user <username> <password> /add (/domain)
```

However, it is possible to automate not only the addition of the user but also the addition of the user to groups and the creation of a template user account directory structure. Many organizations have a basic structure with Word and Excel directories and some template files. This can be automated with a basic script such as the following:

```
addnew.bat
net user %1 password /add /homedir:\\<server>\users\%1
/scriptpath:login.bat /domain
net localgroup "<local group>" %1 /add    Repeat for local groups
```

```
net group "<groups>" %1 /add /domain   Repeat for global groups
xcopy \\<server>\users\template \\<server>\users\%1\ /e
cacls \\<server>\users\%1 /e /r Everyone        Remove the
                                                everyone
                                                permission to
                                                the directory
cacls \\<server>\users\%1 /g %1:F /e
cacls \\<server>\users\%1 /g Administrators:F /e
```

4.0 ONLY

Can I add user accounts from a database?

The Resource Kit utility ADDUSERS.EXE accepts as input a database file (for example, an Excel spreadsheet) and adds users and groups from that file to the database.

You can also use ADDUSERS.EXE to dump out the contents of the domain user database. An example of using ADDUSERS.EXE is shown later in Question 7-31.

Windows 2000 ships with a new utility, LDIFDE.EXE, which can read in LDAP difference files of the following format:

```
dn: CN=john savill,CN=Users,DC=savtech,DC=com
changetype: delete
```

The LDAP difference file can be read in by using the syntax:

```
ldifde -i -f <name>.ldf
```

How do I change my password?

Here's the easiest way to change a password:

1. Press Ctrl+Alt+Delete.
2. Click the Change Password button.

3. Enter your old password. Then enter the new password twice and click OK.

To change your password from the command line, use the net user command, as follows:

```
net user <username> <password> (/domain)
```

To change your password from a program, use the NetUserChangePassword() call.

How do I create a captive account?

"Captive account" is a common term in the VMS world (a Dec Operating System) to indicate an account that restricts a user to a certain task or set of tasks. Although you cannot create a captive account, you can force users to run a certain program and have them be logged out if they close that program.

1. Create a command file similar to the following:

```
<The program you wish to run>
Logout
```

2. Create a mandatory profile for this user.
3. Remove all Start menu groups from this profile except the Startup group.
4. In this group, put the file you created in step 1.

The file LOGOUT.EXE from http://www.ntfaq.com/ntfaq/download/ logout.zip just logs out the user. It is also possible to restrict a user's applications by using the Policy editor. From the Policy editor, you can select which applications a user can run (make sure you give them Explorer).

Microsoft has also created the Zero Administration Kit (download it from http://www.microsoft.com/windows/zak/), which allows you to confine a user to a single application or set of applications.

Where should login scripts go?

Login scripts should be placed in the %SYSTEMROOT%\SYSTEM32\ REPL\EXPORT\SCRIPTS directory under Windows NT 4.0 and earlier. This is because a share, netlogon, is defined on all Domain Controllers that points to the import\scripts directory.

Notice that this directory is under the repl\import\scripts directory because directory replication will copy the contents of the directory repl\export to all other Domain Controllers **and** to the local repl\import directory. You must ensure directory replication is running or the scripts will not be replicated.

Under Windows 2000, logon scripts are in %SYSTEMROOT%\SYSVOL\ SYSVOL\<DOMAIN NAME>\SCRIPTS. Again, this is replicated to all Domain Controllers and netlogon points to this directory.

If you want to check your definition of netlogon, just type

```
net share netlogon
```

What should be in the login script?

This varies from site to site, but generally a login script synchronizes the time of the workstations with the time of the server (providing the server's time is accurate) and perhaps connects a home area (set by using User Manager).

Net use x: /home asks the domain server for your home area location and connects to it. A very basic logon script could be

```
@echo off
net time \\johnserver /set /yes
net use p: /home
```

Are there any utilities that help with login scripts?

With the NT Resource Kit, you get Kix, which enables you to write more advanced login scripts. You can also get a freeware utility called KixTart from http://netnet.net/~swilson/kix/nfKiX.htm.

Microsoft has released the Windows Scripting Host (WSH), which is bound to be the next standard in all cases where scripting is necessary, including login scripts. WSH will be included in NT5 and can be downloaded at http://www.microsoft.com/management/wsh.htm.

Is there a way of performing operations depending on a user's group membership?

In the Resource Kit for NT you'll find a program called IFMEMBER that can test for group membership for a user. You can base your login script on this.

Important safety tip: IFMEMBER works by checking for membership in a group and returning an ERRORLEVEL; hence, you'll have a bunch of IF THENs in your login script.

The following example checks whether the user is in the sales group, with 1 returned if true; if not, exit:

```
ifmember Sales
if not errorlevel 1 exit
echo You are in sales
```

How do I limit the disk space for a user?

There is no way for NT server 4.0 to do this; however, there is third-party software available that can, such as

- Quota Server from http://www.northern.se
- Quota Manager from http://www.softshelf.com/winnt/qm/so02003.htm

- Disk Guard from http://www.spaceguard.com
- QuotaAdvisor from http://www.wquinn.com

Windows 2000 now has built-in per-volume quota software but only on NTFS 5.0 volumes.

What variables are available for use with a user?

Table 7-1 gives a list of variables you can use in login scripts and other batch files. These may only be used on NT client/servers.

Table 7-1. User Variables

%COMPUTERNAME%	Name of computer
%HOMEDRIVE%	User's local drive letter
%HOMEPATH%	Full path of the user's home area
%HOMESHARE%	Share that contains the user's home area
%LOGONSERVER%	Name of the machine that validates the user logon
%OS%	Operating system to which the user is connected
%PROCESSOR%	486, for example
%USERDOMAIN%	Domain containing the user's account
%USERNAME%	Name of the user

Is there a utility that shows who is currently logged on?

The Resource Kit has a utility called WHOAMI.EXE, which displays the domain/workgroup and username.

Alternatively you could just display the %userdomain% and %username% variables, as follows:

```
echo %userdomain%\%username%
```

 ## How can I find out which groups a user is in?

NT provides a means of getting information about your domain account by using the following:

net user <username> /domain

This includes information about group membership; however, the SHOWGRPS.EXE utility, which also ships with the NT Resource Kit, shows only the groups. Its usage is

showgrps <domain>\<user>
(for example, showgrps savilltech\john)

 ## How can I change environment variables from the command line?

The Resource Kit has a utility called SETX.EXE, which enables the user to change environment settings:

```
setx johnvariable 1
setx johnvariable -k
HKEY_LOCAL_MACHINE\...\DefaultDomainName
```

The -k switch sets the variable as a Registry value.

How can I hide drive x from users?

You can do this by using the TweakUI utility from the My Computer tab. (TweakUI is covered in Chapter 35, Utilities, and found in the Control Panel after installation.) Just deselect the check mark next to drives you want to hide. All this does is change the Registry value:

```
HKEY_CURRENT_USER\Software\Microsoft\Windows\CurrentVersion\
Policies\Explorer\NODRIVES
```

This is a 32-bit word. The lower 26 bits of the 32-bit word correspond to drive letters A through Z. Drives are visible when set to 0 and hidden when set to 1.

Drive A is represented by the right-most position of the bitmask when viewed in binary mode, as in the following example, which hides local drives A, C, and E:

```
00000000000000000000010101(0x7h)
```

Drives hidden by using the NODRIVES setting are not available through Windows Explorer, under the My Computer icon, or in the File Open\Save dialog boxes of 32-bit Windows applications. File Manager and the Windows NT command prompt are not affected by this Registry setting.

How do I make the shell start before the logon script finishes?

Normally, when a user logs in, the shell does not start until the logon script has completed.

To allow the shell to start before the logon script has finished, change the Registry value HKEY_CURRENT_USER\software\microsoft\windows nt\ currentversion\winlogon\RunLogonScriptSync to 0 by using a Registry editor.

A value of 1 means the shell will not start until the login script has finished.

FAQ 7.17 I can no longer see items in the common groups from the Start menu. Why?

There is a Registry flag that sets whether the common groups are displayed on the Start menu. To disable this setting, set HKEY_CURRENT_USER\ Software\Microsoft\Windows\CurrentVersion\Policies\Explorer\ NoCommonGroups to 0 by using the Registry editor (REGEDIT.EXE). By default, this value does not exist.

FAQ 7.18 How do I configure users so they can change the system time?

The ability to change the time on an NT system is a right that has to be granted through the User Rights Policy in User Manager, as follows:

1. Start User Manager (Start > Programs > Administrative Tools > User Manager).
2. From the Policies menu, select User Rights.
3. From the drop-down menu, select Change the System Time.
4. Click the Add button and add any users you wish to perform this.
5. Click OK to exit the dialog.
6. Close User Manager.
7. The user will need to log off and log on again.

FAQ 7.19 How do I configure roaming profiles?

When you sit at a computer and change its attributes (the wallpaper, for example), someone else who logs on will still have the same environment as when she last logged on. This is achieved by using a profile for each user, which is stored locally in the %systemroot%/profiles/<username> (for example, d:\winnt\profiles\savillj).

If that user then sits at a different computer, she will not have her setup. To achieve a profile that follows a user to different NT machines (a "roaming profile"), you need to store the user's profile on a network share that can be downloaded each time that user logs on. When the user logs off, the network profile is updated and a copy of the profile is saved locally. To configure roaming profiles, perform the following:

1. Start User Manager for Domains (Start > Programs > Administrative Tools > User Manager for Domains).
2. Double-click on the user.
3. Click the Profiles button.
4. In the User Profile Path, enter the network share location where the profile should go, as follows:

   \\<servername>\<share name>\<user name>
   (for example, \\bugsbunny\profiles\savillj)

5. Click OK to finish.

To make the profile mandatory—so the user cannot change it—rename the file NTUSER.DAT to NTUSER.MAN, which is located at the base of the profile location. As mentioned earlier, profiles are cached locally to machines; however, you can disable this by performing the following:

1. Start the Registry editor (REGEDIT.EXE).
2. Move to HKEY_LOCAL_MACHINE\SOFTWARE\Microsoft\ Windows NT\CurrentVersion\Winlogon.
3. Create a value called DeleteRoamingCache of type DWORD (Edit > New > DWORD Value).
4. Set the value to 1.

Roaming profiles are not saved to the server. Why?

If a user is a member of the Domain Guests group, no changes to profiles are stored. Therefore, you should check that the Domain Guests group does not include those users that are having the problem.

You can check this by starting User Manager, double-clicking the user, and clicking the Groups button.

 ## How do I debug roaming profiles?

It is possible to create a log file of all roaming profile transactions by using the checked version of USERENV.DLL. The checked version of the USERENV.DLL is the same dynamic link library (.DLL) as the retail version except that it contains debug flags you can set and use with the kernel debugger. This file is included in both the Windows NT Device Driver Kit (DDK) and the Windows NT Software Development Kit (SDK).

1. Rename the USERENV.DLL file in the %systemroot%\System32 directory to USERNV.ORG, as follows:

   ```
   rename %systemroot%\system32\userenv.dll userenv.org
   ```

2. Copy the checked version of USERENV.DLL to the %systemroot%\ System32 directory of the client computer you want to debug. The checked version of the USERENV file must match the version of the operating system being used.

   ```
   copy userenv.chk %systemroot%\system32\userenv.dll
   ```

3. Start the Registry editor (REGEDIT.EXE).
4. Move to HKEY_LOCAL_MACHINE\SOFTWARE\Microsoft\ Windows NT\CurrentVersion\Winlogon.
5. From the Edit menu, choose New > DWORD Value.
6. Enter the name **UserEnvDebugLevel** and press Enter.
7. Double-click the new value, set the type to hexadecimal, and set the value to 10002.
8. Click OK and reboot the computer.

A log file of the roaming profile transactions will be written to USERENV.LOG to the root of the C: drive. The following is a profile log:

===

```
LoadUserProfile: Entering, hToken = <0xb0>, lpProfileInfo =
0x12f4e8
LoadUserProfile: lpProfileInfo->dwFlags = <0x2>
LoadUserProfile: lpProfileInfo->lpUserName = <savillj>
LoadUserProfile: lpProfileInfo->lpProfilePath =
<\\titanic\Profiles\savillj>
LoadUserProfile: lpProfileInfo->lpDefaultPath =
<\\TITANIC\netlogon\Default User>
LoadUserProfile: lpProfileInfo->lpServerName = <\\TITANIC>
LoadUserProfile: lpProfileInfo->lpPolicyPath =
<\\TITANIC\netlogon\ntconfig.pol>
ParseProfilePath: Entering, lpProfilePath =
<\\titanic\Profiles\savillj>
ParseProfilePath: Tick Count = 20
ParseProfilePath: FindFirstFile found something with attributes
<0x10>
ParseProfilePath: Found a directory
LoadUserProfile: ParseProfilePath returned a directory of
<\\titanic\Profiles\savillj>
RestoreUserProfile: Entering
RestoreUserProfile: Profile path = <\\titanic\Profiles\savillj>
RestoreUserProfile: User is an Admin
IsCentralProfileReachable: Entering
IsCentralProfileReachable: Testing
<\\titanic\Profiles\savillj\ntuser.man>
IsCentralProfileReachable: Profile is not reachable, error = 2
IsCentralProfileReachable: Testing
<\\titanic\Profiles\savillj\ntuser.dat>
IsCentralProfileReachable: Found a user profile.
RestoreUserProfile: Central Profile is reachable.
RestoreUserProfile: Central Profile is floating.
GetLocalProfileImage: Found entry in profile list for existing
local profile.
GetLocalProfileImage: Local profile image filename =
<%SystemRoot%\Profiles\savillj>
GetLocalProfileImage: Expanded local profile image filename =
<E:\WINNT\Profiles\savillj>
GetLocalProfileImage: No local mandatory profile. Error = 2
GetLocalProfileImage: Found local profile image file ok
<E:\WINNT\Profiles\savillj\ntuser.dat>
Local profile is reachable
Local profilename is <E:\WINNT\Profiles\savillj>
```

```
RestoreUserProfile: About to call UpdateToLatestProfile
UpdateToLatestProfile: Entering. Central =
<\\titanic\Profiles\savillj> Local = <E:\WINNT\Profiles\savillj>
UpdateToLatestProfile: Central and local profile times match.
RestoreUserProfile: About to Leave. Final Information follows:
Profile was successfully loaded.
lpProfile->szCentralProfile = <\\titanic\Profiles\savillj>
lpProfile->szLocalProfile = <E:\WINNT\Profiles\savillj>
lpProfile->dwInternalFlags = 0x112
RestoreUserProfile: Leaving
UpgradeProfile: Entering
UpgradeProfile: Build numbers match.
UpgradeProfile: Leaving Successfully
ApplyPolicy: Entering
ApplyPolicy: PolicyPath is: <\\TITANIC\netlogon\ntconfig.pol>.
ApplyPolicy: Local PolicyPath is:
<E:\WINNT\Profiles\savillj\prf1.tmp>.
ApplyPolicy: Looking for user specific policy. OpenUserKey: No
entry for savillj, using .Default instead.
CopyKeyValues: EnableProfileQuota => 1
COPYKEYVALUES: PROFILEQUOTAMESSAGE => YOU HAVE EXCEEDED YOUR
PROFILE STORAGE SPACE. BEFORE YOU CAN LOG OFF, YOU NEED TO MOVE
SOME ITEMS FROM YOUR PROFILE TO NETWORK OR LOCAL STORAGE.
CopyKeyValues: MaxProfileSize => 48
COPYKEYVALUES: WARNUSERTIMEOUT => 15
ApplyPolicy: Processing group(s) policy.
ApplyPolicy: Failed to get group processing order.
ApplyPolicy: Looking for machine specific policy.
OpenUserKey: No entry for ODIN, using .Default instead.
ApplyPolicy: Leaving with 1
LoadUserProfile: Leaving with a value of 1. hProfile = <0x90>
==========================================================
```

 ## How can I copy a user profile?

User profiles are stored under the %systemroot%\profiles directory, but if you try to just copy this to someone else, the new user will not have permission to use the profile.

Instead, you need to use the following procedure:

1. Log on as an Administrator.
2. Start the System Control Panel applet (Start > Settings > Control Panel > System).
3. Click the User Profiles tab.
4. You will see a list of all the profiles stored on the machine. Select the one you wish to copy.
5. Click the Copy To button.
6. In the Copy Profile To field, enter the location where you want the profile copied. If you want to use it as a roaming profile, enter the netlogon location on a Domain Controller (usually %systemroot%\system32\Repl\ Export\Scripts). You want the Export area—not Import—because anything in Export is copied to the Import by the replication process.
7. In the Permitted To Use dialog box, click Change.
8. Select Everyone and click Add (or select just the user who will use it). Then click OK.
9. Click OK again to start the copy.

You should then check that the file NTUSER.DAT has been created where you selected.

If you have trouble exporting a profile, see Question 32-33 in Chapter 32, Problem-Solving.

 7.23 ## What are the differences between NT and 9x profiles?

The first difference is that different files are used:

Windows NT	Windows 9x
NTUSER.DAT	USER.DAT
NTUSER.DAT.LOG	USER.DA0
NTUSER.MAN	USER.MAN

The Windows 9x USER.DA0 and NT's NTUSER.DAT.LOG files work in different ways. Every time you log off in Windows 9x, a copy of USER.DAT is copied to USER.DA0. Windows NT uses NTUSER.DAT.LOG as a transaction log file to provide fault tolerance, enabling Windows NT to recover the user profile if a problem occurs while Windows NT is updating NTUSER.DAT.

This obviously means you can't share a profile between the two operating systems. Other differences include the following:

- Windows 95 does not support common groups.
- Windows 95 user profiles do not copy all desktop items; copied items are restricted to shortcuts (.LNK) and program information (.PIF) files.
- Windows 95 user profiles don't support a centrally stored Default User profile.
- Windows 95 clients don't use the Windows NT Server profile path to obtain roaming user profiles. They can be retrieved only from the user's home directory.
- To use mandatory user profiles on computers running Windows 95 on a Windows NT Server network, an administrator must create a custom user profile for each user and copy the user profile files to each user's home directory.
- Windows 95 does not support the Application Data folder that makes up the folders structure.

 ## When I log off, all my home directory files are deleted. Why?

The most common cause is if your roaming profile path and your home directory path are the same. It seems that part of the update makes sure the contents of the directories (and subdirectories) are the same. Because the local profile directory does not contain your home directory files, they are deleted.

You should therefore change the location of the roaming profile so it is different from your home directory. It can be a subdirectory if you wish. You can change this by using the User Manager application. Click the Profiles button and change the locations. This has to be done by a domain Administrator; if you are not an Administrator, this will need to be done for you.

How can I delete a local profile?

You can delete any locally stored profile by using the System Control Panel applet:

1. Start the System Control Panel applet (Start > Settings > Control Panel > System).
2. Click the User Profiles tab.
3. Select the profile and click Delete.
4. Click Yes to the confirmation message.
5. Click OK.

Please note that you can't delete a profile if you are currently logged on as that user. A message that the profile is in use will be displayed.

If you want to remotely delete a locally stored profile, you can use the DELPROF.EXE utility supplied with the Windows NT Server Resource Kit. This tool deletes all profiles that have not been used for a given number of days. For example, the following command would delete any profiles that have not been used for three days:

```
delprof /p /q /i /c:\\garfield /d:3
```

The /p prompts for confirmation before deleting each profile and the /q suppresses the starting of the following prompt:

```
Delete profiles on \\garfield that have not been used in
the last 3 days? (Yes /No)
```

The /i ignores errors, /c is the computer name, and /d: is the number of days after which the profile is to be deleted.

 ## I'm having problems locally copying profiles. Why?

If you are not using roaming profiles but are just copying a profile for another domain user on the local machine, you can just create a directory under Profiles for the user and copy it there (see the instructions in Question 7-22).

If you do this, you will find that when the user for whom you copied the profile logs in for the first time, he will not use the directory you created for him, but a <username>.000 will be created instead. This is because a mapping is used for the user to the Profile area. If the user logs in for the first time and a directory of his username already exists, the system doesn't use that directory but instead creates a new area of the format <username>.nnn, where nnn starts at 000.

The workaround to this is to log on as the domain user first and log out again and **then** copy the profile. This sets up the correct mapping of the user to the profile area.

If this has already happened, follow the instructions in Question 7-27 about defining the profile area to use for a user.

 ## How do I define the profile area to use for a user?

By default, when a user logs on for the first time at a machine, a directory is created under %systemroot%\profiles under the name of the user to hold the user's profile. For example, for user saviljo, the area created would be %systemroot%\profiles\saviljo.

Problems arise if the directory already exists and an alternate directory <user name>.nnn is created, starting with 000. This mapping is stored in the Registry HKEY_LOCAL_MACHINE\SOFTWARE\Microsoft\Windows NT\CurrentVersion\ProfileList. You can, therefore, force a user to use a specific profile area by performing the following:

1. Start the Registry editor (REGEDIT.EXE).
2. Move to HKEY_LOCAL_MACHINE\SOFTWARE\Microsoft\Windows NT\CurrentVersion\ProfileList.
3. Find the Security Identifier (SID) that relates to the user (check the ProfileImagePath value).
4. Double-click on ProfileImagePath and remove the .nnn, as in the following example:

```
%SystemRoot%\Profiles\garfield.000
to
%SystemRoot%\Profiles\garfield
```

5. Click OK and close the Registry editor.

The user should now log in, using the profile you originally copied for him. When you are sure it works, you can delete the <username>.nnn directory under %systemroot%\profiles.

You should make sure the user has the right to use the original profile—for example, if you have copied it to the basic name location (such as %SystemRoot%\Profiles\garfield) and granted rights accordingly.

 ## How do I limit user profile space?

Roaming profiles are stored on a central server. With some software placing all of their files as part of a profile, these areas can get very big, very fast. Service Pack 4 introduces PROQUOTA.EXE, which you can use to limit user quotas.

Profile quotas are enabled by using a system policy, as follows:

1. Start the System Policy editor (POLEDIT.EXE).
2. Load the templates COMMON.ADM and WINNT.ADM (from the Options menu, select Policy Template from the %systemroot%\inf directory).
3. Create a new policy (File > New > Policy).
4. Open Default User and then expand Windows NT User Profiles.
5. When you select Limit Profile Size, the following options are available:
   a. Custom Message: The text in the dialog box that appears when the user's profile exceeds the quota.
   b. Max Profile Size: The maximum size of the user profile. This value defaults to 30,000KB, so Administrators will want to carefully consider how low they set this value. This is especially true because users are not able to successfully log off if their profiles are too large.
   c. Include Registry in File List: When the user exceeds the profile quota, an error icon appears in the system tray. Double-clicking the icon brings

up a tool that lists all files in the profile, including the file size from the largest file to the smallest. By default, the list does not include files smaller than 2KB. Users can consult this list to determine which files can be erased, moved to server-based storage, or backed up to offline storage. When Include Registry in File List is checked, the user's Registry settings, NTUSER.DAT, is included in the list. Users cannot delete this file.

    d. Notify User When Profile Storage Space is Exceeded: By default, users get a dialog box informing them that their user profile is too large only when they attempt to log off. With this option selected, a dialog box appears as soon as the profile reaches the quota size, and at a configurable interval thereafter.

6. A second option is to select Exclude Directories in Roaming Profile, which does not include specified directories as part of the user's profile.

7. Name the file NTCONFIG.POL and save it to the netlogon share of the Domain Controller.

Ensure that clients have PROQUOTA.EXE by either installing Service Pack 4 on them or manually copying the file to the %systemroot%\system32 directory.

When the clients log back on, their quotas will now be monitored. You can examine these by clicking the small icon at the bottom right of the taskbar.

Note: Remember that the user will not be able to log off if the user profile quota is exceeded, and, by default, small files are not listed in the dialog that displays the files contained in the profile. If Internet Explorer 4.x is installed, these small files could include the entries in the Temporary Internet Files folder. This cache uses a small percentage of the total drive space but can easily grow to be several megabytes in size. To delete these files, users need to empty the cache through the Internet Explorer Internet Options dialog box.

If quotas are enabled and the user cannot log off, the PROQUOTA.EXE process can be killed in Task Manager. This allows the user to log off.

Table 7-2 lists the Registry keys and values for Profile Quotas in the Registry key HKEY_CURRENT_USER\Software\Microsoft\Windows\CurrentVersion\Policies\System.

Table 7-2. Profile Quota Keys and Values

EnableProfileQuotaREG_DWORD0|1	This setting turns profile quotas on or off.
ProfileQuotaMessageREG_SZ	Default: "You have exceeded your profile storage space. Before you can log off, you need to move some items from your profile to network or local storage."
MaxProfileSizeREG_DWORD0x12C-0x7530	Default is 0x7530. This setting specifies the quota size in kilobytes.
WarnUserREG_DWORD0|1	This setting specifies whether to warn the user as soon as the profile exceeds the quota instead of waiting until the user attempts to log off. In addition, it specifies whether to keep prompting the user to reduce the profile size at the interval set in WarnUserTimeout.
WarnUserTimeoutREG_DWORD0x0-0xFFFFFFFF	Default is 0xF. This setting specifies how often the warning dialog appears if the WarnUser setting is turned on.

I can't log off because my user profile quota is over the limit. What can I do?

Service Pack 4 introduced PROQUOTA.EXE, which allows user profile space to be limited. In the event of an exceeded quota, users cannot log off until the profile size has been reduced to within the limit.

If you need to log off, you can simply stop the PROQUOTA.EXE process.

1. Right-click on the taskbar and select Task Manager.
2. Click the Processes tab.
3. Select PROQUOTA.EXE and press the End Process button.
4. Click Yes to the confirmation.
5. Close Task Manager and log off.

If you have the Resource Kit, you can just enter the following command:

```
kill proquota
```

How can I configure each user to have a different screen resolution?

You can't. The screen resolution is stored in the Registry, in a nonuser-specific area and is therefore not configurable for individual users. The resolution must be manually changed when the user logs on.

How can I create a list of all user accounts?

There a number of ways to produce a list of all user accounts in a domain (or just on a machine):

1. The best way is to use a utility shipped with the Resource Kit called ADDUSERS.EXE, which is used to add users that have been detailed in a text file. This utility can also be used to export the current users and groups into a comma-separated file. (What is a comma-separated file? It's just a file that has commas between fields. When the file is read into a spreadsheet or database, the commas are detected and replaced with a new field.) The format is

   addusers /d <filename>
   (for example, addusers /d johnslis.csf)

   Note: Be very careful not to enter /e instead of /d, because /e will delete all users and groups.
   This file can then be read into a spreadsheet or database (such as Excel). You need to specify the comma as the delimiter.

2. A utility called USRSTAT.EXE is shipped with the NT Server Resource Kit. This utility supplies information on all members of a given domain, including time/date of last login. The syntax is

   usrstat <domain>
   (for example, usrstat savilltech)

3. The Resource Kit utility SHOWMBRS.EXE shows all of the users in a given group, so you can dump out the Domain Users group of a domain by using this command:

showmbrs "<domain>\domain users" command
(for example, showmbrs "savilltech\domain users")

You could add "> <filename>" to output the command to a file, as in showmbrs "savilltech\domain users" > allusers.list.

4. Finally, if you don't have the Resource Kit (go and get it), you can use the NET command, net user /domain, to show all users in a domain. The NET command lists all users in the current domain, and again you can add > <filename> to output to a file. You can then get more information on each user in the list by entering

net user <username> /domain
(for example, net user savillj /domain)

You could easily write a Perl script to automate this task.

It might be that none of these suits your exact needs, or that you need to access the user list from within a program. If so, you can use the NetUserEnum(), NetGroupEnum(), and NetLocalGroupEnum() functions to get the required information. For each of these, the first argument is the name of the computer on which to perform the operation. A null pointer makes it use the current system, or NetGetDCName() gets the computer name of the Domain Controller.

4.0 ONLY

How can I move users from one machine to another?

If you want to replace the Primary Domain Controller (PDC) of a domain with a new machine, the easiest way is to install the new machine as a Backup Domain Controller (BDC) and then promote to the PDC, which removes the need of adding and removing users.

If you want to merge two domains or just move some accounts, the following procedure should help. You will need the Resource Kit utility ADDUSERS.EXE.

1. Log on as an Administrator on the machine that has the accounts you wish to move.

2. Run the following command to create a comma-separated file with details of all accounts and groups:

```
addusers /d <filename>
```

3. You don't want the information about global or local groups (such as Administrators and so on), so edit the file and remove the [Global] and [Local] sections and their content.

4. Copy the file to the machine on which you want to create the accounts or to a network drive.

5. Log on as an Administrator on the machine where the accounts should be added. If a domain, log on to the PDC.

6. Run the following command to read in the file and create the accounts:

```
addusers /c <filename>
```

7. You can then delete the accounts from the original machine by using

```
addusers /e <filename>
```

How can I configure a user to log off at a certain time?

7.33

Basic User Manager functionality allows the setting of working hours for a user and the use of user account policies. You can force NT to log out users who are logged on past their hours.

1. Start User Manager for domains (Start > Programs > Administrative Tools > User Manager for Domains).

2. Double-click on the user; for example, savillj.

3. Click the Hours button.

4. By default, the user has logon time at all hours. Each square in the Hours grid represents one hour. Click on the hour when you want the user to be logged off—say 8 p.m.—and then drag to when you want the user to be able to log on again and click the Disallow button. Notice that you can

drag between days, so you can easily disallow 6 p.m. till midnight for all days and then disallow midnight to 8 a.m. for all days, if you wish.

5. Click OK and then click OK again to close the user dialog.
6. Open the Accounts policy (choose Account from the Policies menu).
7. At the bottom of the dialog is an option to Forcibly Disconnect Remote Users from Server When Logon Hours Expire. Check this and click OK.

 ## How can I grant user rights from the command line?

Usually user rights, such as Logon Locally, are granted by starting User Manager and selecting User Rights from the Policies menu. But perhaps you want to grant rights from the command line for use with account generation scripts, for example. The Windows NT Resource Kit Supplement 2 includes a new utility called NTRIGHTS.EXE that grants user rights from the command line.

The program uses a series of code words for each user right, listed in Table 7-3.

Table 7-3. Code Words for User Rights

Code Word	User Right
SeNetworkLogonRight	Access this computer from the network.
SeTcbPrivilege	Act as part of the operating system.
SeMachineAccountPrivilege	Add workstations to domain.
SeBackupPrivilege	Back up files and directories.
SeChangeNotifyPrivilege	Bypass traverse checking.
SeSystemtimePrivilege	Change the system time.
SeCreatePagefilePrivilege	Create a pagefile.
SeCreateTokenPrivilege	Create a token object.
SeCreatePermanentPrivilege	Create permanent shared objects.
SeDebugPrivilege	Debug programs.
SeRemoteShutdownPrivilege	Force shutdown from a remote system.

Table 7-3. Code Words for User Rights *(continued)*

SeAuditPrivilege	Generate security audits.
SeIncreaseQuotaPrivilege	Increase quotas.
SeIncreaseBasePriorityPrivilege	Increase scheduling priority.
SeLoadDriverPrivilege	Load and unload device drivers.
SeLockMemoryPrivilege	Lock pages in memory.
SeBatchLogonRight	Log on as a batch job.
SeServiceLogonRight	Log on as a service.
SeInteractiveLogonRight	Log on locally.
SeSecurityPrivilege	Manage auditing and security log.
SeSystemEnvironmentPrivilege	Modify firmware environment values.
SeProfileSingleProcessPrivilege	Profile single process.
SeSystemProfilePrivilege	Profile system performance.
SeUnsolicitedInputPrivilege	Read unsolicited input from a terminal device.
SeAssignPrimaryTokenPrivilege	Replace a process level token.
SeRestorePrivilege	Restore files and directories.
SeShutdownPrivilege	Shut down the system.
SeTakeOwnershipPrivilege	Take ownership of files or other objects.

To grant a user right, use the following:

```
ntrights +r SeInteractiveLogonRight -u SavillTech\savillj
```

This example grants savillj of the SavillTech domain the right to log on locally. To grant the right on a remote machine, use the -m switch:

```
ntrights +r SeInteractiveLogonRight -u SavillTech\savillj
-m \\<machine name>
```

How can I configure the system so all users share a common Favorites folder?

It is possible to explicitly define the UNC for the Favorites folder for each user by editing the Registry. The steps would be as follows:

1. Choose a server that will host the Favorites folder and create a Favorites folder on it.
2. Set the required permissions on the folder so users can read it (and add to it if you want that, but probably not). Make sure the folder is shared.
3. Fill the folder with the required links.
4. On the PDC, edit each user entry. Then use the Registry editor (REGEDIT.EXE) to change the Favorites value in the HKEY_CURRENT_USER\Software\Microsoft\Windows\CurrentVersion\Explorer\User Shell Folders key to the path of the common Favorites folder (for example, \\pdcmain\favorites). Click OK.

Is it possible to delete or rename the Administrator account?

It is not possible to delete the Administrator account. If you try to delete it, you'll see the error message "Cannot delete built-in accounts." You can, however, rename the account. In fact, renaming the account is recommended to avoid the possibility of hacking, because most hackers try to enter a system by using an Administrator account. To rename the Administrator account, perform the following:

1. Log on to the machine as an Administrator.
2. Start User Manager (or User Manager for Domains).
3. Select the Administrator account and choose Rename from the User menu.
4. Enter a new name and click OK.

How can I change the local Administrator passwords on machines without going to them?

As you might be aware, it is possible to change your password from the command line by using the Net User command. If you combine this with the AT command, you can run the command on different machines, but you will need Administrator rights on the remote machines for this to work. For example:

AT \\\<machine name> <time> cmd /c net user Administrator anythingyouwant
(for example, AT \\savilljohn 18:00 cmd /c net user Administrator password)

The /c following cmd causes the command window to close after the command has been executed. An alternative to the AT command is the soon command:

soon \\\<machine name> cmd /c net user Administrator password

How can I configure default settings for new users?

When a new user logs on for the first time, a copy of the default user profile (NTUSER.DAT) is copied into the user's profile. To set default settings for a user, you can edit the default NTUSER.DAT file. Anything you define under HKEY_CURRENT_USER can be changed by editing NTUSER.DAT.

To change default settings for a new user on a workstation, perform the following:

1. Start the Registry editor (REGEDT32.EXE).
2. Select the HKEY_USERS on Local Machine window.
3. Select Load Hive from the Registry menu.
4. Move to %systemroot%\Profiles\Default User (for example, d:\winnt\Profiles\Default User).
5. Select NTUSER.DAT and click Open.
6. When you are asked for a key name, enter anything (for example, defuser).

7. Now select the username (defuser) in the HKEY_USERS on Local Machine window and make the changes. For example, you could change the wallpaper by changing defuser\Control Panel\Desktop\Wallpaper. Note: If you add new keys, make sure everyone has at least read access; otherwise, the profile will not be copied.

8. When you have made the changes, select Unload Hive from the Registry menu.

9. Close the Registry editor.

Anyone logging on to the machine will now pick up these default settings.

To configure a default NTUSER.DAT for a domain, perform the previous steps and log on as a user to take these settings. You now need to export these out to the PDC.

1. Log on as an Administrator.

2. Start the System Control Panel applet (Start > Settings > Control Panel > System).

3. Click the User Profiles tab. A list appears of all the profiles stored on the machine. Select the one that has the settings you wish to use as the default for the domain.

4. Click the Copy To button.

5. In the Copy Profile To field, enter the location of the netlogon share of the PDC. This is usually %systemroot%\system32\Repl\Export\Scripts. You want the Export area, not Import, because anything in Export is copied to the Import by the replication process. For example, if h is mapped to the c$ drive of the PDC, use

```
h:\winnt\system32\repl\export\scripts
```

6. In the Permitted To Use dialog box, click Change and select Everyone.

7. Click Add and then click OK.

8. Click OK again to start the copy.

9. Check to see that the NTUSER.DAT file has been created in the location you selected.

If you have trouble exporting a profile, see Question 32-33 in Chapter 32, Problem-Solving.

How can I tell which user has which security identifier (SID)?

Each user has a unique security identifier, and these associations can be viewed in the Registry editor. If you want to view a domain's associations, perform the following on a Domain Controller:

1. Start the Registry editor (REGEDIT.EXE).
2. Move to HKEY_LOCAL_MACHINE\SOFTWARE\Microsoft\ Windows NT\CurrentVersion\ProfileList.
3. Select each SID under this in turn and look at the ProfileImagePath. At the end of this string is the name of the user.
4. Close the Registry editor.

If you know the SID and just want to know the username, you can use the REG.EXE command (with Resource Kit Supplement 2), as follows:

```
reg query "HKEY_LOCAL_MACHINE\SOFTWARE\Microsoft\Windows
NT\CurrentVersion\ProfileList\<SID>\ProfileImagePath"
reg query "HKEY_LOCAL_MACHINE\SOFTWARE\Microsoft\Windows
NT\CurrentVersion\ProfileList\S-1-5-21-1843332746-572796286-
2118856591-1000\ProfileImagePath"
```

Again this shows the ProfileImagePath, giving you the user.

4.0 ONLY

How can I configure NT Server 4.0 to not allow users to log in if their mandatory profile is not available?

This was standard behavior under NT 3.51. To make it work under NT 4.0, in addition to naming the user profile NTUSER.MAN rather than NTUSER.DAT, the user's profile folder also has to be .MAN. To rename the user's profile folder to <name>.man, perform the following:

1. Start User Manager for Domains on the PDC.
2. Select the User and click the Profile button.
3. Check the user's User Profile Path.
4. Start Explorer and move to the user's path.
5. Select the user's folder and press F2 (to rename). Add **.man** to the end of the folder name (as in SAVILLJ.MAN) and press Enter.
6. Back in User Manager, add **.man** to the profile path; for example:

```
\\<server>\<share>\savillj.man
```

7. Close User Manager for Domains.

 ## How do I automatically log off clients after n minutes of inactivity?

In the Registry entry HKEY_LOCAL_MACHINE\SYSTEM\ CurrentControlSet\Services\LanmanServer\Parameters, add a new variable (Edit > New > DWORD Value) and call it Disc. Set the value to the number of minutes of inactivity you want. Some network programs constantly communicate with the server (such as mail), so this does not always work.

This procedure only terminates remote connections. To actually log off from a session, use the WINEXIT.SCR utility that comes with the Resource Kit.

 ## How can I edit the list of connections listed in Explorer when I map a connection?

When you select Tools > Map Network Drive in Explorer and click the drop-down box for the path, Explorer checks the following file:

HKEY_CURRENT_USER\Software\Microsoft\Windows NT\ CurrentVersion\Network\Persistent Connections

This is an area of the Registry for a list of old and current drive mappings (see Figure 7-2). To remove items from the list (or add to it), perform the following:

1. Start the Registry editor (REGEDIT.EXE).
2. Move to HKEY_CURRENT_USER\Software\Microsoft\Windows NT\CurrentVersion\Network\Persistent Connections.
3. In the right-hand pane is a list of values a–z, each having a value such as \\<machine name>\<share>.
4. To remove a map, select the letter associated with it and press Del.
5. You should now edit the Order value and remove the letter you have just deleted.
6. If you wish to add a mapping, select New > String Value. Enter a name from a–z (one that is not in use) and press Enter. Double-click on your new value and set it to the share name (for example, \\johnmachine\d$).
7. Edit the Order value and add your new letter to the end of the string.
8. Close the Registry editor.
9. Start Explorer and your new share or removed share will have taken effect.

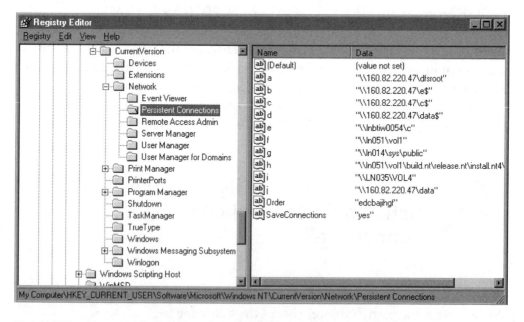

Figure 7-2. An example list of persistent connections. Notice that the Order value represents how the connections are displayed.

How can I exclude the temporary internet files folder from the user profile?

By default, the storage area for temporary internet files is %SYSTEMROOT%\ PROFILES\<USER>\TEMPORARY INTERNET FILES. If you implemented roaming profiles, these files would count as part of your profile, taking up valuable server space. To change the location from the browser, perform the following steps:

1. Start Internet Explorer.
2. Select Internet Options from the View menu.
3. Select the General tab.
4. Click the Settings button.
5. Click the Move Folder button.
6. Click Yes to the confirmation dialog.
7. Select the new location and click OK.

You will need to restart the machine for the new location to take effect. Alternatively, you can create a Registry file to manually update the following Registry values and include it as part of a logon script

- HKEY_LOCAL_MACHINE\SOFTWARE\Microsoft\Windows\ CurrentVersion\Internet Settings\Cache\Paths\path1\CachePath
- HKEY_LOCAL_MACHINE\SOFTWARE\Microsoft\Windows\ CurrentVersion\Internet Settings\Cache\Paths\path2\CachePath
- HKEY_LOCAL_MACHINE\SOFTWARE\Microsoft\Windows\ CurrentVersion\Internet Settings\Cache\Paths\path3\CachePath
- HKEY_LOCAL_MACHINE\SOFTWARE\Microsoft\Windows\ CurrentVersion\Internet Settings\Cache\Paths\path4\CachePath
- HKEY_CURRENT_USER\Software\Microsoft\Windows\ CurrentVersion\Explorer\Shell Folders\Cache
- HKEY_CURRENT_USER\Software\Microsoft\Windows\ CurrentVersion\Explorer\User Shell Folders\Cache

An example .REG file would be:

```
REGEDIT4
[HKEY_LOCAL_MACHINE\SOFTWARE\Microsoft\Windows\CurrentVersion\
Internet Settings\Cache\Paths\path1]
"CachePath"="E:\TEMP\Cache1"
[HKEY_LOCAL_MACHINE\SOFTWARE\Microsoft\Windows\CurrentVersion\
Internet Settings\Cache\Paths\path2]
"CachePath"="E:\TEMP\Cache2"
[HKEY_LOCAL_MACHINE\SOFTWARE\Microsoft\Windows\CurrentVersion\
Internet Settings\Cache\Paths\path3]
"CachePath"="E:\TEMP\Cache3"
[HKEY_LOCAL_MACHINE\SOFTWARE\Microsoft\Windows\CurrentVersion\
Internet Settings\Cache\Paths\path4]
"CachePath"="E:\TEMP\Cache4"
[HKEY_CURRENT_USER\Software\Microsoft\Windows\CurrentVersion\
Explorer\Shell Folders]
"Cache"="E:\TEMP"
[HKEY_CURRENT_USER\Software\Microsoft\Windows\CurrentVersion\
Explorer\User Shell Folders]
"Cache"="E:\TEMP"
```

This sets the cache area to e:\temp, but you can change this to anything you want. Save the above as CACHE.REG and run as follows:

```
regedit /s cache.reg
```

Netscape does not store temp files under the user profile. (If you are interested, it is stored in the HKEY_LOCAL_MACHINE\SOFTWARE\Netscape\ Netscape Navigator\Users\<user>\DirRoot Registry location.)

How can I stop the programs in my Startup folders from running when I log on?

Hold down Shift during your logon, and any programs in the Startup folders will not run.

If Administrators wish to disable this behavior, add the following and set the value to 1:

```
IgnoreShiftOveride of type String to HKEY_LOCAL_MACHINE\
SOFTWARE\Microsoft\Windows NT\CurrentVersion\Winlogon
```

I can't delete user x. Why?

This problem can be caused by a number of things. You can try deleting the user from the command line:

net user <username> /delete [/domain]

If this does not work, try renaming the account and then deleting it:

1. Start User Manager for Domains.
2. Select the user you can't delete.
3. From the User menu, select Rename.
4. Enter the new name and click OK.
5. Now select the new username and press DEL
6. Click OK to the confirmation.

The above solution would also work if you have an invalid username (such as AAAAAAAAAA).

How can I stop users from being able to map or disconnect network drives?

You can accomplish this by using the Policy editor under normal conditions; however, it can also be performed by directly editing the Registry.

1. Start the Registry editor (REGEDIT.EXE).
2. Move to HKEY_CURRENT_USER\Software\Microsoft\Windows\ CurrentVersion\Policies\Explorer.
3. From the Edit menu, select New > DWORD Value.

4. Enter the name NoNetConnectDisconnect and press Enter.

5. Double-click the new value and set to 1.

6. The user will need to log off and on for the change to take effect.

FAQ 7.47   How can I disable a whole group of users?

There is no built-in mechanism for deleting groups, but you can accomplish it with two commands.

The first command uses the Resource Kit utility SHOWMBRS.EXE outputting to a file:

```
showmbrs <domain>\<group> > users.txt
showmbrs savilltech\sales > users.txt
```

The second command iterates through the file and performs a net user <username> /active:no /domain:

```
for /f "skip=2" %I in (users.txt) do net user %I /active:no
/domain
```

An example output is shown in Figure 7-3.

If you want to create a script, enter the following into file DSBLGRP.BAT. The usage is

dsblgrp <group name>
(for example, dsblgrp savilltech\sales)

```
REM
REM dsblgrp <group name>
REM by John Savill, 20th July 1998
REM
showmbrs %1 > users.txt
for /f "skip=2" %%I in (users.txt) do net user %%I /active:no
/domain
```

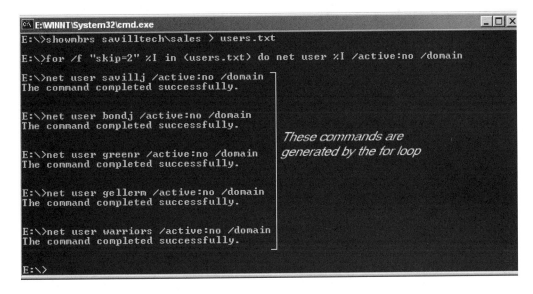

Figure 7-3. This provides a very fast way to disable entire groups of users.

Make sure you use two %% before the I or it won't work.

Because of a problem with SHOWMBRS.EXE, you can only view groups with fewer than seven members. To fix this, download the fixed version from ftp://ftp.microsoft.com/bussys/winnt/winnt-public/reskit/nt40/i386/ Shombrs.exe/.

 ## 7.48 How can I rename a user from the command prompt?

You can download the RENUSER.EXE utility from http://www.ntfaq.com/ ntfaq/download/renuser.zip, which has the following usage:

renuser <old username> <new username> [<domain name>]
(for example, renuser savillj johns savilltech)

I have made user shares hidden, but now the connection fails. Why?

To hide a share, all you need to do is add the $ sign to the end, as in \\server\share$.

If in your logon scripts you previously had the following command, it will no longer work with the $ now that the share is hidden.

```
net use f: \\<server>\%username%
```

To connect, you need to specify the $, so change the command to

```
net use f: \\<server>\%username%$
```

2000 ONLY

How do I grant user rights in Windows 2000?

In Windows NT 4.0, user rights are assigned via User Manager > Policies > User Rights. User Manager has been replaced in Windows 2000, and the way to assign user rights is not obvious. Here is an easy way to do it:

1. Start the Computer Management MMC snap-in (Start > Programs > Administrative Tools > Computer Management).
2. Expand the System Tools branch.
3. Go to Group Policy Editor > Computer Settings > Security Settings > Local Policies > User Rights Assignment.
4. Double-click on the user right you wish to grant (see Figure 7-4).
5. Click Add and select the users or groups. When completed, click OK.
6. Click OK again to close the user rights assignment.

This would modify the local group policy of a machine.

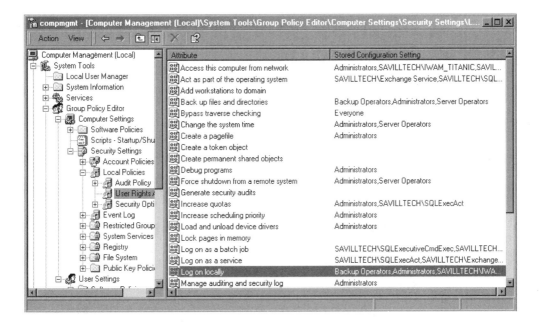

Figure 7-4. Enabling users to log on to the server.

 How can I log off from the command prompt?

The Windows NT 4.0 Resource Kit Supplement 2 ships with the LOGOFF.EXE utility. You can use this utility to log off from the command line.

The syntax is

```
logoff [/f] [/n]
```

where the option /f means running processes will be closed without asking to save unsaved data but will ask for confirmation, and /n will log off without confirmation but will ask to save unsaved data.

Using both together results in no confirmation and all unsaved data being lost.

2000 ONLY

7.52   Where is User Manager for Domains in Windows 2000?

Windows 2000 no longer users User Manager for domain account administration. The new tool is the Directory Management MMC. For more information, see Question 7-53.

2000 ONLY

7.53   How do I administer domain users in Windows 2000?

Windows 2000 has a whole new look for its administration tools with Microsoft Management Console (MMC) snap-ins. The Domain Management MMC snap-in is used for the administration of domain users. Select the snap-in from the Administrative Tools folder (Start > Programs > Administrative Tools > Directory Management). When it starts, expand the domain and users branch to see the users (see Figure 7-5).

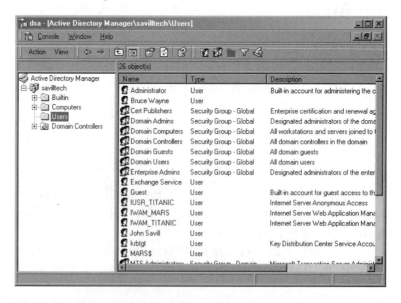

Figure 7-5. Viewing users in Windows 2000.

Context menus are heavily used in Windows 2000. For example, to change a user's password, simply right-click on the user and select Reset Password (see Figure 7-6). Selecting Properties enables you to set other properties of the user, such as group membership and profile location.

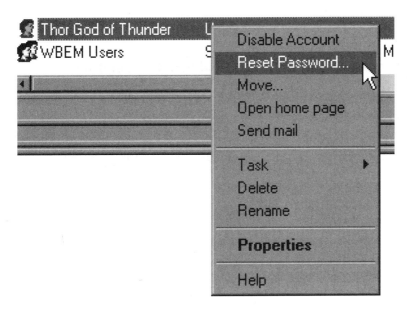

Figure 7-6. Modifying the password is now easy and intuitive.

 ## How do I change the location for temporary files?

There are a number of temp variables, mainly temp and tmp. You can change the values of these as follows:

1. Start the System Control Panel applet (Start > Settings > Control Panel > System).
2. Select the Environment tab.
3. Under User Variables, select temp (or tmp) to display its value. Modify it in the Value box and click Set.
4. When you have made all changes, click Apply and then OK.

Alternatively, you can directly edit the Registry to make these changes:

1. Start the Registry editor (REGEDIT.EXE).
2. Move to HKEY_CURRENT_USER\Environment.
3. Double-click on the variable (temp, for example) and edit the value. When complete, click OK.
4. Close the Registry editor.

A final method is to use the SET command from the command line:

```
set temp=d:\temp
```

Most Windows applications, such as Word, check the variable tmp (not temp) for the location of temporary files, so make sure you modify tmp and not just temp.

8 DESKTOP CONFIGURATION

The desktop can transform your operating system from just usable to a pleasure. Windows NT 4.0 and Windows 2000 allow users to configure the desktop in any way they want. However, this can have a price.

In a corporate environment, a standard desktop might be required, and Administrators might not want users modifying a computer's content. Remember, however, that users have their own desktops, and just changing icons, colors, and so on will not affect other users. This is known as the user's profile.

FAQ 8.1 How do I remove the Goto menu from Explorer?

Under the Tools menu of Explorer is a Goto option that allows the user to jump to a drive or directory.

Service Pack 4 for Windows NT 4.0 and Windows 2000 supports a system policy of Remove Tools > GoTo Menu From Explorer. To configure this via the Policy editor, perform the following:

1. Start the Policy editor (POLEDIT.EXE).
2. Load a policy or create a new one.

3. Select Default User.

4. Expand Windows NT Shell - Restrictions branch.

5. Check Remove Tools > GoTo Menu From Explorer.

6. Click OK and save.

Alternatively, you can perform this procedure directly in the Registry:

1. Start the Registry editor (REGEDT32.EXE).

2. Move to HKEY_CURRENT_USER\Software\Microsoft\Windows\CurrentVersion\Policies\Explorer.

3. From the Edit menu, Choose New > Binary Value.

4. Enter the name **NoGoTo** and press Enter.

5. Double-click the new value and set to 1.

6. Click OK and close the Registry editor.

 ## How can I delete the My Computer icon?

It is not possible to delete the icon, but you can make it invisible.

1. Right-click on the desktop and select Properties.

2. Select the Plus tab.

3. Select My Computer and click Change Icon.

4. Change the filename to **%systemroot%\system32\tweakui.cpl**.

5. Select the fourth icon (a big blank) and click OK.

6. Click Apply and then click OK.

You can then move the icon to the bottom of the screen to hide the My Computer text. Now, if you don't use AutoArrange and don't select a greater screen resolution, you'll never see the icon again.

How do I hide the Network Neighborhood icon?

You can use TweakUI and unselect Network Neighborhood on the Desktop tab. You can also do this by editing the Registry:

1. Start the Registry editor (REGEDIT.EXE).
2. Move to the HKEY_CURRENT_USER\Software\Microsoft\Windows\ CurrentVersion\Policies\Explorer.
3. From the Edit menu, choose New > DWORD Value.
4. Enter the name **NoNetHood** and press Enter.
5. Double-click the new value and set it to 1.
6. Click OK and close the Registry editor.
7. Log off and log on; the Network Neighborhood will be hidden.

How do I delete or rename the Recycle Bin?

When you right-click on the Recycle Bin, its context menu does not display a Rename or Delete option as on other desktop shortcuts and components. To add the Rename option, perform the following:

1. Start the Registry editor (REGEDT32.EXE—don't use REGEDIT.EXE).
2. Move to HKEY_CLASSES_ROOT\CLSID\{645FF040-5081-101B-9F08-00AA002F954E}\ShellFolder.
3. Double-click on the Attributes value in the right-hand pane.
4. Change the value from 40010020 to 50010020.
5. Click OK.

If you right-click on Recycle Bin, you now have a rename option.

If you want to be able to delete the icon, follow the same procedure but change the Attributes value to 60010020. To have both Rename and Delete options, change the Attributes value to 70010020. Click Yes to the confirmation. You can now delete by right-clicking on the icon and selecting Delete.

If you want to avoid manually updating the Registry, you can delete the icon by using the TweakUI utility. If you have TweakUI installed, perform the following:

1. Start the TweakUI control panel applet (Start > Settings > Control Panel > TweakUI).
2. Click the Desktop tab.
3. Unselect the Recycle Bin check box and click OK.

 ## How do I delete or rename the Inbox icon?

When you right-click on the Inbox icon, its context menu does not display a Rename or Delete option as on other desktop shortcuts and components. To add the Rename option, perform the following:

1. Start the Registry editor (REGEDT32.EXE—don't use REGEDIT.EXE).
2. Move to HKEY_CLASSES_ROOT\CLSID\{00020D75-0000-0000-C000-000000000046}\ShellFolder.
3. Double-click on the Attributes value in the right-hand pane.
4. Change from 72000000 to 50000000.
5. Click OK.

If you right-click on the Inbox icon, you now have a Rename option.

If you want to be able to delete the icon, follow the same procedure but change the Attributes value to 60010020. To have both Rename and Delete options, change the Attributes value to 70010020. Click Yes to the confirmation. You can now delete by right-clicking on the icon and selecting Delete.

If you want to avoid manually updating the Registry, you can delete the icon by using the TweakUI utility. If you have TweakUI installed, perform the following:

1. Start the TweakUI control panel applet (Start > Settings > Control Panel > TweakUI).

2. Click the Desktop tab and unselect the Inbox box.

3. Click Apply and then OK.

I have deleted the Recycle Bin. How can I re-create it?

If you have TweakUI, click the Desktop tab and check the Recycle Bin. Click Apply and then OK. If you do not have TweakUI, you can re-add the Recycle Bin by directly updating the Registry:

1. Start the Registry editor (REGEDIT.EXE).

2. Move to HKEY_LOCAL_MACHINE\SOFTWARE\Microsoft\ Windows\CurrentVersion\Explorer\Desktop\NameSpace.

3. From the Edit menu, choose New > Key.

4. Enter the name **{645FF040-5081-101B-9F08-00AA002F954E}**.

5. Select the new key and double-click on (Default). Set to Recycle Bin and click OK.

6. Close the Registry editor.

7. Press F5 on the desktop for the Recycle Bin to appear.

I have deleted Internet Explorer from the desktop. How can I re-create it?

You can use TweakUI, select Desktop, and check the Internet check box. Click Apply and then OK. Alternatively, you can directly edit the Registry:

1. Start the Registry editor (REGEDIT.EXE).

2. Move to HKEY_LOCAL_MACHINE\SOFTWARE\Microsoft\ Windows\CurrentVersion\Explorer\Desktop\NameSpace.

3. From the Edit menu, choose New > Key.

4. Enter the name **{FBF23B42-E3F0-101B-8488-00AA003E56F8}**.

5. Select the new key and double-click on (Default). Set to The Internet and click OK.
6. Close the Registry editor.
7. Press F5 on the desktop for the Internet Explorer icon to appear.

 ## I have deleted the Inbox icon. How can I re-create it?

If you have TweakUI, click the Desktop tab and check the Inbox check box. Click Apply and then OK. If you do not have TweakUI, you can directly update the Registry:

1. Start the Registry editor (REGEDIT.EXE).
2. Move to HKEY_LOCAL_MACHINE\SOFTWARE\Microsoft\ Windows\CurrentVersion\Explorer\Desktop\NameSpace.
3. From the Edit menu, choose New > Key.
4. Enter the name **{00020D75-0000-0000-C000-000000000046}**.
5. Select the new key and double-click on (Default). Set to Inbox and click OK.
6. Close the Registry editor.
7. Press F5 on the desktop for the Inbox icon to appear.

 ## How do I change the My Computer icon?

You can change the My Computer icon by using Themes for NT or the Plus tab of Display settings. You can also change it by using the Registry editor.

1. Start the Registry editor (REGEDIT.EXE).
2. Move to the HKEY_LOCAL_MACHINE\Software\Classes\CLSID\ {20D04FE0-3AEA-1069-A2D8-08002B30309D}\DefaultIcon.

3. Double-click on (Default) and set to the icon required. For example, set it to d:\Prog Files\Plus\Themes\John.ico,0. The 0 shows you have selected icon 1 in the file.
4. Close the Registry editor.

 ## How do I change the Internet Explorer icon?

For Internet Explorer versions prior to 4.0, follow this procedure:

1. Start the Registry editor (REGEDIT.EXE).
2. Move to HKEY_CLASSES_ROOT\CLSID\{FBF23B42-E3F0-101B-8488-00AA003E56F8}\DefaultIcon.
3. Double-click Default on the right-hand side and change to the icon you want (use Browse).
4. Click OK and close the Registry editor.

There is a program called MicroAngelo available from http://www.iconstructions.com that automates this procedure.

The solution I just described does not work for Internet Explorer 4.0 and later. The method for those versions is as follows:

1. Start the Registry editor (REGEDIT.EXE).
2. Move to HKEY_CLASSES_ROOT\CLSID\{871C5380-42A0-1069-A2EA-08002B30309D}.
3. From the Edit menu, choose New > Key.
4. Enter the name **DefaultIcon** and press Enter.
5. Double-click Default on the right-hand side and change to the icon you want (use Browse).
6. Click OK and close the Registry editor.

There are some really nice IE icons at http://www.blably.com/iconstructions.

How do I change the Network Neighborhood icon?

This can be changed by using Themes for NT or the Plus tab of Display settings. You can also change it by using the Registry editor, as follows:

1. Start the Registry editor (REGEDIT.EXE).
2. Move to the HKEY_LOCAL_MACHINE\SOFTWARE\Classes\ CLSID\{208D2C60-3AEA-1069-A2D7-08002B30309D}\DefaultIcon.
3. Double-click on (Default) and set to the icon required. For example, set it to d:\Prog Files\Plus\Themes\John.ico,0. The 0 shows you have selected icon 1 in the file.
4. Close the Registry editor.

 ## How do I change the Recycle Bin icons?

There are two icons for the Recycle Bin—an empty and a full. To change them, use the following:

1. Start the Registry editor (REGEDIT.EXE).
2. Move to the HKEY_LOCAL_MACHINE\SOFTWARE\Classes\ CLSID\{645FF040-5081-101B-9F08-00AA002F954E}\DefaultIcon.
3. To change the Empty icon, double-click on Empty. To change the Full icon, double-click on Full.
4. Set to the icon required; for example, to d:\Prog Files\Plus\Themes\ John.ico,0. The 0 shows you have selected icon 1 in the file.
5. Close the Registry editor.

You can also change the icons by using the Plus tab of Display properties.

How do I change the Briefcase icon?

1. Start the Registry editor (REGEDIT.EXE).
2. Move to the HKEY_LOCAL_MACHINE\SOFTWARE\Classes\ CLSID\{85BBD920-42A0-1069-A2E4-08002B30309D}\DefaultIcon.
3. Double-click on (Default) and set to the icon required. For example, set it to d:\Prog Files\Plus\Themes\John.ico,0. The 0 shows you have selected icon 1 in the file.
4. Close the Registry editor.

How do I create a shortcut on the desktop to a directory or disk?

This procedure works for any file, directory, or disk (even the A: drive):

1. Start Explorer (Start > Programs > Explorer or Win+E).
2. Right-click on the file, directory, or disk and drag to the desktop.
3. Release the right mouse button.
4. From the context menu, select Create Shortcut(s) Here.

How do I disable Task Manager?

You can start Task Manager by right-clicking on the taskbar and selecting Task Manager or by selecting from the Security dialog box that appears when you press Ctrl+Alt+Del.

Task Manager can be dangerous because it allows any process to be stopped. For this reason, you might want to restrict user access to it. You can accomplish this in the Registry, as follows:

1. Start the Registry Editor (REGEDIT.EXE).
2. Move to the HKEY_CURRENT_USER\Software\Microsoft\windows\currentversion\Policies.
3. If the \System key does not exist, create it.
4. Add a new value of type DWORD called DisableTaskMgr and set to 1.
5. Close the Registry editor.

You can also disable the Task Manager by using the Policy editor.

1. Start the Policy editor (POLEDIT.EXE).
2. Select the User or edit the default User.
3. Go to Shell/Restrictions and select Remove Taskbar From User.

To remove Task Manager for all users, rename TASKMGR.EXE to something else. If it is on an NTFS partition, you can set the permissions so ordinary users cannot access it.

How do I disable Window animation?

By using TweakUI on the General tab, you can unselect Window Animation, which disables the animation when a window is minimized or restored. You can also accomplish this by using the Registry:

1. Start the Registry editor (REGEDIT.EXE).
2. Go to the key HKEY_CURRENT_USER\Control Panel\Desktop\WindowsMetrics.
3. Double-click MinAnimate.
4. Set to 1 for normal animation; set to 0 for none.
5. Close the Registry editor.
6. Log out and log in again (if you use TweakUI, you don't need to log out).

4.0 ONLY

How do I reduce or increase the delay for cascading menus?

You can use TweakUI on the Mouse tab and decrease or increase the menu time (see Figure 8-1). You can also use the Registry editor and change the value HKEY_CURRENT_USER\Control Panel\Desktop\MenuShowDelay.

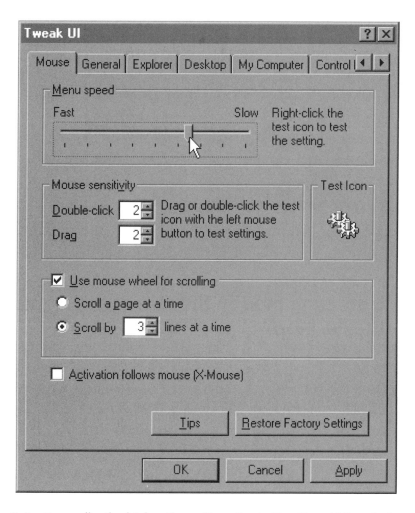

Figure 8-1. Generally, the higher the setting, the better. TweakUI really is a must-have tool.

Why can't I move any icons?

It is possible to configure NT to AutoArrange the icons, which means you can't move them manually. To turn off this feature, right-click on the desktop (any-where where there is not a window). From the context menu, choose Arrange Icons and unselect AutoArrange (see Figure 8-2).

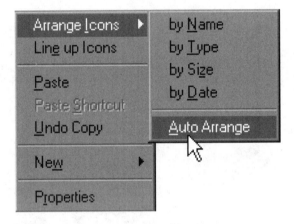

Figure 8-2. This shows AutoArrange disabled.

 ## How can I modify the size of the icons on the desktop?

As you might be aware, you can change the size of icons in Explorer by selecting Large Icons or Small Icons from the View menu. And you can actually make the icons even bigger.

1. Start the Registry editor (REGEDIT.EXE).
2. Move to HKEY_CURRENT_USER\Control Panel\Desktop\ WindowMetrics.
3. Double-click on Shell Icon Size.
4. Modify the icons to the size you want, increasing by 16s (try 48 or 64).

5. Click OK and close the Registry editor.

If you selected Large Icons in Explorer, you will now see the new size. You don't need to log off—just change folders.

The small icons in the Start menu can be enlarged as follows:

1. Start the Registry editor (REGEDIT.EXE).
2. Move to HKEY_CURRENT_USER\Control Panel\Desktop\ WindowMetrics.
3. From the Edit menu, choose New > String.
4. Enter the name **Shell Small Icon Size**.
5. Double-click the new value and set it to the size you want. It's 16 by default, but you can use 32, 48, 64, and so on.

Log off and on again for the change to take effect.

To change the number of colors in the icons, perform the following:

1. Start the Registry editor (REGEDIT.EXE).
2. Move to HKEY_CURRENT_USER\Control Panel\Desktop\ WindowMetrics.
3. Double-click on Shell Icon BPP.
4. Modify to 4 for 16 colors, 8 for 256, 16 for 65,536, 24 for 16 million, and 32 for True Color.
5. Close the Registry editor.

You need to log off for the change to take effect.

How can I configure the Alt+Tab display?

You can configure this through the Registry to change how the running applications are displayed:

1. Start the Registry Editor (REGEDIT.EXE).
2. Move to HKEY_CURRENT_USER\Control Panel\Desktop.

3. Double-click on CoolSwitchColumns to change the number of columns displayed.
4. Double-click on CoolSwitchRows to change the number of rows.
5. Close the Registry editor.

Restart the computer for the change to take effect.

 ## How can I disable the right mouse button menu?

When you right-click on some items, a menu appears that relates to the selected item. This is known as a context menu because it changes depending on the context of the selected item.

For systems running with Service Pack 2 or later, it is possible to disable the context menu as follows:

1. Start the Registry editor (REGEDIT.EXE).
2. Move to HKEY_CURRENT_USER\Software\Microsoft\Windows\CurrentVersion\Policies\Explorer.
3. From the Edit menu, choose New > DWORD Value.
4. Enter the name **NoViewContextMenu** and press Enter.
5. Double-click the new value created. Set the value to 1 and click OK.
6. Close the Registry editor.
7. Log out and log in again.

To reverse this process, delete the value NoViewContextMenu and log out and log in again (or set the value to 0).

You can also accomplish this by using System Policies. Start the System Policy Editor (POLEDIT.EXE), select the user or group policy, and expand the Windows NT Shell - Restrictions branch. There you can disable both the Explorer and the taskbar context menus.

How do I change the color used to display compressed files and directories?

The color is stored in the Registry in hexadecimal format; therefore, before you try to change the color, you need to work out what the value is in hex. Usually you know a color as an RGB value such as 255,0,0 for red. To convert this to hex, use the calculator supplied with Windows NT (CALC.EXE).

1. Start the Calculator (Start > Run > Calc.exe).
2. From the View menu select Scientific.
3. Select Dec and enter the first part of the RGB value.
4. Click Hex to see it displayed in hex. For example, 255 would show as ff.
5. Repeat for the G and B parts of the color.

You now have a hex valuè for the color. For example, 255,128,0 would be ff, 80, 0.

1. Start the Registry editor (REGEDIT.EXE).
2. Move to HKEY_CURRENT_USER\Software\Microsoft\Windows\ CurrentVersion\Explorer.
3. Double-click on the AltColor value in the right-hand pane.
4. The actual value is displayed as something like this:

```
0000 00 00 FF 00 ..y.
```

Ignore the first set of numbers (the four zeros). Modify the three sets after that—the 00, 00, and FF—and ignore the last two. To edit, click once to the right of the value you wish to change. Press the backspace key and delete both parts of the number. Then type in your new value.
5. Click OK and then close the Registry editor.
6. You need to log off and log on again for the change to take effect.

If you prefer to avoid the Registry, you can make the same change by using the TweakUI utility, as follows:

1. Start the TweakUI control panel applet (Start > Settings > Control Panel > TweakUI).

2. Click on the Explorer tab.

3. A box at the bottom of the tab shows the color of compressed files. Click Change Color (see Figure 8-3).

4. You can now just select the color you want and click OK.

5. Click OK again.

6. You need to log off and on again for the change to take effect.

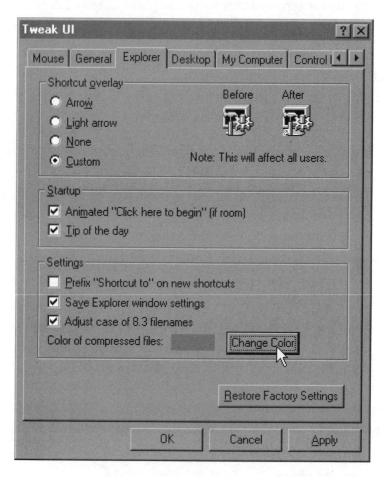

Figure 8-3. Here the color has been modified from the default blue to red.

8.23

How can I configure the wallpaper to be displayed somewhere other than the center of the screen?

It is possible to configure NT to display wallpaper anywhere on the screen, but you have to manually update the Registry.

1. Start the Registry editor (REGEDT32.EXE).
2. Move to HKEY_CURRENT_USER\Control Panel\Desktop.
3. From the Edit menu, select Add Value.
4. Enter the name **WallpaperOriginX** with a type of REG_SZ and click OK.
5. When you're prompted for a value, enter the number of pixels the left side of the image should be from the left side of the screen.
6. Next select Add Value from the Edit menu again. This time enter the name **WallpaperOriginY** and click OK.
7. At the prompt, enter the number of pixels the top of the image should be from the top of the screen.
8. Log off and on to see the change take effect.

 8.24

How can I stop the Click Here to Begin message?

When you first log on, you see a message Click Here to Begin.

There are two ways to remove this message. If you have the TweakUI utility, perform the following:

1. Start the TweakUI control panel applet (Start > Settings > Control Panel > TweakUI).
2. Click the Explorer tab.
3. Unselect Animated Click Here to Begin.
4. Click OK.

If you don't have TweakUI, you need to edit the Registry directly.

1. Start the Registry editor (REGEDIT.EXE).
2. Move to HKEY_CURRENT_USER\Software\Microsoft\Windows\
   CurrentVersion\Policies\Explorer.
3. Double-click on NoStartBanner and change it to 01 00 00 00.
4. Click OK and close the Registry editor.

How can I get more room on the taskbar?

If you move the cursor over the top of the taskbar, it turns into a double-headed arrow. When the cursor is the double arrow, hold down the left mouse button and drag upward. The taskbar's area increases by one row at a time. You can also shrink the taskbar by dragging downward.

Figure 8-4. That's a taskbar!

4.0 ONLY

How do I add the Control Panel to the Start menu?

If you want the Control Panel visible under the main Start menu rather than on the Settings branch, create a new folder under the Start menu you wish to have it on (Administrator or All Users). Name the new folder as follows, complete with the period, braces, and dashes:

```
Control Panel.{21EC2020-3AEA-1069-A2DD-08002B30309D}
```

After you enter this folder name, it will automatically be renamed Control Panel. Unlike the Settings Control Panel, it will cascade, which means all Control Panel applets will be shown as sub-objects.

Figure 8-5. Start menu modified by adding Control Panel to the %systemroot%\
Profiles\All Users\Start Menu directory.

If you have a problem, try pressing F5 to refresh the screen, or log off and on
again.

8.27 How can I remove a program from the Open With menu that appears when I right-click on a file?

Each entry in the Open With menu has an entry in the Registry HKEY_
CLASSES_ROOT called <extension>_auto_file (for example, doc_auto_file
for work). To remove the entry, delete the base <extension>_auto_file tree in the
Registry. If you are unsure, you can perform the following:

1. Start the Registry editor (REGEDIT.EXE).
2. Search for the name of the .EXE file you want to remove from the Open
   With menu.

3. If a match is found and its root is HKEY_CLASSES_ROOT/xxx_ auto_file, delete the tree HKEY_CLASSES_ROOT/xxx_auto_file.

4. Close the Registry editor.

FAQ 8.28 How do I add an item to the right-click (context) menu?

The context menu displayed when you right-click on an item can be modified. Follow the procedures below to add an item to the context menu:

1. Start the Registry Editor (REGEDIT.EXE).
2. Expand the HKEY_CLASSES_ROOT by clicking the plus sign.
3. Scroll down and expand the Unknown subkey.
4. Click on the Shell key and right-click on it.
5. Select New from the pop-up menu and choose Key.
6. Type the name you want displayed (the name of the application) and press Enter.
7. Right-click on the new subkey and click New.
8. Choose Key again. Enter the name Command and click Enter.
9. Click on the newly created command and double-click on (Default).
10. Enter the path and name of the executable with %1:

```
d:\program files\savedit\savedit.exe %1
```

11. Close the Registry editor.

When you right-click on a file now, the new entry will be displayed.

Is it possible to move the taskbar?

The taskbar can be moved to any of the four sides of the screen—left, right, top, or bottom. To move it, single-click on the taskbar and drag it to the side where you want it to reside.

If you have lost the taskbar, just press Ctrl+Esc to redisplay it.

How can I configure NT to display a thumbnail of bitmaps as the icon instead of the Paint icon?

Perform the following actions to make bitmap content show as an icon. For best effect, make Explorer use large icons.

1. Start the Registry editor (REGEDIT.EXE).
2. Move to HKEY_CLASSES_ROOT\Paint.Picture\DefaultIcon.
3. Double-click on Default in the left pane and change to %1. Then click OK.
4. Close the Registry editor. The change takes immediate effect.

Can I remove one of the Startup folders on the Start menu?

Unfortunately, no. One is your own user Startup folder (%systemroot%\Profiles\<Username>\Start Menu\Programs\Startup) and the other is the All Users Startup folder (%system root%\Profiles\All Users\Start Menu\Programs\Startup). Both are system files and therefore undeletable.

It is possible to hide one or both of the Startup folders by setting the hidden attribute on the folder, as follows:

```
attrib +h %system root%\Profiles\<Username>\Start Menu\
Programs\Startup
```

A trick has been found to remove one of the Startup menus by copying the All Users Startup group over the Administrator Startup group, which then deletes the All Users Startup group.

 ## How can I clear the Run history?

The Run history is stored in the Registry in location HKEY_CURRENT_ USER\Software\Microsoft\Windows\CurrentVersion\Explorer\RunMRU as a series of values a–z. To delete an entry from the Run menu, perform the following:

1. Start the Registry editor (REGEDIT.EXE).
2. Move to HKEY_CURRENT_USER\Software\Microsoft\Windows\ CurrentVersion\Explorer\RunMRU.
3. Select the entry you wish to remove (for example, h).
4. Press the Del key (or choose Edit > Delete) and click Yes to the confirmation.
5. Double-click the MRUList value and remove the letter you just deleted. Click OK to save the change.
6. Close the Registry editor.

If you want to clear the whole Run list, you can use the TweakUI utility:

1. Start the TweakUI control panel applet (Start > Settings > Control Panel > TweakUI).
2. Click the Paranoia tab.
3. Check Clear Run History at Logon.
4. Click on Clear Selected Items Now.
5. Then either clear the check on Clear Run History at Logon and click OK, or leave it checked to automatically clear Run at logon.

How can I remove the Documents menu?

There is no way to remove the Documents menu from the Start button; you have to empty it at the start of each session. In Windows 98, you can remove the Documents menu with the following procedure:

1. Start the Registry editor (REGEDIT.EXE).
2. Move to HKEY_CURRENT_USER\Software\Microsoft\Windows\ CurrentVersion\Policies\Explorer.
3. From the Edit menu, choose New > DWORD Value.
4. Enter the name **NoFavoritesMenu** and press Enter.
5. Double-click the new value and set to 1. Click OK.
6. Close the Registry editor.

Log off and on again and the Documents menu is gone.

In NT, the Documents menu is actually the contents of the directory %systemroot%\Profiles\<username>\Recent (for example, d:\winnt\ Profiles\savillj\Recent). If you delete the contents of this folder, nothing will show in the Documents menu. The easiest way to delete the file's contents is to create a batch file and place it in your Startup group, as follows:

1. Start Notepad.
2. Enter the following into the file. Actually type the %systemroot% and %username% unless you are performing this on a Windows 95 machine, in which case you should type in real values.

```
del /q %systemroot%\Profiles\%username%\Recent\*.*
```

3. Save the file as "DELDOC.BAT" (put the filename in quotes or Notepad will add .TXT to the end) in a directory of your choice.
4. Start Explorer.
5. Move to the folder where you saved DELDOC.BAT and right-click on it.
6. Drag the file to the %systemroot%\Profiles\%username%\Start Menu\Programs\Startup (for example, d:\winnt\Profiles\savillj\Start Menu\Programs\Startup) and release the mouse button.
7. From the displayed context menu, choose Create Shortcut(s) Here.

When you log in from now on, the batch file will run and delete your Documents menu.

If you have TweakUI installed, you can gain the same effect by clicking the Paranoia tab and checking Clear Document History at Logon.

 ## How do I disable the context menu for the Start button?

The context menu is displayed when you right-click on an object. If you right-click on the Start button, you get options to start Explorer, Find, and so on. To disable this context menu, perform the following:

1. Start the Registry editor (REGEDIT.EXE).
2. Move to HKEY_CLASSES_ROOT\Directory\shell.
3. Delete the keys under this (for example DosHere, Find).
4. Move to HKEY_CLASSES_ROOT\Folder\shell.
5. Delete the keys under this (for example, Explore, Open).

If you right-click on Start now, these options will have been removed.

To disable the context menu for the Start menu entirely, perform the following:

1. Start the Registry editor (REGEDIT.EXE).
2. Move to HKEY_CURRENT_USER\Software\Microsoft\Windows\CurrentVersion\Policies\Explorer.
3. From the Edit menu, choose New > DWORD Value.
4. Enter the name **NoTrayContextMenu** and press Enter.
5. Double-click the new value and set it to 1.

To reenable the Context menu, set the value to 0. Log out and in again for this change to take effect.

How can I add a shortcut to launch a screen saver on the desktop?

Screen savers are just programs with a .SCR extension. To create a shortcut for a screen saver, perform the following:

1. Start Explorer (Win+E, or Start > Programs > NT Explorer).
2. Move to the %systemroot%\system32 directory (for example, d:\winnt\ system32).
3. Find the .SCR file of the screen saver. You could perform a search by choosing Tools > Find > Folders or Files. Type ***.scr** and unselect Include Subfolders. Then click Find Now.
4. When a list of filenames appears, right-click on one of them, drag it to the desktop, release the right mouse button, and select Create Shortcut(s) Here.
5. Next, right-click on the new shortcut and select Properties.
6. In the target box, add **-s** to the end (for example, C:\WINNT\system32\ sspipes.scr -s).
7. Click OK.

How can I stop and start Explorer (the shell)?

Explorer is just a process, so you can stop the Explorer process and start a new one. You should use caution with this, though. Also, you will lose the icons that are normally created by services on the taskbar when Explorer restarts.

1. Right-click on the taskbar and select Task Manager.
2. Click the Processes tab, select Explorer, and click End Process (See Figure 8-6).
3. Click the Applications tab and click New Task.
4. Enter the name **Explorer** and click OK.
5. Close Task Manager.

After you stop Explorer, it might automatically restart. If not, select the Applications tab and click New Task.

```
┌──────────────────────────────────────────────────────────────┐
│ 🖥 Windows NT Task Manager                        [ _ ][ □ ][ X ] │
│ File  Options  View  Help                                        │
│ ┌─────────────┬─────────────┬──────────────┐                    │
│ │ Applications │  Processes  │ Performance  │                    │
└──────────────────────────────────────────────────────────────┘
```

Image Name	PID	CPU	CPU Time	Mem Usage
mstask.exe	166	00	0:00:00	80 K
sens.exe	173	00	0:00:00	668 K
NDDEAGNT.EXE	192	00	0:00:00	20 K
alertsvc.exe	211	00	0:00:00	200 K
PCMWIN32.EXE	215	00	0:00:00	336 K
rundll32.exe	224	00	0:00:00	28 K
DDHELP.EXE	230	00	0:00:00	0 K
OSA.EXE	242	00	0:00:00	28 K
EXPLORER.EXE	250	00	0:01:19	3032 K
navapw32.exe	253	00	0:00:00	240 K
mswheel.exe	260	00	0:00:00	80 K
point32.exe	271	00	0:00:00	24 K
TASKMGR.EXE	279	01	0:00:00	2328 K
KEAVT.EXE	286	00	0:00:03	984 K
WINWORD.EXE	290	00	0:36:21	13864 K
Psp.exe	294	00	0:01:36	6576 K
systray.exe	300	00	0:00:00	20 K
KEASYS.EXE	306	00	0:00:00	460 K
CMD.EXE	310	00	0:00:00	16 K

End Process

Processes: 43   CPU Usage: 1%   Mem Usage: 95976K / 156552K

Figure 8-6. Stopping Explorer by using the Processes tab in Task Manager.

How do I enable the Mouse SnapTo?

Is it possible to configure Windows to move the mouse to the default button of dialog boxes to speed up general operations. To enable this, perform the following:

1. Start the Registry editor (REGEDIT.EXE).
2. Move to HKEY_CURRENT_USER\Control Panel\Mouse.
3. If the value SnapToDefaultButton exists, go to step 4; otherwise, choose New > String Value From Edit Value and enter the name SnapToDefaultButton (watch the case).
4. Double-click on the value and set it to 1. Click OK.
5. Close the Registry editor.
6. Log off and on for the change to take effect.

You can also accomplish this by using the Mouse control panel applet. Select the StepSavers tab and check the SnapTo box if you have the IntelliMouse software installed (see Figure 8-7). For other devices, select the Motion tab and check Snap Mouse to the Default Button in Dialog Box. Click Apply and then OK; you don't have to reboot.

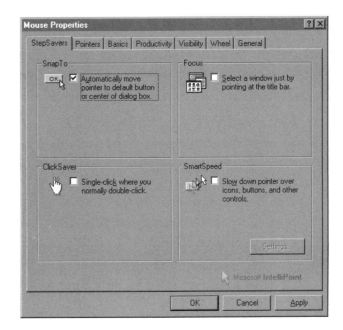

Figure 8-7. You can also configure other mouse options, such as Window Selection.

How do I enable X Windows-Style AutoRaise?

It is possible to configure Windows so a window comes into focus when you move the mouse over it.

1. Start the Registry editor (REGEDIT.EXE).
2. Move to HKEY_CURRENT_USER\Control Panel\Mouse.
3. If the value ActiveWindowTracking exists, go to step 4; otherwise, choose New > DWORD Value from Edit Value and enter the name **ActiveWindowTracking** (watch the case).
4. Double-click on the value and set to 1. Click OK.
5. Close the Registry editor.
6. Log off and on for the change to take effect.

How do I remove a template from the New menu?

If you select New—for example, from within Explorer—you are given a large list of document templates that have registered themselves on your machine.
   If you would like to trim away some of these, perform the following:

1. Start the Registry editor (REGEDIT.EXE).
2. Move to HKEY_CLASSES_ROOT.
3. Move to the file extension of the template you no longer want displayed (for example, .S3D for Simply 3D, .PSP for Paint Shop Pro, .DOC for Word).
4. If the template appears on the New menu, there will be a subkey, ShellNew. Select this key and press Del. Click YES to the confirmation.
5. Close the Registry editor.

The file extension will now be removed from the New menu (you have to restart Explorer if it is running so it reloads the Registry information).

I don't have the New item on my desktop context menu. Why?

If there is no New item when you right-click on the desktop, perform the following:

1. Start the Registry editor (REGEDIT.EXE).
2. Move to HKEY_CLASSES_ROOT\Directory\Background\shellex\ ContextMenuHandlers.
3. From the Edit menu, choose New > Key and enter **New**. Press Enter.
4. Move to New. Double-click on the default value and enter

    `{D969A300-E7FF-11d0-A93B-00A0C90F2719}.`

5. Click OK and close the Registry editor.

You should now have a New item on the Desktop context menu. You don't need to reboot.

How do I remove the Favorites branch of the Start menu?

If you wish to remove your Favorites from the Start menu, perform the following:

1. Start the Registry editor (REGEDIT.EXE).
2. Move to HKEY_CURRENT_USER\Software\Microsoft\Windows\ CurrentVersion\Policies\Explorer.
3. From the Edit menu, choose New > DWORD Value.
4. Enter the name **NoFavoritesMenu** and press Enter.
5. Double-click the new value and set it to 1. Click OK.
6. Close the Registry editor.

Log off and on again and the Favorites menu is gone.

How do I disable the Log-Off buttons?

If you wish to disable the Log-Off buttons on the Start menu or NT Security dialog, perform the following:

1. Start the Registry editor (REGEDIT.EXE).
2. Move to HKEY_CURRENT_USER\Software\Microsoft\Windows\CurrentVersion\Policies\Explorer.
3. From the Edit menu, choose New > DWORD Value.
4. Enter the name **NoLogoff** and press Enter.
5. Double-click the new value and set it to 1. Click OK.
6. Close the Registry editor.

The change takes immediate effect. To undo, simply set the value to 0.

How do I stop the default "Shortcut to" text added to new shortcuts?

When you create a shortcut, the text "Shortcut to" is automatically added to the name. You can stop this by performing the following Registry change:

1. Start the Registry editor (REGEDT32.EXE, **not** REGEDIT.EXE).
2. Move to HKEY_CURRENT_USER\Software\Microsoft\Windows\CurrentVersion\Explorer.
3. Double-click on Link.
4. Change the value to **00000000** and click OK.
5. Close the Registry editor.
6. Log off and on again for the change to take effect.

How can I get rid of the arrow over the shortcuts?

You can remove the overlay by using TweakUI.

1. Start the TweakUI Control Panel applet (Start > Settings > Control Panel > TweakUI).
2. Click the Explorer tab.
3. Select the arrow type (Arrow, Light Arrow, None, or Custom).
4. Click Apply and then OK.
5. Close the TweakUI applet.

You can also remove the arrow by editing the Registry, as follows:

1. Start the Registry editor (REGEDIT.EXE).
2. Move to HKEY_CLASSES_ROOT\lnkfile.
3. Select IsShortcut and choose Delete from the Edit menu.
4. Log off and on again for the change to take effect.

 ## How do I modify the shortcut arrow?

Perform the Registry change described here to modify the arrow used on shortcuts:

1. Start the Registry editor (REGEDT32.EXE or REGEDIT.EXE).
2. Move to HKEY_LOCAL_MACHINE\SOFTWARE\Microsoft\Windows\CurrentVersion\Explorer\Shell Icons.
3. Double-click on 29.
4. Change to the name of the icon and icon number. For example, shell32.dll,30 is a big arrow.
5. Choose OK and close the Registry editor. The change takes effect at the next logon.

To avoid the logoff, you could modify an icon-related entry and make the screen repaint by changing the background and then setting the background back to the original. For example, change HKEY_CURRENT_USER\Control Panel\ Desktop\WindowMetrics\Shell Icon Size.

A better way is to use TweakUI to perform the arrow change on shortcut icons.

How do I change the icon associated with a shortcut?

To modify the icon for a shortcut to something other than the target's icon, perform the following actions:

1. Right-click on the shortcut and choose Properties.
2. Click the Shortcut tab and click Change Icon.
3. Select your new icon. Several sets of icons you can use come with NT: SHELL32.DLL, PIFMGR.DLL, MORICONS.DLL, and PROGMAN.EXE.
4. Click OK and exit.

How can I set the default view for all drives and folders?

Set the view to what you want in Explorer (perhaps Details) and close the window while holding down the Ctrl key.

9 SYSTEM INFORMATION

Gathering information about your systems is a vital aid to performing diagnostics and upgrades. Following are some useful hints.

This chapter looks at ways to gather information about your machine by using built-in NT tools and third-party applications. It also looks at the familiar problem of non-expiry installations expiring.

How can I determine the role of my NT machine?

NT machines can have a number of roles, such as a Primary Domain Controller, a Backup Domain Controller, a standalone/member server, or just a workstation. The easiest way to determine the machine's role is to type the following command:

```
net accounts
```

At the bottom of the output, the computer role is shown as one of the following:

WORKSTATION: A normal NT workstation machine
SERVER: A standalone NT server machine
PRIMARY: A Primary Domain Controller (PDC)
BACKUP: A Backup Domain Controller (BDC)

241

How can I tell who has which files open on a machine?

To view which files are currently open and which user has them open, use

```
net file
```

The Net File command displays information in the form ID <path> <username> <# locks>, as follows:

ID	Path	User name	#Locks
9	D:\index.lnk	savillj	0
11	D:\john.lnk	savillj	0
23	D:\www.savilltech.com\images\me.gif	savillj	0
27	D:\www.savilltech.com\images\mcse.gif	savillj	0
31	D:\www.savilltech.com\images\mvp.gif	savillj	0
35	D:\www.savilltech.com\images\40179.JPG	savillj	0
39	D:\www.savilltech...\goldeneye.gif	savillj	0
43	D:\www.savilltech...\Rita1sml.jpg	savillj	0
47	D:\www.savilltech...\Rita2sml.jpg	savillj	0
49	D:\www.savilltech.com\me.html	savillj	0

The command completed successfully.

You can also delete a file lock by using Net File:

```
net file 47 /close
```

To use Net File (see Figure 9-1), you must have the server service running on the machine. Check Start > Settings > Control Panel > Services or use the Server Control Panel applet on the Domain Controller.

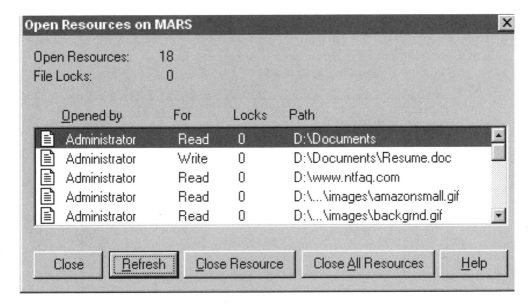

Figure 9-1. Along with showing the user who is opening the file, Net File shows the status (Read or Write).

You can get a freeware utility called Open File List (OFL) from http://www.merxsoft.com/; it provides more information. The best third-party applications I have found are NTHandle (a command-line file-use utility) and NTHandleEx (a GUI version of NTHandle). Both of these utilities are available from http://www.sysinternals.com.

 ## How do I view all of the applications and processes on the system?

You can use Task Manager, which is a standard part of NT. Right-click on the taskbar and select Task Manager. Then choose the Applications tab (see Figure 9-2). You can see that if you have a process that is not working, you can stop the process by selecting it and clicking End Task.

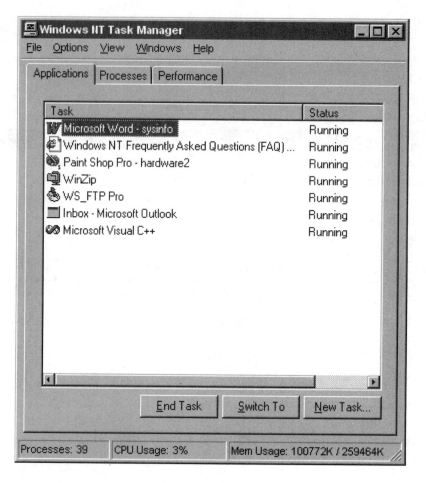

Figure 9-2. Viewing all of the applications on the Applications tab in Task Manager.

Selecting the Processes tab enables you to view all of the processes, and a wide selection of information is available about each of them. By default, the information shown is

- Process ID: Identification of the process
- CPU: Percentage of the CPU being used by the process
- CPU Time: Total amount of CPU used
- Mem Usage: Amount of memory currently being used
- Page Faults: The number of page faults

You can also view other items by choosing Select Columns from the View menu (see Figure 9-3). A whole host of information is shown.

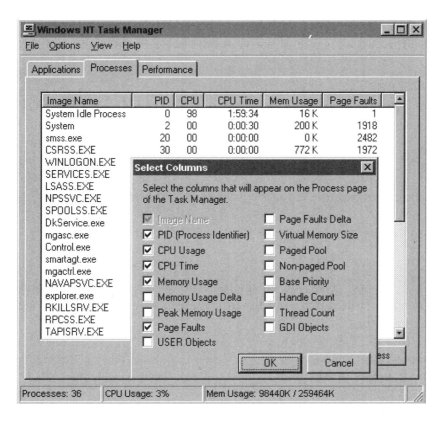

Figure 9-3. Select other process information to show in Task Manager.

There is also the PVIEW program that comes with Visual C++ and the NT Resource Kit. It shows thread and process details about the selected process, but this is overkill except for programmers. For command line viewing, you can use the TLIST command that comes with the Resource Kit to show the process ID, name, and executable.

Where can I get information about my machine?

Several utilities are available; however, WINMSD is good and can produce a full printed report about your computer, including IRQ and DMA settings for devices.

A command line version of WINMSD is called WINMSDP. It is a good idea to run this utility, which is part of the Windows NT Resource Kit, regularly.

How can I tell when NT was last started?

From the command prompt, enter the following command:

```
net statistics workstation
```

At the top, the output says "statistics since…." You need to be quick with Ctrl+S to pause the output (Ctrl+Q starts it again). Now you get the time since the workstation service was started, but the time up will be incorrect if someone has performed one of these:

```
net stop workstation
net start workstation
```

The time NT has been up is also displayed from the PVIEW utility, and a set of applications called 3UPTIMES displays this information. These applications are available from http://barnyard.syr.edu/~vefatica/ (including both a command line and a Windows version). Be aware that 3UPTIMES gives incorrect information if the system has been up for more than 50 days.

The last line of output from the Windows NT Resource Kit utility SRVINFO.EXE displays the total uptime, as well, in this format:

```
System Up Time: 24 Hr 3 Min 29 Sec
```

ElWiz from http://www.heysoft.de/nt/eventlog/ep-elwiz.htm always gives the right uptime (among lots of other useful information), and it is free, too. System Internals now provides an uptime utility obtainable at http://www.sysinternals.com/misc.htm.

FAQ 9.6   I have lost my NT Installation CD-ROM case that had the Key number. How can I find out what it is?

The easiest way is to run WINMSD (Start > Run > Winmsd) and look at the Version tab (see Figure 9-4). On the line above the register information is a number in the form of 50036-xxx-yyyyyyy-71345. The xxx-yyyyyyy is the number on the back of the CD case.

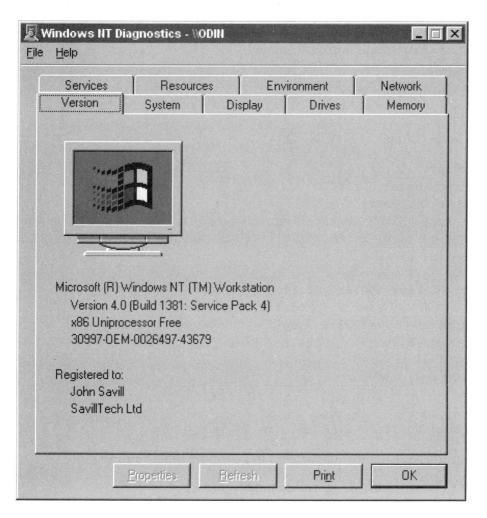

Figure 9-4. WINMSD in action.

This is also the same as the registry entry HKEY_LOCAL_MACHINE\
SOFTWARE\Microsoft\Windows NT\CurrentVersion\ProductId.

 ## How can I get detailed system information from the command prompt?

The Windows NT Server Resource Kit supplies SRVINFO.EXE. This is an excellent tool for gaining a picture of your system, including details about

- Version
- Service packs and hotfixes installed
- Services
- Domain information
- Hardware

Here is an example of SRVINFO:

```
srvinfo
Server Name: GARFIELD
Security: Users
NT Type: WinNT WorkStation
Version: 4.0, Build = 1381, CSD = Service Pack 4, RC 1.99
Domain: SVILLUK
PDC: \\SVLON1
IP Address: 160.82.220.19
CPU[0]: x86 Family 6 Model 3 Stepping 3
Hotfixes: [Q147222]:
Drive: [FileSys] [ Size ] [ Free ]
Services:
[Stopped] Alerter
..
..
System Up Time: 23 Hr 51 Min 43 Sec
```

The utility has a number of switches to give more or less information:

SRVINFO [[|-ns|-d|-v|-s] \\computer_name]

-ns: Do NOT show any service information.
-d: Show service drivers and service.

-v: Get version info for Exchange and SQL.
-s: Show shares.

 # How can I tell when NT was installed?
9.8

NT stores its install time—in seconds from January 1, 1970—in the registry key HKEY_LOCAL_MACHINE\SOFTWARE\Microsoft\Windows NT\ CurrentVersion\InstallDate. I've written a utility you can use to display this (in converted form) along with some other information (see Figure 9-5). You can download it from http://www.savilltech.com/download/wininfo.zip.

```
Windows Information                                    [x]

Windows NT Version          Microsoft Windows 2000
Build Number                1946
Service Pack                Not available
Plus Version Number         Not Available
Processor Type              Uniprocessor Free
Product Type                Windows Terminal Server Edition
Installation type           Time Limited Version (240 days)
Registered Organisation     SavillTech Ltd
Registered Owner            John Savill
Installation Date           18 December 1998, 22:40:17
Source Path                 G:\build1946\i386
System Root                 E:\WINNT


Copyright © 1999 SavillTech Ltd, http://www.savilltech.com
```

Figure 9-5. Basic information such as build, installation date, and type are shown in the Windows Information utility. By the time this book is released, it will include other information.

How can I tell if my NT installation is a 120-day evaluation or full?

If you install NT by using setup disks created with an evaluation CD, your installation will expire, even if you enter a fully registered product ID code. Microsoft does not provide a method to tell if your installation will expire, and only gives you one hour's notice before shutting down, which is very annoying.

The Win Info utility from http://www.savilltech.com/download/wininfo.zip shows the value of Installation Type as either

```
Full version
Time limited version (xxx days)
```

10 THE REGISTRY

The Registry is the core of Windows NT and provides a centralized storage area for both operating system and application configuration information. Editing the Registry allows many hidden parts of NT's functionality to be realized. For successful management of a Windows NT environment, you first need a basic understanding of the Registry and its workings.

Backing up the Registry is vital and is covered in Chapter 12, Backups. Before you make any change to the Registry, you should make sure you have an up-to-date backup.

What is the Registry?

10.1

Originally there were .INI files in Windows; however, the problems with .INI files are many, including size limitations, no standard layout, slow access, and no network support. The .INI files were used to store configuration and initialization instructions for the operating system and some applications.

Windows 3.1 had a Registry that was stored in the file REG.DAT and could be viewed by using REGEDIT.EXE. It was used for DDE, OLE, and File Manager integration.

The Registry is at the heart of Windows NT and is where nearly all information is stored. It is split into a number of subtrees, each starting with HKEY_ to indicate a handle that can be used by a program. The subtrees are listed in Table 10-1.

Table 10.1. Registry Subtrees

HKEY_LOCAL_MACHINE	Contains information about the hardware configuration and installed software.
HKEY_CLASSES_ROOT	A link to HKEY_LOCAL_MACHINE\SOFTWARE\Classes. Contains links between applications and file types (file associations) as well as information about OLE.
HKEY_CURRENT_CONFIG	A link to HKEY_LOCAL_MACHINE\SYSTEM\CurrentControlSet\Hardware Profiles\Current. Contains information about the current configuration.
HKEY_CURRENT_USER	A link to HKEY_USERS\<SID of User>. Contains information about the currently logged on users, such as environment, network connections, printers.
HKEY_USERS	Contains information about actively loaded user profiles, including .default, which is the default user profile.

Each of the subtrees has a number of keys, which in turn have a number of subkeys. Each key or subkey can have values containing three parts:

1. The name of the value (for example, Wallpaper)
2. The type of the value (for example, REG_SZ, which is a text string)
3. The actual value of the value (for example, c:\winnt\savilltech.bmp)

To edit the Registry, a number of tools are available. The two core utilities are REGEDT32.EXE and REGEDIT.EXE. REGEDIT.EXE has better search facilities, but does not support all of the Windows NT Registry value types and is basically an NT port of the Windows 9x Registry editor.

Also supplied with Windows NT Server is POLEDIT.EXE, which is normally used to create policy files for domains. It can also be used to edit the local

Registry (although it is limited to the settings defined in certain template or adm files).

If you want to just have a look around the Registry, perform the following:

1. Start a Registry editor (REGEDIT.EXE or REGEDT32.EXE).
2. In REGEDT32.EXE, you can set the Registry to read-only mode (Options > Read Only Mode), which means you won't corrupt anything (see Figure 10-1).
3. Select the HKEY_USERS subkey.
4. Move to .default > Control Panel > Desktop, where you can see a number of values in the right-hand pane. One of them is wallpaper—the background that is displayed before you log on.

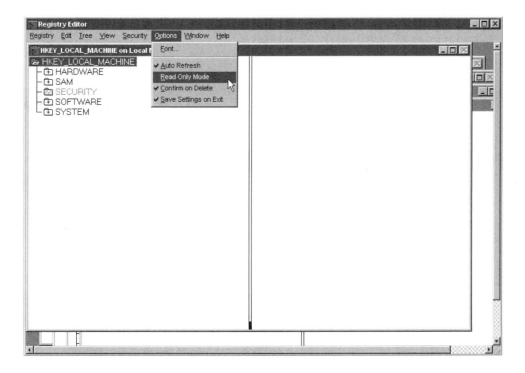

Figure 10-1. Setting REGEDT32.EXE to read-only mode.

What files make up the Registry, and where are they?

The files that make up the Registry are listed here. They are stored in %systemroot%/system32/config directory (see Figure 10-2).

1. **SAM:** HKEY_LOCAL_MACHINE\SAM
2. **SECURITY:** HKEY_LOCAL_MACHINE\Security
3. **SOFTWARE:** HKEY_LOCAL_MACHINE\Software
4. **SYSTEM:** HKEY_LOCAL_MACHINE\System & HKEY_CURRENT_CONFIG
5. **DEFAULT:** HKEY_USERS\.DEFAULT
6. **NTUSER.DAT:** HKEY_CURRENT_USER (this file is stored in %systemroot%\profiles\%username%)

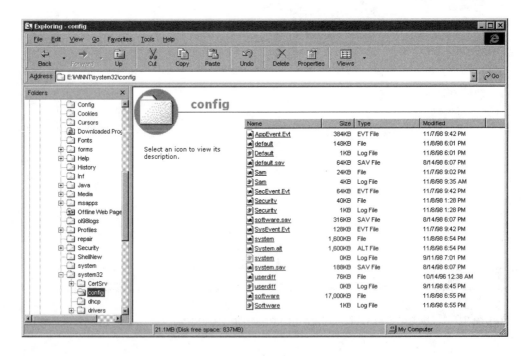

Figure 10-2. Using Explorer to view the files that make up the Registry.

There are also other files with different extensions for some of them, as follows:

.ALT: Contains a backup copy of the HKEY_LOCAL_MACHINE\System hive. Only System has an .ALT file.
.LOG: A log of changes to the keys and values for the hive.
.SAV: A copy of the hive as it looks at the end of the text mode stage in setup.

How do I restrict access to the Registry editor?

The Registry editor is a very powerful tool. A user with access to the Registry via an editor could undo any restrictions you have imposed.

To remove a user's ability to use Registry tools, perform the following on either the profile server (if you use roaming profiles, the user's profile will be stored here) or a local machine (if you use local profiles):

1. Start the Registry editor (REGEDT32.EXE).
2. Highlight HKEY_USERS and load Hive from the Registry menu.
3. Browse to the profile directory of the user you want to restrict and select NTUSER.DAT.
4. When prompted for Key Name, input the user's name.
5. Navigate to \Software\Microsoft\Windows\CurrentVersion\Policies.
6. If no System subkey exists, choose Add Key. Then choose Add Value of DisableRegistryTools (under the System key), using type REG_DWORD, and set it to 1.
7. Unload Hive from the Registry menu.

If you want to set this restriction for everyone or for a certain group of users, you can use a system policy (for more information on system policies, see Chapter 15, System Policies). The preferred method is to set the key under the Default User, System, Restrictions branch (see Figure 10-3).

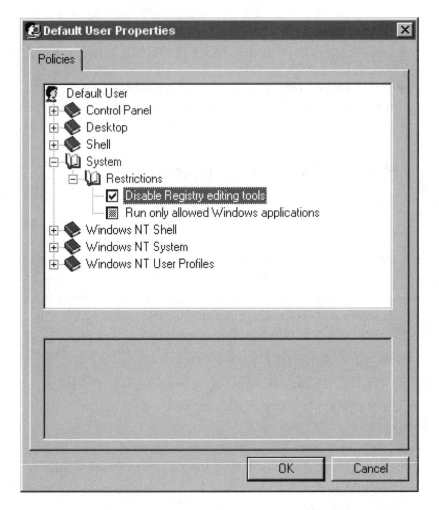

Figure 10-3. Disabling Registry tools for users.

 What is the maximum Registry size?

The maximum size is 102MB; however, the issue is slightly more complicated than this.

The Registry entry that controls the maximum size of the Registry is HKEY_LOCAL_MACHINE\SYSTEM\CurrentControlSet\Control\ RegistrySizeLimit. By default, this entry does not exist, so you need to create it.

1. Start the Registry editor (REGEDIT.EXE).
2. Move to the HKEY_LOCAL_MACHINE\SYSTEM\ CurrentControlSet\Control key.
3. From the Edit menu, select New > DWORD Value and enter the name **RegistrySizeLimit**.
4. Double-click the new entry and enter a value.

The minimum size is 4MB. If you enter anything less than this in the Registry, it will be forced up to 4MB. The maximum is 80% of the paged pool, or 102MB, which is 80% of 128MB, the maximum size of the paged pool. If no entry is made, the maximum size is 25% of the paged pool. (The paged pool is an area of physical memory used for system data that can be written to disk when not in use.)

An important point to note is that the RegistrySizeLimit is a maximum, not an allocation. Setting a high value does not reserve the space and does not guarantee that the space will be available.

You can also configure the Registry size by using the System Control Panel applet (see Figure 10-4). Click on the Performance tab and set the maximum Registry size there. You then need to reboot. This is the safest option and therefore the recommended method.

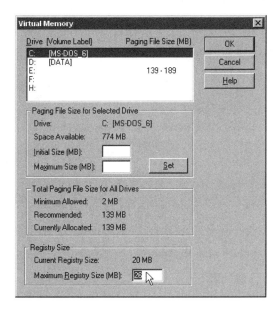

Figure 10-4. Modifying the maximum Registry size on a system by using the System Control Panel applet.

For more information, see Knowledge Base Article Q124594, available on the Microsoft Support Web site at http://support.microsoft.com/support/.

There is another complication. During early boot, NTLDR loads some code, allocates working memory, and reads in parts of the Registry. All of this has to fit in the first 16MB of physical memory, regardless of how much memory is physically installed.

Following are some related problems:

- The Registry contains wasted space (sometimes a lot). Try saving the SYSTEM key from REGEDT32 and then comparing the saved file size with that of the SYSTEM hive in \%systemroot%\system32\config\. On one machine, I reduced the SYSTEM hive from 9,720KB to 864KB in this manner.

- Creation of the LastKnownGood Control Set (usually #2) soon after boot almost doubles the size of the file. Depending on circumstances—such as reclaimable space in the "gas" or wasted space—additions to the Registry might require new space to be allocated beyond the end of the combined Current and LastKnownGood SYSTEM hive. After the next boot, another LastKnownGood is tacked onto the end of the file, adding about a third to its size. In my case, a Registry with a "true" size of 4MB was thus inflated to 12MB and caused boot failure. To turn this off and prevent creation of the LastKnownGood Control Set, use REGEDT32 to add the value "ReportBootOk:REG_SZ:0" [zero] to HKEY_Local_Machine\ SOFTWARE\Microsoft\WindowsNT\CurrentVersion\Winlogon.

Following are a number of ways to get rid of the excess space, but try these only after a full system backup and only if you are confident of what you are doing.

- If FAT, merely boot from a DOS floppy and then replace the SYSTEM file.
- If NTFS, boot from another NT partition and replace the file in the previous partition.
- Use REGBACK/REGREST from the NT Resource Kit (this might be easiest of all).
- Run RDISK, shut down the system, and repair it.
- Use ERD Commander from Winternals Software.

If a boot fails because the 16MB limit with NTLDR is exceeded, no dump can be produced and Microsoft will not solve the problem. This 16MB problem has not been remedied in Windows 2000.

Should I use REGEDIT.EXE or REGEDT32.EXE?

You can use either for NT. REGEDIT does have a few limitations, the most significant being that it does not support the full REGEDIT data types, such as REG_MULTI_SZ. If you edit this type of data with REGEDIT, it will change the file type and possibly corrupt any contained data.

REGEDIT.EXE is based on the Windows 95 version and has features that REGEDT32.EXE lacks (such as Search). In general, REGEDIT.EXE is nicer to work with. Also, REGEDIT.EXE shows your current position in the Registry at the bottom of the window, which helps you keep track of where you are when you're working deep in tree branches.

REGEDIT.EXE allows searches on the Registry, which REGEDT32.EXE does not support. On the other hand, REGEDT32.EXE allows you to set permissions on elements of the Registry, which REGEDIT.EXE does not support.

How do I restrict access to a remote Registry?

Access to a remote Registry is controlled by the Access Control List (ACL) on the key WINREG, which basically is a list of who can perform what actions. The following steps show you how to control access for a given user.

1. Start the Registry editor (REGEDT32.EXE). You have to use REGEDT32.EXE and not REGEDIT.EXE because you will be modifying permissions on keys that are only supported by the native NT Registry editor.
2. Move to HKEY_LOCAL_MACHINE\SYSTEM\CurrentControlSet\Control\SecurePipeServers.
3. Check for a key called WINREG. If it does not exist, create it by using Edit > Add Key.
4. Click on the WINREG key to select it.
5. From the Security menu, select Permissions.

6. Click the Add button and give the user read access.

7. Click on the user and select Special Access (see Figure 10-5).

8. Double-click on the user and select which actions the user can perform.

9. Click OK when finished.

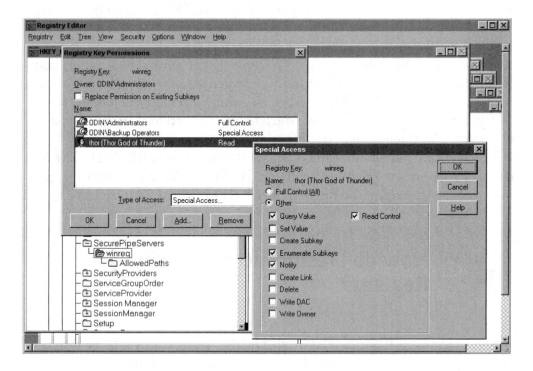

Figure 10-5. Setting special access for a user.

It is possible to set up certain keys to be accessible even if the user does not have access (see Figure 10-6). You do this by editing the value HKEY_LOCAL_ MACHINE\SYSTEM\CurrentControlSet\Control\SecurePipeServers\ winreg\AllowedPaths\Machine (use REGEDT32.EXE). You can add paths to this list, with one path per line.

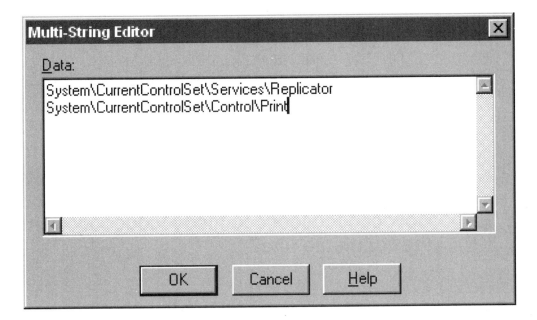

Figure 10-6. Exceptions to the user restriction.

FAQ 10.7 How can I tell what changes have been made to the Registry?

By using the REGEDIT.EXE program, it is possible to export portions of the Registry. This feature can be used as follows to find changes:

1. Start the Registry editor (REGEDIT.EXE).
2. Select the key you want to monitor.
3. From the Registry menu, choose Export Registry File.
4. Enter a filename (if you want to export the whole Registry, just select Export Range > All) and click OK.
5. Perform the change (install some software or change a system parameter, for example).
6. Rerun steps 2 through 4, using a different filename.
7. The export files are just text files and as such can be run through a comparison utility (for example, WINDIFF.EXE, which is supplied with the Resource Kit).

8. If you are using WINDIFF, choose Compare Files from the File menu. At the prompt, select the two files you want to compare.

9. When WINDIFF is finished with the comparison, a summary is displayed. If there are differences, you can view the changes by double-clicking on the message.

10. Press F8 to view the next change (or choose Next Change from the View menu).

11. You have now found what changed.

 ## How can I delete a Registry value/key from the command line?

By using the Windows NT Resource Kit Supplement 2 utility REG.EXE, you can delete a Registry value from the command line or batch file with this command:

```
reg delete HKLM\Software\test
```

This deletes the HKEY_LOCAL_MACHINE\Software\test value. When you enter the command, you are asked if you really want to delete. Press Y to confirm. To avoid the confirmation, add /f to the command, as follows:

```
reg delete HKLM\Software\test /f
```

A full list of the codes to be used with reg delete follows:

HKCR	HKEY_CLASSES_ROOT
HKCU	HKEY_CURRENT_USER
HKLM	HKEY_LOCAL_MACHINE
HKU	HKEY_USERS
HKCC	HKEY_CURRENT_CONFIG

To delete an entry on a remote machine, add the name of the machine, \\<machine name>, like this:

```
reg delete HKLM\Software\test \\johnpc
```

An updated REG.EXE is available from ftp://ftp.microsoft.com/bussys/winnt/winnt-public/reskit/nt40/i386/reg_x86.exe.

How can I audit changes to the Registry?

By using the REGEDT32.EXE utility, it is possible to audit changes in certain parts of the registry. I should note that any type of auditing is very sensitive lately. To avoid any legal problems, you might want to add some sort of warning to let people know their changes are being audited.

1. Start the registry editor (REGEDT32.EXE).
2. Select the key you wish to audit (for example, HKEY_LOCAL_MACHINE\Software).
3. From the Security menu, choose Auditing.
4. If you want subkeys to be audited, check Audit Permission on Existing Subkeys.
5. Click the Add button and select the users you want to audit. Then click Add and click OK.
6. The selected names now appear in the Names box, where you can select which events will be audited, whether success or failure.
7. When you have filled in all of the information, click OK.

You need to make sure that Auditing for File and Object Access is enabled (choose User Manager > Policies > Audit).

To view the information, use the Event Viewer and look at the Security information.

How can I clean up/remove invalid entries from the Registry?

Microsoft has released a utility called RegClean, which can go through your machine's Registry and delete any unused or unnecessary keys. The current version is 4.1a, and you can download it from http://support.microsoft.com/download/support/mslfiles/RegClean.exe.

After the download, click on the executable to check your Registry. When the check is complete, you are asked if you want to fix errors. Click the Fix Errors button or click the Cancel button to exit (see Figure 10-7).

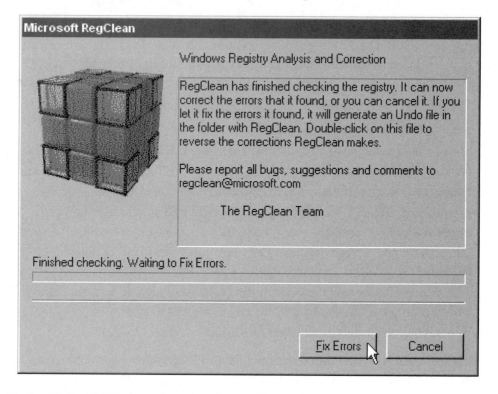

Figure 10-7. Fixing errors found with RegClean.

RegClean creates an uninstall file in the directory where the image is located. The name of the file is Undo <machine name> <yyyymmdd> <hhmmss>.reg. For example, use this:

```
Undo workstation 19980320 104323.reg
```

To undo the changes, double-click this file (or single-click, depending on your configuration). For more information, see http://support.microsoft.com/support/kb/articles/q147/7/69.asp.

When I make changes to HKEY_LOCAL_MACHINE/Hardware, they are lost on reboot. Why?

HKEY_LOCAL_MACHINE/Hardware is a volatile key that is re-created by the system at boot time. This means any settings—such as Access Control Lists (ACLs)—are lost.

What data types are available in the Registry?

Table 7-3 lists the data types supported by REGEDT32.EXE. REGEDIT.EXE does not support REG_EXPAND_SZ or REG_MULTI_SZ.

Table 7-3. Data types supported by REGEDT32.EXE

REG_BINARY	Raw binary data.
REG_DWORD	A double word (4 bytes). It can be displayed in binary, hexadecimal, or decimal format.
REG_EXPAND_SZ	An expandable text string that contains a variable (for example, %systemroot%).
REG_MULTI_SZ	A multiple line string. Each "line" is separated by a null.
REG_SZ	A text string.

Several other Registry data types are used by NT, such as REG_FULL_RESOURCE_DESCRIPTOR and REG_LINK, but these are not visible by using the Registry editors.

How can I automate updates to the Registry?

There are two main methods you can use to create scripts that can be run to automate updates to the Registry. The first is to create a .REG file, which you can then run by using this command:

```
regedit /s <reg file>
```

The format of the file follows:

REGEDIT4

[<key name>]	
"<value name>"="<value>"	A string value
"<value name>"=hex:<value>	A binary value
"<value name>"=dword:<value>	A DWORD value

Here's an example of a script that would set the default background and color before anyone logs on:

```
REGEDIT4

[HKEY_USERS\.DEFAULT\Control Panel\Desktop]
"Wallpaper"="E:\\WINNT\\savtech.bmp"
"TileWallpaper"="0"

[HKEY_USERS\.DEFAULT\Control Panel\Colors]
"Background"="0 0 0"
```

The second method is to use a Windows 95 style .INF file, which can be run by using this command:

```
rundll32 syssetup,SetupInfObjectInstallAction DefaultInstall
128 <inf file>
```

The format of the file is as follows:

```
[Version]
Signature = "$Windows NT$"
```

```
Provider=%Provider%
[Strings]
Provider="SavillTech Ltd"
[DefaultInstall]
AddReg = AddReg
DelReg = DelReg
UpdateInis = UpdateInis
[AddReg]
[DelReg]
[UpdateInis]
```

The AddReg section adds or updates Registry entries, the DelReg section specifies values that should be deleted, and UpdateInis allows you to modify text-based .INI files.

Following are the keys to be used:

HKCR   HKEY_CLASSES_ROOT
HKCU   HKEY_CURRENT_USER
HKLM   HKEY_LOCAL_MACHINE
HKU   HKEY_USERS

The following file is an .INF file, which performs the same as the .REG file described earlier:

```
[Version]
Signature = "$Windows NT$"
[DefaultInstall]
AddReg = AddReg
[AddReg]
HKU,".DEFAULT\Control
Panel\Colors","Background",0000000000,"0 0 0"
HKU,".DEFAULT\Control
Panel\Desktop","Wallpaper",0000000000,"E:\WINNT\savtech.bmp"
HKU,".DEFAULT\Control
Panel\Desktop","TileWallpaper",0000000000,"1"
```

You can generate .INF files automatically by using the SYSDIFF utility if you have a difference file (sysdiff /inf <name of difference file> <dir to create to>).

FAQ 10.14 How do I apply a .REG file without the Success message?

To apply a .REG file (a Registry information file), you would usually enter the following from the command prompt:

```
regedit <Registry file>.reg
```

This applies the change and gives the confirmation message seen in Figure 10-8.

Figure 10-8. The update confirmation dialog.

If you would like to avoid this confirmation message and apply the change silently, use the /s switch, like this:

```
regedit /s <Registry file>.reg
```

11 RECOVERY

As with any other operating system, NT is prone to problems whether they are caused by system corruption or user error. When an error occurs, you need recovery methods and functionality to help you resolve the problems.

In this chapter are some of the most important recoverability steps. The first one—creating an Emergency Repair Disk—is not optional. Every system should have a recent ERD.

In addition to normal single-machine recovery options, this chapter looks at domain recovery options and the complex relationship between a PDC (Primary Domain Controller) and its BDCs (Backup Domain Controllers).

How do I create an Emergency Repair Disk?

4.0 ONLY

11.1

The Emergency Repair Disk (ERD) contains details of your Registry, disk, and user configuration and, in the event of a corruption, can restore your settings. But obviously it's only as up-to-date as you make it, so every time you make a change to your system, you should update your ERD.

From the Start Menu, select Run and type **RDISK**. Click on Update Repair Info to re-create the repair information stored in the winnt\repair directory (see Figure 11-1).

When asked if you want to create a repair disk, insert a blank formatted disk and choose Yes.

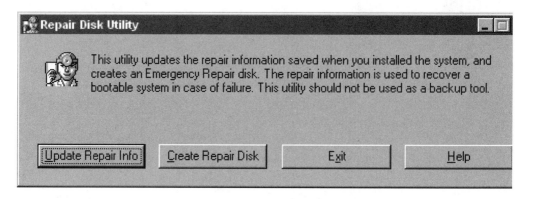

Figure 11-1. Running the RDISK utility.

If you just click Create Repair Disk, you'll create a disk but won't update the repair information, so you'll keep updating the disk with the old information.

RDISK /s updates the information in the %systemroot%/repair and also the SAM and SECURITY keys. Permissions on the repair should be strict, because a user with access to the files could create a repair disk and use it to crack the system passwords.

If you want to update the information in the %systemroot%\repair directory without creating a disk or requiring input, use the /s- qualifier, like this:

```
RDISK /s-
```

2000 ONLY

FAQ 11.2 Where is RDISK in Windows 2000?

The RDISK.EXE utility has been replaced with an option in the NTBACKUP.EXE utility.

1. Start NTBACKUP.EXE (Start > Run > NTBACKUP.EXE).
2. From the Tools menu, choose Create an Emergency Repair Disk (see Figure 11-2).

3. Insert a blank formatted disk in drive A: and click OK.

4. Click OK to the completion message and click OK again to end.

Recovery disks can no longer be used to restore user accounts. You need to backup/restore the Active Directory, which is covered in Chapter 12, Backups.

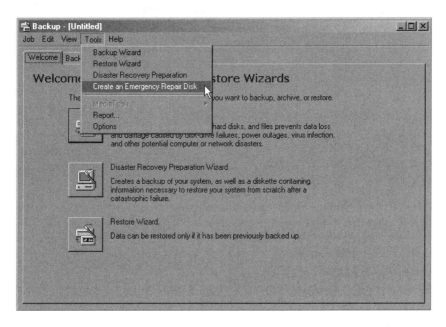

Figure 11-2. Creating a repair disk in Windows 2000.

4.0 ONLY

How do I create an NT boot disk?

NT usually boots off of the active partition; however, you can create a disk that has the basic files needed for OS startup. To create the disk, follow the steps given here. This disk is useful in the event of an active partition problem that leaves the system unbootable.

1. Format the disk, using NT, so the boot sector of the disk can find NTLDR (puts NT boot loaded into sector 0).

2. Copy NTLDR, NTDETECT.COM, and BOOT.INI.

3. If you have a non-SCSI-enabled BIOS and use a SCSI adapter, you also need NTBOOTDD.SYS. For example, if you have an AHA154X.SYS SCSI driver, copy it to the disk as NTBOOTDD.SYS.

You can boot off of this disk, which looks at the existing NT partition and loads the kernel as usual. This is useful for a mirrored system, because you can edit the BOOT.INI file and change the disk. For example, if the mirror is the first partition on the second NT disk, the following

```
multi(0)disk(0)rdisk(0)partition(1)\WINNT="Windows NT
Workstation Version 4.00"
```

could be changed to

```
multi(0)disk(0)rdisk(1)partition(1)\WINNT="Windows NT
Workstation Version 4.00"
```

Notice that the RDISK parameter has changed. On an IDE system, this is the physical disk number (starting at 0 for disk 1).

 11.4 # I get the error "Can't find NTLDR." Why?

NTLDR is a core file that must be in the root directory. If it cannot be found, other files might also be missing. To fix this problem, perform the following:

1. Boot the system with a DOS bootable floppy disk (if it is a FAT partition). If it is an NTFS partition, use the NT boot disk discussed in Question 11-3.
2. In the i386 directory of the CD-ROM, find the file NTLDR._, which is the compressed version of NTLDR.
3. You can expand this file by using EXPAND.EXE, which comes with DOS and Windows for Workgroups:

```
expand d:\i386\ntldr._ c:\ntldr
```

How do I recover a lost Administrator password?

If there are no other accounts in the Administrator group, the only way to recover a lost Administrator password is to reinstall NT into a new directory (not the same one, because it will upgrade and see the old password), and it will let you enter a new Administrator password. If you have an old ERD for which you knew the password at time of making, you could use this to restore the SAM and security portions of the Registry.

There is also a piece of software (LockSmith) from http://www.winternals.com/ that can break into an NT system and change any password. The software is not free—it costs around US$100. Their new product, ERD Professional, can also change passwords and is available from the same site.

A similar piece of software is available from http://www.mirider.com/. With NTAccess, you can boot off of a set of disks and change the Administrator password.

The following instructions require a second installation of NT on the machine for which you have forgotten the password. This method uses the SRVANY.EXE Resource Kit utility.

1. Install a second copy of NT onto the machine into a different directory/drive (it has to be only a minimal installation) and boot into this installation.
2. Copy SRVANY.EXE from the Resource Kit into a directory (for example, c:\temp).
3. Start the Registry editor (REGEDT32.EXE).
4. Move to HKEY_LOCAL_MACHINE and select the root.
5. From the Open menu, select Load Hive.
6. Move to %systemroot%\system32\config of the **main** NT installation. In other words, if your main installation (the one whose password you are trying to change) is installed at d:\winnt, move to d:\winnt\system32\config.
7. Choose System > Open.
8. When you are asked for a key name, enter **Mainreg** and click OK.
9. Select the Select branch and write down the Default value, 0xn (for example, 0x1). This will be used to load the ControlSet00n.

10. Move to HKEY_LOCAL_MACHINE\Mainreg\ControlSet00n\Services\Spooler and take note of the ImagePath value (it is usually %SystemRoot%\system32\spoolss.exe).

11. Change ImagePath to c:\temp\srvany.exe (or wherever you copied the file) and click OK.

12. Move to Parameters and add a Value of type REG_SZ called Application. Then double-click the new value and set it to

```
%systemroot%\system32\net.exe
```

13. Add another Value of type REG_SZ called AppParameters. Double-click the new value and set it to

```
user Administrator password
```

14. Move back to HKEY_LOCAL_MACHINE\Mainreg and choose Open > Unload Hive. Click Yes to the confirmation.

15. You should now reboot and boot off of your original NT installation. Wait a few minutes and then log on as the Administrator with a password of **password**.

You now need to do the following to correct the changes you've made:

1. Start the Registry editor (REGEDT32.EXE).

2. Move to HKEY_LOCAL_MACHINE\SYSTEM\CurrentControlSet\Services\Spooler\Parameters and delete Application and AppParameters values.

3. Move down to HKEY_LOCAL_MACHINE\SYSTEM\CurrentControlSet\Services\Spoole and change ImagePath back to its original value (%SystemRoot%\system32\spoolss.exe).

You may now delete the second installation of NT if you wish and remove it from the boot menu (edit BOOT.INI after removing the hidden, read-only, and system attributes by using **attrib c:\boot.ini -r -s -h**).

All this actually does is change the spooler service to use the SRVANY.EXE program, which runs NET as the service with parameters "user Administrator password." This is the same as typing "net user Administrator <password>", which is a way to change the password. Check the Resource Kit for more information on SRVANY.

I have set a drive to no access and now no one can access it. What can I do?

Log on as an Administrator and then perform the following:

1. Start Explorer (Run > Explorer).
2. Right-click on the drive and choose Properties.
3. Select the Security tab and click on Ownership.
4. Click Take Ownership.
5. The message will be displayed "You do not have access to the directory, do you wish to set the protection to Full Access?" You should click Yes.

With Service Pack 4 installed, the procedure is slightly different because the owner can now be set to a user (see Figure 11-3).

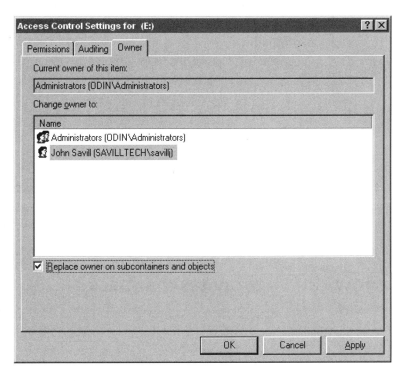

Figure 11-3. Setting ownership with Service Pack 4 installed.

1. Start Explorer (Run > Explorer).
2. Right-click on the drive as before and choose Properties.
3. Select the Security tab and click Advanced.
4. Select the Owner tab.
5. Select the new owner and check the box for Replace Owner on Subcontainers.
6. Click Apply.
7. Click OK and close all dialog boxes.

 ## If I copy a file with Explorer or from the command line, the permissions get lost. Why?

The only time a file keeps its permissions is if it is moved on the same partition. If it is copied, it inherits the protection of the owning directory (a move across drives is a Copy and Delete). Also, FAT does not support permissions, so anything copied to FAT loses protections.

If you wish the files to keep their permissions, you can use the Resource Kit command line tool SCOPY.EXE. The basic usage is

```
scopy <source> <destination> [/o] [/a] [/s]
```

where

/o   Copies owner security information.
/a   Copies auditing information. Requires that you have the Manage Auditing User Right on both the source and destination computers.
/s   Copies all files in subdirectories.

How can I get my taskbar back?

Sometimes Explorer will crash and not restart, leaving you with no taskbar. To restart Explorer and get your taskbar back, just press Ctrl+Alt+Del. Then select Task Manager, click the Applications tab, select New Task, and type **Explorer**.

You might wonder how NT can run without Explorer, but Explorer is just the shell—the interface, not the main operating system kernel. It's possible to actually change the shell to other applications.

I get the error "NTOSKRNL.EXE missing or corrupt" on bootup. Why?

This is usually due to an error in the BOOT.INI file. The entry for NT is either missing or incorrect. Edit the BOOT.INI file and check that the entry for NT is correct. For example, the entry for an IDE disk should look something like this:

```
multi(0)disk(0)rdisk(0)partition(2)\winnt="Windows NT
workstation"
```

Check that the disk and partition are correct. If you have recently added a new disk or altered the partitions, try changing the disk() and partition() values. If you are sure everything in BOOT.INI is OK, the actual file might be corrupt, so copy NTOSKRNL.EXE off of the installation CD onto the %systemroot%/system32 directory.

4.0 ONLY

How do I configure Directory Replication?

Directory Replication is the process of replicating directories and their contents from one machine to one or more other machines. The only machines that can be export servers are Windows NT Server machines. An import server can be an NT server, NT workstation, or OS/2 LAN Manager machine.

The main use for Directory Replication is for the export of login scripts from the PDC to the BDC(s), where the PDC is the export server and the BDC the import server. This means when you log in, the BDC can supply the login script as well as authentication of the user, leaving the PDC free. You must add an account that will be used for the Directory Replication and name it RepUser (you cannot use the name Replicator because there is a user group of this name). The following explains this:

1. Start User Manager for Domains (Start > Programs > Administrative Programs > User Manager for Domains).
2. From the User menu, choose New User.
3. Name the user RepUser, with a full name and description. Set the password.
4. Unselect User Must Change Password at Next Logon and select Password Never Expires.
5. Click Groups and add to Backup Operators group.
6. Click Hours and ensure that the user has 24 hours for all days.
7. Close User Manager for Domains.

The user has been added to the domain, and you now need to configure the export server.

1. Log on to the Export Server machine, the Primary Domain Controller, as an Administrator.
2. Start the Services Control Panel applet (Start > Settings > Control Panel > Services).
3. Select Directory Replicator and click Startup. Select Automatic (see Figure 11-4).
4. For Log On As, click the continuation (...) button. Select the RepUser account and click Add.
5. Type in the password you set for the RepUser and click OK.
6. When you click OK, you should see a message "User <domain>\Repuser has been granted the Logon as a Service right and added to the local Replicator local group."
7. Close the Services control panel applet.
8. Double-click the Server Control Panel applet and click the Replication button.
9. In the export, the default shows %systemroot%/system32/Repl/Export, which is where login scripts should be held. Clear any entries in the Export or Import Machine list.
10. Make sure Export Directories and Import Directories are checked, and close the Replication applet (see Figure 11-5).

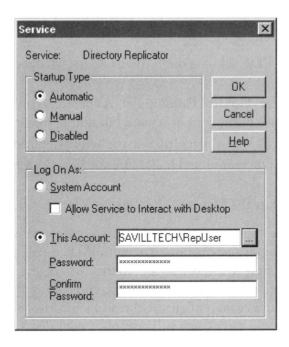

Figure 11-4. Setting the Directory Replicator service.

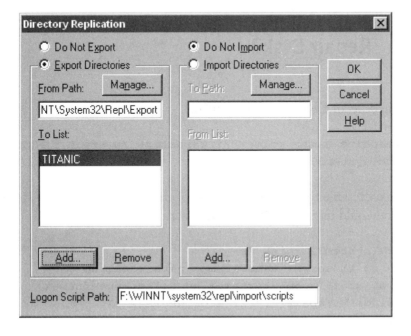

Figure 11-5. Export only for this machine to Titanic.

11. From the Services Control Panel applet, click on Directory Replication and then click Start.

12. Log off of the PDC and log on to the BDC (or whatever the import machine is).

13. Start the Services Control Panel applet. As before, enable the Replication service to automatically start at reboot, but do not manually start it now.

14. Start the Server Control Panel applet and select Replication.

15. Select Import Directories and make sure the list of machines to import from is blank.

16. Click OK to start the Directory Replication service.

You might be wondering why you should keep your login scripts in the export area when your netlogon share is import/scripts. Well, it will actually replicate itself from export/scripts to import/scripts so they will be the same.

Some people have problems with replication, and adding RepUser to the Domain Administrators group might fix the problem. Also, only directories directly under the /export directory will be replicated. Files will not be—they have to be in a subdirectory of export.

4.0 ONLY
How do I remotely create an Emergency Repair Disk?

You can schedule an ERD creation by using

```
AT \\<machine name> <time> /interactive /every:M,T,W,Th,F
%windir%\system32\rdisk /s-
```

It might be preferable to store the contents of this disk on a location at the server, so you could use the following batch script:

```
%windir%\system32\rdisk /s-
net use z: \\<server name>\temp /persistent:no
if not exist z:\%computername% md z:\%computername%
copy %windir%\repair\*.* z:\%computername%\
net use z: /delete
exit
```

This would then be submitted as

```
AT \\<machine name> <time> /interactive /every:M,T,W,Th,F
\\<server>\<share>\ERD.BAT
```

You could also just put the call to ERD.BAT in the login script so the contents of the repair disk are updated every time the user logs on and then stored centrally.

4.0 ONLY

11.12

How do I promote a Backup Domain Controller to the Primary Domain Controller?

When possible, you should always promote a BDC to the PDC while the main PDC is still active. This way, the original PDC is demoted to a BDC and no information is lost. Sometimes, however, the PDC is unavailable (that is, it crashed) and a BDC needs to be promoted in the absence of a PDC. A BDC does not automatically promote itself.

1. Log on to a BDC as an Administrator.
2. Start Server Manager (Start > Programs > Administrative Tools > Server Manager).
3. If the PDC is not available, a warning is displayed: "Cannot find Primary DC for <domain>."
4. Click on the BDC you want to promote to the PDC.
5. From the Computer menu, choose Promote to Primary Domain Controller (see Figure 11-6).
6. Again, if the PDC is not available, you see this warning: "Cannot find Primary for <Domain>." Click OK to continue.
7. The Netlogon service is stopped on the BDC, and it is changed to a PDC. Then the Netlogon service starts again.
8. This machine is now the domain PDC.

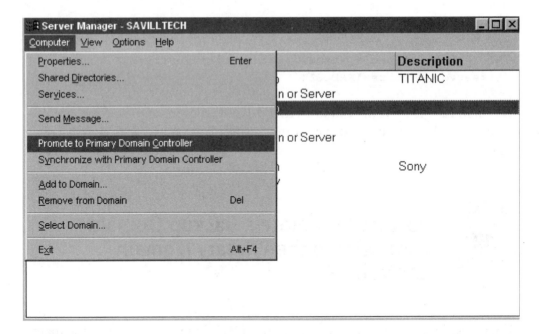

Figure 11-6. Promoting a machine to Primary Domain Controller.

How do I reinstate my old PDC back into the domain as the PDC?

It is not possible to have two PDCs in a domain, so assuming the machine crashed (that is, was not demoted to a BDC before being shut down), it will still be configured to be a PDC when it starts.

1. Start up the old PDC machine.
2. Log on to the machine as an Administrator.
3. Start Server Manager (Start > Programs > Administrative Tools > Server Manager).
4. The machine is still described as a Primary Domain Controller; however, its icon is just a wireframe and it is not acting as a PDC (that is, it does not authenticate logons because the netlogon service is restrained from started).
5. Select the machine. From the Computer menu, choose Demote to Backup Domain Controller.

6. Click Yes to make the change.
7. Now that the machine is a BDC, click on it again. From the Computer menu, select Promote to PDC.
8. Click Yes to make the change.
9. Server Manager then automatically demotes the temporary PDC back to its BDC status and promotes this machine back to the PDC.

 What tuning can be performed on Directory Replication?

You can update a number of Registry entries. These are all values under HKEY_ LOCAL_MACHINE\System\CurrentControlSet\Services\Replicator\ Parameters, as described in Table 11-1.

Table 11-1. Updatable Registry Entries

GuardTime	Amount of time during which the export folder must have had no changes before files are replicated (default, 5 minutes)
Interval	How often an export server looks for changes in the replicator folders (default, 2 minutes)
Pulse	Number of times the import computer repeats the change notice after the initial announcement (default, twice)
Random	Maximum time import servers wait before requesting an update (default, 60 seconds but can be between 1 and 120)

Windows 2000 allows much greater control on replication between domain controllers and using the Active Directory Sites and Services Manager, as follows:

1. Start the Active Directory Sites and Services MMC snap-in (Start > Programs > Administrative Tools > Active Directory Sites and Services Manager).
2. Expand the site name, expand the servers, and expand the server whose replication you wish to set.
3. Select the NTDS Settings branch. In the right-hand window, select one of the NTDS connections. There is one connection for each replication link

between each pair of domain controllers. Right-click on it and select Properties (see Figure 11-7).

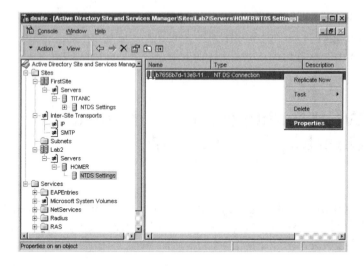

Figure 11-7. Selecting the domain controller for which to configure replication.

4. Click the Change Schedule button.
5. You can then select the replication on a per hour basis of every hour of the week, to be done once, twice, four times an hour, or not at all (see Figure 11-8).

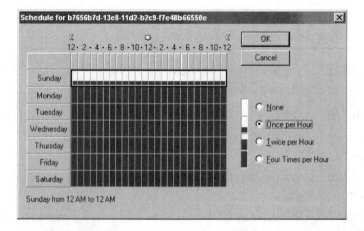

Figure 11-8. Setting the replication schedule for the particular replication link.

4.0 ONLY

I am unable to perform a repair without a CD-ROM drive. What can I do?

Performing any repair requires a CD-ROM in the drive; however, this limitation was fixed in Service Pack 2 and later service packs. You can therefore update your installation/repair disks so they will not check for a CD-ROM drive.

1. Extract the SETUPDD.SYS file from the service pack installation file:

   ```
   nt4sp3_i /x
   ```

2. Answer the prompt for an installation directory.
3. Create a new set of NT installation disks. To do so, go to the i386 structure and run WINNT32 /OX (if from an NT box) or WINNT /OX (if from another OS).
4. When all three disks are created, insert disk 2 and replace the file SETUPDD.SYS from Service Pack 2 (or 3). To do this, you first need to set the file A:\SETUPDD to writable:

   ```
   attrib a:\setupdd.sys -r
   ```

5. Copy the file to the a: drive:

   ```
   copy <service pack expansion drive and dir>\setupdd.sys a:
   ```

You will now be able to boot off of these disks and repair the Registry/boot sector without a CD-ROM. Replacing system files without a CD-ROM is detailed in the procedure Q150497, which you can view from http://support.microsoft.com/support/.

12 BACKUPS

Windows NT has powerful data mirroring and recoverability options, but there is no substitute for good backup procedures. The information in this chapter should help you configure your system for optimum recoverability options.

This chapter covers backing up Registry, which should be completed regularly, before any new software is added or any major system configuration is undertaken.

FAQ 12.1 What backup software is available for Windows NT?

Windows NT 4.0 ships with NTBACKUP.EXE. Although it is suitable for backing up most installations, its features are quite basic and only allow backups to a tape drive. Windows 2000's offering is not much better, but it has built-in wizards and allows backups to tape drives as well as to removable and permanent storage devices. For the larger, more complex installations, one of the following might be worth a look:

- ARCserve from http://www.cheyenne.com
- Back Again II from http://www.cds-inc.com/

- Backup Exec from http://www.nsmg.seagatesoftware.com
- Legato NetWorker from http://www.legato.com/
- NovaBack+ from http://www.novastor.com
- OpenView OmniBack from http://www.hp.com
- Replica from http://www.stac.com/replica/
- UltraBac from http://www.ultrabac.com
- SM-arch from http://www.moguls.com/

 ## How do I add a tape drive?

Before you can add a tape drive, you should first ensure that the correct SCSI driver is loaded for the card to which the tape drive is connected. You can install and check SCSI drivers by using the SCSI control panel applet.

After the SCSI driver is loaded, you should perform the following:

1. Start the Tape Devices Control Panel applet (Start > Settings > Control Panel > Tape Devices).
2. Click the Detect button for NT to detect your tape drive. If this works, go to step 5.
3. If the drive could not be detected, click the Drivers tab.
4. Click the Add button and select your tape drive from the list, or click the Have Disk button and select the location for the driver.
5. Click OK and restart the computer.

When the computer has been restarted, the tape drive should be available to NT Backup, allowing you to do backups and restorations.

NT 4.0 also detects and installs certain tape drivers (such as 4mm DAT), which means there is no need for a reboot after the installation.

12.3 What types of backup does NTBACKUP.EXE support?

NTBACKUP.EXE supports five different types of backups, each used to meet different requirements. They are described here:

- Normal backup: Backs up the selected files and marks them as backed up.
- Incremental backup: Backs up files that have changed since the last backup. After the files have been backed up, they are marked as backed up.
- Differential backup: Backs up files that have changed since the last backup but does not mark the files as backed up.
- Copy backup: Same as a normal backup but does not mark files as backed up.
- Daily backup: Backs up selected files that have been modified on that day; the files are not marked as backed up.

12.4 What backup strategies are available?

There are numerous backup strategies you can use. Depending on the type of data you are backing up, you might need a tailored schedule. The most popular backup strategy is a weekly plan, as follows:

- Monday - Incremental backup
- Tuesday - Incremental backup
- Wednesday - Incremental backup
- Thursday - Incremental backup
- Friday - Normal backup

An incremental backup only backs up files that have changed since the last backup and then tags them as backed up, so it should be quite fast. In the event of a failure, you would have to first restore the normal backup and then any subsequent incremental backups. For example, if the system crashed on Thursday, June 12, you would have to restore

- Friday's normal backup (June 6)
- Monday's incremental backup (June 9)
- Tuesday's incremental backup (June 10)
- Wednesday's incremental backup (June 11)

An alternative backup methodology works as follows:

- Monday - Differential backup
- Tuesday - Differential backup
- Wednesday - Differential backup
- Thursday - Differential backup
- Friday - Normal backup

Differential backups and incremental backups are the same except that differential does not mark the files as backed up. This means files backed up on Monday will still be backed up on Tuesday, and so on. To restore the backup, you only need to restore the normal backup and the latest differential backup.

It is important to have more than one week's worth of tapes. You should have a tape rotation with maybe 10 tapes that you rotate on a biweekly basis. Larger organizations often have 30 or more tapes in rotation. Tapes do wear out, so replace them with new tapes periodically.

If you want an extra backup for special archiving, you would use a "copy backup." This does a full backup but does not mark files as backed up and therefore does not interfere with other backup schemes in use.

 ## What options are available when using NTBACKUP.EXE?

After you start NTBACKUP, a list of all drives on the machine is shown. You can select a whole drive or double-click on the drive and then select directories (see Figure 12-1). After you have selected the drives or directories, click the Backup button.

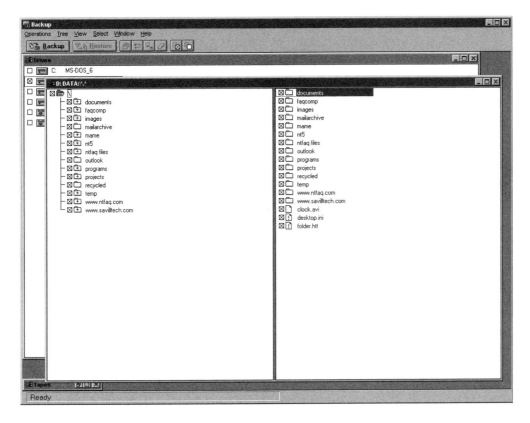

Figure 12-1. Selecting individual directories to be backed up rather than a whole drive.

When you're performing a backup, a number of fields should be completed.

- **Current Tape:** The name of the inserted tape is shown. You cannot edit this field.
- **Creation Date:** Date the original backup set was created. You cannot edit this field.
- **Owner:** The owner of the tape. You cannot edit this field.
- **Tape Name:** A 32-character string describing the tape.
- **Operation Append/Replace:** If you choose Append, the new saveset is added to the end of the tape. If you choose Replace, any information on the current tape is overwritten.
- **Verify after Backup:** With this selected, any files copied to tape are verified against the file on disk.

- **Backup Local Registry:** Backs up the computer's local Registry; you cannot back up a remote computer's Registry.
- **Restrict Access to Owner or Administrator:** If you select this option, the tape is made Secure. Only the owner of the tape or a member of the Administrator or Backup Operators group can access the tape.

 ## Can I run NTBACKUP from the command line?

NTBACKUP is fully usable from the command line by using this format:

```
ntbackup <operation> <path> /a /b /d "text" /e /hc:<on/off>
/l "<filename>" /r /t <backup type> /tape:n /v
```

The meanings for the parameters are shown in Table 12-1.

Table 12.1. NTBACKUP Parameters

<operation>	This parameter will be *backup*. If you want to eject a tape, you can enter *eject* (but you must also include the /tape parameter).
<path>	The list of drives and directories to be backed up. You may not enter filenames or use the wildcard character. To back up multiple drives, put a space between them (for example, ntbackup backup c: d:).
/a	Append backup sets to the end of the tape. If /a is omitted, the tape is erased before the new backup.
/b	Back up the local Registry.
/d "text"	A description of the tape.
/e	Logs only exceptions.
/hc:<on/off>	If set /hc:on, hardware compression is used; if /hc:off, no hardware compression is used.
/l "<filename>"	Location and name for the logfile.
/r	Restricts access (ignored if /a is set).

Table 12.1. NTBACKUP Parameters *(continued)*

/t \<backup type\>	The type of backup: Normal, Incremental, Differential, Copy, or Daily.
/tape:n	Which tape drive to use (from 0 to 9). If omitted, tape drive 0 is used.
/v	Performs verification.

How do I schedule a backup?

Before a backup can be scheduled (or anything else for that matter), you must ensure that the Schedule service is running on the target machine (that is, the machine that will run the task). The Schedule service does not have to be running on the machine issuing the command.

For information on the Schedule service, see Question 6-4 in Chapter 6, System Configuration.

After the Schedule service has been started, you can submit a backup command by using the ntbackup.exe image (*image* is a name for an executable).

```
AT 22:00/every:M,T,W,Th,F ntbackup backup d: /v /b
```

This would schedule a backup at 10 p.m. on weekdays of drive D: and the local Registry with verification.

How do I restore a backup?

Restoring a backup set is simple and depends on what was backed up; however, here are the basics:

1. Start NTBACKUP (Start > Administrative Tools > Backup).
2. Double-click on the tape unit that has the backup set you want. Select the saveset.

3. Check the Restore File Permissions if the set was backed up off of a NTFS volume.

4. Click OK.

4.0 ONLY

FAQ 12.9   How do I back up open files?

Sometimes files become corrupted as the backup program is trying to back up an open file and, when restored, the file is corrupt. To stop NTBACKUP from backing up open files, perform the following:

1. Start the Registry editor.
2. Move to HKEY_CURRENT_USER\Software\Microsoft\Ntbackup\ Backup Engine.
3. Check Backup Files in Use. If it is set to 1, double-click on the value and set it to 0.
4. Click OK and close the Registry editor.

If you have Backup Files in Use set to 1, you should also set the following parameter:

```
HKEY_CURRENT_USER\Software\Microsoft\Ntbackup\User
Interface\Skip open files
```

The values for this are

0 - Do not skip the file; wait till it can be backed up.
1 - Skip files that are open or unreadable.
2 - Wait for open files to close for Wait time (which is another Registry value in seconds).

For more information, have a look at Knowledge Base Article Q159218 from http://support.microsoft.com/support/kb/articles/q159/2/18.asp.

To back up open files without corruption, you should look at a third-party software package such as Open File Manager from http://www.stbernard.com/. You can download Open File Manager for a 15-day free trial.

4.0 ONLY

What permissions do I need to perform a backup?

The operator performing the backup requires the "back up files and directories" user right. This can be given directly by using User Manager, but the preferred way is to make the user a member of either the Administrators group or the Backup Operators group.

How do I back up the Registry?

When the OS is running, most of the Registry hives are open and cannot be copied in the normal way. However, several methods are available to you, as shown here:

- If you have a tape drive attached to NT, the NTBACKUP utility performs a full backup of the Registry if you choose Backup Local Registry when performing the backup. Please note that NTBACKUP cannot back up Registries on remote machines.
- RDISK /s backs up the Registry to the %systemroot%/repair directory. Use RDISK /s- from the command prompt to avoid confirmation messages.
- REGBACK.EXE, which comes with the Resource Kit, backs up the open files that make up the Registry but not the unopened ones. You need to manually copy these by using XCOPY.EXE or SCOPY.EXE. The utility REGREST.EXE can be used to restore the Registry. To back up the registry to directory d:\regbackup use

```
regback d:\regback
```

Remember, NT does not automatically rename the old Registry to .da0 as Windows 95 does. However, you can use RDISK, the Emergency Recovery Disk utility, to generate fresh duplicates of the Registry and then use this script to keep three old versions on hand:

```
REM REGBACK.BAT note: change M: to home directory on LAN
REM pkzip25 is a product of PKWARE, see www.pkware.com for
details
rdisk /s-
if exist m:regback.old del m:regback.old
ren m:regback.sav regback.old
ren m:regback.zip regback.sav
pkzip25 -lev=0 -add -attr=all m:regback %systemroot%\
repair\*.*
exit
```

4.0 ONLY
12.12 How can I erase a tape using NTBACKUP if it reports errors?

When NTBACKUP starts and a tape is inserted, a scan of the device is performed. If any errors are found, one of the following messages is displayed:

Tape Drive Error Detected.
Tape Drive Not Responding.
Bad Tape.

You then cannot perform any actions on the tape (including erasing it). It is possible to force NT not to check a tape when it's inserted. To do this, you use the /nopoll parameter, as follows:

ntbackup /nopoll

You can now erase the tape within NTBACKUP. If you have multiple tape drives, you might want to use the /tape:n parameter to instruct NTBACKUP to ignore a certain tape drive, but no other parameters should be used.

After you have erased the tape, exit NTBACKUP and restart to use the tape (without specifying /nopoll).

4.0 ONLY
FAQ 12.13 How can I remove a dead submitted backup process?

If you submit a backup by using the AT command (the Schedule command) and the NTBACKUP program has a problem, you can't kill the process by running Task Manager. Instead, an error appears along the lines of "you don't have authority to end the process." The only solution is to reboot the server.

If you submit the NTBACKUP command with the /interactive switch, you will see some kind of error.

Instead of rebooting the server, you can create a "special" version of Task Manager that can kill the rogue NTBACKUP process. Simply use the AT command to submit Task Manager to start one minute in the future. Even better, use the Resource Kit's SOON.EXE utility:

```
soon 30 /interactive taskmgr
```

After 30 seconds, Task Manager is displayed and you can kill the NTBACKUP process.

The AT syntax would be

```
at [\\<computer name>] <time in future> /interactive taskmgr
```

The \\<computer name> is optional and would start Task Manager on another machine.

13 NETWORK

A network is now an essential component of any business. When correctly configured and optimized, networks can enable entire organizations to communicate and share information as though they were in the same room. The sharing of information and resources is good; however, control is needed to enable and maintain privacy.

This chapter also looks at managing resources over the Internet, such as your domain, and configuring other Net-based services, such as FTP servers.

FAQ 13.1 How do I hide a machine from the network browse list (Network Neighborhood)?

By default, your computer broadcasts its existence to the Browse Masters, machines that store the lists of computers on the network. One way this list can be viewed is by double-clicking on Network Neighborhood.

To hide your machine from being visible on the browse list, perform the following:

1. Start the Registry editor (REGEDIT.EXE).
2. Move to HKEY_LOCAL_MACHINE\System\CurrentControlSet\ Services\LanManServer\Parameters.

3. Double-click on Hidden and change from 0 to 1. Click OK.

4. Close the Registry editor and reboot the machine.

Typing the following on the command line has the same effect as modifying the Registry:

```
net config server /hidden:yes
```

You can still connect to the computer, but it is not displayed in the browsers.

4.0 ONLY

FAQ 13.2 How do I remote-boot NT?

NT does not support remote boot (Windows 2000 does). It is possible to reboot a machine from another computer by using the Shutdown Manager that comes with the NT Resource Kit, SHUTGUI.EXE (see Figure 13-1).

Figure 13-1. Shutting down Titanic by using SHUTGUI.EXE.

You can also reboot by using the SHUTDOWN.EXE Resource Kit utility and specifying another machine name:

```
shutdown \\<machine name> /l /r /y /c
```

Software such as PC Anywhere can also remotely reboot machines.

4.0 ONLY

How do I install the Remoteboot service?

The Remoteboot service allows a "dumb" terminal to get its operating system from an NT Server.

Before installing the Remoteboot service, you must have both the NetBEUI and Data Link Control (DLC) protocols installed. The Remoteboot service will run only on NT Server.

1. Open the Control Panel (Start > Settings > Control Panel).
2. Double-click the Network icon.
3. Click on the Services tab and click Add.
4. Select Remoteboot Service.
5. Check the path where Remoteboot will be installed (by default, it is %systemroot%\RPL).
6. Click OK and complete the installation.
7. After installation has completed, start Remoteboot Manager.

Click Fix Security from the Configuration menu. This creates the RPLUSER local group and assigns the permissions to the RPL directory.

How can I get a list of users that are currently logged on?

Use the net sessions command; however, this will only work if you are an Administrator. You can also go to the Control Panel and choose Server.

How do I configure NT to be a gateway to an ISP?

FAQ 13.5

First, the hardware required would be a network and a modem. You need a network card so other clients in the network will be able to communicate with the gateway, and the modem to connect to the gateway. Dial-up networking is not covered here, and you should first be confident with dial-up networking before attempting this procedure.

1. Start the Registry editor (REGEDIT.EXE).
2. Move to HKey_Local_Machine\System\CurrentControlSet\Services\ RasArp\Parameters area.
3. Add a value of type DWORD called DisableOtherSrcPackets and set to a value of 0. With this value, packets that are sent through the NT gateway retain the original IP address stored in each packet. That is, if Machine A is sending a packet through B, the packet retains the IP address of A rather than being automatically changed to B.
4. Also change HKEY_LOCAL_MACHINE\SYSTEM\ CurrentControlSet\Services\Tcpip\Parameters\IPEnableRouter to a value of 1.
5. On the gateway machine, ensure that TCP/IP is installed with a static IP address and a correct subnet address (usually 255.0.0.0 for class a, 255.255.0.0 for class b, and 255.255.255.0 for class c). Make sure the default gateway address is blank.
6. Install Dial-Up Networking and configure for NT to dial out only. Now reboot before continuing.
7. Add a phone book entry for your ISP as you would normally, but uncheck the box for Use Default Gateway.
8. You need to enable the PC to forward IP packets. To do so, open the Control Panel, double-click Network, and choose the Protocols tab. Select TCP/IP and then Routing. Check the box for Enable IP Forwarding. Now reboot before continuing.
9. If you are given an IP address when you connect to your ISP, you now need to connect to your ISP and find out which IP address you are given. To get the address, type the command below from a command window:

```
(CMD.EXE)
IPCONFIG
```

Look for a Wan adapter and write down the IP address. If you know your IP address before you connect, you can skip this step.

10. Add a route for the IP address used when connecting to your ISP (the one identified in step 6).

```
route add 0.0.0.0 mask 0.0.0.0 <ip address> metric 2
```

11. Configure All Clients Gateway as the network card IP address of the NT gateway.

Although this procedure enables machines to send out IP packets to the Internet, the packets would have no way of finding their way back because the ISP would not know to route them through the gateway. Therefore, your ISP will have to do one of the following:

1. Have host entries for each of the machines.
2. Point to the gateway as another DNS.

Other things to check are as follows:

- Make sure your ISP routes packets to you; otherwise, you will be able to send packets out but the replies will never get to you.
- Make sure your local IP networks (check that each machine can ping the others) and that all PCs have a valid Internet address. If you do not have Internet addresses for each PC that have been assigned from InterNIC, you need something like Proxy Server instead.

For more information, have a look at http://support.microsoft.com/support/kb/articles/q121/8/77.asp.

FAQ 13.6 How can I get the Ethernet (MAC) address of my Network card?

Type **ipconfig /all** from a command line. One of the returned items is the MAC address of the Network card (see Figure 13-2).

```
E:\WINNT\System32\cmd.exe                                          _□

Microsoft(R) Windows NT(TM)
(C) Copyright 1985-1996 Microsoft Corp.

E:\>ipconfig /all

Windows NT IP Configuration

        Host Name . . . . . . . . : taz.savilltech.com
        DNS Servers . . . . . . . : 200.200.200.50
        Node Type . . . . . . . . : Broadcast
        NetBIOS Scope ID. . . . . :
        IP Routing Enabled. . . . : No
        WINS Proxy Enabled. . . . : No
        NetBIOS Resolution Uses DNS : No

Ethernet adapter E190x1:

        Description . . . . . . . : 3Com 3C90x Ethernet Adapter
        Physical Address. . . . . : 00-10-4B-49-B4-35
        DHCP Enabled. . . . . . . : No
        IP Address. . . . . . . . : 200.200.200.40
        Subnet Mask . . . . . . . : 255.255.255.0
        Default Gateway . . . . . : 200.200.200.50

Ethernet adapter NdisWan4:
```

Figure 13-2. Notice the circled item, which is the MAC address.

Is it possible to protect against Telnet port 135 attacks?

Recently there was a well-known problem involving a Telnet client connecting to an NT machine on port 135—type 10 characters and it would hang NT. There is no *simple* way to protect NT from a certain port attack. It is possible to configure NT to accept incoming packets only from a set of configured ports; however, you have to name the ports from which you want to accept input, as follows:

1. From the Control Panel, double-click on Network.
2. Click the Protocols tab.
3. Select TCP/IP and click Properties.
4. Click Advanced (bottom right of the Properties window).
5. Check the box for Enable Security and click Configure.
6. For TCP, select Permit Only and enable only the ports you want to work (for example, Web Browser is 80, FTP 21).
7. Exit and reboot NT.

To protect against the port 135 attack, install the RPC hotfix from Service Pack 2.

Service Pack 3 and some of its hotfixes are also highly desirable and address a number of Internet attack methods.

What Telnet servers and daemons are available for Windows NT?

A Telnet server on NT allows connection to an NT machine using a Telnet client from any hardware platform. Products are available from the following locations:

- http://www.ataman.com
- http://www.georgiasoftworks.com
- http://www.hummingbird.com/realindex.html
- http://www.pragmasys.com
- http://www.seattlelab.com
- There is a beta version of a Telnet server on the Resource Kit, and an updated oemsetup.inf is available from ftp://ftp.microsoft.com/bussys/winnt/winnt-public/reskit/nt40/telnetd/oemsetup.inf, which fixes an installation problem.

How can I secure a server that will be a Web Server on the Internet?

Following are points to be aware of:

- Disable the creation of Admin shares.
- Use NTFS and remove everyone's access except for the directories that are part of the Web documents. For those directories, have Read access only.
- It is possible to disable TCP ports on NT, and you can restrict the NT server to accept packets only on port 80 (Web browser). This is discussed in Question 13-7.
- If the server is part of your internal intranet, use a firewall.

What firewall products are available for NT?

Table 13-1 lists a selection of firewall systems for NT, with sources.

Table 13-1. Firewall Systems

FireWall/Plus	http://www.network-1.com
Interware	http://www.consensys.com
KyberPASS	http://www.kyberpass.com
Open Sesame	http://www.csm-usa.com/sesame.htm
SessionWall	http://www.AbirNet.com
Firewall-1	http://www.checkpoint.com
Guardian	http://www.ntguard.com
AltaVista FireWall	http://altavista.software.digital.com/firewall/index.htm
Microsoft Proxy Server 2.0	http://www.microsoft.com/proxy/default

How many connections can NT Workstation have?

NT Workstation can have up to 10 concurrent connections. The one exception is Peer Web Services, which allows unlimited concurrent connections.

How do I get a list of all connections to my PC?

Use the command netstat -a for a list of connections with protocol, name, and IP address information. You will see many local connections on this list.

How can I stop a user from logging on more than once?

There is no way in NT to stop a user from logging on more than once. It is possible, however, to restrict a workstation so that only a certain user can log in, and with this method each user can be tied to one workstation and thus can log on only once.

1. Log on to the workstation as the Domain Administrator.
2. Start User Manager (Start > Administrative Tools > User Manager).
3. Double-click the Users group. Select Domain\Everyone and click Remove.
4. Next click Add. Select the specific domain user and click Add again.
5. Close User Manager.
6. Log off, and only that specific user will be able to log on. (Be careful that Administrators still include Domain Administrators or you will not be able to log on.)

This solution is far from ideal. It might be possible to write a login script that checks if a user is currently logged on and, if so, logs them off immediately (using the logout command line tool).

How can I get information about my domain account?

From the command prompt, type

```
net user <username> /domain
```

All of your user information will be displayed, including last logon time, password change, and more.

```
E:\WINNT\System32\cmd.exe                                          _ □ ×
E:\>net user john /domain
The request will be processed at the primary domain controller for domain
SAVILLTECH.

User name                     john
Full Name                     John Savill
Comment
User's comment
Country code                  000 <System Default>
Account active                Yes
Account expires               Never

Password last set             12/18/98 11:33 PM
Password expires              Never
Password changeable           12/18/98 11:33 PM
Password required             Yes
User may change password      Yes

Workstations allowed          All
Logon script
User profile
Home directory
Last logon                    12/30/98 5:58 PM

Logon hours allowed           All
```

Figure 13-3. The results from a net user execution.

4.0 ONLY

13.15

A machine is shown as Inactive in Server Manager when it is not. Why?

Sometimes Server Manager fails to see that a machine has become active. You can attempt to force it to see the machine by typing

```
net use \\<machine name>\IPC$
```

If this fails, the machine might have been configured to be invisible to the network (see Question 13-1).

4.0 ONLY

13.16

How do I install the FTP Server service?

In prior versions of NT, the FTP Server service was installed as part of TCP/IP. As of NT 4.0, however, it became part of IIS/PWS, so you need to install it manually. (Before you install the FTP Server, TCP/IP must be installed.)

1. Start the Network Control Panel applet (Start > Settings > Control Panel > Network) or right-click on Network Neighborhood and select Properties from the context menu.
2. Select the Services tab and click Add.
3. If you are using NT Workstation, click Microsoft Peer Web Services. If you are using NT Server, click Microsoft Internet Information Server 2.0.
4. Click OK and type the path for the Windows NT source files. For example, if you are using the Windows NT CD in drive E, type **E:\i386**.
5. Click OK to start the Microsoft Peer Web Services Setup or Internet Information Server.
6. The FTP Service is selected by default, but you should clear the check boxes for options you do not want to install.

I get errors when accessing a Windows NT FTP Server from a non-Internet Explorer browser. Why?

If you run the Microsoft FTP Server service, you might have problems accessing an area other than the root from a non-Internet Explorer browser. This happens because most other FTP Servers use the UNIX naming conventions so that is what browsers such as Netscape expect; however, the Microsoft FTP service uses DOS naming conventions. You can resolve this by forcing the FTP Server service to use UNIX conventions rather than DOS.

1. Start the Registry editor (REGEDIT.EXE).
2. Move to HKEY_LOCAL_MACHINE\SYSTEM\CurrentControlSet\Services\ftpsvc\Parameters.
3. If the value MsdosDirOutput exists, double-click on it and set it to 0. Then click OK.
4. If the value MsdosDirOutput does not exist, choose Edit > New > DWORD Value. Enter the name **MsdosDirOutput** and click OK.
5. Now perform step 3.

You need to stop and start the FTP Server service for this change to take effect (Start > Settings > Control Panel > Services > FTP Service > Stop > Start).

FAQ 13.18   How do I automatically FTP when using NT?

I use a basic script to update my main site and the mirrors, using two batch files. The first file consists of these few lines:

```
d:
cd \savilltechhomepage
ftp -i -s:d:\savmanagement\goftp.bat
```

The -i suppresses the prompt when performing a multiple put and the -s defines an input file for the FTP. Table 13-2 shows an input file and explains it.

Table 13-2. Sample Input File for FTP

open ftp.savilltech.com	Name of the FTP server.
johnny	Username.
secret	Password.
cd /www	Remotely move to a base directory.
lcd download	Locally change directory.
cd download	Remotely move to a subdirectory of the current directory.
binary	Set mode to binary.
put faqcomp.zip	Send a file.
cd ..	Move down a directory remotely.
lcd ..	Move down a directory locally.
cd ntfaq	
lcd ntfaq	
mput *.html	Send multiple files (this is why we needed -i).
close	Close the connection.

How can I change the time period used for displaying the password expiration message?

A few days before your password is going to expire, Windows displays a warning. It is possible to change this time period as follows:

1. Start the Registry editor (REGEDIT.EXE).
2. Go to the key HKEY_LOCAL_MACHINE\SOFTWARE\Microsoft\ Windows NT\CurrentVersion\Winlogon.
3. From the Edit menu, click New > DWORD.
4. Type the name **PasswordExpiryWarning** and press Enter.
5. Double-click on the new value you have created and set it to the number of days prior to the expiration when you want the message to appear.

How can I modify share permissions from the command line?

The Windows NT Resource Kit ships with a utility called RMTSHARE.EXE, which you can use to modify permissions on shares. The syntax to grant access to a share is as follows:

rmtshare \\<server name>\<share> /grant <username>:<permission>
(for example, rmtshare \\bugsbunny\movies /grant savillj:f)

Valid permissions are f for full, r for read, c for change, and n for none. To revoke access to a share, type

rmtshare \\<server name>\<share> /grant <username>
(for example, rmtshare \\bugsbunny\movies /grant savillj)

This would remove savillj's access to the share. To view share permissions, type

rmtshare \\<server name>\<share> /users
(for example, rmtshare \\bugsbunny\movies /grant)

RMTSHARE.EXE also enables the creation and deletion of shares. Type **rmtshare /?** for help.

13.21 ## How can I change the protocol binding order?

Network bindings are links that enable communication between the network adapter(s), protocols, and services. If you have multiple protocols installed on a machine, you can configure NT to try a certain protocol first for communication.

1. Log on to the machine as a member of the Administrators group.
2. Start the Network Control Panel applet (Start > Settings > Control Panel > Network) or right-click Network Neighborhood and select Properties.
3. Click the Bindings tab.
4. Select All Services from the drop-down list of bindings.
5. To select the service for which you wish to change the binding order, click on its plus sign (usually you should change the Workstation service because this is used for connecting to resources, services, and such).
6. A list appears, showing all of the protocols installed (see Figure 13-4). You can change the order by selecting a protocol and clicking Move Up or Move Down.
7. When everything is the way you want it, click OK.

You have to reboot for the changes to take effect.

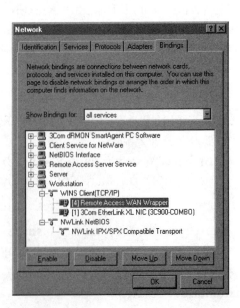

Figure 13-4. Even different adapters for a protocol can be moved in the order.

What criteria are used to decide which machine will be the Master Browser?

A given machine can have one of five roles. In Question 13-23, you'll find instructions for setting a machine as a certain type of browser.

1. **Master Browser:** This machine maintains the list of resources on the network and listens for announcements from other machines to add to the Browse list.
2. **Preferred Master Browser:** When this machine starts, it forces a browser election and will win unless one of the other machines is the PDC or also has the Preferred Master Browser flag set.
3. **Backup Browser:** This type receives a copy of the Browse list from the Master Browser. If it cannot find the Master Browser, it forces an election.
4. **Potential Browser:** This machine does not receive a copy of the Browse list but can be promoted to a Backup Browser by the Master Browser. Or it can actually become the Master Browser as the result of an election.
5. **Non-Browser:** A non-browser does not maintain a Browse list.

When an election takes place, a number of criteria are used. First is the browser type:

- Preferred master
- Master
- Backup browser
- Potential browser

If two machines have the same role, then a determination is made based on which operating system is used.

- Windows NT Server that is the PDC
- Windows NT Server that is a BDC
- Windows NT Server
- Windows NT Workstation
- Windows 95
- Windows for Workgroups

If there is still a tie, the Windows NT version is used:

- 4.0
- 3.51
- 3.5
- 3.1

13.23 How can I set a machine as a certain type of browser?

To set a machine as a certain type of browser, perform the following:

1. Start the Registry editor (REGEDIT.EXE).
2. Move to HKEY_LOCAL_MACHINE\SYSTEM\CurrentControlSet\ Services\Browser\Parameters.
3. Double-click on MaintainServerList and set it to one of these:

   No   The computer will be a Non-browser.

   Yes   The computer will be a Master or Backup Browser.

   Auto   The computer will be a Master, Backup, or Potential Browser, depending on the number of browsers currently in action.
4. Click OK.
5. Close the Registry editor and reboot.

13.24 How can I configure the Preferred Master Browser?

On the NT server you want to use as the Preferred Master Browser, change the following Registry setting to True:

```
HKEY_LOCAL_MACHINE\SYSTEM\CurrentControlSet\Services\Browser\
Parameters\IsDomainMaster
```

How can I view which machines are acting as Browse Masters?

Two utilities that are shipped with the NT Resource Kit (one GUI, one command line) can be used to view current Browse Master status.

BROWMON.EXE: Select from the Diagnostics Resource Kit menu to display the Master Browser for each domain. Double-clicking on a machine then lists the other machines that are browsers. A subsequent double-click on these machines tells their status (for example, Backup Browser).

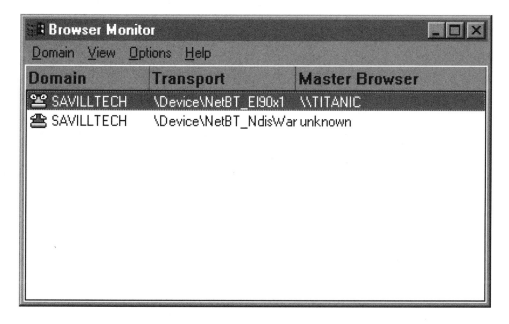

Figure 13-5. BROWMON.EXE in action (not much on this domain).

BROWSTAT.EXE: Start a command session. A number of commands are available, but to get a general view, enter the following command. The Master Browser name is shown, as are backup servers.

```
browstat status <domain name>
Browsing is active on domain.
Master browser name is: PDC.
```

```
Master browser is running build 1381.
2 backup servers retrieved from master PDC
\\PDC
\\WORKSTATION
```

How can I get a list of MAC-to-IP addresses on the network?

An easy way to get a list of MAC-to-IP addresses on the local subnet is to ping every host on the subnet and then check your Address Resolution Protocol (ARP) cache. However, pinging every individual node would take ages, and the entries only stay in the ARP cache for two minutes. An alternative is to ping the broadcast mask of your subnet, which then pings every host on the local subnet. (You can't ping the entire network because you only communicate directly with nodes on the same subnet. All other requests are via the gateway, so you would just get an ARP entry for the gateway.)

What is the broadcast mask? The broadcast mask is easy to calculate if the subnet mask is in the format 255.255.255.0, 255.255.0.0, and so on (multiples of 8 bits). For example, if the IP address is 134.189.23.42 and the subnet mask is 255.255.0.0, the broadcast mask will be 134.189.255.255. You will notice that where 255 is in the subnet mask, the IP address number is used; where 0, it is replaced by 255. Basically, the network ID part is kept. All you need is the IP address and the subnet mask. If the subnet mask is not the basic 255.255 format, you should use the following:

1. For each bit set to 1 in the subnet mask, copy the corresponding bit from the IP address to the broadcast mask.
2. For each bit set to 0 in the subnet mask, copy a 1 into the corresponding bit of the broadcast mask.

For example, IP address 158.234.24.98 and subnet mask 255.255.248.0 would look like this:

```
Subnet mask      11111111 11111111 11111000 00000000
IP address       10011110 11101010 00011000 01100010
Broadcast mask   10011110 11101010 00011111 11111111
```

The first row is the subnet mask 255.255.248.0, the second row is the IP address 158.234.24.98, and the third row is the broadcast mask, 158.234.31.255.

Now, using the broadcast mask, you can perform the following to get the MAC-to-IP addresses:

```
ping <broadcast mask>
arp -a
```

Voila, you have a list of IP addresses and their MAC addresses (you can add > filename to send the list to a file, as in **arp -a > iptomac.lst**). You can repeat this exercise on the various subnets of your organization.

Unfortunately, because of limitations in NT's implementation of ping, the previous command will not work correctly, so put the following into a file:

```
REM arpping.bat
ping -n 1 -l 1 %1.%2
arp -a %1.%2
```

You can then call the batch file as follows:

```
for /l %i in (1,1,254) do arpping 160.82.220 %i
```

This example would generate a list of all MAC-to-IP addresses for 160.82.220.1 to 160.82.220.254. Again, you can put all this in a file, redirect it to a file, and then search, like this:

```
REM test.bat
for /l %%i in (1,1,254) do arpping.bat 160.82.220 %%i
```

Notice you have to use two %%. You can run it as

```
test.bat > file.txt
```

Then search LISTING.TXT for a string. For example, search for "dynamic" and get a list of all related addresses:

```
findstr dynamic file.txt
160.82.220.1 00-00-0c-60-8b-41 dynamic
160.82.220.9 00-60-97-4b-bf-4c dynamic
160.82.220.13 00-10-4b-49-94-e1 dynamic
```

```
160.82.220.17  00-80-5f-d8-a4-8b  dynamic
160.82.220.22  00-a0-d1-02-a4-cf  dynamic
160.82.220.25  00-60-08-75-0d-7a  dynamic
160.82.220.26  00-10-4b-44-e4-73  dynamic
160.82.220.33  00-10-4b-44-d6-33  dynamic
160.82.220.34  00-10-4b-4e-67-6a  dynamic
160.82.220.35  00-60-97-4b-c4-53  dynamic
160.82.220.39  00-10-4b-44-eb-ae  dynamic
160.82.220.41  00-10-4b-49-7b-f7  dynamic
160.82.220.42  00-00-f8-21-7a-7f  dynamic
160.82.220.43  08-00-20-88-82-57  dynamic
160.82.220.221 00-80-5f-88-d0-55  dynamic
```

FAQ 13.27 How can I control the list of connections shown when mapping a network drive?

When you map a network drive (Explorer > Tools > Map Network Drive), clicking the downward arrow on the path displays a list of previous connections. These are stored on the Registry and can be edited, as follows:

1. Start the Registry editor (REGEDIT.EXE).
2. Move to HKEY_CURRENT_USER\Software\Microsoft\Windows NT\CurrentVersion\Network\Persistent Connections.
3. In the left pane, look for a number of string values called a, b, c, and so on. For the connections you do not want shown, click on the entry and then either press the Del key and say Yes to the confirmation or choose Delete from the Edit menu.
4. After you delete entries, you need to update which ones Explorer will show by double-clicking on Order and removing the letters of the entries you deleted.
5. Click OK and close the Registry editor.

How can I create a share on another machine over the network?

From a Windows NT Server machine, you can create a share by opening Server Manager, highlighting the target system, selecting Computer, Shared Directories, and clicking on New Share.

The Windows NT Resource Kit comes with a RMTSHARE.EXE utility that you can use to create shares on other machines, providing you have sufficient privilege. The basic syntax is as follows:

rmtshare \\<computer name>\"<share name to be created>"="<path>"
/remark="<share description>"
(for example, rmtshare \\savillmain\miscfiles=d:\files\misc /remark="General files")

You need to use double quotes around the share and path only if there are spaces in the share/filename. For example, if the share is to be called misc files instead of miscfiles, you must put it in quotes, like this:

rmtshare \\savillmain\"misc files"="d:\my files\misc "/remark="With space share"

Is there any way to improve the performance of my modem connection to the Internet?

By default, NT uses a Maximum Transmission Unit (MTU)—packet size—of 576 over the path to a remote host. Problems can arise if the data is sent over routes that cannot handle data of this size and the packets get fragmented.

Setting the parameter EnablePMTUDiscovery to 1 forces NT to discover the maximum MTU of all connections that are not on the local subnet. To change this parameter, perform the following:

1. Start the Registry editor (REGEDIT.EXE).
2. Move to HKEY_LOCAL_MACHINE\SYSTEM\CurrentControlSet\ Services\Tcpip\Parameters.

3. From the Edit menu, choose New > DWORD Value.
4. Enter the name EnablePMTUDiscovery and press Enter.
5. Double-click on this new value and set it to 1. Then click OK.
6. Close the Registry editor and reboot the machine.

By discovering the path MTU and limiting TCP segments to this size, TCP can eliminate fragmentation at routers along the path that connect networks with different MTUs. Fragmentation adversely affects TCP throughput and network congestion.

How can I remotely tell who is logged on at a machine?

The easiest way to tell who is logged on at a remote machine is to use the NBTSTAT command. There are two ways to use this command, depending on whether you know the machine's name or just its IP address. If you know the machine's name, enter the following command:

nbtstat -a <machine name>
(for example, nbtstat -a pdc)

The output will be of the format:
NetBIOS Remote Machine Name Table

Name	Type	Status
PDC	<00>	UNIQUE Registered
PDC	<20>	UNIQUE Registered
SAVILLTECH	<00>	GROUP Registered
SAVILLTECH	<1C>	GROUP Registered
SAVILLTECH	<1B>	UNIQUE Registered
SAVILLTECH	<1E>	GROUP Registered
PDC	<03>	UNIQUE Registered
SAVILLJ	<03>	UNIQUE Registered

SAVILLTECH	<1D>	UNIQUE Registered
INet~Services	<1C>	GROUP Registered
.._MSBROWSE__.	<01>	GROUP Registered
IS~PDC	<00>	UNIQUE Registered

MAC Address = 00-A0-24-B8-11-F3
MAC Address = 00-A0-24-B8-11-F3
The user name is the <03>.
If you know only the IP address, use this command:

nbtstat -A <IP address>
(For example, nbtstat -A 10.23.23.12)

The output is the same. Notice that you should use a capital A instead of a lowercase a.

 # How do I remove an NT computer from a domain?

The first way would be to log on to the machine you wish to remove from the domain and start the Network Control Panel applet (Start > Settings > Control Panel > Network) or just right-click on Network Neighborhood and select Properties. Select the Identification tab and click Change. Just enter a different domain or workgroup; you will receive a notice, welcoming you to the new domain or workgroup. The problem with this method is that the machine can still rejoin the domain because its account has not been removed from the domain.

To actually remove the computer account from the domain, perform the following:

1. Log on to the PDC as an Administrator.
2. Start Server Manager (Start > Programs > Administrative Tools > Server Manager).
3. Select the machine you wish to remove and click Delete (or choose Remove From Domain from the Computer menu).
4. Click Yes to the confirmation.

In Windows 2000, you can accomplish this by using the Active Directory Users and Computers MMC snap-in and removing the computer from the Computers branch.

Alternatively, you can remove a computer from the command line by using the Resource Kit utility NETDOM, as follows:

netdom /Domain:<domain> MEMBER <machine name> /delete
(for example, netdom /Domain:savilltech MEMBER kevinpc /delete)

You can use this command from any machine, workstation, or server as long as you are logged on as an Administrator. When you enter the command, it will find the PDC and delete, with the output as follows:

```
Searching PDC for domain SAVILLTECH ...
Found PDC \\PDC
Member \\KEVINPC successfully deleted.
```

13.32 How can I shut down a number of machines without going to each machine?

I have a number of machines set up in my lab. At the end of an entertaining evening of computing, I don't want to have to go to each machine and shut it down, so I wrote a small batch file that uses the SHUTDOWN.EXE Resource Kit utility. Enter the following into a file with a .bat extension:

```
rem Batch file to shutdown local machine and the PDC, BDC
shutdown \\pdc /t:2 /y /c (This shuts down a machine called PDC in 2
seconds, repeat with other machine names.)
shutdown \\bdc /t:2 /y /c (This shuts down a machine called BDC in 2
seconds.)
shutdown /l /y /c /t:5 (This shuts down the local machine in 5 seconds.)
```

Now just right-click the file in Explorer and drag it onto the desktop. Release it and select Create Shortcut(s) Here. Clicking this icon will now shut down all of the machines in the file.

How can I close all network sessions or connections?

The following command will close all network sessions to your machine, such as connections to a share on your machine:

```
net session /delete
```

 ## How can I connect to a server, using different user accounts?

It is possible to specify a user account to use when connecting to a share by using the /user switch, like this:

```
net use k: \\server\share /user:domain\user
```

If you then attempt to connect to the server again with a different username, an error message will be given. A workaround is to connect to the server by using its IP address rather than its NetBIOS name, like this:

```
net use l: \\<ip address>\share /user:domain\user
```

 ## How do I set the comment for my machine that is displayed in Network Neighborhood?

There are three ways to set the comment: via the command line, the Registry, or the GUI.

The easiest way is to use the Server Control Panel applet:

1. Start the Server Control Panel applet (Start > Settings > Control Panel > Server).

2. Enter the new description of the machine in the Description field.

3. Click OK.

An alternative method is to use the net config command from the command prompt.

```
net config server /srvcomment:machine comment
```

Note that even if you are performing this task on a workstation machine, you use net config server because this is a configuration on the server service of the machine.

Both of the previous methods update a single Registry value, so you can also edit this directly, as follows:

1. Start the Registry editor (REGEDIT.EXE).

2. Move to HKEY_LOCAL_MACHINE\SYSTEM\CurrentControlSet\ Services\LanmanServer\Parameters.

3. Double-click on Srvcomment.

4. In the Value data box, enter the new description and click OK.

5. Close the Registry editor.

You can remotely change the comment of other machines by using the NT Server Manager utility. Double-click on the remote machine to see the same dialog box as with the Server Control Panel applet. This has the advantage of enabling the Administrator to set a common description format.

13.36 How can I define multiple NetBIOS names for a machine?

This would be useful if, for instance, you wanted to migrate a number of shares to a different machine. Rather than having to switch all clients to the new machine instantly, you can define the new machine to also answer to the old machine's NetBIOS name and then slowly migrate the machines. To define extra names for a machine, perform the following:

1. Start the Registry editor (REGEDT32.EXE).

2. Move to HKEY_Local_Machine\System\CurrentControlSet\Services\ LanmanServer\Parameters.

3. From the Edit menu, choose Add Value.

4. Set the type to REG_SZ if you want one extra name or REG_MULTI_SZ if you want more than one. Then enter **OptionalNames** and click OK.

5. When prompted for a value, enter the other name you want the machine to be known by (or names, one on each line, if type REG_MULTI_SZ) and click OK.

6. Close the Registry editor and reboot the machine.

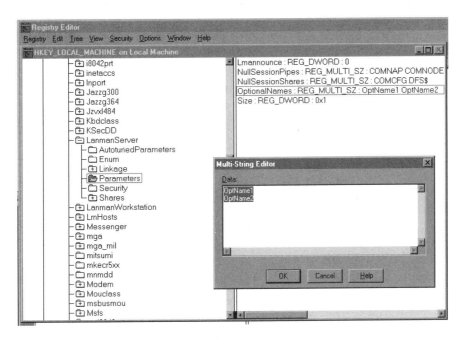

Figure 13-6. Establishing two extra NetBIOS names (although not very useful ones).

 ## How can I manage my NT domain over the Internet?

Microsoft has released Web Administrator 2.0 for Microsoft Windows NT Server. It enables you to do the following via the Web:

- Account Management
- RAS Management

- Share Management
- Session Management
- Server Management
- Printer Management

The additional software required has to be installed on a Server (though it does not have to be a Domain Controller) with

- Service Pack 3 or later (it does not currently work with the beta versions of Service Pack 4)
- Internet Information Server 4.0

Internet Information Server 4.0 is available as part of Option Pack 4, which you can obtain from http://www.microsoft.com/windows/downloads/contents/updates/nt40ptpk/default.asp or as part of MSDN. Option Pack 4 has its own requirement that Internet Explorer 4.0 be installed.

After you have installed all of the software, you can download the Web Admin tools from

- http://www.microsoft.com/windows/downloads/bin/NTSwebadmin20_x86.exe for i386
- http://www.microsoft.com/windows/downloads/bin/NTSwebadmin20_axp.exe for Alpha

To begin the installation, execute the required executable to begin the Installation Wizard. When the installation is complete, you will be able to administer your domain by connecting to http://<the server name>/ntadmin/default.asp. For example, if I had installed the software on the Titanic server in the savilltech.com domain, I would connect to http://titanic.savilltech.com/ntadmin/default.asp.

You need Internet Explorer 4.0 or later to use the site. While you're connected, you can select from a number of options. Figure 13-7 is an example of viewing and changing users.

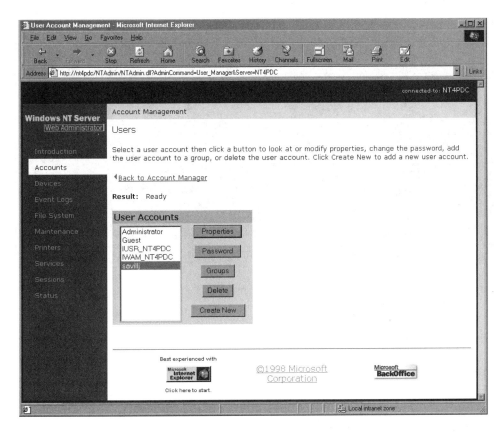

Figure 13-7. Viewing the User accounts on a domain via the Web.

How can I remotely manage services?

The Windows NT Resource Kit has two utilities, SC.EXE and NETSVC.EXE, that allow you to manage remote services. The Resource Kit has help on both of these, but this answer looks only at NETSVC.EXE.

To view the services on a remote machine, use this command:

```
netsvc /query \\<server name> /list
```

```
E:\WINNT\System32\cmd.exe                                    _ □ ×

E:\>netsvc /query \\titanic /list
Installed services on \\titanic:
        <Abiosdsk>.   No separate display name
        <ACPI>.   No separate display name
        <ACPIEC>.   No separate display name
        <AFD>.   Display name is <AFD Networking Support Environment>
        <agp440>.   Display name is <AGP Bus Filter>
        <Aha154x>.   No separate display name
        <Aha174x>.   No separate display name
        <aic116x>.   No separate display name
        <aic78u2>.   No separate display name
        <aic78xx>.   No separate display name
        <Alerter>.   Display name is <Alerter>
        <Always>.   No separate display name
        <ami0nt>.   No separate display name
        <amsint>.   No separate display name
        <AppMgmt>.   Display name is <Application Management>
        <Arrow>.   No separate display name
        <asc>.   No separate display name
        <asc3550>.   No separate display name
        <ASP>.   No separate display name
        <AsyncMac>.   Display name is <RAS Asynchronous Media Driver>
        <atapi>.   Display name is <Standard IDE/ESDI Hard Disk Controller>
        <Atdisk>.   No separate display name
```

Figure 13-8. Listing all services on a remote machine.

To see the current state of a service, use

```
netsvc <service name> \\<server> /query
```

You can then modify the state of the service by using the /start, /stop, /pause, and /continue switches, like this:

```
netsvc <service name> \\<server> /stop
```

How can I make NET.EXE use the next available drive letter?

13.39

The normal syntax for mapping a network drive is

```
net use <drive letter>: \\<server>\<share>
```

However, modifying this to * makes the net use command utilize the next available drive letter:

```
net use * \\<server>\<share>
```

13.40 How can I check if servers can communicate via Remote Procedure Calls (RPCs)?

Microsoft Exchange ships with RPINGS.EXE and RPINGC32.EXE, which you can use to test RPC communication between two servers. These programs are located in the SERVER\SUPPORT\RPCPING directory of the Exchange CD. Test RPC as follows:

1. On one server, start a command line (CMD.EXE) and enter

   RPINGS

2. On the other server, run the RPINGC32.EXE utility.
3. Then enter the name of the Exchange server with which you want to test communication. For example,

   NT4PDC

4. Click Start.

The connection will now be checked. When the check is completed, close the RPINGC32.EXE utility by clicking Exit. On the target machine, enter the sequence **@q**. Figure 13-9 is an example of a successful test.

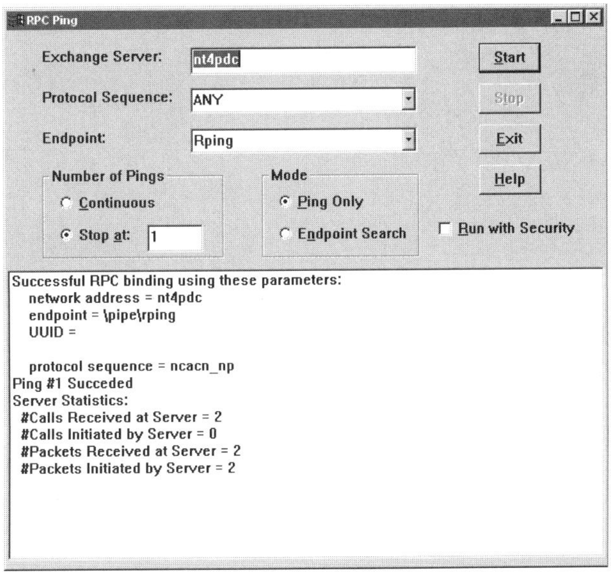

Figure 13-9. RPC ping can be used only when the server end is running on another machine.

14 DOMAINS

Domains are the core of the Windows NT networking administration model and are at the center of the Windows NT security management model. A domain is basically a collection of machines that share a common authentication (user) database, enabling them to more easily interact with one another.

You create a domain at the time when you install a Windows NT Server machine by selecting a machine to be a Primary Domain Controller (PDC). A 15-character NetBIOS name is configured as the name of the domain.

Under Windows 2000, domain names are no longer NetBIOS names but are domain name service (DNS) names—for example, sales.savilltech.com would be a valid domain name. However, a NetBIOS name is also configured for backward compatibility with older clients and Domain Controllers.

This section also looks at Trust Relationships, which allow domains to communicate with other domains in a trusted manner. This leads to a number of domain models, or basic configurations of domains.

4.0 ONLY
FAQ 14.1 What is a PDC and what is a BDC?

A PDC is a Primary Domain Controller, and a BDC is a Backup Domain Controller.

You must install a PDC before any other domain servers or workstations are made members of the domain. The Primary Domain Controller maintains the master copy of the directory database (SAM) and validates users.

A Backup Domain Controller contains a read-only copy of the directory database and can validate users. If the PDC fails, a BDC can be promoted to PDC level, although user changes that have not yet been replicated from the PDC to the BDC may be lost. A PDC can be demoted to a BDC if one of the BDCs is promoted to PDC.

Without a PDC and with only BDCs present, no changes can be made to the domain, because only the PDC has a writable copy of the database. It should be noted that changes can be made when you use User Manager for Domains on a BDC, because the BDC actually passes the changes to the PDC where its SAM is updated.

4.0 ONLY

FAQ 14.2

How many BDCs should I have?

Microsoft says one BDC for every two thousand users.

This is fine when you consider that a 486DX2 with 32MB of RAM can, on average, perform at least 10 logons per minute. However, if everyone in your company arrives at 9 a.m. on the dot and logs on (except for the helpful people who arrive half an hour late), there will be a surge of logon requests to deal with, resulting in large delays.

To try to improve on this, you can configure the Server service to throughput for network applications rather than file applications. Remember, the more powerful the processor, the more logons it can handle (for example, a Pentium 133 would be able to log on at least 30 people).

Geographical considerations are also important. If you have users connected over slow WAN links, having a BDC at each location connected over the WAN might improve performance. Users can be authenticated faster by using the local BDC, thus cutting traffic sent over the WAN link. The BDC has to synchronize with the PDC over the WAN link, so a balance should be found between the traffic caused by authentication requests and that caused by the synchronization.

4.0 ONLY

How do I change domain names?

This is not so much a procedure but things to think about:

1. NT stores both the textual name and the security ID (SID) associated with the name. When you change the domain name, you change only the textual part of the name and not the SID.
2. All users should log off before you start the domain name change.
3. Break all Trust Relationships with other domains.
4. If possible, all BDCs should have the domain name changed and be waiting to reboot. You will be asked if you want to reboot now or later. Choose Reboot Later, shut down the machine, and power it off.
5. On the PDC, open the Control Panel and change the domain name through Network. When the computer prompts for a reboot, choose Reboot Now.
6. After the PDC is up, let it stabilize for a few minutes. Then bring up each BDC with a minute gap between them, so each BDC can validate and synchronize the SAM with the PDC.
7. Re-create Trust Relationships with other domains.
8. Move all clients to the new domain. For moving Workstations, see Question 14-4.

4.0 ONLY

How do I move a workstation to another domain?

Moving a workstation from one domain to another is fairly simple. Before you move the workstation, however, you must ensure that it has a machine account set up. Use Server Manager for this (Start > Programs > Administrative Tools > Server Manager). Alternatively, you can create an account as you change the workstation's domain.

1. Log on to the Workstation locally as Administrator.
2. Start the Network Control Panel applet by either right-clicking on Network Neighborhood and selecting Properties or double-clicking on Network in the Control Panel.
3. Select the Identification tab. Notice that your current domain name is shown.
4. Click Change and enter the new domain name.
5. If no computer account has been set up, check the Create a Computer Account box (see Figure 14-1). Enter an Administrator's name (or an account with the Add Workstations to Domain user right) and the password of that domain.
6. Click OK. A message should appear, welcoming you to the domain.
7. Reboot the machine and you are part of the new domain.

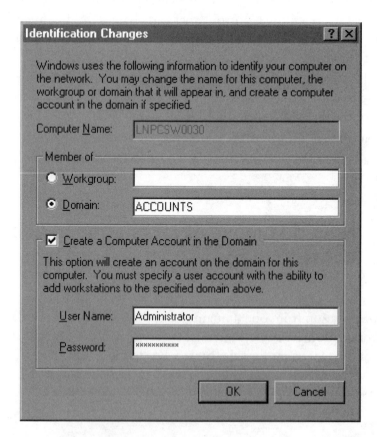

Figure 14-1. Example of moving to a new domain.

How many user accounts can I have in one domain?

The real problem is that each user account and machine account takes up space in the SAM file, and the SAM file has to be memory resident.

A user account takes up 1024 bytes of memory (a machine account half as much), so for each person—assuming each has one machine—you need 1.5KB. This means for a 10,000-user domain, each PDC or BDC needs 15MB of memory just to store the SAM. Imagine a network with 100,000 people. This is one of the reasons to have multiple domains and then set up Trust Relationships.

An accepted limit that has been given by Microsoft is 40,000 accounts for a single domain. Windows 2000 increases this to 10 million per domain.

How do I change my server from standalone to a PDC or BDC?

When you install Windows NT Server, you are asked what role the machine will take:

- Primary Domain Controller
- Backup Domain Controller
- Standalone Server

This is set at installation time because domains use Security Identifiers (SIDs) and all Domain Controllers in a single domain share a common SID. Therefore, if you install a machine as a standalone server, you cannot convert it to a Domain Controller. You need to reinstall the machine.

With Windows 2000, a machine's role can be changed from Domain Controller to a normal server by simply running a new utility, DCPROMO.EXE. In fact, Windows 2000 servers are all installed as normal standalone member servers. You then have to upgrade them to Domain Controllers by running the DCPROMO.EXE utility.

How do I configure a Trust Relationship?

Domains by default are unable to communicate with other domains, which means someone in Domain X cannot access any resource that is part of Domain Y. Before a Trust Relationship is configured, the following is true:

- An Administrator in X cannot give permission to any user of Domain Y for files or printers.
- A user of Domain Y cannot sit at a Workstation that is part of Domain X and log on.

After a Trust Relationship is defined such that X trusts Y, the following happens:

- Users of Domain Y can sit at a Workstation that is part of Domain X and log on to their own Domain Y (it will be displayed in the domain drop-down box).
- An Administrator of Domain X can grant permission to any user of Domain Y to file and print resources.
- Users of Domain Y are included in the Everyone group of Domain X.

In this example, X is the *trusting* domain and Y is the *trusted* domain. Also, this is a one-way Trust Relationship. That is, although Domain Y users can use Domain X resources, users of Domain X cannot use Domain Y resources. A two-way relationship would allow each domain to access resources of the other (if given permission).

The basics of a Trust Relationship are to first configure Domain Y to allow Domain X to trust it, and then configure Domain X to trust Domain Y, as follows:

1. Log on to Domain Y as Administrator.
2. Start User Manager for Domains (Start > Programs > Administrative Tools).
3. Select Trust Relationships from the Policies menu.
4. For the Trusting Domains box, click the Add button.
5. Enter the name of the domain you want to be able to trust you—in this case, Domain X.

6. You can type a password in the Initial Password and Confirm Password boxes; however, this is only used when the Trust Relationship is started, so for now you can leave it blank. Click OK to complete the addition.

7. Close the Trust Relationship dialog box.

8. Log off of Domain Y and log on to Domain X as Administrator.

9. Start User Manager for Domains and choose Trust Relationships from the Policies menu.

10. For the Trusted Domains box, click the Add button.

11. Enter the name of Domain Y (and the password if one was configured in step 6).

12. Click OK and close the User Manager for Domains application.

13. Domain X now trusts Domain Y.

 # How do I terminate a Trust Relationship?

The steps are to stop Domain X from trusting Domain Y and then remove Domain X's ability to trust Domain Y. Follow this procedure:

1. Log on as Administrator to Domain X.

2. Start User Manager for Domains and choose Policies > Trust Relationships.

3. Select Domain Y from the Trusted Domains list. Click Remove and confirm.

4. Log off of Domain X and log on to Domain Y as Administrator.

5. Start User Manager for Domains and choose Policies > Trust Relationships.

6. Select Domain X from the Trusting Domains list. Click Remove and confirm.

7. Exit User Manager.

4.0 ONLY
FAQ 14.9   What are domain models?

There are four domain models, each with advantages and disadvantages. Domain models are just ways of joining domains with the different types of trusts.

While reviewing the types, try to identify the models you have in your network. You might have a composite of several of the basic types described here.

Single Domain Model

This is the simplest of the domain models. In this situation, you have only one domain with one or more optional BDCs. The single domain model can contain up to 40,000 users (the domain can in theory hold up to 40MB; however, this depends on the machine's physical memory), with the actual logon authentication spread over the PDC and a number of BDCs.

Also remember that resource browsing is on a per domain basis. If you have 10,000 machines in a single domain, when you browse, the Browse Master will have to send you information about all the machines. This leads to slower browsing, and the second model might help.

Advantages

- Easy to maintain for companies with a small number of users.
- No management of Trust Relationships is needed.

Disadvantages

- Your company might be too large for this model.
- Browsing the domain is slow if you have a large number of servers.
- Grouping resources or users into departments is not possible.

Master Domain Model

Building on the single domain model, the master domain model still keeps the centralized account management but enables you to split the resources into one or more resource domains.

In this model you have one master domain where all account information is stored and managed, plus several resource domains that trust the master domain (the resource domains are therefore the *trusting domains*). This means users and global groups from the master domain can be granted access to resources in the resource domain. This configuration also allows the resource domains to control access to the resources in their domains without having to manage the actual accounts.

Because all accounts are in the master domain, it is not necessary for the resource domains to trust each other.

Global groups containing certain types of users are usually created in the master domain. These users are then placed in local groups in the resource domains, and the local groups are granted permission to resources in the resource domain. This means that if a user changes departments or leaves the company, only the global group on the master domain needs to be updated, with no action needed in the resource domains.

Advantages

- Good choice if your company does not have too many users.
- Departments can manage their own resources without having to control accounts.
- User accounts can be centrally managed into global groups, and global groups can then be used by the resource domains.
- Resources can be browsed by domain, leading to faster browse times.

Disadvantages

- As with the single domain model, performance may be if you have too many users.
- In each resource domain, local groups need to be defined that include global groups from the resource domain.

Multi-Master Domain Model

If a single master domain is not sufficient to contain all of your users but you still want centralized administration, the multi-master domain model will allow you to do this.

As the name suggests, a multi-master domain includes several master domains, each with a number of accounts (see Figure 14-2). Each of these master domains trusts the others, which means any user account in a domain can access resources in any of the other domains.

As in the master domain model, there will also be a number of resource domains that house resources such as printers and shares, but using global groups is not as easy as in the master domain model, because global groups may contain only users from the local domain. This means it might be necessary to have a number of duplicate global groups on each master domain (they can have the same name). For example, you might have an Accounts global group in each master domain, containing users who work for accounting departments. You would then assign the Accounts global group from each domain access to accounting resources in the resource domains.

Continuing the example, if you have Master1 and Master2—both master domains—and create an Accounts global group in each, you would have global groups Master1\Accounts and Master2\Accounts. You would then assign both of these groups access to accounting resources in the resource domains.

To minimize this problem, you should distribute the users among your master domains by organization rather than by (for example) alphabetical order. This should reduce the need for similar global groups from different master domains.

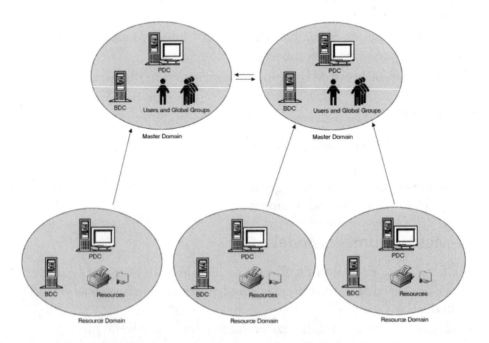

Figure 14-2. Example of a multi-master domain model.

Advantages

- Best choice for companies with a large number of users and a centralized IT department.
- Highly scalable; other master domains can be added to the domain to increase the number of users possible.
- As with the master domain model, resource domains can control access to their resources without managing the accounts.

Disadvantages

- Global groups in the master domains might have to be duplicated.
- Involves many Trust Relationships to manage.
- Not all of the user accounts are in one domain.

Complete Trust Model

The complete trust model offers no central account management; rather, each domain manages its own users and resources. You can use this model if you have multiple departments who each want to manage their own resources and accounts.

Each domain in a complete trust model trusts the others, so you have n*(n-1) Trust Relationships to manage (where n is the number of domains). This means that for 10 domains, you would need 90 Trust Relationships (remember, you have to have a trust each way), and if you want to add a new domain you would need to define 20 trusts.

The idea of a Trust Relationship is that you trust a domain to authenticate the users and to enforce security. With the complete trust model, you are only as good as your worst System Administrator, because he might add users to global admin groups (for example) who should not have that access and who may cause security problems for the whole of the domain structure.

Advantages

- Best choice for companies with no central administration.
- Flexible for users.
- Departments have full control over users and resources.

Disadvantages

- No central management of accounts.
- Need to manage all the Trust Relationships.
- Need to trust each domain not to put inappropriate users into global groups.

By now you should have an idea of the advantages and disadvantages of the domain models and in what circumstances they should be used, such as using resource domains to allow departments control of access to their own resources.

Windows 2000 introduces several new core concepts that make the need for many of the domain models redundant; however, you should note that you do not have to change the structure of your organization with NT 5.0. NT 5.0 is fully backward compatible, so you can maintain the current structure of your NT domain(s) and still move to NT 5.0.

 14.10

How can I join a domain from the command line?

The NT Resource Kit Supplement 2 ships a new utility called NETDOM.EXE that you can use to not only join domains but create computer accounts and Trust Relationships.

To join a domain, there are two paths. The first is to add the computer to the domain and create the computer account simultaneously. This is okay if you are logged on as a domain Administrator, but if you are not a domain Administrator, the account needs to be added in advance and then you join the domain.

If you are logged on as a domain Administrator, enter the following command to create the account and join the domain, where <computer name> is the name of your machine (for example, johnstation):

```
netdom /domain:savilltech /user:savillj /password:nottelling
member <computer name> /joindomain
```

If you are not an Administrator, the domain admin people will have to set up an account for you first, using either Server Manager or NETDOM.EXE.

```
netdom /domain:savilltech /user:savillj /password:nettelling
member <computer name> /add
```

After the account has been added, the member user can join the domain by using the first command shown.

How do I demote a PDC to a BDC?

Normally, when you promote a BDC to the PDC, the existing PDC is automatically demoted to a BDC. Sometimes the PDC is taken offline before a BDC is promoted. In such a case, when the old PDC is restarted, it will still think it's the PDC, and when it detects another PDC, it will simply stop its own netlogon service.

If this happens, you should be able to demote the PDC by using Server Manager, choosing the option Demote to Backup Domain Controller. If this fails, however, you can also demote the PDC by editing the Registry. I strongly advise caution if you use the following information because it involves not only editing the Registry but changing Registry protections.

1. Log on to the machine as an Administrator.
2. Start the Registry editor (REGEDT32.EXE).
3. Move to HKEY_LOCAL_MACHINE\Security.
4. Select Permissions from the Security menu.
5. Select Administrators and change the access type to Full Control.
6. Check Replace Permission on Existing Subkeys and click OK. Then click Yes to the confirmation dialog box.
7. You can now navigate the Security menu and move down to Policy\PolSrvRo.
8. Double-click on the default <no name> value and change the second digit (which should be 3 for a PDC) to a **2** (which means BDC). For example, 03000000 should change to 02000000. Click OK.
9. Now reset the Security on the Security part of the Registry, using the same method as before but changing back to Special Access for Administrators.
10. When you restart the machine, it will come up as a BDC.

4.0 ONLY

FAQ
14.12

How can I configure a BDC to automatically promote itself to a PDC if the PDC fails?

There is no way to do this. The assumption in the event of a crash is that the PDC would be configured to write out the dump information and then reboot itself, thus coming back online. You configure this behavior by using the System Control Panel applet's Startup/Shutdown tab.

4.0 ONLY

FAQ
14.13

How do I rename a PDC/BDC?

To rename a Primary Domain Controller, perform the following:

1. Log on to the PDC as an Administrator.
2. Start the Network Control Panel applet (Start > Settings > Control Panel > Network).
3. Click the Identification tab.
4. Click the Change button, enter the new computer name, and click OK.
5. Restart the PDC for the name change to take effect.
6. After the machine has rebooted, start Server Manager (Start > Programs > Administrative Tools > Server Manager). If the old name still appears as a Backup, or if there is no entry for the new name, perform the following steps.
7. Create an entry for the new name. To do this, select Add to Domain in the Computer menu of Server Manager.
8. Add the new computer account as a Windows NT Backup Domain Controller (it will be added and displayed as a Primary).
9. Remove the old name by selecting the entry and then choosing Remove from Domain on the Computer menu.

To rename a Backup Domain Controller, perform the following:

1. Log on to the PDC as an Administrator and start Server Manager (Start > Programs > Administrative Tools > Server Manager).

2. Add an account for the BDC's new name.

3. Log on to the BDC as an Administrator.

4. Start the Network Control Panel applet (Start > Settings > Control Panel > Network).

5. Click the Identification tab.

6. Click the Change button and enter the new computer name. Then click OK.

7. Restart the BDC for the name change to take effect. The netlogon service will not yet start on this server.

8. On the PDC, open Server Manager and select the new BDC name.

9. From the Computer menu, choose Synchronize With Primary. This starts the netlogon service.

10. In Server Manager, select the old BDC name from the list and then choose Computer > Remove From Domain.

Note: If the BDC begins to receive 7023 or 3210 errors after you synchronize the domain in Server Manager, do the following: on the PDC, choose the BDC, and then synch that specific BDC with the PDC. After an event indicating that the synch is complete, restart the BDC.

4.0 ONLY

Can I move a BDC to another domain?

No. The BDC shares a common SID with the PDC of the domain, so there is no way to move a BDC to another domain. You would need to reinstall the BDC.

System Internals has released NewSID 3.0 (see http://www.sysinternals.com), which has a SID-synchronizing feature that lets you have one machine copy the SID of another. This makes it possible to move a BDC to a new domain. On the BDC, start NewSID and click Synchronize SID. Then enter the name of the PDC and click OK.

Under Windows 2000, you don't have the concept of BDCs and PDCs, but you can move a Domain Controller to another domain by demoting it to a member server and then promoting it to a Domain Controller in the new domain. You can do all of this by using the DCPROMO.EXE utility.

Can I change a PDC/BDC into a standalone server?

4.0 ONLY
14.15

No. The PDC/BDC Registry is different from that of a standalone server, so as with changing a standalone to a Domain Controller, you need to do a reinstallation.

You could disable the machine's netlogon service so it does not act as a Domain Controller, as follows:

1. Start the Services Control Panel applet (Start > Settings > Control Panel > Services).
2. Select Net Logon and click Stop.
3. Click Startup and change to Manual.

Under Windows 2000, you can do this by running DCPROMO.EXE and choosing to demote the machine to a member server.

Can I administer my domain from an NT Workstation?

4.0 ONLY
14.16

It might be that the Domain Controllers are all locked safely away so you need a way to administer your domain from normal workstation machines. If you install the NT Server client-based Administration tools, this is possible.

1. Insert the NT Server CD-ROM into your NT Workstation.
2. Run the file <CD-ROM drive>:\clients\srvtools\winnt\setup.bat. This detects your processor and installs the correct executables into the %systemroot%\system32 folder. Now press Enter.
3. Remove the CD-ROM.
4. You now need to create shortcuts for these applications, on either the desktop or the Start menu:
   - DHCPADMN.EXE   DHCP Manager
   - POLEDIT.EXE   System Policy Editor

- RASADMIN.EXE   Remote Access Administrator
- RPLMGR.EXE   Remoteboot Manager
- SRVMGR.EXE   Server Manager
- USRMGR.EXE   User Manager for Domains
- WINSADMN.EXE   WINS Manager

An alternative is to connect to a Domain Controller's admin$ share, move to the system32 folder, and directly run the applications. For example, use

\\<server>\admin$\system32\usrmgr.exe

It is better to install locally, though.

4.0 ONLY

In what order should I upgrade my PDC and BDCs from 3.51 to 4.0?

The two versions can coexist happily, so you can upgrade in any order you want; however, the following schedule might be the safest:

1. Upgrade a BDC from 3.51 to 4.0.
2. Leave it for a week and check that it is okay.
3. Promote the BDC to the PDC.
4. Leave it for another week and check that everything is okay.
5. Upgrade the other BDCs to 4.0.
6. Promote the old PDC back to the main PDC (the current PDC will automatically be demoted to a BDC).

This luxury of upgrading a BDC to the new version of the operating system will not be possible with the upgrade from 4.0 to Windows 2000. With that upgrade, the first machine to be upgraded will have to be the PDC. Backups, here we come!

What tuning can I perform on PDC/BDC synchronization?

The PDC has to pass account database (SAM) changes to the BDCs in a process known as "synchronization." The several Registry settings that can be configured for PDC/BDC synchronization in Windows NT 4.0 are shown in Table 14-1.

These are all values under HKEY_LOCAL_MACHINE\System\ CurrentControlSet\Services\Netlogon\Parameters.

Table 14-1. Registry Settings for PDC/BDC Synchronization

ChangeLogSize (REG_SZ)	Default size for the Change Log. By default, 64KB with a maximum of 4MB.
Pulse	Determines the gap in seconds between replication from the PDC to the BDCs. The lowest value is 60 and the max is 3600 (1 hour); the default is 300 (5 minutes). You might want to increase this time if the BDCs are over a slow WAN link.
PulseConcurrency	Number of BDCs to which the PDC sends pulses concurrently. By default, 10.
PulseMaximum	The PDC performs periodic checks that the BDCs are still there. This is in seconds, with minimum 60 and maximum 86,400.
Randomize	Number of seconds a BDC waits after an announcement before answering. By default, 1.
ReplicationGovernor	Percentage of the 128K blocks that are sent. If you have a slow link, you might not want the PDC sending 128K blocks, so you could change this to 25, meaning only 32K would be sent at a time. This also means the blocks are sent more frequently (25 would mean four times as often).
Update	By default, set to No, which means only changes are replicated. Setting to Yes causes everything to be replicated even if there is no change. This needs to be set on the import server.

Windows 2000 allows this information to be set graphically and on a per machine/per site basis, using the Active Directory Sites and Services Manager. By using this tool, you can configure replication to occur once, twice, four times, or not at all for every hour of the week.

4.0 ONLY
14.19

I cannot add a BDC over a WAN. Why?

To add a BDC to a domain, the PDC has to be contactable. Therefore, the first task is to check that communications are working.

If you are using TCP/IP, ensure that you can ping the PDC, as follows:

```
ping <ip address of the PDC>
```

If this is okay, the problem is at the NetBIOS level (NetBIOS is explored further in several FAQs in this chapter). If you have WINS on the network, ensure that the BDC is configured to use the WINS server. When the PDC starts, it will register the WINS name <domain><1Bh>, which is used to identify the Domain Controller.

Alternatively, you can update the LMHOSTS file.

1. Start Notepad (or another text editor).
2. Open the file %systemroot%\system32\drivers\etc\lmhosts.
3. Add a line with the following syntax
   <IP address> <machine name> #PRE #DOM:<domain name>
4. Save the file.

To use the LMHOSTS file during installation, you should create the file on another machine and copy it over when the BDC is being installed. Alternatively, add it to the i386 folder, if possible.

How can I synchronize the domain from the command line?

To force a domain synchronization on a BDC with the PDC, use this command from the command line:

```
net accounts /sync
```

This can also be performed by selecting Synchronize with Primary Domain Controller from the Computer menu of Server Manager on the BDC.

How can I force a client to validate its logon against a specific Domain Controller?

Before I answer, you need to understand what happens when a logon occurs.

When a logon request is made to a domain, the workstation sends out a discovery request to find a Domain Controller for the domain. The domain name is actually a NetBIOS 16-character name, with the 16th character used by Microsoft Networking Services to identify the NetBIOS type.

The type used for a Domain Controller is <1C>, so the NetBIOS name for Domain Controller of domain Savilltech would be Savilltech <1C>. The NetBIOS type has to be the 16th character, so the name of the domain has to be filled with blanks to make its length up to 15 characters.

If the client is WINS-enabled, a query for the resolution of <domain name> <1C> is sent to the WINS server, as defined in the client's TCP/IP properties. The WINS server returns up to 25 IP addresses that correspond to Domain Controllers of the requested domain, and a \mailslot\net\ntlogon is broadcast to the local subnet. If the workstation receives a response, it attempts logon with the local Domain Controller.

If WINS is not configured, it is possible to manually configure the LMHOSTS file on the workstations to specify the Domain Controller. This file is located in the %systemroot%\system32\drivers\etc directory.

An example entry in LMHOSTS would be as follows:

```
200.200.200.50 titanic #PRE #DOM:savilltech #savilltech
Domain Controller
```

This entry sets up IP address 200.200.200.50 to be host Titanic—the Domain Controller for Savilltech—and instructs the machine that this entry is to be pre-loaded into the cache.

To check the NetBIOS name cache, you can use command nbtstat -c, which shows all of the entries, including their type. If WINS is not configured and there is no entry in LMHOSTS, the workstation sends out a series of three broadcasts. If no response is received and WINS is configured to use DNS for WINS resolution, a request is sent to the DNS server, and finally the HOSTS file is checked. If all of this fails, you'll see this error message:

A Domain Controller for your domain could not be found.

To force a client to use a specific Domain Controller, you need only do the following:

1. Start the Registry editor (REGEDIT.EXE).
2. Move to HKEY_LOCAL_MACHINE\SYSTEM\CurrentControlSet\ Services\NetBT\Parameters.
3. From the Edit menu, select New > DWORD Value.
4. Enter the name NodeType and press Enter.
5. Double-click on the new value and set to 4 (see Figure 14-3). This sets the network to an M-mode/mixed, which means it will perform a broadcast before querying name servers for resolution. By default, a system is 1 if no WINS servers are configured (B-node/broadcast) or 8 if at least one WINS server is configured (H-node/queries name resolution first and then broadcasts).
6. Double-click on the EnableLMHOSTS value and set it to 1. If it does not exist, select New > DWORD Value from the Edit menu and enter the name **EnableLMHOSTS**.
7. Close the Registry editor and reboot the machine.

The machine is now configured to broadcast for a Domain Controller on a local subnet and then query a name server. If no Domain Controllers are found on the WINS server, or if WINS is not used, it will then search the LMHOSTS file. The next stage is to edit this file, as follows:

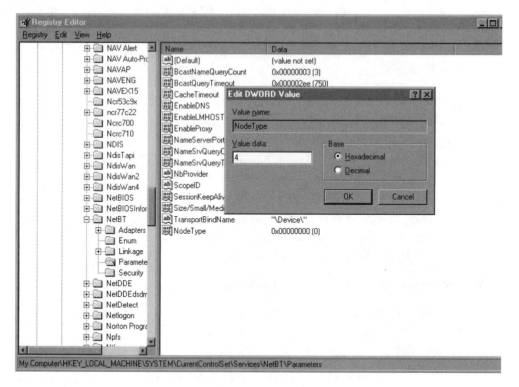

Figure 14-3. Modifying the node type.

1. Check for the LMHOSTS file.

```
dir %systemroot%\system32\drivers\etc\lmhosts
```

2. If the file does not exist, copy the sample host file.

```
copy %systemroot%\system32\drivers\etc\lmhosts.sam
%systemroot%\system32\drivers\etc\lmhosts
1 file(s) copied
```

3. Edit the file by using EDIT.EXE (don't use NOTEPAD.EXE).

```
edit %systemroot%\system32\drivers\etc\lmhosts
```

4. Go to the end of the comments and add a new line of the format

```
<ip address> <name of DC> #PRE #DOM:<domain name>
#<comment>
```

(for example, 200.200.200.50 titanic #PRE #DOM:savilltech #savilltech Domain Controller)

5. Save the changes to the file and exit EDIT.EXE.

6. Force the machine to reload the LMHOSTS file (or just reboot):

nbtstat -R

Note: The **-R** must be uppercase because the command is case sensitive.

7. Check the cache:

nbtstat -c

8. At this point the configuration is complete and a reboot is advisable.

Service Pack 4 includes a new utility, SETPRFDC.EXE, that directs a secure channel client to a preferred list of Domain Controllers. The syntax is

SETPRFDC <domain name> <DC1, DC2, ..., DCn>

SETPRFDC tries each domain controller in the list in order until a secure channel is established. If DC1 does not respond, DC2 is tried, and so on. After you run SETPRFDC on a WinNT 4.0, SP4 computer, the list is remembered until you change it. You can run SETPRFDC in batch, via the scheduler or even in a logon script (for future logons). Don't forget to undo any LMHOSTS entries you might have set.

2000 ONLY

14.22 How do I promote a Windows 2000 server to a Domain Controller?

Windows 2000 ships with the DCPROMO.EXE utility, which is used to promote a standalone/member server to a Domain Controller and vice versa.

In Windows NT 2000, domains are DNS names, which means you can have a hierarchy of domains leading to parent-child domain relationships.

The advantage of these parent-child relationships is their bidirectional transitive trust. In other words, if domain b is a child of domain a, and domain c is a child of domain b, domain c implicitly trusts domain a (see Figure 14-4). This is very different from the way trusts work in earlier versions of Windows NT.

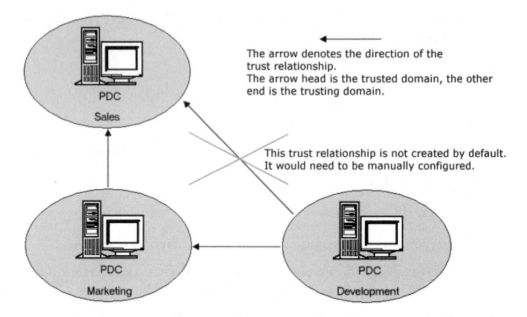

The arrow denotes the direction of the trust relationship.
The arrow head is the trusted domain, the other end is the trusting domain.

This trust relationship is not created by default. It would need to be manually configured.

Figure 14-4. Trust relationships under Windows NT 4.0. Under Windows 2000, if Development is a child of Marketing, and Marketing is a child of Sales, Development implicitly trusts Sales.

Because Windows NT 5.0 domains rely on DNS, it is vital that DNS is correctly configured to enable the domain to be created (if you are creating a new top-level domain). Information on configuring DNS for a domain can be found in Chapter 17, Domain Name System (DNS).

A final prerequisite is that an NTFS 5.0 volume is required to house the SYSVOL volume, so ensure that you have at least one NTFS 5.0 volume (use CHKNTFS to check the versions of your partitions).

To upgrade a standalone/member server to a domain controller, perform the following:

Start the DCPROMO utility (Start > Run > DCPROMO).

Click Next to go to the introduction screen.

You have a choice of New Domain or Replica Domain Controller in Existing Domain. There is no concept of a BDC in NT 5.0, and all domain controllers are equal (more or less). Select New Domain and click Next to continue.

A new concept is trees, which enable child domains. If you are starting a new top-level domain, select Create New Domain Tree. To create a child domain, select Create New Child Domain. Then click Next to continue.

If you choose to create a new domain tree, you are asked if you want to create a new forest of domain trees or put this new domain tree in an existing forest. Forests enable you to "join" a number of separate domain trees, and again a transitive Trust Relationship is created among them. If this is your first NT 5.0 domain tree, you should create a new forest. Then click Next to continue.

You are asked for the DNS name of your domain; for example, Savilltech.com is a valid domain name. This must match the information configured on the DNS server. Click Next to continue.

You are asked for a NetBIOS domain name. By default, this is the left-most part (up to the first 15 characters) of the DNS domain name—for example, Savilltech—however, this can be changed. Click Next to continue.

You have to provide a storage area for the Active Directory and the Active Directory log. Accept the defaults and click Next.

Finally, you must select an area on an NTFS 5.0 partition for the SYSVOL volume for storage of the server's public files. By default, this is %systemroot%\SYSVOL. Click Next to continue.

A summary screen is displayed. Click Next to start the upgrade, which sets security and creates the Directory Server schema container. Information from the default directory service file and the old SAM is then read in if the machine is an upgraded PDC.

Click Finish and reboot the machine.

You now have a Windows NT 5.0 domain controller. You can add additional Domain Controllers (old BDCs) by performing these same steps except for selecting Replica Domain Controller in Existing Domain in step 3 and providing the name of the domain to replicate.

2000 ONLY

14.23 How can I verify my Windows 2000 domain creation?

To verify that the TCP/IP configuration is okay, check for the ldap.tcp.<domain> service record (for example, ldap.tcp.savilltech.com).

```
nslookup
set type=srv
ldap.tcp.savilltech.com
```

The system returns the following:

```
Server: [200.200.200.50]
Address: 200.200.200.50
ldap.tcp.savilltech.com SRV service location:
priority = 0
weight = 0
port = 389
svr hostname = titanic.savilltech.com
titanic.savilltech.com internet address = 200.200.200.50
```

Also make sure that the NetBIOS computer name is okay:

net view \\<computer name>

Finally, check that the NetBIOS domain name works:

usrmgr <domain name>

The NetBIOS domain name is used for backward compatibility.

How can I generate a list of all computer accounts in a domain?

The normal method under Windows NT 4.0 and earlier is to use Server Manager (Start > Programs > Administrative Tools > Server Manager). By this method, you can view, add, or delete computer accounts.

Under Windows 2000, you can view this information by using the Active Directory MMC (Microsoft Management Console) snap-in to browse the domain/computers group. Of course, under Windows NT 5.0 and the Active Directory, computers can also be created in Organization Units (OUs) and not all would be shown under this tree. As shown in Figure 14-5, the computer account in the law OU would not be listed in the Computers group. A more complete method is to use the Windows NT Resource Kit NETDOM.EXE utility (which runs under Windows NT 5.0) to generate the list, like this:

```
netdom member
```

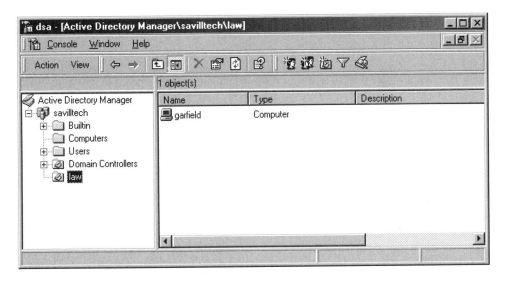

Figure 14-5. Viewing computers in Windows 2000.

This brings the following return:

```
Searching PDC for domain SAVILLTECH ...
Found PDC \\TITANIC
Listing members of domain SAVILLTECH ...
Member 1 = \\ODIN
Member 2 = \\garfield
```

It is also possible to list other domains by using a mixture of command line switches, like this:

netdom /d:<domain name> [/u:<domain>\<user to which query> / p:<password] member

The information in the brackets is only needed if your account does not have privileges in the requested domain. The advantage of the command line tool is that it lists all computer accounts, even those in OUs in the Active Directory.

An alternative method is to use the net view /domain:<domain> command, which has the advantage that you can pipe the output to a file or to another command, like this:

```
net view /domain:savilltech
```

15 SYSTEM POLICIES

System policies allow settings to be configured for users and computers of a domain, including logon warning messages, background pictures—anything you like.

The advantage of policies is that you can also define templates by creating your own .ADM files, which is covered in this chapter. You'll also find information on setting policy values in other chapters, where a policy fulfills a requirement.

Remember that policies are basically a list of Registry entries, so anything that can be defined with a policy can also be accomplished by directly editing the Registry. The advantage of a policy is that clients download the policy at each logon and it applies to the entire domain.

You can find more information on Windows 9x policies in Chapter 29, Windows 95/98 Administration.

4.0 ONLY
FAQ 15.1 How do system policies work?

You will probably have two policies on each domain. You need a different system policy for Windows 95 machines and Windows NT machines because of incompatibilities between the formats.

The Windows NT Policy editor is shipped with Windows NT Server, and the Windows 95 System Policy editor is on the Windows 95 CD in the \admin\apptools\poledit directory. Policies alter Registry settings on the target machine, and when the Registry settings have been changed, the changes remain until changed by something else. Therefore, if you implement restrictions, they remain even if the policy file is deleted.

By default, Windows clients look for policy files in the Net Logon share on the Domain Controller. (For NT, that's the machine that validates the logon; for Windows 95, it's the PDC unless you implement load balancing.) Windows NT looks for the policy file NTCONFIG.POL, and Windows 95 machines look for CONFIG.POL.

An important thing to note is that NTCONFIG.POL and CONFIG.POL are, by default, not copied to BDCs, and you have to set up directory replication so all clients receive the policy file.

4.0 ONLY

How can I install the Policy editor on a workstation?

The Policy editor consists of an image, POLEDIT.EXE, and a number of .ADM files. To install the Policy editor on a workstation, perform the following:

1. Copy POLEDIT.EXE from the %systemroot% (e.g., c:\winnt) on a Windows NT Server machine to the %systemroot% folder on the workstation.

2. Copy COMMON.ADM, WINDOWS.ADM, and WINNT.ADM from %systemroot%/inf on the NT Server to the %systemroot%/inf folder on the workstation.

You will now be able to run the Policy editor on a Windows NT Workstation. You might want to create a shortcut to POLEDIT.EXE in your Administrative Tools folder.

4.0 ONLY

How do I modify a policy?

In this example, you modify the Logon Banner:

1. Start the System Policy editor (Start > Programs > Administrative Tools > System Policy Editor).
2. From the File menu, choose New Policy.
3. Double-click on Local Computer.
4. Double-click on Windows NT System and then double-click on Logon.
5. Click on Logon Banner until it changes to a tick.
6. Enter a caption and text and click OK (see Figure 15-1).

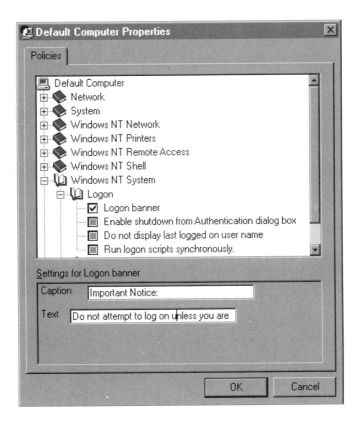

Figure 15-1. The default text for a logon banner.

7. From the File menu, choose Save As. Save in the %system root%/ system32/repl/Export/Scripts as NTCONFIG.POL. You save in the Export directory because directory replication copies the file to the /Import/Scripts directory both on the local machine and on any backup Domain Controllers.

8. Close the System Policy editor.

It is essential to have the policy replicated to all Domain Controllers, because anyone may validate the logon. For information on configuring directory replication, see Question 11-10, in Chapter 11, Recovery.

How do I create my own policy template?

When the System Policy editor is running, you can select which templates to include. These three are supplied with NT and are stored in the %systemroot%/inf directory.

COMMON.ADM
WINDOWS.ADM
WINNT.ADM

Typically, the only templates you will use are COMMON.ADM and WINNT.ADM (see Figure 15-2). WINDOWS.ADM was supplied for compatibility with Windows 95 machines; however, policies created with Windows NT won't work on Windows 95, so this template is not used.

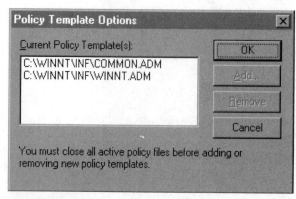

Figure 15-2. Currently, COMMON.ADM and WINNT.ADM are in use.

To select which templates to use, choose Policy Template from the Options menu. The structure of an .ADM file is simple and follows the structure shown here:

```
CLASS MACHINE or USER
CATEGORY !!<string for first level>
  CATEGORY !!<string for second level>  This is optional.
    POLICY !!<string for name to be displayed next to check
box>
    KEYNAME !!<string for the keyname where the value is, do
not include the first part of the Registry location, e.g.
HKEY_LOCAL_MACHINE>
        VALUENAME !!<actual value name>
        VALUEON "1" VALUEOFF "0"
        PART !!<displayed in the bottom of the system policy
screen> TEXT
        END PART
      END POLICY
  END CATEGORY
END CATEGORY
[strings]
<strings defined>="Windows NT Network"
```

The !! introduces a string that has to then be defined in the [strings] section, basically, but you don't have to use strings. An alternative is to actually type the full strings; however, if any string contains a space, you must enclose it in quotes. Using the !! syntax is useful for long key names if they're used repeatedly. Every keyword (except class) must have an end keyword. That is, category needs an end category, if needs endif, and so on.

For examples, look at the COMMON.ADM and WINNT.ADM files. Compare them to how they look in the System Policy editor to get the display and effect you want.

Below is a basic .ADM file that just updates the Registry entry HKEY_LOCAL_MACHINE\SYSTEM\CurrentControlSet\Control\ FileSystem\ NtfsDisable8dot3NameCreation. Notice that you don't enter the HKEY_LOCAL_MACHINE as part of the keyname. This is implied because it's part of the MACHINE class.

```
CLASS MACHINE
CATEGORY !!SavillTech
  CATEGORY !!Update
```

```
KEYNAME SYSTEM\CurrentControlSet\Control\FileSystem
      POLICY !!8dot3create
      VALUENAME "NtfsDisable8dot3NameCreation"
      END POLICY

   END CATEGORY; File System

END CATEGORY; SavillTech

[strings]
SavillTech="SavillTech Entries"
Update="File System"
FileSystem="Name Creation Control"
8dot3create="Disable 8.3 File name creation"
```

You can accomplish many other combinations and effects, such as a drop-down box, by using the following:

```
PART !!<string> DROPDOWNLIST
VALUENAME ""<actual value>
   ITEMLIST
      NAME "<string>" VALUE NUMERIC n
      NAME "<string>" VALUE NUMERIC n
      NAME "<string>" VALUE NUMERIC n
   END ITEMLIST
END PART
```

How can I control the policy updates?

You can dictate how policies are applied to a Windows NT machine, either from the Domain Controller authenticating the logon or by a manual path.

This is usually configured by using the System Policy editor. Go to Default Computer > Network > System Policies Update and check Remote Update. You now have two options. You can choose Automatic Update, which means the NT client makes a connection to the Net Logon share of the Domain Controller that validated the logon, or you can choose Manual and then enter a path and name where the policy is located.

You can also configure the machine to display any error messages and enable load balancing (see Figure 15-3).

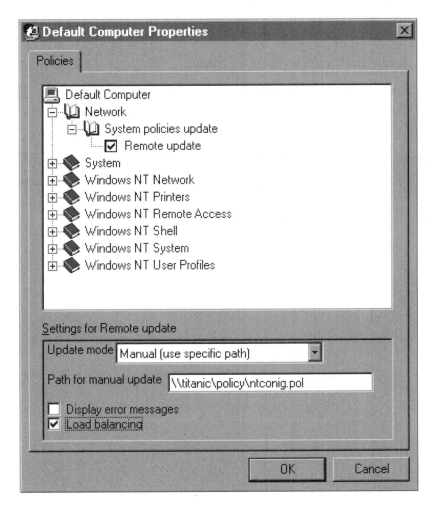

Figure 15-3. Specifying the options for the policy update.

All of these changes can also be configured directly through the Registry.

1. Start the Registry editor (REGEDIT.EXE).
2. Move to HKEY_LOCAL_MACHINE\SYSTEM\CurrentControlSet\ Control\Update.

3. Double-click on UpdateMode (if it does not exist, create it of type DWORD by choosing File > New > DWORD Value).

4. Set to 1 for Automatic Update (the default), 2 for Manual, or 0 for No Update. Click OK.

5. If you set UpdateMode to 2, you should then double-click on NetworkPath (or create it of type REG_SZ or String Value).

6. Set the location and name of the policy file to use.

7. Click OK and close the Registry editor.

You can also create these two other values under HKEY_LOCAL_ MACHINE\SYSTEM\CurrentControlSet\Control\Update.

Value	Type	Setting
Verbose	DWORD value	1 enables error messages
LoadBalance	DWORD value	1 enables load balancing

16 TCP/IP

Unless you have a single computer that never connects to the Internet, you are probably using TCP/IP.

TCP/IP is a suite of related protocols and utilities used for network communications. For basic connectivity, TCP/IP is actually two protocols, Internet Protocol (IP) and Transmission Control Protocol (TCP). IP provides the basic connectivity, and TCP provides error correction, guarantee of delivery, and so on. Related protocols are then used for such operations as File Transfer Protocol (FTP) and Domain Name Server (DNS), all of which rely on IP as the transport mechanism.

There are many different implementations of TCP/IP, but they all conform to a standard, which means the various implementations can communicate with each other.

The explosion of the Internet is in part thanks to TCP/IP with its powerful addressing scheme and enormous industry support.

Each machine that uses TCP/IP must have a unique TCP/IP address. This is a 32-bit number, usually displayed in the *dotted quad* (or dotted decimal) format xxx.xxx.xxx.xxx, where xxx is a number from 0 to 255. For example, here is the IP address 147.98.26.11 in its 32-bit form to show how it breaks down into the dotted quad format:

10010011	01100010	00011010	00001011
147	98	26	11

TCP/IP was originally used on ARPAnet, a military network. It then grew to universities and is now used on virtually every computer system. Have a look at http://rs.internic.net/nic-support/15min/modules/arpanet/sld01.html for more information on ARPAnet.

Companies or institutions are usually given a range of IP addresses, and when you connect to the Internet via an Internet service provider (ISP), they supply you with an IP address from their range. IP addresses are controlled and distributed by InterNIC (http://www.internic.net).

What is the subnet mask?

As explained in the introduction, the IP address consists of four octets and is usually displayed in the format xxx.xxx.xxx.xxx; however, this address on its own does not mean much. A subnet mask is required to show which part of the IP address is the network ID and which part is the host ID.

Imagine the network ID as the road name and the host ID as the house number. With "54 Grove Street," 54 would be the host ID and Grove Street the network ID.

Similarly, with an address of 200.200.200.5 and a subnet mask of 255.255.255.0, the network ID is 200.200.200 and the host ID is 5. This is calculated by using the following grid:

IP Address	11001000	11001000	11001000	00000101
Subnet Mask	11111111	11111111	11111111	00000000
network ID	11001000	11001000	11001000	00000000
host ID	00000000	00000000	00000000	00000101

What happens is a bitwise logical AND operation between the IP address and the subnet mask, as seen here:

1 AND 1=1
1 AND 0=0
0 AND 1=0
0 AND 0=0

There are default subnet masks, depending on the class of the IP address, as follows:

Class A: 001.xxx.xxx.xxx to 126.xxx.xxx.xxx uses subnet mask 255.0.0.0 as default

Class B: 128.xxx.xxx.xxx to 191.xxx.xxx.xxx uses subnet mask 255.255.0.0 as default

Class C: 192.xxx.xxx.xxx to 224.xxx.xxx.xxx uses subnet mask 255.255.255.0 as default

Where's 127.xxx.xxx.xxx ? This is a reserved address that is used for testing purposes. If you ping 127.0.0.1, you will ping yourself. This is known as the local Host Address.

You would obviously not stick to these subnet masks on large networks and would instead "subnet" your IP addresses into smaller groups of IP addresses, linking the subnets via gateway machines or routers.

The subnet mask is used when two hosts communicate. If the two hosts are on the same network, Host A will talk directly to Host B. However, if they're on different networks, Host A and Host B have to communicate via a gateway, and they know if they're on the same network by using the subnet mask. This is called an "adjacency test."

Here's an example:

Host A 200.200.200.5
Host B 200.200.200.9
Host C 200.200.199.6
Subnet Mask 255.255.255.0

Host A and Host B both have network ID 200.200.200, so Host A communicates directly with Host B. But Host A and Host C are on different networks—200.200.200 and 200.200.199, respectively—so Host A communicates with Host C via a gateway.

My Network is not connected to the Internet. Can I use any IP address?

The basic answer would be Yes; however, it is advisable to use one of the following ranges, which are reserved for use by private networks:

10.0.0.0-10.255.255.255	A single class A network
172.16.0.0-172.31.255.255	A group of 16 contiguous class B networks
192.168.0.0-192.168.255.255	A group of 256 contiguous class C networks

The addresses above are detailed in RFC 1918 (Request for Comment). The advantage of these addresses is that they are automatically filtered out by routers, thus protecting the Internet. Obviously, if you someday want part of your network on the Internet, you will need to apply for a range of IP addresses (from InterNIC or from your ISP).

How do I install TCP/IP?

There are two methods, depending on whether Dynamic Host Configuration Protocol (DHCP) dynamically allocates an IP address for your machine or if it has a static IP address. Below are the instructions for installing non-DHCP (static) clients:

1. Start the Network Control Panel applet (Start > Settings > Control Panel > Network).
2. Click the Protocols tab and click Add.
3. Select TCP/IP Protocol and click OK.
4. When you are asked if there is a DHCP server on the Network, click NO for DHCP.
5. After installing files and binding protocols, the TCP/IP configuration dialog box opens (see Figure 16-1).
6. Click the IP Address tab and enter the IP address and subnet mask. When you enter the IP address and press the Tab key, a default subnet mask appears. However, you can configure a different subnet mask if you choose.
7. You can also configure DNS servers by clicking on the DNS tab and entering a domain name (such as Savilltech.com) and a host name.
8. Then click OK and reboot the machine.

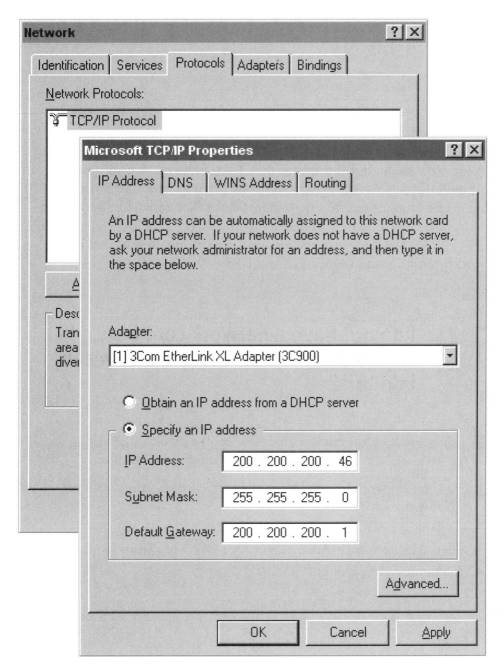

Figure 16-1. Configuring the TCP/IP protocol.

Is there a way to trace TCP/IP traffic by using NT?

As part of the Systems Management Server, a Network Monitor module enables the entire network to be monitored, as well as traffic over a modem.

A limited version of this comes with NT 4.0 Server; however, only communications between the server and other computers on the same subnet can be monitored. You have to install the Network Monitor Service (Control Panel > Network > Services > Add).

The NT 4.0 bundled version is also missing key features, such as the capability to retransmit frames and connect to other agents.

I do not have a network card but would like to install TCP/IP. How can I do this?

Microsoft provides a loopback adapter that can be used for the testing of TCP/IP. To install the loopback adapter, perform the following:

1. Start the Network Control Panel applet (Start > Settings > Control Panel > Network).
2. Click on the Adapters tab and click Add.
3. Select MS Loopback Adapter and click OK (see Figure 16-2).
4. You now need to configure TCP/IP as usual.

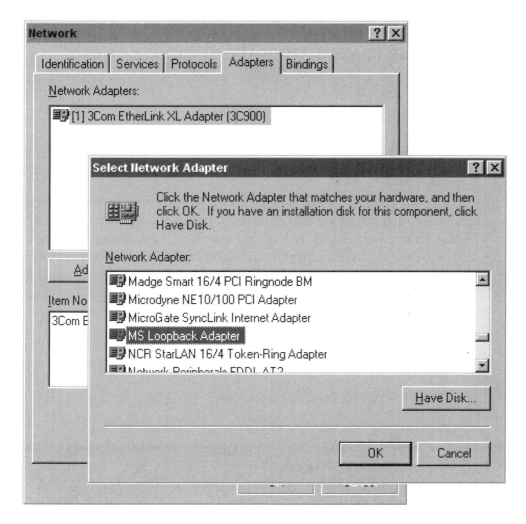

Figure 16-2. Adding the MS loopback adapter.

Obviously, with this adapter you will not be able to communicate with other hosts (there's no physical connection), but you will be able to practice the configuration.

FAQ 16.6 I have installed TCP/IP. What steps should I use to verify that the setup is correct?

To verify your TCP/IP setup, follow these steps:

1. From a command prompt, type

   ```
   ipconfig /all
   ```

   This shows such information as IP address, subnet mask, and the physical (MAC) address (see Figure 16-3). Make sure the IP address and subnet mask are what you would expect. It also shows information of any remote access service (RAS) adapters, if they are configured.
2. A special IP address is used for loopback testing, so try to ping it:

   ```
   ping 127.0.0.1
   ```

   You should get four lines like this:

   Reply from 127.0.0.1: bytes=32 time<10ms TTL=128

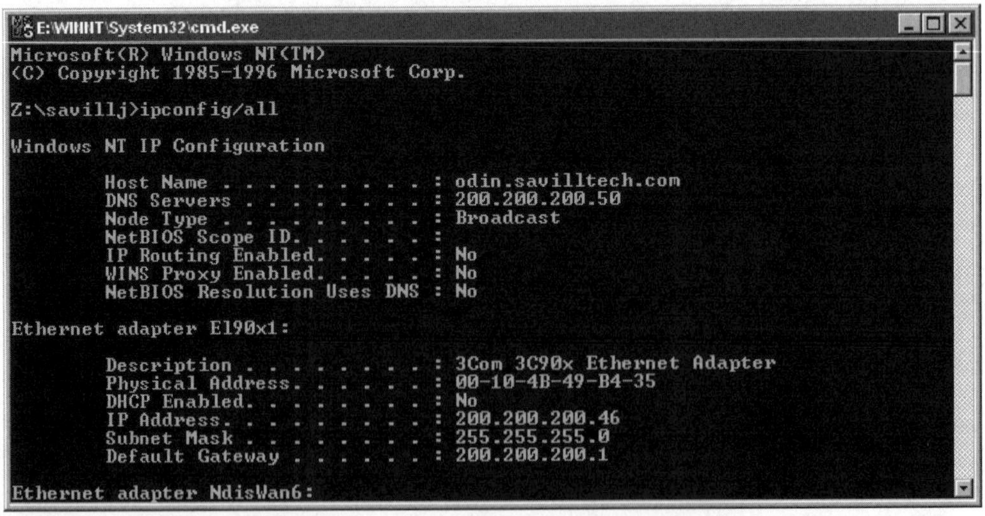

```
E:\WINNT\System32\cmd.exe
Microsoft(R) Windows NT(TM)
(C) Copyright 1985-1996 Microsoft Corp.

Z:\savillj>ipconfig/all

Windows NT IP Configuration

        Host Name . . . . . . . . . : odin.savilltech.com
        DNS Servers . . . . . . . . : 200.200.200.50
        Node Type . . . . . . . . . : Broadcast
        NetBIOS Scope ID. . . . . . :
        IP Routing Enabled. . . . . : No
        WINS Proxy Enabled. . . . . : No
        NetBIOS Resolution Uses DNS : No

Ethernet adapter E190x1:

        Description . . . . . . . . : 3Com 3C90x Ethernet Adapter
        Physical Address. . . . . . : 00-10-4B-49-B4-35
        DHCP Enabled. . . . . . . . : No
        IP Address. . . . . . . . . : 200.200.200.46
        Subnet Mask . . . . . . . . : 255.255.255.0
        Default Gateway . . . . . . : 200.200.200.1

Ethernet adapter NdisWan6:
```

Figure 16-3. Example execution of IPCONFIG/ALL. Notice the information on the last line corresponding to RAS adapter devices.

Pinging 127.0.0.1 does not send any traffic out onto the network. If this does not work, it means the TCP/IP stack is not loaded correctly, so go back and check your configuration.

3. Next try to ping your own IP address. Once again, this does not send any traffic out onto the Network, but it confirms the software:

```
ping 200.200.200.53
```

Once again you should get four reply messages. If this does not work but the loopback did, you have probably typed the IP address incorrectly. Go back and check your configuration.

4. Now try to ping the gateway.

```
ping 200.200.200.1
```

This is the first traffic going out over the network. The gateway should be on your subnet. If you fail to ping the gateway, check that the gateway is up and that your network is correctly connected.

5. Ping something on the other side of the gateway—that is, something not on your subnet, like this:

```
ping 158.234.26.46
```

If this does not work, the gateway might not be functioning correctly.

6. If all of the above worked, you should test Name Resolution by pinging by name. This will test the HOSTS and/or DNS. For example, if your machine name were john and the domain savilltech.com, you would use

```
ping john.savilltech.comft5 cvr
```

If this does not work, check in the Network Settings > Protocols > TCP/IP that the domain name is correct. Also check the HOSTS file and the DNS.

7. Next try to ping a name outside the network (if you're connected to the Internet):

```
ping ftp.microsoft.com
```

If this does not work, check with your ISP.

8. If all of the above works, get down to the serious stuff and start surfing.

How can I trace the route the TCP/IP packets take?

In general, TCP/IP packets do not always take the same route to a destination; however, the start of the journey is likely to be the same (to your gateway, to the firewall, and so on). The command to use is tracert and the syntax is as follows (200.200.200.24.1 is the gateway):

```
tracert <host name or IP address>
```

For example:

```
tracert news.savilltech.com
Tracing route to news.savilltech.com [200.200.8.55]
over a maximum of 30 hops:
1 <10 ms <10 ms <10 ms 200.200.24.1
2 <10 ms 10ms <10 ms 200.200.255.81
3 30 ms 10 ms 10 ms news.savilltech.com [200.200.8.55]
Trace complete
```

The first column is the hop count. The next three columns show the time taken for the cumulative round-trip times (in milliseconds) for the three packets sent. The fourth column is the hostname if the IP address was resolved, and the last column is the IP address of the host. It is really like a street map telling you each turn to take. An important thing is to look for looping routes. If Host A goes to B, then C, and then back to A, this usually indicates a problem.

Tracert does not always work with some firewalls for hosts outside the firewall. This is because firewalls limit which ports TCP/IP can communicate over and filter out the ping packets.

What diagnostic utilities are available for TCP/IP?

With a protocol as powerful and configurable as TCP/IP, routing/communication problems **will** occur. Luckily, a number of extensive utilities are available.

Questions 16.6 and 16.7 talk about PING and TRACERT, and Table 16-1 gives a more complete list.

Table 16-1. TCP/IP Diagnostic Utilities

arp	Displays and modifies the IP to physical address translation tables used by the ARP (Address Resolution Protocol).
finger	Displays information about a user on a specified system that is running the Finger service.
hostname	Displays the name of the current host.
ipconfig	Displays information about the current TCP/IP configuration, including details about DNS servers. Can also be used to renew and release DHCP address leases.
nbtstat	Displays protocol statistics and current TCP/IP connections using NBT (NetBIOS over TCP/IP).
netstat	Displays protocol statistics and current TCP/IP connections.
ping	Used to check if a destination host is receiving TCP/IP packets.
route	Used to maintain and display routing tables.
tracert	Used to view the route packets take to a destination host.

For more information on these commands, enter the command, followed by a question mark; for example:

```
netstat -?
```

 # What is routing and how is it configured?

When Host A wants to send to Host B on the same local network, the IP protocol resolves the IP address to a physical address by using ARP. The physical addresses of the source and destination hosts (for example, 00-05-f3-43-d3-3e) are added to the IP datagram to form a frame, and by using the frame, the two hosts can communicate directly with each other.

If the two hosts are not on the same local network, they cannot communicate directly with each other and instead have to go through a *router*. You have probably already come across a router when you installed TCP/IP, because the default gateway is just a router you have chosen to use as a means of communicating with hosts outside your local network if no specific route is known. A router can be a Windows NT computer with two or more network cards (one card for connection to each separate local network) or it can be a physical hardware device, such as a Cisco router.

Assuming our two hosts are not on the same local network, Host A checks its routing table for a router that connects to the local network of Host B. If it does not find a match, the data frames are sent to the "default gateway." In most cases, there is no one router that connects straight to the intended recipient. Instead, the router knows of another route to pass on your packet, which then goes to another router, and so on.

For example:

```
Host A 200.200.200.5
Host B 200.200.199.6
Subnet Mask 255.255.255.0
Router 200.200.200.2 and 200.200.199.2

Host A's routing table - Network 200.200.199.0; use router
200.200.200.2
```

In this example, Host A deduces that Host B is on a separate network because its network ID is 200.200.199. Host A then checks its routing table and sees that for network 200.200.199 (the zero means all) it should send to 200.200.200.2. The router receives the packets and then forwards them to network 200.200.199.

What actually happens is that each router has its own routing table that will point to other routes.

To configure a route, you use the route command. For example, to configure a root for network 200.200.199 to use router 200.200.200.2, you type

```
route -p add 200.200.199.0 mask 255.255.255.0 200.200.200.2
```

The -p makes the addition permanent; otherwise, it will be lost with a reboot.

To view your existing information, type **route print**.

FAQ 16.10 What is ARP?

ARP stands for Address Resolution Protocol. It was touched on in Question 16.9 as a means of resolving an IP address to an actual physical network card address (MAC).

All network cards have a unique 48-bit address that is written as six hexadecimal pairs (for example, 00-A0-24-7A-01-48). This address is hard-coded into the network card. You can view your network card's hardware address by typing

```
ipconfig /all

..

Ethernet adapter Elnk31:

Description . . . . . . . . : ELNK3 Ethernet Adapter.
Physical Address. . . . . . : 00-A0-24-7A-01-48
DHCP Enabled. . . . . . . . : No
IP Address. . . . . . . . . : 200.200.200.5
Subnet Mask . . . . . . . . : 255.255.255.0
Default Gateway . . . . . . : 200.200.200.1
Primary WINS Server . . . . : 200.200.50.23
Secondary WINS Server . . . : 200.200.40.190
```

As discussed in Question 16-9, if a packet's destination is on the same local network as the sender's, the sender needs to resolve the destination's IP address into a physical hardware address; otherwise, the sender needs to resolve the router's IP address into a physical hardware address. When an NT machine's TCP/IP component starts, it broadcasts an ARP message with its IP-to-hardware address pair. The basic order of events for sending to a host on the local network is as follows:

1. ARP checks the local ARP cache for an entry for destination's IP address. If a match is found, the hardware address of the destination is added to the frame header and the frame is sent.

2. If a match is not found, an ARP request broadcast is sent to the local network (remember it knows the destination is on the local network by working out the network ID from the IP address and the subnet mask). The ARP request contains the sender's IP address and hardware address and the IP address that is being queried and is sent to 255.255.255.255 (everyone, but it won't get routed).

3. When the destination host receives the broadcast, it sends an ARP reply with its hardware address and IP address.

4. When the source receives the ARP reply, it updates its ARP cache and then creates a frame and sends it.

If you are sending to a destination not on your local network, the process is similar except that the sender resolves the route's IP address instead.

To inspect your machine's ARP cache, type

```
arp -a
```

The system responds with a list of IP-address to hardware-address mappings. Try pinging a host on your local network and then displaying the ARP cache again; the response is an entry for the host. Also, try pinging a host outside your local network and check the ARP cache; an entry for the router will have been added. Notice that the word "dynamic" is listed with the records, because they were added as needed and are volatile and will be lost on reboot. In fact, the entries will be lost more quickly than that—if an entry is not used again within 2 minutes, it is deleted from the cache. If an entry is used within 2 minutes, it is deleted after an additional 10 minutes, unless used again. Then it would be 10 minutes from when used.

You might wish to add static entries for some hosts (to save time with the ARP requests). The format is

```
arp -s <IP address> <hardware address>
```

For example, the following would add a static entry for IP address 200.200.200.5 to a physical card with address 00-A0-24-7A-01-48.

```
arp -s 200.200.200.5 00-A0-24-7A-01-48
```

 16.11 **How can I increase the time during which entries are kept in the ARP cache?**

The default of two minutes can be changed by performing the following:

1. Start the Registry editor (REGEDIT.EXE).

2. Move to HKEY_LOCAL_MACHINE\SYSTEM\CurrentControlSet\ Services\Tcpip\Parameters.
3. From the Edit menu, choose New > DWORD Value and enter the name **ArpCacheLife**. Then click OK.
4. Double-click the new value and set to n seconds (for example, 60). Then click OK.
5. Close the Registry editor and reboot.

What other Registry entries are there for TCP/IP?

There is a whole Knowledge Base Article on them that might be useful at http://support.microsoft.com/support/kb/articles/q120/6/42.asp.

How can I configure more than six IP addresses?

Using the TCP/IP configuration GUI, you are limited to six IP addresses. You can add more, however, by directly editing the Registry:

1. Log on as an Administrator.
2. Start the Registry editor (REGEDT32.EXE).
3. Move to HKEY_LOCAL_MACHINE\SYSTEM\CurrentControlSet\ Services and scroll down to the service for your adapter card (look at the Adapter's tab on the Network control panel applet). For example, the Etherlink 3 card is Elnk3; however, you want the first occurrence, so go to Elnk31.
4. Move to the Parameters\TCPIP subkey.
5. Double-click the IPAddress value. Enter additional IP addresses, separated by a new line (see Figure 16-4).
6. When finished, click OK.

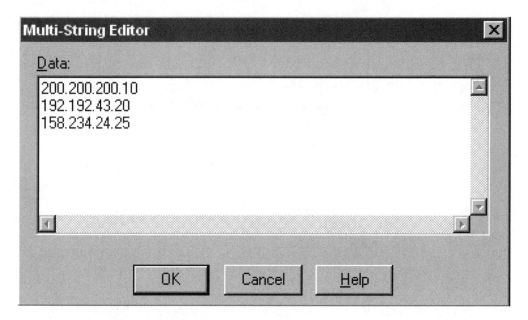

Figure 16-4. Only three addresses here, but you can add lots more.

7. Next, edit the Subnet mask and again add an entry for each IP address (in the same order). Click OK when finished.

8. Close the Registry editor and reboot the machine.

What are the common TCP ports?

Table 16-2 gives a list of some common TCP ports.

Table 16-2. TCP Ports

Keyword	Port	Description
echo	7	Echo
systat	11	Active Users
qotd	17	Quote of the Day

Table 16-2. TCP Ports *(continued)*

Keyword	Port	Description
msp	18	Message Send Protocol
ftp-data	20	File Transfer (Data Channel)
ftp	21	File Transfer (Control)
telnet	23	Telnet
smtp	25	Simple Mail Transfer
name	42	TCP Nameserver
bootps	67	Bootstrap Protocol Server
bootpc	68	Bootstrap Protocol Client
tftp	69	Trival File Transfer
gopher	70	Gopher
finger	79	Finger
http	80	World Wide Web
kerberos	88	Kerberos
pop	109	TCP Post Office
nntp	119	USENET
nfs	2049	Network File System

How can I perform a migration to DHCP?

Only a few basic Registry entries define a client as a DHCP client, so an easy way to migrate clients to DHCP is to create a Registry script that sets the required values via logon script. You should obviously be careful that there is no overlap between the addresses in the DHCP address pool and those statically assigned.

TCP/IP parameters are defined to each NIC (Network Interface Card).

The following is an example Registry script you might consider using:

```
REGEDIT4
[HKEY_LOCAL_MACHINE\SYSTEM\CurrentControlSet\Services\<card
service>\Parameters\Tcpip]
"EnableDHCP"=dword:00000001
"IPInterfaceContext"=dword:00000001
"IPInterfaceContextMax"=dword:00000001
```

You should then add something into the logon script to detect the NIC installed in the computer, run the reg script, and request an IP address, like this:

```
if reg=elpc575 (for the 3com575tx) goto dhcp
..
..
..
:dhcp
regedit /s NIC_dhcp.reg
ipconfig /renew
net send %computername% Congrats Your computer has been
configured for DHCP!
endif
```

A quick way to find out which network card you are using is described here, because you might have various types of NIC on your LAN.

For instance, you might have the 3c89d, netflx3, 3c575tx cards on your network. When the install takes place on the NT 4.0, it adds a Registry key in the HKEY_LOCAL_MACHINE\systems\Current control set\system\services\ cpqNF31 with the following parameters:

```
[HKEY_LOCAL_MACHINE\SYSTEM\CurrentControlSet\Services\CpqNF31\
Parameters\Tcpip]
"EnableDHCP"=dword:00000000.
```

You have to find out what the key name is because it is different for each NIC. Then you can run KIX32.EXE and use the following argument, which checks for the existence of a Registry key, where Key identifies the key you want to check.

```
EXISTKEY (
"Key"
)
```

The command returns one of these parameters:

0   The key specified exists *(Note: this is different from the way the EXIST function works.)*

>0   The key does not exist; the returncode will represent an errorcode.

Below is some sample code to test for the existence of the Registry entries, to determine if the key exists and then execute accordingly for that specific card:

```
$ReturnCode = ExistKey(
"HKEY_LOCAL_MACHINE\SYSTEM\CurrentControlSet\Services\
CpqNF31" )
If $ReturnCode = 0
? "Key exists...."
Endif
```

17 DOMAIN NAME SYSTEM (DNS)

Modern networks use TCP/IP as their principal protocol, but the addressing scheme of dotted-quad—158.234.63.45, for example—is not exactly user-friendly. With IP also being used as the protocol of the Internet, customers and clients cannot be expected to remember a company Web site by its IP address.

The solution is to map a "friendly" or host name to the IP addresses and let the storage of these mappings be handled by DNS servers. DNS is a hierarchical namespace with top-level domains such as .com and .edu pointing to other DNS servers that resolve names for lower DNS domains (for instance, .com would point to a DNS server at Microsoft that would resolve names for microsoft.com).

Windows NT Server provides a built-in DNS server; however, third-party alternatives are available. For Windows 2000, using Microsoft's built-in offering is more important because 2000 relies on new features of DNS 5.0—namely, service records and dynamic DNS. These are explained in later chapters.

 ## How do I install the DNS Service?
17.1

The DNS Service can only be installed on NT Server and is installed as follows:

1. Start the Network Control Panel applet (Start > Settings > Control Panel > Network) or right-click on Network Neighborhood and choose Properties.
2. Choose the Services tab and click Add.

3. Choose Microsoft DNS Server and click OK.

4. The software installs and the machine reboots.

When the machine has rebooted, the DNS Administrator utility will have been added to the Administrative Tools folder. This is the utility used for configuring the DNS service.

One point to remember is that the DNS server should have a static IP address and not one dynamically assigned by DHCP. Otherwise, clients might be unable to find the DNS server because its IP address would be subject to change.

Under Windows 2000, you install the DNS Service via the Add/Remove Programs Control Panel applet in the Configure Windows Components section.

 FAQ 17.2

How do I configure a domain on the DNS server?

DNS Manager is used to configure any new domains. Following is an outline of the procedure:

1. Start the DNS Manager (Start > Programs > Administrative Tools > DNS Manager).

2. From the DNS menu, choose New Server. Enter the IP address of the DNS Server (for example 200.200.200.3) and click OK. If you are unsure of the machine's IP address, you can use this command from the command prompt:

```
IPCONFIG
```

3. The server should now be displayed with a CACHE subcomponent.

4. Next, you want to add the domain (savilltech.com, for example) from the DNS menu, so choose New Zone.

5. Choose Primary and click Next.

6. Type the name (in this case, **savilltech.com**) and press the Tab key. The Zone filename fills in. Then click Next and click Finish.

7. Next, you need to create a zone for reverse lookups, so choose New Zone from the DNS menu.

8. Choose Primary and click Next. Type the name of the first three parts of the domain IP plus in-addr.arpa. For example, if the domain were 158.234.26, the entry would be 26.234.158.in-addr.arpa. In my example, it would be **200.200.200.in-addr.arpa**.

9. Press the Tab key for the filename to be filled. Then click Next and click Finish.

10. Add a record for the DNS server by right-clicking on the domain and choosing New Host.

11. Now enter the name of the machine (for example, BUGSBUNNY) and enter an IP address (for example, 200.200.200.3).

12. Click OK. Now if you press F5 (to refresh the view) and examine 200.200.200.in-addr.arpa, a record has been added for BUGSBUNNY there as well (see Figure 17-1).

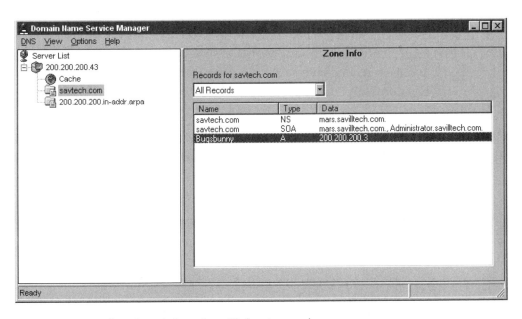

Figure 17-1. A functional domain with host records.

You have a functional name-resolving DNS server. Now you just need to add records to it.

How do I add a record to the DNS?

A blank DNS server is useless. Records must be manually added to the DNS server, mapping IP addresses to the DNS name. To add a record (for example, TAZ with IP address 200.200.200.4), perform the following:

1. Start the DNS Manager (Start > Programs > Administrative Tools > DNS Manager).
2. Double-click on the name of the DNS server to display the list of zones.
3. Right-click on the domain and choose New Record.
4. Enter the name and IP address (**TAZ** and **200.200.200.4** for our example). Choose the record type. For adding a new host, accept the default—record type A.
5. If you have the reverse ARPA zone configured and want the pointer (PTR) record automatically added, make sure Create Associated PTR Record is checked. The reverse ARPA zone is used for reverse name resolution (IP address to hostname, in this case).
6. Click OK.

Windows 2000 allows clients to automatically add records to DNS and removes the need for WINS in a pure Windows 2000 network.

How do I configure a client to use DNS?

The client machines have to be told the IP address (or IP addresses) of the DNS server(s) so they know where to forward name-resolution requests. For an NT machine (and Windows 95), perform the following:

1. Start the Network Control Panel applet (Start > Settings > Control Panel > Network).
2. Choose the Protocols tab.
3. Choose TCP/IP and choose Properties.

4. Click the DNS tab.

5. Make sure the machine's name is entered in the first box and the domain name (for example, savilltech.com) in the Domain box (see Figure 17-2).

6. In the DNS Server section, click Add.

7. In the dialog box, enter the IP address of the DNS Server and click Add again.

8. In the Domain Suffix Search Order section, click Add.

9. Enter the domain (for example, **savilltech.com**) and click Add.

10. Finally, click OK.

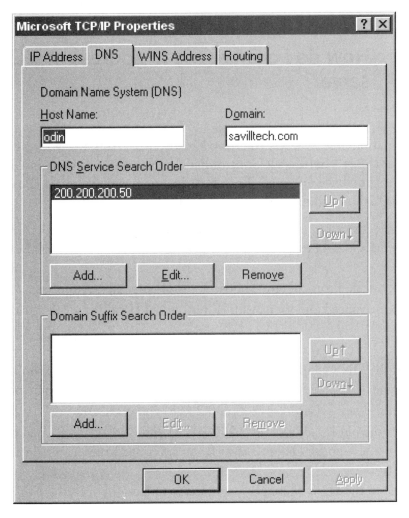

Figure 17-2. Setting TCP/IP to use DNS server 200.200.200.50.

To test, you can start a command prompt and use **nslookup <host name>**. For example, enter

```
nslookup taz
```

The IP address of TAZ will be displayed if DNS is configured correctly. Also try the reverse translation by entering

nslookup <ipaddress>
(for example, nslookup 200.200.200.4)

If reverse translation is working, the name TAZ should now be displayed.

 ## How do I change the IP address of a DNS server?

The information here assumes you have already changed the IP address of the DNS server (Start > Settings > Control Panel > Network > Protocols > TCP/IP > Properties) and have rebooted. The scenario assumes that the old IP address was 200.200.200.3 and the new is 200.200.200.8.

1. You need to configure a second IP address for the network card. Start the Network Control Panel Applet (Start > Settings > Control Panel > Network).
2. Click on the Protocol tab. Choose TCP/IP and click Properties.
3. Click Advanced and then Add. Enter the old IP address (200.200.200.3) and click Add.
4. Click OK until you are back at the Control Panel and then reboot.
5. Start the DNS Manager (Start > Programs > Administrative Tools > DNS Manager). Right-click the Server List and choose New Server.
6. Enter the new IP address (200.200.200.8) and click OK.
7. Select the old IP address (200.200.200.3) and right-click to open the context menu. Choose Delete Server from the context menu and click Yes to confirm.
8. While in the DNS Manager, you need to update the record for this server. Select the IP address of the DNS server (200.200.200.8) and select the domain name (SAVILLTECH.COM).

9. Double-click the entry for the server and update the IP address. Note: It would have had 200.200.200.3 to BUGSBUNNY, so change it to 200.200.200.8.

10. Click OK.

11. Now you need to delete the secondary IP address you added. Start the Network Control Panel applet (Start > Settings > Control Panel > Network).

12. Click on the Protocol tab. Choose TCP/IP and click Properties.

13. Click Advanced and select the address 200.200.200.3. Then click Remove.

14. Click OK until you're back at the Control Panel.

15. You will need to reboot at some point to remove the 200.200.200.3 from being active.

Update all of the clients to use the new DNS server IP address. This would be best done by using a logon script. Or if you're using WINS, just update the WINS server.

The above procedure is the most complete way to change an IP address; however, performing only steps 5–10 should work.

 ## 17.6 How can I configure DNS to use a WINS server?

It is possible to configure the DNS to use a WINS server to resolve the host name of a fully qualified domain name (FQDN). WINS servers are used for clients to dynamically register their NetBIOS names to their IP addresses. Allowing DNS to use WINS means DNS requests can be serviced by WINS records.

1. Start DNS manager (Start > Programs > Administrative Tools > DNS Manager).

2. Right-click on the zone you wish to communicate with the WINS server and choose Properties.

3. Click the WINS Lookup tab (see Figure 17-3).

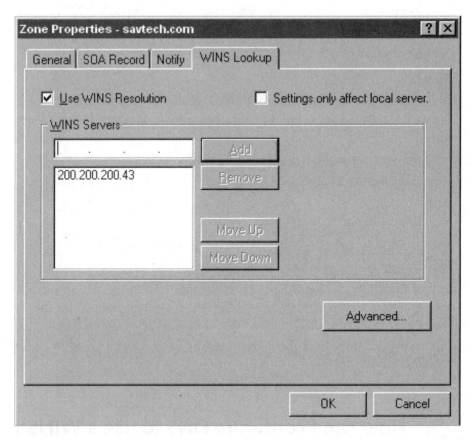

Figure 17-3. Enabling WINS Resolution.

4. Check the Use WINS Resolution check box. Then enter the WINS server IP address and click Add.
5. Click OK when finished.

 ## Where in the Registry are the entries for the DNS servers located?

The entries for the DNS servers are stored in the Registry in the location
HKEY_LOCAL_MACHINE\SYSTEM\CurrentControlSet\Services\Tcpip\

Parameters, under the NameServer value. Entries should be separated by a space.

Using the Resource Kit utility REG.EXE, the command to change would be as follows:

```
reg update
HKLM\System\CurrentControlSet\Services\Tcpip\Parameters\
NameServer="158.234.8.70 158.234.8.100" \\<machine name>
```

where 158.234.8.70 and 158.234.8.100 are the addresses of the DNS servers you want to configure. Note that this sets the value—it does not append the servers—so be sure you enter the existing DNS servers as well as the new ones.

This might be useful for granting users access to the Internet by remotely updating their Registry to know which DNS servers to use.

4.0 ONLY

I receive the error message "No More Endpoints." What should I do?

This can be caused by installing DNS on a machine that has previous settings contained in the %systemroot%\system32\dns directory. To correct the problem, perform the following.

1. Stop the Microsoft DNS server by using the Services Control Panel applet (Start > Settings > Control Panel > Services). Choose Microsoft DNS and then click Stop.

2. Back up any zone files from the %systemroot%\system32\dns directory that you might want later.

3. Remove the DNS server by right-clicking on Network Neighborhood and choosing Properties.

4. Click the Services tab, choose DNS, and click Remove.

5. Delete all files in the %systemroot%\system32\dns folder.

6. Reinstall the DNS server by using the Services tab of the Network Control Panel applet, or restart from the command prompt by using the following:

```
net stop dns
net start dns
```

Setting a secondary DNS server as primary results in errors. What next?

If you have a secondary DNS server configured to duplicate all entries from another DNS server, trying to set it as a primary DNS server results in failure to start the service and an error message saying that the data is wrong:

> "Event ID: 7023
> The MS DNS Server service terminated with the following error:
> The data is invalid."

> "Event ID: 130
> DNS Server zone zone name has invalid or corrupted Registry data.
> Delete its Registry data and recreate with DNSAdmin."

> "Event ID: 133 DNS
> Server secondary zone zone name has no master IP addresses in Registry.
> Secondary zones require masters."

The DNS Manager forgets to set the correct value for the DNS type in the Registry (secondary remains), but it erases the address of the primary DNS, where the data came from. To correct this, perform the following:

1. Start the Registry editor (REGEDIT.EXE).
2. Locate and move to the following key: HKEY_LOCAL_MACHINE\
   SYSTEM\CurrentControlSet\Services\Dns\Zones\< zonename >, where
   < zonename> is the domain (for example, savilltech.com).
3. Double-click on the TYPE value and change it from 2 to 1.
4. Close the Registry editor.

You should now be able to successfully start the DNS service, as follows:

```
net start dns
```

The TYPE value can have one of two values:

0x1 specifies primary zone.
0x2 specifies secondary zone.

A fix for this problem can be downloaded from ftp://ftp.microsoft.com/bussys/winnt/winnt-public/fixes/usa/NT40/ hotfixes-postSP3/dns-fix.

2000 ONLY

FAQ 17.10 How do I configure DNS for a Windows 2000 domain?

Windows 2000 domains rely on DNS and—to work optimally—dynamic DNS, which is an update to the basic DNS specification. You can find details about dynamic DNS in RFC 2136, which can be viewed at ftp://ftp.isi.edu/in-notes/rfc2136.txt.

Another major update in DNS 5.0 is the addition of service (SRV) records (these have already been seen in Chapter 2, Windows 2000) as a mechanism for publishing the LDAP server _ldap._tcp.<domain>. It is through these records that domains can be looked up through the DNS service.

You could perform this on a separate NT 5.0 machine. The Domain Controller and the DNS server will probably not be the same machine; it just has to exist before you can upgrade the server to a Domain Controller. To install DNS 5.0 on the server, perform the following:

1. Start the Install/Remove Programs Control Panel applet (Start > Settings > Control Panel > Add/Remove Programs).
2. Click the Configure Window's left pane.
3. Click the Components button.
4. Choose Networking Options and click Details.
5. Choose Microsoft DNS Server and click OK.
6. Click Finish.

Now you need to configure the DNS service:

1. Start the DNS Management MMC snap-in (Start > Programs > Administrative Tools > DNS Management).
2. It detects that this is the first time it has been run and starts the configuration applet. Click Next.
3. It detects that there are no root servers, so choose This Is the First DNS Server on This Network and then click Next.

4. Check Yes, add a Forward Lookup Zone, and click Next. This zone is used for the storage of host name-to-IP addresses.

5. You should now choose the zone type. Select Standard Primary and click Next. Active Directory Integrated stores the DNS database in the Active Directory, but there is no Active Directory at this point. You can set this option later.

6. Enter the name of the zone (for example, **savilltech.com**) and click Next.

7. Choose New > File and click Next. If you have an existing .DNS file, you may import this.

8. Check Yes, add a reverse lookup zone, and click Next. The reverse lookup zone is used to find the IP address from a host name. When you create a host record, you can also choose to create a PTR record, which adds a record in the reverse lookup zone.

9. Again choose Standard Primary and click Next.

10. Enter the first parts of your subnet, such as **200.200.200.0** (subnet is filled in for you). If your subnet mask is 255.255.0.0, you enter the first two parts of your IP address; if 255.255.255.0, you enter the first three. Click Next.

11. Again check New File and click Next.

12. When the summary is displayed, click Finish to complete the installation.

Now the basic zone is configured and you need to add the required entries for the domain:

1. Start the DNS Management MMC snap-in (Start > Programs > Administrative Tools > DNS Management).

2. Expand the DNS server, expand the Forward Lookup Zones, and choose the domain (for example, savilltech.com).

3. Right-click on the domain and choose New > Host from the context menu.

4. Leave the Host name blank. Enter the IP address of the Domain Controller (to be) and click Add Host.

The final stage is to configure the zones to be dynamic update-enabled. This allows hosts to add records in the DNS server.

1. Start the DNS Management MMC snap-in (Start > Programs > Administrative Tools > DNS Management).

2. Expand the DNS server, expand the Forward Lookup Zones, and select the domain (savilltech.com).

3. Right-click on the domain and choose Properties from the context menu.
4. Choose Allow Updates from the Dynamic Update drop-down box.
5. Click Apply and then OK.
6. Now expand the Reverse Lookup Zones and select the reverse lookup zone (for example, 200.200.200.x Subnet).
7. Right-click the zone and choose Properties from the context menu.
8. Again choose Allow Updates from the Dynamic Update drop-down list.
9. Click Apply and then OK.

DNS is now configured for a domain, and you can create the domain by using the DCPROMO.EXE utility.

2000 ONLY

How do I configure Active Directory integrated DNS?

It is possible to configure DNS servers that are also Domain Controllers to store the contents of the DNS database in the Active Directory, which will then be replicated to all Domain Controllers in the domain. The option to store the DNS database in the Active Directory is not available on DNS servers that are not Domain Controllers.

1. Start the DNS Management MMC snap-in (Start > Programs > Administrative Tools > DNS Management).
2. Expand the DNS server, expand the Forward Lookup Zones, and choose the domain (for example, savilltech.com).
3. Right-click on the domain and choose Properties from the context menu.
4. Under Type, click Change.
5. Choose Active Directory Integrated Primary and click OK (see Figure 17-4).
6. When asked if you're sure you want this zone to become an Active Directory Integrated Primary, click OK.
7. Click Apply and then OK.

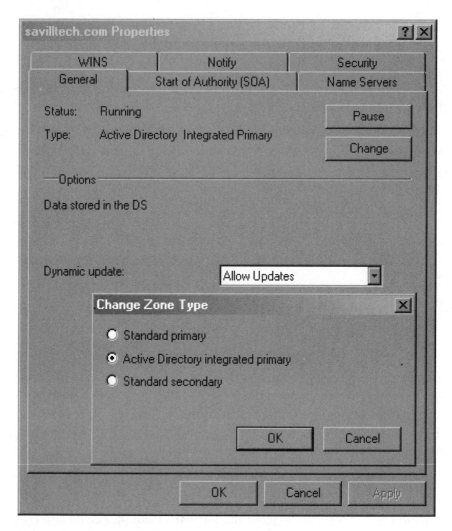

Figure 17-4. Enabling Active Directory integrated DNS.

 2000 ONLY **17.12** ## How do I turn off dynamic DNS?

By default, the TCP/IP stack in NT 5.0 Beta 2 (and later builds) attempts to register its Host (A) record with its DNS server. This makes sense in an all-NT (Windows 2000) environment. If you are using a static, legacy DNS server, however, the DNS folks might not like all the "errors" this shows on their server because the DNS servers do not understand these "updates."

To make the clients stop attempting to publish their DNS names and addresses to the DNS server, perform the following:

1. Log on to each client as Administrator.
2. Start the registry editor (REGEDIT.EXE).
3. Move to HKEY_LOCAL_MACHINE\SYSTEM\CurrentControlSet\ Services\Tcpip\Parameters.
4. From the Edit menu, choose New > DWORD Value.
5. Type **DisableDynamicUpdate** and press Enter.
6. Double-click on the new value and set it to 1. Then click OK.

If you have multiple adapters in the machine, you might not want to disable for all of them. Instead of setting HKEY_LOCAL_MACHINE\SYSTEM\ CurrentControlSet\Services\Tcpip\Parameters\DisableDynamicUpdate to 1, set it as 0. Then move to the Subkey Interfaces\<interface name>, create the DisableDynamicUpdate value there, and set it to 1.

If you need to perform this on a large number of machines, you should create a reg script or set it from the login script.

17.13 How do I configure a forwarder on DNS 5.0?

If you create a DNS server on your network but are not the main DNS server (say your company has a central main DNS server), you want to forward queries your DNS server cannot service to that DNS server.

You do this because only certain servers in your network have access to DNS servers outside your network (due to firewalls, for example) and thus your (departmental?) DNS server cannot access the DNS servers higher in the DNS hierarchy. To configure a forward, perform the following:

1. Start the DNS Management MMC snap-in (Start > Programs > Administrative Tools > DNS Management).
2. Right-click on the DNS server and choose Properties.

3. Choose the Forwarders tab.

4. Check the Enable forwarder(s) box (see Figure 17-5).

5. Enter the IP address of the DNS server and click Add.

6. Click OK and close the DNS Management snap-in.

If you are missing the Forwarders tab, see Question 17-14.

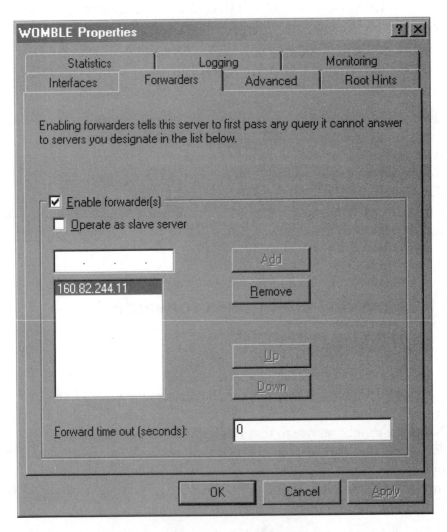

Figure 17-5. Setting a forwarder to a higher DNS server.

2000 ONLY

17.14 I am missing the Forwarders and Root Hints tabs in DNS 5.0. What can I do?

This happens if your server thinks it is the root server in the domain and has a "." zone. To enable the Forwarder, you need to delete this zone from your server, as follows:

1. Start the DNS Management MMC snap-in (Start > Programs > Administrative Tools > DNS Management).
2. Expand the server and expand Forward Lookup Zones.
3. Choose "." and right-click (see Figure 17-6). From the context menu, choose Delete.
4. Click Yes to the confirmation.
5. Stop and start the DNS Manager. The tabs are now available.

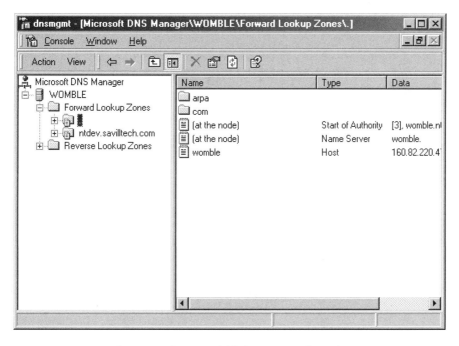

Figure 17-6. Remove this "." tab to enable the Forwarder tab.

18 DYNAMIC HOST CONFIGURATION PROTOCOL (DHCP)

Dynamic Host Configuration Protocol (DHCP) is used to automatically configure a host during bootup on a TCP/IP network and also to change settings related to TCP/IP (such as DNS servers) during the host initialization.

This means you can store all of the available IP addresses in a central database, along with the subnet mask, gateways, DNS servers, and so on. Then the DHCP server can assign an unused address to the requesting client.

DHCP addresses the problem of trying to keep track of your network's IP addresses and the problems of wasted or duplicated addresses. You are no doubt aware of the problems of statically assigning IP addresses—if the machine is reinstalled and the original IP address is not known, you have to give it a new one.

The basics behind DHCP are that the clients are configured to use DHCP instead of being given a static IP address. When the client boots up, it sends out a BOOTP request for an IP address. A DHCP server offers an unassigned IP address from its database; the address is then leased to the client for a predefined time period, usually three days. Periodically this lease is renewed before it expires, so an active client's IP address stays the same unless it is off for more than three days.

18.1 # How do I install the DHCP Server service?

The DHCP Server service can be installed only on a Windows NT Server machine. The machine, however, does not need to be a Domain Controller (and for performance reasons, it should not be).

1. Start the Network Control Panel applet (Start > Settings > Control Panel > Network) or right-click on Network Neighborhood and select Properties from the context menu.
2. Select the Services tab and click Add (see Figure 18-1).

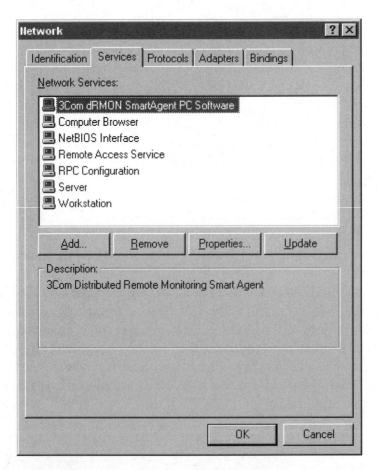

Figure 18-1. Viewing the current NT services.

3. Select Microsoft DHCP Server and click OK (see Figure 18-2).

4. When you're prompted to insert the NT Server installation CD or enter the location of the i386 directory, do so.

5. At the warning that all local adapters must use a static IP address, click OK.

6. Click Close and then click Yes to reboot.

After the machine has rebooted, you can start configuring the new DHCP server, using the newly installed DHCP Manager application that has been placed in the Administrative Tools program folder.

Under Windows 2000, you install the DHCP Server service via the Add/Remove Programs Control Panel applet in the Configure Windows Components section.

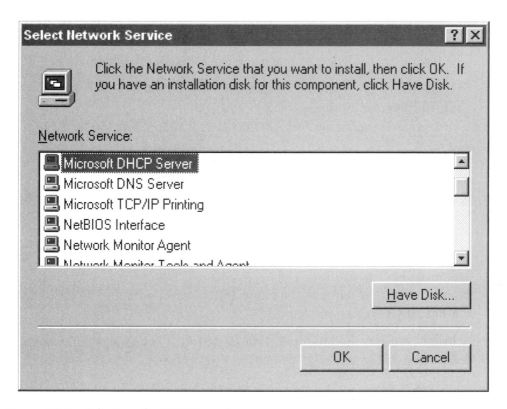

Figure 18-2. Selecting the DHCP service.

FAQ 18.2 How do I configure the DHCP Server service?

You configure the DHCP Server service by using the DHCP Manager, a GUI tool that is complete in its functionality but sometimes lacking in intuitiveness.

The procedure is that you create scopes, which are basically groups of IP addresses that can be assigned to machines. Then you can use the scope to configure various optional settings.

1. Start the DHCP Manager (Start > Programs > Administrative Tools > DHCP Manager).

2. Double-click *Local Machine*.

3. From the Scope menu, select Create. This starts the process of creating a new scope (see Figure 18-3).

4. The Create Scope dialog is shown and the following fields should be filled:

    Start Address (for example, 200.200.200.10)
    End Address (for example, 200.200.200.100)
    This would mean addresses 200.200.200.10 to 200.200.200.100 would be available.
    Subnet Mask (for example, 255.255.255.0)
    Exclusion - Start and End (for example, 200.200.200.20 and 200.200.200.30)
    This would mean available addresses would be 200.200.200.10–200.200.200.20 and 200.200.200.30–200.200.200.100.
    Lease duration (By default, three days; however, you can set it to unlimited.)
    Name (This is the name of the scope; for example, subnet 200.200.200.)
    Comment (Anything you want.)

For Exclusion, you can also enter just a value in Start. That single address is then excluded instead of a range.

5. Click OK.

6. A message appears, saying that the scope has been added but is not active. When asked if you would like it to be active, click Yes.

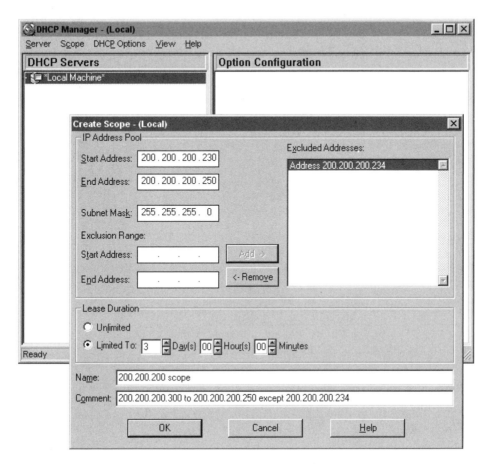

Figure 18-3. Example of creating a scope.

In Windows 2000, you configure the DHCP Server service by using the new DHCP MMC snap-in, but the procedure is basically the same.

Usually items such as DNS servers or WINS servers are configured on a global scale, also by using DHCP Manager. This means clients that get their IP address from the DHCP server can also be set up with other network information. To configure multiple servers, perform the following:

1. Select the Scope and choose Global from the DHCP Options menu.
2. Select 0006 DNS Servers and click Add (see Figure 18-4).
3. Click the Value button. This allows you to assign a value to the DNS Servers.
4. At the bottom of the Global dialog box, click Edit Array.

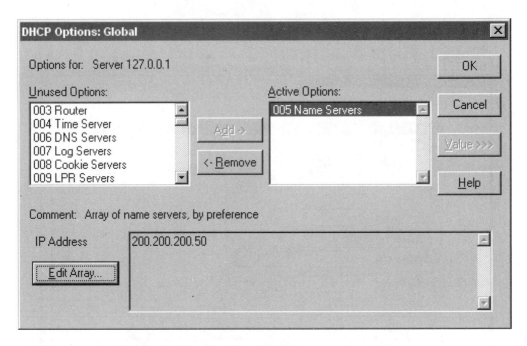

Figure 18-4. Setting the DNS server for all scopes.

5. Enter the IP address and click Add. Continue adding addresses until all are added.
6. Click OK to close the Edit Array dialog box.
7. Now select 015 Domain Name and click Add.
8. In the Active Options box, select 015 Domain Name.
9. Edit the string at the bottom (for example, savilltech.com) and then click OK to exit.

 # How do I configure a client to use DHCP?

After a DHCP server has been configured, the clients have to be set to use it. For NT Workstation and Windows 95 configurations, follow these instructions:

1. Start the Network Control Panel applet (Start > Settings > Control Panel> Network), or right-click on Network Neighborhood and select Properties.

2. Click on the Protocol tab.

3. Select TCP/IP and click Properties.

4. Choose the Obtain an IP Address from a DHCP Service option. Note that DHCP settings will override only a locally configured IP address and subnet mask. If you have configured DNS, WINS, and so on locally, the DHCP configuration will not overwrite it.

5. You now have to reboot the machine for the change to take effect. On bootup, the machine requests its IP address from the DHCP server.

 How can I compress my DHCP database?

Compressing is needed because wasted space creeps into the DHCP database and causes performance problems. NT Server ships with a utility called JETPACK.EXE that you can use to compact DHCP and WINS databases. To compact your DHCP database, perform the following:

1. Start a command prompt (CMD.EXE).

2. Enter the following commands:

```
cd %SystemRoot%\SYSTEM32\DHCP
(for example, cd d:\winnt\system32\dhcp)
net stop DHCPSERVER
jetpack DHCP.MDB TMP.MDB
net start DHCPSERVER
```

Note: While you are stopping the DHCP service, clients using DHCP to receive a TCP/IP address will not be able to start the TCP/IP protocol and might hang.

Jetpack actually compacts DHCP.MDB into TMP.MDB and then deletes DHCP.MDB and copies TMP.MDB to DHCP.MDB.

For more information, see Knowledge Base article Q145881 at http://support.microsoft.com/support/kb/articles/q145/8/81.asp.

How can a DHCP client find its IP address?

Obviously, this address can change. To find the current address, use the following:

On a Windows NT machine, type **ipconfig** from the command prompt.
On a Windows 95 machine, run WINIPCFG.EXE.

How can I move a DHCP database from one server to another?

A number of important steps are involved, and they must be carried out in the order specified. Perform these steps on the server that currently hosts the DHCP Server service. Be warned that no DHCP clients will be able to start TCP/IP while you're moving the database, so you should do it outside of working hours.

1. Log on as an Administrator and stop DHCP (Start > Settings > Control Panel > Services > Microsoft DHCP Server > Stop). You can also stop DHCP from the command prompt, like this:

```
net stop dhcpserver
```

2. You also need to stop DHCP from starting again after a reboot. To do this, first start the Services Control Panel applet (Start > Settings > Control Panel > Services).

3. Select Microsoft DHCP Server and click Startup. From the Startup dialog box, choose Disabled and click OK.

4. Copy the DHCP directory tree %systemroot%\system32\DHCP to a temporary storage area for use later.

5. Start the Registry editor (REGEDT32.EXE) and move to HKEY_LOCAL_MACHINE\SYSTEM\CurrentControlSet\Services\DHCPServer \Configuration.

6. From the Registry menu, click Save Key. Create a name for this key (for example, DHCPCFG.BCK).

7. Close the Registry editor.

Optional: If you want to totally remove DHCP from the source machine, delete the DHCP directory (%systemroot%\system32\dhcp) and then delete the DHCP Service (Start > Settings > Network > Services > Microsoft DHCP Server > Remove).

On the new DHCP server, perform the following:

1. Log on as an Administrator.

2. If the server does not have the DHCP server service installed, install it (Start > Settings > Control Panel > Network > Services > Add > DHCP Server).

3. Stop the DHCP service (Start > Settings > Control Panel > Services > Microsoft DHCP server > Stop).

4. Delete the contents of %systemroot%\system32\dhcp.

5. Copy the backed up DHCP directory tree from the storage area to %systemroot%/system32/dhcp, but rename the file SYSTEM.MDB to SYSTEM.SRC.

6. Start the Registry editor (REGEDT32.EXE).

7. Move to HKEY_LOCAL_MACHINE\SYSTEM\CurrentControlSet\Services\DHCPServer\Configuration and select it.

8. From the Registry menu, choose Restore.

9. Locate the file DHCPCGF.BCK you saved from the original machine, and click Open.

10. At the warning, click Yes.

11. Close the Registry editor and reboot the machine.

4.0 ONLY

FAQ 18.7

How do I create a DHCP Relay Agent?

If you have routers separating some of your DHCP clients from the DHCP server, you might have problems if the routers are not RFC compliant. This means the routers will not forward or route low-level BOOTP requests.

You can solve this by placing a DHCP Relay Agent on the local network area, which is not a DHCP server but communicates on behalf of the DHCP server. The DHCP Relay Agent must be a Windows NT Server computer.

1. On the NT Server, log on as an Administrator.
2. Start the Network Control Panel applet (Start > Settings > Control Panel > Network).
3. Click the Services tab and click Add.
4. Select DHCP Relay Agent and click OK.
5. Type the path of the files (for example, d:\i386) and click OK.
6. When you are asked if you wish to add an IP address to the DHCP servers list, click Yes.
7. Click the DHCP Relay tab and click Add.
8. In the DHCP Server field, type the IP address of the DHCP server and click Add.
9. Click OK and restart the computer.

4.0 ONLY

18.8 How can I stop the DHCP Relay Agent?

The DHCP Relay Agent is just a service. To stop the Relay Agent, stop the DHCP Relay Agent service, as follows:

1. Log on as an Administrator.
2. Start the Services Control Panel applet (Start > Settings > Control Panel > Network).
3. Select DHCP Relay Agent.
4. Click the Startup button.
5. Click Disabled and click OK.
6. Close the Services Control Panel applet.
7. You can now reboot or just stop the service.

How can I back up the DHCP database?

The DHCP database backs itself up automatically every 60 minutes to the %systemroot%\system32\Dhcp\Backup\Jet directory. You can change this interval, as follows:

1. Start the Registry editor (REGEDIT.EXE).
2. Move to HKEY_LOCAL_MACHINE\SYSTEM\CurrentControlSet\ Services\DHCPServer\Parameters\BackupInterval.
3. Double-click on BackupInterval and set to the number of minutes after which you want the backup to be performed.
4. Click OK and close the Registry editor.
5. Stop and restart the DHCP Server service (Start > Settings > Control Panel > Services > DHCP Server > Start and Stop).

Optional: For additional safety, you could back up the %systemroot%\system32\ Dhcp\Backup\Jet directory.

How can I restore the DHCP database?

A number of methods exist for restoring the DHCP backup. Perform one of the following:

- When the DHCP Server service starts, if an error is detected in the database, it will automatically restore the backup version.
- Edit the Registry and set HKEY_LOCAL_MACHINE\SYSTEM\ CurrentControlSet\Services\DHCPServer\Parameters\RestoreFlag to 1. Restart the DHCP Server service. This will restore the backed-up version and set RestoreFlag back to the default 0.
- Stop the DHCP Server service, copy the files from %systemroot%\ system32\Dhcp\Backup\Jet to %systemroot%\system32\Dhcp, and then start the DHCP Server service.

18.11 How do I reserve a specific address for a particular machine?

Before performing this, you need to know the hardware address of the machine. You can find the address by entering the command:

```
ipconfig /all
```

Look for this line:

```
Physical Address. . . . . . : 00-60-97-A4-20-86
```

Now perform the following at the DHCP server:

1. Log on as an Administrator.
2. Start the DHCP Server management software (Start > Programs > Administrative Tools > DHCP Manager).
3. Double-click on the DHCP Server (for example, *Local Machine*).
4. Select the lightbulb icon next to the scope you wish to modify.
5. From the Scope menu, select Add Reservations.
6. In the Add Reserved Clients dialog box, enter the IP address you wish to reserve (see Figure 18-5). In the Unique Identifier box, enter the hardware address of the client machine (which you can get by using ipconfig /all). Do not enter the hyphens.

   006097A42086

7. Also enter a name for the machine (and a comment, if you wish) and click Add.
8. Click Close when you have added all of the reservations.

Add Reserved Clients	☒
IP Address:	200 . 200 . 200 . 232
Unique Identifier:	006097A42086
Client Name:	marge
Client Comment:	Marge machine

Add   Close   Help   Options...

Figure 18-5. Setting a reservation for a specific machine.

19 WINDOWS INTERNET NAME SERVICE (WINS)

Previous chapters have looked at DNS. In current versions of Windows, DNS is a static, manually updated database that resolves host names to IP addresses. Keeping the database up-to-date is obviously a large amount of work, so the Windows Internet Name Service (WINS) was created as a NetBIOS Name Server that enables clients to register their NetBIOS names with their IP addresses dynamically—meaning with no Administrator intervention. Other clients can then query the database to resolve NetBIOS names to the relevant IP address.

Because NT uses NetBIOS over TCP/IP, you need to have WINS running so that each machine can ascertain the correct IP address of the other to facilitate communication. This is important with domains, because each domain is a NetBIOS name; if the LMHOSTS file has no entries, the clients will be unable to locate the Domain Controllers without WINS.

Clients have to be made aware of the WINS servers and therefore need to be configured with the IP address of one or more WINS machines.

If you need to browse over an interdomain network, WINS is your answer.

 ## How does WINS work?
19.1

After your machine is configured to point at a WINS server (and maybe a second backup WINS server), the following happens:

On startup, your machine registers its NetBIOS name with the WINS Server and provides its IP address for resolution actions. This dynamic update means you will **always** get the most current name/IP mapping.

If a machine is already out there with the same name, a request is sent to it by WINS. If the machine doesn't respond, you get the OK. If the machine is out there and alive, you get a negative name acknowledgment.

When you need to communicate with a machine whose NetBIOS name is known, a name query is sent to the WINS server and the resolved IP address returned—no broadcast, no LMHOSTS.

A WINS lookup is also performed at logon time, and special WINS records exist for Domain Controllers. The domain name is actually a NetBIOS name that is a 16-character name with the 16th character used by Microsoft networking services to identify the NetBIOS type. The type used for a Domain Controller is <1C>, so the NetBIOS name for the Domain Controller of domain SavillTech would be SAVILLTECH <1C>.

The NetBIOS type has to be the 16th character; therefore, the name of the domain has to be filled with blanks to make its length up to 15 characters, which is the NetBIOS maximum.

If the client is WINS-enabled, a query is sent for the domain name <1C>. The WINS server returns up to 25 IP addresses that correspond to Domain Controllers of the requested domain. A \mailslot\net\ntlogon is then broadcast to the local subnet, and if the workstation receives a response, it attempts to log on with the local Domain Controller.

How do I set up WINS?

WINS is a server service and, as such, can be installed only on an NT Server machine. Apart from installing the service, very little configuration is required for WINS because it is all dynamically updated.

To install the WINS service, perform the following:

1. Start the Network Control Panel applet (choose Start > Settings > Control Panel > Network or right-click Network Neighborhood and select Properties from the context menu).

2. Select the Services tab.

3. Click the Add button.

4. Select Windows Internet Name Service.

5. Enter the location of the i386 NT installation area (likely the CD-ROM).

6. Now click the Close button and the machine will reboot.

After the server is installed, there are various other steps, all covered later in the chapter:

- If you have any non-WINS clients, add them as static name->IP mappings.
- Configure a WINS Proxy Agent, if needed.
- Configure WINS support on your DHCP server.
- Configure the clients to use WINS by choosing NT Workstation TCP/IP > Properties > WINS and adding the IP address of the WINS server (and your secondary, if you have one).

 # What is a WINS Proxy Agent?

If you have non-WINS machines on a subnet and want them to be visible browsing participants, you want a Proxy Agent to be active within this subnet.

A WINS Proxy Agent is a WINS client that—by listening for broadcast name registrations and requests and then forwarding them to a WINS server—enables non-WINS clients to participate.

In Windows NT 3.51 you could configure a Proxy Agent by simply checking the Enable WINS Proxy Agent box in the Advanced Properties of the TCP/IP protocol in the Network Control Panel. This was removed in NT 4.0.

To set up a machine as a Proxy Agent in NT 4.0, perform the following:

1. Start the Registry Editor (REGEDIT.EXE or REGEDT32.EXE).

2. Move to HKEY_LOCAL_MACHINE\SYSTEM\CurrentControlSet\Services\NetBT\Parameters.

3. Double-click on EnableProxy.

4. Set to 1 and click OK (see Figure 19-1).

5. Reboot the machine for the change to take effect.

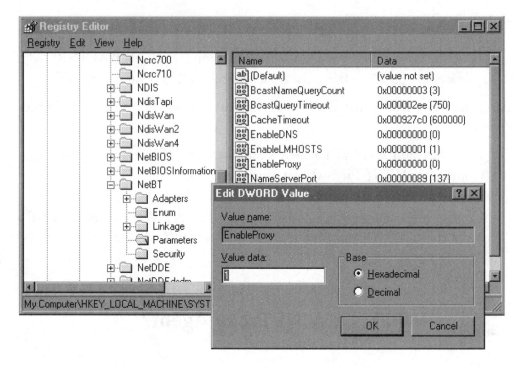

Figure 19-1. Enabling the client to act as a WINS Proxy Agent.

You should have multiple Proxy Agents or dedicated machines in case the computer is turned off, leaving the other non-WINS machines without a resolution mechanism.

How do I configure WINS static entries for a non-WINS client?

You might have clients that do not support WINS and require an entry in the WINS database. Obviously, use a WINS Proxy Agent instead, where possible, because it's less Administrative effort. These static entries can be entered as follows:

1. Start the WINS Manager (Start > Programs > Administrative Tools > WINS Manager).
2. From the Mappings menu, select Static Mappings.

3. Select Add Mappings and enter the Name and IP Address of the machine in question (see Figure 19-2).

4. Under Type, usually you'll just choose Unique.

5. Click Add.

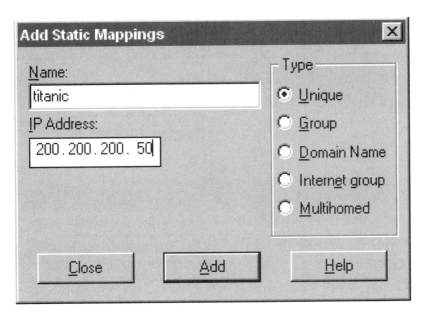

Figure 19-2. Adding a static entry in the WINS database for the Titanic machine.

 ## How do I configure WINS to work with Dynamic Host Configuration Protocol (DHCP)?

If you use DHCP on the network, the DHCP server can be configured with the WINS server information so as to automatically configure the clients with the WINS server information. To configure the DHCP server, perform the following:

1. Start the DHCP Manager (Start > Programs > Administrative Tools > DHCP Manager).

2. Two new scope options should be configured on the global scope. Click Global from the DHCP Options menu.

3. Make the following additions, as in Figure 19-3:

044 WINS/NBNS Servers >   *Add the address of WINS server(s).*
046 WINS/NBT Node Type >   *Configure as 0x8 (H-node).*

4. Click OK.

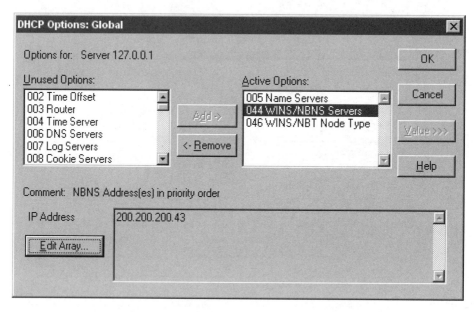

Figure 19-3. Setting the WINS options in DHCP.

 ## How can I compress my WINS database?

NT Server ships with a utility called JETPACK.EXE, which you can use to compact DHCP and WINS databases. To compact your WINS database, perform the following:

1. Start a command prompt (CMD.EXE).

2. Enter the following commands (in the form cd %systemroot%\system32\ WINS):

```
cd d:\winnt\system32\wins
net stop WINS
jetpack WINS.MDB TMP.MDB
net start WINS
```

Note: While you are stopping the WINS service, clients using WINS to resolve addresses will fail unless another mechanism of name resolution is in place.

Jetpack actually compacts WINS.MDB into TMP.MDB and then deletes WINS.MDB and copies TMP.MDB to WINS.MDB.

For more information, see Knowledge Base Article Q145881 at http:// support.microsoft.com/support/kb/articles/q145/8/81.asp.

4.0 ONLY

19.7 WINS Automatic Backup does not run every three hours. Why not?

By default, WINS backup actually takes place 24 to 27 hours after the last backup was completed. To work around this, perform the following:

1. Create a batch file that stops and starts the WINS service. Here's an example:

```
WINSRSTR.BAT
@net stop wins
@net start wins
exit
```

2. Configure WINS to back up the database on exit.
3. Schedule the WINSRSTR.BAT to run whenever you want the database backed up. For example:

```
AT 22:00 cmd /c %systemroot%\winsrsrt.bat
```

The location of the backup can be configured as follows:

1. Start WINS Manager.
2. Select the Mappings menu, and select Backup Database. The Select Backup Directory dialog box appears.
3. Select the backup location from the Drives drop-down list box and the Directories list box.
4. Click OK.

19.8 How can I manually restore the WINS database?

In the event of a corruption, the WINS database should automatically restore itself. However, you can carry out a manual restore, as follows:

1. Stop the WINS server:

   ```
   net stop wins
   ```

2. Move to the \%systemroom%\system32\WINS directory:

   ```
   winnt\system32\wins
   ```

3. Delete the files JET.LOG, JET*.LOG, WINS.TMP, and SYSTEM.MDB.
4. Copy the file SYSTEM.MDB from the installation source to the \%systemroom%\system32\WINS directory.
5. Move to the location of the WINS database backup file. The backup location of the WINS database is specified in the Database Backup Path box of the WINS Server Configuration dialog box.
6. Copy the backup file WINS.MDB to the \%systemroom%\system32\ WINS directory.
7. Start the WINS server:

   ```
   net start wins
   ```

19.9 The WINS log files are created in incorrect locations. What should I do?

The WINS service creates a number of log files, J50.LOG or J50.CHK, in the %systemroot%\system32\WINS directory. This is normal. If these files are being created in other directories, it might cause a problem and stop the WINS service from starting. The log files can be created in incorrect directories for one of the following reasons:

- JETPACK.EXE is being run from the wrong directory. To run JETPACK, you should always set the default directory to be %systemroot%\system32\WINS. If you use the following command, the logs will be created in the wrong directory:

```
C:\winnt\system32\jetpack.exe
c:\winnt\system32\wins\wins.mdb tmp.mdb
```

- The Enable Logging check box in WINS Administrator is not selected. This results in creation of the log files in the %systemroot%\system32 directory.

Note: For the correct way to perform JETPACK, see Question 19-6.

If your system now has the log files in the wrong place and the WINS service will not start, copy the log files to the %systemroot%\system32\WINS directory and restart the service, as follows:

```
net start wins
```

If the WINS service is running, it will lock the files and you will not be able to delete them, so you should perform the following:

1. Stop the WINS service

```
net stop wins
```

2. Back up the WINS data by using the Backup Database function in the WINS manager.
3. Remove the files that are in the wrong directory and restore the data back to the directory.
4. Run JETPACK.
5. Restart the WINS service:

```
net start wins
```

6. Turn on Logging Enabled (WINS Manager > Server > Configuration > Advanced).

4.0 ONLY

FAQ 19.10

The WINS server is not being queried for entries in LMHOSTS after Service Pack 4 was installed. Why?

Before Service Pack 4, a resolution request was always passed to a WINS server and the LMHOSTS file was checked only if no entry was found.

After Service Pack 4, any entry in the LMHOSTS file that has the #PRE qualifier (preloaded) is used and the WINS server is not queried. This means any incorrect entries in your LMHOSTS file will prevent the WINS server from being queried. You should therefore edit the file %systemroot%\system32\drivers\etc\lmhosts (for example, d:\winnt\system32\drivers\etc\lmhosts) and remove the offending entries.

20 INTERNET INFORMATION SERVER (IIS)

Internet Information Server (IIS) is a World Wide Web server, a Gopher server, an FTP server, and much more—all rolled into one. IIS means you can publish WWW pages and extend into the realm of ASP (Active Server Pages), where Java or VBScript (server-side scripts) can generate the pages on the fly. IIS has fun things such as application development environment (FrontPage Express), integrated full-text searching (Index Server), multimedia streaming (NetShow), and site management extensions.

IIS has matured in recent versions, with the Windows 2000 version offering a number of enticing features. On the whole, the various UNIX third-party solutions still have the edge, mainly because of UNIX's consistently superior stability record and the freely available Apache software—but this is changing.

 ## 20.1 How do I install Internet Information Server?

IIS 2.0 is supplied with Windows NT Server 4.0. You can install it at the time you install NT 4.0 by checking the Install Microsoft Internet Information Server box. Alternatively, you can install it later by performing the following:

1. Insert the NT 4.0 Server CD-ROM.
2. Run <CD-ROM>:\I386\Inetsrv\Inetstp.exe.

3. Close all currently running programs and click OK to start the installation (see Figure 20-1).

4. Select the services you want to install and click OK.

5. A message appears, asking for the publishing directories for FTP, WWW, and Gopher. You can change them or accept the defaults. Click OK to continue the installation.

6. If you elected to install ODBC drivers, a dialog box appears, showing the SQL Server driver. Click OK to continue.

7. A message appears, saying that the installation has finished. Click OK.

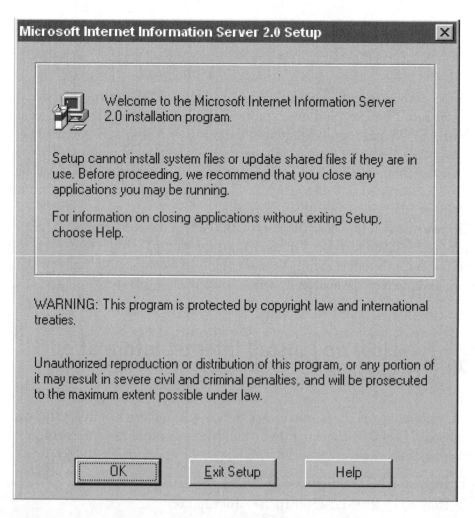

Figure 20-1. Starting the Internet Information Server installation.

Internet Information Server 3.0 is supplied on the Service Pack 2 CD-ROM and as part of Service Packs 3 and 4. It is supplied as an upgrade, so you must already have IIS 2.0 installed before applying the service pack. Internet Information Server 4.0 is supplied as part of the Windows NT 4 Option Pack.

Windows 2000 includes IIS 5.0, which you can install by using the Add/Remove Programs Control Panel applet.

What is Internet Service Manager (ISM)?

If you look under Programs > Microsoft Internet Server, you will find the Internet Service Manager. ISM is used to configure and monitor IIS. With ISM, you can define user connections, user logon and authentication, the home directory location for each IIS service, logging, and security.

If you have IIS 4.0 installed (see Figure 20-2), the programs are in the Windows NT 4.0 Option Pack Start menu folder.

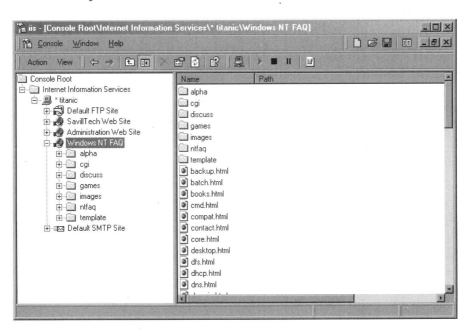

Figure 20-2. The basic view of a Web site, using IIS 5.0 (Windows 2000 version, with the same interface as IIS 4.0).

Each of the three core IIS services—WWW, FTP, and Gopher (though Gopher is not supplied in IIS 4.0 and above)—is an actual NT service. As such, they can be stopped and started through the ISM or the normal Services Control Panel applet.

What is Index Server?

Index Server basically builds a database of Web and document content and enables you to perform full-text searches and retrieve information by using a Web browser. It can search HTML, text, and all Microsoft Office documents. Extensions can be added for other types of documents, such as Adobe Acrobat.

When started, Index Server builds an index of the virtual roots and subdirectories on your Web server. You can select certain directories and file types to be skipped. The index is updated automatically whenever a file is added, deleted, or changed on the server.

Index Server is now built into Office 2000 and replaces the basically useless Find Fast application. Even if you are not running a Web site, you can run Index Server on your computer to aid in the location of local documents.

What are Active Server Pages (ASP)?

ASP is server-side scripting. You can use ASP to create and run dynamic, interactive Web applications. When your scripts run on the server, the **server** does all of the work involved in generating the HTML pages.

One advantage to ASP is that the code is not visible to the user in the browser, eliminating code theft. You can spot an ASP page because it has an .ASP extension as opposed to .HTM or .HTML.

20.5 # How can I configure the connection limit?

If you want to limit the number of simultaneous connections, you can configure the connection limit by using the Internet Service Manager. The limit can be anywhere between 1 and 32,767 (although IIS 4.0 has increased this limit).

1. Start the Internet Service Manager (Start > Programs > Microsoft Internet Server).
2. Double-click on the computer whose connection limit you wish to configure.
3. Select the Service tab.
4. Enter the number of connections you want in the Maximum Connections field (see Figure 20-3).

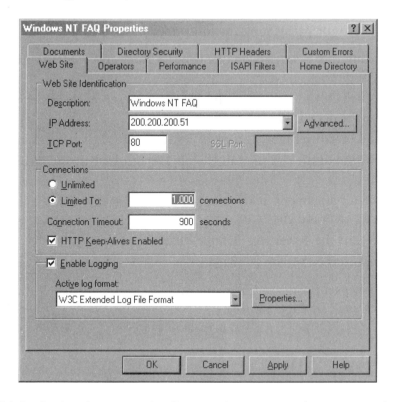

Figure 20-3. Setting the connection limit in IIS 5.0. Notice that you can also set the IP address of the connection, the TCP port, and more.

5. Click OK.

6. Stop and start the service whose limit you changed.

7. Close the Internet Service Manager.

In IIS 5.0, right-click on the Web site you wish to modify (normally, Default) and select Properties from the context menu. Then select the Web Site tab and set the connection limit.

 ## How do I change the default filename?

The default filename is the file searched for if only a directory name is specified. For example, http://www.ntfaq.com would by default search for DEFAULT.HTM or DEFAULT.HTML and display it. You can change the default filename by performing the following:

1. Start the Internet Service Manager (Start > Programs > Microsoft Internet Server).

2. Double-click on the computer name of the Web server for which you wish to modify the default filename.

3. Click the Directories tab.

4. At the bottom of the screen is an Enable Default Document check box. Select this.

5. In the default document field, enter a filename (for example, INDEX.HTM) and click OK.

6. Stop and start the server you just updated.

7. Close the Internet Service Manager.

In IIS 5.0, you can set the default filename on the Documents tab of the Properties on the Web site (see Figure 20-4).

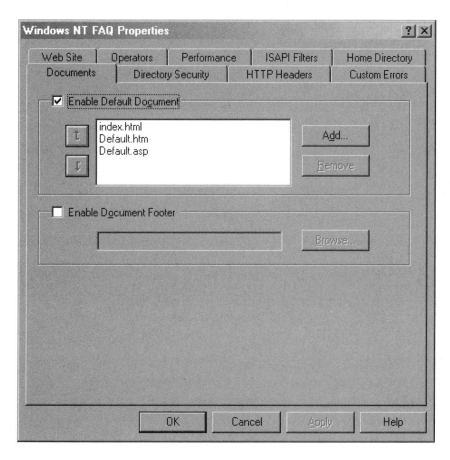

Figure 20-4. The multiple default documents shown here will be used in the order shown. In other words, INDEX.HTML will be used before DEFAULT.HTM.

How can I enable browsers to view the contents of directories on the server?

By default, if you select a directory on a server and no default filename exists (such as DEFAULT.HTM), an error is returned. It is possible to change this behavior so that a directory listing is displayed. This is called directory browsing.

1. Start the Internet Service Manager (Start > Programs > Microsoft Internet Server).

2. Double-click on the computer name of the Web server you wish to modify.

3. Click the Directories tab.

4. Select the Directory Browsing Allowed box and click OK (see Figure 20-5).

5. Close the Internet Service Manager.

You can only set this for the whole site, not on a per-directory basis. If you want to set it on a per-directory basis, enable Directory Browsing and make sure the default filename exists in directories where you do not want people to be able to browse. IIS 4.0 has changed this to be configurable on a directory basis.

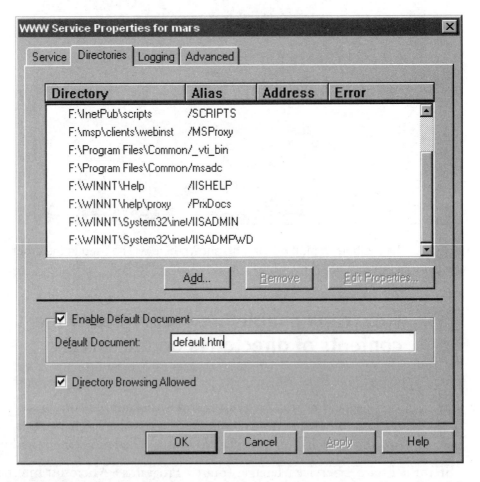

Figure 20-5. Clients can now view the directory contents unless a document of the default name exists (in which case, that document will be shown).

How do I configure a virtual server?

It is possible, using Windows NT, to bind multiple IP addresses to one network card, and for each IP address, it is possible to run a virtual domain server. This means multiple Web sites can be hosted on one server, such as http://www.savilltech.com and http://www.ntfaq.com. The following procedure adds an IP address, adds the new IP address as a domain, and sets up the new IIS virtual server.

To bind an additional IP address to your network card, perform the following:

1. Start the Network Control Panel applet (Start > Settings > Control Panel > Network).
2. Select the Protocols tab.
3. Select TCP/IP and click Properties.
4. On the IP Address tab, click the Advanced button.
5. In the IP Address section, click Add.
6. Enter the additional IP address and subnet mask to which you want the machine to respond and click Add (see Figure 20-6).
7. Click OK until you leave the Network Control Panel applet.
8. Reboot the machine.

You now need to configure the DNS server to respond to the new name with the new IP address.

1. Start the DNS Manager (Start > Programs > Administrative Tools > DNS Manager).
2. From the DNS menu, select New Server and enter the IP address of the DNS Server (for example, **200.200.200.3**). Click OK.
3. The server is now displayed with a CACHE subpart.
4. Next you want to add the domain (for example, savilltech.com). From the DNS menu, select New Zone.
5. Select Primary and click Next.
6. Enter the name (for example, **savilltech.com**). Then press the Tab key to fill in the Zone filename.
7. Click Next and then click Finish.
8. Next, you need to create a zone for reverse lookups, so select New Zone from the DNS menu.

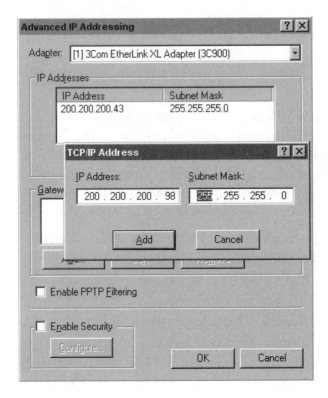

Figure 20-6. Adding a second IP address to a Network Interface Card.

9. Select Primary and click Next.

10. Type the name of the first three parts of the domain IP plus in-addr.arpa. For example, if the domain were 158.234.26, the entry would be **26.234.158.in-addr.arpa**. In my example, it would be **200.200.200.in-addr.arpa**.

11. Press the Tab key for the filename to be filled. Then click Next and click Finish.

12. From the DNS menu, select New Host. Enter the machine name and IP address and select Create Associated PTR Record.

13. Click Add and then Done.

14. Next, create the www.<domain>.com record. From the DNS menu, select New Record.

15. Select record type CNAME. Enter an alias name of www and the actual host name (for example, **www.server.shadow.com**).

16. Click OK and exit the DNS server.

Next you need to update the IIS server to support the new domain.

1. Start the Internet Service Manager (Start > Programs > Microsoft Internet Server).
2. Double-click on the computer name of the Web server that will display the properties.
3. Click the Directories tab and click Add.
4. Enter the directory name and select the Home Directory check box.
5. Now check the Virtual Server box and enter the IP address you added in the first step (see Figure 20-7).
6. Click OK and click OK again to close.

You can now browse to this domain.

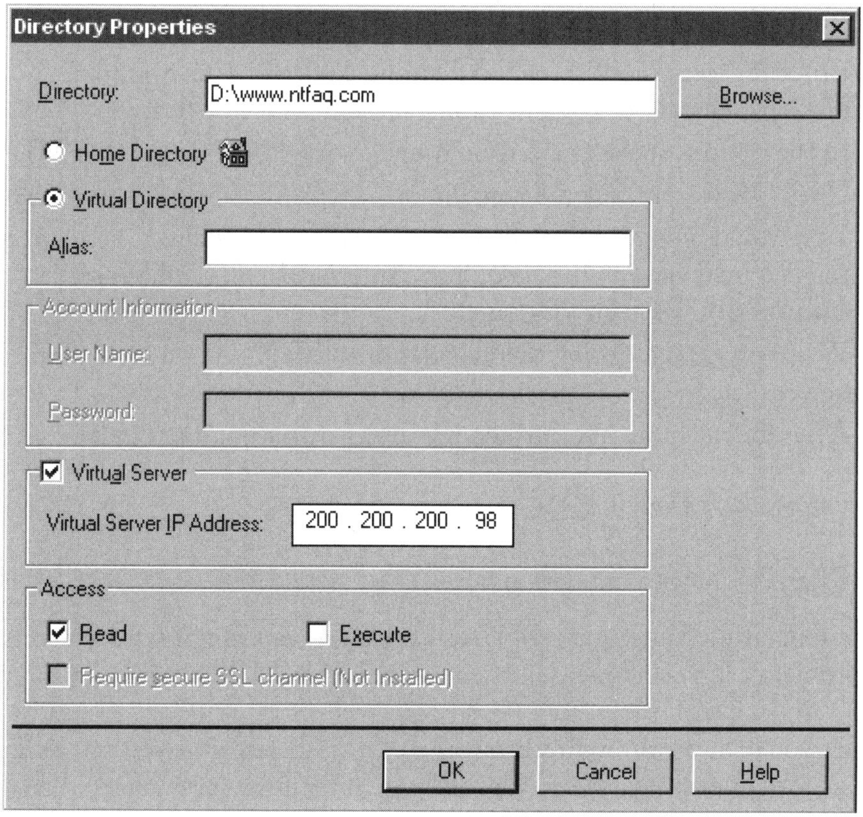

Figure 20-7. The creation of a new virtual server, using the directory d:\www.ntfaq.com.

How can I administer my IIS server by using a Web browser?

IIS comes with a built-in HTML version of Internet Services Manager, with an address of <server name>/iisadmin/default.htm. WebAdmin does have to be installed separately. To check if it's installed, start the browser and move to \iisadmin\default.htm. If you see the Internet Server Manager page but with no graphics, WebAdmin is not installed.

To install, perform the following:

1. Log on to the IIS server as an Administrator.
2. Start the Internet Information Server Setup (Start > Programs > Microsoft Internet Server > Internet Information Server Setup).
3. Click OK in the first dialog box and then select Add/Remove.
4. Enter the location of the setup files and click OK (this would be d:\i386\inetsrv if d: is your NT installation CD-ROM drive).
5. In the options shown, select the Internet Service Manager (HTML).
6. Click OK to continue the installation.
7. You should now reapply your service pack if you installed WebAdmin from the NT installation CD. If you have Internet Explorer 4.0 installed you get a warning. Click Run Program.
8. When prompted during the installation, click No to All for replacing newer files.
9. After the machine has finished rebooting, run this command:

```
regsvr32 rsabase.dll
```

10. Click OK in the completion box.

If your default filename is not DEFAULT.HTM, you might have a few navigation problems. If this happens, just enter DEFAULT.HTM after any directory name.

After you connect through a browser to the iisadmin area, you might have to enter a username and password (depending on the browser you use). You can then perform actions to administer the site (see Figure 20-8).

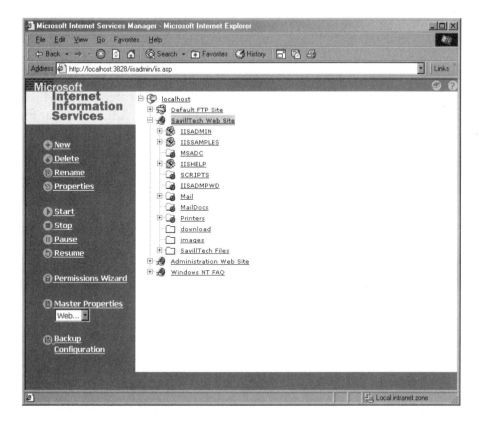

Figure 20-8. The IIS 5.0 Web-based Internet Services Manager.

How can I configure FTP to use directory annotation?

Directory annotation gives a help file display every time a client changes directories on the FTP server. Follow the procedure below:

1. Log on to the IIS server machine as an Administrator.
2. Start the Registry editor (REGEDIT.EXE).
3. Move to HKEY_LOCAL_MACHINE\SYSTEM\CurrentControlSet\ Services\msftpsvc\Parameters.
4. From the Edit menu, select New > DWORD Value.

5. Enter the name **AnnotateDirectories** and press Enter.

6. Double-click on the new value and set the value to 1.

7. You should now stop and restart the FTP Server service.

You now need to create a file called **~ftpsvc~.ckm** for each directory in which you wish the annotation to appear. The file is just a normal ASCII-format file.

   You might want to make the file hidden so it does not get shown on a directory listing on the FTP directory. To hide the file, right-click on the filename. Select Properties from the context menu and check the Hidden box.

 ## How can I configure the FTP welcome message?

By using the IIS ADMIN utility, you can configure Welcome, End, and Connection Refused messages to be displayed when a client connects to or disconnects from your FTP service.

1. Start the Internet Service Manager (Start > Programs > Microsoft Internet Server).

2. Select the FTP service on the machine you wish to configure.

3. From the Properties menu, select Service Properties.

4. Click the Messages tab.

5. Enter text in the Welcome Message, Exit Message, and Maximum Connections fields (see Figure 20-9).

6. Click the Apply button and then click OK.

7. Stop and restart the FTP service.

8. Close the Internet Service Manager.

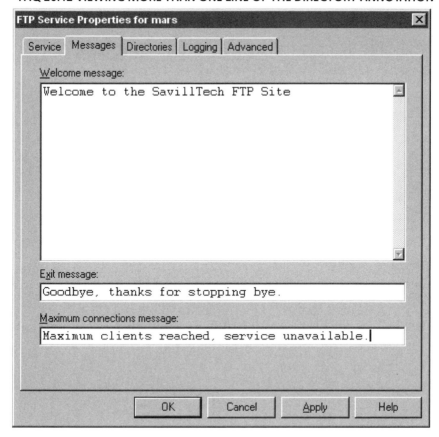

Figure 20-9. Say anything you want in your welcome message. It might be good to include a legal warning outlining usage details of the service.

20.12 Only the first line of the directory annotation is shown. Why?

This is happens if you have no Welcome message. To correct it, add a Welcome message as described in Question 20.11.

How can I configure the amount of IIS cache?

20.13

By default, InetInfo—the process responsible for WWW, FTP, and Gopher—uses a 3MB cache for all of the services. This cache is used to store files in memory, thus providing faster access than from disk. To change the amount of memory available for the cache, perform the following:

1. Start the Registry editor (REGEDIT.EXE).
2. Move to HKEY_LOCAL_MACHINE\System\CurrentControlSet\Services\InetInfo\Parameters.
3. From the Edit menu, select New > DWORD Value.
4. Enter the **MemoryCacheSize** and click Enter.
5. Double-click the new value and set it to the amount of memory you wish to use for the cache. Set it in bytes (for example, 5000000 for 5MB).
6. Click OK and close the Registry editor.
7. Stop and start all IIS services.

If you wish to disable caching, set the value to 0; however, this could have a serious effect on performance.

How do I create a virtual directory?

20.14

Before I describe how to create a virtual directory, it is first important to understand what a virtual directory is. For those who remember DOS, there was a command called join that enabled you to treat a different disk as a directory on the current drive. A virtual directory is the same kind of thing; you can treat a directory or disk as a subdirectory of your Web site. This differs from a virtual server, which basically offers an entirely separate Web site on the same box.

For example, your default Web area might be c:\InetPub\wwwroot, which you could access as http://www.savilltech.com. If you had a subdirectory off of wwwroot called ntfaq (for example, c:\InetPub\wwwroot\ntfaq), you could access this as http://www.savilltech.com/ntfaq. What if I run out of space on C: and want the

FAQ to be on d:? I would create a virtual directory called ntfaq that would point to d:\pages\ntfaq. The procedure for creating a virtual directory is shown here.

1. Start the Internet Service Manager (Start > Programs > Microsoft Internet Server).
2. Double-click on the computer name of the Web server that will display the properties.
3. Click the Directories tab and click the Add button to display the Directory Properties box.
4. In the Directory field, type the name of the disk and directory to which you want the new area to point (or click Browse to select a directory).
5. Next, select the Virtual Directory check box and enter the alias you want the directory to be seen as (for example, **ntfaq**). Click OK.
6. Click OK again and close the Internet Service Manager application.

2000 ONLY
20.15 How do I install FrontPage Server Extensions on Windows 2000 Beta 2?

The FrontPage Server Extensions are not installed during the Beta 2 NT/IIS setup. To install the extensions, perform the following steps:

1. Completely remove any previous FrontPage or FrontPage Extensions installations from the server. You can do this by using the Add/Remove Programs Control Panel applet.
2. Open a command prompt and change directory to SYSTEM32:

```
cd %systemroot%\system32
```

3. Start the Windows NT setup for the FrontPage Server Extensions:

```
sysocmgr /i:fp.inf /n /x
```

4. Ensure that the FrontPage 99 Server Extensions are selected and click Next (see Figure 20-10).
5. Select the location of your NT 5.0 I386 structure and click OK to install the files.

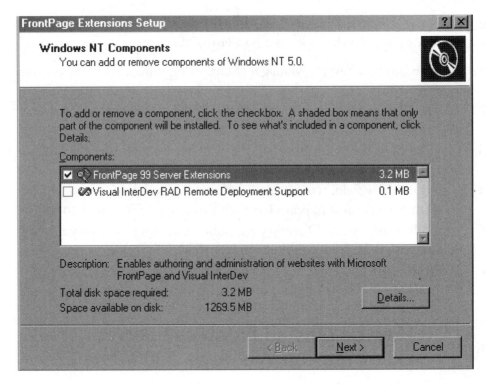

Figure 20-10. Installing the Windows 2000 FrontPage Server Extensions.

FAQ 20.16   What fixes are available for IIS?

Microsoft has released the first NT Option Pack QFE (Quick Fix Engineering) Update, but this actually only updates IIS 4.0 at this time.

The update includes every hotfix made to IIS from its release. This is a cumulative hotfix, and you should only install this if you are experiencing specific problems with IIS. The new intent is to release a new fix pack about every month or so or, when appropriate, so customers won't need to wait for such a long time between service packs. Also, customers who are experiencing problems don't need to hunt down individual hotfixes anymore but can just download this update and get all available fixes at once.

The uninstall is very clean, so if something goes wrong, simply remove the fix. Something new here is letting customers know up front what DLLs are being replaced. During installation of the update, the file IIS_HOTFIX.HTM is dropped into the users \inetsrv directory. This file contains all of the information about the fix and should make it very easy for Product Support Services to determine what version of IIS the customer is using.

Download the QFE Update from http://www.microsoft.com/windows/ downloads/contents/updates/ntopqfe/default.asp.

21 INTERNET EXPLORER

Internet Explorer (IE) is quickly becoming the standard browser and offers lots of good features, such as the Active Desktop. Some of these features can be annoying, however, so this section looks at advanced configuration and component removal.

Microsoft is providing more content in HTML format. Their new Help format is HTML Help, which uses components of IE 4.0.

How can I remove the Active Desktop?
21.1

You can turn off the Active Desktop without removing it by performing the following:

1. Right-click on the desktop.
2. Select Active Desktop.
3. Unselect View as Web Page (by clicking it).

To actually remove Active Desktop completely while leaving the browser intact:

1. Start the Add/Remove Programs Control Panel applet (Start > Settings > Control Panel > Add/Remove Programs).

2. Select Microsoft Internet Explorer 4.0 and click the Add/Remove button.

3. Click the Remove the Windows Desktop Update component but keep the Internet Explorer 4.0 Web Browser option. Click OK.

4. When a dialog box appears to explain the change, click the Restart Windows button.

5. After the restart, the Active Desktop will have been removed.

How can I get past the Active Desktop Recovery page?

This can usually be fixed by deleting the DESKTOP.HTT file, as follows:

1. Start Explorer (Run > Explorer).

2. Move to %systemroot%\Profiles\<your username>\Application Data\Microsoft\Internet Explorer.

3. Select DESKTOP.HTT and delete it. (Because this is a hidden file, you will first need to change the view by choosing View > Folder Options > View).

4. Close Explorer.

5. Right-click on the desktop and choose Refresh.

What keyboard commands can I use with Internet Explorer 4.0?

Table 21-1 shows a list of common keyboard commands for IE 4.0.

Table 21-1. Internet Explorer 4.0 Keyboard Commands

Alt + left arrow (or backspace)	Go back
Alt + right arrow	Go forward
Tab	Move to next hyperlink
Shift + Tab	Move to previous hyperlink

Table 21-1. Internet Explorer 4.0 Keyboard Commands *(continued)*

Enter	Move to page referenced by hyperlink
Down arrow	Scroll down
Page Down	Scroll down in greater jump
End	Move to bottom of document
Up arrow	Scroll up
Page Up	Scroll up in greater jump
Home	Move to top of document
F5	Refresh
Ctrl + F5	Refresh not from cache
Esc	Stop download
F11	Full screen/normal toggle

 # How can I create a keyboard shortcut to a Web site?

It is possible to create your own keyboard shortcuts with a Ctrl+Alt+<letter> combination, as follows:

1. Start Internet Explorer.
2. Select Organize Favorites from the Favorites menu.
3. Right-click on the link and choose Properties.
4. In the Shortcut Key dialog box, type the keyboard combination you want—any combination of Ctrl + Shift + Alt plus a key that is not used.
5. Click OK.

You can also use these steps to create a keyboard shortcut to a desktop item by right-clicking on the shortcut and then choosing Properties.

21.5 How can I customize folders with Web view enabled?

If you have installed the Windows Desktop Update and have enabled View as Web Page (View > As Web Page), you can customize the folder (View > Customize this Folder) and then select the type (Background Picture or a whole HTML file). You can also change the default, which is stored in a hidden HTML file (%systemroot%\Web\folder.htt), by editing this file.

In FOLDER.HTT is the line "Here's A Good Place To Add A Few Lines Of Your Own." You can add your own links, which will then appear on all folders.

Here are four other templates you can edit:

CONTROLP.HTT	Control Panel
PRINTERS.HTT	Printers
MYCOMP.HTT	My Computer
SAFEMODE.HTT	Safe Mode

These templates are hidden, so you will need to either remove the hidden attribute (attrib <file> -h) or just enter the name specifically in the edit utility you use to change these files. A word of warning: make a backup of these files before you break them.

21.6 How can I change the icons on the Quick Launch toolbar?

The icons on the Quick Launch toolbar (Internet Explorer, Outlook Express, Show Desktop, and Channels by default) are all stored in %systemroot%/profiles/<user>/Application Data/Microsoft/Internet Explorer/Quick Launch. You can add files to or remove them from this directory by using Explorer.

You can copy any shortcut to the Quick Launch folder. Updates are done immediately, with no need to log off or reboot. As you can see in Figure 21-1, I have added a shortcut for Word and FrontPage just by copying the shortcut to the Quick Launch directory.

Figure 21-1. A modified Quick Launch toolbar with Word and FrontPage added.

An alternative method is to just drag a shortcut over the Quick Launch bar and the shortcut is added for you. All of the files in the Quick Launch folder are shortcuts except for Show Desktop and View Channels. See Question 21.7 for their contents.

I have lost Show Desktop/View Channels from the Quick Launch toolbar. Help!

As was discussed in Question 21.6, these icons are just files in the %systemroot%/profiles/<user>/Application Data/Microsoft/Internet Explorer/Quick Launch directory. To get the Show Desktop/View Channels icons back, create the following files in the Quick Launch directory (or copy them from another user).

For Show Desktop, create SHOW DESKTOP.SCF with the following contents:

```
[Shell]
Command=2
IconFile=explorer.exe,3

[Taskbar]
Command=ToggleDesktop
```

For View Channels, create VIEW CHANNELS.SCF with the following contents:

```
[Shell]
Command=3
IconFile=shdocvw.dll,-118

[IE]
Command=Channels
```

How do I change the default search engine?

21.8

The URL for the search engine used with Go > Search the Web is stored in the Registry, so you can easily change it, as follows:

1. Start the Registry editor (REGEDIT.EXE).
2. Move to HKEY_CURRENT_USER\Software\Microsoft\Internet Explorer\Main.
3. Double-click on Search Page.
4. Change to the search page you want. For example, you could use http://www.altavista.digital.com.
5. Click OK and close the Registry editor.

When you next select Search, you will be taken to this revised URL. If you want to change back to the default, enter http://www.msn.com/access/allinone.htm.

How do I remove the Internet Explorer icon from the desktop?

21.9

You remove the icon by using the Advanced Options of Internet Explorer, as follows:

1. Start Internet Explorer.
2. From the View menu, choose Internet Options (in IE 5.0, it is under the Tools menu).
3. Click the Advanced tab.
4. Deselect Show Internet Explorer on Desktop (see Figure 21-2).
5. Click OK and restart the machine.

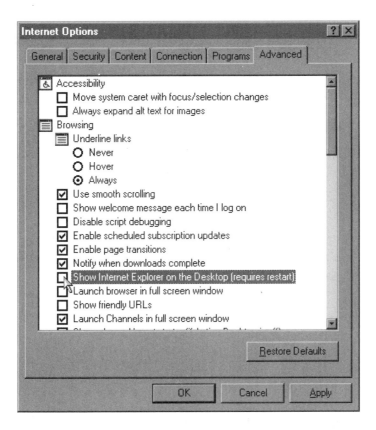

Figure 21-2. Disabling the Internet Explorer icon on the desktop.

How can I browse offline?

FAQ 21.10

As you might be aware, when you connect to a site, the information you view is cached locally to speed up future visits to the site (you can set the cache size in View > Internet Options > General > Temporary Internet Files > Settings). It's actually possible to view the Web by using only the cache when you're not connected (obviously, you can view only the sites that are stored in the cache). To work offline:

1. Start Internet Explorer.
2. From the File menu, choose Work Offline.

You can now enter URLs and link as normal, but you'll receive an error if you attempt to link to a site that is not cached. To stop working offline, deselect Work Offline.

21.11   How can I reclaim space wasted by Microsoft's Internet E-mail readers?

Microsoft's Internet e-mail clients (both Internet Mail under IE3 and Outlook Express under IE4) waste a large amount of disk space due to their methods of storing mail. The reason behind this is to improve performance; however, if you want to reclaim some of the lost space, perform the following:

1. Select one of the folders (Inbox, Outbox, Sent Items).
2. From the File menu, choose Folder > Compact All Folders.

You can also set up Outlook to automatically delete the Deleted Items folder contents. Obviously, when you delete them from this folder, you have lost them unless you have a backup.

1. Select Options from the Tools menu.
2. Select the General tab.
3. Check the box next to Empty Messages From the Deleted Items Folder on Exit.
4. Click OK.

21.12   I cannot specify a download directory when I download a file. Why?

When you download a file, you are asked if you want to open the file from its current location or save the file to a disk. If you take the latter option, you are asked for a storage location. Enter the location and then click Save. Also on the selection screen at that time is an option of Always Ask Before Opening This Type of File. You apparently cleared this check mark, which means downloads of this type are now downloaded to the Temporary Internet Files folder and opened by the program associated with the file type.

If you want to specify download directories, perform the following:

1. Double-click on My Computer.
2. From the View menu, choose Folder Options.
3. Select the File Types tab.
4. In the Registered File Types box, select the file type with which you have the problem and click Edit.
5. In the bottom-right corner is an option to Confirm Open after Download. Check the box and click OK.
6. Click OK again to close the Folder Options dialog box.
7. Close My Computer.

Internet Explorer opens .EXE files instead of downloading them. Why?

As in Question 21.12, if you deselect Always Ask Before Opening This Type of File for an executable, the Registry is updated so you are not asked. However, you can reverse this setting by performing the following:

1. Start the Registry editor (REGEDT32.EXE).
2. Move to HKEY_CLASSES_ROOT\exefile.
3. Double-click on EditFlags.
4. Change the third pair of numbers from 01 to 00 (for example, change D8070100 to D8070000).
5. Close the Registry editor.

For files such as .WAV, .MOV, and .AVI (ActiveMovie files), modify the entry HKEY_CLASSES_ROOT\AMOVIE.ActiveMovieControl.2\EditFlags to be 00000000.

How can I change the default Start page?

21.14

When you first start Internet Explorer, a page is loaded. By default this is a Microsoft MSN Start page (http://home.microsoft.com); however, you can change this, as follows:

1. Start Internet Explorer.
2. Choose Internet Options from the View menu.
3. Select the General tab (see Figure 21-3).

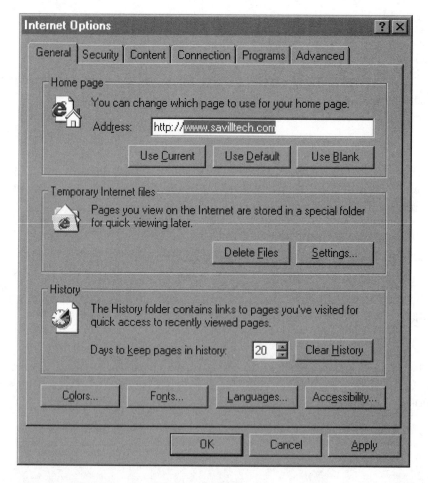

Figure 21-3. Modifying the Start page through the Internet Explorer interface.

4. In the Home Page section at the top, enter the page you wish to be displayed when you start Internet Explorer. Click Apply and then OK.

5. If you just want a blank page, click the Use Blank button. Again, click Apply and then OK.

6. Close Internet Explorer.

The previous procedure updates Registry entry HKEY_CURRENT_USER\ Software\Microsoft\Internet Explorer\Main\Start Page.

You could also create a Registry script that updates a machine's Registry to set your page up as the client's home page. The Registry script would have the following:

```
REGEDIT4
[HKEY_CURRENT_USER\Software\Microsoft\Internet Explorer\Main]
Start Page=http://www.ntfaq.com/
[HKEY_LOCAL_MACHINE\Software\Microsoft\Internet
Explorer\Main] Default_Page_URL=http://www.ntfaq.com/
```

You would then set up a link on your page to the script, and people would select Open from Current Location. The official Microsoft image for this link is shown in Figure 21-4.

Figure 21-4. The official Set As Home Page logo.

You could also run the .REG file as part of a logon script to set for all users in your domain. The Registry section has instructions about running a .REG file.

I have set my Registry file so it sets http://www.ntfaq.com as my Start page. If you want no Start page—a blank—set the value to about:blank.

If you use Netscape, you can use the following to change your default home page:

1. Start Netscape.

2. From the Edit menu, choose Preferences.

3. Select the Navigator category.

4. Enter the required Start page in the Home Page box and click OK.

Netscape does not store the Start page location in the Registry but rather in a JavaScript file PREFS.JS, which is located in the Program Files\Netscape\ Users\<Netscape Profile Name> directory. The line in the file that controls the Start page is shown here, but you should not edit this file.

```
user_pref(browser.startup.homepage, http://www.ntfaq.com/);
```

21.15 I have forgotten the Content Advisor password. What can I do?

The password for the Content Advisor is stored in an encrypted form. Decrypting it, although possible, is too complicated for most people's purposes, so instead just reset the password as if it had never been set.

1. Start the Registry editor (REGEDIT.EXE).
2. Move to HKEY_LOCAL_MACHINE\SOFTWARE\Microsoft\ Windows\CurrentVersion\Policies\Ratings\.
3. If this is a Key value, select it and press Delete. Click OK to the confirmation.
4. If there was not a value but there was instead a subkey .Default, move to the .Default folder and delete the Key value (see Figure 21-5).

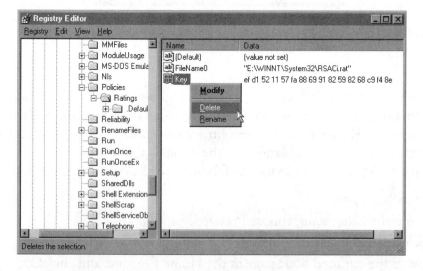

Figure 21-5. Deleting the password Key value.

5. When you restart Internet Explorer, you should be able to set the password with Internet Options > Content.

FAQ 21.16 Where can I download Internet Explorer 5.0 beta?

IE 5.0 beta can be downloaded from http://www.microsoft.com/windows/ie/ie5/default.asp.

Internet Explorer 5.0 does not ship with the Active Desktop, so if you want Active Desktop you need to have IE 4.0 with Active Desktop already installed and then upgrade to IE 5.0.

FAQ 21.17 How do I clear Internet Explorer's history?

Internet Explorer keeps a history of the sites you visit. You can see a list of these by clicking the History button on the toolbar. If you wish to clear this history, perform the following:

IE 4

1. Choose Internet Options from the View menu.
2. In the History section, click Clear History (you can also set the number of days to keep history).
3. Click Yes to the confirmation.
4. Click OK to close the Internet Options dialog box.

IE 5

Same as for IE 4 except Internet Options is under the Tools menu. The History files are stored under the directory %systemroot%\Profiles\<user name>\History\History; however, the permissions on the files are complex, so deleting manually is not advised.

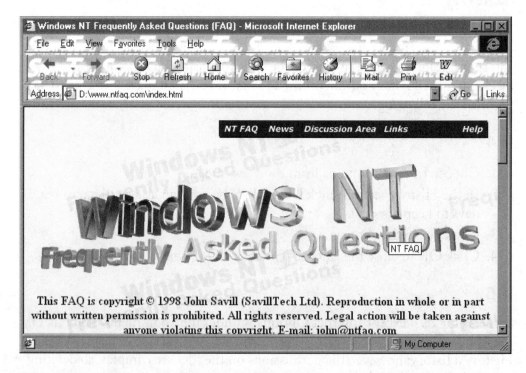

21.18   How can I modify Internet Explorer's toolbar background?

The picture behind the Internet Explorer toolbar buttons can be set to any bitmap you wish. To change the picture, perform the following:

1. Start the Registry editor (REGEDIT.EXE).
2. Move to HKEY_CURRENT_USER\Software\Microsoft\Internet Explorer\Toolbar.
3. From the Edit menu, choose New > String Value.
4. Enter the name **BackBitmap** and press Enter.
5. Double-click the new value (BackBitmap) and set to the name and location of this image. For example, you could set **c:\images\savtech.bmp** (see Figure 21-6).
6. Close the Registry editor and restart IE.

Figure 21-6. Notice the SavillTech logo background to the Internet Explorer toolbars.

FAQ 21.19 How can I restore Internet Explorer's animated logo?

By using the Internet Explorer Admin Kit, it is possible to modify the small E logo in the top-right corner of Internet Explorer (Internet Service Providers such as MSN do this). To restore the default, perform the following:

1. Start the Registry editor (REGEDIT.EXE).
2. Move to HKEY_CURRENT_USER\Software\Microsoft\Internet Explorer\Toolbar.
3. Select BrandBitmap and click Delete. Click Yes to the confirmation.
4. Select SmBrandBitmap and click Delete. Click Yes to the confirmation.
5. Close the Registry editor and restart the computer.

22 REMOTE ACCESS SERVER (RAS)

Remote Access Server (RAS) is an excellent addition to Windows NT 4.0 and enables both Windows NT Server and Workstation machines to act as dial-in servers for machines to access the rest of the network (Workstation is restricted to only a single inbound connection).

RAS is also the tool used to connect to the outside world, and many of us use it to connect to our Internet Service Providers (ISPs) with a modem.

22.1 How do I connect two Workstations using RAS?

NT Workstation supports one inbound RAS connection. One NT station will be the RAS server and one will be the client. Following is the procedure for connecting the two machines.

The Server

If RAS is already installed:

1. Start the Network Control Panel applet (Start > Settings > Control Panel > Network).
2. Click the Services tab.

3. Select Remote Access Server and then click Properties.
4. Click on the port (possibly COM1) and click Configure.
5. Select Dial Out and Receive or just Receive.
6. Click Continue.
7. Select user access: Just Computer or Entire Network for NetBEUI.
8. Click Continue and fill in details for TCP/IP. For this setup, assume the dial-in client will have a TCP/IP address and check the box Allow Clients to Use Preconfigured Address.
9. Click OK and then click Close.
10. At the prompt, restart the computer.

If RAS is not already installed, go to My Computer and double-click Dial-up Networking. It will detect your modem and take you to step 3 as above.

The Client

This assumes RAS is not installed:

1. Double-click My Computer and double-click Dial-up Network.
2. At the prompt, insert the NT CD for installing Modem and RAS.
3. Setup detects any modems. When your modem has been found, click Continue.
4. You are told that the phone book is empty and you should add an entry. Give a name and select Next (do *not* select I Know About Modem Properties unless you do).
5. Select I Am Calling the Internet and click Next.
6. Enter the phone number and click Next. Then click Finish.
7. Select the entry and click More. Then choose Edit Entry.
8. Select the Server tab and check the protocols that apply (for example, NetBEUI and TCP/IP). Click TCP/IP details and fill in valid information such as an IP address, subnet mask, DNS servers.
9. Click OK and then click OK again.
10. Select the phone book entry and click Dial.
11. The first time you connect, you have to supply a username, password, and domain (select Save Password so you won't have to enter the information again).

Is it possible to dial an ISP from the command line?

Yes. You can also use the RASPHONE.EXE utility from the command line. The syntax is

RASPHONE -d <phonebook entry>

 ## How can I keep the RAS connections from disconnecting when I log off?

If you have active RAS connections, they will be closed when you log off. You can change this behavior as follows:

1. Start the Registry editor (REGEDIT.EXE).
2. Move to HKEY_LOCAL_MACHINE\SOFTWARE\Microsoft\ Windows NT\CurrentVersion\Winlogon.
3. Create a new value called KeepRasConnections of type String Value (Edit > New > String Value).
4. Set the new value to 1.
5. Close the Registry editor.

 ## How can I create a RAS Connection script?

It is possible to write a script that will run when you are making a RAS connection to automate such actions as entering your username and password. You may currently enter this information by having a terminal window display after the connection is made.

To specify a script, perform the following:

1. Double-click on My Computer and start up the Dial-Up Networking applet.
2. Select the phone book entry and click More.
3. From the More menu, choose Edit Entry and Modem Properties.
4. Click the Script tab and select Run This Script.
5. Click the Edit Script button to open the SWITCH.INF file.
6. Go to the bottom of the file and create a new connection section. Then click Exit.
7. Answer Yes to save changes.
8. Click the Refresh List button to make sure that the new entry is now displayed.
9. Select the new entry you created and click OK.

An example addition to the SWITCH.INF follows:

```
; the phonebook entry
[Savill1]
; send initial carriage return
COMMAND=<cr>
; wait for : (after username, may be different at your site)
omit the
; U as it may be capitals. You could just have :
OK=<match>"sername:"
LOOP=<ignore>
; send username as entered in the connection dialog box,
alternatively
; you could just enter the username e.g. savillj<cr>
COMMAND=<username><cr>
; wait for : (after password this time, may be different at
your site)
OK=<match>"assword:"
LOOP=<ignore>
; send the password entered in the connection dialog box,
again you
; could just manually enter the password, e.g. password<cr>
COMMAND=<password><cr>
NoResponse
; send the "start ppp" command
COMMAND=ppp default<cr>
OK=<ignore>
```

You can find in-depth information on all of the commands in the %systemroot%\system32\ras\SWITCH.INF file.

How can I debug the RAS Connection Script?
22.5

It is possible to create a log file of the connection by performing the following steps. This log enables you to pinpoint any problems in the script.

1. Start the Registry editor (REGEDIT.EXE).
2. Move to HKEY_LOCAL_MACHINE\SYSTEM\CurrentControlSet\ Services\RasMan\Parameters.
3. Double-click on Logging.
4. Change the value data to 1 and click OK.
5. Close the Registry editor and restart the computer.

Each dial-up session will now be appended to the file %systemroot%/system32/RAS/device.log. To stop logging, perform the same steps but set the value back to 0.

How do I configure RAS to connect to a leased line?
22.6

The method varies, depending on your system's current setup. If you have RAS already installed, the following actions are the ones for configuring your leased line. This procedure assumes that the modems (at both ends) are configured correctly for leased-line usage (&D0 for DTR override).

1. Start the Modems Control Panel applet (Start > Settings > Control Panel > Modems).
2. Click Add.
3. Check Don't Detect My Modem, I Will Select It From a List. Then click Next.

4. In the Manufacturers box, select Standard Modem Types.

5. In the Models area, select Dial-Up Networking Serial Cable Between 2 PCs. Then click Next.

6. Select the port (possibly COM1) and click Next.

7. You now have a modem setup ready for leased-line use.

You should now configure the RAS connection (server to client) in the normal way (using the RAS service properties).

1. Right-click on Network and choose Properties.

2. Click the Services tab and select RAS. Then click Properties.

3. Select the COM port and click Configure.

4. Select the Connection Type (dial-in/dial-out/both) and click OK. Then click Continue.

5. When asked about NetBEUI client access, select the one you want and click OK.

6. If you selected Server, you are now prompted for TCP/IP access and for which IP addresses should be given, either by DHCP (if configured) or from a given pool of addresses. You can also check the box to allow a client to request a specific IP address.

7. In the Network dialog box, click Close. The bindings of the machine update and you are asked if you want to reboot. Click Yes.

After you have configured the RAS connection, you might also want a phone book entry for outgoing use. Create it as you would normally except check the Persistent Connection box in the Dialing section.

 ## How can I disable RAS Autodial?

If you find your machine is constantly trying to dial out, you might want to disable RAS Autodial. The easiest way to do this is to disable the RAS Autodial service:

1. Start the Services Control Panel applet (Start > Settings > Control Panel > Services).

2. Scroll down to Remote Access Autodial Manager and select it.
3. Click the Startup button and change the startup to Manual (see Figure 22-1). Click OK.
4. If you want to stop now, click the Stop button.
5. Click the Close button.

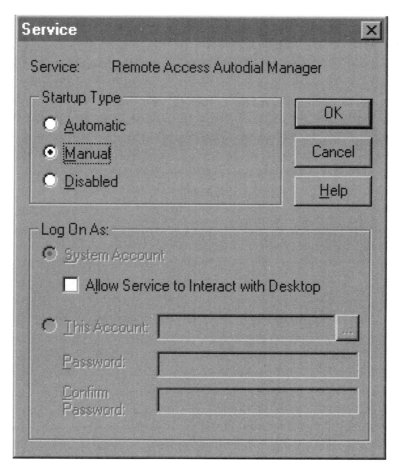

Figure 22-1. Setting the RAS Autodial service to Manual.

To reenable, repeat these steps but change the startup to Automatic.

RAS tries to dial out even on local resources. Why?

22.8

Sometimes the Autodial list of addresses gets confused and RAS attempts to dial out to the Internet even for local resources. Try the following to rectify the situation:

1. Start the Registry editor (REGEDIT.EXE).
2. Move to HKEY_CURRENT_USER\Software\Microsoft\RAS Autodial\Addresses (see Figure 22-2). A better way to view these addresses is to type **rasautou -s** from the command prompt.
3. In the subkeys, look for the local address (and name, if there is one). If you find it, select the subkey and choose Edit > Delete.
4. Close the Registry editor.

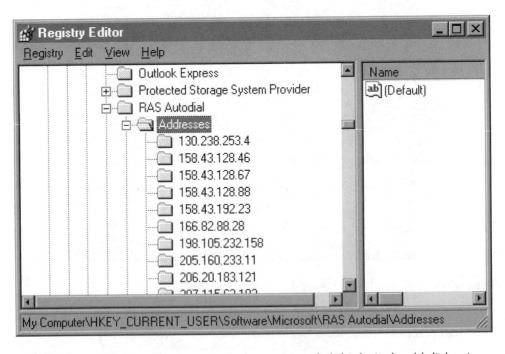

Figure 22-2. Viewing addresses for which RAS Autodial thinks it should dial out.

You might also wish to add addresses to the disabled list by doing the following:

1. Start the Registry editor (REGEDT32.EXE, **not** REGEDIT.EXE).
2. Move to HKEY_CURRENT_USER\Software\Microsoft\RAS Autodial\Control.
3. Double-click on DisabledAddresses and add the address on a new line. Then click OK.
4. Close the Registry editor.

You need to reboot the machine after both of these procedures (or stop and start the RAS Autodial service).

 I have connected to a server via RAS, but the only resources I see are on the machine I connect to. Why?

When you configure the RAS server, you set for each protocol the scope of the connection—the server or the whole network. To change the protocol, perform the following:

1. Start the Network Control Panel applet (Start > Settings > Control Panel > Network).
2. Right-click on Network and choose Properties.
3. Choose the Service tab and select the Remote Access Service. Then click Properties.
4. Select the COM port and click the Network button.
5. Click the Configure button next to the protocol for which you wish to change access (for example, TCP/IP).
6. At the top of the Configure window, check Entire Network.
7. Click OK.

Clients should now be able to view the entire network.

22.10

How do I force Logon Using Dialup Networking to be checked by default on the logon screen?

When you log on, there is an optional check box that enables you to log on using dial-up networking. You might want to have this set by default. You can accomplish this with a Registry change on each client machine.

1. Start the Registry editor (REGEDIT.EXE).
2. Move to HKEY_LOCAL_MACHINE\SOFTWARE\Microsoft\ Windows NT\CurrentVersion\Winlogon
3. From the Edit menu, choose New > String Value (REG_SZ type).
4. Enter the name RASForce.
5. Double-click the new value and set to 1.
6. Close the Registry editor and reboot the machine.

22.11

Where are the RAS phone book entries and settings stored?

The actual phone book entries are stored in the file %systemroot%/system32/ ras/rasphone.pbk (PBK > Phone Book). You can copy this file to another machine to copy the phone book entries.

Another important file is %systemroot%/system32/ras/switch.inf, which is used to create terminal login scripts (as discussed in Question 22.4). You might find that phone book entries refer to an entry in this file:

```
DEVICE=switch
Type=Terminal
```

In this case, Type=Terminal means to bring up a terminal window after connection, so it does not use SWITCH.INF. The following would cause the script Pipex (which is in SWITCH.INF) to be run after a connection has been made:

```
DEVICE=switch
Type=Pipex
```

If these two lines are missing, don't worry; it just means you don't need a terminal window after you have connected (it probably means you're connecting to a Windows NT box). If you connect to a non-NT machine, you usually have to send it a username and password, along with the connection type (protocol), which is PPP on most modern systems (SLIP is an older option).

RAS information relating to phone book entries and outbound connections in the Registry is actually stored under HKEY_CURRENT_USER\Software\ Microsoft\RAS Phonebook. This file contains details about redial attempts, display settings, and so on. Again, you can export this section of the Registry to a .REG file (using REGEDIT.EXE) and import it into another machine to copy the machine-specific settings.

FAQ 22.12 How can I change the number of rings the RAS server waits for before answering?

The normal method is to edit the file %systemroot%\system32\ras\modem.inf. Open the file, find the sections relating to your modem, and find this line:

```
COMMAND_LISTEN=ATS0=1<cr>
```

Change the numeric value to the number of rings to answer after. For example, so it will answer after 10 rings, use the following:

```
COMMAND_LISTEN=ATS0=10<cr>
```

You must restart Windows NT for this change to take effect.

This procedure does not work if RAS is using any Telephony Application Programming Interface (TAPI)/Unimodem-based devices. In this case, perform the following:

1. Start the Registry editor (REGEDIT.EXE).
2. Move to HKEY_LOCAL_MACHINE\SYSTEM\CurrentControlSet\ Services\RasMan\Parameters.
3. From the Edit menu, choose New > DWORD Value.
4. Enter the name NumberOfRings and press Enter.

5. Double-click on this new value and set to the number of rings you want the RAS Server to wait for before answering the phone (1–20). With any number greater than 20 the setting automatically defaults to 1.
6. Click OK and close the Registry editor.

How can I configure how long RAS Server waits before calling back a user when callback is enabled?

22.13

By default, the RAS Server waits 12 seconds before calling back an RAS client; however, you can change this setting by editing the Registry, as follows:

1. Start the Registry editor (REGEDIT.EXE).
2. Move to HKEY_LOCAL_MACHINE\SYSTEM\CurrentControlSet\ Services\RasMan\PPP.
3. From the Edit menu, choose New > DWORD Value.
4. Enter the name DefaultCallbackDelay and press Enter.
5. Double-click on this new value and set it to the number of seconds you want the RAS Server to wait before dialing the client (1–255).
6. Click OK and close the Registry editor.

Whenever I connect via RAS, I cannot connect to local machines on my LAN. Why?

22.14

To enable WWW and FTP browsing when you connect via RAS, you enable the Use Default Gateway on Remote Network option. This has the effect of adding a new route to the route list, superseding the existing LAN routes so any traffic destined for a node outside your local subnet will attempt to be sent by using the RAS route. This happens because a metric is used to identify the number of hops needed. When connected to RAS, the RAS connection will have a metric of 1 and existing routes will be bumped out to a metric of 2.

To solve this, you can manually add a persistent route for your LAN's subnet and the associated subnet gateway. When you're not connected via RAS, you can examine your route information by using the ROUTE PRINT command. For example, if your network were 160.82.0.0 (meaning your company has a class B address) and the gateway were 160.82.220.1 for your local subnet, you could add a route for the LAN only. Then all addresses outside of 160.82.0.0 would be routed by using the RAS gateway.

route -p add <ip network> mask <subnet mask> <local gateway for the route>
(for example, route -p add 160.82.0.0 mask 255.255.0.0 160.82.220.1)

This means that all addresses from 160.82.1.1 to 160.82.254.254 would be routed via 160.82.220.1, and anything else via the RAS gateway.

If you want to add a route for a single host (maybe your Internet firewall, which is on another subnet), use the following:

```
route -p add 192.168.248.8 mask 255.255.255.255 160.82.220.1
```

Notice the subnet mask of 255.255.255.255, which means "only for this single host."

When connected via RAS, you will still be able to access resources outside of your local subnet on the LAN with no problems.

22.15 How can I disable the Save Password option in dial-up networking?

When you connect via RAS, you can cache the password. If you feel this is a security problem, you can disable the option for enabling the password to be saved.

1. Start the Registry editor (REGEDIT.EXE).
2. Move to HKEY_LOCAL_MACHINE\System\CurrentControlSet\Services\RasMan\Parameters.
3. From the Edit menu, choose New > DWORD value.
4. Enter **DisableSavePassword** and press Enter.
5. Double-click the new value and set it to 1.

If you disable Save Password, make sure Redial on Link Failure is not activated as one redial attempt. Because Redial does not save user information, it will attempt to connect as Administrator, which will not work (unless the ISP has very poor security).

22.16 How can I set the number of authentication retries for dial-up connections?

By default, the dial-up networking (DUN) component hangs up the line after two unsuccessful authentication attempts. You can change this to between 0 and 10, with 0 meaning the line will be hung up after the first attempt, 1 allowing one retry, and so on.

1. Start the Registry editor (REGEDIT.EXE).
2. Move to HKEY_LOCAL_MACHINE\SYSTEM\CurrentControlSet\ Services\RemoteAccess\Parameters.
3. Double-click on AuthenticateRetries and set to the required value. Click OK.
4. Close the Registry editor.
5. Reboot the machine for the change to take effect (or stop and restart the RAS services).

22.17 How can I set the authentication time-out for dial-up connections?

In addition to changing the allowed number of authentication retries, you can configure the amount of time between attempt. After that time has elapsed, it counts as a logon failure. This can be between 20 and 600 seconds.

1. Start the Registry editor (REGEDIT.EXE).
2. Move to HKEY_LOCAL_MACHINE\SYSTEM\CurrentControlSet\ Services\RemoteAccess\Parameters.

3. Double-click on AuthenticateTime and set it to the required value. Click OK.

4. Close the Registry editor.

5. Reboot the machine for the change to take effect (or stop and restart the RAS services).

FAQ 22.18 How do I enable 128-bit RAS Data Encryption?

Service Pack 3 (128-bit version) introduced the capability to use 128-bit RAS data encryption with a Windows NT 4.0 RAS server as opposed to the normal 40-bit encryption.

To enable this 128-bit encryption, perform the following:

1. Start the Network Control Panel applet (Start > Settings > Control Panel > Network).

2. Select the Services tab.

3. Choose Remote Access Service and click Properties.

4. Click Network and then choose Require Microsoft Encrypted Authentication.

5. Click Require Data Encryption and click OK.

6. Click Continue and close the Network Control Panel applet.

7. Do not restart the computer at this point.

It is now necessary to enable the 128-bit setting:

1. Start the Registry editor (REGEDIT.EXE).

2. Move to HKEY_LOCAL_MACHINE\SYSTEM\CurrentControlSet\ Services\RasMan\PPP\COMPCP.

3. From the Edit menu, choose New > DWORD value.

4. Enter the name **ForceStrongEncryption** and press Enter.

5. Double-click the new value and set to 1. Click OK.

6. Close the Registry editor and reboot the computer.

After reboot is completed, clients connecting via RAS or PPTP have to authenticate, using 128-bit key encryption. A number of event logs can be viewed by using Event Viewer (Start > Programs > Administrative Tools > Event Viewer).

If a successful connection is made, the log appears, like this:

Event ID: 20107
Source: RemoteAccess
Description: The user RAS connected to port COMx using strong encryption

If the connection is unsuccessful, you see this warning message:

Event ID: 20077
Source: RemoteAccess
Description: An error occurred in the Point to Point Protocol module on port COMx. The remote computer does not support the required encryption type.

The client attempting connection would also receive a 629 error, informing him or her of an encryption problem.

 22.19 # Why does my RAS client have the wrong IP configuration?

The only parameter from DHCP that the RAS client uses is the IP address. Other parameters come as follows:

Subnet mask: The subnet mask is that used by the NIC in the workstation, if fitted. IPCONFIG shows the mask as being the default mask for the class of IP address in use, but this is irrelevant. MS used to display it as 0.0.0.0; that's clearly wrong, but the default is more subtly wrong. If there is no NIC in the client, the subnet mask is irrelevant because all traffic is passed through the dial-up connection.

Default router: The default router is displayed as the same as the address of the client RAS interface. What is actually used as default router is the RAS server itself.

Server addresses: WINS server addresses and DNS server addresses for use by the client similarly do not come from the parameters set on the DHCP server but rather are those used by the RAS server itself.

Node type: Node type is not taken from the DHCP parameters but can change on the RAS client, depending on WINS information. If the RAS server has no WINS servers defined locally, a B-node Windows NT RAS client remains a B-node client (which mean it uses broadcasts for resolution). If the RAS server has WINS servers defined locally, a B-node Windows NT RAS client switches to H-node (it queries name resolution first and then broadcasts) for the duration of the connection.

More information can be found in Knowledge Base Article Q160699 at http://support.microsoft.com/support/kb/articles/q160/6/99.asp/.

23 FILE SYSTEMS

Windows NT natively supports a number of file systems, File Allocation Table (FAT) and New Technology File System (NTFS); Windows 2000 also supports FAT32 and NTFS 5.0.

FAT is only supported for backward compatibility and offers none of the fault-tolerant security of NTFS. Only NTFS should be used on file servers and Domain Controllers.

Many file system problems can occur when dual-booting NT with other operating systems, but just remember that Windows NT 4.0 can read NTFS and FAT, Windows 9x can read FAT and FAT32, and Windows 2000 can read all of them. Remember to always use the lowest common file system when access to a partition is required from multiple operating systems.

23.1 How can a FAT partition be converted to an NTFS partition?

Conversion from FAT to NTFS is possible. From the command line, enter this command:

```
convert d: /fs:ntfs
```

This command is one way only, and you cannot convert an NTFS partition to FAT. If the FAT partition is the system partition, the conversion will take place on the next reboot.

After the conversion, File Permissions are set to Full Control for everyone, but if you install directly to NTFS, the permissions are set on a stricter basis. For help on setting the correct NTFS permissions, see Question 30.4, in Chapter 30, Security.

How much free space do I need to convert a FAT partition to NTFS?

The calculation below can be used for disks of a standard 512 bytes per sector:

1. Take the size of the partition and divide by 100. If this is less than 1,048,576, use 1,048,576; if greater than 4,194,304, use 4,194,304.
2. To the number calculated in step 1, add the size of the partition divided by 803.
3. To the number calculated in step 2, add the total number of files and directories, multiplied by 1280. You can work out the total number of files and directories by using the dir /s command at the base of the partition. It would look something like this:

   dir /s d:
   Total Files Listed:
   3397 File(s) 300,860,372 bytes

4. To the number calculated in step 3, add 196096.

To summarize:

Free space needed = (<size of partition in bytes>/100) + (<size of partition in bytes>/803) + (<no of files & directories> * 1280) + 196096

For more information, see Knowledge Base Article Q156560 at http://support.microsoft.com/support/kb/articles/q156/5/60.asp.

23.3 How can an NTFS partition be converted to a FAT partition?

A simple conversion is not possible. The only course of action is to back up all data on the drive, reformat the disk to FAT, and then restore your data backup.

23.4 What cluster size does a FAT/NTFS partition use?

The default cluster sizes for FAT partitions are shown in Table 23-1.

Table 23-1. FAT Partitions

Partition Size	Sectors per Cluster	Cluster Size
<32MB	1	512 bytes
<64MB	2	1K
<128MB	4	2K
<255MB	8	4K
<511MB	16	8K
<1023MB	32	16K
<2047MB	64	32K
<4095MB	128	64K

Notice the amount of potentially wasted space on the larger partitions, due to the 16KB-and-above cluster sizes. This is why FAT volumes larger than 511MB are not recommended.

The default cluster sizes for NTFS are shown in Table 23-2.

Table 23-2. NTFS Partitions

Partition Size	Sectors per Cluster	Cluster Size
<512MB	1	512 bytes (or hardware sector size if greater than 512 bytes)
<1024MB	2	1K
<2048MB	4	2K
<4096MB	8	4K
<8192MB	16	8K
<16384MB	32	16K
<32768MB	64	32K
>32768MB	128	64K

NTFS better balances the trade-off between the disk defragmentation that results from small cluster sizes and the wasted space of large cluster sizes.

When formatting a drive, you can change the cluster size by using the /a:<size> switch, like this:

```
format d: /a:1024 /fs:ntfs
```

How do I run HPFS under NT 4.0?

If you want NT support for High Performance File System (HPFS), you can upgrade from NT 3.51 to 4.0, which will retain HPFS support. You can manually install the 3.51 driver under NT 4.0; however, this is not supported by Microsoft.

1. Copy the 3.51 PINBALL.SYS to the NT 4.0 %SystemRoot%\system32\drivers directory.
2. Start the Registry editor (REGEDIT.EXE).
3. Go to the HKEY_LOCAL_MACHINE\SYSTEM\CurrentControlSet\Services.

4. From the Edit menu, select New Key.

5. In the form entry box that appears, enter Pinball as the Key Name. Leave the class field blank and click OK.

6. Highlight the new Pinball key in the editor's left panel and select New DWORD from the Edit menu.

7. Enter the name **ErrorControl** and click OK.

8. Double-click ErrorControl and set to **0x1**.

9. Highlight Pinball again. Select New String from the Edit menu with name Group and click OK.

10. Double-click Group and set to Boot File System.

11. Highlight Pinball again. Select New DWORD from the Edit menu with name Start and click OK.

12. Double-click Start and set to **0x1**.

13. Highlight Pinball again. Select New DWORD from the Edit menu with name Type and click OK.

14. Double-click Type and set to **0x2**.

15. Close the Registry editor and reboot the machine.

 # How do I compress a directory?

Windows NT has a built-in compression utility for files and folders. Follow these instructions (you can do this only on an NTFS partition):

1. Using Explorer or My Computer, select a drive.

2. Right-click on a directory and choose Properties.

3. On the General tab, select the Compress check box and click Apply (see Figure 23-1).

4. When you're asked if you want to compress subdirectories, click OK.

5. Click OK to exit.

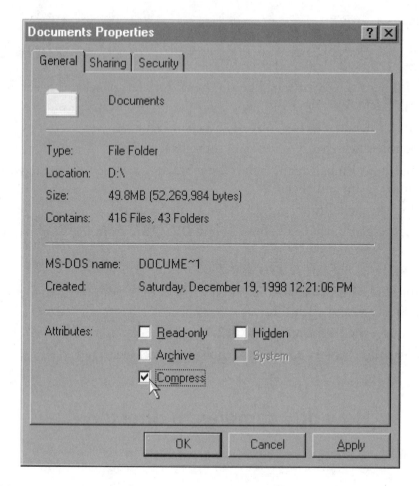

Figure 23-1. Notice you also have a Security tab where you can set permissions on the files and folders. This is only visible on an NTFS partition.

Windows NT cannot read drives that were compressed by using the Windows 95/98 method.

How do I uncompress a directory?

Follow the same procedure outlined in 23.6, but uncheck the compress box.

How can I compress files and directories from the command line?

A COMPACT.EXE utility is supplied with the Resource Kit. You can use it to view and change the compression characteristics of a file or directory.

To compress a single file, use the following command and get results as shown:

```
compact /c hfwmsg.txt
```

Compressing files in D:\temp\

HFWMSG.TXT   14898 :8192 = 1.8 to 1 [OK]

1 files within 1 directories were compressed.
14,898 total bytes of data are stored in 8,192 bytes.
The compression ratio is 1.8 to 1.

For full help, type **compact /?** at the command line.

Is there an NTFS defragmentation tool available?

A number of NTFS defragmentation tools are available for NT. Here are some that I know of:

Diskeeper (http://www.diskeeper.com)
This is available from Executive Software. Diskeeper has the advantage of having a free full-function version for download, Diskeeper Lite.

Norton Utilities for NT   http://www.symantec.com
This contains a disk defragmentation package.

PerfectDisk NT   http://www.raxco.com
I have not tried it.

O&O Defragmentation   http://www.oo-defrag.com/index-e.html
I have been informed works well.

VoptNT   http://www.goldenbow.com
I have not tried it.

Windows 2000 has a limited built-in defragmentation tool that can be used as follows:

1. Start the MMC (Start > Run > MMC).
2. From the console menu, select Add/Remove Snap-in and click Add.
3. Select Disk Defragmenter and click Add. Then click Close.
4. Click OK in the main Add/Remove dialog box.
5. Select the Disk Defragmenter option from Console Root.
6. Select a partition. Then select Analyze and Defragment (see Figure 23-2).

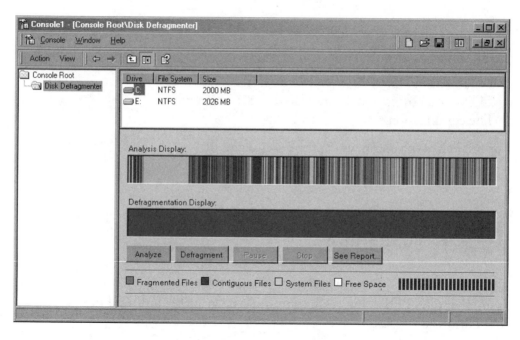

Figure 23-2. Selecting Defragment will unfragment this disk.

Can I undelete a file in NT?

23.10

It depends on the file system. NT has no Undelete facility; however, if the file system is FAT, you can boot into DOS and then use the DOS

UNDELETE.EXE utility. With the NT Resource Kit, the DiskProbe utility enables users to view the data on a disk, which can then be copied to another file. It is possible to search sectors for data by using DiskProbe.

If the files are deleted on an NTFS partition, booting from a DOS disk and using UNDELETE.EXE is not possible because DOS cannot read NTFS partitions. NTFS does not perform destructive deletes, which means the actual data is left intact on the disk (until another file is written in its place). A new Network Undelete application from Executive Software can be used to undelete files from NTFS partitions—you can download a free 30-day version from http://www.networkundelete.com/.

Important: After any file is deleted by mistake, you need to stop all activity on the machine to reduce the possibility that other files might overwrite the data you want to recover.

FAQ 23.11 Does NT support FAT32?

Native NT does not support FAT32, but NT 5.0 provides full FAT32 support. NT Internals has released a read-only FAT32 driver for Windows NT 4.0 (go to http://www.sysinternals.com/fat32.htm). You can purchase a full read/write version from http://www.winternals.com.

FAQ 23.12 Can you read an NTFS partition from DOS?

You can't read an NTFS partition with standard DOS; however, a product called NTFSDos enables a user to read from an NTFS partition. The home page for this utility is http://www.sysinternals.com.

FAQ 23.13   How can I delete an NTFS partition?

You can boot off of the three NT installation disks and follow these instructions:

1. Read the license agreement and press F8.
2. Select the NTFS partition you wish to delete.
3. Press L to confirm.
4. Press F3 twice to exit the NT setup.

Usually you can delete an NTFS partition by using FDISK (delete non-DOS partition); however, this will not work if the NTFS partition is in the extended partition.

You can delete an NTFS partition by using Disk Administrator—select the partition and press Del (as long as it is not the system/boot partition).

There is also a DELPART.EXE utility that will delete an NTFS partition from a DOS bootup. This is part of the NT Resource Kit.

FAQ 23.14   Is it possible to repartition a disk without losing data?

There is no standard way to repartition a disk in NT. A third-party product called Partition Magic will repartition FAT, NTFS, and FAT32; however, a bug in the product makes the boot partition unbootable if it is repartitioned. A fix is available for this from their Web site (http://www.powerquest.com).

FAQ 23.15   What is the biggest disk NT can use?

The simple answer to this question is that NT can view a maximum partition size of 2 terabytes (or 2,199,023,255,552 bytes); however, there are limitations that restrict you to well below this number.

FAT has internal limits of 4GB because it uses 16-bit fields to store file sizes. Because 2^{16} is 65,536, with a cluster size of 64KB, that gives us the 4GB limit. HPFS uses 32-bit fields and can therefore handle greater-size disks, but the largest single file size is 4GB. HPFS allocates disk space in 512-byte sectors, which can cause problems in Asian markets where sector sizes are typically 1024 bytes (this means HPFS cannot be used in Asia).

NTFS uses 64 bits for all sizes, leading to a maximum size of 16 exabytes (18,446,744,073,709,551,616 bytes); however, NT cannot handle a volume this big because of other limits.

For IDE drives, the maximum is 136.9GB, but this is constrained to 528MB on a standard Integrated Drive Electronic (IDE) drive. The new enhanced (EIDE) drives can access much larger sizes.

It is important to note that the system partition (holding NTLDR, BOOT.INI, and such) **must** be entirely within the first 7.8GB of any disk (if this is the same as the boot partition, this limit applies). This is true because of the BIOS int 13H interface used by NTLDR to bootstrap up to the point where it can drive the native HDD IDE or SCSI. The int 13H interface presents a 24-bit cylinder/head/sector parameter for a drive. If by defragmentation, for example, the system is moved beyond this point, you will not be able to boot the system.

FAQ 23.16 Can I disable 8.3 filename creation on NTFS?

To stop the 8.3 alias creation (namedF~1.FIL) on NTFS partitions, perform the following:

1. Start the Registry editor (REGEDIT.EXE).
2. Move to HKEY_LOCAL_MACHINE\SYSTEM\CurrentControlSet\ Control\FileSystem.
3. Double-click NtfsDisable8dot3NameCreation.
4. Change from 0 to 1.
5. Close the Registry editor.

You might experience problems installing Office 97 if you disable 8.3 name creation, and you might have to reenable it during installation of the software.

FAQ 23.17 How do I disable 8.3 filename creation on VFAT?

Start the Registry editor (REGEDIT.EXE) and set the value HKEY_LOCAL_MACHINE\SYSTEM\CurrentControlSet\Control\FileSystem\Win95TruncatedExtensions to 0.

FAQ 23.18 How can I stop NT from generating long filenames (LFNs) on a FAT partition?

Follow the instructions in Question 23.17, but this time use the Registry editor to change the value HKEY_LOCAL_MACHINE\SYSTEM\CurrentControlSet\Control\FileSystem\Win31FileSystem from 0 to 1. Now only 8.3 filenames will be created.

The reason for not wanting LFNs to be created is that some third-party disk utilities that directly manipulate FAT can destroy the LFNs. Utilities such as SCANDISK and DEFRAG that come with DOS 6.x and later do not harm LFNs.

FAQ 23.19 How do long filenames (LFNs) work?

Long filenames are stored by using a series of linked directory entries. An LFN uses one directory entry for its alias (the alias is the 8.3 name automatically generated) and a hidden secondary directory entry for every 13 characters in its name. If you have a 200-character filename, it would use 17 entries.

The alias is generated using the first six characters of the LFN followed by a tilde (~) and a number for the first four versions of files with the same first six characters. For example, for the file JOHN SAVILLS FILE.TXT, the names generated would be JOHNSA~1.TXT, JOHNSA~2.TXT, and so on.

After the first four versions of a file, only the first two characters of the filename are used and the last six are generated, as in JO0E38~1.TXT.

 ## 23.20 I can't create any files on the root of a FAT partition. Why?

The root of a FAT drive has a coded limit of 512 entries, so if you have exceeded this, you will not be able to create any more files.

Remember that long filenames take up more than one entry (see Question 23.19 for more about LFNs), so if you have many LFNs on the root, this drastically reduces the number of files you can have.

23.21 How do I change access permissions on a directory?

You can only set access permissions on an NTFS volume. Follow these instructions:

1. Start Explorer (Win key + E or Start > Programs > Explorer).
2. Right-click on a directory and choose Properties.
3. Click on the Security tab.
4. Click the Permissions button and enter the information required.
5. Click OK and then click OK again to exit.

23.22 How can I change access permissions from the command line?

A CACLS.EXE utility comes as standard with NT and can be used from the command prompt. (To read the Help with the CACLS.EXE program, use **cacls /?**). For example, to give user john read access to a directory called files, type the following, where /e is used to edit the ACL instead of replacing it (therefore, other permissions on the directory will be kept) and /p sets permission for user:<permission>.

```
CACLS files /e /p john:r
```

I have a CHKDSK scheduled to start at next reboot, but I want to stop it. How do I do it?

If the command chkdsk /f /r (which will find bad sectors, recover information from bad sectors, and fix errors on the disk) is run, the check disk is scheduled on the next reboot. However, you might want to cancel this check disk. To do so, perform the following:

1. Run the Registry editor (REGEDT32.EXE, **not** REGEDIT.EXE).
2. Go to HKEY_LOCAL_MACHINE\SYSTEM\CurrentControlSet\ Control\Session Manager.
3. Change the BootExecute value from this:

```
autocheck autochk * /r\DosDevice\<drive letter>
```

to this:

```
autocheck autochk *
```

How can I stop CHKDSK at boot time from checking volume *x*?

When NT boots, it performs a check on all volumes to see if the "dirty bit" is set; if so, it then runs a full chkdsk /f. To stop NT from performing this dirty-bit check, you can exclude certain drives. (You might want to do this for some types of removable drives, such as an Iomega drive.)

1. Run the Registry Editor (REGEDT32.EXE, **not** REGEDIT.EXE).
2. Go to HKEY_LOCAL_MACHINE\SYSTEM\CurrentControlSet\
   Control\Session Manager.
3. Change the BootExecute value from this:

```
autocheck autochk *
```

to this:

autocheck autochk /k:x *

where *x* is the drive letter. For example, if you want to stop the check on drive F:, type **autocheck autochk /k:f***.

To stop the check on multiple volumes, enter the drive names one after another. For example, to stop the check on e: and g: at the same time, type **autocheck autochk /k:eg***. Note that you do not retype the /k each time.

If you are using NT 4.0 with Service Pack 2 or later, you can also use the CHKNTFS.EXE command. This utility excludes drives from the check and updates the Registry for you. The syntax for disabling a drive is

chkntfs /x <drive letter>:

For example, **chkntfs /x f:** would exclude the check of the F: drive.

To set the system back to checking all drives, just type

chkntfs /d

How can I modify the CHKDSK timer?

Service Pack 4 introduces a new feature. Before performing a chkdsk of a disk, if the disk's dirty bit is set, a countdown timer starts. As a default, this timer allows you 30 seconds to cancel the chkdsk from running.

If you want to modify this 30-second value, perform the following:

1. Start the Registry editor (REGEDIT.EXE).
2. Move to HKEY_LOCAL_MACHINE\SYSTEM\CurrentControlSet\
   Control\Session Manager.

3. From the Edit menu, choose New > DWORD Value. Enter the name **AutoChkTimeOut** and press Enter.

4. Double-click this new value and set it to 0 to disable the timer or to set the time in seconds you wish to be given to cancel the chkdsk.

5. Close the Registry editor.

The change will take effect at the next reboot.

23.26 My NTFS drive is corrupt. How do I recover?

To restore an NTFS drive by using the following information, it must have been created by using Windows NT 4.0. If the drive was not created by using NT 4.0, you should refer to Knowledge Base Article Q121517.

To restore an NTFS partition, you must locate the spare copy of the boot sector and copy it to the correct position on the drive. You need the NTdiskedit utility, which is available from Microsoft Support Services. (You can also use DiskProbe, which comes with the Resource Kit, or Norton Disk Edit.)

1. Using NTdiskedit for Windows NT 4.0, choose Open on the File menu.

2. Type the Volume Name as

    `\\.\PhysicaldriveX`

    where *X* = the ordinal of the disk that appears in Disk Administrator.

3. Click OK.

4. On the Read menu, click Sectors. Select **0** for Starting Sectors and select **1** for Run Length. Click OK.

5. On the View menu, click Partition Table. You should see a table that has four sections—Entry 0 through Entry 3—referring to the order of partitions. If the partition in question is Partition 2 on the disk, you need the data in Entry 1. If the partition in question is Partition 1 on the disk, you need the data from Entry 0, and so on.

6. Write down the values of Starting Sector and Sectors. Note: All of the values you see will be in hexadecimal format. Do not convert to decimal.

7. Using a calculator that can add hexadecimal numbers (you can use the one from the Accessories group if one is available), add the values for Starting Sector and Sectors and subtract 1 from the sum. For example:

STARTING SECTOR = Ox3F
SECTORS = 0x201c84 +

———————

0x201CC3
Less 1 0x1 -

———————

Copy of NTFS bootsector = 0x201CC2

8. On the Read menu, click Sectors. In Starting Sectors, type the value from the equation in step 7. Then type **1** in Run Length and click OK.

9. You now should be at your copy of the NTFS boot sector. Visually inspect the boot sector for completeness: NTFS header at first line, text in the lower region (for example, "A kernel file is missing from the disk"), and so forth.

10. Click Relocate Sectors. This is the sector you are going to write to the boot sector. This will be the value of your starting sector with the run length of 1. Click OK.

11. Quit NTdiskedit and use Disk Administrator to assign a drive letter if one is not already assigned.

12. Restart the computer; the file system should be recognized as NTFS.

How can I delete a file without sending it to the Recycle Bin?

When you delete the file, hold down the Shift key. You can permanently stop files from going to the Recycle Bin by right-clicking on Recycle Bin, selecting the Global tab, and checking Do Not Move Files to the Recycle Bin.

FAQ 23.28 How can I back up the Master Boot Record?

The Master Boot Record on the hard disk is used to start the computer (the system partition) and is the most critical sector, so make sure this is the sector you back up. The boot partition is also very important (where %systemroot% resides). You need the DiskProbe utility that comes with the Resource Kit.

1. Start DiskProbe.
2. From the Drives menu, choose Physical Drive. In the Open Physical Drive dialog box, click on the drive that is the system partition.
3. The clicked disk will be displayed in the Handle 0 section. Click Set Active and then click Close.
4. From the Sectors menu, choose Read. Accept the default sectors of Starting Sector 0 and Number of Sectors 1.
5. From the File menu, choose Save As and enter a filename.

The Windows NT Resource Kit supplies a DISKSAVE.EXE utility that enables you to save a binary image of the Master Boot Record (MBR) or boot sector.

You have to run DISKSAVE from DOS, so you will need to create a bootable DOS disk and copy DISKSAVE.EXE to the disk. To create a DOS bootable disk, just use the following command from a DOS machine (do not do it from a Windows NT command session):

```
format a: /s
```

After you boot with the disk, you will have a number of options, as follows:

F2 - Backup the Master Boot Record: This function will prompt for a path and filename to which to save the MBR image. The path and filename are limited to 64 characters. The resulting file will be a binary image of the sector and will be 512 bytes in size. The MBR is always located at Cylinder 0, Side 0, Sector 1 of the boot disk.

F3 - Restore Master Boot Record: This function will prompt for a path and filename for the previously saved Master Boot Record (MBR) file. The only error-checking is for the file size (must be 512 bytes). Copying an incorrect file to the MBR will permanently destroy the partition table information. In addition, the machine will not boot without a valid MBR. The path and filename string is limited to 64 characters.

F4 - Backup the Boot Sector: This function will prompt for a path and file-name to which to save the boot sector image. The path and filename are limited to 64 characters. The resulting file will be a binary image of the sector and will be 512 bytes in size. The function opens the partition table, searches for an active partition, and then jumps to the starting location of that partition. The sector at that location is then saved under the filename entered by the user. There are no checks to determine if the sector is a valid boot sector.

F5 - Restore Boot Sector: This function will prompt for a path and filename for the previously saved boot sector file. The only error-checking is for the file size (must be 512 bytes). Copying an incorrect file to the boot sector will permanently destroy boot sector information. In addition, the machine will not boot without a valid boot sector. The path and filename string is limited to 64 characters.

F6 - Disable FT on the Boot Drive: This function might be useful when Windows NT will not boot from a mirrored system drive. The function looks for the bootable (marked active) partition. It then checks to see if the SystemType byte has the high bit set. Windows NT sets the high bit of the SystemType byte if the partition is a member of a Fault Tolerant set. Disabling this bit has the same effect as breaking the mirror. There is no provision for reenabling the bit after it has been disabled.

 ## How do I restore the Master Boot Record?

Follow the instructions below, but be very careful!

1. Start DiskProbe.
2. From the File menu, choose Open and select the file in which the information was saved.
3. From the Drives menu, click Physical Drive and click the disk on which you want to replace the boot partition.
4. In the Handle 0 box, clear the Read-Only box and click Set Active. Then click Close.
5. From the Sectors menu, choose Write and set the starting sector to **0**. Then choose Write It.

6. Verify and close DiskProbe.

7. Keep your fingers crossed.

The DOS FDISK utility also has an /MBR which simply wipes the Master Boot Record—this would render your NT system unbootable.

What CD-ROM file systems can NT read?

NT's primary file system is CDFS, a read-only file system; however, NT can read any file system that is ISO9660 compliant.

4.0 ONLY

How do I create a volume set?

A volume set enables you to take all of the unused space on one or more drives (up to 32 drives per volume set) and combine it into a single, large, system-recognizable drive. To create a volume set, follow this procedure:

1. Log on as an Administrator and start Disk Administrator (Start > Programs > Administrative Tools > Disk Administrator).

2. Click on the first free area of disk space. Then hold down the Ctrl key and select all other areas of unpartitioned space.

3. With all of the parts selected, choose Create Volume Set from the Partition menu.

4. A dialog box appears. Choose the size of the partition to be created and click OK.

5. After the partition is created, the areas that are part of a volume set show in yellow on the disk display area.

6. Close Disk Administrator (or choose Commit Changes New).

7. Click Yes at the Confirmation dialog box. Now you need to reboot.

8. After the reboot has completed, you can format the volume. You should format the volume as NTFS, because DOS and Windows 95 clients will not be able to read it anyway.

The main problem with volume sets is that if one drive in the volume set fails, the entire volume set becomes unavailable.

4.0 ONLY

How do I extend a volume set?

23.32

Extending a volume set is very simple, but a reboot will be required.

1. Start Disk Administrator (Start > Programs > Administrative Tools > Disk Administrator).
2. Click on the existing volume set and hold down the Ctrl key.
3. Click on the area (or areas) of free space to be added (a black border appears around them).
4. From the Partition menu, choose Extend Volume Set, or right-click on one of the selected areas and choose Extend Volume Set from the context menu.
5. A dialog box appears, asking how large the drive should be. By default, it shows the largest possible size. You can change this, but click OK this time.
6. From the Partition menu, select Commit Changes Now.
7. Answer the further dialogs and reboot the server.

The reboot will take longer than usual because the new area you added has to be formatted to the same file system as the rest of the volume set.

Note: Only NTFS volume sets can be extended.

4.0 ONLY

How do I delete a volume set?

23.33

When you delete a volume set, all of the stored data will be lost. Do the following to delete a volume set:

1. Start Disk Administrator (Start > Programs > Administrative Tools > Disk Administrator).
2. Click on part of the volume set.

3. From the Partition menu, choose Delete.

4. Click Yes at the dialog box.

 ## 23.34 What is the maximum number of characters a filename can have?

This depends on whether the file is being created on a FAT or an NTFS partition. The maximum file length on an NTFS partition is 256 characters, and the maximum on FAT is 11 characters (8-character name and 3-character extension, separated by a dot). NTFS filenames keep their case, whereas FAT filenames have no concept of case (however, case is ignored when you perform a search or other procedures on NTFS). The new VFAT also has 256-character filenames.

NTFS filenames can contain any uppercase or lowercase characters, including spaces, except for the following:

   * : / \ ? < > |

These characters are reserved for NT; however, the filename must start with a letter or number.

VFAT filenames can also contain any characters except for the following:

   / \ : | = ? ; [ ] , ^

Again, the filename must start with a letter or number.

NTFS and VFAT also create an 8.3 format filename (for more about LFNs, see Question 23.19).

23.35 What protections can be set on files and directories on an NTFS partition?

When you right-click on a file in Explorer and choose Properties (or choose Properties from the File menu), you are presented with a dialog box telling you the file's size, ownership, and so on. If the file or directory is on an NTFS partition, there will be a Security tab and, on that tab, a Permissions button. If you click the Permissions button, you can grant access to that file or directory to users or groups at various levels.

There are six types of basic permissions:

R   Read
W   Write
D   Delete
X   Execute
P   Change permissions
O   Take ownership

These can be assigned to a resource; however, they are grouped for ease of use, as shown in Table 23-3.

Table 23-3. Permission Groups

No Access	User has no access to the resource.
List - R	User can view directory and filenames in directory.
Read - RX	User can read files in directory and execute programs.
Add - WX	User can add files to the directory but cannot read or change the contents of the directory.
Add & Read - RWX	User has read and add permissions.
Change - RWXD	User has read, add, change contents, and delete files permissions.
All - RWXDPO	User can do anything she wants.

These permissions can be set on a directory. For a file, however, the list of permissions is limited to only No Access, Read, Change, and Full Control.

There is another type of permission called Special Access (on a directory there will be two—one for files and one for directories). From Special Access, you can set which of the basic permissions should be assigned.

23.36 How can I take ownership of files?

Sometimes you might want to take ownership of files or directories—usually because someone has removed all access on a resource and can't see it. You would log on as the Administrator and take ownership. You can only take ownership;

you cannot give ownership to someone else, using standard NT functionality in Windows NT 4.0.

1. Log on as Administrator or as a member of the Administrators group.
2. Start Explorer (Win key + E or Start > Programs > Explorer).
3. Right-click on the file or directory and choose Properties.
4. Select the Security tab and click Ownership.
5. Click Take Ownership and then click Yes at the confirmation prompt.

The Administrator group gets the ownership of the files—not the Administrator who clicked the button. This is not the same as if a normal user with the Take Ownership privilege takes ownership.

Under Windows 2000, you can actually set the owner to a different person. Follow the previous steps until step 4. Then click the Advanced button on the Security tab and select the Owner tab from the displayed dialog box.

 23.37

How can I view, from the command line, the permissions a user has on a file?

The PERMS.EXE utility supplied with the Resource Kit can be used to view permissions on files and directories. The usage is

perms <domain>\<user> <file>
(for example, perms savilltech\savillj d:\file\john\file.dat)

You can add /s to also show details of subfiles or subdirectories. Table 23-4 shows the types of permissions.

Table 23-4. Permissions

R	Read
W	Write
X	Execute
D	Delete
P	Change permission
O	Take ownership

Table 23-4. Permissions (continued)

A	All
None	No access
*	User is the owner.
#	A group of which the user is a member owns the file.
?	Permissions cannot be determined.

To output the return to a file, just add > **filename.txt** at the end, like this:

```
perms <user> <file> > file.txt
```

How can I tell the total amount of space used by a folder (including subfolders)?

Here are two ways of doing this (there are more). One way uses Explorer and one is from the command line. If using Explorer, perform the following:

1. Start Explorer (Win key + E or Start > Programs > Explorer).
2. Right-click on the required folder and choose Properties.
3. Under the General tab, a size is displayed. This is the total size of the folder and all subfolders and their contents.

From the command line, you can just use the dir command with /s qualifier, which also lists all subdirectories. For example, the following command would list all files and folders in the savilltechhomepage directory, with the total size given at the end.

```
dir/s d:\savilltechhomepage
```

There are files beginning with $ at the root of my NTFS drive. Can I delete them?

NO!!! These files hold the information of your NTFS volume. Table 23-5 shows all the files used by the file system.

Table 23-5. NTFS Files

$MFT	Master file table
$MFTMIRR	A copy of the first 16 records of the MFT
$LOGFILE	Log of changes made to the volume
$VOLUME	Information about the volume, serial number, creation time, dirty flag
$ATTRDEF	Attribute definitions
$BITMAP	Drive cluster map
$BOOT	Boot record of the drive
$BADCLUS	List of bad clusters on the drive
$QUOTA	Quota information (used on NTFS 5.0)
$UPCASE	Maps lowercase characters to uppercase version

If you want to have a look at any of these files, use this command:

```
dir /ah <filename>
```

It's basically impossible to delete these files, anyway, because you can't remove the hidden flag. And if you can't remove the hidden flag, you can't delete the file.

What file systems do Iomega Jaz or Zip disks use?

23.40

By default, the formatted Zip disks are FAT; however, you can format these with NTFS if you want. NTFS has a higher overhead than FAT on small volumes (an initial 2MB), which is why you don't have NTFS on 1.44 floppy disks.

23.41 NT becomes unresponsive during an NTFS disk operation such as a dir. Why?

When you perform a large NTFS disk operation (such as dir/s *.* or ntbackup :*.*), NT can sometimes become unresponsive. NT updates NTFS files with a last-access stamp. When viewing thousands of files, the NTFS log file can become full. It then waits to be flushed to the hard disk, which can cause NT to become unresponsive. To stop NTFS from updating the last-access stamp, perform the following:

1. Start the Registry editor (REGEDIT.EXE).
2. Move to HKEY_LOCAL_MACHINE\SYSTEM\CurrentControlSet\ Control\FileSystem.
3. From the Edit menu, choose New > DWORD Value.
4. Enter **NtfsDisableLastAccessUpdate** and click OK.
5. Double-click the new value and set it to 1. Click OK.
6. Close the Registry editor and reboot the machine.

This should improve the performance of your NTFS partitions.

23.42 I have missing space on my NTFS partitions (Alternate Data Streams). Why?

It's possible to hide data from both Explorer and the dir command within an NTFS file, which—although it takes up space—you cannot see unless you know its stream name. NTFS allows multiple streams to a file in the form of <filename>:<stream name>. A stream is basically data within the file, and by default, most files have one stream per file. You can experiment with multiple streams as follows:

1. Start a console window (CMD.EXE).
2. Run Notepad as normal.txt; enter some text and save. This has to be on an NTFS partition.

3. Now edit the file again, but this time with a different stream: notepad normal.txt:hidden. When you're prompted to create a new file, enter some text and save.

4. When you perform a dir command, you will see only NORMAL.TXT, with its original size.

You can have as many streams as you want. If you copy a file, it keeps the streams, so if you copy NORMAL.TXT to JOHN.TXT, the file JOHN.TXT:HIDDEN will exist. You cannot use streams from the command prompt because it does not allow a colon (:) in filenames except for drive letters.

Microsoft provides no way of detecting or deleting these streams. There are two ways to delete. The first one is to copy the file to a FAT partition and back again. The second is to use the following commands:

```
REN <FILE> TEMP.EXE
CAT TEMP.EXE > <FILE>
DEL TEMP.EXE
```

One application I have found that can detect alternate datastreams is LADS by Frank Heyne, which can be downloaded from http://www.heysoft.de/nt/ep-lads.htm/.

One way to delete these streams is to edit them in Notepad and delete all of the text. When you quit Notepad, NT tells you that the file is empty and will be deleted, and you only have to confirm.

If you want to write your own programs to detect streams, have a look at

- http://www.brilig.demon.co.uk/nt/streams.html
- http://www.mvps.org/win32/ntfs/streams.html

The only reliable way of handling streams is to use the BackupRead() function, but BackupRead() requires SeRestorePrivilege/SeBackupPrivilege rights, which most users do not have. BackupRead() actually turns a file and its associated metadata (extended attributes, security data, alternate streams, links) into a stream of bytes. BackupWrite() converts it back.

How can I change the Volume ID of a disk?

Windows NT provides functionality to change the volume name of a disk by using the following command:

```
label <drive>: <label name>
```

Windows NT does not provide built-in functionality to change volume IDs; however, NT Internals has produced a free utility that can be downloaded from http://www.sysinternals.com/misc.htm. It is called VolumeID and it can change the volume ID of a FAT or NTFS volume. To view a drive's current volume ID, you can just perform a dir <drive>: to display the volume serial number on the second line down, like this:

Volume in drive E is system
Volume Serial Number is BC09-8AE4

To change, enter command looks like this:

```
volumeid <drive letter>: xxxx-xxxx
```

The serial number is located in the boot sector for a volume. For FAT drives, it's 4 bytes, starting at offset 0x27; for NTFS drives, it's 8 bytes, starting at offset 0x48. You could use a sector-level editor to modify the number (such as the Resource Kit's DiskProbe).

4.0 ONLY

How do I read NTFS 5.0 partitions from Windows NT 4.0?

Service Pack 4 includes a read/write driver for NTFS 5.0 volumes (an updated NTFS.SYS driver). It does not offer all of the NTFS functionality, such as quotas or encrypted file system.

23.45 How do share and file system permissions interact?

In general, when you have protections on a share or on a file or directory, the privileges are added. For example, if user John is a member of two groups—one with read access and another with change—John will have read and change access. The exception is if a group has no access. In that case, no matter what other group memberships a person has, if he is a member of the no-access group, he will have no access.

The opposite is true when protections are set on the file system and on the share where the most restrictive policy is enforced. For example, if the file has full control set for a user but the share only has read, the user is limited to read-only privileges. Likewise, if the file had read-only but the share has full, the user would still be limited to read-only.

Share protections are used only when the file system is accessed through a network connection. If the user is using the partition locally, the share protections are ignored.

23.46 Is it possible to map a drive letter to a directory?

You can use the SUBST command to map a pseudo drive letter to a drive or directory, as follows:

```
subst r: d:\winnt\system32
```

This would map the letter r to the directory winnt\system32 on the d: drive.

2000 ONLY

23.47 How do I convert an NTFS partition to NTFS 5.0?

Windows NT 5.0 introduces NTFS 5.0, which enables a number of new features. By default, installing Windows NT 5.0 automatically converts any NTFS 4.0 partitions to NTFS 5.0 (however, this might change).

During the installation of Windows NT 5.0, if it detects any Windows NT 4.0 installations, it upgrades their NTFS.SYS (providing the systems are Service Pack 3 or later) so they too will be able to read the NTFS 5.0 partitions. Service Pack 4 also has an updated NTFS.SYS that can read NTFS 5.0 partitions.

To check the version of an NTFS partition, use the CHKNTFS.EXE utility:

chkntfs <drive>:
(The type of the file system is NTFS 5.0.)

or

The type of the file system is NTFS 4.0
<drive>: is not dirty

If the file system is not NTFS 5.0 and you want to upgrade it, use this command:

```
chkntfs /e <drive>:
```

You will need to reboot for the upgrade to take place.

FAQ 23.48 I cannot compress files on an NTFS partition. Why?

If you try to compress files on an NTFS partition by using Explorer (right-click on a file or directory, choose Properties, and check the Compress box), the option is not available.

If you try from the command prompt, using this command:

```
compact /c ntfaq.txt /s
```

you get the following error:

"The file system does not support compression."

The cause is usually that the cluster size of the NTFS partition is greater than 4096. To check the cluster size of your NTFS partition, use the chkdsk command, like this:

```
chkdsk <disk>: /i /c
```

The /i /c is used to speed up the chkdsk, and at the end of the display, it tells you the bytes in each allocation unit:

2048 bytes in each allocation unit.
1012032 total allocation units on disk.
572750 allocation units available on disk.

If the number of bytes is greater than 4,096, you need to back up all the data on the disk and then reformat the partition, using any of the following methods:

- Start Explorer (Win key + E or Start > Programs > Explorer) and make sure the partition is not being used. Right-click on the partition and choose Format. Set the allocation unit size to 4,096 or less.
- Start Disk Administrator (Start > Programs > Administrative Tools > Disk Administrator). Right-click on the partition, choose format, and set the unit size to 4,096 or less.
- Format from the command prompt, like this:

```
format <drive>: /fs:ntfs /a:4096
```

After reformatting, you can restore your backed-up data.

To understand more about the 4,096 limit, read Knowledge Base article Q171892 at http://support.microsoft.com/support/kb/articles/q171/8/92.asp.

23.49 How can I view the current owner of a file?

The usual method would be to right-click on the file in Explorer, choose Properties, click the Security tab, and click Ownership. This shows the current owner and gives the option to take ownership.

To view the current owner from the command line, you can use the SUBINACL.EXE utility that is shipped with the Windows NT Resource Kit Supplement 2. To view the current owner, use the following command:

```
subinacl /file <filename>
//++++
// D:\Documents\<filename>
//—
+ Owner = builtin\administrators
+ Primary Group= lnautd0001\domain users
+ System ACE count =0
+ Disc. ACE count =1
lnautd0001\saviljo ACCESS_ALLOWED_ACE_TYPE FILE_ALL_ACCESS
```

You can use *.* (the wildcard) in your command to list owners for all files in all subdirectories (no need for any /s switch).

4.0 ONLY
FAQ 23.50 How can I view/defrag pagefile fragmentation?

System Internals has released PageDefrag, a free utility that shows fragmentation in the pagefile and then offers the option of defragmentation at boot time (see Figure 23-3). You can download this utility from http://www.sysinternals.com/pagedfrg.htm. After you download, unzip the file and run PAGEDFRG.EXE. Below is a sample output.

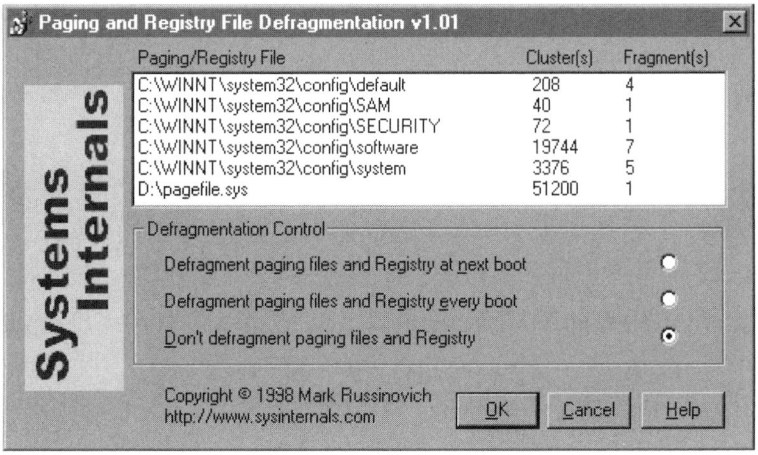

Figure 23-3. The System Internals pagefile defragmenter in action.

I understand that Executive Software's Diskeeper 4.0 can also defragment (http://www.diskeeper.com).

4.0 ONLY

FAQ 23.51 I get a disk maintenance message during setup. Why?

You might get this message during setup:

> "Setup has performed maintenance on your hard disk(s) that requires a reboot to take effect. You must reboot and restart Setup to continue. Press F3 to reboot."

This message appears when the Autochk part of the installation was able to repair the partition but requires a reboot.

For a FAT partition, this could mean that corruption of extended attributes was fixed, the dirty bit was cleared, orphaned long filename entry was fixed (or any other fixing of LFNs), directory entry was fixed, cross-linked files were fixed, non-unique filename was made unique, or any other structural issues were fixed.

In short, this is not a problem as long as the setup does not get stuck in a loop and keep running this stage.

2000 ONLY

FAQ 23.52 Where is Disk Administrator in Windows 2000?

As with every other Administration tool in Windows 2000, Disk Administrator has been replaced with a Microsoft Management Console (MMC) snap-in. By default, it is accessible via the Computer Management MMC snap-in.

1. Start the Computer Management MMC snap-in (Start > Programs > Administrative Tools > Computer Management).
2. Choose the Storage branch.
3. Choose Disk Management.
4. Things should now look familiar (see Figure 23-4).

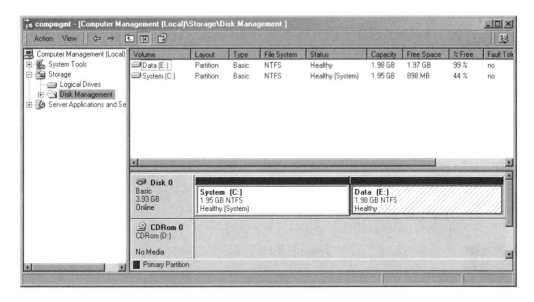

Figure 23-4. Windows 2000's Disk Administrator is basically the same as the old 4.0 Disk Administrator, but it is now an MMC snap-in.

Alternatively, you can create your own MMC console:

1. Start the MMC (Start > Run > MMC).
2. Select Add/Remove Snap-in from the Console menu and click Add.
3. Choose Disk Management and click Add.
4. Choose Local Computer and click Finish.
5. Click Close.
6. Click OK in the main dialog box.

You now have your own MMC with just the Disk Management component.

You could save by choosing Save As from the Console menu, entering Disk Admin as the name, and clicking Save. You will now see under the Programs menu a new folder, My Administrative Tools, with Disk Admin as an MMC snap-in.

23.53 How do I convert a basic disk to dynamic?

Windows 2000 introduces the idea of a dynamic disk needed for fault-tolerant configurations. To convert, perform the following:

1. Start the Computer Manager MMC snap-in (Start > Programs > Administrative Tools > Computer Management).
2. Choose Expand Storage > Disk Management.
3. Right-click on the disk and select Upgrade to Dynamic Disk.
4. Select the disks to upgrade and click OK.
5. When the summary is displayed, click Upgrade.

Converting basic disks to dynamic disks doesn't require a reboot; however, any volumes contained on the disks after the conversion will generate a pop-up that says a reboot is necessary before the volumes can be used. I generally say no, do not reboot, until all the volumes are identified and all the pop-ups finish. Then I perform a single reboot.

If you get a message that says you are out of space, you might not have enough unallocated free space at the end of the disk for the private region used by database dynamic disks to keep volume information. To be dynamic, the disk needs about 1MB of this space. Sometimes the space is not visible to you in the GUI, but it is still there.

You might not have the space if the partitions on the disk take up the entire disk and were created with Setup, an earlier version of NT, or another OS. If partitions are created within Windows 2000, the space is reserved. Partitions created with Setup will reserve the space in a later release.

To undo this conversion, run DMUNROOT.EXE, which will revert the boot and system partition back to basic but will destroy all other volumes. Alternatively, you should back up any data on the disk you wish to preserve and then delete all partitions—that should activate the menu choice Revert to Basic Disk. The entire disk **has** to be unallocated or free space.

How do I import a foreign volume in Windows 2000?

If you take a disk from another machine and place it in a Windows 2000 box, it will be shown as foreign and its partitions not available. However, the disk's partition information can be imported and its volumes used. Any volumes that were part of a set will be deleted during the import phase unless the whole set of disks is imported.

1. Start the Computer Management MMC (Start > Programs > Administrative Tools > Computer Management).
2. Expand the Storage branch and select Disk Management.
3. Right-click on the volume to be imported and choose Import Foreign Disks from the context menu (see Figure 23-5).

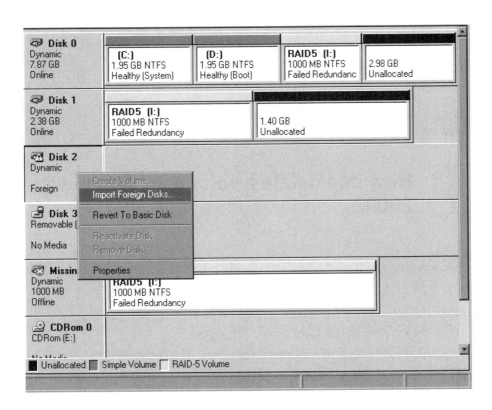

Figure 23-5. Importing a foreign disk.

4. Click OK to the displayed dialog for the disk to import. If you import multiple disks, they will be grouped by the computer from which you moved them and can be selected by clicking the Select Disk button. If the disks imported are not dynamic, they will all be imported, regardless of your choices.

5. A dialog box appears, showing the volumes to import (see Figure 23-6). Click OK.

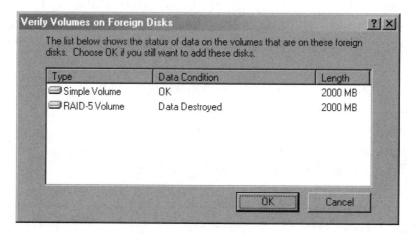

Figure 23-6. Notice that the partition that was part of a RAID 5 set is not usable.

The data on the imported volumes is now accessible, but you have to refresh in Explorer to see them (press F5).

2000 ONLY

How do I delete a volume in Windows 2000?

23.55

To delete a volume, just perform the following, but be warned that you will lose any data on these volumes.

1. Start the Computer Management MMC snap-in (Start > Programs > Administrative Tools > Computer Management).

2. Expand the Storage branch and select Disk Management.

3. Right-click on the volume to be deleted and choose Delete Volume from the context menu.

4. Click Yes to the confirmation.

24 RAID

RAID stands for Redundant Array of Inexpensive Disks. It's a methodology for providing a high level of availability and redundancy by using a number of inexpensive disks chained together logically.

Hardware RAID solutions are available, which are always preferable to software RAID; however, NT Server has a built-in software RAID implementation of RAID 0, RAID 1, and RAID 5. Software RAID is obviously cheaper because no new special hardware is needed.

FAQ 24.1 Does NT Workstation support RAID?

Workstation does not support fault-tolerant RAID, such as RAID 1 or RAID 5; however, it does support RAID 0 (stripe set without parity). Hardware RAID will work, because it is transparent to the operating system.

There is much talk about changing the ProductType Registry key to enable fault tolerance on NT Workstation. This can be done, but it violates Microsoft licensing and would therefore be unsupported by Microsoft. Recent service packs have stopped this entry from being updated by the user.

You should look at the FTEDIT.EXE Resource Kit utility that allows fault-tolerant sets to be created. All that would be left is to manually load the fault-tolerant driver at boot-up time by setting the following to 0: HKEY_LOCAL_MACHINE\System\CurrentControlSet\Services\FtDisk\Start

24.2 What RAID levels does NT Server Support?

NT Server supports RAID 1 (disk mirroring) and RAID 5 (stripe sets with parity check). NT also supports RAID 0, which is striping without parity; this offers no data redundancy but does offer performance gains.

4.0 ONLY

24.3 How do I create a stripe set with parity?

Follow these instructions to create a stripe set with parity. A stripe set with parity (RAID 5) allows for a disk to fail without losing any data.

1. Start the Disk Administrator (Start Menu > Programs > Administrative Tools).
2. Select at least three areas of free space on different physical disks.
3. From the Fault Tolerance menu, select Create Stripe Set With Parity.
4. Fill in the size wanted, and click OK.

Note: A stripe set will only use the lowest common disk space on each physical drive. In other words, with three disks of 100MB, 50MB, and 40MB free, each part of the stripe set would be only 40MB with a maximum of 120MB partition in total.

4.0 ONLY

How do I re-create a broken stripe set?

24.4

When a member of a stripe set with parity fails, you do not get a warning and everything continues to work. As indications, a system event log would be generated when you start Disk Administrator and a space would be marked where the partition should be on the event log. Follow these instructions to re-create the stripe set:

1. Replace the faulty disk and start NT.
2. Start the Disk Administrator (Start Menu > Programs > Administrative Tools).
3. Select the stripe set to be repaired and select an area of unpartioned space on the new physical disk.
4. From the Fault Tolerance menu, choose Regenerate.

4.0 ONLY

How do I remove a stripe set?

24.5

Follow these instructions to remove a stripe set:

1. Start Disk Administrator (Start Menu > Programs > Administrative Tools).
2. Select the stripe set you wish to delete.
3. From the Partition drop-down menu, choose Delete.
4. Confirm the action.

Warning: You will lose ALL data on the stripe set.

Can NT be on a stripe set?

If NT is providing software RAID 0 or RAID 5 (stripe set or stripe set with parity), neither the NT boot nor system partition may be on a RAID 0 or RAID 5 volume. Using this type of volume requires the fault-tolerant driver, and that is loaded during NT's bootup. If you require NT to be on a stripe set, you need to purchase hardware RAID.

4.0 ONLY

How do I create a mirror set (RAID 1)?

To create a mirror, you should first create the prime, and then you can create a mirror of it, as follows:

1. Start Disk Administrator (Start > Programs > Administrative Tools > Disk Administrator).
2. Click on the existing partitions that make up the prime and hold down the Ctrl key.
3. Click on an unpartitioned area of disk space. You must select an unpartitioned area of space and not an existing partition.
4. From the Fault Tolerance menu, choose Establish Mirror (see Figure 24-1).

Figure 24-1. Creating a mirror set.

5. From the Partition menu, choose Commit Changes Now, and the duplication begins.

6. You will need to reboot when it finishes.

4.0 ONLY

How do I break a mirror set?

24.8

If part of a fault-tolerant set is lost (by hardware failure, for example), a message is displayed to say "A disk that is part of a fault-tolerant volume can no longer be accessed." The drive will still be usable, but the mirroring will have been suspended because there is no second disk to which it can write. To break the mirror set, perform the following:

1. Start Disk Administrator (Start > Programs > Administrative Tools > Disk Administrator).

2. When a message is displayed that a disk is missing, click on the Mirror.

3. From the Fault Tolerance menu, choose Break Mirror.

4. Confirm the action.

4.0 ONLY

How do I repair a broken mirror set?

24.9

Make sure you have an area of unpartitioned space that is at least the size of the primary partition. Then perform the following:

1. Start Disk Administrator (Start > Programs > Administrative Tools > Disk Administrator).

2. Click on the working part of the mirror, hold down the Ctrl key, and select the area of unpartitioned space.

3. From the Fault Tolerance menu, choose Establish Mirror.

I am unable to boot by using the mirror disk. Why?

When you create a mirror disk, the partition is automatically created for you, but the Master Boot Record (MBR) of the disk is not updated with the NT boot loader.

To install the NT boot loader, first partition and format the drive with Disk Administrator, which will write the MBR to the shadow (to-be) disk. Then delete this partition and continue creating the mirror as usual.

If you already have a mirror disk that you need to boot off of and do not wish to use a modified NT boot disk, you can write the MBR record to the shadow disk by using the repair process. (For details about creating an NT book disk, see Question 11.3 in Chapter 11, Recovery.)

1. Boot the machine, using the three NT installation disks.
2. At the options after disk 2, press R for Repair.
3. Deselect all options except Inspect Boot Sector, and continue.
4. Press Enter to detect hardware and then insert disk 3.
5. When asked if you have an Emergency Repair Disk (ERD), say Yes and insert the ERD.
6. The machine reboots and the MBR record has been written.

4.0 ONLY

I have reinstalled NT but now I have lost all RAID/volume sets. What can I do?

Windows NT stores information about volume/mirror/stripe sets in the HKEY_LOCAL_MACHINE\System\Disk Registry key. If you reinstall Windows NT, it will lose this information and not recognize the volumes as fault-tolerant sets.

The best way to avoid this problem is to perform the following **before** you reinstall:

1. Start Disk Administrator (Start Menu > Programs > Administrative Tools).

2. From the Partition menu, choose Configuration > Save.

3. Insert a blank formatted disk and click OK.

4. Click OK to the Success message.

This creates a single file, SYSTEM, on the disk. Keep the disk safe. You should label it with the system name and the date made.

When you reinstall NT, you can then start Disk Administrator and choose Configuration > Restore from the Partition menu. Insert the disk and your original volume/RAID sets will be restored, along with any drive letter assignments.

If you are simply adding another installation of NT on the machine and keeping the original, you can perform a Configuration > Search from the Partition menu. It will attempt to find any other copies of Windows NT and then give you the option to duplicate its configuration.

If none of the above is possible and you have already lost your configuration, the only option is to use the FTEDIT.EXE Resource Kit utility, which enables the editing of fault-tolerant sets. Full help is given with the utility, but use FTEDIT.EXE carefully or you may actually lose the data.

2000 ONLY

24.12 How do I create a RAID 5 set in Windows 2000?

Windows 2000 introduces dynamic disks, and all members of a RAID volume set have to be on a dynamic disk. To convert a disk from basic to dynamic, see Question 23.53 in Chapter 23, File Systems.

You need disk areas from three separate disks to create a RAID 5 set. To create a RAID 5 set, perform the following:

1. Start the Computer Management MMC (Start > Programs > Administrative Tools > Computer Management).

2. Expand the Storage branch and select Disk Management.

3. Right-click on an area of unallocated space. From the context menu, select Create Volume (see Figure 24-2).

4. In the Volume Creation Wizard, click Next.

5. Select a volume type of RAID-5 volume and click Next (see Figure 24-3).

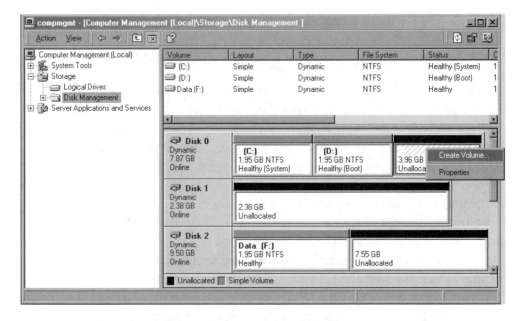

Figure 24-2. Creating a new volume using the context menu.

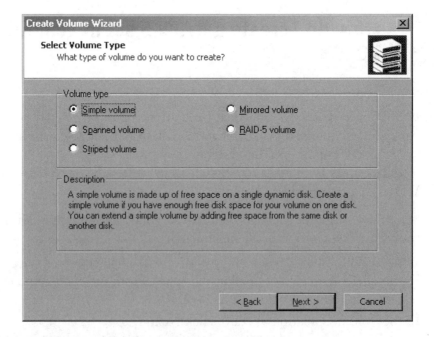

Figure 24-3. Selecting the volume type. Notice you can also create stripe and mirror sets from here.

6. On the left side of the snap-in, select the disks you want to use (at least three in total) and click Add to use them.

7. Next, select the amount of space to use from each disk. This has to be equal for each disk, so the largest space you can use is the smallest free space on any of the disks.

8. When you have selected the size, click Next. Notice that if you select 1000MB (for example) from each disk, the total size is only 2000MB because a third of the space is used for parity information.

9. Select a drive letter to use and click Next.

10. Select the file system to use and the label. You may also select whether to enable file and folder compression. Click Next.

11. When the summary screen is displayed, click Finish.

The disk areas should now be shown as RAID 5 and in Regenerating mode.

You might get a message from the Logical Disk Manager saying, "The operation did not complete because the partition/volume is not enabled. Please reboot the computer to enable the partition/volume." Click OK to this message but do not reboot until the regeneration has completed and the volume is shown as healthy; otherwise, you will have to reformat the partition after the reboot.

2000 ONLY

24.13 How do I delete a RAID 5 set in Windows 2000?

Deleting a RAID 5 set will result in all contained data being lost, so make sure you back up first.

To delete a RAID 5 set, perform the following:

1. Start the Computer Management MMC (Start > Programs > Administrative Tools > Computer Management).

2. Expand the Storage branch and select Disk Management.

3. Right-click on an element of the RAID 5 volume and choose Delete Volume from the context menu.

4. Click Yes to the confirmation.

All space used by the RAID 5 volume will now be listed as unpartitioned.

2000 ONLY

24.14

How do I regenerate a RAID 5 set in Windows 2000?

If one part of a RAID 5 set is replaced as a result of faulty hardware, the volume will not lose any data, thanks to the stored parity information. However, you must replace the broken disk to reenable the fault-tolerant capability of RAID 5.

After you have replaced the bad disk, perform the following:

1. Start the Computer Management MMC (Start > Programs > Administrative Tools > Computer Management).

2. Expand the Storage branch and select Disk Management. Notice that the removed disk is still shown as Missing.

3. Right-click on an element of the RAID 5 volume and choose Repair Volume from the context menu (see Figure 24-4).

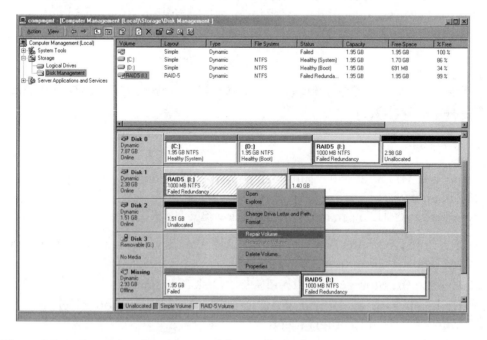

Figure 24-4. Repairing the volume of the RAID 5 set.

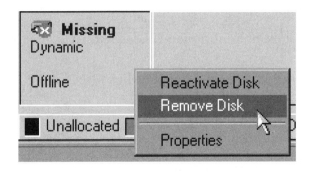

Figure 24-5. Removing a disk from the Logical Disk Manager service after that disk has been physically removed from the system.

4. Select a disk from the list to use as the replacement and click OK. Every disk on the system that is capable of becoming part of the set (dynamic and with enough unpartitioned space) but is not already part of the set will be listed as DISK 1, DISK 2, and so on.

5. The RAID 5 set will now be shown as regenerating.

You are now fault-tolerant again. The RAID5 partition will have been removed from the "missing" disk.

If you had other partitions on the disk that was removed, delete the partitions by right-clicking on the partition and selecting Delete Volume. You should now right-click on the missing text and choose Remove Disk from the context menu (see Figure 24-5).

If you ever put back the original disk, it would be displayed as Foreign. To learn how to read in (import) this disk, see Question 23.54 in Chapter 23, File Systems.

2000 ONLY

24.15 How do I create a mirror set (RAID 1) in Windows 2000?

As with a RAID 5 set, all members of a RAID 1 volume set have to be on a dynamic disk. To convert a disk from basic to dynamic, see Question 23.53 in Chapter 23, File Systems.

To create a RAID 1 set, perform the following:

1. Start the Computer Management MMC (Start > Programs > Administrative Tools > Computer Management).

2. Expand the Storage branch and select Disk Management.

3. Right-click on the partition you want to mirror and choose Add Mirror from the context menu.

4. Select the disk that will host the mirror and click Add Mirror (see Figure 24-6).

5. If you are mirroring the boot partition, a dialog box appears, detailing changes to be made to BOOT.INI to enable mirror booting. Click OK.

The mirror set will show as Regenerating (see Figure 24-7).

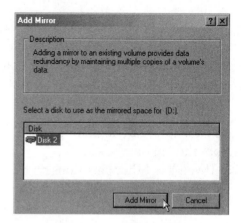

Figure 24-6. Only disks capable of becoming part of the mirror are shown.

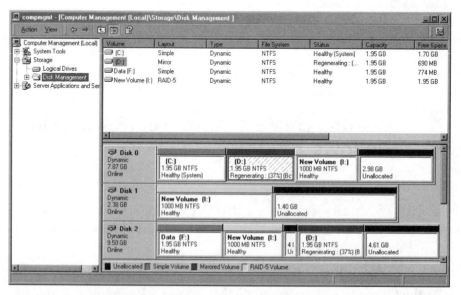

Figure 24-7. Notice the combination of normal volumes, members of a RAID 5 set, and members of a mirror set.

FAQ
24.16

How do I break a mirror set (RAID 1) in Windows 2000?

Breaking a mirror will not result in data loss. You will be left with two single volumes with duplicate data.

To break a RAID 1 set, perform the following:

1. Start the Computer Management MMC (Start > Programs > Administrative Tools > Computer Management).
2. Expand the Storage branch and select Disk Management.
3. Right-click on the mirror volume to be removed and choose Break Mirror from the context menu.
4. Click Yes to the confirmation dialog.
5. Another dialog might be shown, warning of possible data loss on the broken mirror and asking if you want to continue. Click Yes.

You will be left with two volumes; you might want to delete the now-unwanted ex-mirror to avoid any confusion.

On the context menu in step 3, you probably noticed a Delete Mirror option. Clicking this removes both volumes making up the mirror, and you will lose any data on them.

25 DISTRIBUTED FILE SYSTEM (DFS)

The Distributed File System (DFS) was introduced as an add-on for Windows NT 4.0. DFS allows Administrators to hide a network's physical topology and display it as a logical hierarchy.

Windows 2000 includes the Distributed File System as a core component, so understanding its principles and application will aid you in your Windows 2000 migration.

 ## What is Distributed File System?

25.1

Distributed File System (or DFS) is a new tool for NT Server that was not completed in time for inclusion as part of NT 4.0 but is now available for downloading. It enables Administrators to simulate a single server share environment that actually exists over several servers—basically a link to a share on another server that looks like a subdirectory of the main server.

Allowing a single view for all of the shares on your network can simplify your backup procedures. With DFS, you simply back up the root share, and DFS takes care of gathering all the information from the other servers across the network.

You are not required to have a single tree (DFS directory structures are called trees). Rather, you can have separate trees for different purposes—perhaps one for each department—but each tree can have exactly the same structure (sales, information, and so on).

For more information on DFS, see http://www.microsoft.com/ntserver/nts/downloads/winfeatures/NTSDistrFile/AdminGuide.asp.

Where can I get DFS?

DFS is available for downloading from Microsoft at http://www.microsoft.com/ntserver/nts/downloads/winfeatures/NTSDistrFile/default.asp. Follow the instructions at the site and fill in the form about your site. The file you want for the i386 platform is DFS-V41-I386.EXE.

After the download, double-click on the file and agree to the license to begin installation of files to your drive.

DFS is a standard component of Windows 2000.

How do I install DFS?

First, download and expand the file DFS-V41-I386.EXE. Then follow these instructions:

1. Right-click on Network Neighborhood and choose Properties (or double-click Network in the Control Panel).
2. Click the Services tab and then click Add.
3. Click the Have Disk button. When asked where, enter %systemroot%/system32/dfs. Do not actually type %systemroot%, but rather what it points to (that is, d:\winnt). The full path would be

```
d:\winnt\system32\dfs
```

4. Click Enter and then click OK for DFS installation (see Figure 25-1).

5. A dialog box appears. Check the Host a DFS On Share check box and click New Share (see Figure 25-2).

6. Type the name of the required root (for example, **c:\dfsroot**) and click Create Share to create the directory. Click Yes to the confirmation.

7. Select Shared As, fill in the required information, and click OK (see Figure 25-3).

8. Close the dialog boxes and reboot the machine.

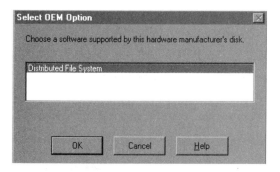

Figure 25-1. Choosing to install DFS.

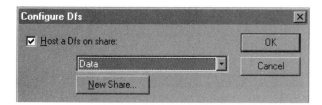

Figure 25-2. Hosting a DFS share.

Figure 25-3. An example of information needed for the DFS root share.

4.0 ONLY
FAQ 25.4 How do I create a new folder as part of the DFS?

When DFS is installed, a new application—the DFS Administrator—is created in the Administrative Tools folder. You should use this application to manage DFS. To add a new area as part of the DFS tree, follow these procedures:

1. Start the DFS Administrator application (Start > Programs > Administrative Tools > DFS Administrator).
2. From the DFS menu, choose Add to DFS.
3. Enter the folder name by which you want an existing share to be known.
4. Select what the name should point to—you can either type the path or use Browse (see Figure 25-4).
5. Click OK and close the DFS Administrator.

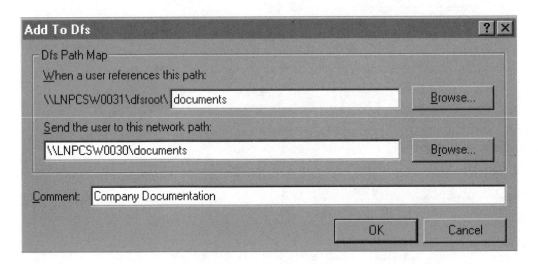

Figure 25-4. Creating a DFS branch to a share on another machine.

4.0 ONLY
FAQ 25.5 How do I uninstall DFS?

Follow these procedures:

1. Start the Network Control Panel applet or right-click on Network Neighborhood and choose Properties.
2. Click the Services tab.
3. Select Distributed File System and click Remove.
4. At the prompt to continue, click Yes.
5. In the Network dialog box, click Close.
6. A reboot is required. When prompted, click Yes.

26 COMMAND PROMPT CONFIGURATION

Although Windows NT has a powerful Graphical User Interface (GUI), the command prompt can still be a vital tool for an experienced administrator, enabling you to complete complex tasks in a minimum amount of time with maximum configurability.

I still use the command line all the time. If you're fluent with its use, you can perform tasks there faster than with the GUI.

26.1 How can I configure the command prompt?

When you are in a CMD.EXE or COMMAND.COM session, it is possible to change the prompt to display information other than the default drive and directory (such as time, date, OS version).

The basic command and syntax to change the prompt is

prompt <text>

For example, to modify the prompt to johns prompt>, type

```
prompt johns prompt$g)
```

Notice that the specified $g has been changed to the > sign. A number of these symbols are available, as shown in Table 26-1.

Table 26-1. Symbols for Command Prompt

$a	& Ampersand
$b	| Pipe
$c	(Open parenthesis
$d	Current date
$e	Escape code (ASCII code 27)
$f	) Close parenthesis
$g	> greater than sign
$h	Backspace (erases previous character)
$1	< Less than sign
$n	Current drive
$p	Current drive with path
$q	= Equal sign
$s	Space
$t	Current time
$v	Windows NT version number
$_	Carriage return and linefeed
$$	$ sign

Command extensions are new to Windows NT 4.0 and are explained in Question 26.2. If you have command extensions enabled, you can also use the following:

$+ Zero or more + characters, depending on the depth of the PUSHD directory stack.

$M Displays the remote name associated with the current drive letter if the drive is on a remote directory. If the current drive is not remote, it returns blank.

How do I enable/disable command extensions?

26.2

When you use CMD.EXE, there are various extensions that enhance the command environment. These enable more advanced batch processing, such as additional IF statement capabilities.

These "extensions" to the command environment are enabled by default. To permanently enable/disable the extensions, perform the following on the local machine. This change makes a change to the Registry, so you should be comfortable with using the Registry (and ensure you have an up-to-date backup before you ever modify the Registry). Read Chapter 10, The Registry, before proceeding.

1. Start the Registry editor (REGEDIT.EXE).
2. Move to HKEY_CURRENT_USER\Software\Microsoft\Command Processor.
3. Double-click on EnableExtensions (see Figure 26-1).
4. Set to **1** for extensions to be enabled, or set to **0** for extensions to be disabled.
5. Click OK.

You can also enable or disable extensions for a specific command session by using the appropriate qualifier to CMD.EXE, as follows:

cmd /y   Disables command extensions for this cmd session
cmd /x   Enables command extensions for this cmd session

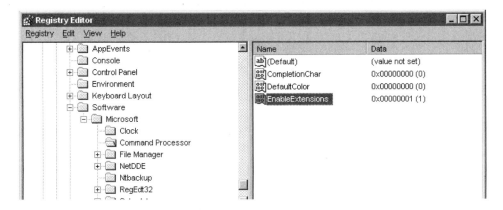

Figure 26-1. The default setting of 1 means the new extensions to the command environment in NT 4.0 will be available.

How can I configure a scrollbar on my command window?

It is possible to increase the line buffer for the command windows above the normal 25. To change the "history," perform the following:

1. Start a command session (CMD.EXE).
2. Right-click on the title bar and select Properties.
3. Click the Layout tab.
4. In the Screen Buffer Size section, increase the Height value and click OK (see Figure 26-2).
5. When you're asked if you want to "Apply properties to current windows only" or "Save properties for future windows with same title," select the latter and click OK.

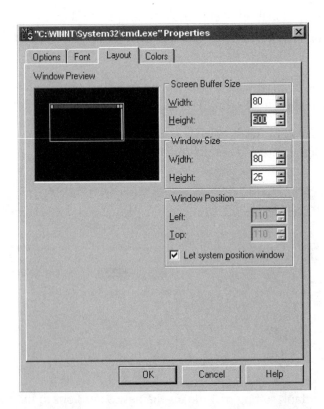

Figure 26-2. These settings will result in a 500-line history buffer.

What this procedure actually does is create HKEY_CURRENT_USER\ Console\E:_WINNT_System32_cmd.exe key with a value ScreenBufferSize in which the first part is the buffer height in hexadecimal.

From the command line itself, you can set the number of lines and columns by using these commands:

mode con lines=n   Where *n* is the number of lines to keep (if *n* is larger than can fit on the screen, a scrollbar will be added).

mode con cols=n   Where *n* is the number of columns to show (again, a scrollbar will be added).

 26.4 ## How do I cut and paste information in a command box?

To copy the entire contents of a command window, you can maximize the window (Alt+Enter) and press the PrintScrn key. This is very awkward, and the command environment has a far more flexible method.

1. Right-click the title bar.
2. From the Edit menu, choose Mark.
3. Click the left mouse button at the start of the text you wish to copy, and drag until the end of the selection (see Figure 26-3).
4. Press Enter to copy the selection. Or right-click the title bar again and choose Copy from the Edit menu. This places the selected text into the Windows Clipboard for pasting into any Windows application.

To paste information into a command window, right-click on the title bar and choose Paste from the Edit menu

Alternatively, you can enable QuickEdit mode by right-clicking on the title bar and selecting Properties. Select the Options tab and check the QuickEdit Mode box. Now you can select text with the left mouse button and just press Enter or right-click on the selection to copy into the Clipboard. Right-clicking when information is already in the Clipboard pastes into the command window.

```
Select C:\WINNT\System32\cmd.exe                                    _ □ ✕
01/09/98   08:57           <DIR>              other FAQs
01/09/98   08:58           <DIR>              SavillTech
21/09/98   09:02           <DIR>              Scripts
              12 File(s)                      0 bytes
                        1,697,605,632 bytes free

D:\Documents>cd nt faq book

D:\Documents\nt faq book>dir *.tif
 Volume in drive D is Data
 Volume Serial Number is 885C-D7F1

 Directory of D:\Documents\nt faq book

05/10/98   14:42                  24,740  cmdconf1.tif
05/10/98   14:46                  26,102  cmdconf2.tif
05/10/98   15:30                  31,866  cmdconf3.tif
05/10/98   15:37                  18,638  cmdconf4.tif
05/10/98   15:46                   7,634  cmdconf5.tif
05/10/98   15:49                   5,230  cmdconf6.tif
05/10/98   15:53                  23,204  cmdconf7.tif
              7 File(s)          137,414  bytes
                        1,697,605,632 bytes free

D:\Documents\nt faq book>_
```

Figure 26-3. As you can see, the selection is not on a per-line basis; it is a square.

How do I enable Tab to complete filenames?

26.5

Users of UNIX will be familiar with pressing the Tab key to force the operating system to complete any filename you are typing. NT has this functionality built in; however, it is disabled by default. To enable this Tab function, perform the following:

1. Start the Registry editor (REGEDIT.EXE).
2. Move to HKEY_CURRENT_USER\Software\Microsoft\Command Processor.
3. Double-click on the value CompletionChar.
4. Make sure the base is hexadecimal and then set the value to **9** and click OK.
5. Close the Registry editor.
6. Log off and on again.

Now pressing Tab from a command prompt will complete filenames. Repeated pressing of Tab will cycle through any filenames matching the characters you have entered manually.

Other keys can be set for the completion of characters by setting CompletionChar to the appropriate key code in Hex (for example, 8 is the backspace key).

How do I create a shortcut from the command prompt?

You will no doubt be used to creating shortcuts by just dragging objects; however, you might want to create these useful links from the command prompt—perhaps from a login script or the like.

The SHORTCUT.EXE utility supplied with the Windows NT Server Resource Kit Version 4.0 Supplement 1 can be used to create .LNK files. The application is quite powerful and enables you to specify not only the resource to link to but also an icon and other parameters. Here is an example:

```
shortcut -t "d:\program files\johnsapp\test.exe" -n "Johns
App.lnk" -i "d:\program files\johnicon\icon1.ico" -x 0 -d
"e:\johns\data"
```

Table 26-2 shows what this command means.

Table 26-2. SHORTCUT.EXE

-t	The location of the resource to be linked to
-n	The name of the link file to be created
-i	The icon file
-x	The icon index to use in the icon file
-d	The starting directory for the application

You can copy SHORTCUT.EXE from the CD that comes with the Resource Kit; it is located in <processor>\desktop (e.g. i386\desktop). You do not need any other files.

How can I redirect the output from a command to a file?

The most basic method is using the greater than symbol (>), as follows:

\<command> > \<filename>
(for example, dir/s >list.txt)

In this example, the output from the directory command will be sent to the file LIST.TXT.

However, with this approach, errors can still get output to the screen. To rectify this, use the 2> for the errors, as follows:

\<command> >\<filename> 2>\<error file>
(for example, dir/s >list.txt 2>error.txt)

If you want the errors and output to be sent to the same file, use the following:

\<command> >\<filename> 2>&1

What this says is, for the 2> parameter, use the first parameter entered, which was \<filename>.

How can I get a list of the commands I have entered in a command session?

You can press the up- and down-arrow keys in a command session to display your previous commands (same as the old DOSKEY software). If you press the F7 key, however, a list of all the commands entered is displayed. You can then select a specific command and press Enter to run it (see Figure 26-4).

You can configure the history by right-clicking on the title bar, selecting Properties, and then selecting the Options tab. Update the command history section, indicating the number of commands to store.

Figure 26-4. Here you can use the up- and down-arrow keys to move through the command history. Press Enter to select a command to execute.

Keys you can use are as shown in Table 26-3.

Table 26-3. Function Keys for Accessing Command History

F2	Searches for a character in the previous command and displays up to that character
F3	Recalls the last command issued
F7	Displays a list of all the commands entered
F8	Moves backward through the command history
F9	Lets you return to a command by its number as given by pressing F7

How can I start Explorer from the command prompt?

You can start Explorer by simply typing Explorer at the command prompt; however, Explorer can also be started in different modes. To start Explorer in your current directory, enter the following command:

```
explorer /e
```

To bring up the single-pane version of Explorer, use the following command:

```
explorer
```

If you add a location to the command, Explorer will start in that location:

```
explorer d:\temp
```

 ## 26.10 How can I change the title of the command window?

By default, the title display name is the location of CMD.EXE; however, this can be changed by either of two methods, depending on the situation.

If you currently have a command session and you wish to change its title, use the title command:

title <title>
(for example, title John Savill's Command Window)

Alternatively, if you want to start a new command session from an existing command prompt, use the start command:

start "<title>"
(for example, start "John Savill's Command Window")

 ## 26.11 What keyboard actions can I take to navigate the command line?

Rather than just using the left- and right-arrow keys to move one character at a time through the command, you can use any of the keys shown in Table 26-4.

Table 26-4. Command Line Keys

Home	Start of the line
End	End of the line
Left arrow	Move back one character
Right arrow	Move forward one character
Ctrl+left arrow	Move back one word
Ctrl+right arrow	Move forward one word
Insert	Toggle between insert and overstrike mode
Esc	Delete current line

You can also use the Tab key to complete filenames, as described in Question 26.5.

 How can I change the default DIR output format?

The DIR command has many switches. You can configure your own default behavior for the command instead of using the normal format. For example, you might want to view the output one page at a time (/p), in lowercase (/l), with file times listed by time of creation rather than last write (/tc), and sorted first by extension and then by name (/oen). Normally, you would type

```
dir /p /l /tc /oen
```

However, this is slightly tedious, so to set this as your default, perform the following:

1. Start the System Control Panel applet (Start > Settings > Control Panel > System).
2. Select the Environment tab (see Figure 26-5).
3. Create the Variable dircmd and set the value to your qualifiers. For example, type **/p /l /tc /oen** and click Set.
4. Click Apply and then OK.

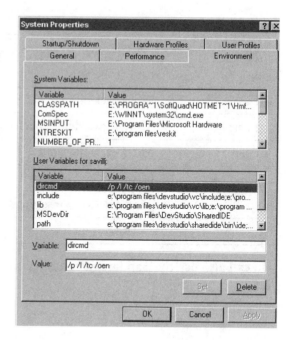

Figure 26-5. All DIR commands will now output as if the switches /p, /l, /tc, and /oen had been specified.

Any new command session will now use the new DIR output format.

It is possible to modify dircmd for the current session only. To do so, enter this command:

```
set dircmd = <switches>
```

26.13 How do I pause output from a command to one screen at a time?

To pause output, add |**more** to the end of the command. For example, the following command would display the Help one screen at a time:

```
findstr /? |more
```

How can I increase the environment space for a single command session?

Although you can update the CONFIG.NT with a larger shell= to affect all command sessions, you can set the environment space for just a single session by calling the command with the /e switch, as follows, where /e:nnnnn sets the initial environment size to nnnnn bytes:

```
command /e:2048 myapp.exe
```

How can I stop a process from the command line?

To stop a process, you usually start Task Manager, select the Processes tab, select the process, and then click End Process. However, you can also accomplish this from the command prompt by using two Resource Kit utilities.

First you need to get a list of all processes on the system. You can do this by using the TLIST.EXE utility, which has the plus of also showing relationships between processes, if applicable. The command and sample output are shown here:

```
tlist
0 System Process
2 System
20 smss.exe
26 csrss.exe
34 WINLOGON.EXE
42 SERVICES.EXE
45 LSASS.EXE
72 SPOOLSS.EXE
91 Nettime.exe
64 navapsvc.exe
...
198 Notepad.exe Untitled > Notepad
214 TLIST.EXE
```

The first part, the number, is the process ID (for example, 198 is the process ID of the NOTEPAD.EXE process that is running). When you know the process ID (PID), you can stop it by using the KILL.EXE utility:

kill 198
(process #198 killed)

You can optionally use the -f switch, which forces the process kill even if busy.

You might, if you wish, kill a process by its name instead of its process ID, like this:

```
kill notepad.exe
```

With this command, you should take care in case more than one instance of Notepad is running. Killing by process ID is safer.

How can I open a command prompt from my current directory in Explorer?

It might be a normal situation. Say you are browsing directories in Explorer and want to open a command prompt from the current location without typing a long change directory command to get to the correct directory. It is possible to add a Context Menu option that will be displayed when you right-click on a folder, containing a Command Prompt Here option to open a command prompt at your current Explorer location.

A power toy (which is a generic term for a small Microsoft add-on product to Windows NT or 9x), Command Prompt Here, can be downloaded from Microsoft (and it's also included with the Resource Kit as CMDHERE.INF). This power toy adds the capability to start a command session from the current Explorer directory. All this does, however, is update a couple of Registry entries, so it can be accomplished manually, allowing greater flexibility.

1. Start the Registry editor (REGEDIT.EXE).
2. Move to HKEY_CLASSES_ROOT\Folder\shell (you could use HKEY_CLASSES_ROOT\Directory\shell, but then it would not apply to folders, whereas Folder does both).

3. From the Edit menu, choose New > Key and enter **CmdHere** (or anything else).

4. Under the new key, choose New > Key and enter **command** (lowercase).

5. Under the key CmdHere, double-click on Default and enter a name that will be displayed when you right-click on the directory (for example, enter **Command Prompt Here**).

6. As an extra, if you add an ampersand (&) in front of a character, the character will be underlined (for example, typing **&John Prompt here** would produce "John Prompt here").

7. Move to the command key and again double-click on (Default). Then enter the following:

   ```
   <system dir>\System32\cmd.exe /k cd "%1"
   ```
   (for example, c:\winnt\System32\cmd.exe /k cd "%1")

8. Close the Registry editor.

There is no need to reboot the machine; the new option will be available when you right-click on a folder (see Figure 26-6).

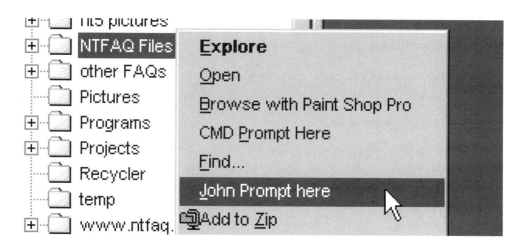

Figure 26-6. Example of the new Context menu option.

How can I open a command prompt at my current drive in Explorer?

The answer is exactly the same as for Question 26.16, but this time you create a command prompt for a base drive. This has a separate context menu, so a different Registry entry needs updating.

1. Start the Registry Editor (REGEDIT.EXE).
2. Move to HKEY_CLASSES_ROOT\Drive\shell.
3. From the Edit menu, choose New > Key and enter the name **CmdHere** (or anything else)
4. Under the new key, choose New > Key and enter the name **command** (lowercase).
5. Under the key (CmdHere), double-click on (Default) and enter a name that will be displayed when you right-click on the directory (for example, enter **Command Prompt Here**).
6. As an extra, if you add an ampersand (&) in front of a character, the character will be underlined (for example, typing **&John Prompt here** would produce "John Prompt here").
7. Move to the command key and again double-click on (Default). Then enter the following:

   ```
   <system dir>\System32\cmd.exe /k cd "%1"
   ```
   (for example, c:\winnt\System32\cmd.exe /k cd "%1")

8. Close the Registry editor.

Below is an .INF file that incorporates the creation of the Command Here for drives and directories if you don't have CMDHERE.INF that comes with the Resource Kit. Save this file with an .INF extension and then right-click on it and choose Install.

```
; Command Here
[Version]
Signature = "$Windows NT$"
Provider=%Provider%

[Strings]
Provider="SavillTech Ltd"
```

```
[DefaultInstall]
AddReg = AddReg
[AddReg]
HKCR,Directory\Shell\CmdHere,,,"Command Here"
HKCR,Directory\Shell\CmdHere\command,,,"%11%\cmd.exe /k cd
""%1"""
HKCR,Drive\Shell\CmdHere,,,"Command Here"
HKCR,Drive\Shell\CmdHere\command,,,"%11%\cmd.exe /k cd ""%1"""
```

 ## How can I change the editor used to edit batch or command files?

If you right-click on a .BAT or .CMD file and choose Edit from the context menu, the file opens in Notepad; however, you might want to use a different editor as the default. You can accomplish this by making the following two small Registry modifications:

1. Start the Registry editor (REGEDIT.EXE).
2. First, change the editor used for .BAT files.
3. Move to HKEY_CLASSES_ROOT\batfile\shell\edit\command.
4. Double-click on the Default value and change to the executable you want to use to edit the batch files. For example, if you want to use Microsoft Development Editor, type

   Program Files\DevStudio\SharedIDE\BIN\msdev.exe "%1"

5. Click OK. Now perform the same for .CMD files.
6. Move to HKEY_CLASSES_ROOT\cmdfile\shell\edit\command.
7. Double-click on the (Default) value and again change to the editor you want to use.
8. Click OK.

No reboot is required, and the changes take immediate effect.

You can also perform the above via a GUI front end by choosing View > Folder Options > File Types from Explorer. You then select the file type (for example, MS-DOS Batch File) and click Edit. The context menu options available are listed and you can modify them. All this does is update the Registry values you have looked at.

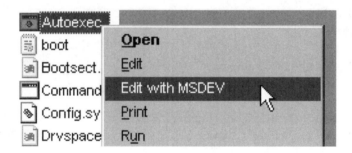

Figure 26-7. The additional option to edit with the Microsoft Visual Studio editor might be useful.

If you want to leave the existing option and add a new Edit option (for example, Edit with MSDEV), perform the following. In this example, you only update .BAT with a second edit option, but the same could be performed on .CMD files (see Figure 26-7).

1. Start the Registry editor (REGEDIT.EXE).
2. Move to HKEY_CLASSES_ROOT\batfile\shell.
3. From the Edit menu, choose New > Key and enter **editms**.
4. Double-click on the Default value under editms and set the name to be displayed on the context menu (for example, type **Edit with MSDEV**).
5. Click OK.
6. Select editms and choose New > Key from the Edit menu. Then enter the name command.
7. Double-click the Default under Command and set to the required value (see Figure 26-8). For example, type

```
C:\Program Files\DevStudio\SharedIDE\BIN\msdev.exe "%1" for
msdev.
```

8. Click OK and close the Registry editor.

You will now have two options when you right-click on a batch file: Edit and Edit with MSDEV.

You can use this on any type of file—.TXT files, for example—by editing HKEY_CLASSES_ROOT\txtfile\shell\open\command. Just look through HKEY_CLASSES_ROOT\xxxfile, where xxx is the extension. (Actually, to find the correct file type, use the assoc command, as in ASSOC.TXT. This will return the file type, as in TXTFILE.)

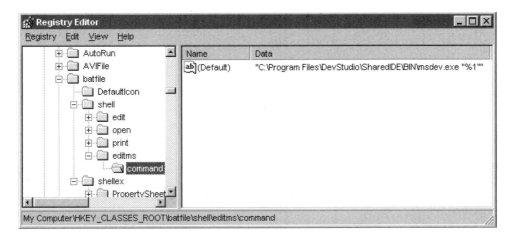

Figure 26-8. Example of the Registry modification.

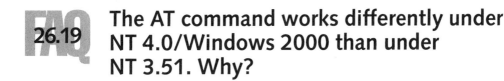

The AT command works differently under NT 4.0/Windows 2000 than under NT 3.51. Why?

To better support long filenames, the parsing algorithm was changed in NT 4.0 so that only the target file should be surrounded by quotes. Examples are given here:

Under Windows NT 3.51, use

AT 20:00 "Notepad d:\documents\bonde\maxfactor.txt"

Under Windows NT 4.0, use

AT 20:00 Notepad "d:\documents\bonde\maxfactor.txt"

This can cause a problem, because if you surround the whole command in double quotes (a batch file, for example), it will not run correctly.

Support for a Registry key has been improved in Windows NT 4.0 Service Pack 4, which enables you to force the parse of the AT command to behave in the same manner as in 3.51. To achieve this, perform the following:

1. Start the Registry editor (REGEDIT.EXE).
2. Move to HKEY_LOCAL_MACHINE\SYSTEM\CurrentControlSet\ Services\Schedule.

3. From the Edit menu, choose New > Key. Type **Parameters** and press Enter.

4. Move to this new Parameters key.

5. From the Edit menu, choose New > DWORD value. Type **UseOldParsing** and press Enter.

6. Double-click on the new value and set it to 1.

7. Reboot the machine.

How can I append the date and time to a file?

26.20

You can use the following batch file to rename a file to filename_ YYYYMMDDHHMM. This can be useful in a number of situations.

```
@Echo OFF
TITLE DateName
REM DateName.CMD
REM takes a filename as %1 and renames as %1_YYMMDDHHMM
REM
REM ───────────────────────────────────────────
IF %1.==. GoTo USAGE
Set CURRDATE=%TEMP%\CURRDATE.TMP
Set CURRTIME=%TEMP%\CURRTIME.TMP
DATE /T > %CURRDATE%
TIME /T > %CURRTIME%
Set PARSEARG="eol=; tokens=1,2,3,4* delims=/, "
For /F %PARSEARG% %%i in (%CURRDATE%) Do SET
YYYYMMDD=%%l%%k%%j
Set PARSEARG="eol=; tokens=1,2,3* delims=:, "
For /F %PARSEARG% %%i in (%CURRTIME%) Do Set HHMM=%%i%%j%%k
Echo RENAME %1 %1_%YYYYMMDD%%HHMM%
RENAME %1 %1_%YYYYMMDD%%HHMM%
GoTo END
:USAGE
Echo Usage: DateName filename
Echo Renames filename to filename_YYYYMMDDHHMM
GoTo END
:END
```

```
REM
TITLE Command Prompt
```

Example:

```
D:\Exchange> datetype logfile.log
RENAME logfile.log logfile.log_199809281630
```

Other date options include LOGTIME.EXE, which enables you to specify a string and then writes the time, followed by the string, to the file LOGTIME.LOG at the current default directory. For example, say you had the following commands from a batch file:

```
Logtime "Backup Started"
..
ntbackup ….
..
Logtime "Backup Finished"
```

A file, LOGTIME.LOG, would be created with these contents:

```
10/05/98 16:15:25  Backup Started
10/05/98 19:13:33  Backup Finished
```

This record would help diagnose and identify at what point various parts of the command file were executed.

The other option is NOW.EXE, which just replaces itself with the date and time, like this:

```
D:\temp>now Batch complete
Mon Sep 28 15:54:19 1998 – Batch complete
```

Both of these utilities are part of the Windows NT Resource Kit.

27 BATCH FILES

A batch file is just a text file with a .BAT or .CMD extension that adheres to a syntax and a set of valid commands and instructions. To run a batch file, just enter the name of the file—you don't need to enter the .CMD or .BAT extension. In line with programming tradition, the first batch file we write here will output Hello World.

1. Start Notepad.
2. Type the following (everything after echo will be output to the screen):

```
@echo hello world
```

3. The @ suppresses the command from being printed to the screen; try it with and without the @ sign.
4. To stop commands from being displayed in the whole batch file, put the following at the top of the file:

```
@echo off
```

5. From the File menu, choose Save As. Save the file as **<name>.cmd** (for example, testfile.cmd). Make sure you enter the name in quotes or notepad will add .TXT to the end.
6. Start a command session (run CMD.EXE).

7. Enter the name of the batch file, with no extension. For example, use

`testfile`

8. The words "Hello world" are displayed, and you have written a batch file.

Under normal conditions you should not use Notepad as the editor, because it can put stray characters into files that might cause problems with logon scripts. Use the EDIT.EXE utility.

 ## What commands can be used in a batch file?

Windows NT 4.0 introduced some extensions to CMD.EXE. To use these make sure HKEY_CURRENT_USER\Software\Microsoft\Command Processor\EnableExtensions is set to 1. Table 27-1 gives a list of the more common commands you can use.

Table 27-1. Batch File Commands

call <batch file>	Used to call one batch from inside another. The execution of the current batch file is suspended until the called batch file completes.
exit	Used to stop batch file execution. If a batch file is called from inside another and exit is called, both batch files are stopped.
findstr <string> <filename(s)>	Used to find a string in a file. There are a number of parameters from this, and it is quite powerful.
for	Standard for loop. To print 1 to 10, use for /L %n IN (1,1,10) DO @ECHO %n
goto <label>	Causes the execution of a program to skip to a given point. The actual label name must be preceded with a colon (:), for example goto label1 ... :label1 ...

Table 27-1. Batch File Commands (continued)

if <condition> ..	The if statement has a great deal of functionality, most commonly if /i <string1> <compare> <string2> <command> The /i makes the comparison case insensitive and compare can be one of: EQU equal NEQ not equal LSS less than LEQ less than or equal GTR greater than GEQ greater than or equal if errorlevel if exists <filename>
rem <string>	A comment.
start <window title> <command>	Starts a new command session and runs a given command. Unlike call, the execution of the current batch file is not halted.

Some extra utilities are supplied with the NT Resource Kit that can be useful. These are all detailed in the Resource Kit Help file (which is very good).

How can I perform an action that depends on the arrival of a file?

This is a common request because users on hosts have files FTP'd from a host and need to take action on them when they arrive. The following simple batch file checks for FILE.TXT every 100 seconds:

```
:filecheck
if exist e:\upload\file.txt goto actionfile
sleep 100
goto filecheck
:actionfile
...
```

The program SLEEP.EXE is supplied with the Resource Kit, so you need the Resource Kit installed.

How can I access files on other machines?

You can use the UNC naming conventions:

```
\\<server name>\<share name>\<dir>\<file>
```

Alternatively, you can map the drive, access the file by using a drive letter, and then unmap the drive, like this:

```
net use g: \\savilltech\filetosee
<some action>... g:\dir\file.txt
net use g: /d
```

 ## How can I send a message from a batch file?

Use the NET SEND command:

```
net send <machine> <message>
```

The machine specified must have its Messenger service started to receive the message and avert any errors. Start the Messenger service by using the Services control panel applet or by entering the following from the command line:

```
net start messenger
```

 ## The command I enter asks for input. Can I automate the response?

Most commands have a switch to confirm an action; however, some commands require a response when run. For example, a logon might want you to enter a password. Try the following:

```
echo <password> | logon savillj
```

This runs the command logon savillj. If it asks for a password, the echo command then echoes the password with a return—thus entering your password for you.

 ## How can I pass parameters to a batch file?

When you call a batch file, you may enter data after the command that the batch file refers to as %1, %2, and so on. For example, the batch file sayhello.bat

```
@echo hello %1 boy
```

would output

hello john boy

if called as sayhello john.

Table 27-2 shows the ways in which you can modify the passed parameter:

Table 27-2. Parameter Modifications

Parameter	Description
%1	The normal parameter
%~f1	Expands %1 to a fully qualified pathname. If you only pass a filename from the current directory, it expands to the drive/directory as well.
%~d1	Extracts the drive letter from %1.
%~p1	Extracts the path from %1.
%~n1	Extracts the filename from %1 without the extension.
%~x1	Extracts the file extension from %1.
%~s1	Changes the meaning of n and x options to reference the short name. You would therefore use %~sn1 for the short filename or %~sx1 for the short extension.

You can combine some of the parameters, like this:

%~dp1   Expands %1 to a drive letter and path only.
%~nx1   Expands %1 to a filename and extension only.

To see all of these in action, put this into a batch file named
TESTING.BAT:

```
@echo off
echo fully qualified name %~f1
echo drive %~d1
echo path %~p1
echo filename %~n1
echo file extension %~x1
echo short filename %~sn1
echo short file extension %~sx1
echo drive and directory %~dp1
echo filename and extension %~nx1
```

Run the file with a long filename; for example, running the batch file on file
c:\temp\longfilename.long produces the following output:

```
fully qualified name c:\TEMP\longfilename.long
drive c:
path \TEMP\
filename longfilename
file extension .long
short filename LONGFI~1
short file extension .LON
drive and directory c:\TEMP\
filename and extension longfilename.long
```

Obviously, all of this also works on the second parameter, third parameter, and
so on. Just substitute 1 for the parameter; for example, use %~f2 for the second
parameter's fully qualified pathname.

How can I stop my batch file from outputting the command to the screen as it runs?

This is stopped by placing the following at the top of your batch file:

```
@echo off
```

To stop a single command from being output to the screen, put @ in front of the command.

 ## How do I call a batch file from within another batch file?

It is possible to just enter the name of one batch file in another batch file, which runs the called batch file. When the called file completes, however, it does not pass control back to the calling batch file, leaving the rest of the calling batch file unexecuted. For example, suppose you had these two batch files:

```
calling.bat
@echo off
echo Calling bat here
called.bat
echo Back to Calling bat
```

```
called.bat
@echo off
echo called bat here
```

If you run CALLING.BAT, you do not get the line Back to Calling bat displayed, because CALLED.BAT does not return to CALLING.BAT after terminating. To call a batch file and have it return to the calling batch file after completing, use **call**.

For example, if CALLING.BAT is modified to include *call called.bat* instead of *called.bat*, the line Back to Calling bat is displayed. With **call**, control returns to CALLING.BAT when CALLED.BAT has completed. This is how it looks:

```
calling.bat
@echo off
echo Calling bat here
call called.bat
echo Back to Calling bat .
```

 ## My .bat files have lost their association. What should I do?

This is easily fixed. Enter these commands:

```
ftype batfile=%1 %*
assoc .bat=batfile
```

The ftype command sets up a new type of file and the associated action (which in this case is just to run it). The assoc command associates an extension with a file type.

 ## How do I search files for a string from a batch file/command line?

You could use the basic find command, which allows you to search one file at a time for string; however, findstr is far more versatile. The command has the following switches, defined in Table 27-3:

```
FINDSTR [/B] [/E] [/L] [/R] [/S] [/I] [/X] [/V] [/N] [/M]
[/O] [/F:file] [/C:string] [/G:file] [strings]
[[drive:][path]filename[ ...]]
```

Table 27-3. Switches for the Findstr Command

Parameters	Meaning
/b	Match pattern if at the start of a line.
/e	Match pattern if at the end of a line.
/l	Search literally.
/r	Use text as a regular expression (default).
/s	Search current directory and all subdirectories.
/i	Ignore case.
/x	Selects lines that are an exact match.
/v	Selects lines that do not match.
/n	Displays the line number before the matched line.
/m	Display only the matching filenames.
/o	Displays the offset of the match before the matched line.
/g:<file>	Gets the search string from the specified file. /g:argument.txt
/c:<string>	Use text as a literal. /c:string
/f:<file>	Get the file list from the specified file. /f:filelist.txt
strings	The search string (in double quotes if multiple words).
files	Files to be searched.

Use spaces to separate multiple search strings unless /c is used. For example, to search for Windows, NT, or FAQ in ntfaq.html, use

```
findstr Windows NT FAQ ntfaq.html
```

To search for Windows NT FAQ in ntfaq.html, use

```
findstr /c:Windows NT FAQ ntfaq.html
```

FAQ 27.11 How can I delete files that are over *x* days old?

There is a utility called DELOLD, which is used in the form of

```
delold <location>\*.* n
```

where n is the number of days old the files need to be for them to be deleted.

You can download this utility from ACI Software at http://www.michna.com/ software.htm/.

28 WINDOWS SCRIPTING HOST (WSH)

The Windows Scripting Host (WSH) is a tool that enables you to run Visual Basic Scripting Edition and JScript (JavaScript) within the base operating system on Windows 95, Windows 98, or Windows NT 4.0. By using scripting languages, you can now write script to automate common tasks and create powerful macros and logon scripts.

Windows 2000 natively supports the Windows Scripting Host, but NT and 9x clients need the software installed.

 ## Where can I get the Windows Scripting Host?

The Windows Scripting Host software can be downloaded from http://msdn.microsoft.com/scripting/ along with a large amount of help files and samples. It is also supplied in the Windows NT 4 Option Pack.

The JScript and VScript engines you need are supplied with Internet Explorer 3.01 and later; however, the latest versions are supplied with Internet Explorer 4.01. These engines can be downloaded separately from the same address as the WSH. Beta versions of the newest engines are supplied with Internet Explorer 5.0.

How do I install the Windows Scripting Host software?

Downloading the software from http://msdn.microsoft.com/scripting/ fetches a single file, WSH.EXE. Switches for WSH.EXE are

/Q	Quiet mode
/T:<full path>	Specifies a temporary working folder
/C	Extract files only to the folder when used also with /T
/C:<CMD>	Overrides Install command defined by author

To install WSH, perform the following:

1. Start WSH.EXE by either running it or clicking it in Explorer.
2. Click Yes to the installation confirmation.
3. Click Yes to the license agreement.
4. Click OK to the install success message.

If you want to install WSH as part of a logon script or the like, use

```
wsh /q
```

This command asks no questions and gives no confirmations. If you want to check to see if WSH is installed and only install if it's not found, use

```
if not exist %systemroot%\system32\wscript.exe
\\<server>\<share>\wsh.exe /q
```

where \\<server>\<share> is a share that holds the WSH.EXE executable.

Where can I get more information on WSH?

Here are a number of sites for getting more information:

- http://msdn.microsoft.com/scripting/
- http://msdn.microsoft.com/scripting/windowshost/docs/reference/whitepaper.htm

- http://msdn.microsoft.com/scripting/windowshost/docs/reference/ objectmodel.htm
- http://wsh.glazier.co.nz/frame.asp?target=faq/wshfaq.asp

Two books are available that I know of:

- *Introducing Windows Scripting Host for Microsoft Windows 98*
- *Sam's Teach Yourself Windows Scripting Host in 21 Days*

For more FAQs, see the WSH FAQ at http://wsh.glazier.co.nz/frame.asp? target=faq/wshfaq.asp.

How do I create a new user in NT by using ADSI?

To create a new user, use the following Active Directory Scripting Interface (ADSI) script:

```
On Error Resume Next
strUser="UserID"
Set oDomain=GetObject("WinNT://YourDomain")
Set oUser=oDomain.Create ("user", strUser)
If (err.number=0) Then 'If not 0 then user ID already exists
oUser.SetInfo
oUser.SetPassword "mypassword"
oUser.SetInfo
End If
```

To update other elements of information, you can use

```
set user=GetObject("WinNT://domain/user")
User.FullName=FirstNameVar
User.HomeDirectory=UserHome
User.Profile="\\Server\Share\user"
User.LoginScript=LogonScript
User.Description="Description"
User.setinfo
```

For more information on ADSI (Active Directory Scripting Interface), see http://www.15seconds.com/focus/ADSI.htm/.

29 WINDOWS 95/98 ADMINISTRATION

In a perfect world, every machine would be NT; however, you might have to deal with a number of Windows 9x clients. The following questions are about the most common problems or issues you might see.

 29.1 How can I create a spare set of Windows 95 disks?

Microsoft distributed Windows 95 by using a new method—storing 1.68MB of data on a normal disk—which makes copying impossible with the usual methods. From http://www.sydex.com, you can download CopyQM, which performs an image copy. You can duplicate a Windows 95 installation disk by using the following command:

```
copyqm a: bios blind silent tracks=80 sides=2 convert=1.68m
```

At the prompt, insert the master disk. CopyQM will read in the information and ask you to insert the target disk.

How do I communicate with a Windows 9x client?

By "communicate," I mean send a message to and with Windows NT machines. The Messenger service can be used to receive any messages sent by using the net send command.

Windows 9x machines don't have the Messenger service, but they have an alternative, WINPOPUP.EXE, which can display delivered messages (see Figure 29-1). The best way to use the WinPopup utility is to place it in the Startup group under Program Files so it is always running.

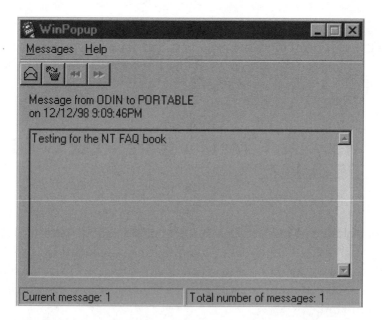

Figure 29-1. The Windows 98 WinPopup application. You can also send messages by clicking the Mail button.

Other options include using Microsoft's System Management Server product and Hewlett Packard's Desktop Administrator (DTA) (http://www.openview.hp.com/dta/).

How can I administer my domain from a Windows 95 client?

Install the server tools that are part of the Windows NT installation CD. Right-click on the file <CD ROM>:\clients\srvtools\win95\srvtools.inf.

Other options are the Hyena product from http://www.adkins-resource.com/index.html. I have not used this but have been advised it is very good.

How do I install the Windows 9x Policy editor?

To install the Windows 9x Policy editor on a Windows 9x machine, perform the following:

1. Start the Add/Remove Programs Control Panel applet (Start > Settings > Control Panel > Add/Remove Programs).
2. Click the Windows Setup tab.
3. Click Have Disk.
4. Click the Browse button and select the Netadmin\poledit directory of the Windows 98 Resource Kit. Click OK.
5. Check the System Policy Editor box and click Install.
6. Close the Add/Remove Control Panel applet.

The System Policy editor will now be available under Start > Programs > Accessories > System Tools > System Policy Editor.

To install the Windows 9x Policy editor under an NT machine, just copy the Netadmin\poledit directory to a folder on the Windows NT machine (for example, 98poledt) and create a shortcut on your desktop or Start menu to the newly copied POLEDIT.EXE. When you first run the Policy editor, it will load the NT .ADM files. Remove these by using Options > Policy Template and then re-add the files located in the 98poledt folder (normally COMMON.ADM and WINDOWS.ADM).

Be aware: Profiles created under NT, even with the Windows 9x version of the Policy editor, will not be read correctly from a Windows 9x machine. The

CONFIG.POL file needed for Windows 9x machines should be created under a Windows 9x machine and then copied to the netlogon share of the Domain Controller.

Installing under NT is only useful for experimentation and will not load profiles created by a Windows 9x machine.

How do I force a 95 machine to log on to a domain?

Using the Policy editor, create a new profile or edit your existing profile. Although NT has a Windows 9x template for its Policy editor, Windows 9x clients can't read a profile created by using the NT profile editor. You must use the Windows 9x Profile editor.

1. Double-click the Default Computer.
2. Move to the Network directory.
3. Move to the Logon tree and select Require Validation By Network For Windows Access.
4. You can also add a legal warning notice if you wish.
5. Save the policy in the Netlogon share (%systemroot%\system32\ repl\import\scripts) as CONFIG.POL.

How do I enable Windows 9x machines to use Group policies?

Copy the file GROUPPOL.DLL from the Windows 9x installation CD to the system folder of each Windows 9x machine (c:\windows\system). You also need to apply the changes as supplied in the GROUPPOL.REG file (in the same directory as GROUPPOL.DLL). You run this by entering the following:

```
regedit grouppol.reg
```

This adds the following entries (if you have problems, be sure the entries exist):

```
- Registry key: HKEY_LOCAL_MACHINE\Network\Logon
Value name (STRING): PolicyHandler
Value data: GROUPPOL.DLL, ProcessPolicies
- Registry key: HKEY_LOCAL_MACHINE\System\CurrentControlSet\
Services\ MSNP32\NetworkProvider
Value name (STRING): GroupFcn
Value data: GROUPPOL.DLL, NTGetUserGroups
- Registry key:
HKEY_LOCAL_MACHINE\System\CurrentControlSet\Services\
NWNP32\NetworkProvider
Value name (STRING): GroupFcn
Value data: GROUPPOL.DLL, NWGetUserGroups
```

This could be automated by adding the copy and the Registry update to a logon script. A GROUPPOL.INF is also supplied, which enables you to install completely by right-clicking on GROUPPOL.INF and selecting Install.

All of the above actions are performed if you install the Windows 9x system Policy editor on a machine.

How do I enable load balancing on a Windows 95 machine?

With load balancing, the logons, authentication, and so on are shared between the numerous Domain Controllers and not just the Primary Domain Controller. Follow these procedures to implement load balancing:

1. Start the Policy editor (POLEDIT.EXE).
2. From the Network branch, choose Logon and Validation.
3. Choose Remote Update and Load Balance.

This enables a Windows 95 machine to look for the logon script and such from the logon server.

How can I stop a Windows 95 machine from acting as a Browse Master or Backup Browser?

To stop a Windows 95 machine from acting as a Browse Master (or a Backup Browser), perform the following:

1. On the Windows 95 machine, start the Network Control Panel applet (right-click on Network Neighborhood and choose Properties).
2. Click the Configuration tab.
3. In the list of installed network components, locate File and Printer Sharing for Microsoft Networks. If you find it, go to step 7.
4. If this is not installed, click the Add button, select Service, and click Add.
5. Select Microsoft and select File and Printer Sharing for Microsoft Networks. Then click OK.
6. Click OK to the Configuration tab and reboot the machine at the prompt.
7. Select File and Printer Sharing for Microsoft Networks and click Properties.
8. In the Property dialog box, click Browse Master.
9. In the Value box, select Disabled and click OK.

Some of the Windows 95/98 clients do not show up in Network Neighborhood. Why?

This is usually caused if the machines don't have File and Print Sharing installed.

1. Start the Network Control Panel applet (right-click on Network Neighborhood and choose Properties).
2. Click the File and Print Sharing button and then enable them (see Figure 29-2).

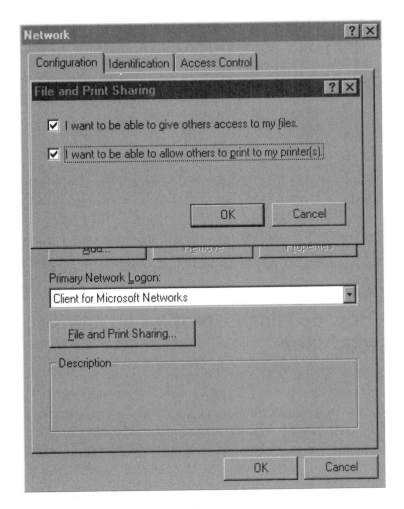

Figure 29-2. Enabling File and Printer Sharing.

 How can I stop my Windows 9x clients from having to enter a separate Windows password when logging on to a domain?

29.10

In the old Windows for Workgroups days, the ADMINCFG.EXE utility was used to disable password caching. A similar functionality exists in Windows 95 and Windows 98.

1. Start the Registry editor (REGEDIT.EXE).
2. Move to HKEY_LOCAL_MACHINE\Software\Microsoft\Windows\CurrentVersion\Policies\Network.
3. From the Edit menu, choose New > DWORD Value.
4. Enter **DisablePwdCaching** and press Enter.
5. Double-click on the new value and set to 1. Click OK.
6. Close the Registry editor and reboot the machine.

After reboot, clients will no longer have to enter a local password—just the domain password.

When clients use the Password Control Panel applet, the Change Windows Password button under Windows Password will be grayed out and only Other Passwords can be set. Clients should then select Microsoft Networking as usual.

FAQ 29.11 How do I enable profiles on a Windows 9x machine?

By default, all users of a Windows 9x machine share the same profile; however, machines can be configured so that each logon name can have individual settings for background, colors, and so on. To enable multiple profiles, perform the following:

1. Start the Passwords Control Panel applet (Start > Settings > Control Panel > Passwords).
2. Click the User Profiles tab.
3. Check the Users Can Customize Their Preferences box. You can also choose these options:
   • Include Desktop Icons and Network Neighborhood.
   • Include Start Menu and Program Groups in User Settings.
4. Click OK.
5. You will have to reboot the computer.

After reboot, the first logon on the machine will be given the option to retain options. Click Yes.

The profiles are stored in the C:\windows\profiles\<username> directory (or wherever Windows is installed).

If you want to automate this process, you can create a system policy by using the Windows 9x Policy editor.

How do I enable roaming profiles for Windows 9x machines?

After you have enabled individual profiles on the Windows 9x machines, a copy of the profile is automatically stored in the user's home directory (which is normally on a network server). The profile consists of a number of files and a USER.DAT, which is the Windows 9x equivalent of NTUSER.DAT.

Therefore, to enable roaming profiles for Windows 9x machines, here's all you need to do:

1. Ensure that all users are configured with a home directory on a network server. (This is configured by using the User Manager - Profiles button in Windows NT 4.0 or the Directory Management MMC - Profile tab in Windows NT 5.0.)
2. Make sure users have permissions to at least read, write, and modify to their home directory areas. If not, the profile cannot be copied but no error is given.

Can Windows NT and Windows 9x share a roaming profile?

No. The main problem is that Windows 9x clients store the profile in the root of their home directory, but Windows NT clients store the profile in the profile path location.

Even if you made these the same, it would still not work because there are differences in the Registry structure. Also, Windows NT stores the user portion of the Registry in the file NTUSER.DAT and Windows 9x stores it in USER.DAT.

How can I stop Windows 9x profiles from being copied to the home directory?

By default, if individual profiles are configured on a Windows 9x machine, the profile is also copied to the user's home directory (usually a network share). This means the user has the same desktop settings on any 9x machine on the network. If you don't want this behavior but still want individual settings, perform the following on each machine:

1. Start the Registry editor (REGEDIT.EXE).
2. Move to HKEY_LOCAL_MACHINE\Network\Logon.
3. From the Edit menu, choose New > DWORD Value.
4. Enter **UseHomeDirectory** and press Enter.
5. Double-click the new value and set to 0.
6. Close the Registry editor and reboot the machine.

After the reboot, the user's profile will no longer be copied to the network share.

30 SECURITY

Security is one of the most important considerations of any operating system. This is true for NT—especially its file system.

Any operating system has to be able to address C2, a major U.S. Department of Defense (DOD) standard. The Windows NT Resource Kit has a utility, C2CONFIG.EXE, that enables you to view and "fix" any problems with a click of the mouse (see Figure 30-1).

C2 Configuration Manager

File   View   Help

C2	Security Feature	Current Setting
	File Systems	2 Volumes do not use the NTFS File System.
	OS Configuration	MS-DOS is installed on the System.
	OS/2 Subsystem	OS/2 Subsystem is installed.
	Posix Subsystem	Posix Subsystem is installed.
	Security Log	The Security Log will overwrite events when full.
	Halt on Audit Failure	The System will not halt when the Security Log is full.
	Display Logon Message	A Logon Message will not be displayed.
	Last Username Display	The previous username will be displayed at logon.
	Shutdown Button	The shutdown button is displayed on the logon dialog.
	Password Length	The minimum password length is 7 characters.
	Guest Account	The Guest user account is disabled.
	Networking	One or more network services are installed on the system.
	Drive Letters & Printers	Only Administrators may assign Drive Letters and Printers.
	Removable Media Drives	The CD-ROM and Floppy Drives will be allocated at logon.
	Registry Security	Unable to read the current status of this item.
	File System Security	Unable to read the current status of this item.
	Other Security Items	Unable to read the current status of this item.

Figure 30-1. C2Config in action. Hmmm—not very secure, am I?

4.0 ONLY

How do I enable auditing?

A necessary function is viewing an audit trail of actions on a system (file system changes, user changes, and so on). With NT you can configure auditing on nearly every aspect of the operating system.

To configure auditing, log on as the Administrator (or a member of the Administrators group) on a machine and perform the following actions:

1. Start User Manager (Start Menu > Programs > Administrative Tools > start User Manager).
2. From the Policies menu, choose Audit.
3. Enable the events you want to audit and click OK (see Figure 30-2).
4. Exit User Manager.

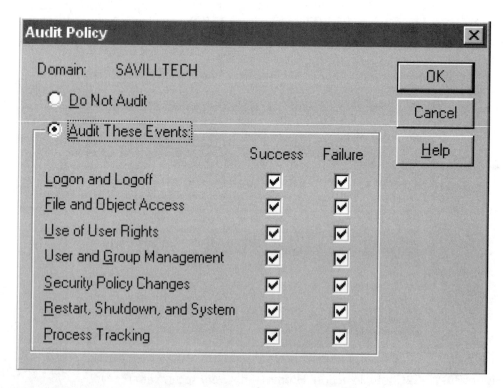

Figure 30-2. Selecting the system components to be audited.

It is also possible to configure auditing on a file or directory. Right-click on the file or directory and choose Properties. Select the Security tab and then choose Auditing. Be aware that if auditing for the objects is not turned on via User Manager, auditing on files or directories is not possible.

 ## How do I view or clear the security log?

Log settings on each log can be configured by selecting Log Settings from the Log menu of Event viewer. For the most security, you should configure it not to overwrite old settings, so you will need to clear the log manually (see Figure 30-3).

Log on as the Administrator (or a member of the Administrators group) and perform the following:

1. Start Event Viewer (Start Menu > Programs > Administrative Tools > Event Viewer).
2. From the Log menu, choose Security.

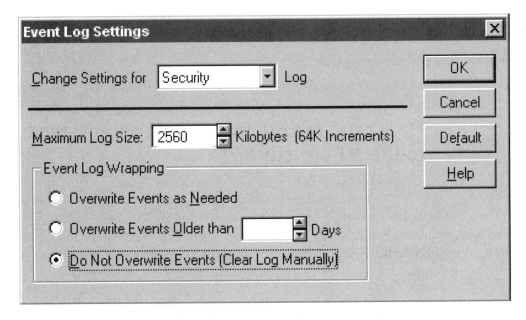

Figure 30-3. Configuring the log settings. You will want to go over security settings to check for problems.

3. Double-click any entry for more information.

4. Close the individual event information window.

5. To clear, select Log and clear all events. When asked if you want to save the information, click No.

6. When asked if you are sure, click Yes.

7. Close Event Viewer.

Where can I get information on NT security problems?

There are various sites that are updated with security problems and their fixes. To the credit of Microsoft, although NT has had its problems, a fix is generally available in a matter of days.

- http://www.ntsecurity.com
- http://www.ntsecurity.net
- http://www.microsoft.com/security
- http://www.ntfaq.com
- http://www.iss.com
- http://www.ntbugtraq.com

4.0 ONLY

How can I restore the default permissions to the NT structure?

When you install NT on an NTFS partition, strict file system protections are set; however, if you installed to a FAT partition and then converted to NTFS (by using the CONVERT.EXE utility), everyone will have full access to all files.

Use the following procedure to restore the default NTFS permissions:

1. Log on as Administrator (or a member of the Administrators group).

2. The built-in SYSTEM account needs access to the Windows NT default directories and subdirectories. To get this access, do the following:

a. In File Manager, use Security/Permissions to grant the SYSTEM account full control of the root directory of the NTFS volume that contains Windows NT.

b. Select the option to Replace Permissions on Subdirectories, which gives SYSTEM access to the entire volume.

3. Start Registry Editor (REGEDIT.EXE).

4. Go to HKEY_LOCAL_MACHINE\System\CurrentControlSet\ Control\SessionManager.

5. Double-click the value BootExecute.

6. Under BootExecute, you might find a few entries (such as autocheck autochk *). After any entries, add the following on a separate line, where <systemdrive> is the drive on which Windows NT is installed and <winnt_root> is the Windows NT root directory on that drive.

setacl /a \DosDevices\<systemdrive>:\<winnt_root>\System32\ winperms.txt \DosDevices\<systemdrive>:

7. Save your changes by clicking OK.

8. Exit the Registry editor and restart the computer.

9. On restart, the system will set security on the system files to the norm.

This procedure only works on an NT 3.51 system. To perform it on an NT 4.0 system, you need the Windows NT Resource Kit Supplement 2, and you should perform the following:

1. Log on as an account that has Backup Files and Folders privilege.

2. Run the FIXACLS.EXE utility (Start > Run > Fixacls).

3. Click the Continue button.

4. Click OK when completed.

FIXACLS sets the permissions to the values defined in %systemroot%\ INF\PERMS.INF. Therefore, access to this file is also required to run FIXACLS.

How can I copy files and keep their security and permissions?

By default, when you copy files from one NTFS partition to another, the files inherit their protections from the parent directory. It is possible to copy the files and keep their settings by using the SCOPY program that comes with the NT Resource Kit. SCOPY can copy owner and security audit information, as in the following example:

```
SCOPY c:\savilltech\secure.dat d:\temp\ /o /a
```

You can also use /s to copy information in subdirectories.

The restriction for this command is that both the origin and the target drives **must** be NTFS, or the command will fail.

How do I enable auditing on certain files and directories?

Auditing is only available on NTFS volumes. Follow these instructions:

1. Start Explorer (Win key + E, or Start > Programs > Explorer).
2. Right-click on the file or directory you want to audit and choose Properties from the context menu.
3. Select the Security tab and choose Auditing.
4. If you have selected a directory, check the Replace Auditing on Subdirectories option.
5. Click the Add button. Add any users you wish to audit by selecting them and clicking Add (see Figure 30-4). When you finish adding users, click OK.
6. Select the events you wish to audit and then click OK.

With Service Pack 4, this has moved and is now accessed by clicking Advanced under the Security tab and selecting the Auditing tab.

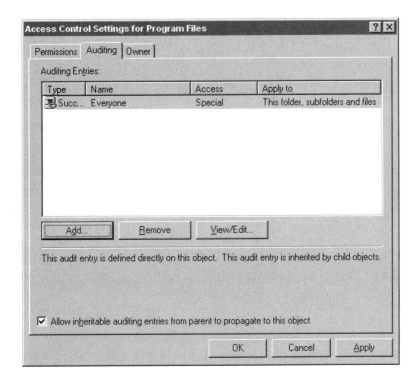

Figure 30-4. Selecting Auditing for everyone.

You must be sure that File Access auditing is enabled (Start > Programs > Administrative Tools > User Manager > Policies > Audit). You can then view these events by using the Event Viewer (Start > Programs > Administrative Tools > Event Viewer > Log > Security).

4.0 ONLY

How do I use the System Key functionality of Service Pack 3?

Service Pack 3 introduced a new feature in NT—the capability to increase security on the SAM database. You do this by introducing a new key in one of the following three modes:

1. A secure key generated by the system, which is used to encrypt the SAM stored on the local hard disk.
2. A secure key generated by the system, which is stored on a floppy disk you need to place in the computer at bootup.
3. A password given by the user, which is used to encrypt the SAM and must be entered on bootup.

To generate the system key, you use the System Key Generation utility, SYSKEY.EXE. Be warned that after you activate the encryption, you cannot turn it off without performing a system recovery by using an Emergency Repair Disk (ERD) that was produced before SYSKEY was enabled. To enable encryption, perform the following:

1. Make sure Service Pack 3 is installed.
2. Log on to the system as a member of the Administrators group (only Administrators can run SYSKEY.EXE).
3. Create a new ERD (rdisk /s) and store it somewhere safe. Label the disk "Pre System Key ERD."
4. Run the System Key Generation utility (Start > Run > SYSKEY.EXE).
5. A dialog box is displayed with encryption disabled. Select Encryption Enabled and click OK (see Figure 30-5).

Figure 30-5. Enabling security.

6. Click OK at the Warning message.

7. Select which of the three encryption modes you require (see Figure 30-6). If you select Password, enter a password and then enter it again for verification. If you choose Stored on Floppy Disk, insert a disk at the prompt and then click OK.

8. Click OK. When the Success message is displayed, click OK again.

9. You now need to reboot the machine.

10. After reboot, you should create a new ERD (rdisk /s).

If you chose to use a password, a dialog box is displayed after the GUI phase of NT starts. Enter the password you gave and click OK. Then you may log on as usual. If you chose Stored on Floppy Disk, insert the disk at the prompt and then click OK.

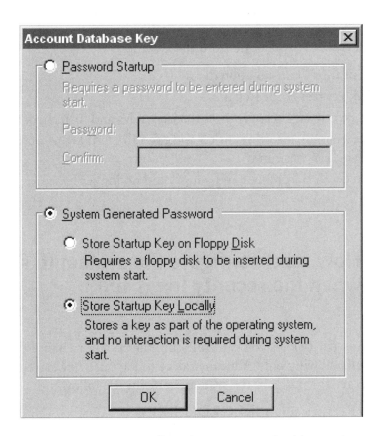

Figure 30-6. Store Startup Key Locally is the easiest method for storing a password.

Although you cannot remove the system key, you can change the mode by running SYSKEY.EXE and clicking Update. You will be asked to either enter the existing password or insert the system key floppy if you're changing from one of these modes.

For more information, see Knowledge Base article Q143475 at http://support.microsoft.com/support/kb/articles/q143/4/75.asp.

How do I remove the System Key functionality of Service Pack 3?

As stated in Question 30-7, there is not a simple Remove function. However, if you restore the SAM from an ERD that was taken before the system key was enabled, it will remove this feature from the system.

1. Boot off of the NT installation disks.
2. After disk 2, press **R** for Repair.
3. Deselect everything except Inspect Registry Files and then choose Continue.
4. Continue as usual, inserting disk 3 and then the ERD (the one created before SYSKEY was run).
5. After you do all this, reboot and you should no longer have the system key in use.

How can I configure the system to stop when the security log is full?

To avoid losing security logs, you can configure the system to halt if the security log becomes full, allowing only Administrators to log on. They can then archive the log and purge. To configure the system, perform the following:

1. Start the Registry editor (REGEDIT.EXE).
2. Move to HKEY_LOCAL_MACHINE\SYSTEM\CurrentControlSet\Control\Lsa.

3. If CrashOnAuditFail exists, skip to step 4. If it doesn't exist, choose New > DWORD Value from the Edit menu and enter CrashOnAuditFail. Then click OK.

4. Double-click on CrashOnAuditFail and set to either:
   1 - Stop if the audit log is full.
   2 - This is set by the operating system just before the system crashes due to a full audit log. (When set to 2, only the Administrator can log on.)

5. Close the Registry editor.

When the security log fills, the OS will display a BSOD (Blue Screen of Death).

 30.10 # How can I clear the pagefile at shutdown?

As you are probably aware, the pagefile contains areas of memory that were swapped out to disk and might be in a secure environment. You want this pagefile cleared when the machine is shut down, because parts of memory containing passwords or other sensitive information might have been mapped out to the pagefile.

1. Start the Registry editor (REGEDIT.EXE).

2. Move to HKEY_LOCAL_MACHINE\SYSTEM\CurrentControlSet\ Control\Session Manager\Memory Management.

3. If the value ClearPageFileAtShutdown does not exist, choose New > DWORD Value from the Edit menu and enter ClearPageFileAtShutdown (see Figure 30-7). If it does exist, go to step 4.

4. Double-click on ClearPageFileAtShutdown and set to 1.

5. Reboot the machine. Next time you shut down, the pagefile will be cleared.

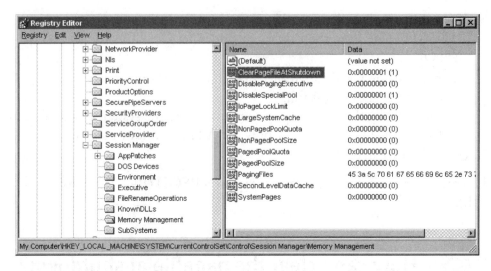

Figure 30-7. Set the value back to 0 to disable the clear effect.

30.11 How do I enable strong password filtering?

Windows NT 4.0 Service Pack 2 introduced a new password filter, PASSFILT.DLL, which implements the following new restrictions:

- Passwords must be at least 6 characters long.
- Passwords must meet at least three of the following criteria:
- Uppercase letters A–Z
- Lowercase letters a–z
- Numbers 0–9
- Nonalphanumeric character (such as !)
- Password may not contain your username or any part of your full name.

To enable this functionality, perform the following on all PDCs (and standalones, if used). You do not need to install this on BDCs; however, it's a good idea in case the BDC is promoted to a PDC.

1. Start the Registry editor (REGEDT32.EXE; do **not** use REGEDIT.EXE).
2. Move to HKEY_LOCAL_MACHINE\SYSTEM\CurrentControlSet\ Control\Lsa.
3. Double-click on Notification Packages.
4. Add PASSFILT on a new line (there might be a FPNWCLNT, so you should add this after this value). Click OK.
5. Close the Registry editor and reboot the machine.

Note that you will still be able to set passwords in User Manager that do not meet the criteria. This is by design, because direct SAM updates are not filtered.

 # How do I set what happens during a crash?

A crash dump file will be produced by default, but there are two other options that can be configured.

The first option is to enter a log entry in the system log. You can set this by using the Startup/Shutdown tab of the System Control Panel applet in NT 4.0. In Windows 2000, choose the Startup and Recovery button under the Advanced tab of the System Control Panel applet and check the box for Write an Event to the System Log.

You can also achieve this by setting the following Registry key to 1. HKEY_LOCAL_MACHINE\SYSTEM\CurrentControlSet\Control\ CrashControl\LogEvent.

The other option is to send an Administrative Alert (you need the Alerter service to be running to enable this option). Using the same dialog box, check Send An Administrative Alert.

You can also achieve this by setting the HKEY_LOCAL_MACHINE\ SYSTEM\CurrentControlSet\Control\CrashControl\SendAlert Registry key to 1.

FAQ 30.13   How can I configure the system to automatically reboot in the event of a crash?

You can set this by using the Startup/Shutdown tab of the System Control Panel applet in NT 4.0. In Windows 2000, choose the Startup and Recovery button under the Advanced tab of the System Control Panel applet and check the box for Automatically Reboot.

You can also achieve this by setting the HKEY_LOCAL_MACHINE\ SYSTEM\CurrentControlSet\Control\CrashControl\AutoReboot Registry key to 1.

31   PERFORMANCE

With an operating system as big as NT, you can set a number of tuning parameters. Compared to OpenVMS (both VMS and NT were designed by Dave Cutler), your control is quite limited. However, if you want to monitor and identify bottlenecks, NT's built-in Performance Monitor tool is fantastic.

A bottleneck is the component of the system that is limiting performance. There will **always** be a bottleneck; otherwise, tasks would finish instantly. Your task is to find the bottleneck and work on it until the performance of the system meets your expectations. The term "bottleneck" comes from visualizing a bottle when you're pouring water. The liquid is slowed down by the narrow part of the bottle—the neck—which is limiting the amount of liquid that can leave the bottle.

Physicist Werner Heisenberg's uncertainty principle states that measuring the exact position and the exact momentum of a particle at the same time is physically impossible—the act of observing interferes with the observation. This principle also applies to performance monitoring. When you monitor performance, you use additional CPU time; if you enable disk monitoring, you will experience slower disk access. However, the resource use is negligible and rarely affects your results significantly.

If you plan to install new servers, you should create a baseline performance monitor of the system for later comparison when the server is running other software or greater loads. You can thus compare the baseline to current use to detect large changes, such as high disk access.

How do I move my pagefile?

A "pagefile" is a file on disk that the operating system can use to dump out parts of its memory. It's also known as virtual memory and allows your machine to consume more than the amount of physical RAM.

Obviously, the pagefile is on a disk and many times slower than physical RAM. Whenever possible, make sure your servers have plenty of RAM, minimizing the amount of paging (the act of reading and writing memory to the pagefile).

Pagefiles can be moved, but make sure you have a 2MB pagefile on your boot partition or some crash information will be unavailable in the event of a problem. To move a pagefile, perform the following:

1. Open the Control Panel and double-click the System icon.
2. Click Performance and then Virtual Memory Change.
3. Select the current pagefile disk and change the initial size to 0. Then click Set.
4. Select a different disk and change Initial Size and Max Size. Then click Set.
5. Click OK and then close and reboot.

How big and where should my pagefile be?

To determine this, consider the following:

- There is no point in having two pagefiles on the same physical disk.
- The pagefile should be the size of memory + 11MB (or 2.5 times the size of the SAM file, whichever is larger).
- If possible, have multiple pagefiles on separate physical disks.
- Some performance gains can be had by placing the pagefile on a stripe set; however, not as much as on separate disks.
- Defragment the disk on which you put the pagefile.

- Try to make the drive NTFS.
- Minimum pagefile size should be 2MB.

To enhance performance, you can create a second pagefile on another physical disk. Moving, however, is never advised, because it disables the option to create a memory dump file at a crash (System Control Panel applet > Startup tab). In addition, so that you can dump the RAM content to the pagefile (saved as MEMORY.DMP), the pagefile **must** be located on the boot partition.

 # How can I change the size of the pagefile?

In Question 31.1, we discussed moving the pagefile; however, you might just need to modify the size of an existing pagefile or add a new one as an addition to your existing one.

Remember: The more disk heads, the better the performance, so moving your pagefile to a RAID 0 disk arrangement would give excellent performance (RAID 0 is a stripe set without parity). On the other hand, writing to a RAID 5 disk might adversely affect performance because of the extra parity information that needs to be written (RAID 5 is a stripe set with parity).

There is little point to adding a second pagefile to another partition if it is on the same physical disk. A better way would be to increase the size of the existing file; however, two smaller pagefiles on different physical disks will give even better results.

1. Start the System Control Panel applet (Start > Settings > Control Panel > System).
2. Click the Performance tab.
3. Under the Virtual Memory section, find the currently configured amount and click Change.
4. A list of all partitions appears, with the size of any existing pagefiles listed next to them. To modify the size of an existing pagefile, first select the drive (for example, C:).
5. For Paging File Size for Selected Drive, enter new Initial and Maximum sizes. Click Set when you have changed the values. The minimum size

is 2MB, but the total size of all pagefiles should be at least the size of memory + 11MB.

6. If you want to add an additional pagefile, select a drive that does not currently have a pagefile (for example, D:). Enter Initial and Maximum sizes and then click Set.

7. When you have completed all changes, click OK (see Figure 31-1).

8. Click OK again to close the System Control Panel applet.

9. You will have to reboot the machine for the change to take effect.

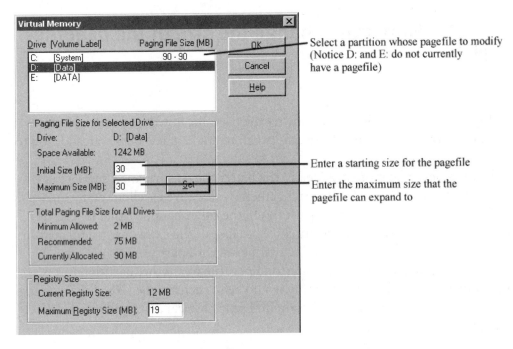

Figure 31-1. You can have as many pagefiles as you want.

Users complain server response is slow, but when I use the server everything is fine. What can cause this?

It could be the server screen saver. The OpenGL screen savers (especially the pipes) can use every CPU cycle off the server. In general, you should always use the blank screen saver on a server.

Is there a RAM disk in NT 4.0?

No. But Microsoft produced a RAM disk called NTRamdsk, which still works on NT 4.0. Download it from http://www.ntfaq.com/ntfaq/download/ntramdsk.zip.

A commercial package SuperDisk-NT is now available from EEC Systems (http://www.eecsys.com/).

How can I monitor disk performance?

NT's built-in Performance Monitor can be used to monitor disk activity, but this is not active by default. To activate it, type the following from the command prompt:

```
diskperf -y
```

You will need to reboot, and then disk activity can be viewed by using Performance Monitor.

You should use the following command if you have drives in a software RAID or striped set.

```
diskperf -ye
```

Performance Monitor is disabled by default because it slows down performance slightly.

How can I tell if I need a faster CPU?

To see how much time the computer is waiting to use the CPU, use Performance Monitor as follows:

1. Start Performance Monitor (Start > Programs > Administrative Tools > Performance Monitor).
2. Click the + button (if you cannot see a title bar, press Ctrl+T).
3. From the drop-down Object box, select System.
4. From the counters, select Processor Queue Length.
5. Monitor the system for a typical day of work. If the counter exceeds 2, you should consider a faster processor.

 ## I need to run a number of 16-bit applications. What is the best way to do this?

The best way is to create a shortcut to the 16-bit application and then right-click on the shortcut and choose Properties. Click on the Shortcut tab and check the box for Run In Separate Memory Space. This makes the application run in its own Virtual DOS Machine (VDM) with its own memory space, which improves performance and system stability because one 16-bit application can no longer affect another one.

An application can also be forced to run in its own memory space if you use

```
start /separate <application name>
```

 ## How can I run an application at a higher priority?

It is possible to start an application at a priority other than normal; however, if you run applications at high priority, they might slow performance. Priorities range from 0 to 31, with 0–15 used by dynamic applications (such as user applications and most of the operating system parts) and 16–31 used by real-time applications (such as the kernel, which cannot be written to the pagefile). Normal priority is level 8 (NT 3.51 normal was 7). Here is the full list:

- realtime   priority 24
- high   priority 13
- normal   priority 8
- low   priority 4

To start an application at a priority other than the default, use the Start command:

start /<priority> <application>
(for example, start /high winword)

Be warned that if you run applications at high priority, this might slow performance because other applications will get less I/O time. To use the /realtime option, you have to be logged on as a user with Administrator privileges.

To modify the privilege of a currently running application, use Task Manager:

1. Start Task Manager (right-click on the Start bar and open Task Manager).
2. Click on the Processes tab.
3. Right-click on the required process and choose Set Priority.
4. You can now select a different priority (see Figure 31-2).
5. Close Task Manager.

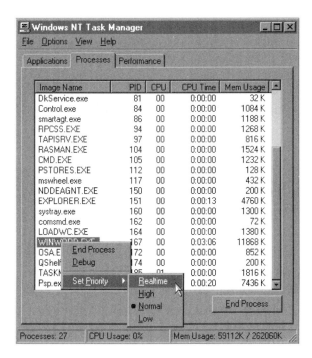

Figure 31-2. Don't click here—running Word at realtime is not a good idea.

It is also possible to increase the priority of whichever application is currently in the foreground, as opposed to the background processes, by using the following procedure:

1. Start the System Control Panel applet (Start > Settings > Control Panel > System).
2. Click the Performance tab.
3. In the Application Performance tab, move the arrow to choose one of the following:
   None: The foreground application runs the same as background applications.
   Middle: The foreground application has its priority increased by one; background applications stay the same.
   Maximum: The foreground application has its priority increased by two (for example, from 8 to 10); background applications stay the same.

 ## How can I monitor processes that start after I start the Performance Monitor?

Say you are running Performance Monitor in Log mode. Then after the log is closed, you wish to view certain processes in the drop-down list but you see only processes that were running at the time you started the log. You are not getting a true picture of the processes' performance.

1. Start Performance Monitor (Start > Programs > Administrative Tools > Performance Monitor).
2. Select Log View (choose View > Log or press Ctrl+L).
3. Add to the log the objects you wish to monitor, including Process (Edit > Add to Log). When you're finished, click Done.
4. From the Options menu, choose Log. Enter a filename and a period of time and click Start Log.
5. When you have logged enough, switch to Performance Monitor. From the Options menu, choose Log > Stop Log.
6. Move to Chart view (choose View > Chart or press Ctrl+C).
7. To load in the log you created, choose Options > Data From. Then select the file and click OK.

8. From the Edit menu, choose Add and add the counters you wish to see. Notice that under Processes, the instances are only those running when you started. But don't worry.

9. There will probably be an area you wish to investigate, such as a spike in CPU use or disk I/O. You need to alter the Timeframe window to start from the peak. Start by choosing Timeframe window from the Edit menu.

10. Move the left bar until the left line is in the correct place on the chart—the spike or whatever you want to investigate—and click OK (see Figure 31-3).

11. From the Edit menu, choose Add and look under Processes. You will now see processes that were running at **this** point, allowing you to diagnose the problem process.

12. Now you can also put the Timeframe window back to normal and this process will still show.

What this means is that the instances shown are only those running at the start of the Timeframe window. To add other processes running at other times, you might need to continue moving the start of the Timeframe window.

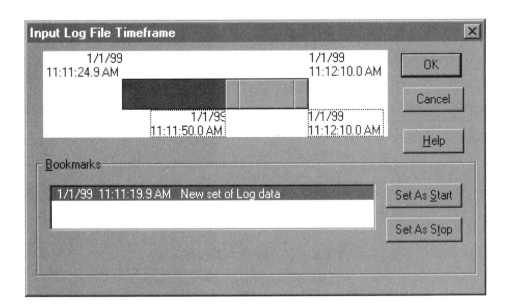

Figure 31-3. Moving the Timeframe window to when the application is running.

FAQ 31.11 How can I view information in the Event Log from the command line?

The DUMPEL.EXE utility supplied with the Windows NT Resource Kit outputs a comma- or tab-separated file, enabling the events from all three logs to be dumped on the local or remote computer. For full information, see the NT Resource Kit Tools Help, but here is the basic syntax, where <which log> could be system, application, security.

dumpel -f <filename for output> [-s \\<servername>] [-l <which log>] -c
(for example, dumpel -f applog.txt -l application -c)

This would dump out the application log as a comma-separated file (use -t instead of -c for a tab-separated file).

Another useful switch is -e <event>, which allows you to output only a given event. For example, the following would display all information about winlogon (you don't need the quotes if the event is one word).

```
dumpel -f winlogon.txt -l application -c -m "winlogon"
```

Another application is NTLast, which you can download from http://www.ntobjectives.com. This utility does two major things that Event Viewer does not: It can distinguish remote/interactive logons, and it matches logon times with logoff times. Table 31-1 gives example uses for NTLast. The final one is the most useful.

Table 31-1. The NTLast Command

ntlast	Gets a default list of the last 10 successful logons against the local machine.
ntlast /f	Gets the last 10 failed logon attempts.
ntlast /f /i	Gets the last 10 failed interactive logon attempts.
ntlast /f /r	Gets the last 10 failed remote logon attempts.
ntlast /i	Gets the last 10 successful logons.
ntlast /r	Gets the last 10 successful remote logons.
ntlast /n 6	Gets the last 6 logons.
ntlast /m machinename /f /r	Gets the last 10 failed remote attempts against machinename.

FAQ 31.12 Is there anything available to help diagnose performance problems?

You can use the Excel macro PERFMON.XLA, which you can download from http://www.ntfaq.com/ntfaq/download/perfmon.zip. Use the macro as follows:

1. Start Performance Monitor by choosing Start > Programs > Administrative Tools (Common) > Performance Monitor.
2. Move into Chart Mode (choose View > Chart or press Ctrl+C).
3. Add the following Counters by choosing Edit > Add to Chart (or click the big + on the toolbar). The first part (for example, Memory) is the Object, and the second part (for example, Pages/sec) is the Counter. Click Done when you have added all of them.

   - Memory - Pages/sec
   - Memory - Available Bytes
   - PhysicalDisk - % Disk Time
   - PhysicalDisk - Current Disk Queue Length
   - Processor - % Processor Time
   - Processor - Interrupts/sec
   - System - Processor Queue Length

4. Let the monitor run for a while and perform your normal day-to-day operations.
5. After it has run for a while, choose Export Chart from the File menu. From the Save As Type drop-down list, select Export CSV Files (*.csv).
6. Enter a filename (.csv is added automatically for you) and click Save.
7. Exit Performance Monitor.
8. Start Excel, open a new blank spreadsheet, and choose File > Open.
9. In the Files of Type box, select Add-Ins and then move to the directory to which you extracted PERFMON.XLSelect PERFMON.XLA and click Open.
10. Choose Open from the Planning menu. Move to the directory in which you saved the file in step 6. Select the file and click Open.

11. Choose Bottlenecks from the Planning menu to see a list of possible bottlenecks. Selecting one will give more detail in the Suggestions area. Click OK when you are finished.

12. You can also create a chart by choosing Create Chart from the Planning menu. Select the counters you want to show on the chart and click OK.

This macro is only basic, but it might give you some starting points to investigate, and it automates the line of thinking you should be following.

 Is there any way to output performance logs directly to a comma-separated file?

The Windows NT Resource Kit ships with the PerfLog service, which can output data directly to a file in comma- or tab-separated format. To install PerfLog, perform the following:

1. Copy the following files from the NT Resource Kit installation dir\PerfTool\LogTools to the %systemroot%\system32:
   PDLCNFIG.EXE
   PDH.DLL
   PDLSVC.EXE
   PERFLOG.HLP
   PERFLOG.CNT

2. Run PDLCNFIG to install the service.

3. Click OK to install the service.

4. The Performance Data Log Service dialog box is displayed with two tabs, enabling you to add Counters and to designate the location of the file for output.

To start the service, select it from the Services Control Panel applet and click Start. You can also start from the command prompt by typing

```
net start performance data log
```

To change the configuration later, just rerun PDLCNFIG.EXE.

How can I control the amount of memory NT uses for file caching?

31.14

Windows NT does not allow much tuning of caching except for one Registry entry, as follows:

1. Start the Registry editor (REGEDIT.EXE).
2. Move to HKEY_LOCAL_MACHINE\SYSTEM\CurrentControlSet\ Control\ Session Manager\Memory Management.
3. Double-click on LargeSystemCache and set to **0** to reduce the amount of memory used for file caching.
4. Click OK and close the Registry editor.

If you start the Network Control Panel applet and select the Services tab, you can select Server, click Properties, and then choose Maximize Throughput for Network Applications to use less memory (this actually sets LargeSystemCache to 0). System Internals has released CacheSet (http://www.sysinternals.com), which allows you to more specifically set the memory used for caching.

How can I stop Windows NT system code and drivers from being paged?

31.15

Normally, user-mode and kernel-mode drivers and kernel-mode system code is written to either pageable or nonpageable memory. It is possible to configure NT never to page out drivers and system code to the pagefile if they are in the pageable memory area; however, you should only do this on systems with large amounts of RAM to prevent severe performance problems.

1. Start the Registry editor (REGEDIT.EXE).
2. Move to HKEY_LOCAL_MACHINE\SYSTEM\CurrentControlSet\ Control\Session Manager\Memory Management.
3. Double-click on DisablePagingExecutive and set to **1**. Click OK (it is of type DWORD, so create it if it does not exist).
4. Reboot the machine.

FAQ 31.16 How can I speed up the performance of my OS/2 applications?

Many applications written for OS/2 will run faster under a Virtual DOS Machine (VDM) because NT allocates more resources to a VDM than to the OS/2 subsystem. Therefore, you should disable the OS/2 subsystem as follows:

1. Start the Registry editor (REGEDIT.EXE).
2. Move to HKEY_LOCAL_MACHINE\SYSTEM\CurrentControlSet\ Control\Session Manager.
3. Double-click on GlobalFlag and change from 0 to **20100000**. Click OK to save.
4. Close the Registry editor and reboot the machine.

32 PROBLEM-SOLVING

Many items of this book resolve problems, but this chapter addresses specific problems that require resolution. This chapter covers such problems as deleting reserved system filenames, installing a CPU, and debugging NT.

4.0 ONLY
FAQ 32.1 I have installed Office 97 and now I can no longer use Desktop Themes. Why?

Desktop Themes will be familiar to Windows 95/98 users. They are basically a method of saving the desktop's background, icons, colors, pointers, and sounds as a package and then applying the package to change the whole look of the desktop.

There was a bug with Office 97 that corrupted the JPEG loader used with Themes. To repair the bug, download the THEMEFIX.EXE patch from ftp://ftp.microsoft.com/bussys/winnt/winnt-public/reskit/nt40/themes/i386/ThemeFix.exe.

I cannot delete a file called AUX.BAT or COM1. Why?

A file of which the name (or a part of it) is equal to a DOS device (including NUL, COMx, AUX, LPTx, PRN) cannot be deleted with Explorer or the usual DEL syntax.

Instead, use DEL \\.\drive:\path\AUX.BAT, replacing drive and path with appropriate values, as in this example:

```
del \\.\c:\tempfiles\aux.bat
```

These files might be the remains of a failed installation. You can create them, for example, by typing COPY "some existing file" \\.\drive:\path\COM1.

 ## I can't delete a directory called CON. Why?

CON is a reserved name. To delete it, you must use the Uniform Naming Convention (UNC), like this:

rd \\.\\<drive letter>:\\<dir>
(for example, rd \\.\c:\john\con)

 ## The AT command does not work. Why?

A sine qua non for using AT is a running Scheduler service. To start the service, type **net start schedule** on the command line or use Control Panel/Services. (If you want to use it regularly, set the Startup Type to Automatic.)

A common problem is that people try to use the example given in the online help: AT sometime CMD /C DIR > TEST.OUT. Unfortunately, in NT 4.0 this does not work anymore. You must use AT sometime CMD /C "DIR > TEST.OUT" instead. The execution of the command starts by default in

%systemroot%\system32, as can be seen from the output of the previous example. You should specify the complete path if the command is in a different directory (for example, AT sometime C:\TEMP\TEST.BAT).

A further problem is that the command is executed in the security context of the LOCAL SYSTEM account, and not the caller. However, the SYSTEM account does not have access to network resources, so your program cannot reside on or access files on mapped drives (even if they are mapped from the local machine). Also, environment variables (such as PATH) might be set differently. You can test the environment interactively by using AT sometime /INTERACTIVE CMD.

What is USER.DMP?

USER.DMP is created by Dr. Watson when a program crashes. This file is there to help you fix the problem. You can examine it by using \support\debug\i386\ dumpexam.exe or windbg -z user.dmp. You can delete this file without any worries. The syntax for DUMPEXAM.EXE is

dumpexam -y <symbol file location> <dumpfilename and location>
(for example, dumpexam -y d:\winnt\symbols d:\winnt\memory.dmp)

The output from dumpexam will be placed at %systemroot%\MEMORY.TXT.

To stop this file from being created, start the System Control Panel applet, select the Startup/Shutdown tab, and uncheck the Write Debugging Information To check box.

4.0 ONLY

I can't format a disk or create an Emergency Repair Disk. Why?

There are a number of possible explanations. First, if you're using Service Pack 2, ensure that you have applied the kernel fix. Also, some virus killers (such as Dr. Solomons) lock up drives, making a format impossible because NT recognizes the drive as locked (this is why you can't create an Emergency Repair Disk). Stop the virus process by choosing Control Panel > Services, clicking on the Virus Killer process, and clicking Stop. After the disk is formatted or you've created the Emergency Repair Disk, go back to the Control Panel and start the Virus Killer process again.

When I change CDs or access the floppy drive, NT crashes. Why?

This is probably caused by the bug in Service Pack 2. If you have Service Pack 2, apply the kernel fix from ftp://ftp.microsoft.com/bussys/winnt/winnt-public/fixes/usa/nt40/hotfixes-postSP2/krnl-fix/KRNL40I.EXE.

After a new installation of NT, I can log on, but no shell starts. Why?

Usually a normal user will have this problem, not an Administrator, because the problem is security on files. To cure this problem, the security on the %systemroot% needs to be set so the Everyone group has Read, Execute (RX) access.

If the shell does not start from any account, you need to do one of these:

- Reformat the drive and reinstall.
- Boot from another installation of NT that does not have this problem.
- Install onto another volume that does not have security set.

For more information see http://support.microsoft.com/support/kb/articles/q155/5/79.asp.

4.0 ONLY
32.9 I have a Matrox Millennium graphics card, and the windows blink and flash when moved. Why?

If you are using the graphics card at 1600x1200 resolution in True Color 24-bit or True Color 32-bit mode, a window's frame might blink or flash when you drag the window across the screen. This is a known problem, and to resolve it, enable the Show Window Contents While Dragging option from the Plus tab in the Display control dialog box (Start > Settings > Control Panel > Display).

4.0 ONLY
32.10 When I start NT, I get NTDETECT twice. Why?

This is caused by a missing or corrupt NTDETECT.COM. To resolve this problem, copy the latest NTDETECT.COM from either the latest service pack or—if no service packs have been applied—from NT installation disk 1.

32.11 My desktop disappears after a crash. Why?

By default, if Explorer crashes, it automatically restarts; however, Explorer might have been corrupted or changed. Use the Registry editor change the value of the following HKEY_LOCAL_MACHINE\SOFTWARE\Microsoft\Windows NT\CurrentVersion\Winlogon\AutoRestartShell to 1.

4.0 ONLY

32.12 I have installed a second CPU; however, NT will not recognize it. Why?

When moving from a single CPU to dual CPUs, you must install multiprocessor versions of a number of NT files, including the HAL and the OS kernel. The UPTOMP.EXE utility, contained in the NT Resource Kits, installs the multi-processor files. The files can be installed manually (see the MS Knowledge Base Articles Q156358, "How to Manually Add Support for a Second Processor," and Q168132, "After Applying Service Pack NT Reports Single Processor").

The MS Knowledge Base Article Q142660, "Upgrade from Uni- to Multi-processor (Uptomp.exe) and Win32k.sys," describes a known problem that occurs when UPTOMP.EXE is used on a version 4.0 NT system. The fix described in the article is to add the following line to the file UPTOMP.INF, located at the base directory of the Resource Kit installation (reskit):

```
win32k.sys=0, 2, win32k.sys
```

Finally, if you install the multiprocessor files on a system to which a service pack has been applied, you probably need to reapply the service pack after running UPTOMP.EXE and before rebooting. Until you reapply the service pack, your disk contains a mix of file versions, with the multiprocessor files at the revision level of the distribution media and files already present at the service pack revision level. Such a mix of versions can cause your reboot to fail.

For Compaq Proliant servers, Compaq has provided a very automated method of changing the HAL that does not require the NT Resource Kit and is distributed on the Compaq SmartStart CD. The time from opening the case until the last reboot seems to be 45 minutes (and that was by a user).

32.13 I reinstalled NT and now I cannot log on. Why?

When you reinstall NT, a new security identifier (SID) is created for the machine. It is therefore necessary to remove the computer account for the machine from the NT server and then add a new entry.

Domain Controllers keep track of the SIDs of workstations that are allowed to be part of the domain. When you reinstall the machine, even if you use the same computer name and IP address, a new SID is generated and thus you are refused access to the domain's resources.

You can remove an account from a domain by using Server Manager (Start > Programs > Server Manager). Select the computer and then choose Computer > Remove From Domain. To then re-add the computer, choose Computer > Add To Domain, select the machine's type, and enter its name—the same as before (see Figure 32-1).

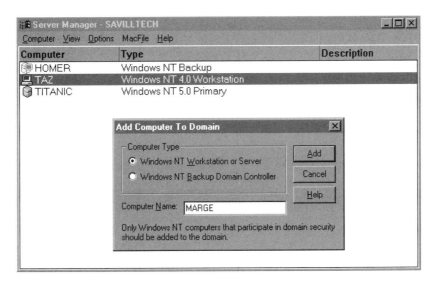

Figure 32-1. A distinction between Domain Controllers and normal servers or workstations has to be made (as Domain Controllers all share a common SID).

4.0 ONLY

32.14 I have Windows 95 installed and I am trying to start the NT installation, but it fails. Why?

If you want to install NT from within Windows 95, start a command session (COMMAND.COM) and type **lock**. This enables direct disk access for the NT installation program. Remember to use WINNT.EXE (not WINNT32.EXE).

32.15 ## An application keeps starting every time I start NT. Why?

Sometimes when an application is installed, the setup program adds the program in such a way that it starts automatically each time a user logs on or the machine starts.

Applications can be started from a number of places, as listed in Table 32-1. Try looking at each until you find the application. When you find the application, simply delete it.

Table 32-1. Startup Locations for Applications

In the Startup folder for the current user and for the All User group.
In the Registry (use a Registry editor, such as REGEDIT.EXE):
HKEY_LOCAL_MACHINE\Software\Microsoft\Windows\CurrentVersion\Run
HKEY_LOCAL_MACHINE\Software\Microsoft\Windows\CurrentVersion\RunOnce
HKEY_LOCAL_MACHINE\Software\Microsoft\Windows\CurrentVersion\RunServices
HKEY_LOCAL_MACHINE\Software\Microsoft\Windows\CurrentVersion\RunServicesOnce
HKEY_LOCAL_MACHINE\Software\Microsoft\Windows NT\CurrentVersion\Winlogon\Userinit
HKEY_CURRENT_USER\Software\Microsoft\Windows\CurrentVersion\Run
HKEY_CURRENT_USER\Software\Microsoft\Windows\CurrentVersion\RunOnce
HKEY_CURRENT_USER\Software\Microsoft\Windows\CurrentVersion\RunServices
HKEY_CURRENT_USER\Software\Microsoft\Windows\CurrentVersion\RunServicesOnce
HKEY_CURRENT_USER\Software\Microsoft\Windows NT\CurrentVersion\Windows, Run and Load keys

4.0 ONLY

FAQ
32.16

Each time I start NT, I get a file-delete sharing violation. Why?

There is a problem with TweakUI and the Clear Document History At Logon option that can result in an error message of "Cannot delete <filename>, there has been a sharing violation." Disable the TweakUI Document History Clear option (see Figure 32-2)—or just press OK each time the error message appears.

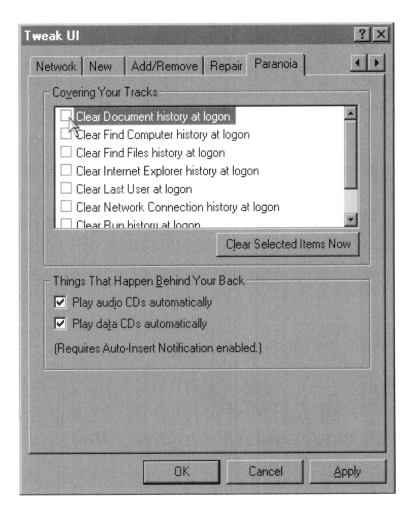

Figure 32-2. Disabling the Clear Document history at Logon option.

32.17 Sometimes when I run a program or Control Panel applet, I get a "No disk in drive a:" message. Why?

It is possible that the NT path statement includes an "a:," which means whenever the program searches for something, it tries the disk drive. Check these locations. If you find a: defined in any path, remove it.

- Registry entry HKEY_LOCAL_MACHINE\SYSTEM\Setup\WinntPath
- Registry entry HKEY_LOCAL_MACHINE\SYSTEM\CurrentControlSet\Control\Session Manager\Environment\Path
- Control Panel > System > Environment > the global and user path statements
- AUTOEXEC.BAT
- %systemroot%/system32/Autoexec.nt

4.0 ONLY

32.18 When I try to create an Emergency Repair Disk, I get an error message of "One or more configuration files missing." Why?

Run the rdisk /s a few times, and this error will fix itself. Adding /s also stores user information to the repair area.

4.0 ONLY

32.19 I have installed Service Pack 3 and now I cannot run Java programs. Why?

Download the latest version of Internet Explorer, which includes the latest virtual machines.

A hotfix for Service Pack 3 is available from Microsoft at ftp://
ftp.microsoft.com/bussys/winnt/winnt-public/fixes/usa/nt40/
hotfixes-postSP3/archive/java-fix/JAVAFIXI.EXE
Service Pack 4 also includes this fix.

4.0 ONLY
FAQ 32.20 Every time I start NT, Explorer starts, showing the system32 directory. Why?

This is caused by an incorrect program call at startup. Look for an incorrect entry in one of the areas from which a program can be started. These are listed at Question 32.15.

4.0 ONLY
FAQ 32.21 I have removed my IDE CD-ROM drive and now NT will not boot. Why?

Unless it is hardware-related—for example, you have not connected the cable correctly or you have not set the master/slave correctly—you need to perform the following actions before disconnecting the CD-ROM drive. Therefore, if you have already disconnected the CD-ROM drive, you should reconnect it temporarily and perform this procedure:

1. Start the SCSI Control Panel applet (Start > Settings > Control Panel > SCSI) and click the Drivers tab.
2. Select the IDE CD-ROM (ATAPI 1.2) and click Remove.
3. Start the Devices Control Panel applet (Start > Settings > Control Panel > Devices). Select the ATAPI device and click Startup. Set the Startup type to Disabled.
4. Select the ATDISK device and choose Startup. For the type, select Boot and click OK.
5. Copy ATDISK.SYS from the i386 directory on the NT installation CD to the %systemroot%\system32\drivers directory.

6. Shut down Windows NT and remove the CD-ROM drive.

You should now be able to boot normally. See Knowledge Base Article Q125933 for more information.

4.0 ONLY
32.22   I get an error message, "WNetEnumCachedPasswords could not be located in MPR.DLL." Why?

This is usually caused by an incorrect MAPI32.DLL. Sometimes the software installs the Windows 95 version. Copy MAPI32.DLL from your NT installation CD to %systemroot%/system32.

32.23   What information is shown on the Blue Screen of Death (BSOD)?

The NT operating system has two basic layers: the user mode and the kernel mode. The user mode cannot directly access hardware, is limited to an assigned address space, and operates at Ring 3 (lower priority). If a user mode program has an error, NT just halts the program's process and generates an operation error. Because the application runs in its own virtual address, it cannot affect any other program. The following components commonly run in user mode:

- Logon Process
- Security Subsystem
- Win32 Application and Subsystem
- OS/2 Application and Subsystem
- POSIX Application and Subsystem

NT 4.0 introduced a change in the NT architecture. Because the kernel mode process runs much faster (Ring 0), they moved video and printer drivers from user mode to kernel mode. Kernel mode is a privileged processor mode, allowing direct access to the memory and hardware. Kernel mode errors are not usually recoverable, and a reboot of the system is required.

The BSOD is a built-in error-trapping mechanism that is used to halt any further processing to avoid system and data corruption. This means a faulty graphics or printer driver could now crash NT. Components in kernel mode are

- Various managers, handling I/O, objects, security, interprocess communication (IPC), graphics, window, and virtual memory
- Microkernel that provides the basic operating system functionality
- Hardware abstraction layer
- Device drivers

But what does the BSOD (or STOP message screen) show? Following is the basic structure of the BSOD; however, what you see will differ and you might not have some of the sections, as I explain after the example.

```
Section 1: Debug Port Status Indicators
DSR CTS SND


Section 2: BugCheck Information
*** STOP: 0x0000000A (0x00000002,0x00000000,0xDB30442D)
IRQL_NOT_LESS_OR_EQUAL *** Address db30442d has base at
db300000 > matrxmil.SYS

CPUID: GenuineIntel 5.2.4 irql:1f SYSVER 0xF0000565


Section 3: Driver Information
Dll Base  DateStmp > Name    Dll Base    DateStmp > Name
80100000  2cd348a4 > ntoskrnl.exe 80400000    2cd348b2 >
hal.dll
80010000  2cd348b5 > ncrc810.sys  80013000    2cda574d >
SCSIPORT.SYS
and so on.


Section 4: Kernel Build and Stack Dump
Address dword dump Build [1381] -Name
xxxxxxxx xxxxxxxx xxxxxxxx xxxxxxxx xxxxxxxx xxxxxxxx
xxxxxxxx > matrxmil.SYS
xxxxxxxx xxxxxxxx xxxxxxxx xxxxxxxx xxxxxxxx xxxxxxxx
xxxxxxxx > ntoskrnl.exe
```

```
xxxxxxxx xxxxxxxx xxxxxxxx xxxxxxxx xxxxxxxx xxxxxxxx
xxxxxxxx > ntoskrnl.exe
etc.
```

Section 5: Debug Port Information

Restart and set the recovery options in the system Control Panel or the /CRASHDEBUG system start option. If this message reappears, contact your system administrator or technical support group.

OR if your system is started with /debug or /crashdebug:

Kernel Debugger Using : Com2 (Port 0x2f8, Baud Rate 9600)
Beginning Dump of physical memory
Physical memory dump complete. Contact your system administrator or technical support group.

Section 1: This section is shown only if the system was started with /debug or /crashdebug. To tell if your system is debugger-enabled, look at the boot menu when you start the machine—you'll see the words [debugger enabled] next to the Windows NT menu choice. To enable /debug, follow these instructions:

1. Modify BOOT.INI to be editable by typing

   `attrib c:\boot.ini -r -s`

2. Edit the file and edit the Windows NT start line to include /debug (to tell the system to load the kernel debugger into memory at bootup) or /crashdebug (to tell the system to load the kernel debugger but swap it out to the pagefile). Other options are /debugport to tell which COM port to use (by default, COM2) and /baudrate for the speed (by default 19200, but better to be 9600), like this:

   ```
   [operating systems]
   multi(0)disk(0)rdisk(0)partition(0)\WINDOWS="Windows NT"
   /debug /debugport=com3 /baudrate=9600
   ```

3. Save the file.
4. Set the BOOT.INI attributes back:

   `attrib c:\boot.ini +r +s`

The three-letter combinations are signals. For example, RTS means Ready to Send, DSR means Data Send Ready, CTS means Clear to Send, and SND means data is being sent to the COM port.

Section 2: This section contains the error (or BugCheck) code with up to four developer-defined parameters (defined in the KeBugCheckEx() function call). In this case, the BugCheck was 0x0000000A IRQL_NOT_LESS_OR_EQUAL, which means a process attempted to access pageable memory at a process level that was too high (usually caused by a device driver).

A BugCheck of 0x00000077 or 0x0000007A means the pagefile could not be loaded into memory. The second hexadecimal value helps you diagnose the cause, as shown in Table 32-2.

Table 32-2. Hexadecimal Values in BugCheck

0xC000009A	STATUS_INSUFFICIENT_RESOURCES, caused by lack of nonpaged pool.
0xC000009C	STATUS_DEVICE_DATA_ERROR, generally due to bad block on the drive.
0xC000009D	STATUS_DEVICE_NOT_CONNECTED, bad or loose cabling, termination, or controller not seeing drive.
0xC000016A	STATUS_DISK_OPERATION_FAILED, also caused by bad block on the drive.
0xC0000185	STATUS_IO_DEVICE_ERROR, caused by improper termination or bad cabling on SCSI devices.

For a full list of what the codes mean, see Knowledge Base Article Q103059 at http://support.microsoft.com/support/kb/articles/q103/0/59.asp.

Section 3: This lists all drivers that were loaded at the time of the crash. It is split into two sides, with three columns to each side. The first column is the link time stamp (in seconds since the year 1970) and can be converted into real time by using the CVTIME.EXE application (f$cvtime on VMS).

Section 4: This includes the build number of the operating system and a stack dump that shows the addresses used by the failed module. The top lines might show the offending code/driver—not always, however, because the kernel trap handlers might execute last to preserve error information.

Section 5: This depends on whether you have the /debug setup, but it basically shows the communication settings and whether a .DMP file has been created.

32.24 I have created my own application service; however, when the user logs off, the application stops. Why?

When a user logs off, a number of messages are sent. For graphical applications, the messages WM_QUERYENDSESSION and WM_ENDSESSION are sent, and for console (character mode) applications, the message CTRL_ LOGOFF_EVENT is sent. If your application responds to these messages, the application might cause itself to stop. You will need to modify your program to either ignore the messages or handle them differently. There is more information on this topic in the Resource Kit.

 4.0 ONLY

32.25 I can't install any software. Why?

Sometimes the file CONFIG.NT becomes corrupted, specifically the files= line. Therefore, perform the following:

1. Start Notepad (Start > Programs > Accessories > Notepad).
2. Open %systemroot%/system32/config.nt. For example,

   `d:/winnt/system32/config.nt`

3. Check at the bottom for this line:

   ```
   files=40
   ```

4. If it is something like files=20$%THY, CONFIG.NT has been corrupted and you should change it to have only a number after the equals sign.
5. Save the file and reboot.

I get an error message, "This application is not supported by Windows NT." Why?

Sometimes this happens because the following files do not have everyone:full access protection if the boot partition is NTFS.

```
%SystemRoot%\system32\config.nt
%SystemRoot%\system32\autoexec.nt
```

To check or change this protection, perform the following:

1. Start Explorer (Win key + E, or Start > Programs > Explorer).
2. Move to %systemroot%\system32 (for example, d:\winnt\system32).
3. Right-click on the file (CONFIG.NT or AUTOEXEC.NT) and choose Properties.
4. Click the Security tab and click Permissions.
5. You can now view or change the protection.
6. Click OK when you're finished.

I have installed IE 4.0 and now my shortcut icons are corrupt. Why?

This is caused by an incompatibility between the final version of Internet Explorer 4.0 and TweakUI. To fix this, you need to uninstall TweakUI.

1. Start the Add/Remove Control Panel applet (Start > Settings > Add/Remove Programs).
2. Select TweakUI and click Add/Remove.

If you get an error saying it could not be removed, you can manually remove it by entering the following command:

```
rundll32 syssetup.dll,SetupInfObjectInstallAction
DefaultUninstall 4 e:\winnt\inf\tweakui.inf
```

Now reboot the computer.

Another method to try is to delete the hidden file %systemroot%\shellIconcache as follows and restart Windows NT. The "correct" desktop icons will be re-created when you log on.

```
attrib %systemroot%\shelliconcache -h
del %systemroot%\shelliconcache
```

If you find after the reboot that the icons are still corrupt, install TweakUI again and then remove it. TweakUI can be downloaded from www.microsoft.com/windows/downloads/contents/WUToys/NTTweakUI/default.asp.

4.0 ONLY
32.28 I have lost access to the root of the boot partition, so now I can't log on. What can I do?

If you set the root of the boot partition to No Access, you will be unable to log on. To get around this, perform the following:

1. Log on to the NT machine as Administrator.
2. When you get the blue screen and "Path too Long," click the OK button.
3. Press Ctrl+Alt+Del. The Windows NT Security dialog box appears.
4. Click the Task Manager button. The Task Manager appears.
5. Select the Applications tab and click the New Task button.
6. Enter the path **%systemroot%\system32\cmd.exe**.
7. Enter the following command, where d is the boot partition.

```
CACLS d:\ /e /g everyone:F
```

8. Select Task Manager again and click New Task.
9. Enter **%systemroot%\explorer.exe**, and the desktop should now appear.
10. Log off and log on again to confirm that everything is OK.
11. You should now set the permissions on the root.

For more information, see Knowledge Base Article Q155315 at http://support.microsoft.com/support/kb/articles/q155/3/15.asp.

4.0 ONLY

I received the error message, "WNetEnumCachedPasswords could not be located in MPR.DLL." Why?

This problem is caused when the file MAPI32.DLL has been replaced by an application installation, usually with the Windows 95 version. To correct the problem, reinstall the MAPI32.DLL file from the NT installation CD, as follows:

1. Insert the NT installation CD.
2. Back up your current MAPI32.DLL by typing

```
copy %systemroot%\system32\mapi32.dll
%systemroot%\system32\mapi32.old
```

3. Move to the installation directory for your processor type on the CD; for example, **cd i386**.
4. Enter the following command:

```
expand -r mapi32.dl_ %systemroot%\system32
```

If you have applied service packs, be aware that MAPI32.DLL was redelivered in some of the service packs, so you should take MAPI32.DLL from the service pack delivery (expand the service pack and then copy the file over).

4.0 ONLY

How can I perform a kernel debug?

Before you perform a kernel debug, the computer should be connected via a null modem cable or a modem connection for dial-in purposes. I'll refer to the computers as Host for the machine that performs the debug and Target for the machine that has the problem and is being debugged.

The computers should both be running the same version of Windows NT, and the symbol files for the Target machine should be installed on the Host machine. The symbol files are supplied on the Windows NT installation CD in the Support\Debug directory.

The Target computer's BOOT.INI entry needs to be modified as follows to allow debugging:

1. Modify BOOT.INI to be editable:

   ```
   attrib c:\boot.ini -r -s
   ```

2. Open the file and edit the Windows NT start line to include **/debug** (to tell the system to load the kernel debugger into memory at bootup). Other options are **/debugport** to tell which COM port to use (by default COM2) and **/baudrate** for the speed (by default 19200, but better to be 9600). For example:

   ```
   [operating systems]
   multi(0)disk(0)rdisk(0)partition(0)\WINDOWS="Windows NT
   Debug" /debug /debugport=com2 /baudrate=9600
   ```

3. Save the file.
4. Set the BOOT.INI attributes back:

   ```
   attrib c:\boot.ini +r +s
   ```

In this example, the Target machine will allow a debug connection, using COM2 at a speed of 9600 bps.

The Host computer needs to be configured with the information necessary to perform the debug and the installation of the symbol files.

To install the symbol files, move to the \support\debug directory on the CD and enter this command:

expndsym <CD-ROM>: <target drive and directory>
(for example, expndsym f: d:\symbols)

This might take some time. Remember that if you have installed service packs on the Target machine, the symbol files for these also need to be installed on the Host computer. The symbol files for service packs need to be downloaded from Microsoft separately.

The next stage is to configure the environment variables needed for the debugging, such as the symbol file location. These are shown in Table 32-3.

Table 32-3. Environment Variables for Debugging

_NT_DEBUG_PORT	COM port to be used (for example, COM2).
_NT_DEBUG_BAUD_RATE	Speed for the connection (for example, 9600). Make sure this matches the /baudrate specified on the target machine.
_NT_SYMBOL_PATH	Location of the symbols files (where you expanded them to by using the expndsym utility).
_NT_LOG_FILE_OPEN	Name of the file used for the log of the debug session (optional).

It might be worth putting the definition of the environment variables into a command file to avoid having to type in the commands every time. Do so like this:

```
echo off
set _nt_debug_port=com2
set _nt_debug_baud_rate=9600
set _nt_symbol_path=d:\symbols\i386
set _nt_log_file_open=d:\debug\logs\debug.log
```

Next you should copy over the kernel debug software, which is located in the support\debug\<processor> directory on the NT installation CD (for example, **support\debug\i386**). It is easiest just to copy over the entire directory, because it is not very large (around 2.5MB). The actual debugger for the i386 platform is i386KD.EXE, and you would just enter i386KD to start the debugger. To enter a command, press Ctrl+C and wait for the kd> prompt.

4.0 ONLY

32.31

How do I configure remote kernel debugging?

If you find you do not have the knowledge to debug a Windows NT problem, you might need to get Microsoft to perform the debug for you. In this scenario, three computers will be involved—the computer at Microsoft, the host machine, and the target machine.

The Microsoft machine will need to connect via RAS to either the host machine or a computer on the same network, so one machine will need to run the RAS Server service.

The configuration is the same as in Question 32.30, except that on the Host machine, instead of entering the command i386kd.exe, enter the following command, where debug is the name of the session (this can be anything):

```
remote /s "i386KD -v" debug
```

At the Microsoft end, after they have connected to the network, they would enter this command:

```
remote /c <computer name of the host> debug
```

Again, debug is the name of the session and must match the session name configured at the Host machine.

4.0 ONLY

I get the error message, "Not enough server storage is available to process this command." Why?

This problem might happen because the machines have a non-zero PagedPoolSize in the Registry. You can set the paged pool size by performing the following:

1. Log onto the server as an Administrator.
2. Start the Registry editor (REGEDIT.EXE).
3. Move to HKEY_LOCAL_MACHINE\SYSTEM\CurrentControlSet\ Control\Session Manager\Memory Management.
4. Double-click on PagedPoolSize and set to **0**.
5. Click OK.
6. Close the Registry editor and reboot the machine.

A PagedPoolSize of 0 allows NT to dynamically allocate memory. The installation of software such as ARCServe is known to cause this "Not enough server storage" error.

This can also happen when you are accessing a Windows NT Server share from a Windows NT client if IRPstackSize is too small. To correct, try the following:

1. Log onto the server as Administrator.
2. Start the Registry editor (REGEDIT.EXE).
3. Move to HKEY_LOCAL_MACHINE\SYSTEM\CurrentControlSet\ Services\LanmanServer\Parameters.
4. Double-click on IRPstackSize.
5. Increase the value. Valid ranges are between 1 and 12. Click OK.
6. Reboot the machine.

After setting this, you might find that other connections, such as those to NetWare volumes, gain a performance boost.

Another cause for the "Not enough server storage" error is if you installed Service Pack 3 or later before installing any network components. If this is the case, reapply Service Pack 3 and any subsequent hotfixes. A good practice is to reapply a service pack whenever you modify or add components to the system.

4.0 ONLY

32.33

I get an error when I try to export any profile other than the Administrator profile. Why?

This is usually due to insufficient privilege on the Protected Storage System Provider\<SID> key. To be able to export your profile, perform the following:

1. Log on as you.
2. Start the Registry editor (REGEDT32.EXE).
3. Select the HKEY_CURRENT_USER on Local Machine window.
4. Move to Software\Microsoft\Protected Storage System Provider\<SID>.
5. Select Permissions from the Security menu and click Add.
6. Select Domain Admins (or whatever you want), access type READ, and click Add. Then click OK.

You should now be able to export this profile. To be able to export someone else's profile, perform the following:

1. Log on as an Administrator.
2. Start the Registry editor (REGEDT32.EXE).
3. Select the HKEY_USERS on Local Machine window.
4. From the Registry menu, choose Load Hive.
5. Move to the person's profile area in the %systemroot%\Profiles\<name> (for example, d:\winnt\Profiles\batman).
6. Select the NTUSER.DAT file and click Open.
7. When asked for a key name, enter the person's name (for example, John) and click OK.
8. Move to <user name>\Software\Microsoft\Protected Storage System Provider\<SID>.
9. Choose Permissions from the Security menu and click Add.
10. Select Domain Admins (or whatever you want), access type READ, and click Add. Then click OK.
11. Choose Unload Hive from the Registry menu.
12. Close the Registry editor.

You will now be able to export this user's profile.

4.0 ONLY

32.34

I have chosen a screen resolution that has corrupted the display and now I can't change it back. What can I do?

When you attempt to change screen resolution, Windows NT asks you to test it. If you ignore this and set the display to a resolution that causes a problem, your only course of action is to boot in VGA mode. While in VGA mode, set the resolution back to something you know works.

1. Reboot the machine.
2. Select the following option:

    Windows NT Workstation Version 4.00 [VGA mode] (or Server)

    If you find you don't have this option, edit BOOT.INI and add a line similar to your normal NT Workstation startup with the /basevideo /sos. For example, use the following:

```
multi(0)disk(0)rdisk(0)partition(2)\WINNT="Windows NT
Workstation Version 4.00 [VGA mode]" /basevideo /sos
```

3. The machine boots in base 16-color VGA mode.
4. Open the Display Control Panel applet (Start > Settings > Control Panel > Display).
5. Click the Settings tab and change to a resolution you know works (use the test).
6. Click OK.

I get the error message "Boot record signature AA55 not found (1079 found)." Why?

If Windows NT is installed on a logical drive in an extended partition (the fourth partition is usually the extended start), the following error message will appear after you select the OS choice and NTDETECT runs:

> OS Loader 4.0 Boot record Signature AA55 Not Found, xxyy Found.
> Windows NT could not start because of a computer disk hardware configuration problem.
> Could not read from the selected boot disk. Check boot path and disk hardware.
> Please check the Windows NT Documentation about hardware disk Configuration and your hardware reference manuals for additional information.

The Master Boot Record (MBR) consists of boot code that is used by the system BIOS to read the partition table. From data contained in the partition table, the MBR can determine which partition is set to be bootable (active) and also the starting sector of that partition. After that location is determined, the BIOS jumps to that sector and begins the next phase of the boot process by executing additional code that is operating-system specific.

If you have files required for boot located above 1024 cyl, it will fail. If you're running SCSI, there's a chance you can get around it by using the SCSI driver as NTBOOTDD.SYS. If you're on IDE, you're out of luck.

Windows NT 5.0 gets around the boot failure if any files needed for boot are above cylinder 1024 with an updated NTLDR. This file can be copied to a Windows NT 4.0 installation on the active partition without any ill effects—just make sure you have Service Pack 4 applied to the system before you copy the NT 5.0 NTLDR.

If the only thing wrong with sector zero is that the last two bytes are not AA55, you can fix this with a disk editor such as Norton Diskedit. However, this message is usually indicative of something overwriting or destroying the entire boot sector (sector zero), including the partition table entries.

When you install Windows NT on a logical drive in an extended partition, OSLOADER needs to "walk the extended partition table" through BIOS calls to get to the partition in which you have Windows NT installed. Each of these logical drives is addressed in a "daisy chain" of partition tables. Each sector that contains a partition table entry **must** end with AA55 as the last two bytes in the sector.

The best way to determine how to recover is to use a disk editor to see if the partition table entries are still intact. Each sector occupies 512 bytes. The first 446 bytes of sector zero contain the MBR boot code, followed by the partition table entries and ending with AA55. If the partition table entries are still intact at offsets 1BE through 1FD, manually record their values and then write AA55 starting at offset 1FE. After the signature AA55 is written, you can regenerate the MBR boot code by using the FDISK.EXE program from MS-DOS version 5.0 or later, as follows:

FDISK /MBR

Warning: This process will repair the bootstrap code and the AA55 signature by rewriting sector zero, but it will also overwrite the partition table entries with all zeros, rendering your logical drives useless (unless, that is, you manually enter the AA55 signature by using a disk editor prior to performing the FDISK /MBR).

If the partition table entries are not intact or were overwritten with unreadable characters, the problem is more involved and entails locating the Master Boot Sector (MBS) for each partition and manually rebuilding the partition table entries. This process is beyond the scope of this book.

To speed recovery from future MBR corruption, use the Windows NT 4.0 Resource Kit utility DISKSAVE.EXE to save a copy of the MBR to a floppy disk. You can use this if needed at some future date to restore the MBR by using DISKSAVE.EXE.

In the case where Windows NT is installed on a logical drive in an extended partition, you will need a disk-editing utility such as Norton Diskedit so you can examine each sector containing an extended partition logical drive entry to make sure it ends with AA55. This process is beyond the scope of this book.

A virus in your boot sector might also cause this "Boot record signature AA55 not found" problem, so run an anti-virus program on your boot sector if in doubt.

When I boot up NT, it pauses for about 30 seconds on the blue screen. Why?

Each dot is part of the boot-time chkdsk (AUTOCHK.EXE), and every three dots represents one drive, so the number of dots should equal three times the number of drives. Sometimes if something is wrong with the drive, represented by a pause in the startup dots, the startup will be delayed. However, there is a known problem with NT such that if your computer has one or more IDE disks and one or more SCSI disks, the result is a pause of around 30 seconds. This problem is due to the detection code used by NT and is currently being investigated by Microsoft.

When I run RDISK, I receive a "Disk is Full" error. Why?

When you run RDISK.EXE, it updates the directory %systemroot%\repair with the files shown in Table 32-4.

Table 32-4. RDISK Update 5Files

File	Registry Hive
AUTOEXEC.NT	This is not a Registry hive but rather a copy of the AUTOEXEC.NT file located in the %systemroot%\system32 directory.
CONFIG.NT	This is not a Registry hive but rather a copy of the CONFIG.NT file located in the %systemroot%\system32 directory.

Table 32-4. RDISK Update 5Files (continued)

DEFAULT._	HKEY_USERS\.Default
NTUSER.DA_	New user profile
SAM._	Parts of HKEY_LOCAL_MACHINE\Security
SECURITY._	HKEY_LOCAL_MACHINE\Security
SETUP.LOG	Details of location of system and application files along with cyclic redundancy check information for use with a repair
software._	HKEY_LOCAL_MACHINE\Software
system._	HKEY_LOCAL_MACHINE\System

As the system is used, the files SETUP.LOG, SAM._, and SECURITY._ will grow. The SAM._ and SECURITY._ files are only updated if RDISK.EXE is run with /s qualifier (rdisk /s).

If the contents of the %systemroot%\repair directory exceed 1.44MB, you will receive the error "The Emergency Repair Disk is full. The configuration files were saved in your hard disk." You should look at the contents of the repair directory and ascertain which file is the problem—for example, SETUP.LOG might be 1MB.

If SETUP.LOG is the problem, you can perform the following:

1. Create a copy of SETUP.LOG in the repair directory, as follows:

```
copy %systemroot%\repair\setup.log
%systemroot%\repair\setup.backup
```

2. Edit the SETUP.BACKUP file, using Notepad.
3. Move to the [Files.WinNt] section and remove all entries except those starting with %systemroot%\system32 (or whatever %systemroot% equates to, such as winnt).
4. Save the modified file.
5. Run RDISK.EXE.
6. When completed, delete the SETUP.LOG that was created:

```
del %systemroot%\repair\setup.log
```

7. And copy the backup version back:

```
copy %systemroot%\repair\setup.backup
%systemroot%\repair\setup.log
```

If the problem is not SETUP.LOG but is that the SAM._ and SECURITY._ files are too large, the problem is too many accounts on the system, so you need to examine your users and groups and it might be possible to remove old/unused accounts.

What you can do is locate an ERD that was created early in the computer's life on which the SAM._ and SECURITY._ files are small and copy these to the %systemroot%\repair directory. Then in the future, do not run RDISK.EXE with the /s option. This does mean that account information will not be recoverable and you will need to know what the Administrator password was when the original ERD was created (if the ERD is used, accounts will be set back to their state when originally created, including the Administrator password).

Obviously, you will still want to be able to restore accounts in the event of a disaster, so I suggest doing one of the following:

- Use NTBACKUP.EXE with the option of backing up local Registry.
- Use the REGBACK.EXE and REGREST.EXE that come with the resource kit to back up the entire Registry to file and then restore, like this:

```
REGBACK d:\Registry.bku
```

For more information, see Knowledge Base Article Q130029 at http://support.microsoft.com/support/kb/articles/q130/0/29.asp.

32.38 My shortcuts try to resolve to UNC paths. Why?

When you create shortcuts, they are automatically created with an UNC with \\<Computer name>\<file> in the .LNK file. This is usually a problem if you copy shortcuts to other machines; however, there are a number of ways to fix this.

To fix a single shortcut, you can use the SHORTCUT.EXE program supplied with the Windows NT Resource Kit Supplement 1.

To dump out a shortcut, use the following:

```
shortcut -u <file>.lnk
```

To alter the shortcut not to track the machine before you copy it to others, use the command

```
shortcut -c -s -n <shortcut name>.lnk
```

To change the target and working directory on a moved shortcut, use

```
shortcut -c -t d:\www.ntfaq.com\index.html -d
d:\www.ntfaq.com -n ntfaq.lnk
```

To disable link tracking for all shortcuts, perform the following:

1. Start the Registry editor (REGEDIT.EXE).
2. Move to HKEY_LOCAL_MACHINE\SOFTWARE\Microsoft\
    Windows\CurrentVersion\Policies.
3. If the Explorer key exists, move to it. If it does not exist, create it by using
    Edit > New Key Explorer. Select the new key.
4. Create a new value LinkResolveIgnoreLinkInfo of type DWORD (Edit >
    New DWORD Value).
5. Double-click the new value and set to 1.
6. Close the Registry editor.
7. Log on and off for the change to take effect.

4.0 ONLY

32.39

When I select a hyperlink or open a channel, the system32 folder opens. Why?

This has now been fixed in Service Pack 4.

As a workaround, you should either remove the Active Desktop or wait one minute before logging on when the Logon box is displayed.

4.0 ONLY

32.40 When I try to use WinAT, I get a Dr. Watson error. Why?

This is usually caused if the Resource Kit is installed in a long filename directory (for example, d:\program files\reskit). To solve this problem, install the Resource Kit in a short-name directory (8 characters or fewer).

32.41 Drive mappings are being created by themselves. Why?

One known cause of this behavior is the FIND FAST.EXE application that is supplied with Office 97. If **both** parts of either of the following sets of conditions are true, drive mappings might be created automatically.

Condition Set 1

1. You perform a search in either the Open dialog box or the Advanced Find dialog box in any Microsoft Office 97 program.
2. The drive you search contains shortcuts specifying a target location that uses a network drive letter instead of a universal naming convention (UNC) path (for example, \\<Server>\<Share>).

Condition Set 2

1. Find Fast is installed in your Startup group.
2. You index a drive that contains shortcuts specifying a target location that uses a network drive letter instead of a UNC path.

A number of resolutions are possible:

- Install Service Pack 3 or later.
- Avoid searching folders that contain shortcuts (.LNK files).
- Change shortcut target locations to UNC paths (for example, d:\folder\ john.txt to \\<server>\<folder>\john.txt).
- Disable Find Fast.

My experience with Find Fast is that it uses up a great deal of system resources and is not worth the resource use for what it does, so option 4 might be your best bet.

See Knowledge Base Article Q150604 (http://support.microsoft.com/support/kb/articles/q150/6/04.asp) for more information.

I can't create a partition over 1GB when using an Adaptec 2940 SCSI controller. Why?

As the machine boots up, you should be able to press Alt+A to take you into the SCSI BIOS. Under Advanced Host Adapter Settings, enable Extended BIOS Translation for DOS Drives >1GB.

I get a STOP 0x00000078 error. Why?

This can be caused by a bug in Windows NT; the error is produced if the NonPagedPoolSize is greater than 7/8 of your physical memory. To correct this, perform the following:

1. Start the Registry Editor (REGEDIT.EXE).
2. Move to HKEY_LOCAL_MACHINE\SYSTEM\CurrentControlSet\Control\Session Manager\Memory Management.
3. Double-click on NonPagedPoolSize.
4. Change this to less than 7/8 of your physical memory (or set to 0 to let NT set it dynamically). Click OK.
5. Close the Registry editor and reboot the computer.

4.0 ONLY

32.44

A file TESTDIR.TMP is created on a shared volume that cannot be deleted. Why?

When a file or folder is copied to a shared NTFS volume, a file TESTDIR.TMP is created and then automatically deleted. Sometimes the user performing the copy does not have Delete permission on the shared NTFS volume. In this case, the file is not deleted and has to be manually deleted by someone who has the Delete privilege.

To fix this, give the Delete permission to the user or group who performs the copies.

1. Log on as an Administrator to the machine that hosts the NTFS volume.
2. Start Explorer (Win key + E, or Start > Programs > Explorer).
3. Right-click on the NTFS volume and choose Properties from the context menu.
4. Select the Security tab and click the Permissions button.
5. Click the Add button, select the user or group required, and click OK.
6. In the main Permissions dialog box, select the new user. For Type of Access, choose Special File Access.
7. Check the Delete box and click OK.
8. Click OK to close the Permissions dialog box and OK again to close the Drive Properties dialog box.

32.45

How can I replace an in-use NT system file?

If you attempt to replace any of the core NT system files, you'll get a message that the file is currently locked. The Windows NT Resource Kit ships with MV.EXE, which is a 32-bit version of the POSIX MV utility. This utility enables file moves to be scheduled for the next reboot, which means the system files will not be locked by the operating system.

The basic format of MV follows:

```
mv /x /d d:\temp\ntfs.sys d:\winnt\system32\drivers\ntfs.sys
```

The /x means do not save a copy of the file that is replaced. If you do not specify /d, a hidden system subdirectory called "deleted" will be created under the destination directory and a copy of the original file will be placed there.

The /d means do not copy the file until reboot time. The first filename is the file to be copied, and the second is the destination name and directory of the copy.

You can do this rescheduling without using the MV.EXE utility by just manually updating the Registry (which is all MV does).

1. Start the Registry editor (REGEDT32.EXE, **not** REGEDIT.EXE).
2. Move to HKEY_LOCAL_MACHINE\SYSTEM\CurrentControlSet\ Control\Session Manager.
3. Double-click on PendingFileRenameOperations (or create of type multi_str if it does not exist).
4. On the first line is the name of the file that will replace the current file, with \??\ in front, like this (see Figure 32-3):

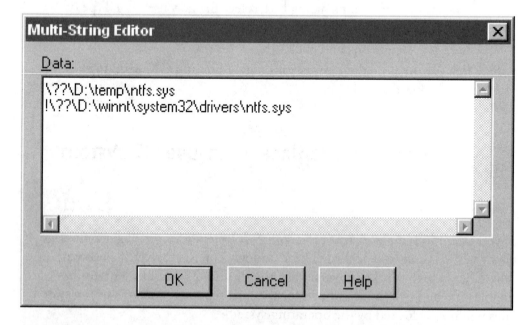

Figure 32-3. This would replace the default NTFS.SYS with the version in the d:\temp directory.

```
\??\d:\temp\ntfs.sys
```

5. On the second line is the file to be replaced, with !\??\ in front, like this:

```
!\??\d:\winnt\system32\drivers\ntfs.sys
```

6. Click OK and reboot.

After the reboot is complete and the file replaced, the PendingFileRenameOperations value will be deleted from the Registry.

 # I removed my folder association and cannot open any folders. What can I do?

Fortunately, you can fix this with two simple commands, which should be run from a command session (CMD.EXE), as follows:

1. From the Start menu, choose Programs and then Command Prompt (or choose Run and enter **cmd.exe**).

2. Enter the following commands:

```
ftype folder=%SystemRoot%\Explorer.exe /idlist,%I,%L
assoc folder=folder
```

3. Close the command session.

The first command creates a new file type, folder, and the action associated with it. The second command creates the association between the "extension" and its file type.

 # The batch file I schedule to run does not work with the /every switch. Why?

You might find that if you submit a batch file without the /every switch, it works fine, like this:

```
AT 22:00 /interactive command.bat
```

However, if you try the following, it fails:

```
AT 23:00 /every:M,T,W,Th,F /interactive command.bat
```

To correct this, add cmd /c "<batch file>", like this:

```
AT 23:00 /every:M,T,W,Th,F /interactive cmd /c "command.bat"
```

4.0 ONLY
32.48 I have a volume of type Unknown in Disk Administrator. Why?

If you have a partition in Disk Administrator that is of type unknown, it does not necessarily mean the partition is corrupt. If the user has no permissions on the root of the drive, the file type will be shown as Unknown. To correct this, perform the following:

1. Start Explorer (Win key + E, or Start > Programs > Explorer).
2. Right-click on the root of the partition and choose Properties.
3. Select the Security tab.
4. Click the Ownership button.
5. Click the Take Ownership button.
6. Click Yes for all confirmation dialog boxes.

The file system type of the partition will now be visible in Disk Administrator.

32.49 I am unable to use Start from the command line for files with spaces in them. Why?

The Windows NT Start command enables users to create a separate window/process to run a specified program. If you try to run something that consists of a long filename with a space in quotes, it fails and just brings up an empty CMD.EXE window. For example, the following command will fail:

```
start "d:\documents\ntfaq book\contents.doc"
```

To make it work, put only the part that has the long name in quotes, like this:

```
start d:\documents\"ntfaq book"\contents.doc
```

It will now work okay. This applies to anything, including a server or share, as in this example:

```
start \\"<server with space>"\"<share with space>"\"<dir with
space>"\"<file with space>"
```
(for example, start \\"johns server"\"docs share"\"ntfaq dir"\"table of contents.doc")

The first item in quotes should be the title of the window, so a better way to work around the problem is to use the following:

```
start "" "d:\documents\ntfaq book\contents.doc"
```

This will work fine, and there can be as many spaces as you want in any part.

32.50 I am not offered the option to install from an INF context menu. Why?

The options given from a context menu are derived from its file type entry under HKEY_CLASSES_ROOT\inffile. The first item to check is that .INF is associated with inffile, and you can check this with

```
assoc .inf
.inf=inffile
```

If you do not get the response shown here, enter this command:

```
assoc .inf=inffile
```

The next step is to check that the context menu item "Install" exists for inffile:

1. Start the Registry editor (REGEDT32.EXE).
2. Move to HKEY_CLASSES_ROOT\inffile\shell.
3. Check for a subkey Install. If it does not exist, choose Add Key from the Edit menu and enter the name **Install.**

4. The default entry from Install (called <No Name>) should be &Install. If it does not exist, choose Add Value from the Edit menu. Do **not** enter any name, but select type REG_SZ and click OK.

5. When asked for a string, enter **&Install** and click OK.

6. Under the Install key should be another key, Command. If this does not exist, again create it by using Add Key from the Edit menu.

7. Under the command key should be a default value (called <No Name>), which should have the data "%systemroot%\system32\rundll32.exe setupapi,InstallHinfSection DefaultInstall 132 %1" in it. If the default key is missing, choose Add Value from the Edit menu. Do **not** enter any name, but select type REG_EXPAND_SZ and click OK.

8. When asked for a string, enter the following:

```
%SystemRoot%\System32\rundll32.exe
setupapi,InstallHinfSection DefaultInstall 132 %1
```

9. Click OK and close the Registry editor.

You should now have an install option for .INF files.

4.0 ONLY 32.51 How can I deallocate corrupt memory?

If you get the blue screen or Dr. Watson often, your memory might be corrupt or you have mixed the memory.

For testing this FAQ, I have mixed two EDO-SIMMs (2x16MB) with two normal SIMMs (2x16MB) on an ASUS-Board P55 TP4-XE (this board can use mixed memory). After this, I often received Dr. Watson errors.

You should use the MAXMEM switch in BOOT.INI to deactivate the corrupt memory bank until such time as mixed memory is no longer in the main board. The MAXMEM switch always uses the lowest physical memory addresses and therefore always uses bank0+. During the NT boot process, NT probes the memory hard to make sure it is really there and working—generating a blue screen if any memory tests fail.

1. First, set the attributes on BOOT.INI so you can edit it:

```
attrib c:\boot.ini -r -s -h
```

2. Edit BOOT.INI and add the Switch (for example, /MAXMEM=32) to
   the end of your Windows NT option:

```
multi(0)disk(0)rdisk(0)partition(1)\WINNT="Windows NT
Workstation Version 4.00" /maxmem=32
```

3. Save the file and reset the attributes:

```
attrib c:\boot.ini +r +s +h
```

4. Reboot the machine.

Windows NT uses this switch and limits the whole memory from 64 to 32MB
and chooses only the good memory bank. You can also use this switch to observe
the swapping process if you're limiting the whole memory.

I am unable to run certain 16-bit applications. Why?

32.52

Certain 16-bit applications won't run under Windows NT—for example, if they
try to directly access hardware. However, if you're receiving any of the following
errors, you might be able to do something about it:

- Cannot run 16-bit Windows program. This program requires a newer
  version of Windows.
- Cannot run the 16-bit program. The application is not supported by
  Windows NT.
- Can't run 16-bit Windows program. One of the library files needed to run
  <program> is damaged. Please reinstall this application.

A possible cause for these errors is if any of the following dynamic link libraries
are missing, corrupt, or simply the wrong version:

- compobj.dll
- ddeml.dll

- ole2.dll
- ole2disp.dll
- storage.dll
- ctl3dv2.dll
- ole2nls.dll
- stdole.tlb
- typelib.dll
- ver.dll

To fix this, expand and copy the missing files from the latest service pack or hot-fix you have applied or—if the files are not in the latest service pack—from your Windows NT installation CD.

Another cause might be that the file NTVDM.EXE has been deleted from your %systemroot%\system32 directory, so check this.

I have a service stopping NT from booting. What can I do?

Normally you can modify the start behavior of services by using the Services Control Panel applet (or Computer Management MMC Snap-in > System Tools > Services in Windows 2000). When you modify the startup of a service, you actually change a value, Start, under the Services Registry key (HKEY_LOCAL_MACHINE\SYSTEM\CurrentControlSet\Services).

The first action to try is to choose the LastKnownGood configuration when Windows NT boots. If this does not work, keep reading.

The Start value of a service can have a number of values, as defined in Question 6.32 in Chapter 6, System Configuration.

To modify the startup state of a service from outside of NT, you need to install a second copy of Windows NT on the machine. If you can get the System file from the machine onto another machine by using a tool such as ERD Commanded (from http://www.winternals.com), the extra copy is not necessary.

1. Install a second copy of NT (minimal) to a different partition.
2. Boot into the second copy of NT and start REGEDT32.EXE.
3. Select the HKEY_LOCAL_MACHINE window.
4. From the Registry menu, choose Load Hive.

5. Move to your **original** NT installation partition and folder and then to system32\config (for example, c:\winnt\system32\config).

6. Select System file and click Open.

7. Enter a name for this temporary opening of the hive (for example, **OrigSystemHive**).

8. Select the new hive—which you perhaps named OrigSystemHive—and click Select.

9. Check the value of Default, which is usually 1. This number is *x* (you'll see what I mean).

10. Now move to OrigSystemHive\ControlSet00x (for example, OrigSystemHive\ControlSet001).

11. Under this key, choose Services. Then find your problem service and select it.

12. Double-click the service's Start value and modify it (4 will disable the service, 2 will set it to autostart). If you have a more complex problem, you might need to alter the Type value to change the time when the service attempts to load.

13. Move back to the base (OrigSystemHive) and choose Unload Hive from the Registry menu. Click Yes in the warning box.

14. Reboot into your original NT installation, and your service problem should be resolved.

You can now delete your second copy of NT if you wish; however, it is always useful and takes up a minimal amount of space.

Another solution is to use ERD Professional, which allows you to specify startup options for services and drivers from outside of NT. Have a look at http://www.winternals.com.

If I run winfile d:, it starts Explorer. Why?

If you try to pass a drive to WINFILE.EXE (the old File Manager, pre 4.0), expecting it to start by default on that drive, you will find that it starts WINFILE as normal and then opens an Explorer view of the specified drive.

For example, the following command would start a File Manager session and an Explorer session pointing to the D: drive:

```
winfile d:
```

This behavior is not a bug but is caused by a misunderstanding of the parameters expected by WINFILE.EXE. If you pass any parameters to WINFILE.EXE, it interprets that it should run the parameters as a program. For example, typing the following will start a File Manager session and a Notepad session editing FILE.TXT:

```
winfile notepad c:\file.txt
```

Explorer starts if you specify a drive letter, because under NT and 95/98, any directory listings are executed by Explorer. Try typing C: from Run—it will start Explorer, pointing to the C: drive.

4.0 ONLY
32.55 I have problems with tips after Service Pack 4. Why?

If you receive an access violation from IntelliPoint Productivity Tips (TIPS.EXE) when starting Windows NT 4.0 SP4, it is recommended that you install the latest version of IntelliPoint software, available from the Microsoft Web site at http://www.microsoft.com/products/hardware/mouse/. Version 2.2c should fix the problem.

If IntelliPoint does not solve the problem, perform the following:

1. Start the Registry editor (REGEDIT.EXE).
2. Move to HKEY_LOCAL_MACHINE\SOFTWARE\Microsoft\Windows\CurrentVersion\Run.
3. Look for a Tips value. If you find one, delete it.

4.0 ONLY
32.56 After installing Service Pack 4, my ATAPI/IDE Zip drive is not available. Why?

This seems to happen because the drive is not assigned a drive letter. To resolve, perform the following:

1. Insert a Zip disk into the drive.
2. Start Disk Administrator (Start > Programs > Administrative Tools > Disk Administrator).
3. Right-click on the Zip drive and choose Assign Drive Letter.
4. Select a drive letter (H, for example) and click OK.
5. The change takes effect, and the drive should now be visible from Explorer.

32.57 Disk Power Management does not work after Service Pack 4. Why?

After Service Pack 4 is applied, the Windows NT operating system accesses the disk every five minutes, interfering with Disk Power Management features. This disk access is caused by a time stamp used by the Event Log service and was intended for NT Server only but has been enabled on Workstation.

To fix the time stamp, perform the following:

1. Start the Registry editor (REGEDIT.EXE).
2. Move to HKEY_LOCAL_MACHINE\SOFTWARE\Microsoft\Windows\CurrentVersion\Reliability.
3. From the Edit menu, choose New > DWORD Value and enter the name **TimeStampInterval**.
4. Double-click the new value and set it to 0.
5. Close the Registry editor.
6. Reboot the machine.

4.0 ONLY
32.58 I get the error message "Your password must be at least 0 characters long." What can I do?

If you enable the strong password filter (for information on this, see Question 30.11 in Chapter 30, Security) but your domain account policy has no password restrictions and allows blank passwords, you will get the following error:

> Your password must be at least 0 characters long. Your new password cannot be the same as any of your previous 0 passwords. Also, your site might require passwords that must be a combination of uppercase, lowercase, numbers, and non-alphanumeric characters. Type a password that meets these requirements in both text boxes.

To resolve this, you need to turn off the secure password filter, as follows:

1. Start the Registry editor (REGEDT32.EXE).
2. Move to HKEY_LOCAL_MACHINE\SYSTEM\CurrentControlSet\ Control\Lsa.
3. Double-click on Notification Packages.
4. Remove the value PASSFILT.
5. Click OK and close the Registry editor.
6. Reboot the machine.

Alternatively, turn off the capability to have blank passwords:

1. Start User Manager.
2. Choose Account from the Policies menu.
3. Set the minimum password length to 6 or above.
4. Click OK.

What is Remote Explorer?

Remote Explorer is a new NT-specific virus. If you wish to check your Windows NT system for this virus, you can look in the Service applet in the Control Panel. If you see a service called Remote Explorer, you might be infected by this virus.

The virus has been known to hit MCI Worldcom and results in .EXE, .TXT, and .HTML file damage.

A virus killer is available from http://www.nai.com/products/antivirus/remote_explorer.asp.

33 PRINTING

In any medium to large organization, each computer will not have its own printer but will instead share with a number of other client machines. This section looks at the configuration and optimization of printing with Windows NT.

FAQ 33.1 How do I create a queue to a network printer?

If you have a printer that has its own network card and IP address, such as a JetDirect card, you can create a queue to the device by following these instructions:

1. Log in as a member of the Administrators group.
2. Open the control panel (Start > Settings > Control Panel).
3. Double-click Network and select the Services tab (or right-click on the Network Neighborhood icon and choose Properties from the context menu).
4. Click Add and select Microsoft TCP/IP printing.
5. Click OK and then Close.
6. Click Yes to the reboot.
7. After the reboot, double-click My Computer.

8. Double-click Printers and choose Add Printer. The Add Printer Wizard opens. Click Next.

9. Indicate that you're installing a local printer and then click Next.

10. Click Add Port, and select LPR port.

11. Click New Port. Fill in the IP address of the printer in the top box and a name in the bottom box.

12. Click OK and ignore the error message about not being able to communicate.

13. Click Next and then select the printer driver.

14. Click Next and choose whether you want to share it. Then click Finish.

The device will now be available to be used by clients via the server for which the queue has been configured

How can I restart the Print Spooler service?

The Print Spooler service can be restarted in either of two ways:
The first method is via the Service Control Panel applet, as follows:

1. Start the Services Control Panel applet (Start > Settings > Control Panel > Services).

2. Select Spooler and click Stop.

3. After the service has stopped, click Start.

An alternate method is from the command line:

```
net stop spooler
net start spooler
```

You could combine the above commands into a command file to enable simpler restarting of the print spooler service.

How do I delete a network port (for example, LPT3)?

Network ports are defined in the Registry at HKEY_LOCAL_MACHINE\
SOFTWARE\Microsoft\Windows NT\CurrentVersion\Ports. To delete a
port, perform the following:

1. Start the Registry editor (REGEDIT.EXE).
2. Move to HKEY_LOCAL_MACHINE\SOFTWARE\Microsoft\
   Windows NT\CurrentVersion\Ports.
3. Select the port you wish to delete (see Figure 33-1).
4. From the Edit menu, choose Delete.

An alternative method is to delete a port from the command line by using the
net.exe command, like this:

```
net use lpt3: /del
```

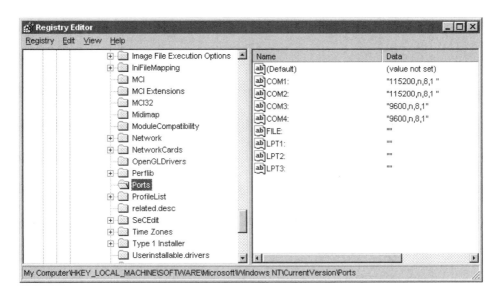

Figure 33-1. Example of the typical ports defined in a Windows NT installation.

33.4 # How do I configure my print jobs to wait until after business hours?

If you have large print jobs you would rather run at a less busy time, you can configure usage hours on the print queue, as follows:

1. Double click My Computer.
2. Choose Printers.
3. Right-click on your printer and choose Properties.
4. Click the Scheduling tab. At the top, in the Available section, enter From and To times, such as 6:00 a.m. and 10:00 p.m. (see Figure 33-2).
5. Click OK to save your changes.

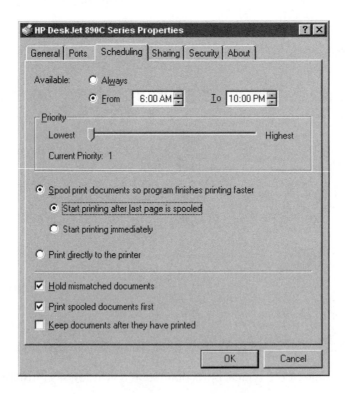

Figure 33-2. Setting the available hours for printing.

Jobs submitted to this print queue will now be printed only between the hours specified. If you want some jobs to be printed immediately, you can define two queues, one for overnight and one for all hours. Both queues can be assigned to the same printer.

How can I disable the printer pop-up message?

A sometimes-useful feature is for the print server to send an alert to a client when a submitted print job has completed. This feature can be disabled in two ways. If the printer is a local printer, perform either of the following actions on the local machine. If the printer is on a print server, the actions should be performed on the print server.

Method 1

1. Start the Registry editor (REGEDIT.EXE).
2. Move to HKEY_LOCAL_MACHINE\SYSTEM\CurrentControlSet\Control\Print\Providers.
3. Double-click on NetPopup and set to **0**. Then click OK.

Method 2

1. Start the Printer Control Panel applet (Start > Settings > Control Panel > Printers).
2. From the File menu, choose Server Properties.
3. Select the Advanced tab.
4. Uncheck the box for Notify When Remote Documents Are Printed.
5. Click OK.

Whichever method you use, you will need to restart the machine for the change to take effect. Alternatively, restart the Print Spooler service.

33.6 # How do I change the print spool location?

The print spooler is where messages waiting to be printed are stored. You might wish to move this to a faster disk to improve performance.

To move the print spool location, perform the following actions:

1. Start the Registry editor (REGEDIT.EXE).
2. Move to HKEY_LOCAL_MACHINE\SYSTEM\CurrentControlSet\ Control\Print\Printers.
3. Double-click on DefaultSpoolDirectory.
4. Modify the directory specification to the required location. Click OK.
5. Close the Registry editor.

For the change to take effect, you will need to stop and start the Print Spooler service.

This procedure will change the print spool area for all printers. To change the print spool for only one printer, move down to a printer key and create a value of type REG_SZ called SpoolDirectory. Set this as where the spool files should be for this particular printer.

 33.7 # How do I enable drag-and-drop printing?

To enable drag-and-drop printing, all you have to do is create a shortcut to the printer on your desktop.

1. Start the Printers Control Panel applet (Start > Settings > Control Panel > Printers).
2. Right-click on the printer and drag to the desktop. Release and choose Create Shortcut(s) Here.

You can now just drag files over the printer and they will be printed (providing they are registered file types that NT knows how to print).

How do I configure a print separator page?

A print separator page is configured by creating a text file, using a number of special control codes. The basic codes that can be used in the separator page are shown in Table 33-1.

Table 33-1. Control Codes for Printer Separator Page

$	This can be any character, and it must be the first character on the first line. Choose a character not normally used as the control character—in this case, choose $.
$LUser Name $N	$L is used to display normal text until another code is found. $N displays the username.
$L, Job Number $I	$I displays the job number.
$E	$E means end of page.
BS	Turns on block character printing.
$D	Data job printer.
$F<filename>	A file to print.
$H	Printer-specific control code.
$x	Where x is a number of blank lines to print.
$T	Time when job was printed.
$U	Turns off block character printing.
$Wxx	Width of the separator page.

To configure the printer to use the separator file, perform the following:

1. Start the Printers Control Panel applet (Start > Settings > Control Panel > Printers).
2. Right-click on a printer and select Properties.
3. Click the Separator Page button.
4. Enter the path and filename of the separator pagefile and click OK.
5. Click OK again to exit the Printer Setup.

How can I restrict which users can install local printer drivers?

It is possible to restrict print-driver installation so that only Administrators and Print Operators (on a server) or Power Users (on a workstation) can install local printer drivers.

1. Start the Registry editor (REGEDIT.EXE).
2. Move to HKEY_LOCAL_MACHINE\SYSTEM\CurrentControlSet\ Control\Print\Providers\LanMan Print Services\Servers.
3. From the Edit menu, choose New > DWORD Value. Enter the name **AddPrinterDrivers** and click OK.
4. Double-click on the value and set to 1. Click OK.
5. Close the Registry editor and reboot the machine.

 ## How do I grant users access to a network printer?

Just as files have security information, so do printers, and you need to establish which users can perform actions on each network printer.

1. Log on as an Administrator.
2. Double-click My Computer and then select Printers.
3. Right-click on the printer whose permissions you wish to change and choose Properties.
4. Click the Security tab and select Permissions.
5. You can now add users or groups and grant them the appropriate privilege.
6. Click OK when finished.

FAQ 33.11 How many printers can be hosted on one NT Server?

You are only limited by how large the Registry grows. I know of sites with 990 print queues, all LPR, on one NT server, with no performance problems (NT Server 4.0 with Service Pack 3 and dual Pentium Pro 200, 256MB of RAM, FDDI). There are some variables, but each queue adds about 30–35KB to the Registry.

FAQ 33.12 How can I print to an ASCII text file?

The print driver Generic/Text Only can be used to print to an ASCII text file with the file output capability as its default.

1. Start the Printer Control Panel applet (Start > Settings > Control Panel > Printers).
2. Click Add Printer to start the Add Printer Wizard.
3. Select My Computer and click Next.
4. Under Ports, check File and click Next.
5. Under Manufacturers, select Generic and choose Generic/Text Only as the printer. Then click Next.
6. Enter a printer name and designate whether you want it to be the default printer. Then click Next.
7. Select Not Shared and click Next.
8. Select No to print a test page and then click Finish.
9. Insert your NT installation CD and click OK.

To use the ASCII print driver, go into your application and print as usual, except select the Generic/Text Only printer and click OK. In the displayed dialog box, enter the filename to which you want the output directed and click OK. You will now be able to view the file by using Notepad or the like.

How do I set security on a printer?

33.13

The following levels of security can be set on a printer:

No Access	Users may not print to the device.
Print	Users may print to the device and pause, resume, and delete their own jobs.
Manage Documents	Enables users to change the status of **any** print job submitted by any user. The user may not change the status of the printer.
Full	Enables complete access and administrative control of the printer.

By default, all users have Print access (the Everyone group). Also, the Creator Owner name has Manage Documents access. The Creator Owner is the user who printed the document, which means users have the ability to delete their own entries on the print queue.

To change print permissions, perform the following:

1. Double-click on My Computer.
2. Double-click on Printers.
3. Right-click the printer whose permissions you wish to change and select Properties.
4. Select the Security tab.
5. Click the Permissions tab.
6. You can now set permissions for users.

4.0 ONLY

When installing a printer, I get the error message "The print processor is unknown." Why?

33.14

There are two causes for this error message.

1. The default print processor WINPRINT.DLL is missing from the directory %systemroot%\system32\Spool\Prtprocs\W32x86.

2. The Winprint key in the Registry is missing or corrupt.

If the WINPRINT.DLL is not found, you should expand WINPRINT.DL_ from your Windows NT installation CD by using the EXPAND command, as follows:

```
expand -r <cd-rom drive>:\i386\winprint.dl_
%systemroot%\system32\spool\prtprocs\w32x86
```

If the file is there, you need to check the Registry:

1. Start the Registry editor (REGEDIT.EXE).
2. Move to HKEY_LOCAL_MACHINE\SYSTEM\CurrentControlSet\ Control\Print\Environments\Windows NT x86\Print Processors.
3. If the Winprint key exists, go to step 4. If it does not exist, choose New > Key from the Edit menu and enter the name **winprint**.
4. Under Winprint, check for a value called Driver. If this does not exist from the Edit menu, choose New > String Value and enter the name **Driver**.
5. Driver should have a value of WINPRINT.DLL. If it does not, double-click on Driver and set it to WINPRINT.DLL. Then click OK.
6. Close the Registry editor and restart the computer.

33.15 Where in the Registry is the default printer set?

The default printer is set on a per user basis and so is part of the HKEY_ USERS hive. To view the default printer for the currently logged-on user, view the following value:

HKEY_CURRENT_USER\Software\Microsoft\Windows NT\ CurrentVersion\Windows\Device

It is of the format

\\LN014\LN.S651.CSP001.HPLJ5,winspool,Ne01:

where the first part is the actual printer share, then the spooler, and finally the connection (network or parallel port).

To view a different user or view remotely, you would view HKEY_USERS\ <SID of user>\Software\Microsoft\Windows NT\CurrentVersion\Windows\ Device. To check which user has which SID, see Question 7.39 in Chapter 7, User Configuration.

If no default printer is manually defined, the first printer alphabetically will be set as the default.

4.0 ONLY

33.16 When I try to print to a parallel device (LPT1), I receive this error message: "System could not find the file." Why?

This is usually caused because the parallel service is not running. To check and fix, perform the following:

1. Start the Registry editor (REGEDIT.EXE).
2. Move to HKEY_LOCAL_MACHINE\SYSTEM\CurrentControlSet\ Services\Parallel.
3. Double-click on Start.
4. If the value is 0, it means the service will start too early in the bootup, so change this to **2** and click OK.
5. Close the Registry editor and reboot the machine.

If you still have problems, also check the Parport and ParVdm services under HKEY_LOCAL_MACHINE\SYSTEM\CurrentControlSet\Services\ (these are also needed for parallel printing).

Another cause for this error is if LPT1 is disabled via the system BIOS, so you should also check this.

33.17 How can I allow members of the Printer Operators group to add printers?

Members of the Print Operators group can stop and restart the print spooler, modify jobs, and perform other administrative functions, but they cannot add or modify the actual printers. You can change their access by performing the following:

1. Start the Registry editor (REGEDT32.EXE, **not** REGEDIT.EXE).
2. Move to HKEY_LOCAL_MACHINE\SYSTEM\CurrentControlSet\ Control\Print\Monitors.
3. From the Security menu, select Permissions.
4. Click the Add button.
5. Select Printer Operators and give them Full Control access. Click OK.
6. Close the Registry editor.

Stop and start the machine for the change to take effect. Alternatively, just stop and start the Print Spool service.

4.0 ONLY
33.18 How can I configure NT as a print server for UNIX systems?

The Windows NT Server that will be acting as the print service must have the following:

- TCP/IP installed
- Microsoft TCP/IP printing service installed (Start > Settings > Control Panel > Network > Services tab > Add > Microsoft TCP/IP Printing)
- TCP/IP Print server service set to start automatically (Start > Settings > Control Panel > Services > TCP/IP Print Server > Startup > Automatic)

After all of this is completed, it is necessary to add a Registry key. For UNIX to successfully pass data to an NT server, the data type must be set to RAW.

1. Start the Registry editor (REGEDIT.EXE).
2. Move to HKEY_LOCAL_MACHINE\SYSTEM\CurrentControlSet\ Services\LPDSVC\Parameters.
3. From the Edit menu, choose New > DWORD Value.
4. Type the name **SimulatePassThrough** and press Enter.
5. Double-click the new value and set to 1. Click OK.
6. Close the Registry editor.

The default value for SimulatePassThrough is 0, which informs LPD to assign data types according to the control commands.

You should now shut down and restart the server. After the restart, the NT box will be able to accept UNIX print jobs. At the UNIX end, you need to use the following commands (example only for SCO Open Server 5).

1. The following command needs to be entered only once by technical staff:

```
# mkdev rlp
```

2. You can now add a remote printer via SCOADMIN Printers for ordinary use.

On the SVR system you would use the following commands:

1. This command needs to be entered only once, by technical staff:

```
# /usr/sbin/lpsystem -t bsd -R 1 -T 1 <remote system>
```

2. The final stage is to actually configure the link to the NT printer:

```
# lpadmin -p <local printer> -s<remote NT system>!<NT
printer name>
# enable <local printer>
# accept <local printer>
```

An example would be NT server name SAVPDC and printer HP4SI. The UNIX command would be:

```
# lpadmin -p p0 -sSAVPDC!HP4SI
```

4.0 ONLY

33.19

How can I audit the number of pages printed by any particular user on an NT network?

If you need only basic information for NT-based workstations, you can extract this from the print server's event log. The event log records each job, including the page count. However, the page count is always 0 for Windows 98, Windows 95, Windows 3.x, and non-Windows workstations, as well as for print jobs from console or MS-DOS applications—and it does not take into account the number of copies requested by the user.

To enable the auditing of print jobs, perform the following:

1. Start the Printers Control Panel (Start > Settings > Control Panel > Printers).
2. From the File menu, choose Server Properties.
3. Click the Advanced tab.
4. Check the Log Spooler Information Events box and click OK.
5. You will need to restart the server for the auditing to start (or stop and start the Print Spool service).

When auditing is enabled, you can view the audit logs by using the Event Viewer application, System Log. To view only print logs, choose Filter Events from the View menu and set the Source to Print. Each print job will be logged with its size in bytes and number of pages.

If you need to have accurate page counts, you will need to purchase a third-party package for monitoring and managing the printing activities.

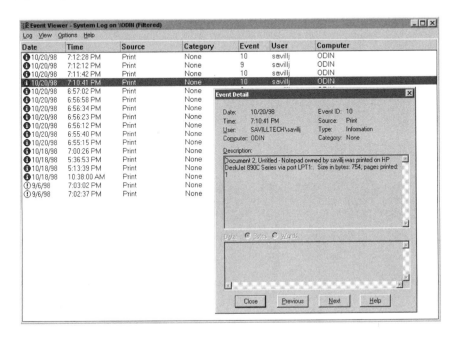

Figure 33-3. Viewing a sample print log by using Event Viewer. Event 10s are print jobs.

34 MULTIMEDIA

NT has not really been renowned for its multimedia capabilities. Although Windows 2000 will change this with its new driver model, true USB, and plug-and-play support, Windows NT 4.0 does have some good multimedia features, mainly because hardware vendors are now supplying NT-specific drivers for multimedia-specific hardware.

This section describes the configuration of multimedia devices, including soundcard settings, joystick installation, and various autoplay settings supported by NT, as well as the resolution of multimedia-related problems.

How do I disable CD AutoPlay?

When you insert a CD that has some special files at the root (an AUTORUN.INF file), it launches an application or Web page automatically.

You can use the TweakUI utility (which is basically a GUI front to some of the more popular Registry entries) to disable this automatic launch of applications. Just start TweakUI (Start > Settings > Control Panel > TweakUI), go to the Paranoia tab, and uncheck the Autorun boxes (see Figure 34-1).

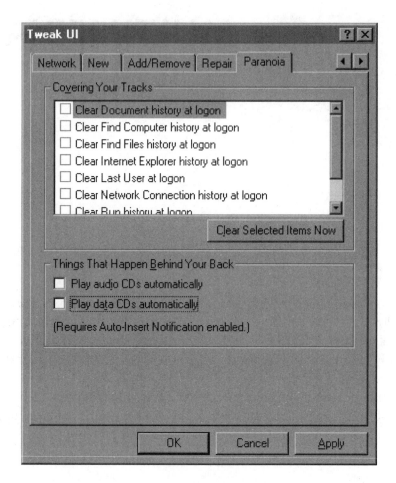

Figure 34-1. You can be selective about disabling audio and data Autorun.

You can also disable Autorun by editing the Registry. Go to HKEY_LOCAL_MACHINE\SYSTEM\CurrentControlSet\Services\Cdrom and change Autorun 0x1 to 0x0.

If you use TweakUI, it only affects the current user, whereas the Registry entry sets it for all users.

To achieve the same as TweakUI, go to HKEY_CURRENT_USER\Software\Microsoft\Windows\CurrentVersion\Policies\Explorer and set the value NoDriveTypeAutoRun from 0x95 to **0xff**.

How do I install a joystick in NT?

Windows NT ships with a basic, generic joystick driver that might work with your joystick.

On the NT installation CD, go to the directory drvlib\multimed\joystick\x86. Right-click OEMSETUP.INF and select Install. You will need to reboot, after which the joystick will be enabled.

Some joysticks are now supplied with their own native drivers for NT, so you should always install these drivers before using the generic NT joystick driver.

How do I change my soundcard's settings (IRQ, DMA, and so on)?

If the card is not plug-and-play, it has to be configured manually with settings such as its interrupt value, which enables a piece of hardware to get the CPU's attention.

To change the soundcard's settings, perform the following:

1. Start the Multimedia Control Panel applet (Start > Settings > Control Panel > Multimedia).
2. Select the Devices tab and expand the Audio Devices (see Figure 34-2).
3. Click on the appropriate soundcard and click Properties.
4. Click Settings. Scroll to the setting you wish to change and click Change Setting.
5. Change the setting, click OK, and reboot.

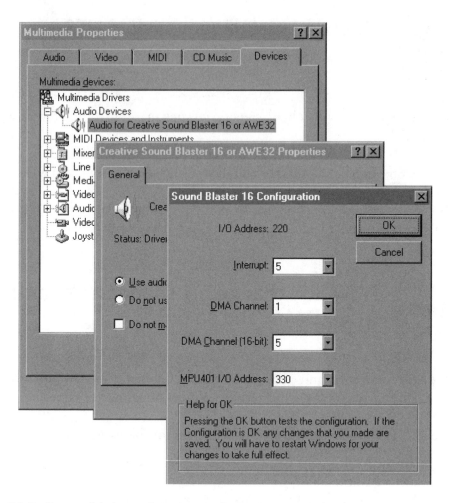

Figure 34-2. Be careful about changing Audio Device settings values. A wrong setting can cause hardware conflicts.

Does NT 4.0 support Direct X?

Direct X is built into NT 4.0, although in a limited way. There is no way to upgrade the Direct X part of NT; however, Service Pack 3 has complete Direct X 3.0 support. NT 4.0 pre Service Pack 3 supports the DirectDraw,

DirectSound, and DirectPlay components of Direct X. Service Pack 4 includes Direct X 5.0 support.

Many games that rely on Direct X will not work correctly under Windows NT 4.0.

 ## Does NT have a speaker driver?

There is no NT speaker driver like there was in DOS; however, this used to badly impact performance and it is better to buy a cheap soundcard.

The very nature of this driver prohibits its use. A preemptive multitasking operating system will not allow enough CPU cycles to generate the sound. The sound is generated by pulse with modulation, which requires 100% of CPU time while the sound is being played. Soundcards offload this to their DAC chips.

 ## How do I install my SoundBlaster soundcard?

If you have one of the newer plug-and-play SoundBlaster cards, the installation is simple.

1. Insert the NT installation CD.
2. Go to the drvlib\pnpisa\x86 directory.
3. Right-click on the PNPISA.INF file and choose Install.
4. Reboot the machine.
5. After reboot, NT detects any ISA plug-and-play (PNP) devices, including your soundcard. The drivers are on the CD in directory drvlib\audio\ sbpnp\i386.

If you have one of the older non-PNP soundcards, go to http://www.creaf.com/ creative/drivers/sb16awe/awent40.exe and download the file AWENT40.EXE. Expand the file and follow the instructions.

34.7 # I have lost the speaker icon from my taskbar. What can I do?

When you have an audio device, a small speaker icon is shown on your taskbar that allows you to change the volume or mute it altogether. To show the speaker icon on the taskbar, start the Multimedia Control Panel applet (Start > Settings > Control Panel > Multimedia) and make sure Show Volume Control on the Taskbar is checked (see Figure 34-3).

If this option has been checked but you still do not have a speaker icon, you can easily re-create the icon by running SYSTRAY.EXE. To ensure that you have the speaker icon every time you start Windows, you can place it in your Startup group.

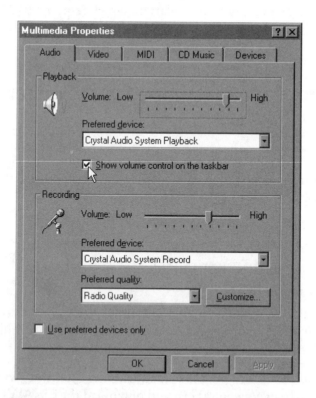

Figure 34-3. Selecting Show Volume Control on the taskbar should add the speaker icon to your taskbar.

35 UTILITIES

Windows NT's built-in offerings are not among the best (except for Performance Monitor).

Microsoft realized this and began offering an additional collection of tools and resources called the Windows NT Resource Kit. Often throughout the book I refer to a Resource Kit. In my opinion, the Resource Kit is **not** optional—in my opinion, it should be supplied as a standard part of the operating system, and for any serious user or administrator, it's a must.

Various other good utilities and resources are out there, and this chapter covers the most useful of them.

Where can I find the Resource Kit?

The Resource Kit is available from most large computer and bookstores. The Windows NT Workstation Resource Kit is around US$50, and the NT Server Resource Kit is around US$150. You can purchase it online from a number of sources, such as http://www.amazon.com.

A number of utilities are supplied on the Server Resource Kit that are not on the Workstation Resource Kit.

The Supplements provide additional tools and resources and are cumulative, so if you want only the utilities and not the printed books, just buy Supplement 2 for everything. Here is the entire list:

- Windows NT Workstation Resource Kit
- Windows NT Server Resource Kit
- Windows NT Server Supplement 1
- Windows NT Server Supplement 2

Updates to the Resource Kits are available from ftp://ftp.microsoft.com/bussys/winnt/winnt-public/reskit/.

A free support version of the Resource Kit can be downloaded from http://www.microsoft.com/ntserver/nts/downloads/recommended/ntkit/. Released in December 1998, this version uses the new Microsoft Management Console snap-in, but not all of the tools and resources are supplied.

 ## How do I run an application as a service?

The NT Resource Kit includes a utility called SRVANY.EXE that enables you to run an application as a service. There is more information on this at http://support.microsoft.com/support/kb/articles/q137/8/90.asp. Also read the file that comes with the Resource Kit (Start > Resource Kit > Configuration > Running An Application As A Service).

 ## How can I shut down a computer remotely?

Use SHUTDOWN.EXE, the Shut Down Workstation utility supplied with the NT Resource Kit. It has a number of switches to enable rebooting, closing of applications, and so on. An example is shown here:

```
shutdown \\titanic /r /y /t:5 "Shutting you down in 5
seconds."
```

This would cause the machine Titanic to reboot (the /r switch), without asking (/y switch), in 5 seconds (/t:5), with the message "Shutting you down in 5 seconds."

You can shut down the local machine by omitting the machine name and adding the /l switch, like this:

```
shutdown /y /t:5 /l
```

Where can I find a UNIX SU (substitute user) utility?

Background for those unfamiliar with UNIX: it is a good idea for System Administrators to do everyday work with a low-privileged account and only change to an account that is a member of the Administrators group if they really have to do administrative work. To avoid closing all open applications and log off, it is useful to have a utility that allows you to temporarily start applications running in the security context of a different account.

The Resource Kit ships SU.EXE, and a free equivalent is SU.ZIP (on Cica in /admin <LINK>). Both require setting system privileges for the caller. An alternative is SUSRV.ZIP (also from Cica), which has to be installed as a service but does not require privileges. There is no equivalent to UNIX SUID programs (a file attribute with the objective that the file is run in the security context of the owner instead of the caller, without specifying a password).

4.0 ONLY

I'm running NT on Alpha. Can I run Intel programs?

Digital has produced a special on-the-fly binary translator available at http://www.digital.com/amt/fx32/index.html to allow Intel-based programs to run on Alpha (this URL might change because Digital was purchased by Compaq, but it is correct at the time of this writing).

FAQ 35.6   What is TweakUI?

TweakUI is part of the powerToys set released for Windows 95; however, TweakUI (and a number of the other utilities) also runs on NT 4.0.

The utility basically puts a graphical front end to some of the more useful Registry settings and enables the user to remove icons from the desktop (such as Recycle Bin), automatically log in, and many other useful config options (see Figure 35.1).

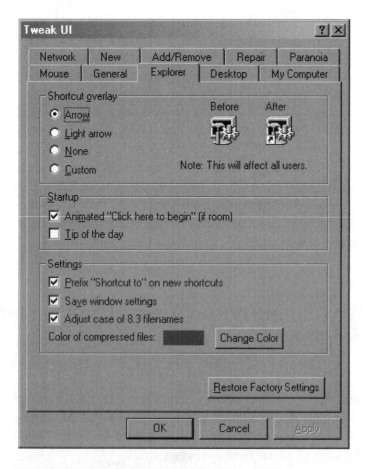

Figure 35-1. With TweakUI, you can modify the Explorer window settings such as the shortcut arrow without touching the Registry.

Download TweakUI from http://www.microsoft.com/windows/downloads/
contents/WUToys/NTTweakUI/default.asp. Then run the file, and a number of
files will be created. Right-click on TWEAKUI.INF and select Install to place a
TweakUI option in the control panel.

Windows 98 has an updated version. A special version is also available that
runs under Windows 2000.

Do Windows 95 powerToys work in NT?

Some of them do, and I suspect as time goes on, they all will. The ones that currently work on NT 4.0 are

- Desktop menu
- Find X
- Send to X
- Target menu
- TweakUI
- Explore from here
- Command prompt here

As part of the powertoys for Windows 95, there is also a QUICKRES utility that
allows a change of resolution without a reboot. This utility does not work in NT,
but the NT Resource Kit includes an identical utility called QUICKRES.EXE.

Where is File Manager?

File Manager is still shipped with NT 4.0—just run WINFILE.EXE (see Figure 35-2). Windows 2000 does **not** ship WINFILE.EXE, but if you upgrade
from Windows NT 4.0, the executable is not deleted. It is thus still available, but
it is not supported.

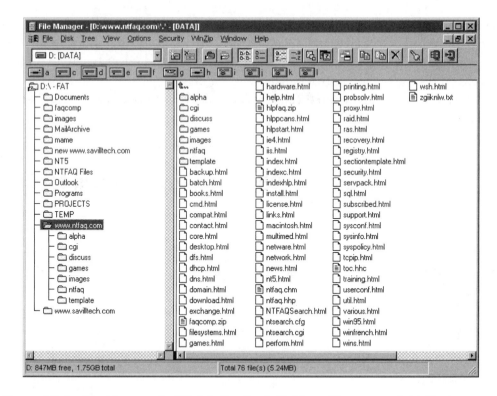

Figure 35-2. File Manager in NT 4.0. For the initial transition, you might like to see a "friendly face."

Where do I get themes for NT?

Desktop themes are supplied on the NT Resource Kit; however, if you have Windows 95 installed with the Plus Pack, you can copy the files THEMES.CPL and THEMES.EXE to the %systemroot$/system32 directory and reboot your machine. These files are contained in Plus_3.cab on the Windows 95 CD.

Where can I get UNIX tools for NT?

There are two selections of UNIX utilities that I know of, at the following locations:

- http://www.cygnus.com/misc/gnu-win32/
- http://www.datafocus.com

 How can I fix, replace, or copy files on an NTFS partition from outside Windows NT?

NT Internals has released ERD Commander, which enables you to perform read and write operations on NTFS/FAT and CDFS partitions. You can purchase ERD Commander from http://www.winternals.com/erdcmndr.htmlor or get a free read-only version from http://www.sysinternals.com/erdcmndr.htm.

After you download, just run the executable ERDCMNDR.EXE and it will self-install to a directory of your choosing. It will also create an ERD Commander program group. After ERD Commander is installed, it will ask if you want to create the ERD Commander disks. ERD Commander works by altering a set of NT installation disks with special versions of certain files so that it brings up a DOS-like command prompt instead of installing NT. You can either modify an existing set of installation disks or let ERD Commander create a new set (you will need to insert your NT installation CD). The following instructions are for creating the disks.

1. If you are booted in NT, run ERD Commander setup32 (Start > Programs > ERD Commander). If you are running a 16-bit OS, you could run ERD Commander setup16.
2. Click Next and then Next again to confirm the license agreement.
3. If you have a set of NT installation disks you want to modify, check the box for I Already Have NT Setup Floppies. If you don't and want the installation to create them, leave the box unchecked. Click Next.
4. Insert your NT installation CD and click Next.

5. Click Next at the next screen. Then in the dialog box, enter the location of your installation files: **<CD-ROM>:\i386**.

6. At the prompts, insert three blank formatted disks, following the onscreen instructions. You insert the disks in reverse order, so do disk 3 first, then disk 2, and disk 1 last. This is so if you were installing, you could just leave disk 1 in the machine after it's created and reboot.

7. After the disks are created, make sure disk 1 is in the disk drive. Then click Next on the ERD Commander window. It alters the disk, asks you to put in disk 2, and again alters a number of files. You do not have to put in disk 3 (this disk contains only drivers).

When the disk creation is complete, you can insert disk 1 and reboot the machine to boot into ERD Commander. At the prompts, insert disk 2, then disk 3, and finally disk 2 again.

There is a pause of about 30 seconds when the Microsoft Windows NT first displays—don't worry, this is normal. Next, you are shown a list of all the drives (see Figure 35-3).

Pay attention to the drive letters, because they might not match your usual drive assignments. Windows NT grants letters on active partitions of each disk

```
Microsoft (R) Windows NT (TM) Version 4.0
1 System Processor [128 MB Memory]

ERD Commander V1.0
Copyright (C) 1998 Winternals Software LLC

http://www.winternals.com

Drive letter mappings:
A: \Device\Floppy0\                              FAT
C: \Device\Harddisk0\Partition1\ WINDOWS         FAT      1015744 KB
D: \Device\Harddisk0\Partition2\ WINNT           NTFS      205600 KB
E: \Device\Harddisk0\Partition3\ SRC             FAT       870640 KB
F: \Device\Harddisk0\Partition4\ TEST            NTFS       20128 KB
G: \Device\Cdrom0\                               CDFS

C:\>dir
 Volume in drive C is WINDOWS
 Volume Serial Number is 3764-13ED

 Directory of C:\

03/21/96   01:12p        <DIR>          Program Files
03/21/96   01:12p        <DIR>          TEMP
08/27/96   10:57a        <DIR>          WINNDOWS
09/10/96   09:13a        <DIR>          bin
11/20/97   01:17p        <DIR>          eudora
03/09/98   04:08p        <DIR>          test
               7 File(s)          0 bytes
                        59,965,440 bytes free

C:\_
```

Figure 35-3. Full access is available to NTFS drives. This highlights the importance of keeping your servers secure, because anyone with disk access can get all of your files.

first, whereas ERD Commander assigns them as it comes across them from floppy disk 0, hard disk 0, and then CDRom 0 onward. For example, if you had two hard disks—harddisk 0 and harddisk 1—with harddisk 0 having two partitions, here is how Windows NT would assign the letters:

Harddisk 0, partition 1 c:
Harddisk 1, partition 1 d:
Harddisk 0, partition 2 e:

This is because active partitions are assigned drive letters first. ERD Commander, however, would label the partitions like this:

Harddisk 0, partition 1 c:
Harddisk 0, partition 2 d:
Harddisk 1, partition 1 e:

This is not a problem, so just be aware of it and don't panic that your files have disappeared.

You can now enter normal commands such as dir, rename, or copy. When you are finished, Ctrl+Alt+Del won't work. Just remove the ERD Commander disk and type **exit**.

How can I save a file in Notepad without the .TXT extension?

When you save the file, just put the filename in double quotes. For example, **"johns.bat"** will save the file as JOHNS.BAT with no .TXT extension.

4.0 ONLY

What are the Windows NT Support Tools?

They are a set of tools used to aid debugging and diagnosis of Windows 3.51 and 4.0 systems.

The current version is 1.0. These tools are free and can be downloaded from ftp://ftp.microsoft.com/bussys/winnt/winnt-public/tools/OEMSupportTools/OEMTools.exe (5.29MB).

The support tools consist of three programs:

- **Kernel Debugger:** New debugger extensions to facilitate examination and analysis of a wider range of kernel data structures than is conveniently possible today, especially when dealing with crash dumps.
- **Pool Enhancements:** Tools for caller-tracking/tail-checking the memory pool and increasing available pool statistics.
- **Kernel Memory Space Analyzer:** A heuristics-based kernel-memory crash-dump analysis tool to aid in diagnosing memory corruption problems. This tool discovers and analyzes anomalies in the kernel memory space.

The download file is self-extracting, and detailed instructions are provided in the README.TXT file.

36 HARDWARE

One of the biggest reasons people choose Windows 9x over NT is NT's very strict hardware requirements and limited compatibility. However, with NT becoming mainstream, more manufacturers of hardware producing NT drivers, and the merging of the device driver model between Windows 2000 and Windows 98, hardware and compatibility issues are becoming less of a problem.

Following are some of the more usual hardware-related questions.

4.0 ONLY
FAQ 36.1 How can I get NT to recognize my second hard disk?

Sometimes the Enhanced IDE (EIDE) adapter is misidentified as an ATAPI controller; this loads the ATAPI.SYS driver, which does not support the second hard disk. To fix this, disable the ATAPI driver (Control Panel > Devices > Startup > Disable) and load the correct EIDE driver.

If the second disk is on a different SCSI controller, you should make sure the driver for the second SCSI adapter is loaded (by using the SCSI Control Panel applet).

How do I install dual screens?

Windows 2000 has full support for multiple graphics adapters (you can even mix and match); however, in the meantime you are limited to certain graphics cards with specialty drivers, such as two Matrox Millennium cards.

Multi-monitor support is also provided by #9, Diamond MM, Dynamic Pictures, and STB. Some graphics cards even have single PCI slot solutions, such as certain STB cards and Diamond FireGL 3000.

How much memory can NT support?

NT is a 32-bit operating system, which means it can support 2^{32} amount of memory (4GB); however, NT splits memory into two parts—2GB for the programs and 2GB for the operating system. There are known to be some problems when you have more than 64MB even in NT 4.0; please see Q117373 from the Microsoft Knowledge Base (http://support.microsoft.com).

Windows NT 4.0 Service Pack 3 and Windows 2000 allow you to modify the split to 3GB for the user applications and 1GB for the operating system by using the /3GB BOOT.INI switch. To take advantage of this, the system must be part of the NT Enterprise suite and the application must be flagged as a 3GB-aware application.

How much memory do I need for NT?

For NT Workstation on Intel, 12MB is the minimum; however, 16MB is the recommended minimum, and 24MB will reduce virtual memory usage and increase performance. For RISC-based processors, 24MB is recommended—and 32MB to improve performance. Most NT people say the most acceptable performance numbers are 40MB for NT Workstation and 64MB for NT Server. It really does depend on what you will be running on the server.

For NT Server, 16MB is the minimum; however, most sites have 32MB.

These days, memory is so cheap there is no excuse not to have 64MB in your workstations and 128MB in a server.

I cannot see my CD-ROM drive from NT. Why?

If it is an IDE CD-ROM drive, do the following to ensure that you have the ATAPI CD-ROM driver installed (or one supplied with the drive).

1. In the Control Panel, double-click SCSI Adapters (I know it's IDE, but trust me).
2. There should be an ATAPI CD-ROM driver; if there is not, continue.
3. Click on the Drivers tab.
4. Add Standard Mass Storage Device and select the ATAPI driver. If it is SCSI and you have a disk, click Have Disk and then select your drive.
5. Click OK and reboot.

If it is a SCSI CD-ROM, ensure that the correct SCSI driver is loaded. You can do so on the Drivers tab of the SCSI Control Panel applet.

What are Interrupt request lines (IRQs) used for?

An interrupt allows the piece of hardware to get the CPU's attention. For something like a network card, this is important. The card has limited buffer space so the CPU must move the data out of the buffer or it will get lost. Table 36-1 gives the common IRQ uses.

Table 36-1. IRQ Uses

IRQ Level	Common Use	Comments
0	Timer	Hardwired on motherboard.
1	Keyboard	Hardwired on motherboard.
2	Cascade from IRQ 9	Might be available, depending on motherboard.
3	COM2 or COM4	
4	COM1 or COM3	
5	LPT2	This is usually free, as not many people have two parallel ports. SoundBlaster cards usually use this.
6	Floppy disk controller	
7	LPT1	SoundBlaster cards can use this.
8	Real-time clock	Hardwired on motherboard.
9	Cascade to IRQ 2	Wired directly to 2; can be used in configuration of software to mean 2.
10	Unused	Usually used by network cards, with many of them not allowing it to be changed.
11	Unused	Usually used by SCSI controllers.
12	PS/2, bus mouse	If you are not using a PS/2 or bus mouse, this can usually be used by another device.
13	Math coprocessor	Used to signal errors.
14	Hard disk controller	If you are not using an IDE hard disk, you may use this for another device.
15	Some computers use this for the secondary IDE controller.	If you do not use the secondary IDE controller, you may use this for another device.

Note about attempting to free IRQs used by unused motherboard devices: If your BIOS lets you disable the device manually and doesn't get reset by any plug-and-play software you have (for instance, Windows 95), you are probably okay. Otherwise, you'll just have to experiment to determine whether you can use the IRQ occupied by the unused motherboard device.

Sometimes IRQ conflicts can be the cause of system bottlenecks when two components are using the same interrupt, causing chaos on the system.

 ## How many CPUs does NT support?

By default, NT Workstation can support two CPUs, NT Server supports four CPUs, and NT Server Enterprise edition supports eight. The OEM version of NT Server can support up to 32 CPUs. I've heard of installations that use many more than this.

The new Windows 2000 family will break down as follows (from current information):

Windows 2000 Professional	2 processors
Windows 2000 Server	2 processors (4 if you upgrade from NT 4.0 Server)
Windows 2000 Advanced Server	4 processors (8 if you upgrade from NT 4.0 Enterprise Server)
Windows 2000 Datacenter Server	16 processors

 ## Is there a list of hardware that is supported by NT?

Microsoft has an NT hardware compatibility list at http://www.microsoft.com/hwtest/hcl/. Obviously, other hardware does work under NT with manufacturer-supplied drivers, but Microsoft has not confirmed these.

 4.0 ONLY

Can I test my hardware to see if it is compatible with NT?

It is possible to create an NT Hardware Qualifier Disk. Boot to DOS and insert the NT installation CD and a blank formatted floppy disk. On the CD, go to \SUPPORT\HQTOOL and run makedisk. Then just boot off of the floppy disk.

The Qualifier Disk will only spot hardware that NT is not "aware" of "and if NT is not aware of a piece of hardware it does not necessarily mean there will be a problem."

36.10 How do I disable mouse detection on a COM port (for UPS usage)?

Follow the steps below, after first removing the uninterruptible power supply (UPS) from the computer.

1. Start a command prompt (Start > Run > Command).
2. Move to the boot partition:

```
c:
cd\
```

3. Change the attributes of BOOT.INI so it can be edited:

```
attrib boot.ini -r -s
```

4. Edit BOOT.INI as follows: for each line with multi(x), for IDE, and scsi(x), for SCSI, drives, add this at the end (where *x* is the COM port number):

```
/noserialmice=comx
```

5. Exit edit and set the permissions back on BOOT.INI:

```
attrib boot.ini +r +s
```

6. Shut down NT, power off, and attach the UPS.
7. Boot the machine and start NT. NTDETECT will no longer try to search for a mouse on that COM port.

The /NoSerialMice switch only disables the Microsoft Serial Mouse device driver.

If you have installed any third-party mouse drivers, go to Control Panel > Devices and disable their serial mouse drivers as well. For example, if you installed the Logitech Mouseware V8.0 for a Trackman Marble, you must also disable the Logitech Serial Mouse device, called lsermous (note that this is a lowercase l, not an uppercase i).

36.11 My U.S. Robotics 56K modem only connects at 19200. Why?

The U.S. Robotics .INF that is supplied with NT defaults to and has a limit of 19200. Download the latest MDMUSR.INF from http://www.usrobotics.com, which will allow the top speeds.

36.12 Can I use the IDE interface on my soundcard?

It depends on whether it is ATAPI 1.2 compliant. If it is, there should be no problems; however, if it is not, the IDE interface will not work and you will be unable to use this port.

36.13 Does NT support plug-and-play?

In a limited sense. There is a driver that can be installed that will detect plug-and-play devices; however, it is not supported and you will receive no support. Here's how to install the driver:

1. On the NT installation CD, go to the DRVLIB/PNPISA/I386 (or whatever your processor is).
2. Right-click on the file PNPISA.INF and select Install.
3. Reboot the machine.

Installing the driver sets the following Registry values:

```
HKEY_LOCAL_MACHINE\SYSTEM\CurrentControlSet\Services\pnpisa\E
num\Type > 0x1
HKEY_LOCAL_MACHINE\SYSTEM\CurrentControlSet\Services\pnpisa\E
num\Start > 0x1
```

```
HKEY_LOCAL_MACHINE\SYSTEM\CurrentControlSet\Services\pnpisa\E
num\ErrorControl > 0x0
HKEY_LOCAL_MACHINE\SYSTEM\CurrentControlSet\Services\pnpisa\E
num\DisplayName > Pnp ISA Enabler Driver
HKEY_LOCAL_MACHINE\SYSTEM\CurrentControlSet\Services\pnpisa\E
num\ImagePath > system32\DRIVERS\pnpisa.sys
```

Windows 2000 has full plug-and-play support.

How do I install an uninterruptible power supply (UPS)?

An uninterruptible power supply is useful on mission-critical servers and work-stations and allows machines to keep running and perform a clean shutdown in the event of a power failure.

The UPS connects to the PC not only via the power supply but also via a COM port so it can communicate with the operating system.

Follow these instructions:

1. Open the Control Panel (Start > Settings > Control Panel).
2. Double-click UPS.
3. Check the box for Uninterruptible Power Supply Is Installed On.
4. From the drop-down list, select the COM port to which the UPS is attached.
5. Enter the settings in the UPS Configuration control group.
6. Enter any command line entries you want, such as a command to page the manager of the machine if there is a loss of power.
7. Click OK.

How do I give my tape drive a letter so it is visible from Explorer?

NT on its own cannot do this; however, there is a third-party "driver" that provides this functionality. For more information, see http://www.tapedisk.com.

How can I force NT to use a mouse on a given port?

36.16

When NT boots, its hardware detection component checks all hardware and updates the Registry. Sometimes it might not detect the mouse, but you can force NT to use a mouse on a given port by performing the following:

1. Start the Registry editor (REGEDIT.EXE).
2. Move to HKEY_LOCAL_MACHINE\SYSTEM\CurrentControlSet\Services\Sermouse\Parameters.
3. From the Edit menu, choose New > DWORD Value.
4. Enter **OverrideHardwareBitstring** and click OK.
5. Double-click on the new value and set it to **1** if the mouse is on COM1 or **2** if on COM2.
6. Click OK and close the Registry editor.
7. Reboot.

For more information, see Knowledge Base article Q102990 at http://support.microsoft.com/support/kb/articles/Q102/9/90.asp.

How can I view which resources are being used by devices under NT?

36.17

The easiest way to view resource use by devices is to use the built-in WINMSD.EXE utility supplied with Windows NT:

1. Start the WINMSD.EXE utility (Start > Run > winmsd).
2. Click on the Resources tab (see Figure 36-1).
3. You can now view any of the following by clicking the appropriate button:

   IRQ   Memory
   I/O Port   Devices
   DMA

4. When you're finished, click OK to close WINMSD.

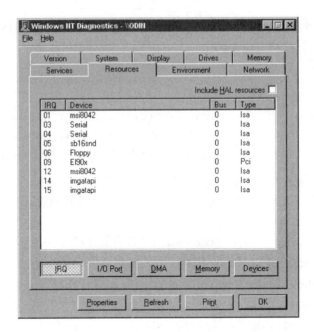

Figure 36-1. Listing the IRQ usage of the system components.

You could also use the WINMSDP.EXE utility that is supplied with the Resource Kit.

The following command will output the IRQ usage information to the file MSDRPT.TXT:

```
winmsdp /i
```

When I disconnect one of my devices (such as my Zip drive), I get errors when I boot NT. How can I stop them?

The warnings are there for a reason; however, if you want to stop them, perform the following:

1. Start the Registry editor (REGEDIT.EXE).
2. Move to HKEY_LOCAL_MACHINE\SYSTEM\CurrentControlSet\ Services\<device>.

3. Double-click on ErrorControl.

4. Change to **0** to disable error reporting or **1** to reenable it.

5. Click OK and close the Registry editor.

As an example, you would perform the following to stop the Iomega Zip service (PPA3NT):

1. Start the Registry editor (REGEDIT.EXE).

2. Move to HKEY_LOCAL_MACHINE\SYSTEM\CurrentControlSet\ Services\ppa3nt.

3. If ErrorControl does not exist, choose Edit > New > DWORD Value.

4. Enter **ErrorControl** and press Enter.

5. Double-click the ErrorControl value and set to 0.

6. Close the Registry editor.

Reboot the machine for the change to take effect.

 # How can I tell if I am using the Compaq Hardware Abstraction Layer?

36.19

Compaq has its own HAL.DLL, designed in conjunction with Microsoft. The Compaq version of the HAL.DLL takes advantage of Compaq's hardware more effectively than the default Microsoft Windows NT HAL.DLL.

This special HAL.DLL can be downloaded from http://www.compaq.com or from their download area at 713-518-1418. The current version is 1.20A and the filename is SP2465.EXE.

To check which version of the HAL.DLL you have, perform the following:

1. Start Explorer (Win key + E or Start > Programs > Explorer).

2. Move to %systemroot%\system32 (for example, use **d:\winnt\system32**).

3. Right-click on HAL.DLL and choose Properties.

4. Click the Version tab (see Figure 36-2).

5. Examine the File Version. If this value is 3.1, 3.5, 3.51, or 4.00, your HAL.DLL is the Microsoft version. Any other version means you are using a non-Microsoft HAL.DLL—in other words, Compaq.

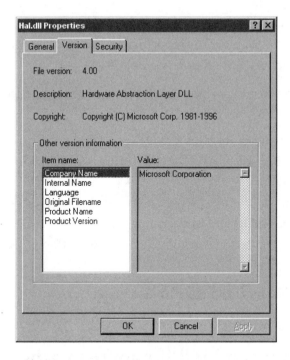

Figure 36-2. The normal Vanilla Windows NT 4.0 HAL.DLL is installed on this system.

 How do I get a dual monitor Matrox Millennium system not to split dialog boxes across the screens?

36.20

If you use a split screen, any dialog boxes will pop up in the center of the screen—between the two monitors, making the dialog hard to read. To modify this behavior, perform the following:

1. Start the Registry editor (REGEDT32.EXE).
2. Move to HKEY_LOCAL_MACHINE\SYSTEM\CurrentControlSet\Services\mgax64\Device.
3. Double-click User.CenterDialogs.
4. Change from 00000000 to **00000001** and click OK.
5. Close the Registry editor and reboot the machine.

4.0 ONLY

36.21 Does Windows NT 4.0 support USB?

Universal Serial Bus (USB) is the new external bus standard for the connection of PC peripherals. The idea behind USB is that it will be plug-and-play and will automatically detect and install devices as they are connected.

Windows NT 4.0 does not provide built-in USB support—you will need to wait for Windows NT 5.0 or switch to Windows 98. Some boxes convert the USB devices into serial ports.

Inside Out has produced USB cards and hubs for NT 4.0 (see http://www.ionetworks.com/press/nt.html).

4.0 ONLY

36.22 Why can't I hot-swap my PCMCIA card with Windows NT 4.0?

Windows NT 4.0 does not support hot-swap capabilities for PCMCIA cards—the card must be inserted at bootup. This will be supported in Windows 2000. If you need these capabilities with Windows NT 4.0, you can use a third-party package, such as SystemSoft's CardWizard product. For more information, check out their Web site at http://www.systemsoft.com.

4.0 ONLY

36.23 How do I install the Iomega parallel disk drive?

Service Packs 3 and later provide built-in support for the internal ATAPI versions of the Zip drive, but follow these steps to install the parallel version:

1. Before you do this, make sure your parallel Zip drive is plugged in and make sure you **do not** have a Zip disk in the drive.

2. Go to Iomega's Web site at http://www.iomega.com/software/ and download the software. Download the Windows NT Tools for Windows NT 3.51 and 4.0 version 1.5 IOMGNT15.EXE (3.3MB).

3. Execute this program. It decompresses the files and then starts the SCSI Control Panel applet. Click the Drivers tab and click Add (see Figure 36-3).

4. On the right side, look at the list of Iomega drivers. Select the relevant one and click Add.

5. After restarting, your system should see the Zip drive. You do not have to install the Zip tools; you can use the drive without them. To install the tools anyway, run the setup program again.

Note: When you start up your PC, make sure there is no Zip disk in the drive. If there is, NT might run checkdisk on the drive, which can take an eternity.

If you do not have the Zip drive attached when you boot up, you will get an error message at bootup that a service did not start.

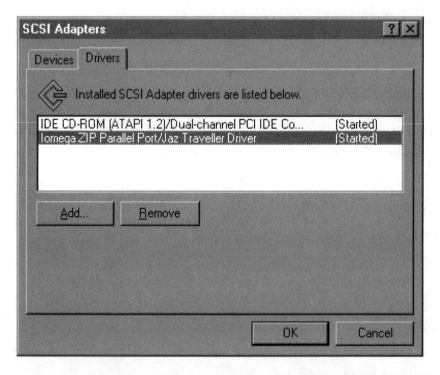

Figure 36-3. The Zip and Jaz drives share a common parallel driver.

4.0 ONLY

FAQ 36.24 How do I enable bus mastering in Windows NT?

Windows NT 4.0 has native bus mastering support with Service Pack 3. To enable bus mastering in Windows NT 4.0, perform the following:

1. Ensure that you have Service Pack 3 installed and that you have the Service Pack 3 CD.
2. Run the DMACHECK.EXE utility in the support\utils\i386\ directory of the CD or download it from http://support.microsoft.com/download/support/mslfiles/Dmachcki.exe.
3. When DMACHECK.EXE is run, it indicates whether DMA is enabled on either IDE channel. Click on the Enabled radio button to enable DMA for each drive and any other DMA-capable devices in the system.
4. Reboot the system.
5. Execute the DMACHECK utility again to check that DMA was enabled.
6. If the drive is DMA-capable and DMA is not enabled at this point, you must correct this failure before proceeding

See also the following sites for more information:

- http://www.microsoft.com/hwtest/faqs/storqa.htm
- http://support.microsoft.com/support/kb/articles/q191/7/74.asp
- http://www.bmdrivers.com
- http://www.benchtest.com/

DMACHECK.EXE IDE BusMaster is very important: you can read or write on disk without using 100% of your CPU (like SCSI).

36.25 I said no to a PNPISA device when it was detected, but now I want to install it. What can I do?

If you have installed the PNPISA driver that enables NT to use some plug-and-play devices, and on reboot you said no to installing some devices, NT will not ask you again.

If you later decide you do want to install a device, it is necessary to make NT "forget" it has ever seen the device before. Each PNPISA device has an entry in HKEY_LOCAL_MACHINE\SYSTEM\CurrentControlSet\Services\pnpisa, so to make NT forget about a device, just delete its key.

1. Start the Registry editor (REGEDIT.EXE).
2. Move to HKEY_LOCAL_MACHINE\SYSTEM\CurrentControlSet\ Services\pnpisa.
3. Each device that uses PNPISA.SYS should have a subkey under ISAPNP. Creative Labs uses a prefix of CTL for the subkey name. You'll be able to tell which key is for what device by looking at a description value defined in the subkey.
4. Delete the subkey whose hardware you want to install.
5. Close the Registry editor and reboot the machine.

On reboot, you will be able to install the device.

For more information on installing the driver, see Question 36.13.

4.0 ONLY

36.26 How do I perform unattended installations on machines with AGP graphics cards?

An updated HAL.DLL is needed to support machines with AGP graphics cards and a PCI bridge. One such HAL is supplied with Service Pack 3, so you need to replace the standard HAL.DLL shipped with NT with the Service Pack 3 version.

1. Create a share with the Windows NT installation files.
2. Rename the HAL.DLL file to **HAL.OLD**.
3. From the Service Pack 3 (or later) CD, copy HAL.DLL into the directory.
4. Install as normal.
5. When that is complete, install Service Pack 3.

 # Does NT support DVD drives?

Windows NT 4.0 does not natively support DVD drives. Windows 2000 supports them, but only for data reading and not for playing movies.

Creative Labs has released a Windows NT 4.0 driver for their DVD product. You can download the driver from http://www.soundblaster.com/creative/drivers/cdrom/dvdent4.exe.

After you download the file, you should expand it by using this command:

```
dvdent4 -d
```

This creates two directories, Drivers and Appl. To install the drivers, just run SETUP.EXE from the Drivers directory. Reboot and then run SETUP.EXE from the Appl directory.

37 PROXY SERVER 2.0

A Proxy Server is a server service that sits between the client applications (such as Internet Explorer) and the connection to the Internet. It intercepts the requests to the server to see if it can perform the action in place of the client. This improves performance by filtering requests that go out to the Internet and responding with cached information when it's available.

Basically, the client requests a page from the Proxy Server, and the Proxy Server checks its cache of pages. If the page content is available, the Proxy Server returns the page. If it does not have the page in its cache, it must go out to the Internet, retrieve the page, and forward it to the requesting client. It then stores the page in its cache for a finite time.

The Proxy Server can cache files it downloads from the Internet for a client by using this method. If someone else asks for the same page, the Proxy Server can send back the version it's holding in its cache rather than sending a request out on the Internet. A Proxy Server can also act as a firewall by filtering IP traffic by port or IP address.

Proxy Server 2.0 performs all of this, but also has extra functions. One of these is WinSock Proxy for use by WinSock-based clients (such as Windows 95) to enable IP-type access even if the local network protocol is, for example, IPX. The WinSock Proxy does this by replacing the WinSock on the client machines. WinSock Proxy can also be used to hide your network's TCP/IP configuration by allowing you to have any TCP/IP addresses on your intranet — only the Proxy Server's IP address is used on the Internet.

Proxy Server 2.0 also has the Socks proxy service for non-WinSock clients such as UNIX-based machines.

FAQ 37.1 How do I install Proxy Server 2.0?

Before you install Proxy Server 2.0, make sure your system meets the following prerequisites:

- The machine is Windows NT Server 4.0.
- The server has at least two network interface cards (NICs). You might have one network card connected to your network and the second adapter could be a modem or ISDN port. (The server might have only one NIC, but it then functions as an "optional" proxy. In that configuration, clients don't have to go through it to gain access but use it as a caching Proxy Server.)
- You are logged in as an Administrator account.
- TCP/IP is installed and configured.
- Service Pack 3 is installed.
- Internet Information Server 3.0 is installed and configured.
- You have an NTFS partition if you are going to use proxy caching.

If your system meets these criteria, you can start the installation, as follows:

1. Insert the Proxy Server 2.0 installation CD.
2. Start the Proxy Server 2.0 setup program (SETUP.EXE from the MSPROXY directory).
3. Click Continue at the first dialog box.
4. Write down the displayed Product ID and click OK.
5. To change the installation directory, click the Change Folder button and move to the directory to which you wish to install (for example, e:\msp). Click OK.
6. To start the installation, click the large button.
7. Select the installation options you require—by default, all are selected. Click Continue.

8. The next dialog box is the Caching dialog box. Check the Enable Caching box and select a partition and size (only NTFS partitions are selectable). Click Set and then click OK.

9. The next step is to configure the Local Address Table (LAT). This is used to specify which addresses are on your local network as well as which ones should not be used on the Internet. Enter an address range and click Add (for example, 200.200.200.1 to 200.200.200.255).

10. When you have entered all of the addresses, click Construct Table. Accept the defaults and click OK. Then click OK at the LAT dialog box.

11. Now you have to configure the Client installation part of Proxy Server. By default, the current machine will be selected as the computer name. You can also configure an automatic configuration script by checking Configure Web Browsers To Use Automatic Configuration. Click OK.

12. Finally, you need to choose whether you will use Access Control on the WinSock Proxy service and the Web Proxy service. By default, both are enabled. Click OK.

13. The Proxy server files are copied to the machine.

14. Click OK at the Packet Filtering dialog box.

15. Click OK to the Proxy Server installation completion message.

How do I install the client for the WinSock Proxy Service?

There are two methods—the easiest to use is the Web-based installation method described here. Before you start this, make sure the IIS server has DEFAULT.HTM as one of the default document types:

1. Start up the browser.

2. Connect to the server as http:\\<server>\MSProxy.

3. Select the link on the line that says Install the WinSock Proxy 2.0 Client for Microsoft Proxy Server Version 2.0.

4. Select Run This Program From Its Current Location. At the dialog box, click OK.

5. Click Continue to the WinSock Proxy Client installation software.

6. Select the installation directory and click the large installation button.

7. Click Restart Windows Now.

Alternatively, you can run the setup manually by connecting to the Mspclnt share on the server and running SETUP.EXE. The installation is as just described.

After the machine has rebooted, confirm that the installation is okay by performing the following:

1. Start the WSP Client Control Panel applet (Start > Settings > Control Panel > WSP Client).

2. Check that the Proxy Server is shown in the Server Name box.

3. Click the Update Now button. At the message, click OK.

4. Click the Don't Restart Windows Now button.

5. Close the Control Panel.

 ## How do I remove the client WinSock Proxy Service?

Just run the Uninstall program in the Microsoft Proxy Client group.

 ## How can I bypass the client WinSock Proxy?

There might be a scenario in which the machine is taken to different locations (such as a portable that is taken home) and in this situation you do not want to use the WinSock Proxy client. Rather than uninstalling every time you take the machine home, you can disable it like this:

1. Start the WSP Client Control Panel applet (Start > Settings > Control Panel > WSP Client).

2. Uncheck the box for Enable WinSock Proxy Client and then click OK (see Figure 37-1).

3. Click Restart Computer Now.

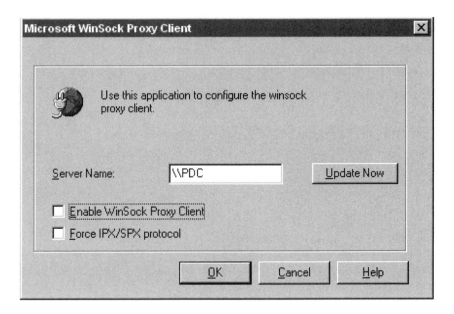

Figure 37-1. Disabling the WinSock Proxy client.

After the computer restarts, it will no longer use the Proxy WinSock. To reenable, perform the same procedure but check Enable WinSock Proxy Client.

How do I configure an Internet browser to use the Web Proxy service?

This procedure is basically the same for all browsers:

Internet Explorer 4.0

1. From the View menu, choose Internet Options.
2. Click the Connection tab.
3. Check the box for Access the Internet Using a Proxy Server.
4. Click the Advanced button. Type the address of the Proxy Server in the HTTP Address box and enter the port (usually 80). If all protocols use the same Proxy Server, check the Use the Same Proxy Server For All Protocols. Then click OK.

5. You will probably want to check Bypass Proxy Server For Local (Intranet) Addresses.
6. Click Apply and then click OK.

Netscape Navigator 4.0

1. Select Preferences from the Edit menu.
2. Expand the Advanced category and select Proxies.
3. Check the Manual Proxy Configuration and click View.
4. Enter the name of the Proxy Server and its port for all protocols for which you wish to use a Proxy Server. Click OK.
5. Click OK to end the configuration.

Mosaic 3.0

1. From the View menu, choose Options > Preferences.
2. Click the Proxy tab.
3. Enter the Proxy Server in the format **http://<server>:<port>,** for example,

   ```
   e.g. http://proxy:80.
   ```

4. Click Apply and then click OK.

You need to do the following to make sure all clients are allowed to use the Proxy Server:

1. Start the Internet Service Manager (Start > Programs > Microsoft Proxy Service > Internet Service Manager).
2. Double-click on the computer name of the Proxy Server next to the Web Proxy service.
3. Click the Permissions tab and select WWW from the Protocols list.
4. Click Edit and add all users or groups who are allowed to access the Proxy Server and thus the rest of the Internet. Click OK.
5. Click Apply and then OK.

How do I administer the Proxy Server?

37.6

Proxy Server uses the Microsoft Internet Service Manager (ISM) as its management interface, so to manage your Proxy Server, start the ISM. The example here examines which clients are currently using the Web Proxy service.

1. Start the ISM (Start > Programs > Microsoft Proxy Service > Internet Service Manager).
2. Double-click on the computer name of the Proxy Server next to the Web Proxy service.
3. Click the Service tab and click the Current Sessions button.
4. A list of connections appears. Click the Refresh button to get an update. As shown in Figure 37-2, you can also select the WinSock and Socks Proxy service by clicking the select area.
5. Click Close when finished.

You use the Internet Service Manager to stop, start, pause, and continue the Proxy services. If a service is running when you select it—for example, the Web

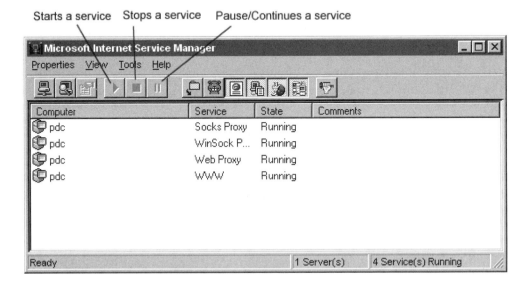

Figure 37-2. The Proxy Server is just another service that can be administered by using the ISM.

Proxy service—the Stop and Pause buttons become active. You can then stop or pause the service and its state changes.

Double-clicking on the services brings up their options. You can also hide certain types of services from the display. In Figure 37-2, I have hidden the FTP and Gopher services by clicking their icons to deselect them.

 ## How can I configure the Proxy Server to automatically dial out to the Internet service provider (ISP) when needed?

This is configured via the Internet Service Manager; however, before Proxy Server is configured, you need to ensure that the correct RAS services are running.

1. Start the Services Control Panel applet (Start > Settings > Control Panel > Services).
2. Select Remote Access Autodial Manager and click Startup.
3. Set to Disabled and click OK.
4. Select Remote Access Connection Manager and click Startup.
5. Set to Automatic and click OK.
6. Close the Services Control Panel applet.

Before you proceed, you need to make sure you have a phonebook entry for your ISP; if not, you should add one.

The WINS client has to be disabled for the Remote Access WAN Wrappers, as follows:

1. Start the Network Control Panel applet (Start > Settings > Control Panel > Network, or right-click on Network Neighborhood and choose Properties).
2. Click the Bindings tab.
3. Select Show Bindings for all adapters.
4. You might have several Remote Access WAN Wrappers. For each of these, perform the following:
   a. Expand it.
   b. If there is a WINS Client (TCP/IP), select it and click Disable.
5. Click OK.

6. Your machine's bindings will now be updated, and you should click Yes to restart your computer.

You can now configure the Proxy Services to Autodial, as follows:

1. Start the Internet Service Manager (Start > Programs > Microsoft Proxy Service > Internet Service Manager).
2. Double-click on a computer name next to either the Socks, WinSock or Web Proxy service
3. Click the Auto Dial button.
4. Select the Configuration tab and check Enable Dialing for WinSock and SOCKS Proxy if you want the server to automatically dial for either of these. Check Enable Dialing for Web Proxy Primary Route if you want dialing for the Web Proxy service.
5. You can also select the hours for which the Autodial is valid. (The connection will not hang up outside of these hours; it will just not initiate a new connection.)
6. Click the Credentials tab.
7. Select the phonebook entry and enter any username and password details required. I would advise creating a connection script if you have to enter logon information in a terminal window during the connection. For more information about connection scripts, see Question 22.4 in Chapter 22, RAS.
8. Click Apply and then click OK.

You should now stop and start all services that will use Autodial.

Any client request that cannot be handled locally will now cause the Proxy Server to dial out to the Internet.

 ## How can I stop and start the Proxy services?

Several options are available to you. The easiest is to use the Internet Service Manager. Just select the service and click the Stop or Start button.

You can also stop the services from the command line by using the following commands:

```
net stop/start w3svc       For the Web Proxy service
net stop/start wspsvc      For the WinSock Proxy service
net stop/start spsvc       For the Socks Proxy service
```

37.9 How can I use the Web-based Proxy Server Administration software?

You can download this software from http://backoffice.microsoft.com/ downtrial/moreinfo/proxyadmin.asp. On the Intel platform, this will download WATX86R.EXE to your machine. You really need IE 4.0 to get the most from the download.

To install the software, follow this procedure:

1. Log on to the Proxy Server as an Administrator.
2. Activate the installation program (double-click on it from Explorer).
3. Click Yes at the Installation dialog box and then click Continue.
4. Specify the installation directory (by default, c:\msp\msp-htm). Click Yes to create the folder and then click OK.
5. Click the large Installation button.
6. The installation stops certain IIS services and performs the installation.
7. If you have no SSL key, you are asked if you want to continue. Click Continue.
8. Click OK at the box asking about Internet Publishing.
9. The IIS services start up again.
10. Click OK at the Installation Completed message.

To administer the Proxy Server from a browser, you would connect to http://<Proxy Server name>/PrxAdmin. Then click the large graphic and enter an Admin username, password, and domain.

You can now perform all the normal functions via the interface (see Figure 37-3).

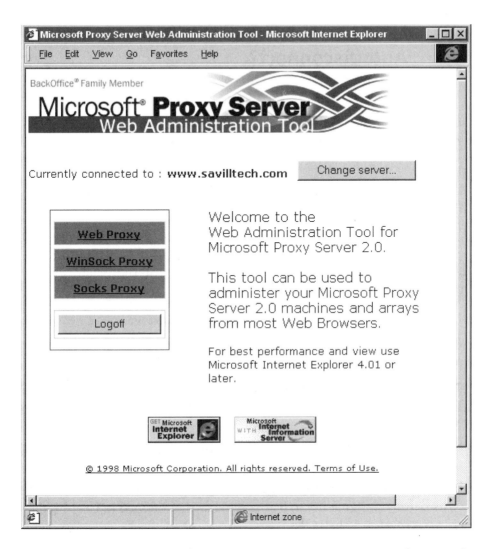

Figure 37-3. You can connect to various servers hosting Proxy servers by using the Proxy Server Web Administration tool.

Which port does WinSock use?

Proxy Server 2.0 uses UDP port 1745; Proxy Server 1.0 used 9321.

FAQ 37.11   How can I configure the RAS Autodisconnect?

You might have RAS Autodisconnect configured, but if it does not disconnect after the assigned time, one of the following might be to blame:

- A WinSock client might be currently connected to the Internet.
- A Web Proxy client (a Web browser) might be open and connected to the Internet, with a Refresh tag.
- If active caching is configured on the Proxy Server, it might be performing page fetches.
- Other TCP/IP traffic might be coming from the Internet, such as router messages from the ISP (ICMP and IGMP messages).

To actually change the idle timeout, perform the following:

1. Open the Dial-Up Networking dialog box (My Computer > Dial-Up Networking).
2. Select User Preferences from the More button menu.
3. Disable Autodial By Location by removing the check from the box next to New Location.
4. Set the idle seconds in the Idle Seconds Before Hanging Up box and click OK.
5. Choose Logon Preferences from the More button menu. Set the Idle Seconds Before Hanging Up to be the same as that defined in User Preferences (step 4) and click OK.
6. Disable the Remote Access AutoDial Manager, as explained in Question 37.7.
7. You can also open RASPHONE.PBK (in %systemroot%/system32/ras) and edit it.
8. Find IdleDisconnectSeconds in the section of the connection you use and set it to the number of seconds after which to disconnect (same as in Logon Preferences in step 5).
9. If OverridePref is present, set the seconds to 4. If OverridePref does not exist, do not create it.
10. Save the file.

FAQ 37.12 How do I ban a Web site by using Proxy Server?

Proxy Server enables you to ban certain sites and IP addresses from being visible. For example, you might want to ban the Dilbert Zone (although this gets you listed in the "Pointy Haired Boss Index," because I think Dilbert is brilliant). To ban a site, perform the following:

1. Start the Internet Service Manager (Start > Programs > Proxy Server > Internet Service Manager).
2. Expand Internet Information Server.
3. Select the server.
4. Double-click on Web Proxy and select the Service tab.
5. Click the Security button and select the Domain Filters tab.
6. Select Enable Filtering.
7. For all sites, select Granted by Default and click Add to create exceptions—IP address, group of IP addresses, or domain (for example, www.dilbert.com). Then click OK.
8. Click OK to all dialog boxes until you return to the basic Internet Service Manager console.
9. Close the Internet Service Manager.

Clients trying to access a banned site will now receive the error message shown in Figure 37-4.

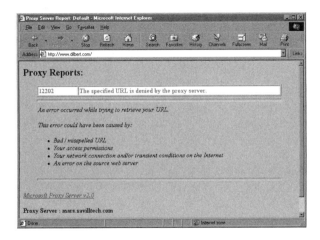

Figure 37-4. Ooops! The Proxy Server's response to a prohibited site.

38 EXCHANGE

Exchange is Microsoft's Messaging and Collaboration Server, but it's much more than that. With built-in public folders and newsgroups (among other things), it is quickly becoming the world's messaging standard.

Early on, Exchange was also the name of the mail client; however, the name has been changed to Outlook. Outlook first shipped as part of the Office suite of applications and is now available in three versions:

- Outlook 98/2000 full client
- Outlook Express with SMTP/POP3 support only, supplied with Internet Explorer
- Outlook Web Access, which is accessed via a Web browser and requires an Exchange 5.5 server, IIS 3.0 or later, and ASP

Exchange 5.5 introduced the advanced Directory Service that is at the heart of Windows 2000, so learning Exchange 5.5 will aid you in learning the NT version. Exchange Server 6.0 will share its database with the Windows 2000 directory service.

The Outlook/Exchange client takes a long time to start. Why?

Sometimes the protocol binding for Exchange can be wrong if more than one protocol is installed. For example, if you have NetBEUI and TCP/IP installed, and you connect to the Exchange server via TCP/IP, you need to ensure that TCP/IP is first in the binding order. Otherwise, Exchange attempts to communicate via NetBEUI initially. To check and set this, perform the following:

1. Start the Registry editor (REGEDIT.EXE).
2. Move to HKEY_LOCAL_MACHINE\SOFTWARE\Microsoft\ Exchange\Exchange Provider.
3. In the right pane, double-click Rpc_Binding_Order.
4. A dialog box appears, containing a text string of the installed protocols, separated by commas. You can move items—for example, you might want to move ncacn_ip_tcp (TCP/IP) to the front if you connect over TCP/IP. Make sure you keep them separated by commas.
5. Click OK and close the Registry editor.
6. Stop and start Exchange/Outlook.

How do I enable the Exchange Outlook Web access?

This functionality is new in 5.0 and enables users to view their Exchange mailbox from an Internet browser such as Internet Explorer or Netscape. Before the Exchange Active Server Pages extension can be installed, there are two prerequisites:

1. Internet Information Server (IIS) 3.0 must be installed
2. Active Server Pages add-on for IIS 3.0 must be installed

NT Server 4.0 ships with IIS 2.0; therefore—assuming you have not upgraded your system since then—you need to perform the following:

1. The upgrade to IIS 3.0 is part of Service Pack 3 for NT 4.0; you should install this service pack and reboot.
2. After you reboot the machine, install the Active Server Pages extensions (included on the Service Pack 3 CD, \winnt400\Iis30\Asp\I386\Asp.exe).
3. Run the Exchange setup program and choose Add/Remove Components.
4. Check the box for Active Server Components and click Continue.
5. The setup program will continue as usual.

When this has finished, you will be able to connect to your Exchange mailbox by entering the following URL:

http://<Exchange server>/exchange

Then enter your Exchange alias and click the Click Here text.

How can I convert my mail system to Exchange?

Exchange is supplied with a Migration Wizard, which can convert the following mail systems to Exchange:

- MsMail for PC Networks
- Lotus cc:Mail
- Novell Groupwise
- Collabra Share

The wizard is in the Microsoft Exchange folder. Following is an example of converting an MsMail post office:

1. Start the Migration Wizard (Start > Programs > Microsoft Exchange > Microsoft Exchange Migration Wizard).
2. Select MsMail for PC Networks and click Next.
3. Click Next to the dialog box that explains how MsMail and Exchange can coexist.
4. Enter the path to the MsMail post office and the Administrator account name and password for the post office. Then click Next.
5. Select One-Step Migration and click Next.

6. Select the type of information you want to import and click Next.

7. Click Select All to migrate all users and click Next.

8. Enter the name of the Exchange server to store the new accounts and messages. Click Next.

9. You now need to select the type of access you want for the shared MS Mail folders (The common one is Author access: read, create, edit items). Click Next.

10. Select the recipient container and template (optional) and click Next.

11. Finally, choose the type of passwords to create for the new Windows NT accounts that will be created from the MS Mail mailboxes. In a multidomain environment, you must select the domain for the new accounts. Click Next to begin the conversion.

12. A process box shows the progress. When it reaches the completion dialog box , click OK to complete.

 ## How can I create a shortcut on the desktop with the To field completed?

As you might be aware, if you enter the following command, you create a blank new message:

```
exchng32 /n
```

This creates a blank new message; however, it is not possible to specify a qualifier from the command line containing information relating to the content of the message. A workaround to this is the following:

1. Start Exchange/Outlook and create a new message.

2. Fill in information for the To field, CC field, and so on.

3. Instead of sending the message, choose Save As from the File menu.

4. For the Save As type, select Message Format and enter a filename and location (the default extension is .MSG). Click Save.

5. Start Explorer (Win key + E, or Start > Programs > Explorer).

6. Move to the directory in which you saved the Message Format file and right-click on the file.

7. While holding down the right mouse button, drag to the desktop and release the button. Choose Create Shortcut(s) Here from the context menu.

If you now double-click on the desktop message icon, you will create a new message that you can edit and then send with information already filled in.

 ## How can I send a mail message from the command line?

You need to use the MAPISEND.EXE utility that is supplied with the Exchange Resource Kit. The Resource Kit can be downloaded from http://www.microsoft.com/msdownload/exchange/rkintel/rkintel.htm (you need to download the AdminNT part).

After the download, double-click on the Zip file and it will expand to a specified location. With the following command, copy the MAPISEND.EXE from the restored path (i386\admin\mapisend) to an area of your choice. The usage is simple as long as the Exchange client is installed on the computer already (Outlook is also okay).

mapisend -u <profile> -p <anything> -r <recipient> -s <subject> -t <text file containing the message>
(for example, mapisend -u john savill -p anything -r john@savilltech.com -s Test message -t c:\message\mail4.txt)

This is just an example, and you might not be sure of your profile name. Instead of using -u and -p, use just -I, which enables interactive login and also enables you to create a profile you can use in the future. Table 38-1 gives the full list of switches.

Table 38-1. Switches for MAPISEND.EXE

-u	Profile name (user mailbox) of sender
-p	Login password.
-i	Interactive login (prompts for profile and password).
-r	Recipient (multiples must be separated by commas and must not be ambiguous in default address book).

-c	Specifies mail copy list (cc: list).
-s	Subject line.
-m	Specifies contents of the mail message; this is ignored if -t is specified.
-t	Specifies text file for contents of the mail message.
-f	Path and filename(s) to attach to message.
-v	Generates an 8-line summary of the sent message.

In all cases, if the passing parameter is more than one word, it should be enclosed in quotes.

 What files does Exchange use?
38.6

Table 38-2 gives a list of the more common files used by Exchange (normally in the Exchsrvr folder).

Table 38-2. Files Used by Exchange

File	Directory	Use
Priv.pat, Pub.pat	Mdbdata	Patch files; safe to delete if no backup is taking place and no startup recovery is in operation.
Dir.pat	DsaData	Patch files, as above.
Dlv.log Snd.log Dlvxxxxx.log Sndxxxxx.log	Mdbdata	These are created when sending and delivering. Diagnostics logging for either the private or public information stores are set. These can be deleted at any time. DLV.LOG and SND.LOG are the most recent logs created.
PUB.EDB PRIV.EDB	MDBdata	Information store.
DIR.EDB	DSAdata	Directory information.
EDB.LOG		Transaction log.

EDB00nn.LOG	Previous transaction logs.
EDB.CHK	Checkpoint file.
RES1.LOG, RES2.LOG	Emergency logs for when disk is full.
TEMP.EDB	In-progress transaction.

 ## 38.7 How can I change the location of my mail file in Outlook 98?

If you are using an Internet-only configuration, your messages are stored in a .PST file, and by default this is kept in your personal profile space (%systemroot%/Profiles/<user name>/Application Data/Microsoft/Outlook). This is fine unless you use roaming files, which means your mail file is stored on a central server, taking up space.

Fortunately, moving your mail file is easy. Perform the following:

1. Stop Outlook if it is running.
2. Move to your profile area and move your .PST file to another location (for example, c:\savillj\outlook). Make sure the .PST file is no longer under your profile.
3. Start Outlook. When you get an error message "The file <filename> could not be found," click OK.
4. You can now browse to where you moved the file. Select the .PST file and click Open.
5. Outlook should now start as normal.

What this actually does is update the Registry key HKEY_CURRENT_USER\Software\Microsoft\Windows NT\CurrentVersion\Windows Messaging Subsystem\Profiles\Microsoft Outlook Internet Settings\14780fd532f9d11181cc00600851c569\001e6700.

Its value is the name and location of the .PST file.

FAQ 38.8 How can I reduce the size of my .PST mail file?

When you delete files from your mail file, the space is usually not cleared away and your mail file might actually grow. To reclaim the wasted space, you can compact the mail database. The following information is for Outlook 98, but previous versions have similar functions.

1. Start Outlook 98.
2. From the View menu, choose Folder List.
3. In the Folder List pane, right-click on the root folder (Personal Folders) and choose Properties from the context menu.
4. Click the Advanced button from the Personal Folders Properties dialog box.
5. Click the Compact Now button to compact the database (see Figure 38-1).
6. Click OK to all dialog boxes to return to Outlook 98.

If you find that the mail file has not been substantially reduced in size, perhaps there is no redundant information. You might need to run the compaction a couple more times because sometimes the process does not work 100%.

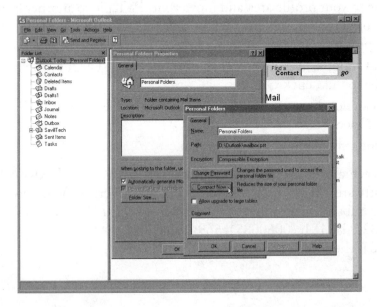

Figure 38-1. You might want to compact a couple of times to ensure all space is freed up.

I have a bad message in my POP3 mail box. How can I remove it/read POP by using TELNET?

It is possible to connect to a POP3 mailbox by using Telnet, so you should connect via Telnet and delete the problem message.

1. Telnet to the POP3 mail server on port 110 by using the following command. When you connect, you get a +OK prompt.

   `telnet <pop3 mail server> 110`
   (for example, telnet pop.savilltech.com 110—this doesn't exist, so don't bother)

2. Tell the POP3 server your username (the name by which you usually log on):

   `user john`

3. Tell the server your password:

   `pass <password>`

4. You should now be logged in. To see how many messages you have, enter the word **STAT** to get the number and size of the messages.
5. To get a list of all messages, type **LIST**.
6. To view the contents of a message, use

   `retr <message number>`

7. To view just the header, type

   `top <message number> 0`

8. When you find the problem, delete it by using the DELE command (see Figure 38-2):

   `dele <message number>`

9. Finally, to exit just type **QUIT**.

```
Telnet - pop.dial.pipex.com                              _ □ ✕
Connect  Edit  Terminal  Help
+OK Ready
user john
+OK Please send PASS command
pass neveryoumind
+OK Maildrop locked and ready
stat
+OK 2 7255
list
+OK scan listing follows
1 2660
2 4595
.
dele 1
+OK message deleted
list
+OK scan listing follows
2 4595
.
quit
+OK
█
```

Figure 38-2. Here I have deleted the first message that was on the POP queue.

This is obviously useful in a number of scenarios. You could even use it just to read your mail if you do not have access to a mail client.

How can I send mail to an SMTP server by using Telnet?

38.10

As with POP3, you can use Telnet to send SMTP messages by connecting to port 25 on the SMTP server. For example, like this:

telnet smtp.savilltech.com 25

When you're connected, you optionally announce to the server who you are (this is needed for some SMTP servers).

helo <domain>
(for example, helo savilltech.com)

vrfy <user account>
(for example, vrfy john)

When you are verified, you can begin to write an e-mail message. The first command is mail and you specify who it is from, like this:

```
mail from:<billg@microsoft.com>
```

The address **must** be in <>. Next you have to specify who will be receiving the message, using rcpt, like this:

```
rcpt to:<john@savilltech.com>
```

When the from and to have been completed, you can start the body of the message by using the data command. You have to create the header information in the first lines of the message.

When you have completed the message, enter a period (.) on a blank line and the message will be sent. Figure 38-3 is an example of creating a message. As you can see in Figure 38-3, I entered a from, date, to, and a subject and then entered the body of the text. Make sure you don't make a mistake—if you press the backspace key, this is interpreted as a bad character and rejected. If a message is rejected, a rejection is sent to the address specified in the mail from area, so you should only ever put your own e-mail address there. Although I have used a different address as a joke in the figure, you should **never** do this.

Figure 38-4 shows how the message would look when received in Outlook 98.

Figure 38-3. An example of SMTP message creation.

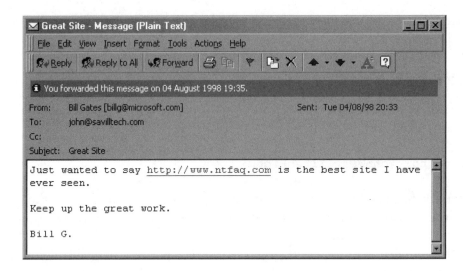

Figure 38-4. Notice that the from line shows the name I entered and the e-mail address.

The above shows how easy it is to send a message and make it appear to be from a different address. If you examine the header, however, you can easily see it was sent from a different mail server and rumble "It's a fake" (and a very bad one).

For full information on SMTP and the commands you can use, see Request For Comments 821 from http://www.internic.net.

Is there a list of known Exchange Directory and Information store problems?

An excellent collection has been compiled and is located at http://support. microsoft.com/support/exchange/content/whitepapers/dsis.asp.

Another great resource is Sue Moscher's Exchange Center, http:// www.slipstick.com.

How do I install Exchange Server 5.5?

These instructions are to install the first Exchange Server in the organization.

Before you install Exchange Server 5.5, you need to decide on two accounts. The first one is the account that you log on as when you perform the installation of Exchange; this account will be automatically granted the Exchange Administrator permission. The second account will be used as the service account for running the Exchange Server services. You can use any name, but the most obvious would be Exchange Service. To create this account, perform the following:

1. Start User Manager (Start > Programs > Administrative Tools > User Manager for Domains).
2. From the User menu, choose New User.
3. Enter the name Exchange Service with a password.
4. Make sure you clear User Must Change Password At Next Logon and Account Disabled and that you set User Cannot Change Password and Password Never Expires.
5. Close User Manager.

Under Windows 2000, you would set this by using the Directory Management MMC. Expand the domain, right-click on Users, and choose New > Users. Enter Exchange Service and click Next. Then select the options as in the previous step 4 and click Finish.

Also, before installing, make sure you have a complete backup of your system.

Now you can start the installation:

1. Log on to the server as the account you want to be the Exchange Administrator.
2. Insert the Exchange Server 5.5 CD. Run LAUNCH.EXE off of the CD if it does not start automatically.
3. Choose Setup Server and Components (see Figure 38-5).

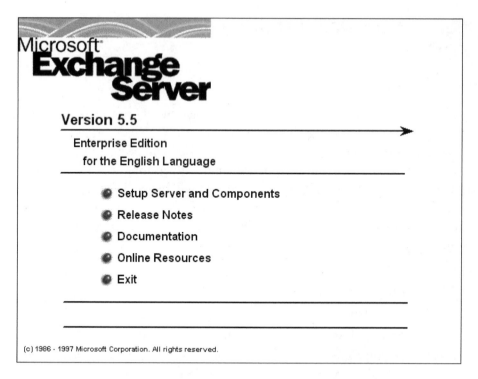

Figure 38-5. Notice that you can also view the documentation and release notes.

4. Select Microsoft Exchange Server 5.5. If you have problems with setup not starting, move directly to EXCHSRVR\SERVER\SETUP\i386 on the CD and run SETUP.EXE.

5. When the Exchange server setup starts to run, click Accept to the license agreement.

6. When offered installation types—Typical, Complete/Custom, or Minimum—click Complete/Custom. You can also change the installation directory if you wish by clicking Change Directory.

7. Select the components to install. Then click Continue.

8. Enter the CD-Key and click OK. This is of the format NNN-NNNNNNN.

9. Click OK to the Product ID dialog.

10. Check I Agree on the licensing dialog box and click OK.

11. Because this is the first Exchange server, select Create A New Site. Enter an organization name and a site name (for example, SavillTech and London). Click OK (see Figure 38-6).

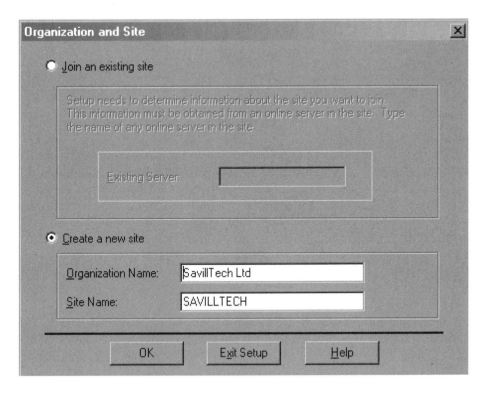

Figure 38-6. These names cannot be changed, so make sure you enter them correctly.

12. Click Yes to create a new site.
13. Now you should select the user account you created as the Exchange Service account. Click Browse to select the account and enter the password you set. Click OK.
14. These rights are automatically granted to the Exchange Service account: Log On as a Service, Restore Files and Directories, and Act as Part of The Operating System. Click OK at the Notification dialog box.
15. Exchange files will now be copied to the local server.

When installation is complete, run the Microsoft Exchange Performance Optimizer (Start > Programs > Microsoft Exchange > Microsoft Exchange Optimizer). You will be given the option to run this automatically if installation is successful.

How do I run the Exchange Optimizer?
38.13

Exchange ships with an Exchange Optimizer utility that enables the program to gather information about the computer and make changes to the Exchange configuration to enhance performance. These performance enhancements are primarily gained by moving the files that make up Exchange to different physical disk drives.

1. Start the Exchange Optimizer (either as part of the installation of Exchange or from the Exchange submenu of Programs).
2. Choose options for the server, as shown in Figure 38-7. You can run this again at a later time if the configuration scaling changes.
3. Disk analysis runs. When it finishes, click Next.
4. Recommended file moves are displayed. Adjust or accept them and click Next.

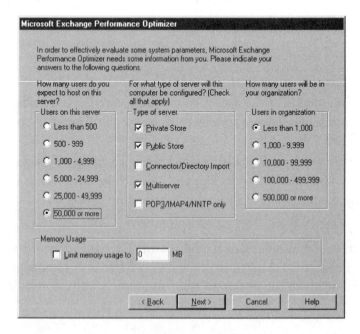

Figure 38-7. The more realistic your user estimates are, the better your performance will be.

5. Select whether the optimizer should copy files automatically (by checking the Move Files Automatically box) and click Next.

6. Services will be restarted. If that's not convenient, check Do Not Restart These Services. Then click Finish.

7. Parameters are saved as calculated by the optimizer. Services are stopped, files moved, and then services started again.

 What service packs are available for Exchange 5.5?

Here is a list of the service packs available for Exchange 5.5.

Get Service Pack 2 from ftp://ftp.microsoft.com/bussys/exchange/exchange-public/fixes/Eng/Exchg5.5/Sp2/Server/. Table 38-3 shows the files to download.

Table 38.3. Service Pack 2

SP2_550A.EXE	Server update for Alpha
SP2_550I.EXE	Server update for Intel
SP2_55CA.EXE	Chat server update for Alpha
SP2_55CI.EXE	Chat server update for Intel
SP2_55DC.EXE	Documentation
SP2_55FO.EXE	HTML form converter
SP2_55SS.EXE	Server support files (cluster, KMS, and so on)
SP2_55XA.EXE	Exchange connector installation (Alpha)
SP2_55XI.EXE	Exchange connector installation (Intel)
SP2S550A.EXE	Server symbols for Alpha
SP2S550I.EXE	Server symbols for Intel
SP2S55CA.EXE	Chat server symbols for Alpha
SP2S55CI.EXE	Chat server symbols for Intel
SP2_55RE.EXE	Readme and HTML file

Get Service Pack 1 from ftp://ftp.microsoft.com/bussys/exchange/
exchange-public/fixes/Eng/Exchg5.5/SP1/Server/. Table 38-4 shows the files to
download.

Table 38-4. Service Pack 2

SP1_550A.EXE	Server update for Alpha
SP1_550I.EXE	Server update for Intel
SP1_55CA.EXE	Chat server update for Alpha
SP1_55CI.EXE	Chat server update for Intel
SP1_55DC.EXE	Documentation
SP1_55FO.EXE	HTML form converter
SP1_55SS.EXE	Server support files (cluster, KMS, and so on)
SP1_55XC.EXE	Exchange connector installation
SP1S550A.EXE	Server symbols for Alpha
SP1S550I.EXE	Server symbols for Intel
SP1S55CA.EXE	Chat server symbols for Alpha
SP1S55CI.EXE	Chat server symbols for Intel
SP1_55RE.EXE	Readme and HTML file

Currently, one hotfix is also available, which fixes a storage problem. Download
it from ftp://ftp.microsoft.com/bussys/exchange/exchange-public/fixes/Eng/
Exchg5.5/PostSP1/Store-fix/PSP1STRI.EXE.

 ## How can I retrieve mail from a POP3 mailbox and forward it to Exchange server?

If your ISP does not support "extended turn" (ETRN), you have to use a third-
party utility to retrieve the mail from a POP3 mailbox. One of these utilities is
POP2exchange (http://www.gficomms.com). For one mailbox, this is a freeware
utility.

A more complete listing of utilities can be found at http://www.slipstick.com.

Outlook can retrieve mail automatically if you add an Internet Mail service (to collect the POP3 mail) but leave the delivery options set to deliver mail to the Exchange Server mailbox (on the server). Outlook will then retrieve the POP3 mail and move it to the mailbox on the server.

FAQ 38.16 How do I upgrade from Exchange 5.0 to 5.5?

The Exchange 5.5 upgrade process actually performs a database upgrade **before** it copies any of the code of 5.5 to the server. This allows for a complete rollback in case the upgrade of the database fails. Following are the steps for performing the upgrade:

1. Start the SETUP.EXE program as per a normal installation.
2. Setup detects the existing installation and asks if you want to Upgrade or Remove the Existing Installation. Click Upgrade.
3. A confirmation that the database will be reformatted is displayed. Click OK.
4. You are shown the Database Upgrade Options. By default, the Fault Tolerant Option is selected; however, this does require extra disk space because it makes a copy of the database; if the Fault Tolerant Option is not selected, it might mean you don't have enough drive space for this method. You might want to change the default location for the Fault Tolerant Upgrade temp files from the C:\temp location to a location on the database drive. Click OK to continue.
5. The upgrade progresses. First the database is upgraded (this might take up to 40 minutes per GB of original database). Next the code is copied to the server, and finally the Registry is modified, the services are installed, and other system changes take place.
6. The Exchange Services are restarted.
7. As with a normal installation, when all is completed, you are asked if you wish to run the Optimizer utility. This is optional.

How do I uninstall Exchange Server?

To uninstall Exchange Server, perform the following. Be aware that you will lose all information.

1. Run Exchange setup (SETUP.EXE).
2. Click Remove All.
3. Click Yes to the uninstall confirmation dialog box.
4. Click Yes to remove the shared components.
5. When the files have been removed, click OK at the Remove Complete confirmation message.

 ## How do I install a duplicate Exchange server?

With the concepts of sites in Exchange, it is possible to install multiple Exchange services in a site. The services will automatically replicate directory and routing information to one another. Duplicate servers in a site provide fault-tolerance and load-balancing. Servers within a site don't have to be in the same domain but must use the same service account (via a trust) and should be connected by a fast connection (128KB is the normal definition of a fast link). To install a duplicate server in a site, perform the following:

1. Log on as an Administrator of the domain currently hosting the Exchange service. If you log on as an account that does not have administrative rights on the current Exchange server, you will be unable to add a duplicate server.
2. Run Exchange's SETUP.EXE.
3. Click Accept to the license agreement. Setup searches for the installed components (such as IIS and ASP).
4. Select the installation type. Click Custom/Complete, set the options, and click OK.
5. Enter the product code number (xxx - xxxxxxx) and click OK.

6. Click OK to the displayed Product ID that is generated by the setup program.

7. Check I Agree for the licensing and click OK.

8. Select Join An Existing Site and enter the name of a server in the site you wish to join (for example, Mars). Then click OK.

9. When you are shown details of the Exchange server on that site, including organization name and site, click Yes (see Figure 38-8).

10. When the service account currently used to address the original Exchange Server is shown, just enter its password—if this is on its own domain, you should create a new service account to address tolerance problems (for example, main Domain Controller not available). Click OK.

11. Files are copied, services installed, the Registry updated, and the relevant services started. After the Directory Service starts, replication takes place between the sites. When this is complete, the other Exchange services start.

12. Click OK in the Replication dialog box.

13. You can now run Optimizer optionally, which is a good idea.

You now have a duplicate Exchange server in the specified site.

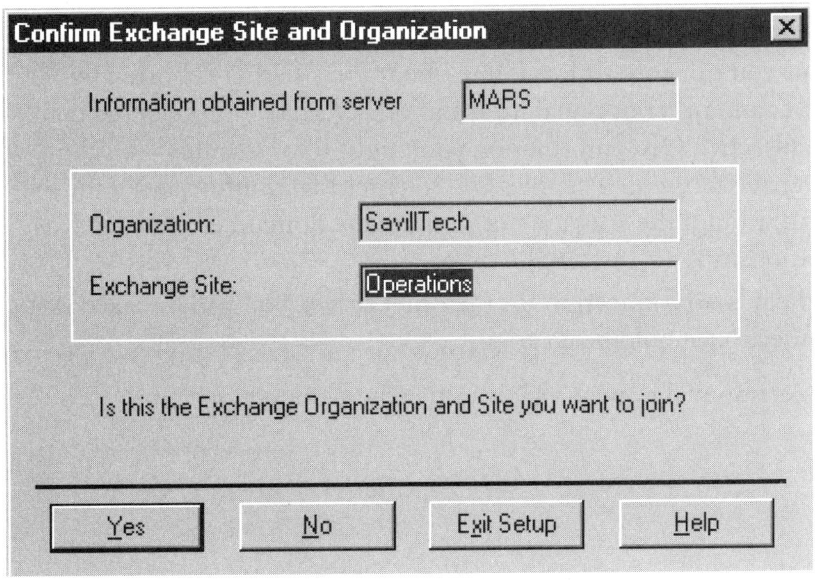

Figure 38-8. The information about the site and organization on the server.

How do I connect Exchange sites?

If you configure multiple sites by installing new servers and entering a different site name (but the same organizational name), you can connect the sites by using Exchange's built-in site connector. To connect sites by using the built-in connector, they must be able to communicate via RPC calls. To test this, see Question 13.40 in Chapter 13, Network. Many routes actually filter out RPCs, so it is important to perform this test.

To add a connector between sites, perform the following:

1. Start the Exchange Administrator program on one of the servers (Start > Programs > Microsoft Exchange > Microsoft Exchange Administrator).
2. You might need to choose an Exchange server to which to connect.
3. Expand the organization, expand the site name and finally expand Configuration.
4. Select Connections.
5. From the File menu, choose New Other > Site Connector.
6. Enter the name of the server that maintains the site to which you wish to connect and click OK.
7. Now you can enter information about the site that is hosted by the server and other optional information. When you have entered all details, click OK. Information you might have to enter is on the Override tab, which enables you to enter logon information for the connection if the sites are not in the same domain or part of a trust relationship.
8. If there is no connection for the other server, you will be asked if such a connection should be created.

The connection will now be visible under the Connections tab.

How do I configure Exchange directory replication?

After you have connected sites by a connector—Exchange, X.400, or Dynamic RAS—no data will be replicated until you configure the directory replication. You must have defined connections between the sites before directory replication can be configured.

The directory replication connector is only necessary between sites; directory replication is automatic within a site.

To configure directory replication between sites, perform the following:

1. Start the Exchange Administrator Program (Start > Programs > Microsoft Exchange > Microsoft Exchange Administrator).

2. Expand the organization and expand the site (for example, the Operations site). Expand Configuration and then choose Directory Replication.

3. From the File menu, choose New Other > Directory Replication Connector.

4. In the first dialog box, you can select (from a drop-down list) the remote site name (only sites that are connected via a connector are shown). You should enter the name of an Exchange server in the selected site. You should also leave the defaults for the Configure Both Sites option. Click OK.

5. On the General tab of the Directory Replicator, you can enter an Administrative note if you wish. You might also click the Schedule tab to select how often you want directory replication to take place. Selecting Always means changes will be replicated as they happen— this is okay if you don't care about bandwidth usage. Click OK.

The Directory Replicator between the sites is now configured. You can modify it by double-clicking on the replicator component, which is part of the Directory Replication folder.

How do I monitor an Exchange link?

It is possible to install link monitors that can be configured to perform a number of actions in the event of a link failure. A link monitor basically works by repeatedly sending messages to a nonexistent address and looking for them to be returned. If the messages stop being returned, the link must be down and the actions you have configured are performed.

1. Start the Exchange Administrator program (Start > Programs > Microsoft Exchange > Microsoft Exchange Administrator).
2. Select the Monitors subfolder of the Configuration folder of the site.
3. From the File menu, choose New Other > Link Monitor.
4. On the General tab shown in Figure 38-9, you must enter a Directory Name (a 64-character name identifying the monitor) and a Display Name (which will be shown in the Exchange Administrator application). Specify a log file and indicate how often the link should be checked (the polling interval).

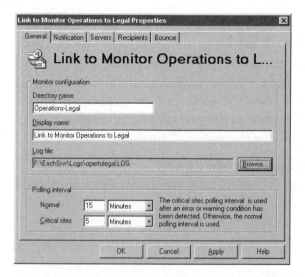

Figure 38-9. Monitoring the link between the legal and operations sites.

5. On the Notification tab, you can add notification methods (such as e-mail), start a process, or write an event log by clicking the New button. You can also test the method you specify by clicking the Test button. Click OK to the Notification dialog box.

6. On the Servers tab, left pane, you should select the servers to monitor and click Add. They will be shown in the Monitor Server pane.

7. The Recipients tab is used with non-Exchange servers that support mail "bounce," whereby e-mail is sent to the server and a reply is expected back.

8. On the Bounce tab, you can choose the times considered reasonable for a round trip.

9. When everything is set, click OK.

 ## How do I delete a server from an Exchange site?

If you have multiple servers in a site and a specific server no longer exists, you can delete it from the Exchange Directory by using the Administrator program. Do so by performing the following:

1. Start the Exchange Administrator program (Start > Programs > Microsoft Exchange > Microsoft Exchange Administrator).

2. Expand the organization and expand the site (for example, Legal). Expand Configuration and then Servers.

3. Select the server you wish to delete and press the Del key.

4. A check is performed to be sure the server can't be found.

5. If the server is not found, click OK at all dialog boxes until you are back to the normal Exchange Administrator view.

The server will now be removed from the directory.

How do I set up an Exchange forward?

A forward can be configured in a number of places. The first place is at the Exchange server:

1. Start the Exchange Administrator program (Start > Programs > Microsoft Exchange > Microsoft Exchange Administrator).
2. Select the Recipients folder of the site (for example, Operations Recipients).
3. From the File menu, choose New > Custom Recipient.
4. Select Internet Address (to forward to an Internet address) and click OK.
5. Enter the e-mail address (for example, colin@travers.com) and click OK.
6. When you are shown the normal Recipient dialog box, enter a name, e-mail address, and so on. The option to set an NT account will not be shown. After you enter all details, click OK.

People will now be able to send mail to this person and it will be forwarded accordingly.

After setting up a Custom Recipient as just described, you could then go to the Delivery Options for your mailbox and set an Alternate Recipient that points to that Custom Recipient. Select the check box for Deliver Messages to Both Recipient and Alternate Recipient. In the Properties dialog box for the Custom Recipient, you can select the option to hide the alternate recipient from the address list.

Other options that can be performed at the client end include

- Use the Inbox Assistant.
- Use the Out of Office Assistant.
- Use the Rules Wizard.

How do I configure an X.400 Exchange connector?

Aside from the native Exchange Site Connector, the X.400 connector is the most common Exchange connector, enabling Exchange to connect to non-Exchange systems. Although X.400 suffers a 20% drop in performance in comparison to the native Exchange Site connector, it is still impressive.

X.400 is a common standard, and Exchange's implementation of X.400 is based on the 1988 standard. X.400 operates on the MTA stack and has to be installed before you install an X.400 connector. MTA stacks are available for TCP/IP, X.25, and TP4. An MTA stack is available for RAS as well, but that stack does not support X.400. This walkthrough looks at implementing X.400 over TCP/IP.

The first step is to install the MTA transport stack:

1. Start the Exchange Administrator program (Start > Programs > Microsoft Exchange > Microsoft Exchange Administrator).
2. From the File menu, choose New Other > MTA Transport Stack.
3. Select TCP/IP MTA Transport Stack from the displayed list. Select the local server and click OK.
4. When a dialog for the configuration of MTA is shown, you can leave the OSI information blank. On the Connectors tab, leave the fields blank. Make sure you enter a display and directory name.
5. Click OK.

If you find you don't have a number of MTA stacks, make sure you installed the X.400 connector at installation time.

1. Rerun Setup and click Add/Remove.
2. Select Exchange Server and click Change Options.
3. Check the X.400 Connector box and click OK.
4. Click Continue.

You will now be able to install the TCP/IP MTA stack.

When the MTA stack is installed, you can install the actual X.400 connector and configure it accordingly.

1. Start the Exchange Administrator program (Start > Programs > Microsoft Exchange > Microsoft Exchange Administrator).
2. Select the Connections container of the required site to which you want to add the connection.
3. From the File menu, choose New Other > X.400 Connector.
4. Accept the default TCP/IP X.400 Connector and click OK.
5. The X.400 configuration dialog is displayed. On the General tab, enter a display and directory name (this can be any string of text). You should enter the remote MTA name (and a password if required), which is used to identify the Message Transfer Agent on the other host/site.
6. Select the Schedule tab to configure replication settings.
7. Select the Stack tab to enter the IP address or name of the system to which you want to connect. Again, you can leave the OSI information blank.
8. Use the Override tab to specify a different local MTA name and password.
9. The Connected Sites tab is used only when connecting Exchange sites via X.400.
10. If you don't enter anything under Connected Sites, you must configure an address space on the Address Space tab.
11. Delivery Restrictions and Advanced all along with other nonessential settings to be set.
12. When you have entered all information, click OK.

You now have a functional one-way X.400 link. You would need to repeat the procedure for the opposite direction.

38.25 How do I allow a user to administer Exchange?

When Exchange is installed, the user who performs the installation is granted Exchange Administrator rights. To grant additional users the ability to administer Exchange, perform the following:

1. Log on as an Exchange Administrator (Start > Programs > Microsoft Exchange > Microsoft Exchange Administrator).

2. Start the Exchange Administrator program.
3. Select the site whose permissions you wish to modify.
4. From the File menu, choose Properties.
5. Click the Permissions tab.
6. Click Add and select the user (or group) to whom you wish to grant Exchange Administrator rights.
7. Click OK. Now choose the role (for example, Permissions Administrator) and click OK again.

The user (or group) will now have rights granted to Exchange. You might want to create a group (perhaps Exchange Admins), grant the group access in Exchange, and then add users to or remove them from this group.

 ## How do I grant or deny permission for people to create top-level public folders?

By default, all users can create top-level folders; however, you can change this if you would like to restrict it.

1. Start the Exchange Administrator program (Start > Programs > Microsoft Exchange > Microsoft Exchange Administrator).
2. Expand the organization, expand the site, and expand Configuration.
3. Select Information Store Site Configuration and then choose Properties from the File menu.
4. Click the Top Level Folder Creation tab (see Figure 38-10).
5. For Allowed To Create Top Level Folders, notice that All is selected by default. Change this to List and click the Modify button.
6. You will be shown a list of Exchange mailboxes. Select the ones that should be allowed to create top-level folders and click OK.
7. Click Apply and then OK.

Alternatively, you can leave it as All and modify the list of people who should **not** be able to create top-level folders.

If people are logged in at this time, they will be able to continue to create top-level folders until they close Outlook/Exchange and restart it.

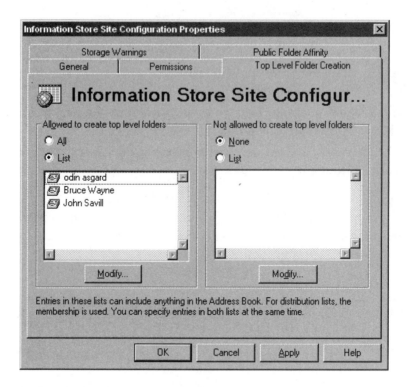

Figure 38-10. Setting top-level folder creation access.

 ## How do I connect my Exchange server to an SMTP server?

Exchange Server 5.5 ships with the Internet Mail Service (IMS), which allows connections to an SMTP server.

You will need a connection method to the SMTP server—for example, an RAS dial-up connection to an ISP. If you are connecting via a firewall, make sure the ports used by POP and SMTP are not disallowed (ports 25, 110, and 995).

Before doing any of this, you should ensure that DNS is correctly configured for your local domain. You configure this by adding an MX record for the Exchange server in DNS (or this might be done by the ISP). This is not needed if you are connecting via a RAS dial-up connection and just connecting to a specific host.

In this example, you connect to an SMTP server at an ISP. This will download all mail for the Exchange server's domain.

1. Start the Exchange Administrator program (Start > Programs > Microsoft Exchange > Microsoft Exchange Administrator).
2. Expand the organization and expand your site. Expand Configuration and select the Connections container.
3. From the File menu, choose New Other > Internet Mail Service.
4. Click Next in the introduction dialog box.
5. Click Next in the dialog box outlining the steps that should have been completed (DNS configuration and so on).
6. Select the Exchange server that will have the IMS installed, and check the box for Allow Internet Mail Through a Dial-Up Connection. Click Next.
7. Select a phone book entry and click Next.
8. Check the box for Route All Mail Through a Single Host and enter the TCP/IP address or hostname of the host (for example, SMTP.DIAL.PIPEX.COM). Click Next.
9. Check the box for All Internet Mail Addresses and click Next.
10. Now specify the name that should be appended to the mailbox names (for example, NTFAQ.COM) and click Next.
11. Select the mailbox to which you want notification or nondelivery reports to be sent. Click Next.
12. Enter the Exchange Service account password and click Next.
13. A number of changes will occur and an extra service will be added.

To configure such items as the dial-up account username and password, double-click on Internet Mail Service under Configuration\Connections. Then select the Dial-up Connections tab and click Logon Information. From this tab, you can also configure timeout and how often to dial out.

If you have problems, try applying Service Pack 1, which I found fixes a number of problems.

FAQ 38.28 How do I connect my Exchange server to a news feed?

Exchange Server 5.5 has the capability to accept a news feed and publish to the Public Folders area. It can also be configured to post back any articles posted by your network's user to the appropriate news server.

1. Start the Exchange Administrator program (Start > Programs > Microsoft Exchange > Microsoft Exchange Administrator).

2. Expand the organization, expand the site, expand Configuration, and choose Connections.

3. From the File menu, choose New Other > Newsfeed to start the Newsfeed Configuration Wizard.

4. Click Next at the Welcome dialog box.

5. From the drop-down list, select the Exchange server to install and enter a USENET site name. You can accept the default, which will be <sitename>.<domain> (for example, operations.savilltech.com). Click Next.

6. Select the type of newsfeed: inbound and outbound, inbound only, or outbound only. You also need to specify the type of feed: push or pull. "Push" means you wait for incoming to be sent to you; "pull" means at a scheduled interval you go and grab the newsposts off of the news server. Click Next.

7. Select the connection type: LAN or dial-up. If dial-up, you need to select a RAS phone book entry and enter the connection username and password (if it supports CHAP) or make sure you have an automated script configured. Click Next.

8. Now select how often to connect to the news server: every 15 minutes, 1 hour, 3 hours, 6 hours, 12 hours, or 24 hours. You can change this setting to be more specific later, if you wish. Click Next.

9. Enter the USENET site name (for example, msnews.microsoft.com). Click Next.

10. Enter the IP address or hostname of the news server and click Next.

11. If you require a password to connect to the news server, enter it here; otherwise, leave the password field blank and click Next.

12. Click Next to the summary dialog.

13. Select an Internet News administrator by clicking the Change button and then click Next.

14. Now you have to tell the configuration program where to get a list of newsgroups on the server. You can choose to import from a current file, download now, or configure it later. Click Next. If you selected Download Now, it connects (if via RAS, it dials out) and retrieves the news list. This could take a while, depending on the news server.

15. When you are shown all of the newsgroups available, select the branches from which you wish to download messages as part of your feed. To select, just click a branch and click Include. The icon for the newsgroup changes to show the connection, as shown in Figure 38-11.

16. When you have selected all of the newsgroups you want, click Next and then click Finish.

The system will now connect for the first time and get an initial feed for all newsgroups selected.

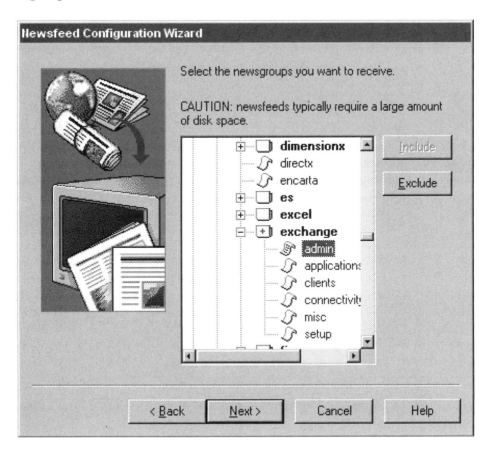

Figure 38-11. Always download the Exchange Admin newsgroup. Don't we all?

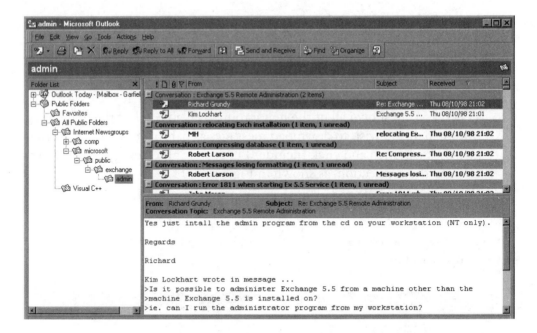

Figure 38-12. That's one question I don't need to answer now. This demonstrates the power of newsgroups, and you will be surprised how willing people are to help.

Via the Folders List in Outlook, clients will now be able to view Public Folders > All Public Folders > Internet Newsgroups > microsoft . . .

You can change any details by double-clicking on the appropriate Newsfeed entry under Connections. For example, clicking Schedule enables you to specify how often to connect at certain times of the day or on certain days of the week.

If you are connecting via dial-up, you can change the timeout parameter as follows:

1. Start the Exchange Administrator program.
2. Expand the organization and expand the site. Then expand Configuration and choose Protocols.
3. Double-click on NNTP (News) Site Defaults.
4. Select the Idle Timeout tab.
5. Change the Close Idle Connections value (between 10 and 32767). Click Apply and then OK.

What Web sites have good Exchange information?

Table 38-5 gives a list of some of the best sites I have found. Table 38-6 gives sources for some good downloads.

Table 38-5. Web Sites About Exchange

http://www.slipstick.com/	Information on the Exchange and Outlook 98 clients
http://www.swinc.com/	Information on connecting Exchange to various other mail systems, as well as downloadable utilities
http://www.exchangestuff.com/	General Exchange information
http://www.microsoft.com/exchange/	Microsoft Exchange home page default.asp
http://support.microsoft.com/support/exchange/content/whitepapers/whitepapers.asp	Various Exchange white papers

Table 38-6. Downloads About Exchange

Migration Wizard	http://backoffice.microsoft.com/downtrial/moreinfo/migrationWizard.asp
Exchange Connector for Lotus Notes	http://backoffice.microsoft.com/downtrial/moreinfo/connectorLotus.asp
Exchange Connector for SNADS	http://backoffice.microsoft.com/downtrial/moreinfo/connectorSNADS.asp
Exchange Connector for IBM OfficeVision/VM	http://backoffice.microsoft.com/downtrial/moreinfo/connectorIBMS.asp
Importers for cc:Mail Archives	http://backoffice.microsoft.com/downtrial/moreinfo/importers_ccMail.asp

FAQ 38.30   How do I download to Exchange from multiple POP3 mailboxes?

Exchange does not really support the downloading of mail from POP3 because you would be asking a server to act like a client. A third-party piece of software called PULLMAIL (from http://www.swsoft.co.uk/pullmail) can be used to download from a POP3 mailbox and deposit in an Exchange mailbox. By using the following command procedure, it can be made to download from multiple POP3 mailboxes and deposit in the correct mailbox.

Enter the following into file GETMAIL.CMD and save:

```
@ECHO OFF
TITLE GetMail
REM getmail.cmd 20-Aug-1997 Luke Brennan
REM
REM Get the POP3 mail in POP3 accounts and deposit into
REM EXCHANGE accounts
REM
REM uses the PULLMAIL program from ->
http://www.swsoft.co.uk/pullmail
REM PULLMAIL specific Info/support -> pullmail@swsoft.co.uk
REM general inquires -> mark@swsoft.co.uk
REM
SET POPUSERS=%SystemRoot%\POPUSERS.DAT
SET PARSEARG=eol=; tokens=1,2,3,4* delims=,
REM RASPHONE -d OzEmail
For /F %PARSEARG% %%i in (%POPUSERS%) Do PULLMAIL %%i %%j %%k
/to:%%l
REM RASPHONE -h OzEmail
REM
TITLE Command Prompt
```

The next step is to create the file that GETMAIL.CMD will read in, POPUSERS.DAT (see the following example). GETMAIL.CMD expects to find the file in the %systemroot% directory (for example, d:\winnt); however, you can change the location by altering the SET POPUSERS= line.

```
POPusers.dat
; space or comma delimited file
```

```
; 1. ISP pop server 2. POP3 account 3. POP3 password 4.
EXCHANGE username
;
savcom.demon.co.uk rita pass savillr
cello.cchs.usyd.edu.au brennan ###### LDB
savill.pipex.co.uk johnsavill pass savillj
```

How do I install the Key Management Server?
38.31

Key Management Server allows secure e-mail via both signed and encrypted messages. To install Key Manager, perform the following:

1. Log on to the Exchange server as an Exchange Administrator.
2. Insert the Exchange Server 5.5 CD.
3. Run the Exchange SETUP.EXE.
4. Click Add/Remove.
5. Select Microsoft Exchange Server and click Change Option.
6. Check Key Management Server and click OK.

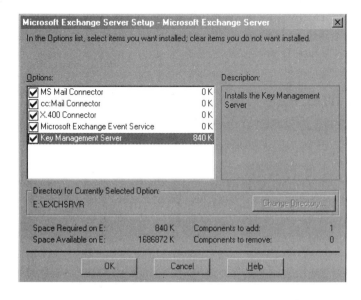

Figure 38-13. Installing the Key Management Service. This could have been done during the initial Exchange installation.

7. Click Continue.

8. Enter the site services account and password and click OK.

9. You now have an option for the special start password to be displayed (only once). You need to securely store it and enter it every time you start, or choose the option to write to a floppy disk and a backup copy and click OK.

10. If you chose to write to a disk, you are now asked where to write to. The default is the A: drive; however, you can change this to a permanent drive. If you do permanently store the secure KM password, anyone will be able to have it.

11. After the setup completes, you should reinstall any service packs you had previously installed.

Whether or not you choose to store the password, a single file KMSERVER.PWD will be created with a single word in it—like this, for example:

SWOBRQSBQZPSPQC

The final step is to configure the Key Management service to start automatically at reboot time:

1. Start the Services Control Panel applet (Start > Settings > Control Panel > Services).

2. Select Microsoft Exchange Key Management Server and click Startup.

3. Select Automatic and click OK.

4. You can also choose to start now by clicking Start. You will have to insert the disk containing the password or manually enter the password.

 ## How do I manage the Certificate Authority
38.32 of Key Management Server?

The Certificate Authority (CA) is managed through the Exchange Administrator program as follows, but make sure that the Microsoft Key Management (KM) service is running (Start > Settings > Control Panel > Services).

1. Start the Exchange Administrator Program (Start > Programs > Microsoft Exchange > Microsoft Exchange Administrator).
2. Expand the organization, expand the site, and expand Configuration.
3. Double-click on CA.
4. When asked for the password, if this is the first time, enter the password (lowercase, no quotes). You can also choose to save the password for up to 5 minutes to avoid having to retype it in the short term. Click OK.
5. When you're logged in, you can perform various functions.

To change your CA password, perform the previous procedure and continue here:

1. Select the Administrators tab.
2. Click Change My KM Server Password.
3. Enter the current password and set a new one. Click OK.
4. Click OK to the main dialog box.

You can also add new KM Administrators from the Administrators tab.

How do I enable advanced security for a user?
38.33

By default, users do not have advanced security after Key Management server is installed. To enable advanced security for a user, perform the following:

1. Start the Exchange Administrator program (Start > Programs > Microsoft Exchange > Microsoft Exchange Administrator).
2. Expand the organization, expand the site, expand Configuration, and select the Recipients container.
3. Double-click on the mailbox for which you want to enable advanced security (for example, Garfield).
4. Click the Security tab. You are asked for your KM server password because only KM Administrators can view the Security tab, not just normal Exchange Administrators. Enter the password and check the Remember box if you want to make multiple changes to mailboxes and don't want to retype the password every time.

5. Notice that the current status is Undefined. Click the Enable Advanced Security button.

6. A dialog appears with the temporary key, or the key will be mailed to the user, depending on your options and configuration. Click OK.

To allow the key to be sent via e-mail to the user, perform the following:

1. Start the Exchange Administrator Program.

2. Expand the organization, expand the site, and expand Configuration.

3. Double-click on CA.

4. Select the Enrollment tab.

5. Check the box for Allow Email To Be Sent To The User.

6. You can also change the welcome message that is sent by clicking Edit Welcome Message.

7. Click OK.

Now notify the user to read e-mail or give the user the password. The user should perform the following:

1. Start the Outlook client.

2. Choose Options from the Tools menu and select the Security tab.

3. In the Secure Email area, click Change Settings.

4. In the Digital IDs section, click Get a Digital ID.

5. Select Set Up Security For Me On The Exchange Server and click OK.

6. Enter the password and click OK.

7. Click OK to the Confirmation message.

The user will then be sent a reply message. The user should open the message and click OK to all dialog boxes and then Yes to the installation of the certificate (see Figure 38-14).

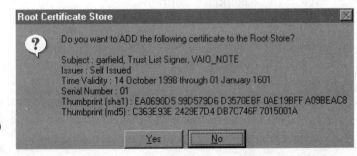

Figure 38-14. Hmmm, looks like a year 2000 problem.

Options for which security to use, signing, or encryption can be set on the Security tab of the client's Options dialog box or on an individual message basis by clicking the Options button.

How do I automatically create an Exchange mailbox for all members of the domain?

38.34

Exchange can import users from a comma-separated-file (CSV) of the following format:

```
Obj-Class,Common-Name,Display-Name,Home-Server,Comment
Mailbox,Administrator,,~SERVER,Built-in account for
administering the computer/domain
Mailbox,batman,Bruce Wayne,~SERVER,
Mailbox,denise,denise van outen,~SERVER,
Mailbox,Exchange Service,Exchange Service,~SERVER,
Mailbox,Guest,,~SERVER,Built-in account for guest access to the
computer/domain
Mailbox,IUSR_ODIN,Internet Guest Account,~SERVER,Internet Server
Anonymous Access
Mailbox,IWAM_ODIN,Web Application Manager
account,~SERVER,Internet Server Web Application Manager identity
Mailbox,krbtgt,,~SERVER,Key Distribution Center Service Account
Mailbox,MTS_ODIN,MTS_ODIN,~SERVER,Transaction Server system
package administrator account
```

Exchange enables you to generate this file from either an NT domain listing or a NetWare account list, as follows:

1. Start the Exchange Administrator Program (Start > Programs > Microsoft Exchange > Microsoft Exchange Administrator).
2. From the Tools menu, choose Extract Windows NT Account List (also notice the NetWare option).
3. Select the domain and a Domain Controller. Then click the Browse button to select a directory and filename for the output. Click OK.
4. A summary appears, listing any errors encountered. Click OK.

The file generated has **all** accounts in the domain (including Exchange service accounts, guest account, IIS accounts, as can be seen in the example), so you might want to edit the generated file and remove the lines for accounts that should not be created.

After you have edited the file to your satisfaction, perform the following:

1. Start the Exchange Administrator Program.
2. From the Tools menu, choose Directory Import.
3. Select the Windows NT domain and the MS Exchange Server (see Figure 38-15). You can also select the container; however, you should leave this as the default Recipients.
4. Click the Import File and enter the location and name of the .CSV file you created earlier. You can also choose to create a Windows NT account, but this is not needed because these accounts were generated by a domain listing. Click the Import button.

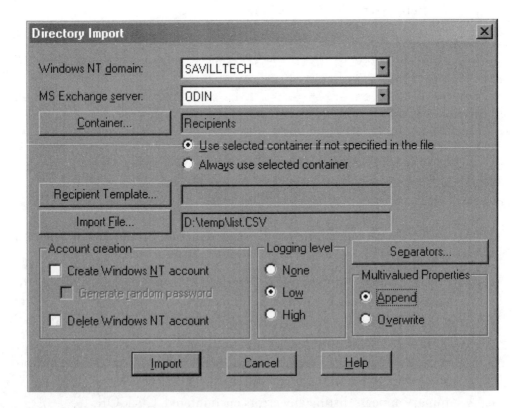

Figure 38-15. Example dialog box for Import from Domain file.

5. The file is read in, mailboxes created, and a summary displayed to show any errors.

Every member of your domain now has a mailbox on the Exchange server. In larger domains with multiple Exchange sites, you might edit the file and import some people into one Exchange site and others into a different site, depending on their geographic location.

 ## How do I avoid having to enter the Key Management password?

If you have the Key Management Server installed, each time you start the KM service, you have to either insert a disk with the password on it or manually enter it, depending on your configuration.

It is possible to configure the service to look on the hard disk, although this is not recommended for security reasons. On development systems, however, this might be okay.

1. Create a directory on your local hard disk (or you could use an existing directory).
2. From the floppy disk you created in Question 38.31, copy the file KMSERVER.PWD to the local directory (for example, d:\exchsrvr).
3. Start the Registry editor (REGEDIT.EXE) and move to HKEY_ LOCAL_MACHINE\SOFTWARE\Microsoft\Exchange\ KMServer.
4. Double-click on MasterPasswordPath.
5. Change from A:\ to the directory you created in step 1 (for example, d:\exchsrvr as in step 2).
6. Click OK and close the Registry editor.

Next time the service is started, it will look for the password file on the local hard disk and not prompt you for a disk to be entered.

FAQ 38.36   I archived some .PST files to a CD but am unable to load the files.

When Outlook opens a .PST file, it needs write access, so you will be unable to load a file from a read-only medium such as a CD-ROM drive.

To resolve this, simply copy the file to a writable medium such as your hard drive and read it accordingly.

Messages can be sent to a .PST file by using Outlook's archive function. To open a .PST file with Outlook 98, choose File > Open > Personal Folders File.

FAQ 38.37   How can I limit the Exchange Server mailbox size?

Exchange comes with the built-in capability to limit mailbox size and notify users of quota violations.

To set the limits, perform the following:

1. Start the Exchange Administrator program (Start > Programs > Microsoft Exchange > Microsoft Exchange Administrator).
2. Expand the organization, expand the site, and expand the Servers branch.
3. Expand the server whose quotas you wish to set and select Private Information Store.
4. From the File menu, choose Properties and click the General tab.
5. You can set a policy for the keeping of deleted items (this will save your having to fish out a backup if you have users who delete mail they wanted to keep). Be careful of setting the Don't Permanently Delete Items until the store has been backed up; if you don't do frequent backups, this could affect performance badly.
6. In the bottom half of the dialog box, you can set actions for quotas, namely
   - A warning to be issued (for example, 900 KB)
   - Stop the user sending mail (for example, 1100 KB)
   - Stop the user receiving mail (for example, 1500 KB)
7. Click Apply and then click OK.

Figure 38-16. You can select to have only certain of the limits—for example, only give a warning but never physically restrict.

Individual limits can be set for users by double-clicking on the username under the Recipients branch and selecting the Limits tab. Under Information Store, in the Storage Limits section, unselect Use Information Store Defaults and set explicit values for the user.

When you have configured the values for the warning, you must tell the system how often to warn the mailbox owner:

1. Start the Exchange Administrator program.
2. Expand the organization, expand the site, and expand Configuration.
3. Double-click on the Information Store Site Configuration.
4. Select the Storage Warnings tab.
5. Select the warning level: Never, Always (which is every 15 minutes), or at Selected Times.
6. Click Apply and then OK.

Clients who exceed the limit will be given warnings like the one shown in Figure 38-17.

Figure 38-17. Office 2000 has a whole new Office Assistant look (and they can be disabled).

If the client does not have the helpful Office Assistants enabled, they will just get a normal dialog box.

A message from the System Administrator with the conditions of the mailbox quotas will also be sent:

> Your mailbox has exceeded one or more size limits set by your administrator. Your mailbox size is 1518KB.
> Mailbox size limits:
> You will receive a warning when your mailbox reaches 900KB.
> You cannot send mail when your mailbox reaches 1100KB.
> You cannot send or receive mail when your mailbox reaches 1500KB.
> You might not be able to send or receive new mail until you reduce your mailbox size. To make more space available, delete any items that you are no longer using or move them to your personal folder file (.pst). Items in all of your mailbox folders, including the Deleted Items and Sent Items folders, count against your size limit. You must empty the Deleted Items folder after deleting items or the space will not be freed. See client Help for more information.

How can I limit message sizes in Exchange?

Maximum size limits can be set on the Message Transfer Agent (MTA) for inter-server traffic by selecting the General tab of the server's MTA Configuration dialog box. If a message is too large, it would then be returned to the sender; however, this limit is not used for people on the same server.

Limits can also be set on a per user basis for all traffic:

1. Start the Exchange Administrator Program.
2. Expand the organization, expand the site, and expand Configuration. Select the Recipients branch.
3. Select the user and select Properties from the File menu.
4. Select the Limits tab.
5. You can now set outgoing and incoming maximum message sizes.
6. Click Apply and then OK.

How can I undelete mail in Outlook?

When you delete an item from the Outlook client (and it's been removed from the Deleted Items folder), it is actually kept on the Exchange server for a set amount of "deleted items retention time" (Exchange Server 5.5 and later, only). This affects any mail on the server, but mail delivered to a .PST file cannot be recovered.

Mail can be recovered as follows:

1. Start the Outlook client.
2. Select the Deleted Items folder.
3. From the Tools menu, choose Recover Deleted Items.
4. Select the message and click the Recover Selected Message button (see Figure 38-18).
5. Close the dialog box.
6. The message will be added to the Deleted Items folder.

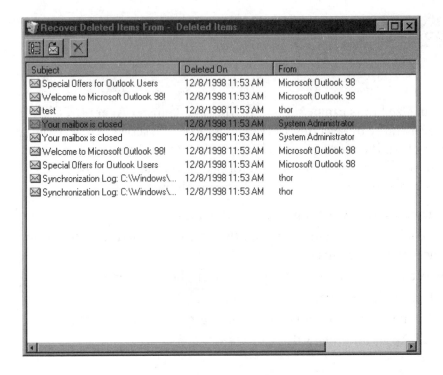

Figure 38-18. This is only available for mail on the server—**not** from POP mailboxes.

To change the number of days Exchange stores deleted items, perform the following:

1. Start the Exchange Administrator Program (Start > Programs > Microsoft Exchange > Exchange Administrator Program).
2. Expand the Organization, Site, Configuration, and Servers branch and select the Server.
3. Select Private Information Store and select Properties from the File menu.
4. Click the General tab (see Figure 38-16).
5. Under Item Recovery, select the number of days for which to keep deleted items. You can also select not to delete items until the store has been backed up.
6. Click OK.
7. Close the Exchange Administrator program.

NT Server hangs at shutdown if User Manager is running. Why?

FAQ 38.40

This is caused by an Exchange .DLL file that is used by User Manager. To fix this, perform the following

1. Start the Registry editor (REGEDIT.EXE).
2. Move to HKEY_LOCAL_MACHINE\SOFTWARE\Microsoft\ Windows NT\CurrentVersion\Network\UMAddOns.
3. Click on Mailumx and click the DEL key.
4. Click yes to the Confirmation message.

APPENDIX A

Places for Support

Newsgroups

Here are the newsgroups I frequent; they are among the most popular:

- http://comp.os.ms-windows.nt.misc
- http://comp.os.ms-windows.net.setup.misc
- http://comp.os.ms-windows.nt.admin.misc
- http://comp.os.ms-windows.nt.admin.security
- http://comp.os.ms-windows.nt.admin.networking
- http://comp.os.ms-windows.nt.software.services
- http://comp.os.ms-windows.nt.announce (moderated)
- http://microsoft.public.windowsnt.misc
- http://microsoft.public.windowsnt.setup
- http://microsoft.public.windowsnt.domain

There are also specific groups for parts of NT. For example, for DNS, go to http://microsoft.public.windowsnt.dns.

Before posting to any of the Microsoft newsgroups, please read the Microsoft policy on Newsgroup posting. You will find an HTML version of this at http://www.ntfaq.com/ntfaq/MSNews.html.

Web Sites

Various sites on the Web have extra information:

- http://www.ntfaq.com
- http://www.microsoft.com/ntworkstation
- http://www.microsoft.com/ntserver
- http://www.microsoft.com/ntserverenterprise/
- http://www.microsoft.com/iis/
- http://www.microsoft.com/windows/
- http://www.microsoft.com/windows98/
- http://support.microsoft.com/support/
- http://www.sysinternals.com
- http://www.jsiinc.com/reghack.htm
- http://www.nthelp.com/
- http://www.it.kth.se/~rom/ntsec.html

APPENDIX B

Net.exe Reference

Following is a summary of all the net.exe usage methods. Net.exe is so powerful, it warrants its own appendix.

net accounts

Used to modify user accounts. If specified on its own, it gives information about the current logon. Options for net accounts are shown in Table B-1.

Table B-1. Options for Net Accounts

/forcelogoff:<minutes or no>	Minutes until the user gets logged off after logon hours expire. *No* means a forced logoff will not occur.
/lockoutthreshold: <number of failed attempts>	Allows you to configure the number of failed logon attempts before the account is locked. The range is 1 to 999.
/lockoutduration:<minutes>	Specifies the number of minutes accounts remain locked before automatically becoming unlocked. The range is 1 to 99999.
/lockoutwindow:<minutes>	Lets you configure the maximum number of minutes between two consecutive failed logon attempts before an account is locked. The range is 1 to 99999.

Table B-1. Options for Net Accounts *(continued)*

/minpwlen:<length>	Minimum number of characters for the password. Default is 6; valid range is between 0 and 14.
/maxpwage:<days>	Maximum number of days a password is valid. Default is 90; valid range is between 0 and 49710.
/minpwage:<days>	Number of days that must pass before the password can be changed. Default is 0; valid range is between 0 and maxpwage.
/uniquepw:<number>	Password may not be reused for <number> attempts.
/sync	Forces a domain sync.
/domain	Performs any of the above actions on the Domain Controller.

net computer

You can use this method to add and remove computer accounts from the domain. Options are shown in Table B-2.

Table B-2 Options for Net Computer

\\<computer name>	Name of the computer to be added or removed.
/add	Adds the specified computer.
/del	Removes the specified computer.

net config server

This one enables you to make modifications to the server service. Entered with no parameters it gives details of the current configuration

Options:

/autodisconnect:<minutes>	Number of minutes an account may be inactive before disconnection. Default is 15, valid range between 1 and 65535. -1 means never disconnected.
/srvcomment:"text"	Set the comment for the machine.
/hidden:<yes or no>	*Yes* means the computer is hidden in the listing of computers.

net config workstation

This one enables modifications to the workstation service. Entered with no parameters, it gives details of the current configuration. Options are shown in Table B-3.

Table B-3. Options for Net Config Workstation

/charcount:	Number of bytes to be collected before data is sent. The default is 16, valid range is between 0 and 65535.
/chartime:<msec>	Number of milliseconds NT waits before sending data. If charcount is also set, whichever is satisfied first is used. Default is 250, valid range is between 0 and 65535000.
/charwait:<seconds>	Number of seconds NT waits for a communications device to become available. Default is 3600; valid is between 0 and 65535.

net continue <service name>

Use net continue to restart the specified paused service.

net file

This one lists any files that are open or locked via a network share. Options are shown in Table B-4.

Table B-4. Options for Net File

id	Identifies the file (given by entering net file on its own).
/close	Closes the specified lock.

For how to know who has which files open on a machine, see Question 9.2 in Chapter 9, System Information.

net group

You can use net group to add or modify global groups on servers. Entered without parameters, it lists global groups. Options are shown in Table B-5.

Syntax:

net group <group name> [/command:"<text>"] [/domain]
net group <group name> [/add [/comment:"<text>"] or /delete] [/domain]
net group <group name> <user name> /add or /delete [/domain]

Table B-5. Options for Net Group

groupname	Name of the global group
/comment:"<text>"	Comment if a new global group is created. Up to 48 characters
/domain	Performs the function on the primary domain controller
username	Username to which apply the operation
/add	Adds the specified user to the group or the group to the domain
/delete	Removes a group from a domain or a user from a group

net localgroup

This performs actions on local groups. It has the same parameters as net group.

net name

You can add or remove a name to which messaging may be directed. Running the command on its own will list all messaging names eligible on the machine. Options are shown in Table B-6.

Table B-6. Options for Net Name

name	The messaging name to be added or removed.
/add	Adds the name.
/delete	Removes the name.

net pause <service name>

This can be used to pause a service from the command line.

net print

You can use this to list or modify print jobs. Options are shown in Table B-7.

Table B-7. Options for Net Print

\\computername	Indicates the computer that hosts the printer queue.
sharename	Name of the printer queue.
job	The job number to modify.
/hold	Pauses a job on the print queue.
/release	Removes the hold status of a job on the print queue.
/delete	Deletes a job from the print queue.

net send

This one sends a message to a computer, user, or messaging name. Options are shown in Table B-8.

Table B-8. Options for Net Send

name	Name of the user, computer, or messaging name. Can also use * to send to everyone in the group.
/domain:<domain name>	All users in the current domain or the specified domain.
/users	All users connected to the server.
message	The message to send.

net session

Use this to list or disconnect sessions. If used with no options, it lists the current sessions. Options are shown in Table B-9.

Table B-9. Options for Net Session

\\<computer name>	The computer whose session you want to close.
/delete	Closes the session to the computer specified. Omitting a computer name closes all sessions.

net share

With this one, you can manage shares from the command line. Options are shown in Table B-10.

Syntax:

net share <sharename>=<drive>:\<directory> [/users=<number> or /unlimited] [/
remark:"text"]
net share <sharename> [/users=<number> or /unlimited] [/remark:"text"]
net share <sharename or device name or drive and path> /delete

Table B-10. Options for Net Share

<sharename>	Name of the share.
<device name>	Used to specify the printer name if specifying a printer share.
<drive>:<path>	Absolute path.
/users:<number>	Number of simultaneous connections to the share.
/unlimited	Unlimited usage.
/remark:"<text>"	Comment for the share.
/delete	Delete the specified share.

net start <service name>

This starts the specified service.

net statistics [workstation or service]

This gives information about either the server or workstation service.

net stop <service name>

This is for stopping the specified service.

net time

You can use this to synchronize the time of a computer. Options are shown in Table B-11.

Table B-11. Options for Net Time

\\<computer name>	The name of the computer to which to synchronize the time.
/domain:<domain>	Synchronizes the time with the specified domain.
/set	Sets the time.

net use

This connects or disconnects a machine to a network share. Used with no qualifiers, it lists the current network mappings. Options are shown in Table B-12.

Syntax:

net use <device name> or * \\<computer name>\<share name> [password or *] [/user:[domain\user] /delete or [persistent:[yes or no]]
net use <device name> /home /delete or /persistent:[yes or no]

Table B-12. Options for Net Use

<device name>	Name of the device to map to. Use * to use the next available device name.
\\computer name	The name of the computer controlling the resource.
\sharename	Name of the share.
\volume	Name of the volume, if on a NetWare server.
password	Password to which to map.
*	Gives a prompt to which to enter the password.
/user:<domain>\<user>	Specifies the user to connect as.
/home	Connects to a user's home directory.
/delete	Closes a connection.
/persistent:[yes or no>	Sets whether the connection should be reconnected at next logon.

net user

Use this one to add/create/modify user accounts. Options are shown in Table B-13.

Syntax:

net user <username> [password or *] [/add] [options] [/domain]
net user <username] /delete /domain

Table B-13. Options for Net User

username	The name of the account.
password	Assigns or changes a password.
*	Gives a prompt for the password.
/domain	Perform on a domain.
/add	Creates the account.
/delete	Removes the account.
/active:[yes or no]	Activates or deactivates the account.
/comment:"<text>"	Adds a descriptive comment.
/counterycode.nnn	nnn is the number operating system code. Use 0 for the operating systems default.
/expires:<date or never>	The expiry date of the account. Date format is mm,dd,yy or dd,mm,yy, which is determined by the country code.
/fullname:"<name>"	The full name of the account.
/homedir:<path>	Path for the users home directory.
/passwordchg:[yes or no]	Used to specify if the user can modify the password.
/passwordreq:[yes or no]	Used to determine whether the account needs a password.
/profilepath:<path>	Used to specify the profile path.
/scriptpath:<path>	Path of the logon script.
/times:<times or all>	Hours user may log on.
/usercomment:"<text>"	A comment for the account.
/workstations:<machine names>	Names the user may logon to. * means all.

net view

This lists any shared resources on a domain. Used with no parameters, it lists all machine accounts in a domain. Options are shown in Table B-14.

Table B-14. Options for Net View

\\computer name	Specifies the computer whose resource should be viewed.
/domain:<domain name>	The domain to be used.
/network:<NetWare network>	A NetWare network to be used.

GLOSSARY

ACL	*Access Control List* A list that controls the access to an object.
API	*Application Programming Interface* An interface through which programs interact with each other, normally through DLL calls.
BDC	*Backup Domain Controller* An NT Server machine that receives a copy of the master user database from the PDC and can validate logons.
COLD	*Computer Output to Laser Disk*
DHCP	*Dynamic Host Configuration Protocol* A service that automatically assigns IP addresses to clients from a given range (scope).
DLC	*Data Link Control* International standard protocol IEEE 802.2. Used with mainframe gateways and to control printers with a JetDirect-card.
FAT	*File Allocation Table* The DOS way of organizing a hard disk. Lots of wasted space on large disks and little file security.
HPFS	*High Performance File System* The OS/2 way of organizing a hard disk.
InterNIC	The organization that assigns domain names and IP-addresses to Internet hosts (http://www.internic.net).
IPX/SPX	*Internetwork Packet Exchange/Sequenced Packet Exchange* Novell NetWare protocol, based on the Xerox protocol XNS (Xerox Networking Services).

MAC-addresses	*Media Access Control layer addresses* 8-bit address that is hardwired into the netcard. DHCP, among others, uses this to identify a machine requesting a certain IP address within its lease duration.
NBT	*NetBIOS over TCP/IP* NetBIOS built on top of the TCP/IP suite.
NDIS	*Network Driver Interface Specification* Microsoft binding standard (interface between netcard driver and protocol). Can load into high memory on DOS systems.
NetBEUI	*NetBIOS Extended User Interface* The actual NetBIOS transport protocol.
NetBIOS	*Network Basic Input/Output System* An API of 18 networking-related commands.
NIC	*Network Interface Card* Such as an ethernet card. Also, a shortened version of InterNIC.
NTFS	*New Technology File System* The NT way of organizing a hard disk. Efficient storage with a high level of security.
ODI	*Open Data-link Interface* Novell binding standard (interface between netcard driver and protocol). Cannot load into high memory on DOS systems.
PDC	*Primary Domain Controller* The NT Server machine that stores the master user database in a domain.
RAID	*Redundant Array of Inexpensive Drives* A number of disks with data distributed all over them to allow for faster access. Can also provide data-recoverability. NT supports RAID level 0, 1, and 5.
RIP	*Routing Internet Protocol* The protocol that takes care of routing on the Internet.
SID number	*Security identification number* Every object in an NT domain has a SID number. Reinstalling NT will not give the same SID number.
SPS	*Standby Power Supply* A device that is installed between the wall outlet and the computer inlet. The power goes directly into the computer with a branch to the batteries. When the power fails, the batteries take over, but with a delay. The delay should be 4 ms or better for proper operation.
TCP/IP	*Transmission Control Protocol/Internet Protocol* The protocol used for Internet and intranet communications.

UDP

User Datagram Protocol Part of the TCP/IP suite. It is used for many things, including communication between DHCP-servers and clients.

UPS

Uninterruptible Power Supply Device installed between the wall outlet and the computer inlet. The power is directed through the batteries, thus stabilizing the variance of the power from the outlet. Because of this, the switch delay is 0 ms.

WINS

Windows Internet Naming Service A dynamic IP-to-Net-BIOS name database.

INDEX

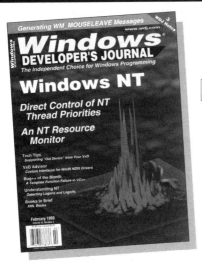

Addison-Wesley Computer and Engineering Publishing Group

How to Interact with Us

1. Visit our Web site

http://www.awl.com/cseng

When you think you've read enough, there's always more content for you at Addison-Wesley's web site. Our web site contains a directory of complete product information including:

- Chapters
- Exclusive author interviews
- Links to authors' pages
- Tables of contents
- Source code

You can also discover what tradeshows and conferences Addison-Wesley will be attending, read what others are saying about our titles, and find out where and when you can meet our authors and have them sign your book.

2. Subscribe to Our Email Mailing Lists

Subscribe to our electronic mailing lists and be the first to know when new books are publishing. Here's how it works: Sign up for our electronic mailing at **http://www.awl.com/cseng/mailinglists.html**. Just select the subject areas that interest you and you will receive notification via email when we publish a book in that area.

3. Contact Us via Email

cepubprof@awl.com
Ask general questions about our books.
Sign up for our electronic mailing lists.
Submit corrections for our web site.

bexpress@awl.com
Request an Addison-Wesley catalog.
Get answers to questions regarding your order or our products.

innovations@awl.com
Request a current Innovations Newsletter.

webmaster@awl.com
Send comments about our web site.

cepubeditors@awl.com
Submit a book proposal.
Send errata for an Addison-Wesley book.

cepubpublicity@awl.com
Request a review copy for a member of the media interested in reviewing new Addison-Wesley titles.

We encourage you to patronize the many fine retailers who stock Addison-Wesley titles. Visit our online directory to find stores near you or visit our online store: **http://store.awl.com/** or call 800-824-7799.

Addison Wesley Longman
Computer and Engineering Publishing Group
One Jacob Way, Reading, Massachusetts 01867 USA
TEL 781-944-3700 • FAX 781-942-3076